RELIGION, LAW AND THE STATE IN INDIA

Religion, Law and the State in India

by

J. Duncan M. Derrett, D.C.L. (Oxon.)

of Gray's Inn Barrister-at-law,
Professor of Oriental Laws
in the University of London

THE FREE PRESS : NEW YORK

Collier-Macmillan Canada, Ltd., Toronto, Ontario
Library of Congress Catalog Card Number 68-20979
Printed in Great Britain

CONTENTS

HINTS ON PRONUNCIATION

Indian words and names are pronounced as they appear, all the vowels being sounded: thus Kāṇe rhymes with 'neigh'. The accent usually falls on the penultimate syllable, unless this is short and is preceded by a long vowel: thus *paramā́nanda*, but *ācā́rya*. In a book of this character it is not necessary or desirable to reduce all words and names to a single diacritical script. Sanskrit words have been shown in a standard system of spelling adopted by most orientalists, but names of persons have been allowed to retain their most usual spelling, modified by such diacritical marks as will prevent the reader from making a bad slip in pronouncing them. It will be a sufficient guide to pronunciation to note the following: vowels marked long in our transliteration are to be sounded as in Italian, thus *ā* is as the a in *father*; the *r* is always sounded; *ṛ* is like the re in *pretty*; *c* is the ch in *church* (in the names of persons an original 'ch' has been allowed to stand since it will mislead no one); unmarked vowels are short, *i* is the i in sit, *a* is the u in *butter*, *u* is the u in *push*; *ś* is like the ssi in *passion*, while *ṣ* or *sh* is the sh in *push*. The *zh* in *tāvazhi* is a peculiar r sound for which there is no European equivalent. Dotted consonants have a somewhat nasal sound, the corresponding undotted consonants a dental quality, neither of which is present in English.

ABBREVIATIONS

A. & N.	Assam and Nagaland
A.B.O.R.I.	Annals of the Bhandarkar Oriental Research Institute
AHL	Anglo-Hindu Law
AIR	All India Reporter
A.O.R.	Annals of Oriental Research
A.R.E.	Annual Report of Epigraphy
A.R.I.E.	Annual Report of Indian Epigraphy
A.R.S.I.E.	Annual Report of South Indian Epigraphy
A.W.N.	Allahabad Weekly Notes
All E.R.	All England Reports
All.	Allahabad
An.P. or A.P.	Andhra Pradesh
An.W.R.	Andhra Weekly Reporter
Ass.	Assam
B.H.C.R.	Bombay High Court Reports
B.K.	Inscriptions gathered from the Bombay Karnatak (now in Mysore State) and published as appendices to the A.R.S.I.E. and A.R.I.E.
B.K. Ins.	Bombay Karnatak Inscriptions
B.S.O.A.S.	Bulletin of the School of Oriental and African Studies
Beng. L.R. or B.L.R.	Bengal Law Reports
Bibl. Ind.	Bibliotheca Indica series
Bom.	Bombay
Bom. L.R.	Bombay Law Reporter
C.S.S.H.	Comparative Studies in Society and History
Cal.	Calcutta
C.W.N.	Calcutta Weekly Notes
E.C.	Epigraphia Carnatica

E.I.	Epigraphia Indica
F.B.	Full Bench (normally of three judges)
For. Not.	K. A. N. Sastri, Foreign Notices of S. India
HAMA	Hindu Adoptions and Maintenance Act
H.D.	History of Dharmaśāstra
H.L.	Hindu Law
HMA	Hindu Marriage Act
HMGA	Hindu Minority and Guardianship Act
H.P.	Himachal Pradesh
HSA	Hindu Succession Act
Hyd. Arch. Ser.	Hyderabad Archaeological Series
I.A.	Law Reports, Indian Appeals series
I.C.L.Q.	International and Comparative Law Quarterly
I.H.Q.	Indian Historical Quarterly
I.M.H.L.	Introduction to Modern Hindu Law
I.R.	Indian Reports (a Madras Law Journal reprint)
I.Y.B.I.A.	India Year-book of International Affairs
J.	Journal section
J. & K.	Jammu and Kashmir
J.A.O.S.	Journal of the American Oriental Society
J.A.S.B.	Journal of the Asiatic Society of Bengal
J.B.O.R.S.	Journal of the Bihar and Orissa Research Society
J.Bih.Res.Soc.	Journal of the Bihar Research Society
J.E.S.H.O.	Journal of the Economic and Social History of the Orient
J.I.L.I.	Journal of the Indian Law Institute
J.Ind.Hist.	Journal of Indian History
J.O.R.	Journal of Oriental Research
J.R.A.S.	Journal of the Royal Asiatic Society
Jur. Rev.	Juridical Review
Kar.	Karachi
K.I.	Karnatak Inscriptions
K.L.T.	Kerala Law Times
Ker.	Kerala
L.Q.R.	Law Quarterly Review

Luck.	Lucknow
M.A.R.	Mysore Archaeological Report
M.B.	Madhya Bharat
M.H.C.R.	Madras High Court Reports
MHL	Modern Hindu Law
M.I.A.	Moore's Indian Appeals
M.L.J.	Madras Law Journal
M.P.	Madhya Pradesh
M.W.N.	Madras Weekly Notes
Mad.	Madras
Madras G.O.Mss.Lib.	Madras Government Oriental Manuscripts Library
Mit.	Mitāksharā
Mys.	Mysore
N.I.A.	New Indian Antiquary
N.U.C.	Notes of Unreported Cases
N.W.P.	North Western Provinces
Nag.	Nagpur
Nag. L.R.	Nagpur Law Reports
Norton	Norton's Leading Cases
Or.	Orissa
P.C.	Privy Council
P.L.D.	All Pakistan Legal Decisions
P.R.	Punjab Record
Pat.	Patna
Punj.	Punjab
RabelsZ.	Rabels Zeitschrift, formerly Zeitschrift für ausländisches und internationales Privatrecht
S.B.	Special Bench (for matrimonial causes or for appeals before fuller benches)
S.C.	Supreme Court
S.C.J.	Supreme Court Journal
S.C.R.	Supreme Court Reports
S.C.W.R.	Supreme Court Weekly Reporter
S.D.A.	Sadr Diwani Adalat (available in the original edition or the India Decisions (O.S.) *Select Reports* reprint)
S.I.I.	South Indian Inscriptions
Sel. Rep.	Select Reports

Suth.W.R.	Sutherland's Weekly Reporter
T.C.	Travancore-Cochin
Trav.L.R.	Travancore Law Reports
W.R. *see* Suth.W.R.	
Yājñ.	Yājñavalkya
Z.D.M.G.	Zeitschrift der deutschen morgenländischen Gesellschaft
Z.f.vergl.Rechtsw.	Zeitschrift für vergleichende Rechtswissenschaft

GLOSSARY OF SANSKRIT TERMS, ETC.

adhikaraṇa	chapter, topic
adṛṣṭa	'unseen', undemonstrable, transcendental
adṛṣṭārtha	having a purpose which is *adṛṣṭa*
agrahāra	settlement or colony of Brahmins
anuloma	natural (of caste-relation of parents of a child)[1]
anyathā	otherwise, wrongly
āpad	misfortune, distress, disaster
artha	profit, material wealth, convenience
arthavāda	declamatory or explanatory adjunct to an injunction
āśrama	'stage', stage of life, status
asvargya	non-conducive to attaining heaven
ātmanas tuṣṭi, *ātma-tuṣṭi*	self-satisfaction (in the sense of a quiet conscience)
aurasa	born of the body, legitimate
bhakti	worship, adoration
caritra	custom, practice
dakṣiṇā	ceremonial present, fee
dāsi-putra	son of a slave-girl or concubine
dattaka	son given, adopted son
dāya	share in ancestral property when divided, or before division
devatā	a deity
dharma	righteousness, duty, sacred law
dharmaśāstra	science of *dharma*
dīkṣā	initiation (for a sacrifice or into a sect)
dṛṣṭa	'seen', obvious, worldly
dṛṣṭārtha	having a purpose which is *dṛṣṭa*

[1] With the husband of the higher caste; *pratiloma* is the reverse.

gotra	paternal (agnatic) lineage
gṛhastha	householder
illatom	adopted son-in-law in Andhra
jāti	caste
jñāna	knowledge (especially esoteric or mystical knowledge)
karma	action or ritual, action seen as involving retribution in the form of transcendental or occult effects
karma-kāṇḍa	the aspect of the *śāstra* which prescribes actions and abstentions
kratvartha	having the sacrifice, or ritual, as its purpose or object
laukika	worldly, secular
lipsā	acquisitiveness
mantra	formula, spell
maṭha (mutt)	seminary
mīmāṃsaka	scholar in hermeneutics
mleccha	non-Hindu
mokṣa	'release', salvation from rebirth and sin
nivṛtti	cessation from being subject to *karma*
niyama	rule, regulation of an action
nyāya	logic, reason, maxim
pāpa	sin (whether or not also a crime)
phala	'fruit', result of an act or ritual, reward
piṇḍa	'body', aggregate, rice-ball
prajā	subjects (of a king)
pratiloma	unnatural (of caste-relation of parents of a child)
pravṛtti	continuance (in search of *phala*)
prāyaścitta	repentance, penance
purāṇa	'history', mythology
puruṣārtha	having the individual as its purpose or object
rāja	ruler, king
sagotra	having the same *gotra*
samaya	convention, agreement
saṅgha	community (especially of monks)
sannyāsī (or 'sanyāsī')	ascetic, one who has renounced the world

sapiṇḍa	close relation, within seven degrees on the father's side or five on the mother's[1]
sapravara	having the same *pravara* or *catena* of names of sages in the pedigree
śāsana	order, decree, grant
śāstra	see *dharmaśāstra*
śāstrī	scholar or professor of the *śāstra*
śiṣṭa	'disciplined', cultured person
smṛti	'recollection', verse or treatise of traditional learning
śrāddha	ceremony in commemoration of and for the feeding of spirits of ancestors
śruti	the Vedas, scripture
sthiti	determination, compromise, decree
śūdra	member of the fourth *varna*
sunna	practice and sayings of the Prophet of Islam
sūtra	aphorism, series of aphorisms
svatva	own-ness, proprietary right
vaiśya	member of the third *varṇa*
varṇa	class, super-category of castes
vidhi	injunction
vyavahāra	'business', litigation
vyāvahārika	recognized by the court
vyavasthā	determination, settlement, opinion
yama	rule, observance
zamīndār	'land-holder', revenue-payer

[1] The degrees are counted inclusively by ascent *and* descent, thus the father's father's father's son's son's son is, according to the Hindu method of computation, a *sapiṇḍa* in the *fourth* degree. A mother's mother's mother's mother's ancestor's descendant, however near or remote by any method of computation, is not a *sapiṇḍa*, being beyond the fifth degree. The Hindu Marriage Act, 1955, introduced a new method of computation and, more significantly, new limits for sapiṇḍaship for marriage: five degrees on the father's side and three on the mother's. Sapiṇḍaship for succession to property is abolished by the Hindu Succession Act, 1956, but sapiṇḍaship for pollution remains untouched in the religious law—see p. 314 below.

PREFACE

The maintenance of Indo-British friendship, according to Lord Butler, should be one of the important objectives of peace-lovers today. Indo-American friendship is no less valuable. But why? Not because India is to be feared, surely. From India something is to be expected which cannot be obtained from elsewhere, something elusive and hard to describe. Writers are increasingly aware of this; publications about India (always numerous) are growing into a flood.[1] The great question, whether India is being 'westernized' and if so with what effect (will it diminish our expectation?), remains an enigma. Enigmas abound in this, the world's greatest democracy, a democracy in which something we affect to value, the principle of equality, does not appear to exist. India calls herself a 'secular state', but a recent symposium of leading Indian statesmen and lawyers[2] reveals some confusion of thought and a

[1] The India Office Library Accessions Lists show the receipt of an average of about thirty-five books on or about India each month. In view of this output the large number of works about India or by Indians on Indian themes reviewed in the *Times Literary Supplement* is not disproportionate.

[2] G. S. Sharma, ed., *Secularism: Its Implications for Law and Life in India* (Bombay, Tripathi for the Indian Law Institute, 1966). The symposium (called 'seminar') was organized at New Delhi in November 1965. The editor says, 'Secularism emerged in the West as a concept antagonistic to religion and as a by-product of materialism and industrialization. The problem of secularism in India is how such a peculiarly intellectual and scientifically empirical concept can be made viable in a community subject to mass illiteracy, superstition and the all-inclusive hold of religion' (p. i). 'For secularism to thrive in India it is necessary to find proper institutions through which the economic motivations of the individual could be channelled into other interest-group organizations. It is hoped that as society becomes economically better ordered and merit and skill become the criteria of selection for jobs in industry and government, the religious motivations will gradually disappear.' P. B. Gajendragadkar (the then Chief Justice of India) said (p. 6), 'Secularism has a very vital impact on the structure of castes which distinguish the Hindu community. Castes are regarded by orthodox Hindus as a religious institution, and this notion has

failure to agree as to the country's fundamental aims with reference to the future status of religion *vis-à-vis* law, except in negative terms. The speakers, some of whom were extremely able, played their roles: what they wanted to say was relevant to the theme and perhaps to the circumstances. Yet the one really outstanding academic approach to the topic neglected the psychology of the Indian people, with which any legal propositions must accord if they are to mean anything at all. To see what India is really doing, one needs the distance of a far planet–one must see all India at a glance and her neighbours not less–and the magnification and steadiness of a microscope. Without access to the grass roots of the civilization one remains at the mercy of the hopes, the apprehensions, and, at times, the self-deception of the vocal classes of educated Indians, whose lack of faith in themselves and fear of criticism or implied criticism from foreigners are, if understandable, depressing. Their addiction to academic works devoted to description (usually uncritical and uncomparative) of the ancient Indian civilization[1] is a symptom of the desperate belief that a rosy view of the past matters as much as, if not more than, an objective committal to the present. And while knowledge of detail is so insecure, a rosy view may as plausibly be taken as any other. The present writer hoped to describe from time to time, for the benefit of those who knew relatively little about

to be completely eradicated if secularism is going to have its full impact on the social structure of the Hindus. . . . It is in that sense that (the) Hindu Code has played a major role in revolutionizing the outlook of the Hindu community in relation to the secular character of personal law.' A. R. Blackshield at p. 11 points out that 'it is perfectly possible to advocate *both* secularism *and* religion'. His rather discursive paper seems, to judge from the minutes of the symposium, to have had little effect on the participants. The very limited notions entertained by many are illustrated at p. 228: 'How effectively has secularism been concretized in India became manifest during the conflict with Pakistan during August–September 1965. . . . The Muslim and other religious minority groups have been in the forefront both in the battlefields and in the civilian defence effort. That the unity and strength of India lies in secularism, and that the adoption of the secular ideal and its pursuit through numerous measures, constitutional, legal, economic and social is the only wise course to a multi-religious society like the Indian, has been amply proved.'

[1] A recent specimen is Sudhākar Chattopādhyaya, *Social Life in Ancient India* (Calcutta, Academic Publishers, 1965).

India or, in any event, about those aspects of India, features of the Indian civilization not usually touched by the general historian. Perhaps they may have stimulated particular reflections, for, to his surprise, he has been asked to reprint some of them in a more convenient form.

This is, therefore, a volume of collected papers, and yet it is something more. Chapters 3 to 12 were published in various periodicals; particulars are given at the commencement of each. The writer owes thanks to the editors and/or proprietors of the journals concerned, for their permission to reprint so much as has been printed. Chapters 13 and 14 were written for this volume but out of material previously gathered and used in somewhat different forms. Chapter 15 was compiled for this volume since, although it is concerned with the perplexing topic of the future of the personal law of Muslims in India, its main object is to prefigure in some manner the Indian Civil Code which Art. 44 of the Constitution of India promises and a few lively minds in India are already envisaging. If such a Code comes to be passed the dimensions of contact between religion and the State in India will suddenly be greatly narrowed. Meanwhile Chapters 1 and 2, and naturally 16 (the Conclusion), were written to subserve the collection itself.

To sketch therein the academic background of the research studies would have been to produce an encyclopedia. Both religion and law are woven into the material of Indian life, and make such elaborate and apparently changing patterns that observers vie with each other in eschewing generalizations while yearning for certainty. To cover all aspects of the background would be beyond the competence of the writer. But some background needed to be written in for the much more modest purpose of showing from what standpoint the author writes.

But some clarification is needed at this point: for that standpoint does not explain the motive or content of the individual research chapters. It throws light on the way these chapters are now seen by their author with fresh eyes. For they now tell, in series, a different tale from that which they told singly, a tale which now surprises their author, who has frequently expressed himself in another sense. The real continuity of Hinduism into the present age, and the significance of historical Hindu methods and presuppositions in an age when Hindus appear to be 'westernized', struck the writer only when the material he had previously gathered was tied up in this bundle.

This would seem to argue a strange blindness. India's nature and history, like her future, are perplexing. Could she so deceive one who had used his microscope at various times and for various purposes? Indeed she could, and yet may. Her contradictions baffle her own scholars, who, as Mr. Nirad C. Chaudhuri has emphasized somewhat ungracefully,[1] prefer, if they can, to look at their own culture through foreign eyes (of a past generation, of course).

The reader will grasp that the research chapters were not written in order to prove any thesis or to make any case, still less to form parts of a hypothetical composite volume. The argumentative tone to be detected occasionally is therefore a matter of style. A quasi-polemical tone both suits Indian readers and attracts the attention of non-Indians who are currently more fashionably engaged in other problems, in other areas of the world, or on other lines of enquiry even if they be Indian. The point is worth the mention, since the aim was to give information, rather than to nourish an established appetite –for no such appetite existed in 1953 when the first of the series was written. And curiosity about the thread that joins the 'Old' India to the 'New', a curiosity which should have sinews tough enough to wrestle with tedious and multitudinous details, must still be fostered.

The author hopes that students and former students, not merely of Indology but also of political science and sociology, and also perhaps a particularly patient kind of historian, will take up the real materials of Indian legal experience and expression, and occupy themselves at first hand with the texts (if only with the aid of translations). As a teacher this writer firmly believes in students' involving themselves with their materials–an experience from which they are bound not to emerge unaffected. Just as no one can become an engineer without occasionally getting his hands dirty with machinery, so a student of Indian society and its history is deceiving himself if

[1] For the author's work see below, p. 571. Apart from those observations it is fair to draw attention to the unconscious and unexplained obsession with India which this writer and lesser examples of the same phenomenon manifest.

he confines himself to what is written at second hand or listens to Indians of this generation chatting about themselves. One cannot know a river by merely stepping into its waters, but there is a sense in which one knows it better so than by studying a map. The repellent features of Indian legal materials (a character they fully share with legal materials anywhere) disperse before an enquirer who has made up his mind to find out at first hand what was going on. So in revising these articles the writer allowed the bulk of the references to remain and even added others, particularly those relating to more recent materials. The references are not placed where they are to give an impression of what is often quaintly called 'scholarship', but to invite the serious reader to go into the sources and see things for himself.

The opportunity for revision was particularly pleasing since some obscurities of style have been ironed out, errors have been corrected, and the typing, retyping and printing mistakes which overseas editors have sometimes encouraged by their failure or even refusal to supply proofs or otherwise failed to detect have been eliminated. Again, when any author is trying to attract attention to a relatively neglected field he often crosses the same ground, for one who wishes to be heard above the din of other people's discussions must needs repeat himself. It would be surprising if the same topic did not recur. The field was crossed from several widely divergent angles, and points reappeared more obtrusively than could have happened had the field been observed at once. While stringing these chapters upon their thread the writer narrowed repetitions considerably and great use is made of cross-references. The original articles are to these extents virtually superseded, with the possible exception of the article on religious endowments in India which appeared in Donald E. Smith's *South Asian Politics and Religion* (1966). That article, though written from a point of view now abandoned by its author, retains a quantity of instances and perhaps a verve of expression not reproduced in the chapter into which corresponding material has been inserted here.

It is important to have confidence in the adequate pronunciation of foreign words and diacritical marks have been used wherever it was felt that the pronunciation was significant.[1]

[1] I have written 'Rāmmohun' for 'Rāma-mohana' by way of compromise, as we know how the celebrated reformer spelt his name.

These marks are not needed for the names of parties in litigation: no one will care if these labels are mispronounced, for it is the volume and page which counts. In the interests of space the citations in the more heavily annotated chapters have been reduced to the names of the first party only, a convention normally observed in writing on criminal law. In the same interests all the citations have been pruned to a proportion of the parties' names which strictly ought to have been reproduced in their original prolixity.

All authors cited in this book may be traced in the index. The bibliographical appendix tells the general reader where he may find most reliably the bulk of the information along the main lines of enquiry covered by this volume. A warning is first needed against the interpretation of their history by such Indian writers of the first half of this century who have not adopted the 'dry as dust' style. Epigraphists, general historians and sociologists had not become used to pooling their skills, and the Anglo-Indian models, such as they were, were virtually the only ones available. Indians are acutely conscious of the reaction of their compatriots to anything which amounts, however inferentially, to criticism–unless it be criticism of an established Aunt Sally, like the caste-system; they find it difficult to believe that their subtle and cryptic civilization can possibly be understood by a foreigner (and not without reason); and yet they aim to supply (as is all too natural) work that superficially resembles contemporary European literature on vaguely comparable topics. An Indian writer will sometimes reflect: 'They like originality. Let us see what original thing can be said about this old matter?' One might refer to the frank Mr. Chaudhuri, who says what any observer can confirm but few have liked to point out, namely that the Indian scholar who deals with Indian topics looks over both shoulders, desiring to be commended by his countrymen for fearless patriotism[1] and

[1] K. A. Nīlakanta Sāstrī, *Studies in Coḷa History and Administration* (Madras, 1932), at p. 98, comments, '. . . to cast a doubt on the democratic nature of ancient Indian society and government is no longer a mortal sin against patriotism'. The writer is in a class by himself as a historian and such remarks, some way ahead of their time, struck the right note when they were written. See R. S. Sharmā, 'Historiography of the ancient Indian social order', in C. H. Philips, ed., *Historians of India, Pakistan and Ceylon* (London, Oxford University Press, 1961).

to be accepted by non-Indians (however inexpert) as a fellow savant and writer. The result of this over the years has been unfair to Indian studies, for the days of European hegemony in Indology are over and the true heirs to the great ones of the past have still to find their feet. Encouragement from the West has still its part to play. This writer hopes that his own participation proves that he is in the battle alongside his Indian colleagues. The tone of gentle mockery which he occasionally adopts is intended only to portend that objectivity which must sooner or later emerge, in which all students of India, whatever their provenance, will be at one.

Meanwhile the bibliographical appendix seeks to indicate where substantial and reliable references to original materials are to be found, and this note has served to put the reader on enquiry as to the motives and limitations of the respective authors.

The merits of the study of India are not prejudiced by the adhesive or agglutinative tendency of Indian scholars and writers, whose powers of expression develop as they become aware of our attention to them. It is the agglutinative power (as contrasted with the de-racination which other races experience, when exposed to the attractions of another culture) which makes Indians, their culture and their contemporary predicaments especially intriguing. They are intriguing to themselves, as Indian observers with genuine academic qualifications abundantly show. And they intrigue the remainder of the world, for though India is sometimes, understandably, accused of being a parrot kept by western Powers, her own nature and identity remain secure, though garbed, it would seem, in a borrowed wardrobe. Indians, though unmovably oriental, are yet not inscrutable asiatics. If they were these present efforts would be in vain. There are Asian societies with whom discussions are impossible or futile: India meets us more than half way. The people's own charm and unique dignity is matched by naturalness, spontaneity and an instinctive desire to 'relate' to the one who approaches. Indian tolerance of oddities and broadness of sympathy are proverbial. The ability to adjust to the novel environment and the novel idea, without abandoning the original standpoint, is unique. Modifications in colour do not affect the substance. The Indian is in no danger of losing his

Indianness. The ability to adjust to environment or ideology was present already when Alexander the Great visited what is now Pakistan, was a remarkable feature of Kerala when the Portuguese rediscovered it (indeed they are the original Utopians of Sir Thomas More's *Utopia*),[1] and can be experienced by any visitor for himself. And these qualities were not acquired overnight or for nothing. They were born of the family, the caste, the village, and the vast plains and the pitiless climate. The Indian characteristics, including their more attractive features, were bred out of the sorrows of civilization in that peninsula, which no other area resembles.

Dialogues with India are real dialogues, provided the 'selves' of our partners are understood. A work which purports to disclose or declare what some of the fundamentals of those 'selves' are should have a place in current research. And so the writer sends his studies off once again, this time in each other's company, hoping that they will, because of (and not in spite of) their abundance of detail, contribute to the discovery of a far too little known aspect of the real India.

[1] Derrett, 'Thomas More and Joseph the Indian', *J.R.A.S.*, 1962, pp. 18–34; 'Gemistus Plethon, the Essenes, and More's *Utopia*', *Bibliothèque d'Humanisme et Renaissance*, 27 (1965), 579–606.

INTRODUCTION

The emperor Aśoka, the famous 'missionary-Caesar' of India, the 'Indian Constantine' as he is sometimes called, ruled in the third century B.C. His edicts, inscribed on pillars and rocks some in the heart and some at the edges of his vast empire,[1] have an ethical motive and it has been posited with some plausibility that he was trying by these means to outshine his contemporaries further westwards, whose inscriptions record less exalted principles. If this is true, and the style of the recently found bilingual inscription appears to confirm it,[2]

[1] New finds of Aśokan edicts were reported from within India and from Afghanistan in 1966. The very remarkable ideas propounded and evidently transmuted into an ideology of the State entirely justify the large bibliography devoted to Aśoka and the Mauryans. N. A. Nikam and Richard McKeon, *The Edicts of Asoka* (University of Chicago Press, 1966) is the handiest and most suitable introduction to the sources and their implications. It has a good bibliography at p. xxii. To this may be added Sachchidānanda Bhaṭṭāchārya, *Select Asokan Epigraphs* (Calcutta, K. L. Mukhopadhyay, 1960) and P. H. L. Eggermont and J. Hoftijzer, *The Moral Edicts of King Aśoka* (Textus Minores, 29) (Leiden, Brill, 1962) which contains the texts without translation. Aśoka was concerned to protect all religions, but so far as Buddhism was concerned he prescribed texts for study (!) (Bhabra Rock Edict), and threatened those that would disrupt any *saṅgha* (Sanchi and Sarnath Pillar Edicts). Judicial officials must conquer their defects in order to administer justice mildly but efficiently: otherwise they are threatened with failure to attain heaven or the king's favour (in that order). Aśoka's desire for moral conquest (*dharma-vijaya*) rather than other kinds of conquest is echoed in the modern outlook of such enlightened Hindus as are concerned with international relations. Of some of the edicts it could be said as H. N. Sinha said of Aśoka (in *Sovereignty in Ancient Indian Polity*, London, 1938, p. 188): 'when he branded certain ceremonies as "useless" and "vulgar", and prohibited the slaughter of animals even for sacrifices, he certainly encroached upon the religious freedom and the liberty of conscience of a large part of the people'. But would this be entirely accurate (see p. 559 below)?

[2] G. P. Carratelli, etc., *Bilingual Graeco-Aramaic edict . . . , new edition* (Rome, 1964) (reviewed by T. R. Trautmann in *J.R.A.S.*, 1966, 1–2, pp. 75–7). Professor Zeph Stewart of Harvard opined (in a lecture delivered in London, May 16th, 1966) that Darius' usage was the model, and compared the inscription of Antiochus at Commagene.

Aśoka seems to have been successful, since his fame rests more on his ethical, perhaps even philosophical, reputation than on his martial prowess. Was Aśoka a freak, a 'sport' amongst Indian rulers? He admonished his subjects and his royal neighbours to obey *dharma* ('righteousness') and made provision for his subjects to be taught what this meant. He set an example himself, abstaining from eating flesh, abstaining from injuring living beings. This is what the classical jurisprudence says the king must do: he must secure the performance of their *dharma-s* by all classes of people (and it is of no importance for our present purpose whether *varṇa* or caste is a factor in the identification of *dharma*), and must set a good example by his own regularity and sincerity. It was obviously of importance to Aśoka that his people should reverence the things he reverenced; and as a self-constituted missionary-prince he sought to send the light of the religion he favoured, Buddhism, a reformed and systematized Hindu faith accompanied by advanced social ideas, to contemporaries abroad as well as to the remotest corners of his own dominions. His sense was unerring. He sent ambassadors of the faith to Greece; as the devotees of Rāmakṛṣṇa Paramahaṃsa in the nineteenth century sent Svāmī Vivekānanda to America. The boundaries of his own dominions received like attention. The State supported Righteousness in numerous highly practical respects, including provisions of a charitable character. That is to say, it did so if we are to believe Aśoka's inscriptions, which we are bound to do unless we are to suppose that they were cut, read and protected in spite of their being a fraud.

The former President of India, Dr. S. Rādhākrishnan, whose sincerity in religious and philosophical matters no one doubts,[1] and whose writings have immense influence within and outside India,[2] displays the Indian conscience in a particular light.

[1] His principal works are *The Hindu View of Life*, *Eastern Religions and Western Thought*, and *Indian Philosophy*, all of which have appeared in more than one edition.

[2] Within India Rādhākrishnan has been less eagerly acclaimed as an Indian philosopher than as a successful propagandist for India abroad; but for his place in the Hindu law relative to the question of 'Hinduness' see below, p. 50. Outside India his work is the subject of secondary investigations and compilations, e.g. P. A. Schilpp, *The Philosophy of Sarvepalli Radhakrishnan* (New York, Tudor Publishing Co., 1952); Surjit Singh, *Preface to Personality: Christology in relation to Radhakrishnan's Philosophy*

'Indian' means, virtually, 'Hindu', as in practice no member of the minority communities cares vigorously to debate–for other reasons, evidently, than the malice or pusillanimity that Mr. Chaudhuri attributes to them. To Dr. Rādhākrishnan it is past doubt but that the greatest wisdom and experience of the West at best merely cross some t's and dot a few i's of Indian traditional beliefs, which in essentials anticipate every advantage that western thought can offer, and excel the West in religious insight. Dr. Rādhākrishnan has placed his view on record, with all the weight of his personal and official authority, in his Foreword to the last volume of Dr. P. V. Kāṇe's monumental *History of Dharmaśāstra*, that the Parliament of modern India, enacting laws for the amendment and codification of the formerly religious law of the Hindus, is entitled morally as well as legally to the obedience and faith to which the laws of the ancient sages of Hinduism were entitled.[1]

The State in India from the time of Aśoka, and perhaps earlier, to the days in which we live has never been afraid to

(Madras, Christian Literature Society, 1952); S. J. Samartha, *Introduction to Radhakrishnan: the Man and his Thought* (New York, Association Press, 1964); Horst Buerkle, *Dialog mit dem Osten. Radhakrishnans neuhinduistische Botschaft. ...* (Stuttgart, 1965).

[1] 'When Manu (I. 85) tells us that different customs prevailed in different ages he suggests that the social code is not a fixed but a flexible one. Social customs and institutions are subject to change. Yājñavalkya tells us that "one should not practise that which, though ordained by the *Smṛti*, is condemned by the people". [See below p. 90, n. 1] What appeals to one's conscience, *ātmanas tuṣṭiḥ*, the conscience of the disciplined, not of the superficial, the forms which the elect praise, should be our standard. Vital changes may be introduced in the habits of the people by *pariṣads* or assemblies of the learned. When such assemblies cannot be constituted even the decision of one learned in *dharma* will be authoritative. The *Āpastamba Dharmasūtra* says: *dharmajña-samayaḥ pramāṇam* ["the Council of knowers of *dharma* is authoritative"]. People who are learned and compassionate, who are practical-minded can decide the issues of right and wrong. They are the conscience of the community. What we are doing by legislative enactments is consistent with our tradition.' It is doubtful whether *ātmanas tuṣṭiḥ* as a source of law actually operated as the learned President here suggests; nor is it certain that the rule cited from Āpastamba was originally intended to provide for an abrogation of established rules of *dharma*, rather than to provide for *lacunae* or the resolution of conflicts between *smṛti-s*. But the proposition that the state may determine what is law within the general framework of *dharma* is genuinely traditional. For M. C. Chagla's view of parliamentary competence see below, p. 557, n. 3.

speak of Righteousness in terms of Law and of Law in terms of Righteousness. A law which cannot speak the language of righteousness can naturally fail to claim obedience, and persons adept at manipulating law may still live not without honour, because they have not necessarily lived unrighteously. The tension between the custom which expresses righteousness close at hand, and the enacted law which expresses a higher but more remote righteousness is ever present and is unresolved. The theme is apt for imaginative writing and the three novels of the Oriya writer Phakīrmohan Senāpati (1843–1918) which are devoted to the subject of justice betray the author's and his readers' preoccupation with the tortures suffered by men who know *dharma*, *karma-phala* ('fruits of *karma*, the accumulated transcendental effects of action'), and *pāpa* ('sin-crime'), and believe in all of them, but have not quite accepted society's official claim that Anglo-Indian law and justice have to do with transcendental realities.[1]

Judges of various faiths have in fact, whatever their personal consciences, never shirked the task of administering, especially in matters of great delicacy, rules of law which are based, or claim to be based, or are thought to be based upon religious principles or upon precepts which have, or appear to have, the authority of religion behind them. The awkward current dichotomy between belief and practice (which some would-be reformers of Islamic law in India have referred to hopefully)[2]–itself hardly a traditional dichotomy in India, is handled by them expertly. Meanwhile a law teacher, dissatisfied with a piece of

[1] Mr. J. V. Boulton kindly supplies the following information. In *Cha māṇa Āṭha Guṇṭha* (1897) the central character, Maṅgarāja, is extolled by ironical appeals to quasi-legal arguments, which indirectly attack British, or rather Anglo-Indian notions of justice. Under the temporal law Maṅgarāja, though vicious and unprincipled, gets off almost scot-free; but violent ends indicate the nemesis brought by *dharma*. Under the old system culprits were brought to justice; now clever rich men with the aid of lawyers were committing crimes with impunity. The author turns his back on Anglo-Indian justice and its narrow conception of crime in the later novels, *Māmũ* and *Prāyaścitta*. In his view the old semi-feudalistic system where law, religion and finance formed a unity was an ideal to which India should return. A virtuous *zamīndār* who dispenses justice to his tenants and loans them money at low interest suggests that Rāma-rājya (the Golden Age of *dharma*) has already arrived.

[2] See below, p. 534.

legislation amending the sacred laws of the Hindus, tells us (with what verisimilitude the reader may imagine) that a return to the *dharmaśāstra*, whose rules have not been practised for at least seven centuries, would command the obedience of the people when the Acts of Parliament do not.[1] That such a notion can be written up and published in a leading legal periodical tells it own tale.

The question whether India is a secular state has occupied many minds. Professor Donald E. Smith and Dr. V. P. Luthera have drawn attention eloquently to the discrepancies between the implications of the word 'secular' (which, as an English word, is supposed to have a meaning appropriate to its Anglo-Saxon provenance) and the facts of modern Indian law and life.[2] Far too readily it is assumed that India, having adopted the word 'secular' for its present condition, ought to study what 'secular' means or ought to mean, and then put that into practice! That would indeed be a strange proceeding, though the principle that the State can determine what its philosophy should be and that the citizen (i.e. what in the old Indian literatures were called the *prajā*, the 'subjects') should accept this obediently is nowhere denied. What is often forgotten is that, whatever the citizen accepts or thinks he accepts, nothing will actually emerge in fact which is inconsistent with the ancient and traditional values, and these are consistent with 'secularism' in a wholly unique, Indian, sense.

In reality India is a multi-religious state in which various faiths, which are in some points incompatible, are entitled to the protection of their religious laws to limited extents. The limits are set by the inescapable fact that each must live, and not merely co-exist, with the others. A multi-religious conglomeration of peoples can allow great freedom of religion, since the very fact of multi-religiosity proves the seriousness with which the majority accept the validity, for the whole, of the sincere beliefs of the minorities. This tolerance does not spring from

[1] V. N. Capoor, Lecturer at the Nagpur University College of Law, 'Rights of the unmarried daughter in father's property under the Hindu law', AIR 1966 Journ. 63–5.

[2] D. E. Smith, *India as a Secular State* (Princeton University Press, 1963). V. P. Luthera, *The Concept of the Secular State and India* (Calcutta, Oxford University Press, 1964). The latter work is usefully reviewed by Professor Hugh Tinker at *B.S.O.A.S.*, 29, pt. 2 (1966), p. 406.

indifference, but from the Hindu attitude to faith, about which more must be said in the appropriate place. But the society as a whole cannot tolerate practices, however associated with religion, which are repugnant to the concept of the society. Since the so-called 'secular state' itself is a recent and still evolving creation, and since even from its inception it was the child of imported notions and prescriptions, it is not surprising that it does not really know what it is, and that the distinction between description and wishful thinking is not evident. This is why the works which concentrate upon holding up the mirror of fact to the Indian self-consciousness have a valuable function, and Smith's and Luthera's books were carefully studied by the symposium to which allusion has already been made.

At this point the question will arise whether law and legal history is a valid path of approach to these problems. Surely law, and especially law since the European powers assumed governmental roles in India, is artificial and fictional? The free flowing of opinion, or, to take the opposite example, the half-conscious presuppositions of 'typical' villagers and villages might be better keys to the Indian mind. To evaluate legal rules in terms of their social reality is, moreover, the task traditionally for the sociologist, not the lawyer. Nice distinctions seem to the uninitiated to exist for the lawyers' employment (as if laymen would do any better). The dry and apparently lifeless formulae, living, if at all, in the activity known as 'adhering to precedent' have few attractions for those not already committed to law. This is why the study of the relations between religion in India and Indian law remains to be tackled comprehensively–and indeed in the chapters that follow some aspects (notably that of caste)[1] are very barely handled. Yet, surely, this was always a possible way of sorting opinions and feelings from fact? As Indian art is convoluted and rococo, and its classical poetry loaded with tiring conceits, it is no coincidence that its law tells a minutely varied tale, so that the material fits the culture. The search for generalizations is indefinitely prolonged: which, most Indologists will comment, is as it should be. But this variety and complexity leads to, and is concerned with, *fact*. In a country

[1] M. Galanter, 'The religious aspects of caste: a legal view', in D. E. Smith, ed., *South Asian Politics and Religion* (Princeton University Press, 1966), pp. 277–310, is highly informative.

where people say and sometimes even think what is expected of them, to find the level at which religion lies in the population cannot be the work of a casual diviner: but law is an index to usage. Law shows what people do and suffer whether they like it or not. The actual decision, more than the reasons which led, or appeared to lead to it, tells us what is going on. Every decision causes money to flow in some direction. How India's law is shaped or shapes itself tells us about her character and her real beliefs–irrespective of her pretensions. What touches the bottom of the purse is not far from the bottom of the heart.

We cannot confine our enquiry to the India of 1967: we must start far off in the earliest strata of Indian history which present materials upon which we can rely with confidence. And before we plunge into the curious history of the *dharmaśāstra* with which all such investigations should start we must define our primary terms and take a distant planet's view of the Indian character and religion's place in it.

I

DEFINITIONS

The definition of 'State' presents no problem: as far as we are concerned 'State' means the governmental organization of India, whereby laws, including legally sanctioned regulations and by-laws, are made and enforced. 'Law', too, is easily defined in a manner familiar to the common lawyers, with whom all lawyers of modern India are in agreement. 'Law' is that aggregate or totality of rules which are or may be enforced upon the subject by the courts of the State. Thus the customs enforced by caste tribunals are not normally 'law', whatever relations law properly so called may have with such or any other customs. The definition of 'religion' is a serious problem which will detain us for some while.

Religion

Law is quite capable of providing a definition of 'religion', and, as we shall see, of making a subtle but effective distinction between it and 'superstition'. Law, as we shall see, protects 'religion' in various contexts, but will not undertake to support 'superstition'. The nature and source of this distinction must be investigated in the proper place. We are hindered here, as so often, by the fact that law does not commence with preconceived principles exhaustively defining and explaining: it has to be inferred from myriads of instances, each of which was decided on its own facts and with reference to its own issues, with the aid of principles or alleged principles put forward by the judges in defence of the attitude which they sometimes adopt quite independently of any conscious principle.[1] Therefore in

[1] In *Imperial Chemical Industries, Ltd.* v. *Shatwell* [1964] 2 All E.R.999, 1005 Viscount Radcliffe said, 'My Lords, it sometimes helps to assess the merits of a decision, if one starts by noticing its results and only after doing that

this book the word 'religion' is not used in any sense understood by any particular judge or judges, but in the author's own sense.

In his view it is a mistaken starting-point to suppose that 'religion' contains an evaluative element. To say 'my observances are religious whilst yours are only superstitious', is to betray the common error of supposing that 'religion' is a commendatory term. There is no doubt but that in a society which has emerged beyond the single tribe it is axiomatic that religious principles and observances which do not harm or offend others must be respected. This does not mean that they must be accepted intellectually. Nor does it mean, as the Hindu outlook has suggested so often, that all religious observances have 'more or less' the same spiritual value and purpose. This is a charitable notion manifesting the Hindu's humane approach to all such problems. Evaluation of a religious belief or observance is certainly possible, perhaps desirable in those who have the necessary talent, but such a belief or observance which is condemned as irrational or absurd does not cease to be religious in *this* writer's view. The definition must relate to the kind of thing, not its appeal, its rationality, its history, or its capacity of attracting another person's sympathy.

The definition in the Oxford English Dictionary which would deny the status of 'religion' to any belief or observance which is founded upon fear or ignorance must therefore be abandoned. In this writer's view 'religion' is not in any way dependent for its nature upon informed opinion, the absence of fear, or indeed 'knowledge' of any kind. The source of the belief, and the authority behind the observance, and, what is much more important, the content and nature of the belief or observance have nothing to do with it. The expression 'higher religion' can be used by those who have a need for it: they are intent upon evaluating, upon praise or blame if only by implication. In this book, however, 'religion' means merely–

> *Recognition* (conscious or unconscious) of a force or power outside man or men, not subject to the control of a man or men, which is nevertheless in a constant relation to a man or men,
>
> which recognition, as a fact, manifests itself in thought action or absten-

allots to it the legal principles on which it is said to depend.' This is quoted with interesting comment by Mr. Justice M. Madhavan Nair in a very frank article entitled 'About the judicial process', [1966] K.L.T., *J*, 1–4.

tion from action in order that (*a*) a benefit may accrue, whether seen, unseen or both, whether in this life openly or secretly or in some other life of state of being, by reason of the thought, action, etc., or (*b*) evil may be averted, whether seen, unseen or both, whether in this life, etc., or (*c*) both benefit may accrue and evil may be averted.

No system, no philosophy is a prerequisite. No priests, no ritual, no temples, no scriptures are necessary. But recognition can take many forms, and may, and indeed usually does develop the aids supplied by all of these–and it is only in our half of this century that religion without props or aids is beginning to be visualized as not only more real but probably more helpful. The distinction between religion and superstition is difficult to find on this footing. And in this book, until chapter 13, no such distinction will be made.

If a European throws salt over his shoulder if some is accidentally spilt, or touches wood after expressing a hope, this is usually said to be a superstition. It is really, from this author's standpoint, a survival of an ancient religion which the doer of the act acknowledged when he performed an observance which betrayed a recognition of the kind set out above. Whether this is inconsistent with his professed beliefs drawn from another systematic religion is neither here nor there. Thus Hindus who slaughter buffaloes or pour oil upon stones in the belief that merit will accrue to them or others would be none the less engaged in a religious activity even if they have conscious knowledge that Hinduism, as a book-religion, knows nothing of these acts. For Jainas to pour a mixture of milk and other fluids over gigantic images may be an absurdity and a waste of valuable objects, but it is an act sanctioned by their religion. In both those cases religion is a 'recognition' which through centuries of use has drawn to itself intellectual and liturgical developments and aids, and has fitted itself out with a system. Multitudes of Hindu 'religions' form conglomerately 'the' Hindu religion. According to our present definition it is no less religious to deprive a child who has caught small-pox of medical care during a short period, out of deference to the goddess who manifests herself through the disease, than it is religious to believe that the god Veṅkaṭeśvara of Tirumalai will cure your muscular pain if you think of him and make a small vow to him. It is religious to abhor the slaughter of cows which are dying from want of pasture, and it is religious to leave money for the feeding of Brahmins who either could feed themselves or would be better employed learning how to do so. It is religious to recognize the force or power, whether the result is rational or irrational, whether it is obviously beneficial or obviously wasteful: and the price of religion must be high in a country which, like India, knows poverty and stress and strain in every one of her many joints. Perhaps this is the reason why songs and poems which express religion, sometimes in very baldly simple forms (as in the recitation of the names of a god), evoke powerful responses from the population as a whole, discriminating and undiscriminating alike.

This definition may have a substantive value, independently of its usefulness for a historical purpose. Much of the difficulty in modern discussions of 'freedom of religion' lies in the failure to observe that evaluation of a religion in terms of the one who 'recognizes', or of others, is irrelevant in a society where religion is a fact of existence; and upon that footing no system or attitude of a religious character has more claims to attention or to support than another. This would be the foundation of a secular state, indifferent to what support was given to any religion, and singling out none for special support. But discussions of whether India is a secular state or not are beside the point of this book.[1]

A person is 'religious', then, if he frequently 'recognizes'; but not particularly religious if he seldom recognizes. Belief in astrology and some kinds of clairvoyance will be religious within our definition, and the fact that the 'recognizer' has no systematic or logical explanation for his recognition makes no difference. At the other extreme one who believes that a teacher should be treated with awe, that one who maltreats his mother, even his adoptive mother, with disrespect is tainted with an unseen stain,[2] that hospitality is a debt (no matter how unde-

[1] The determination of what is meant by 'secular state' by referring to the practice of the United States, proceeding then to ask whether Indian practice agrees or conforms to this precedent, is a futile undertaking. The question, what do Indians mean when they call India a secular state, is legitimate and is to be answered without reference to non-Indian phenomena. See below, pp. 453–4. Also D. E. Smith at *C.S.S.H.*, 7, no. 2 (1965), pp. 166–72.

[2] The tone of a recent Calcutta case in which an adopted son maltreated his parents (the judgement proceeds with a kind of excited horror) is

serving the guest), and that a gift in charity confers no obligation on the taker is, whenever the belief expresses itself, recognizing the forces or powers in no more 'religious' a way –and yet no less–than the seekers for an oracle.

Personal Law

India is a land of personal laws. The 'personal law' is now the system of rules applicable by any court to an individual in respect of the topics covered by that law, determined by reference to the religion which he professes or purports to profess or is presumed to profess; for the law determines what a man's religious affiliation is for purposes of application of the personal law by methods peculiar to itself. As the Privy Council remarked in the celebrated case of *Skinner* v. *Orde*[1] in 1871: 'While Brahmin, Buddhist, Christian, Mahomedan, Parsee, and Sikh are one nation, enjoying equal political rights and having perfect equality before the Tribunals, they co-exist as separate and very distinct communities, having distinct laws affecting every relation of life. The law of Husband and Wife, parent and child, the descent, devolution, and disposition of property are all different, depending, in each case, on the body to which the individual is deemed to belong; and the difference of religion pervades and governs all domestic usages and social relations.' The personal law goes with him, within the territories where it is part of the law of the land,[2] and he is entitled to have it applied and not the law which would be applied in respect of the local land, or other property within the jurisdiction, to persons professing some other personal law, or subject to the residual law (if any), or even that same personal law as declared by a court other than the court of his domicile.[3] Shortly, there is no *lex loci* in India with regard to the topics for which personal law provides.[4] These are in general the family law, with especial reference to marriage and succession.

instructive: *Nanda* v. *Bhupendra* AIR 1966 Cal. 181. On the teacher-pupil relationship see *Deputy* v. *S. M. College* AIR 1962 All. 207.

[1] 14 M.I.A. 309, 323.

[2] Derrett, *Introduction to Modern Hindu Law* (Bombay, Oxford University Press, 1963), §. 26. *Balwant Rao* v. *Baji Rao* (1920) 47 I.A. 213.

[3] See below, p. 529, n. 2.

[4] Mayne, *Hindu Law and Usage*[11], pp. 89–90. *Mitar Sen Singh* v. *Maqbul Hasan Khan* (1930) 57 I.A. 313 (where the property of a Muslim converted

Parsi law is the system applied to Parsis, who are Parsi Zoroastrians born of Parsi Zoroastrian parents or parents one of whom is a Parsi Zoroastrian.[1] Muhammadan law is the system which applies to a Muslim, that is to say one who is born or brought up as a Muslim or has made the Muslim profession of faith.[2] Jewish law is the personal law of the Jews,[3] of whichever community professing the Jewish faith, about the identity of which, in fact, no doubt has been raised. Christians do not have a personal law as such,[4] though their law of marriage, with special exceptions in the case of Christians domiciled in Kerala (a substantial proportion of Indian Christians), is codified in the Indian Christian Marriage Act[5] and the Indian Divorce Act.[6] The Parsis share with the Jews and Christians certain portions of the Indian Succession Act, whilst having certain sections devoted to themselves. They have their own marriage and divorce law.[7]

Hindu law is the personal law of 85 per cent of the population of India (we are not concerned here with Hindus overseas). The definition of Hindu law, if we ask to whom it is applicable, is extremely difficult and complicated. Perhaps we shall do well to

from Hinduism has passed according to Muhammadan law to his descendants, Hindu collaterals cannot claim by virtue of the Caste Disabilities Removal Act, 1850, to succeed under Hindu law).

[1] All Parsis are Zoroastrians. *Petit* v. *Jijibhai* (1909) 11 Bom. L.R. 85. See Phiroze K. Irani, 'The personal law of the Parsis of India', in J. N. D. Anderson, ed., *Family Law in Asia and Africa* (London, Allen and Unwin, 1968). In the Parsi Marriage and Divorce Act, 1936, s. 2 (7) the word 'Parsi' includes not only the Parsi Zoroastrians of India but also Zoroastrians of Iran, whether they are domiciled or merely resident in India: *Jamshed A. Irani* v. *Banu* (1960) 68 (*sic*) Bom. L.R. 794 (where Mody, J., refused to follow *Yezdiar* v. *Yezdiar* (1950) 52 Bom. L.R. 876 on the ground that adequate evidence was not heard and a new issue was tried by the appellate court which had not been properly tried in the court of first instance).

[2] On conversion to Islam see F. B. Tyabji, *Muhammadan Law*[3], §. 9, pp. 54–9.

[3] See Derrett, 'Jewish law in Southern Asia', (1964) 13 *I.C.L.Q.* 288–301.

[4] Nevertheless the Canon law will be applied in connection with capacity to marry, in default of statutory provision.

[5] Act 15 of 1872. [6] Act 4 of 1869.

[7] The Parsi Marriage and Divorce Act of 1865 was repealed and replaced by the Parsi Marriage and Divorce Act of 1936, which sets up a special Parsi matrimonial court, the necessity of which in these days has been doubted (see Irani, cited above).

proceed in this fashion: first we shall ask to whom Hindu law is applicable and from there we may pass to consider who is a Hindu. Whether a person is a Muhammadan, a Parsi or a Jew for the purposes of application to him of a personal law is seldom a problem. There is seldom any doubt whether a person is a Christian for a similar purpose.[1] Within Hindu castes, however, there are persons who do not profess any religion, and there are some who are hostile to certain Hindu orthodox or traditional religious practices.[2] On the other hand there are persons having beliefs resembling those characteristic of Hindus who nevertheless belong to tribes which were or are imperfectly 'Hinduized'.[3] Such nice distinctions require care. It will be found that the clue to them is social rather than religious: but this does not by any means deprive the word 'Hindu' of a content in religious contexts. For Hindu public temples have been thrown open to the Hindu public, and a temple which is not a Hindu temple does not come within the scope of Temple Entry legislation.[4]

Hindu Law

Hindu law is applicable to those whom the law defines as 'Hindus'. It is not the *personal law* for the curious reason that by 'personal law' we invariably mean the Anglo-Hindu (as similarly, *mutandis mutatis*, the Anglo-Muhammadan) law which has been developed from the book-law of the pre-British period. In a general sense the personal law of a given Hindu may not be the *personal law* at all, but some mixture of rules in which the

[1] See below, p. 342, n. 1.

[2] Ārya Samājists, for example, for whose benefit the Arya Marriage Validation Act, 19 of 1937, was passed.

[3] Authorities are cited and distinguished at Derrett, *I.M.H.L.*, §. 18. One may add, however, that in *Mohari* v. *Mokaram* AIR 1963 Pat. 466 it was held that even if some members of a tribe profess to be Hindus it does not raise a presumption that the tribe is governed by Hindu law; while in *Mokka* v. *Ammakutti* (1927) 51 Mad. 1, 22–3, 29 FB., it was held that if the Hindu religion is professed and the persons professing it aim thereby to identify themselves with other Hindus the presumption *is* raised that Hindu law applies.

[4] By the series of statutes introducing Temple Entry (originally for the benefit exclusively of Harijans, formerly outcastes). See, for this subject in general, below, pp. 468–71.

true personal law will play some role. No Hindu is governed by his personal law irrespective of custom. Custom will derogate from it where it is still available for the purpose, subject to the 'Hindu Code'. In the Punjab persons not exempted from the customary law by occupation or residence must be ruled by their ascertained customary law, and by the personal law only in default of proof of this.[1] In Kerala there are several special cross-classifications even of Hindus governed by customary laws, in which the personal law appears in different guises, i.e. in substitution for the basic customs of a caste, as the residual law where custom fails, or as the personal law modified by specific known customs.[2] But leaving these curiosities aside, as also the special régime governing those subject to the provisions of the Special Marriage Act, 1954, or its predecessor,[3] we may proceed to determine the applicability of Hindu law by enquiring who are 'Hindu' by religion, who are 'Hindu' at law, and what is the relation between the two.

[1] Punjab Laws Act, 1872, s. 5 (as amended by Act 12 of 1878) is to be read subject to the Shariat Act (26 of 1937), for which see below, p. 520. The section runs as follows: 'In questions regarding succession, special property of females, betrothal, marriage, divorce, dower, adoption, guardianship, minority, bastardy, family relations, wills, legacies, gifts, partitions, or any religious usage or institution, the rule of decision shall be–(*a*) Any custom applicable to the parties concerned, which is not contrary to justice, equity or good conscience, and has not been by this or any other enactment altered or abolished, and has not been declared to be void by any competent authority; (*b*) the Muhammadan law, in cases where the parties are Muhammadans, and the Hindu law, in cases where the parties are Hindus, except in so far as such law has been altered or abolished by legislative enactment or is opposed to the provisions of this Act, or has been modified by any such custom as is above referred to.' For the residual law see *Ujagar* v. *Jeo* AIR 1959 S.C. 1041.

[2] Ezhavas are governed (apart from statute) by customary law which is presumed to be Mitāksharā law: *Kalyani* v. *Krishnan* [1966] K.L.T. 688 (F.B.). Kuruvas may follow marumakkattayam *or* Hindu law *or* Hindu law modified by custom: *Ayyappan* v. *Kurumpa Mema* [1966] K.L.T. 514. Malayala Kammalas are governed by Hindu Mitāksharā law (see below, p. 414) *modified* by custom, as contrasted with the Panni Kammalas who are governed by Mitāksharā law from which custom may be proved to derogate: *Thankammal* v. *Madhavi Amma* [1966] K.L.T. 181. These decisions are illustrative though (to the newcomer) hardly illuminating: they support the case for the total abolition of all personal laws.

[3] On the Special Marriage Act and its régime see below, p. 332.

To the layman, as to Mr. Chaudhuri,[1] it is evident that 'Hindu' is basically a designation of *nationality*. The inhabitants of the Indus valley were called *indoi* by the Greeks, and the name was extended to comprehend all the dark people who lived beyond the Indus. The cultures of these peoples appear to have been very mixed, but already contained elements which later interpenetrated all the inhabited areas of the continent with the partial exception of the supposedly aboriginal tribes, some of whom are imperfectly Hinduized at this day. Part of the culture was the religion or bundle of religions which was then no more susceptible of creed or system than it is now. The religion(s) of the Hindus were called Hinduism by foreigners for want of another word. The culture of the Indians was Hinduism, until Muslims and other non-assimilating foreigners, such as Jews and Parsis, introduced minority cultures and religions. Hinduism began to stand then, as it does now, for the culture, not of a nation, but of an overwhelming majority of a potential nation, or of any segment of it. The warm bosom of Hinduism harboured the minority religions the more readily because if it were not tolerant of disunity and discrepancy it would have no survival of its own. We shall see presently that the most influential voice in Hinduism in recent centuries, that of the Lord Krishna in the *Śrīmad Bhagavadgītā*, the 'Song Celestial' as Sir Edwin Arnold happily called it, claims as 'Hindu' and as therefore integral to Indian culture *any* and *every* worship of a divinity recognizably identifiable with the Supreme Being (whom Lord Krishna represents in a transfiguration before his friend and worshipper, Arjuna), provided that the approach is that of *bhakti*, personal adoration. It is impossible to go further in sympathy with and in furtherance of the minority religions actually known to Hindus in the period when that Song must have been composed or put into its final shape. But though the religious aspect of Hinduism must have, and has had, sufficient attention, we must not for a moment forget that Hindu religion and Hindu life, social and political, were a unit when minority religious societies began to appear in India, whether or not those societies retained a non-Indian social or political outlook or complexion (which, to a surprising extent, they did not). The

[1] *The Continent of Circe* by Nirad C. Chaudhuri (London, Chatto and Windus, 1965), p. 35.

natural inclination of post-Reformation western man to think of religion as something distinct from social and political life must here be checked unless grave misunderstandings are to be allowed to develop.

Thus it should not surprise us to find that for the purposes of the application of the *codified* parts of the personal law[1] a Hindu is one who is not a Muslim, Parsi, Christian, or Jew! The earlier case-law held a person to be a 'Hindu' for the purpose of application of Hindu law even if he renounced all religion, renounced idols, renounced the Brahminical trinity of gods;[2] he could join a cross-caste community which has a purified monotheistic religion, such as the Brahmo Samaj,[3] and still be a 'Hindu'. Sikhs and Jainas, whatever they themselves think of their relationship to Hindus, are 'Hindus' for legal purposes. But if a Hindu embraces Islam or Christianity (Parsiism, Zoroastrianism, is in practice not open to him), he is automatically outside the Hindu personal law.[4] Having taken up a foreign religion (as Hindus still, with unconscious accuracy, call Islam and Christianity) he may even fall between two stools in a country which, like India at present, applies personal laws of religious origins which have not yet been homologated, and which has hardly a rudimentary *lex loci* in matters of family law.[5]

[1] See below, p. 52.

[2] *Chandrasekhara* v. *Kulandaivelu* AIR 1963 S.C. 185.

[3] *In the goods of Jnanendra Nath Roy* (1922) 49 Cal. 1069 following *Bhagwan* v. *J. C. Bose* (1903) 31 Cal. 11 (P.C.). On the whole subject see Mulla, *Principles of Hindu Law*[13], §§. 6–7.

[4] M. Galanter shrewdly comments (where cited above, at p. 303): 'In the case of individual converts, the question facing the court would seem to be whether the individual convert's acceptance of Christianity, Islam or Buddhism evidences a loss of membership in the caste group to which he belonged at the time of the conversion. This can be treated as a question of fact . . . This was the approach taken in the cases dealing with conversions to sects within Hinduism. . . . However in dealing with these conversions to religions outside Hinduism the courts have forsaken this empirical approach and have treated the conversion as depriving him of his membership as a matter of law. This conclusion derives not from the facts of the individual case but from a view of castes as the components in the sacral order of Hinduism.'

[5] See below, p. 543, n. 3, also the case of *Sundarambal* v. *Suppiah* AIR 1961 Mad. 323, on appeal [1963] 1 M.L.J. 106 (the convert's right to arrears of maintenance). An appeal to 'justice, equity and good conscience' may leave an individual (e.g. an illegitimate child) without adequate rights.

The *uncodified* areas of Hindu law are still to be applied to those who are 'Hindus', positively capable of being identified as such. Of some little help is the remarkable judgement of Gajendragadkar, C.J., in *Shastri Yagnapurushdasji* v. *Muldas*[1] which concerned the identification of an institution as a 'Hindu' institution. It was 'Hindu' if the sect which owned it was 'Hindu'. The sect would be 'Hindu' if the individuals were 'Hindus'. Yet the test of Hinduness for legal purposes was difficult in view of the paucity and oddity of the existing Anglo-Indian case-law, with which the learned Chief Justice deliberately had nothing to do. Those earlier decisions[2] had made it clear that (i) communities which were descended from undoubted Hindu stock could cease to be Hindus by cultural discontinuity and absorption into another religious community, e.g. Burmese Buddhists; (ii) a non-Hindu could become a Hindu by conversion if the society or group into which he or she was admitted accepted him or her as a full member – though it might be doubtful what caste (in the *varṇa* scale) he or she would obtain; (iii) similarly a person of demonstrably other communal origins could be engrafted into a Hindu social unity and either become a Hindu himself by gradual acceptance or at least enable his children to be accepted as Hindus; (iv) meanwhile no amount of personal indifference to traditional Hindu habits, such as veneration for the cow, dietary laws, etc., would exempt the unconverted individual from the Hindu personal law; and (v) communities which sought to be governed by Hindu law though they were known historically to have been descended from non-Hindus (e.g. Aboriginals) in social proximity to Hindus could not be Hindus for the purposes of the law unless it was shown that they had adopted Hindu customs, habits and beliefs – and the distinction was so fine that peoples could have Hindu law applied to them to the extent that they had adopted it, or part of it, as their custom, whilst in other

[1] AIR 1966 S.C. 1119, also (1967) 69 Bom. L.R. 1 (S.C.), [1966] 2 S.C.W.R. 109. The case is discussed at Derrett, 'The Definition of a Hindu', [1966] 2 S.C.J., *J.*, 67–74 or [1966] 2 M.L.J., *J.*, 47–54.

[2] *Ma Yait* v. *Maung* (1921) 48 I.A. 553; *Morarji* v. *Administrator-General* (1929) 52 Mad. 160; *Durga* v. *Sudarsanaswami* AIR 1940 Mad. 513; *Rafail* v. *Baiha* AIR 1957 Pat. 70, 72. *Bhaiya Sher* v. *Bhaiya Ganga* (1913) 41 I.A. 1, Fyzee, *Cases*, pp. 77 ff., is of extraordinary interest, demonstrating society's attitude to religion and the court's reactions to it.

respects they would not be entitled to appeal to that system as their personal law.[1] Thus an adoption of a child by a non-Hindu could be totally invalid if it were not proved that the caste or rather tribe had taken up the institution of adoption as one of their customs.

Whom does the Law regard as a 'Hindu' by Religion?

It was thus evident, before the case we have cited, that it never was a test of 'Hinduness' for the purposes of application of the personal law whether the individual believed in any of those elements which scholars, after infinite pains, have picked upon as characteristic of Hindus. Professor W. Norman Brown's attempt is perhaps one of the most persuasive in a long line of such essays, a line by no means at an end. He suggests[2] that Hindus believe in rebirth, in the behavioural implications of *dharma* in this connexion, in the association between action in this life and the *karma* which influences future births and future potentialities and tendencies. The belief that Hindus universally accept *karma* and the doctrine of a succession of rebirths is widespread and can hardly be an illusion.[3] Professor Brown emphasizes the search for the real, the desire to rise above the phenomenal world, the *bhakti* ideal which is far older than the *Bhagavadgītā*, the constant willingness to think, to listen to thinkers and to search or to reverence others' searches for the ultimate reality. He dwells on the belief in the unity of life, and the doctrine of abstention from injury, with the positive tendency to protect the cow; on the belief that time, as he puts it, is a 'noose', that the universe proceeds through unending eras with perpetual motion, *saṃsāra*; and finally on the reactions to these beliefs (born, though he does not say so, evidently from the dreadful uniformity and inexorableness of life in the Indian

[1] Derrett, *I.M.H.L.*, §. 18.

[2] *Man in the Universe, Some Continuities in Indian Thought* (Berkeley and Los Angeles, University of California Press, 1966).

[3] The notion that *karma* can operate even in this life can have repercussions in court. In *Akbar* v. *State* AIR 1965 J. & K. 126 a gruesome murder took place, the murderer being caught red-handed. Pending his trial 'his legs dried up' and he became unable to stand or walk. The trial court was impressed by this and showed clemency to him. The High Court vigorously objected.

plains), the desperate urge to break the noose of time, to conquer *karma*, to 'overcome', to treat the very doctrines themselves as an obstacle to attainment of the real. In fact in his picture we see the Hindu's minute attention to his *dharma* as a step in the ladder towards absorption, perhaps rather re-absorption, with the Infinite, from which he, in that unexplained moment of 'ignorance', emanated. Professor Brown's view of Hinduism, and many another's, will agree in the essentials, and will put the many inessentials into their more or less orderly places: but can one be a Hindu for legal purposes without any of these? Indeed one can. Nor will the acceptance of all these beliefs by a non-Hindu make him a Hindu for legal purposes if he is not a member of a social unit which is recognizably Hindu. The case of *Yagnapurushdasji*, which may be known as the *Satsang case*, will throw a certain amount of light on this subject if it is read with care.

The steps in the long-drawn-out litigation, which began in the era of hostility to Temple Entry legislation, need not detain us. The plea raised initially was that the Bombay statutes enabling Harijans to enter Hindu public temples could not apply to the temples of the Swāminārāyaṇ sect because the Satsangis, members of that sect, were not Hindus. Alternatively it was argued, at the later stages, that the statutes were *ultra vires* as they contravened Art. 26 (*b*) of the Constitution, to which we must return in due course.[1]

The question, therefore, was whether Satsangis were Hindus, and this meant, in the Court's view, considering what was a Hindu. It would have been possible to restrain the judgement to the exact occasion, but the function of the Supreme Court is to go further than the precise requirements if in the public interest this is desirable. It would have been possible to determine from the very relevant and helpful researches of Sir M. Monier-Williams, who personally questioned Satsangis many years ago, and from published and unpublished literature by leading Satsangis themselves that they were spiritual descendants of a reforming Vaishnava saint, whose campaign of spiritual regeneration of a Vaishnava sect which had become corrupt had placed him within the long line of Hindu reformers, equal in his way to Rāmānuja himself. The leader, who is known as

[1] Below, pp. 467, 477.

Swāminārāyaṇ, is worshipped as the embodiment of Vishnu, for he taught his followers to worship manifestations of Vishnu, in particular Lord Krishna, in purity and truth. That his methods and teachings were nothing more nor less than truly Indian revivals of native religious traditions is entirely apparent from the tenets and code of conduct he required of such devotees as he authorized to be given *dikṣā* (initiation into full membership). In the light of the evidence the temples of the Satsangi sect were obviously Hindu temples.

> Acceptance of the Vedas with reverence, recognition of the fact that the path of Bhakti or devotion leads to *moksha*, and insistence on devotion to Lord Krishna unambiguously and unequivocally proclaim that Swāminārāyaṇ was a Hindu saint who was determined to remove the corrupt practices which had crept into the lives of the preachers and followers of Vallabhāchārya, and who wanted to restore the Hindu religion to its original glory and purity. Considering the work done by Swāminārāyaṇ, history will not hesitate to accord him the place of honour in the galaxy of Hindu saints and religious reformers who by their teachings have contributed to make Hindu religion ever-alive, youthful and vigorous.

But although this would have been sufficient to identify the sect as a Hindu sect the further question, what is a Hindu?, was raised by certain allegations against the Satsangis. It was alleged (i) that women were given *dikṣā*, which is unusual; (ii) that Muslims and Parsis were admitted to *dikṣā* and thus could become full members of the sect without ceasing to be Muslims or Parsis; and (iii) the founder of the sect was worshipped as a god in temples belonging to the sect. The first point was not seriously debated. The second was disposed of in a significant manner: even if Muslims and Parsis become Satsangis,

> . . . this fact . . . merely shows that the Satsang philosophy preached by Swāminārāyaṇ allows followers of other religions to receive the blessings of his teachings without insisting upon their forsaking their own religions. The fact that outsiders are willing to accept Dikshā or initiation, is taken as an indication of their sincere desire to absorb and practise the philosophy of Swāminārāyaṇ and that alone is held to be enough to confer on them the benefit of Swāminārāyaṇ's teachings. The fact that the sect does not insist upon the actual process of proselytizing on such occasions, has really no relevance in deciding the question as to whether the sect itself is a Hindu sect or not. In a sense this attitude of the Satsang sect is consistent with the basic Hindu religious and philosophic theory that many roads lead to God.

His Lordship went further and cited the *Bhagavadgītā* (IX. 23) to the effect that those who are devoted to other deities worship thereby Krishna himself. The Hindu Satsangis, it would seem to follow, are not less Hindus when they allow persons professing other religions to join them, because Hinduism does not deny that worshippers of other deities are, if they are sincere, equally worshippers of the Hindus' own deity. This does not mean, as it would appear at a casual glance, that the Muslims and Parsis are Hindus for legal purposes. They do not cease to be Muslims and Parsis from the Hindu point of view, because the question of conversion to Hinduism is not *necessarily* raised by joining in the Satsangi sect! The Muslims may disown them for their conduct, but to have legal effect this would have to be established by precedent, for the law as at present constituted does not declare a Muslim to have lost the benefit and responsibilities of his personal law merely by joining in a multi-religious spiritual community.[1] The Hindus, consistently with Hinduism, have set an example of religious catholicity, finding a common ground without exacting an impossible price. This is consistent with the Hindu position we shall notice again, namely that a Hindu may accept Christianity, and, in these days, even undergo baptism, without ceasing to be a Hindu in both social and spiritual terms.

The judgement in the *Satsang case* went further. The worship of Swāminārāyaṇ was not inconsistent with Hinduism, as the *Bhagavadgītā* teaches (IV. 7) that whenever religion is on the decline and irreligion is in the ascendant, God is born (literally 'creates himself') to restore the balance of religion and guide the destiny of the human race towards salvation. On that footing

[1] For the case of the Ismāīlī Khojas see below, p. 543, n. 3. The case of the communities dealt with in Fyzee, *Outlines*,[1] p. 52, n. (*i*), in respect of whom there is a real difficulty in determining whether they are Hindus or Muslims, permits the application of Muhammadan law to persons of Hindu beliefs. The Khojas' holy book, the *Dasavatār*, tells of nine Hindu incarnations followed by incarnations of the 'Most Holy Ali' (Fyzee, *Outlines*[1], p. 56, n. (*s*)). Families may indeed be neither Hindu nor Muslim: *Raj* v. *Bishen* (1882) 4 All. 343; but a family of Hindu beliefs may be governed by the Muhammadan law: *Azima Bibi* v. *Shamalanand* (1912) 40 Cal. 378 P.C. In *Bhagwan Bakhsh* v. *Drigbijai* (1930) 6 Luck. 487 the propositus and his ancestors for four generations were Muslims but the propositus observed certain Hindu rituals; the result was that the Muhammadan law applied.

any genuine religious reformer may be treated as an abode of divinity.

Whether a belief is a Hindu belief is therefore open to judicial determination by reference to some standard. In the absence of a creed the opinions of acknowledged experts may be consulted. Whom were the court to consult? The then President, Dr. Rādhākrishnan, was an obvious choice. The Supreme Court, through the mouth of the Chief Justice, liberally quote from Rādhākrishnan's *Hindu View of Life*[1] and *Indian Philosophy*.[2] They also make a reference (scholars may feel somewhat unfortunately) to the work of the patriot and visionary Indologist, B. G. Tilak. The following quotations from the judgement[3] show what at present Indian law conceives to be as near a definition of 'Hinduism' as we can attain, and this writer has no objection to make to it.

> There is no scope for ex-communicating any notion or principle as heretical and rejecting it as such . . .
>
> [Yet] The term 'Hindu', according to Dr. Rādhākrishnan, had originally a territorial and not a credal significance. It implied residence in a well defined geographical area. . . . The Hindu thinkers reckoned with the striking fact that men and women dwelling in India belonged to different communities, worshipped different gods, and practised different rites. . . .
>
> The history of Indian thought emphatically brings out the fact that the development of Hindu religion has always been inspired by an endless quest of the mind for truth based on the consciousness that truth has many facets. Truth is one but wise men describe it differently. . . .
>
> . . . Indian thought . . . 'has a disposition to interpret life and nature in the way of monistic idealism, though this tendency is so plastic, living and manifold that it takes many forms and expresses itself in even mutually hostile teachings.'
>
> Beneath the diversity of philosophic thoughts, concepts and ideas expressed by Hindu philosophers, lie certain broad concepts which can be treated as basic. The first . . . is the acceptance of the Veda as the highest authority in religious and philosophic matters. This concept necessarily implies that all the systems claim to have drawn their principles from a common reservoir of thought enshrined in the Veda. The Hindu teachers were thus obliged to use the heritage they received from the past in order

[1] It appears that the New York (Macmillan) edition of 1931 was used; however, the text agrees with that of the London edition of 1927.

[2] Citing from pp. 22–3, 32, 48 of vol. 1 and pp. 26–7 of vol. 2 of the London edition of 1940 (subsequently reprinted).

[3] From pp. 1129–31 of the AIR report and pp. 11–14 of the Bom.L.R. report.

to make their views readily understood. The other basic concept which is common to the six systems of Hindu philosophy is that 'all of them accept the view of the great world rhythm. Vast periods of creation, maintenance and dissolution follow each other in endless succession. This theory is not inconsistent with belief in progress; for it is not a question of the movement of the world reaching its goal times without number, and being again forced back to its starting-point. . . . It means that the race of man enters upon and retravels its ascending path of realization. This interminable succession of world ages has no beginning.' It may also be said that all the systems of Hindu philosophy believe in rebirth and pre-existence . . .

The development of Hindu religion and philosophy shows that from time to time saints and religious reformers attempted to remove from the Hindu thought and practices elements of corruption and superstition and that led to the formation of different sects. . . .

. . . what according to this religion, is the ultimate goal of humanity? It is the release and freedom from the unceasing cycle of births and rebirths; Moksha or Nirvāṇa,[1] which is the ultimate aim of Hindu religion and philosophy, represents the state of absolute absorption and assimilation of the individual soul with the infinite. What are the means to attain this end? On this vital issue there is great divergence of views; some emphasize the importance of Gyan[2] or knowledge, while others extol the virtues of Bhakti or devotion; and yet others insist upon the paramount importance of the performance of duties with a heart full of devotion and mind inspired by true knowledge. In this sphere, again, there is diversity of opinion. . . .

'Acceptance of the Vedas with reverence; recognition of the fact that the means or ways to salvation are diverse; and realization of the truth that the number of gods to be worshipped is large, that indeed is the distinguishing feature of Hindu religion.' This definition brings out succinctly the broad distinctive features of Hindu religion.

Religion for the Purpose of the Personal Laws

Thus, with this legal recognition of the fundamental character of Hinduism, unorthodoxy, departure from śāstric ideals, social and spiritual association with non-Hindus, absorption of foreign modes of thought and expression – all these are consistent with Hinduism, and the Anglo-Indian case-law on Hinduness for the purpose of application of the personal law was probably correct on the whole. The statutory definition of a Hindu for the

[1] Ludo and Rosane Rocher, '*Mokṣa*: le concept hindou de la délivrance', *Religions de Salut* (Brussels, 1963), pp. 169–202, give an exhaustive picture of Hindu learning on this subject.

[2] Usually spelt *jnāna*, i.e. (esoteric) knowledge.

purposes of the application of the *codified* Hindu law admits of no such approach, because it distinctly contemplates a person being a Hindu for this purpose though he has no beliefs or religion. This aspect of the subject was naturally not touched upon in the *Satsang case* because the subject concerned temples and worship in temples; the possibility of interested parties having no belief or religion was absolutely excluded. We see, therefore, that, apart from the definition provided in the 'Hindu Code' (to which we are about to come) the test of whether a person is a Hindu for legal purposes starts with ethnic and geographical tests, which raise a presumption that can be rebutted not by proof of absence of belief or presence of disbelief but only by proof of exclusive adherence (or conversion) to a *foreign* (i.e. a non-Hindu) faith.

This historical background explains the current definition of a Hindu for legal purposes in, for example, the Hindu Marriage Act, 1955:

Sec. 2. *Application of Act*

(1) This Act applies–

(*a*) to any person who is a Hindu by religion in any of its forms or developments, including a Virashaiva, a Lingayat or a follower of the Brahmo, Prarthana or Arya Samaj,

(*b*) to any person who is a Buddhist, Jaina or Sikh by religion, and

(*c*) to any other person domiciled in the territories to which this Act extends who is not a Muslim, Christian, Parsi or Jew by religion, unless it is proved that any such person would not have been governed by the Hindu law or by any custom or usage as part of that law in respect of any of the matters dealt with herein if this Act had not been passed.

Explanation. The following persons are Hindus, Buddhists, Jainas or Sikhs by religion, as the case may be:

(*a*) any child, legitimate or illegitimate, both of whose parents are Hindus, Buddhists, Jainas or Sikhs by religion;

(*b*) any child, legitimate or illegitimate, one of whose parents is a Hindu, Buddhist, Jaina or Sikh by religion and who is brought up as a member of the tribe, community, group or family to which such parent belongs or belonged; and

(*c*) any person who is a convert or re-convert to the Hindu, Buddhist, Jaina or Sikh religion.

. . . .

(3) The expression 'Hindu' in any portion of this Act shall be construed as if it included a person who, though not a Hindu by religion, is, nevertheless, a person to whom this Act applies by virtue of the provisions contained in this section.

Irrespective of the intricacies of the definition of a 'Hindu' for this purpose, there arises the inconvenience of having personal laws which do not make provision for those who have left their respective folds. There are gaps and interstices between the systems into which an individual can fall, or from which an individual can profit. Conversion from one community's religion to another can have the effect of cutting off even elementary rights;[1] it can also have the effect of enlarging the convert's rights.[2] In both cases public policy in the broadest sense is offended. In neither case does it seem practicable to enquire too closely into the genuineness of a conversion, once it is established as a fact. The policy laid down by the Constitution in Art. 44 that a uniform civil code should be devised, wherein all personal laws will disappear or be merged, is obviously sound, provided we may hope that the task of distinguishing rules of law from their various religious foundations can be carried through successfully. This is a matter we shall investigate in chapter 15.

The oddity of the personal law system stems from two sources, first the history of India, and secondly from the juridical presuppositions of the European rulers of the eighteenth century. The latter were prepared to believe in personal laws based upon religion because they knew that such a system operated in the Ottoman Empire and they viewed the Mughals as a variety of 'Moors' or Muhammadan sovereigns with whom the Christian world had many and various dealings. It is just possible that some jurists of the period remembered the personal laws of the Middle Ages in Continental Europe, whereby citizens of various towns and provinces of the Empire were entitled to have their laws administered to them wherever they were. Yet in such suppositions European visitors to India were merely rationalizing a situation they saw for themselves but imperfectly understood.

In Aśoka's empire there were Indians, and there were Greeks and other foreign visitors and settlers. The Greek colonies established by Alexander the Great must have had their own city-laws, and the Iranians who came under Indian government must have had their own customs, about which Aśoka seems to have had some regrets. India herself had two systems of

[1] See below, p. 333. [2] See below, p. 545, n. 4.

jurisprudence, the *dharmaśāstra*,[1] and the Buddhist. The latter was a development from the former, with special attention to the needs of the *Saṅgha*, in particular its recruitment, discipline and accommodation. With the disappearance of Buddhist law and Greek and Iranian elements under Indian rule, all Indians were in theory governed by the native Indian jurisprudence. Districts and countries eventually overrun by the Muslim invaders continued as before on condition of payment of poll-tax, while the Muslims, including their newly-won converts, were governed by the Islamic law so far as might be, without restriction to topics such as we have envisaged above. The law was a personal law, but was an entire juridical system founded on the *Koran* and the *sunna*, complete in all its parts, as the *dharmaśāstra* had been before it. The Muslims, in order to carry out the requirements of government, introduced in respect of non-Muslims also their own criminal law, and fiscal law, utilizing such facilities as the rich country offered them. To that extent the *śāstra* and such custom as it recognized and authorized were superseded. The law governing the individual was therefore not the law of the locality but, if he were a Muslim, the law of the Kazi to whom he applied for solution of his dispute, which would be the law of the Hanafī school in the vast majority of cases;[2] or if he were a Hindu the dominant school of law recognized in the region from which he himself originally came. This was a sufficient factual basis for the proposition that India was governed by personal laws, and the European's imagination did the rest. The details must be reserved for chapter 9 below.

'Muhammadan law' to this day means the appropriate school of law modified by customs where legally applicable; 'Hindu law' means the appropriate school of law modified by customs, if still applicable, and modified also by statutes. Statutory interference with Muhammadan law has been minimal, though not insignificant. It is thus possible for Muslims to say, as they do, that their personal law is based upon religion;[3] whereas

[1] Then in an early form: see Wagle, cited below, p. 102, n. 1.

[2] For the schools of Islamic law see below, p. 517.

[3] It is worth noting, in comparison with the reluctance of Indian Muslims to contemplate the interference of Parliament with the Shariat (see below, p. 539), that Alberuni, who was in India about A.D. 1030, was able to note the greater accessibility of Hindu law to modification and reform than was

this claim is less often made now for Hindus than it used to be.

The development of the personal laws has depended less upon consciously directed public policy than upon the characters of the laws themselves in their social context; and so it is with these that we must start the long story. The reader must have an opportunity, however confined, to see what the laws were like, and what materials served as the basis for more modern developments. And the first question that confronts us is whether, as it is often said, the distinctions between religion, morality and law were blurred in the system inherited by the vast majority of Indians; and further what role religion actually played in the development of the rules in that system. Only then shall we be able to know whether religion has been affronted by the modifications made to the system of law, by the working of the Constitution relative to religion, or by the way in which other aspects of Indian law are at present developing. Incidentally the value of completely 'secularizing' the system will make itself apparent.

the Islamic system with which he was even better acquainted. Amongst Hindus he notices that 'the abrogation of a law is allowable' (E. C. Sachau, *Alberuni's India*, Indian reprint, 1964, vol. 1, p. 108).

2

RELIGION, CHARACTER AND HISTORY

Many habits and habitual attitudes start as a recognition on someone's part of forces which it is in his interest to obey, and this is imitated by those who merely find it convenient to follow suit. Hinduism, as perhaps other religious systems also, has proliferated supernatural and transcendental reasons for habits which could not call upon a remembered origin. Taboos thus acquire the same outward authority and justification that religious observances have. A man who eats with his left hand would have difficulty in claiming recognition as a Hindu, though the taboo against using the left hand for any 'good' purpose is not confined to Hindus. The rational reason for not using the hand does not determine whether a man uses it or not, for the taboo has led to a habit. Other social taboos are surrounded with mythological and truly religious ideas, so that it is difficult to determine how much habit, mere 'tradition', determines the behaviour and how much true recognition of an unseen power. At a crisis taboo might be more powerful than religion, but it is not into such delicate realms that we need to penetrate at present. But we shall return to such distinctions when we notice the Indian judiciary confidently visualizing, and in fact practising, a sifting of usages, so as to enable some to be classed as 'religious' and some to be classed as 'superstitious'.

Some characteristics of India require to be painted in the broad, because the majority of Indian Muslims and Christians was derived as communities from the Hindu population itself to which their ancestors belonged before they were converted. Broad characteristics of Hinduism belong to the entire population still.[1] Thus the quality of 'religion' in India, if it differs from religion as known in the West, deserves to be explored first.

[1] D. P. Mukerji, *Modern Indian Culture. A Sociological Study* (Bombay, Hind Kitabs, 1948), ch. 2.

Society and Tolerance

The first characteristic, which plays a large part in the Indian make-up, is the non-confinement of 'religion' to personal belief, and its persistence irrespective of personal belief. One is free to have any and every belief or no beliefs at all, without forfeiting one's religious denomination or affiliation. On the other hand, if one's social status is disturbed it would follow that one's religion is likewise in doubt.[1] Religion is thus a social phenomenon, and the character of the religious observance or right to perform a religious observance (the Sanskrit word *adhikāra* 'right', 'authority', is heard in classical Hinduism) depends upon factual membership of a social group. Thus it is not absurd to say that a man's religion may be told by the hat he wears, and if onlookers are told that a man wearing a hat associated with Muslims is in fact a Hindu they will suffer momentary discomfort such as western people suffer when they observe or think they observe that one of their compatriots, really male, is wearing female attire. The right, or perhaps even the duty, to wear a particular costume has as a concomitant other observances which are religious in the sense in which the present writer has defined it, and this explains the horror Hindus of Goa felt years ago when the Portuguese forced them to wear trousers. The present writer remembers an incident in about 1951 which illustrates this as clearly. He was wearing a white homespun cap of the design and material which is associated with members of the Congress Party and is often called a 'Gandhi cap'. He chose it for its convenience and was indifferent to its associations. A deputation of young Hindus called upon him and said, 'Do you intend to insult us by wearing that cap?' Two answers would have satisfied them, that is to say either that by wearing it on his head he was honouring those who wore such a cap (whereas had he polished his shoes with it the opposite inference would have been allowable), or that he was

[1] M. Galanter (where cited) shows that social immobility lessens the effect of conversion *within* Hinduism. At the bottom of the social ladder mass conversions took place to Islam and Christianity, to the consternation of other Hindus (see next note). At the top of the social ladder movement into cosmopolitan patterns of expression and reaction threaten the recognizability of Hinduism in those subject to it.

himself a Hindu. The latter statement would be acceptable on the footing that he had been adopted into a Hindu social group and was admitted to full equality with its members, entitled to all the observances to which it was entitled: a rare event but possible. No one would have questioned him as to his *beliefs*, whether he accepted any particular deities and so on. They would assume that his adoptive associates had satisfied themselves that he shared with them all that was necessary to identify him with their group. Religion is therefore, as we have seen, basically a national or sub-national means of identification. Hinduism is the national religion, Islam is an imported religion which has struck deep roots, Christianity is likewise an imported religion. To tell Hindus that Islam and Christianity are both eastern religions because Muslim and Christian Asians live in Asia is to confuse the issue. Religious affiliation is not a question of an individual's belief, for on that footing he is free to believe or not believe in anything he likes, but of a social *belonging*. The Muslims belonged to a nation different from their predecessors. The Christians, for the most part, decided to detach themselves from their parent Hindu society (which in fact placed most of them in a low prestige position) and to become a new society by being accepted by people who at the time had a high prestige-rating. It is therefore absurd to expect either the Christians to have had or to have adequate theological qualifications as Christians, or to expect Hindus in general to admit those Christians as still members of their social complex, their nation. Hinduism has no objection to castes' hiving off and developing new communities: but they cannot, in social terms, both have their cake and eat it. The resistance of Hinduism to conversion to Christianity, which conversion many missionaries have thought a natural and rational goal for the Hindu who is interested in religious belief, is based simply on the fact that change of personal belief does not automatically mean a change in social belonging. For 'you can believe anything you like'; as the Hindu fathers pathetically assured their sons during the agitation which successful missionary endeavour created in the 1840's in Calcutta[1]–with the result that even significant changes can take, and in fact have taken place within Hinduism so as to

[1] M. Mohar Ali, *The Bengali Reaction to Christian Missionary Activities, 1833–57* (Chittagong, Mehrub Publications, 1965), p. 96.

accommodate every shift of personal predilection rather than to condemn society to a brittle rigidity. The very curious incident of iconoclasm in Kashmir in the time of Harṣa (A.D. 1089–1101) could be taken as an example of mass lunacy. On the other hand it is not impossible that a short-lived programme of religious reform was undertaken by this eccentric monarch under the sincere belief that idolatry was wrong, a belief to which some enterprising teacher of Islam could well have contributed.[1] Such vigorous not to say virulent manifestations of intolerance are hard to parallel in Indian history, except where Muslims have attempted to impose their religion upon Hindus and others.[2]

A Hindu can have Christian or 'reformed' beliefs alongside his ancestral beliefs. This is becoming more common, now that Christian beliefs are not remotely associated with the foreign power and prestige-seeking. The present writer knows a young Hindu who was baptized and confirmed in London and on return to India not only passes as a Hindu but feels discomfort if he cannot be a Hindu in India and a Christian in London. Rammohun Roy had a religion of his own, but used to amuse his visitors by saying that after his death not less than three communities would claim him for themselves: with reason, for his monotheism qualified him as a Unitarian or a Muslim, while his social behaviour kept him on the right side of the line dividing Hindus from others. This was symbolized by his method of entertaining. He put two tables with an inch or so between them. His European guests ate their food at their table and he ate his food at his table, and so there was no 'interdining' (as the phrase goes) and no loss of caste! The present writer recalls the sexton of a prominent church in South India who is a Hindu and has been seen worshipping in a famous temple in the same city. Not all Hindus, even in Madras, bother to visit temples: this man is obviously of a religious turn of mind. The headmaster of a Madras school was obviously a Hindu in social terms: the present writer has his poems before him, which are decidedly Christian in tone and content,[3] and his son heads his

[1] A. L. Basham, 'Harṣa of Kashmir and the iconoclast ascetics', *B.S.O.A.S.*, 12, no. 3 (1948), pp. 688 ff. Cf. B.K. Ins. II (1964), No. 56, p. 73 (Śaivites destroy Jaina temples, twelfth century).

[2] See B.K. Ins. II, No. 695, p. 433 (sixteenth century).

[3] V. Kandaswami Mudaliar, B.A., L.T., *Pearls*, published by the author,

letters with the sign of the Cross where Hindus usually write the symbol for *Śrī*. To be a Hindu, even a pious Hindu, is merely to be a member of a recognized social group, and it is hardly conceivable that one could leave that social group as an individual without being 'converted' to another religion, i.e. to another religious community, as the law has observed.[1] Groups can deny the value of Vedic worship, can renounce 'superstition', can agree amongst themselves to have different marriage ceremonies and improve the tone of their little society in other ways: they are still Hindus, for Hinduism rejoices in never excluding a member for personal heterodoxy, the chief reason why it is contended that Hinduism has no creed. Whatever Hinduism is, its members are supposed to live it as a matter of observance and irrespective of personal opinion. It is not altogether surprising that some Christians who have cross-communal interests and social ambitions should be found to have assumed a position in which, as with many Muslims, it is possible to contend both that they are Hindus and that they are non-Hindus—to the occasional embarrassment of the courts.[2]

Because religion is a social question as well as, or more significantly than a personal question, an opposite tendency manifests itself. The Indian is pre-eminently a family man. The background of the joint-family, which persists to a large extent even amongst some groups of Muslims and Christians,[3] teaches the child to play a multitude of rôles and to learn the parts he must play as son, nephew, grandchild, brother and so on. The rôles are stereotyped and are played irrespective of personal inclinations. The present writer well remembers enquiring how *A* liked *B* and being given the answer which showed clearly that whether *A* liked *B* or not they were cousins, had identical interests, belonged together and therefore for all practical purposes

Chintadripet (Madras), 1942. One poem is entitled 'Magdalene', another 'Judas', another, entitled 'He' is about Christ and the author's life. The same writer painstakingly translated or paraphrased the ancient Sangam poem *Cirupanattuppadai* (in *Tamil Culture*, 5, No. 1, 1956). Similarly 'Kuvempu', poet-laureate of Karṇāṭaka, wrote in 1933 a poem called *Avatār* which depicts an imaginary sermon of Christ from the cross.

[1] See above, p. 45, n. 2.

[2] *Janamma* v. *Joseph* [1967] K.L.T. 105.

[3] For Muslims, see below, p. 527; for an instance of the very few Christian joint-family households left see *Chinnaswami* v. *Anthony* AIR 1961 Ker. 161.

must be treated as a unit, their 'personal relations' (if any existed) being quite irrelevant. In the joint-family your shirt will be borrowed without your permission by anyone who is approximately the right size, and irrespective of whether you like him: in fact the very question, as appeared, whether you like your cousin is fatuous. In such a situation the pressures upon the individual personality must be heavy, and they must have some outlet.

Hence, though religion is a social expression, a social identification, personal religious belief tends to transcend the barriers of caste and even community. Simple poetic appeals to God (often conveniently unnamed) from the individual soul (away from mother and father and uncle and cousins and other demanding people) are at once moving, and appeal to all classes and ages and both sexes. Religious movements aimed to transcend caste barriers and even the bounds, vague as they can be, between the religions are very successful. Associations formed for common religious expression, however quaint, following saints of various clothings (to whom we must return) and adopting various forms of expression are popular and if not actually joined by every other person are held in esteem by all. Tolerance is thus a feature on two planes, within society and across societies. It seems always to have been so and is a feature of the age-old experience of the Hindu civilization. Hindus can give land for a Christian church[1] and Hindus can feel proud that in so doing they are performing a social service, which, in fact, the law allows.

What then of instances of intolerance? The Old India can be intolerant when it becomes excited about the slaughter of cows.[2]

[1] *Kolandai* v. *Gnanavaram* [1943] 2 M.L.J. 664. Chhadama, a Muslim minister of Jayakeśi, a Kadamba king of Goa (a Hindu), constructed a mosque for worship by his community, and the king made certain monetary concessions for its maintenance in A.D. 1053. This was, of course, before the Muslim incursions into South India harmed the mutual respect of the two communities.

[2] W. Norman Brown, 'The sanctity of the cow in Hinduism', *Economic Weekly*, Feb. 1964, pp. 245–55 or *Journal of the Madras University*, 28, no. 2, 1957, pp. 29–49; also *Man in the Universe* (cited above), at pp. 48 ff. The violent agitation in New Delhi against cow slaughter which took place in November 1966 after severe drought stemmed at least on the surface from the traditional belief that sacrifices of ghee (a product of milk) are required for timely and adequate monsoons (see below, p. 119).

The New India can be intolerant when it attempts to purify Hinduism of what it calls, superciliously, accretions and superstitions. The law countenances both sorts of intolerance. One wonders how this is to be reconciled with what was said above. The answer must lie in the concept of religion itself. Religion in India implies observance, positive and negative. Out of religion one wears clothing, takes particular baths, makes particular offerings, abstains from particular foods, and so on. There is the doing and the abstaining from doing. Irrespective of belief things must be done or abstained from–if only the minimum, or the social identification is lost. To lose or to be in danger of losing one's social identification is a horrid prospect. The belief that merit is lost if one permits the slaughter of cows is a social phenomenon, and must be treated seriously as such.[1] If religion is protected by law this belief must be protected, as it is. The belief that merit is gained by dedicating girls to temples, where they will become prostitutes, or by slaughtering animals and/or birds is not a belief that anyone is in a position to deny, if it exists as a fact: but because it is a question of doing, and not abstaining from doing, the deprivation of the opportunity to do it can be achieved, if it is a question of pressure from outside, without a sense of loss of merit from the sufferers' standpoint: for the latter have alternatives. The relatively intolerant Hinduism of the upper classes today derives from two sources, their own westernization which has imparted to their outlook a discrimination which previously was not felt, and their consciousness that in due course the example which they themselves set as the prestige-holding class should draw the others to their point of view. Their paternalistic interference with the religion of others is therefore based ultimately on a very Hindu notion, though upon the surface it looks dramatically foreign. True, these same ruling classes look over their shoulders at the opinions passed on Hinduism by foreigners; yet this does not mean that they are tyrannizing over their co-religionists in an effort to obtain foreign approbation, but rather that their own standards and ways of thinking have been coloured by contact with the West: no one, after all, has outcasted them for being westernized!

[1] See below, p. 450.

Fantasy and Self-control

It is time to turn to some characteristics of Hinduism as it was and is. The role of fantasy is important. The tight social setting, in which action matters much and belief less, is the right soil in which irrational fantasies can grow. Without actually being lunatics Indians are frequently detected in imaginary lives and systematic delusions such as would consign western counterparts to the asylum. Once we admit that the source of the curious inconsistencies is fantasy we can drop the alternative possibility that it is hypocrisy. The fantasies are almost always associated with religion, and marvellous incongruities result.[1] Those who have led lives of ordinary, or middling honesty and efficiency look forward to spending their retirement in religious observances. Some drink whisky by day and perform *pūjā* by night. What is of interest is that this is tolerated as not abnormal. Young people who mock these ways of behaving know that there is every chance that they will go the same way themselves when they are older, and that sobers their reactions. The belief that the old gods and the old ways are still true, whether or not we are in an atomic age, is widespread. The ancient sages, whose cryptic works lend themselves readily to various and fanciful interpretations, are held to have anticipated all modern advances and all science, past, present and future.[2] The prestige-bearing members of society, the natural leaders, feel naked without the clothing of authority which association, in some form, with the ancient culture gives. The sacred language,

[1] Instances from recent history and personal experience are cited in the present writer's article at [1966] 1 M.L.J., *J.*, 43 ff. used below at pp. 117–21. In *King-Emperor* v. *Bharat Bepari* AIR 1921 Cal. 501 (1) the parents whose children died in infancy vowed to offer their next child to the crocodiles of a certain tank. The child was devoured. They were sentenced to two years' rigorous imprisonment under s. 304 of the Penal Code. In *Narayan Das* v. *State* AIR 1952 Or. 149 a man claiming to be a living god had a fanatical disciple who claimed in a public procession that 'the village gods were stone idols and he would pass urine on them'. The disciple was guilty under s. 298 (see below, p. 450); not his preceptor, who believed he was God. In *Ashiruddin Ahmad* v. *The King* AIR 1949 Cal. 182 a Muslim dreamt he was bidden by heaven to sacrifice his five-year-old son in a mosque: held not guilty of murder.

[2] A tendency, amongst others, exposed by Dr. N. Subrahmanian in his admirable *Hindu Tripod* (Madras, Inst. Trad. Cult., 1965).

Sanskrit, cannot so easily evoke pleasure or amusement as awe: it is associated with the unseen powers, for which respect is easier than indifference. Even politicians are expected to be able to call upon personal acquaintance with the *śāstra-s*, the classical systems of instruction, and there are outstanding instances of very successful addiction to such study on the part of public men.[1]

The leading spirit of Hindu belief is self-control, as we should expect of a society such as has been briefly described above. Where the roles which an individual must play are laid down for him irrespective of his personal choice, and where they are so many and constantly in danger of conflict, children are naturally brought up to think that the unseen forces favour one who is entirely and always self-controlled. Self-abnegation was an ancient virtue (it would otherwise be difficult to imagine why) and persists through every strand of social life. The wife who rises at 4.30 when she need not do so, who performs the worship of the family idol personally, though she could easily afford to pay a priest to do it for her, who waits upon her husband like a servant out of regard for the ancient proprieties, symbolizes the religious spirit of Hinduism. The castes that have always yielded to impulses are despised by the higher classes, whose higher status is due to their having more observances, greater purity. The greater the freedom the lower the caste. A man who says, 'I am willing to accept presents from *anybody*', even in fun, announces himself at the very bottom of the social ladder. Purity, which is an entirely religious concept, is firmly intertwined with domestic, matrimonial and occupational restraint and observance. No matter how westernized the family some vestige of observance will be retained, or the social identity will be lost. This is why mixed marriages are a problem, for unless the marriage is orthodox, as planned and arranged marriages are orthodox, the observances of the home will lack continuity or even identity.

Self-restraint is thus part and parcel of social status as it is of religion. But self-restraint need not exist *in vacuo*. Hinduism has always insisted on the merit and value of giving, much to the amusement of cynical observers. The Hindu gains spiritually by

[1] For example the politician Dr. Sampurnanand's contribution to Vol. 3 of the *Jaipur Law Journal* (1963), pp. 1–6.

divesting himself of property, which can be done in favour of the public, as by way of digging wells, tanks, etc., or building shelters and temples, or in favour of a deity by gifts to that diety. The gift to the deity is an act of propitiation of the deity. The notion that gifts in charity and to deities are of religious importance is universally accepted. Indeed the law has always had to set bounds to a man's liberality in the interests of his family, as it used to set bounds to his restraint upon his sexual enjoyment.[1] There is a double social aspect to this also. Gifts to a deity strengthen the communion whose deity it is, and symbolize social identification within that communion. Liberality advertises religious qualities and gains merit and social esteem at the same time. On the whole this aspect of religion continues to weigh much in comparison with observances of a more demanding character, and it is not surprising that while the family law has been altered in such a fashion as to imperil the maintenance of observances in the home by those whose inclination to maintain them is weak enough for them to risk their loss,[2] that part of the law which relates to charitable endowments and related topics remains substantially unaltered.

The Future of Religion

It may be asked, in view of the state of the law, which we shall investigate, what is the outlook of educated youth on religion today. A careful investigation carried out in very recent times reveals that a belief in religion as such is not diminished.[3] The interest in observances decreases; the ancient religious practices fall into contempt, but the belief in the need for recognition of unseen forces continues unabated. Belief in caste is dying out rapidly, that is to say, belief in its rationality as a statement of social hierarchy. It is far from certain whether the

[1] A penance was prescribed for failing to have intercourse with the wife within a week or so after the end of each menstrual period: the concept of *ṛtu* is well known (see e.g. *Yājñavalkya-smṛti*, I, 89) but see U. C. Sarkar's reference to Śūlapāṇi's *Prāyaścitta-viveka* at *Law Review* (Punjab Univ.), 18, no. 2 (1966), p. 25.

[2] See below, p. 442.

[3] Margaret L. Cormack, *She who Rides a Peacock. Indian Students and Social Change* (New York, 1961), ch. 8. Eighty per cent of those questioned replied that love of all mankind was the most important aspect of religion.

ancient belief in social identification has gone, and the competition for employment and for advantages proceeds largely on the footing of social identification as a title,[1] or on the footing of analogous association. The recent difficulties about 'protective discrimination', which was thought, wrongly, to be a system of advantaging individuals on the ground of their caste,[2] illustrate the readiness with which some portions at least of the public believe in social identification as a still justified criterion in that aspect of life which matters most.

Doubts as to the future of the Hindu religion, granted the apparently irreligious attitudes of the young, seem highly exaggerated. It is argued that Hinduism attained a new lease of life from the period of foreign rule; that Hindus braced themselves for the conflict and the pangs of Independence by constant refreshment at the wells of the traditional heritage, with its heavy religious content, and that a patriot without religion could neither make a successful politician nor a plausible patriot. It is argued that now that independence is evidently a fact as well as an expended emotional explosion the role of religion must fade: persecution, or what patriots preferred to regard as persecution, aided faith; and the victory of native faith over foreign dominion should pull from under Hinduism one of its strongest props. Evidence tending to support this argument is abundant. It is possible to live in an Indian town and to search for traces of the old culture without success. For one who sees modern India as a romantic antiquarian it is horrifying to ask young people about *gotra-s* and *śrāddha-s* only to find that they have hardly heard of them. Law students prior to joining their College have never so much as heard of 'Hindu law' (which rules their families from the cradle to the pyre). But the late Professor K. V. Rangaswāmī Aiyangār gave lectures on Hinduism and on the 'true' Hindu law to students who had never had the opportunity of learning about their national and traditional ethos, and he held his audiences spellbound. Chin-

[1] N. C. Chaudhuri's comments on caste in *Continent of Circe* (cited above) are more caustic than, for example, Amlan Datta's in his 'Hinduism, reason and justice', in *Quest*, 49 (1966), pp. 9–15, but the complaint is essentially the same, and is very common.

[2] N. Rādhākrishnan, 'Unities of social, economic and educational backwardness: caste and individual', (1965) 7 *J.I.L.I.*, 262 ff. *Devadasan* v. *Union of India* AIR 1964 S.C. 179.

mayānanda-swāmī the celebrated contemporary preacher, tells his audiences that other faiths are preached, but apart from his 'Mission' and the work of several important *maṭha-s*, Hinduism remains the religion of people who know little about it. But Chinmayānanda, like the great speakers who took and take the *Rāmāyaṇa* and the *Śrīmad-Bhāgavatam* for their themes, finds vast gatherings quickly responsive to what evidently impresses them as keenly as it moved their ancestors, well over a millennium ago. Vedic ceremonies are in vogue, especially on public occasions and in the homes of the pompous if barely orthodox, and there is a level at which the ancient verities, garbed recognizably in traditional forms, appeal to everyone. The fashionable professions of atheism should not be taken too seriously. An advocate in Andhra Pradesh writes about the Indian Penal Code's provisions relative to attempted suicides and argues,

> But the theological notion upon which the punishment was originally based, holds no water at the present day. We have no remnant of faith left in that Being whose existence all scientists are ever at work to disprove. Belief in God is now a harmful delusion leading to bigotry. Nobody made the world, they say. It was simply the result of chemical and electrical processes.

But he is attempting to show that the juridical basis of the penalty should be re-examined, and he does not argue that religion is not a force to be reckoned with. A popular article in a daily paper attacks religion as the cause of narrowness, bigotry, ignorance: but both writers assume that they can appeal from a lower form of religious consciousness to a higher; both evaluate and compare–and at the back of both minds there is a sureness that Hinduism will go on though beliefs in *devatā-s* (gods or even God) fades into a wider framework of religious consciousness. Thus the worldly householder who still allows the traditional formulae to be gabbled in his house at the relevant points in the calendar, though he himself has so little faith in them that he will not bother to greet the officiant Brahmin, is a figure who links the ages: he knows that it is inadvisable to break with the past, and he can accept it only on the footing that the meaning of what is done on his behalf is worth while for fruits much more remote and intangible than the *phala* which the Vedic ritualists promise him. But because he pays the small fee he admits that the religious element is necessary to his welfare, and he leaves time to explain to him in what precisely that necessity consists. Similarly the traditional legal system with all its intricate and antiquated rules and principles stands for the inherited culture and, though it will not be impossible to throw it overboard at the last, this will only be done when it is certain that the spirit which it once put literally into words survives intact in spite of the abandonment of the letter.

The majority of the essays that follow are concerned with Hindu law. The system which was built up over the centuries was based upon religion and the ways in which that religion expressed itself in every walk of life. It is obvious from the texts that their original authors, or perhaps more accurately the society in which such authorship could be envisaged, attributed origins which could be regarded as religious to the customs both of doing, and abstaining from doing, of preferring or of rejecting, actually observed amongst real groups. Even where the custom, as in some commercial matters, appeared to have no importance from a religious point of view, the authority behind every established rule was supposed to be a sanction, which though actually the result of habit and consensus, could be seen by contemporaries only in the same terms as the totality of duty. Later the distinction between the 'seen' and the 'unseen' motive was accepted. Rules based upon a 'seen' motive could be neglected, though it was always meritorious to follow them. There might, however, be some overriding consideration, by reason of which it would be more meritorious to take a different course, and the discretion to make the choice lay with the person authorized to carry the responsibility. And this was seen entirely in social terms. A further distinction was seen between a rule which was good, and another which was less good, though both came down from anterior ages with the sanction of religion behind them. Hinduism early developed the ability to recognize as good even the less meritorious of alternatives.

The Two Paths

A peculiar example will serve because it too has a heavy social content. Hindu *śāstra-s* recognized that a childless widow could and should burn herself alive with the body of her husband, or follow him in such a suicide as soon as practicable after his death. Other Hindu *śāstra-s* deprecated this act, since suicide in itself was a sinful act. This kind of suicide was a survival from a period in which religious suicides were fashionable, and men too threw themselves from high places in a desire to show their devotion to a deity.[1] But the *śāstra* though recognizing and sanctioning both outlooks, also provided a theoretical reconciliation between them. The present writer would not pretend that modern leading Indian societies are aware of this teaching, or have ever come into contact with even the fringes of it (though it is well known to the student of Rāmmohun Roy's struggles against suttee), but he does claim that the attitude which gave birth to it, centuries ago, explains the calm of the Hindu population while their scheme of religious observances undergoes radical attack from the side of law, and while it loses adherence gradually, in some quarters, as a feature of daily life. The theory was this: all the actions of man are derived from desire, but the ultimate goal of man is absence of desire; religious injunctions are of two sorts, those which apply to the individual in the wheel of social life, attached to observances as a social fact and not truly directed to the ultimate release of his personality from *karma* and from rebirth, and those, on the other hand, directed to him who seeks *mokṣa*, *nivṛtti*, the cessation of striving and suffering and experience altogether. This is ultimate merit, and it is subserved by injunctions suited to attaining it. The ability to distinguish between injunctions directed to a better rebirth and injunctions directed to avoiding rebirth is an ability which the *śāstra* would regard as supreme. The rule permitting a woman to commit suttee is a rule of the first kind; she will be reborn in an advantageous position, for her act is done out of a desire, perhaps a desire for merit. But for those who seek *mokṣa* the duties of the household life as a widow, in patient self-abnegation, are appropriate.[2]

[1] Kāṇe, *History of Dharmaśāstra*, II, 924–8. U. Ṭhakur, *History of Suicide in India: an Introduction* (Delhi, 1963). V. Minorsky, 'Gardīzī on India', *B.S.O.A.S.* 12, no. 3 (1948), pp. 625–40.

[2] Rāmmohun Roy, *Abstract of the Argument regarding the Burning of Widows, considered as a Religious Rite* (Calcutta, 1830) in *English Works of Raja Rammohun Roy*, ed. J. C. Ghose, II (Calcutta, 1901), pp. 187–90. He cites Vijñāneśvara, *Mitākṣarā* on Yājñavalkya I, 86 (see the discussion at Kāṇe, *H.D.*, II, 631–3) and a very important group of verses, Manu XII, 88–90, the last pair of which he paraphrases, 'Whatever act is performed for the

This distinction between *pravṛtti* and *nivṛtti* is not mere philosophy divorced from law. In *Kameswara Sastri* v. *Veeracharlu*[1] the question was whether the manager of a joint Hindu family was entitled to burden members of the family (irrespective of their consent) with an alienation of the family's landed assets for the purpose of performing a non-indispensable duty, viz. the marriage ceremony of a male member of the family. Krishnaswami Ayyar, J., said:[2]

> . . . it is necessary to examine the principles on which the obligatory character of the marriage ceremony rests. There are two paths laid down for the Hindu in the sacred texts (see Mahadeva Sastri's *Bhagavat Gita* [sic] with Sankara's commentary, p. 2). One is the path of work or attachment to the things of this world and the other the path of non-attachment or renunciation. The four *āśramas* or stages of life are prescribed for the regenerate classes. . . . The journey from stage to stage in regular order of succession is contemplated as progress along the path of worldly work. [i.e. the whole of the *dharma* of the *gṛhasthāśrama* is a matter of *pravṛtti* if we see it as a question of *karma* and ritual observances.] It is true . . . that if he has conquered his passions and cultivated the feeling of non-attachment he may pass directly . . . to the *āśrama* of the *sannyāsin* (see Medhātithi on Manu VI, 36 and the *Mitākṣarā* on Yājñavalkya III, 56–7). But except for him . . . the stage of householder is practically compulsory.

So it is with the Hinduism of today, which its law subserves: those who value observances and orthodox rituals and marriages which will serve those ends are entitled to pursue the course, and nothing in the law forbids them to do so. It is the

sake of gratification in this world or the next, is called *Pravartaka*, as leading to the temporary enjoyment of the mansions of gods; and those which are performed according to the knowledge respecting God are called *Nivartaka*, as means to procure release from the five elements of this body; that is, they obtain eternal bliss.' Cf. Manu II, 2, III, 12. The *Bhagavad-gītā* confirms this (II. 42–4 and IX. 21, which last should be read in context in IX. 20–34). The *Mahābhārata* obviously refers to Manu when at XII (Śāntiparva), sec. 192, *vv.* 39–40 (Poona edn., 1951) Bhīṣma divides Brahmins and *dharma-s* into two classes; those which are *pravṛtta* and those which are *nivṛtta*. The character depicted claims to be *nivṛtta* (and so in search of *mokṣa*) and thus inhibited from *pratigraha* (the religious acceptance of gifts in ritual acts). He is made to say, 'Give gifts to those, O King, who are *pravṛtta*; I shall not accept any boon. . . .' M. Yamunāchārya, at *Kannada Studies*, 3 (Jan. 1966), pp. 23–32, contends that Śaivism and Vaishnavism in Karṇāṭaka taught that *pravṛtti* might be pursued in *nivṛtti* and vice versa, fostering thereby a sane social philosophy. That the absence of desire (*kāma*) led to *mokṣa* was taught as early as the *Bṛhadāraṇyaka Upaniṣad* (IV, 4).

[1] (1910) 34 Mad. 422.

[2] At 34 Mad. 428.

duty of the State to facilitate and not to hinder religious aspirations, unless their pursuit conflicts with the well-being of others. Those, on the other hand, who seek release, personal salvation, personal absorption into the divine, never to be reborn in a world which is an experience of suffering best construed as a retribution for sins in past lives, may make their own way, fulfilling such injunctions as they regard as binding upon them, not motivated by desire whether for merit or for social prestige, and emerging from the tight nexus of social obligation into the freer and purer air of devotion. For this śāstric Hinduism makes ample provision. The higher learning which is by no means lower-rated than the *karma-kāṇḍa*, about which law is preoccupied, seeks nothing but the *mokṣa* of the individual, without a backward glance at the family or dependants, about whom the law thinks so much.

Thus our modern students, with their freedom from caste prejudice and their happy ignorance about Hindu law, share with all their compatriots the stereotyped admiration for the *sannyāsī*, the man who appears to have thrown off the world, and seeks not that which can be gained, but the absence of desire, the man to whom desire of any kind is meaningless, and in whom, as a result, a special potency and contact with unseen forces can be detected. High Court judges and raw students of the sciences will prostrate themselves before this roguish peasant or that polished actor who wear the garb of the *sannyāsī* and have thought themselves, like R. K. Nārāyan's 'Guide', into the timeless role of the *fakir*, the man who has given up the world. That the man may be bogus does not matter in the least, for it is the prostration that counts.

But that both the *karma-kāṇḍa* and the stages of life including *sannyāsa*, the sum-total of religious observances and the flight from observance, are related to *dharma* as various means are to their common end, was understood at least fifteen hundred years ago. Yājñavalkya (III, 65–6) says, with a frankness disconcerting to the ritualist and the enthusiast alike:

> *nāśramaḥ kāraṇaṃ dharme kriyamāṇo bhaveddhi saḥ*
> *ato yad ātmano 'pathyaṃ pareṣāṃ na tad ācaret:*
> *satyam asteyam akrodho hrīḥ śaucaṃ dhīr dhṛtir damaḥ*
> *saṃyatendriyatā vidyā dharmaḥ sarva udāhṛtaḥ.*

The (outward show of the) *āśrama* [especially of the *sannyāsī*, but *a fortiori* that of the student or householder] is not the efficient cause of *dharma*, for that comes about only by being *done*. Consequently, whatever is not agreeable to one's own self should not be done to others:

Truthfulness, not stealing, absence of anger, modesty, cleanliness, discrimination, courage, equanimity (including humility), the quality of subjugating the senses, and *knowledge*: these comprise all *dharma*!

No doubt this is high-level soteriology, like the Vedānta, looking upon 'works' as wholly subordinate to 'renunciation', and even despising 'works' as more of a hindrance to 'salvation' than a help. No doubt this view-point, which has existed alongside the pursuit of *karma* from pre-historic times, filters very slowly down to the masses. But it is none the less true Hinduism for that.[1] Hinduism is the pursuit of *dharma*, which may be defined at several levels.

And so the two religious paths go on together as they have gone on in all time of which Indian history has any record. Let this chapter end with a story from real life, and let the reader see whether the tales of the law which follow agree with it.

In South Kanara District there are many Brahmin villages in which an orthodox and at the same time businesslike and mobile people are domiciled. A Brahmin householder dies and the time comes when his *śrāddha* must be performed. It is the first *śrāddha* and the eldest son should be there to make the offerings to the dead and to the Brahmins who have assembled by invitation to represent the deceased, the society to which he belonged and the unseen powers, all in one. All the sons are there, the eldest son amongst them, but he is sitting on the veranda and the ceremony goes on with the second eldest acting as if his senior was dead. Why? The Brahmin specialists in ritual who have attended this family from long before memory, even their long and detailed memory, runs, carry on and direct proceedings, and the name of this second eldest brother is used, and that of the eldest is forgotten. They will consider the *second* son's lineage alone as the senior branch; the

[1] 'The Hindu view of life . . . is governed by an implicit faith in the efficacy and validity of both these ways and in the possibility of reconciling the claims of action and renunciation. This faith is indeed the very motive force of Hindu *dharma* . . .' R. N. Dandekar, 'The Role of Man in Hinduism', in K. W. Morgan, ed., *The Religion of the Hindus* (New York, Ronald Press Co., 1953), at p. 134.

senior brother is as good as dead, and the children who play on the veranda with him are as good as strangers. Why? The elder brother, who was the great hope of the family, travelled and studied in Bombay. His intellect and his adaptability took him into many quarters and he chose and married a bride from another community, a Hindu it is true, but the daughter of a man of another *varṇa*. True the Hindu law of the day sanctioned the marriage: he did not have to go before a registrar to have his marriage solemnized in the banal form which the State afforded. In Bombay priests of many kinds can be found and one was available to perform the ceremony, with which, no doubt, the bride's relations were well pleased. But he broke the sacred law as understood in his village. Years ago such a man would not be expected to return, or if he did he must stay in some hotel. Nowadays he can come back to his ancestral home, but as far as the religion is concerned he has ceased to exist at all the major crises of life. As far as his blood relations are concerned his wife is a concubine, and his children are illegitimate. They have no right, except by courtesy, to the family name. They will never participate in family rituals. The eldest son of this man will no doubt perform his own father's funeral; but the Brahmin priests of this family will not assist. Their books and genealogies do not contain the names of these people.[1] The horoscopes which are kept in the family archives do not record the wife's name. Those who step out of the caste *mores* step, so far as the *śāstra* is concerned, into a limbo, where only residual rights remain for them. They are fit to form a new community of their own, whereupon they can employ their own priests, and thus, says the *śāstra*, castes (*jāti-s*) are in fact formed.

The eldest son is content to pay the price for his irregular behaviour. In Bombay he is a man, in his own father's house he is less than a man. Does this mean that his religious life is at an end: must he become an atheist? By no means. He is a sincere student of the *Upaniṣad-s*, a moral thinker of some eminence, and himself plays a role in propagating Hindu doctrines, though it be a minor one. He is a devotee of the Śaṅkarācārya, and is an

[1] On the legal implications of such records see *Kishori* v. *Mst. Chaltibai* (1959) 22 S.C.J. 560. On the genealogist and his practice see A. M. Shah and R. G. Shroff, 'The Vahīvancā Bāroṭs of Gujarat . . .', in Milton Singer, ed., *Traditional India: Structure and Change* (Philadelphia, 1959) pp. 40–70.

exemplary citizen. And on his death bed he will call upon the Lord Hari to stretch out a hand to him, and to take him up into Paradise. The paths are there, and the legislatures know it. While the conflict between religion and the State in India strongly resembles that between the Church and the State in Europe prior to and during the Reformation, there are essential points of difference, which it is hoped this book will clarify.

3

RELIGIOUS COMMANDS AND LEGAL COMMANDS

Many educated Hindus believe that the *dharmaśāstra*,[1] which incorporates classical Hindu jurisprudence, has said the last word on all topics of both religious and legal importance. To them there has never been, in conscience, any distinction between law and religion, whatever force the State may have given to the decisions of the courts set up after the advent of Europeans. This point of view is found even amongst those who have benefited from 'western' education, and is to be detected even in very unexpected quarters. The man who has spent all his working life ignoring the *śāstra* may be found at the last practising austerities, and performing *pūjā* inculcated by śāstric authorities, in the hope, perhaps of atoning for his previous neglect of the perennial truths of the race. In this mood the orthodox do not disrespect the courts, but they see them and what goes on in them as features of a transient world, of practical importance, no doubt, but of no reality in point of conscience.

This attitude, which can be called the 'orthodox' point of view, did not until the 1950's stand in the way of adjustment of the Hindu law to the changing needs of modern life, since the power of interpretation has always been allowed to those who have approached the study of the *śāstra* after preparatory linguistic and philosophical studies. But it tends to weaken the faith of a respectable section of the public in India in the validity and virtue of much Indian legislation, and presented an obstacle in

[1] This chapter corresponds to an article entitled 'The criteria for distinguishing between legal and religious commands in the Dharmaśāstra', AIR 1953 Journal 52–3, 57–62. The wording has been improved in places, and the whole has been slightly expanded.

the way of the Hindu Code Bill throughout its various stages. Mr. V. V. Deshpande may stand as a leading proponent of this point of view. The validity of statutes altering the Hindu Law of the courts is flatly denied, and those whose studies might have been expected to be of the greatest service to contemporary legal draftsmen have stood aside, for the most part, as if that way of proceeding must not be admitted to be relevant or useful. Two quotations from a work of K. V. Rangaswāmī Aiyangār,[1] who in his day combined śāstric knowledge, faith in the *śāstra* and a practical knowledge of government and economics, will illustrate this attitude. The work was published in 1941, when the Hindu Code Bill controversies were very much in the air. He says,[2] 'Medhātithi roundly declared that a king cannot make a law overriding *Dharma*,' and 'The evidence of history does not disclose any exercise of the alleged regal power of independent legislation.' Again,[3] he says of the king, 'He cannot make a new law. The royal edict is merely declaratory, and not innovative.' The same objection would obviously apply to statutes of a modern parliament. The reason for this apparently unpractical point of view is merely this, that law and religion are conceived of as one and undivided, that the tradition and research of millennia are thought to have shaped the religious norm, which, seeing that it is intended to be operative and not merely theoretical, has given once and for all a certain character to the law to which all legislation must conform. If statutes agree with the *śāstra* they may be superfluous. If they deviate from it, they may be wrong. They may be enforced by the officials of the State: but they are not binding in conscience. This takes us back to the position in England during, say, the reign of Elizabeth I, when statutes would bind Roman Catholics in a secular sense, but not necessarily in conscience. Inconvenient, out of tune with the modern world, but paralleled in many oriental countries which possess a written and a religious law: whether this outlook is supported by history is a question which the opponents of legislation do not stop to ask. If we should return to it we must do so in another connexion.[4]

It is obviously in India's interest that the traditional (apart from the technically constitutional) capacity of the national

[1] *Rājadharma* (Madras, The Adyar Library, 1941).
[2] At p. 23. [3] At p. 133. [4] Below, p. 438.

legislature to pass valid statutes should be investigated, since the present 'split mind' on this topic is injurious to public morale. The orthodox scholar, the professor of the *śāstra*, reacts, with increasing impotence, in some such manner as this: 'Let them pass what they choose; for our part we shall do our best to avoid the courts! As for the so-called Hindu Code, they may codify and de-codify what they please, but let them have the courtesy not to call their products "Hindu law", for that is just what they are not!'

It is the purpose of this paper to raise certain points which need to be discussed; a full answer still eludes us, for our present state of knowledge is defective. Even our *interim* results may not harmonize with the wishful thinking about India's past which some eminent and knowledgeable men have been betrayed into evincing. In a tentative conclusion it will be possible to show the distinctions actually observed in the *śāstra* itself, both in theory and in what we know of practice, between what is known in the West as 'legal' commands as opposed to that which is generally understood to be excluded by them, namely (merely) 'religious' commands. At the outset, however, it is necessary to make plain that, as regards *validity*, all commands to be found in the *śāstra* were equally binding, and that no command which was enforceable in the Western sense lacked the character of being 'religious' also. To omit to perform the act enjoined brought sin in any event, and sin brought misfortune in this life and the prospect, if not expiated personally or vicariously, of unhappy births hereafter. To perform an act forbidden could not lead to less awful consequences. The fruitful distinction for us, therefore, is not between 'legal' and 'religious' commands, but between that which was merely binding in conscience, and that which was, apart from the conscientious sanction, capable of being enforced by the king or his officer in the course of judicial proceedings. The possibility of conflict between enforceable and unenforceable commands which is denied by the 'orthodox', and even between different classes of enforceable commands, deserves investigation, and throws no little light on the true nature of the *śāstra* itself. The *śāstra* flatly denied any paramount legal force to customs of a religious character emanating from sources other than the Veda (the source of all knowledge so far as the 'orthodox' are concerned). It must be remembered therefore that rules obeyed by Buddhists such as 'bowing to Chaityas' though viewed as religious commands by that community had no sanction whatever in the eyes of the 'orthodox'[1] whose jurisprudence was the only legal science India knew before the coming of the Muslims. A further opportunity for conflict, between the *dharmaśāstra* and its colleague the *arthaśāstra* (the science of ways and means), was taken seriously by the authors of both classes of writing, but it can be ignored for the purpose of this paper[2] since it is almost certain that the latter never prevailed against the former on its own ground.

The Judicial Committee of the Most Honourable Privy Council, until recently in effect the highest Court of Appeal for British India, were in the year 1898 faced by three cases in which a conflict between law and religion seemed inescapable. In two of them the clash was in fact impossible to ignore. By 1898 it had become axiomatic that Indian religious doctrines and prejudices must be treated with respect, without an attempt to evaluate them. In the first of the cases, *Balwant Singh* v. *Rani Kishori*,[3] it was held, *inter alia*, that the self-acquired immoveable property of a coparcener in a Hindu joint-family was freely alienable by him, the śāstric text to the contrary being merely directory and not flatly mandatory. We read at page 69 of the judgement:

> All these old textbooks and commentaries are apt to mingle religious and moral considerations, not being positive laws, with rules intended for positive laws. In the preface of his valuable work on Hindu Law Sir W. Macnaghten says: 'It by no means follows that because an act has been prohibited it should therefore be considered as illegal. The distinction between the *vinculum juris* and the *vinculum pudoris* is not always discernible.'

The latter truth their Lordships were able easily to illustrate from contemporary English behaviour. The distinction enabled them to solve an extremely difficult problem in *Sri Balusu Gurulingaswamy* v. *Sri Balusu Rama Lakshmamma*,[4] namely whether

[1] Medhātithi on Manu I, 3; Haradatta on Gautama I, 1, 1.

[2] See below, pp. 166f.

[3] (1898) 25 I.A. 54.

[4] (1899) 26 I.A. 113. See also *Ram Harakh* v. *Jagarnath* (1931) 53 All. 815, a case of no little importance as it was cited and followed in *Abhiraj* v. *Debendra* AIR 1962 S.C. 351. At p. 821 their Lordships said, 'It may be stated with confidence as a general, though not a universal rule that where a

an only son might be adopted: the texts were uniformly against such an adoption, but practice and usage and the view of the Presidencies' High Courts seemed equally balanced. It was decided that the rule found in the *śāstra* was intended to be binding in conscience, but that the breach of the rule would not invalidate the adoption. In the judgement it is remarked:[1]

> No system of law makes the province of legal obligation co-extensive with that of religious or moral obligation. A man may, in his conduct or in the disposition of his property, disregard the plainest dictates of duty. . . . And yet he may be within his legal rights. The Hindu sages doubtless saw this distinction as clearly as we do, and the precepts they have given for the guidance of life must be construed with reference to it. If a transaction is declared to be null and void in law, whether on a religious ground or another, it is so; and if its nullity is a necessary implication from a condemnation of it, the law must be so declared. But the mere fact that a transaction is condemned in books like the Smritis does not necessarily prove it to be void. It raises the question what kind of condemnation is meant.

It will be clear from this that their Lordships envisaged the contrast as one between advice, which one *ought* to take, and rules which one *could* not frustrate or circumvent. It will appear presently that this was not an entirely satisfactory diagnosis of the true field of conflict. Their Lordships were unfortunate in not having available to them Hindu texts in which the topic of conflict of rules is distinctly ventilated. But the attitude the Privy Council adopted, entirely intelligible from Europe's own legal history, made its mark on Hindu law and paved the way for the developments we shall review. The third case in the

spiritual penalty has been provided for in the *smṛtis* for the violation of a śāstric duty, the injunction is not one of an imperative character so as to be legally binding upon the conscience.' [This by no means follows.] At p. 822: 'In construing the *smṛtis* texts, one is apt to confound a rule of a commendatory character with a rule which is positive and imperative. The Hindu sages knew and emphasized upon the difference between the two. The technical term *vidhi* or *vidhivākya* connotes a rule of positive law and is distinguishable from *niyama*, which, though a rule of conduct, is not necessarily and in all cases binding upon the conscience. Vijñāneśvara, in his famous commentary, significantly points out that a precept which, upon a proper classification of the text, belongs to the realm of ecclesiastical law has not, in the *vyavahāra* law, the same authority as a *vidhivākya* and cannot be treated there as a positive rule of law.' [The case involved questions of guardianship in marriage and *factum valet*, on which see below, p. 91.]

[1] 26 I.A. 113 at 139.

series, *Bhagwan Singh* v. *Bhagwan Singh*,[1] was not equally difficult to decide since custom and the Indian decisions were in a closer degree of agreement. Notwithstanding the doubt expressed in the earlier cases, the adoption of a mother's sister's son was held to be *void* on the mere formal ground (without regard being had to the merits of the question, at least overtly) that the śāstric texts tended to forbid it. Had the current of the Indian decisions been as disturbed as in *Sri Balusu's case*, the result might well have been otherwise, for the Privy Council always gave great weight to decisions on social matters by judges long resident in India and acquainted with Indian conditions: and had *some* of them thought such adoptions allowable, and had there been no outcry at this finding, the purely formal approach might have been avoided.

The uncertainty thus introduced into the interpretation of the śāstric texts is emphasized for comparative lawyers by the statement of Sir Henry Maine, that ambiguous figure in Indian legal history,[2] that the 'Hindoo Code called the Laws of Manu', whose position in śāstric literature he was in no position to evaluate, was 'in great part an ideal picture of that which, in the view of the Brahmins, ought to be the law.'[3] Thus, in addition to the suggestion of the learned Board of the highest court of appeal that of commands appearing in the *śāstra* phrased in similar language some were directory and some mandatory–no key was ever supplied to the problem of distinguishing which were which, a problem which persisted as late as the year 1954[4] –we are faced by the proposition of an eminent comparative jurist that the entire literature was more visionary than practical and that it was almost impossible to say what part of the *śāstra* was ever administered in practice. These discouragements, excusable in the then state of knowledge, need not deter us today. We now know that every commentator writing in the time of the Hindu dynasties and the earlier Muslim empires in India intended his readers to take his declaration of positive duties and of abstentions seriously, and that every phrase implying a posi-

[1] (1899) 26 I.A. 153.

[2] See Derrett, 'Sir Henry Maine and Law in India', *Jur. Rev.* 1959, pt. 1, pp. 40–55.

[3] *Ancient Law* (edn. of 1916), ch. 1, p. 15.

[4] See *Kasubai* v. *Bhagwan* AIR 1955 Nag. 210, 213.

tive or a negative injunction was intended to be acted upon.[1] We know, moreover, that his readers were the spiritual teachers of their own and coming generations and also the judiciary, whose advice to the king or his deputy was generally, if not universally, accepted and put into effect.[2] If we leave aside for the present the different categories of enforceable injunctions, there was a well-recognized distinction between enforceable and unenforceable injunctions, and the literature, and its readers, were amply aware of this.

At the outset we may do well to point out that the *śāstra* shows signs of having entered into its early formative stages at a period when the king was little more than a commander-in-chief. The conception of the king as the supreme judge is one which was superimposed upon an accepted background of self-help and conscience as the ultimate guide. There is not the smallest doubt but that the king in classical times imposed punishments upon and coerced subjects and strangers who were troublesome to him, whether or not they had committed a sin thereby or otherwise; but it is evident that the king is given by the *śāstra* powers of punishing only a section of the offences, for the sin of committing which the *śāstra* prescribes *prāyaścitta* or penance. Thus, a Hindu committing a theft was obliged to perform his own personal expiation and if the injured party took the matter to the king (theft being a particularly abhorrent crime in the ancient Indian view), he would be bound to make restitution and pay a fine as well. A civil as well as a religious penalty attached to those offences which, in the interests of the developing State, seemed to the jurists of primaeval times insufficiently discouraged by social, that is to say, conscientious penalties alone. It is not possible to enter here into the doubtful question how far the civil penalty could, especially in cases of the death penalty, operate *suo vigore* as a penance, so as to relieve the sinner of the effects of his sin in the after-life or lives. But it is of importance to know that such questions interested jurists at least as much as the questions of the appropriate penalties themselves.

Injunctions enforceable either by the king at the instance of an aggrieved party–the king could only in limited cases initiate

[1] See Kumārila, *Tantravārttika* (Jhā's trans.), p. 247.

[2] On the function of the Brahmin in court see below, p. 183.

litigation, and theoretically might not defer it–or by a caste tribunal partook of both a legal and a religious character, but unenforceable injunctions were quite as numerous. Of these the vast majority have become obsolete as the glamour of a highly organized ceremonial personal life fades before competing images of prestige, and as methods of atoning for failure become easier, whether by the greater facility of pilgrimage to holy places or by the greater ease of making atoning gifts in charity, or because of the corrosive effect of genuine Hindu beliefs witnessed in the *Bhagavadgītā* to the effect that 'salvation' is available to those who may have failed in point of performances but have faith in a personal saviour.[1] Obsolescence therefore has many causes, not by any means all of them discreditable to persons having faith in the *śāstra*.

Injunctions Unenforceable by Nature

In the *Bṛhadāraṇyaka Upaniṣad* (V. 2,3) we read: 'Be subdued. Give (gifts). Be merciful.' The second injunction in particular is often repeated in various contexts, since liberality is a cardinal duty in Hinduism. These are, however, excellent illustrations of unenforceable commands, since no period is stated within which the command is to be fulfilled and, more especially, since the performance of the command is inculcated with the object of increasing the spiritual merit of the individual, who may safely be left to attend to his unseen interests. It is a rule of interpretation that unless the injunction is of a nature which does not immediately coincide with natural inclination it lacks binding (legal and religious) force. On the other hand it is admitted by all writers that the *vyavahāra* (business) part of the *dharmaśāstra* largely codifies practice and is not unenforceable merely because it coincides with what everybody does.

In the *Yājñavalkya-smṛti*, I, 323, we read: 'There is no higher *dharma* for kings than that they should give to Brahmins the wealth they acquire in war, and that they should always give security to their subjects.' Similarly unenforceable, because there is no court to which appeal against him can be lodged, are rules that a king should never reprieve the guilty and should never resume grants to religious uses made by his ancestors or

[1] See above, pp. 71f.

by himself or even by enemy kings whose lands he has taken. It is because of the impossibility of putting the king himself on trial that the sections of *dharmaśāstra* addressed to the king rely chiefly upon his assumed eagerness to acquire and reluctance to lose spiritual merit. Vagueness alone is not, in this case, the principal ground for unenforceability.

Penances, described at length in the third book of that same *smṛti*, are of two kinds: suitable for occasions where the offence is known to others than the perpetrator, and others suitable for secret offences. This curious division, which has not received the study it deserves,[1] makes it possible for even great sins to be expiated by a particular penance, generally less severe than the penance appropriate when the same offence is publicly known. By its very nature, such a rule of penance (see Yājñ. III, 301 and ff.) cannot be enforced. Again certain penances are prescribed for sins *possibly* or *probably* committed, e.g. for destroying minute creatures in fruit, etc. (ibid., 275): since the facts cannot be known and the penance is more or less anticipatory or inspired by abundant caution, it must be unenforceable. Many private matters which seemed to require penance can never have been enquired into by any tribunal.

Injunctions which are Capable of Enforcement by a Caste Tribunal

The caste tribunal had an option whether to enquire into offences of a non-criminal nature. A wide discretion appertained to it, and in pre-British times its jurisdiction was as wide, as important and as effective as that of the civil and criminal court. In early British times caste tribunals and tribunals composed of representatives of various castes still exercised jurisdictions, and the battle of the young Bengalis who wanted religious and social freedom more, perhaps, than they wanted Christianity was fought against an orthodoxy which at that very period was striving to keep the weapon of excommunication sharp *in terrorem.*[2] Vijñāneśvara, who, for all his great age (he lived

[1] Kāṇe, *H.D.*, III, pp. 944–5.

[2] Shown by M. Mohar Ali, *The Bengali Reaction to Christian Missionary Activities 1833–1857* (cited above). This story is of great interest, especially in relation to the balance between education (as a prestige-earning tool) and social sanctions with a religious criterion. Raja Rammohun Roy's constant

about A.D. 1100), remains a prime authority, takes pains (*Mitākṣarā* on Yājñ. III, 300) to illustrate the powers and duties as well as the constitution of caste tribunals. One illustration may be given of an injunction, unquestionably binding in conscience, which might have been enforced in certain localities at certain periods, but which was certainly not universally enforced: *Yājñavalkya* (I, 159) declares that one should not bathe in water belonging to another without first taking out five balls (of mud). The object of this, obviously, is that when bathing in a tank, other than a stone-lined tank, or perhaps even in a stone-lined tank fed from a river liable to silt, one should help to counter-balance soil descending into it (possibly due to one's own descent), not to speak of impurities washed from one's own body. Where permission to bathe has been given by the owner, or where the tank is public property, the need for this conscientious act disappears. The rule is not incapable of being enforced, for small boys notice whether obligatory acts are performed or not, but practice in such contexts must have varied from place to place and from time to time and some communities or villages will have been more concerned about the non-performance of this duty than others. The forum would not be the king's court or that of any deputy of his, but the caste or village council. Similarly more important rules, such as the age within which a child should be tonsured, or within which his initiation (called for convenience 'thread-ceremony') should be performed, or within which a daughter should be given in marriage, must have been applied with differing degrees of vigour and with different emphasis in different regions at various epochs.

Enforceable Injunctions

All the injunctions contained in the *smṛti-s* are *prima facie* binding, since it was universally believed that the authors not only summarized the Veda, but reproduced in practical form parts of the Veda lost since the earliest times. The supposition of a lost Vedic authority as a basis for a *smṛti* rule is not so absurd as it seems, once one has accepted the fact that at some period in the

awareness of the dangers of excommunication is notorious, and relates to the period 1818–30.

history of ancient India a break in continuity of tradition occurred. This break had the effect of shaking the public's confidence in its own power to innovate and make original research into jurisprudence, amongst the sciences in general, and this lack of confidence is evidenced by the accepted theory that all knowledge, past, present and future, is or was to be found in the Veda–a useful hypothesis as it accounted, at second hand, for the passages in *smṛti* texts which would otherwise have been anachronisms if their authors had not had the entire Veda before them. This firm anchorage perhaps saved Indian culture from extinction, but has tended, amongst other factors, to stifle originality.

As Medhātithi says (on *Manu-smṛti* I, 1), 'Manu has said all that has been said in the Ṛgveda, the Yajurveda, the Sāmaveda and the *mantra-s* of the Atharva, as also by the Seven Great Sages.' The authority thus given to Manu, deservedly considered, for all his more curious angularities, the greatest jurist India has produced, is extended in lesser measure to the writers of other *smṛti-s*, and the task of harmonizing the rules contained in these authorities has been the primary task of the legal commentator. The fossilizing tendency of this traditional technique, drawing of necessity upon sources some of which are not less than twenty-eight centuries old, was apparent to these practitioners themselves, and they adopted various expedients to avoid the effects of applying literally what the *smṛti* appeared at first sight to lay down, if that would clearly result in inconvenience. They were fortified by certain elements in the *śāstra* itself, which cannot be examined fully here, but which, in sum, accorded great weight to the conduct of men learned in the Veda, the practice of 'good people', the exigencies of judicial procedure, and the directives of the executive as supplementary sources of law. These require separate investigation.[1] Custom today, at Hindu law, less so at Muhammadan law–for the techniques of the two major oriental systems differ here as elsewhere[2]–can override any written text, once it is proved and established to the court's satisfaction, no matter how glaringly inconsistent it may be with the policy of the *śāstra*. But the

[1] See chapters 6 and 7 below.

[2] On the peculiar place of custom *vis-à-vis* written law in the Islamic system as administered in India see below, p. 519.

orthodox here enter a *caveat*. To them, as to the *mīmāṃsaka-s*, or professors of hermeneutics, of the late classical period, no rule contrary to the tenor of the *dharmaśāstra* could be valid either in conscience or in law. If the *mīmāṃsaka* Kumārila-bhaṭṭa were asked whether the southern custom of marrying one's sister's daughter should be tolerated, since whole castes including virtuous men learned in the Veda practised it, he would at once answer that a custom so flagrantly contrary to the *śāstra* could not be practised by 'good men', whatever their apparent qualifications, and that the custom was bad in law.[1] But, as we shall see, what a *śāstric* scholar thought was bad would not necessarily amount to the same thing as what we mean by 'unenforceable'. However, theory and practice departed from the orthodox view,[2] and lawyers constantly reviewed the law in the light of practical needs.

Expedients for Circumventing the Written Text

(1) Interpretation alone could work marvels. A close study of the methods of the *śāstrī-s* has yet to be published. To a casual reader, however, it is obvious that the meaning which even an early commentator such as Medhātithi obtains from his text is seldom that which would occur to a lay Sanskrit scholar of today. The necessity of interpreting each text in the light of parallel, and often apparently inconsistent texts in equally valuable and binding sources—according to the hermeneutic theory of *ekavākyatā* (all the sages were in harmony)—leaves ample scope for the introduction of alternatives, and the application of conditions, where the text gives no hint of such. One illustration, well known to specialists, will suffice to show to what lengths the art of interpretation could be carried. The chief objection to the marriage of a maternal uncle's daughter, customary in southern India, is that it offends against the paramount śāstric rule that one should not take a *sapiṇḍa* as one's wife, since such a union would be incestuous.[3] Mādhava (c. 1350) takes the trouble to prove that such marriages are in

[1] P. V. Kāṇe, *Hindu Customs and Modern Law* (Bombay, University of Bombay, 1950) gives much attention to the views of Kumārila-bhaṭṭa.

[2] On relations between *mīmāṃsā* and practical law see chapter 6 below.

[3] Kāṇe, *H.D.*, II, pp. 459 ff. See below, p. 108.

fact not objectionable, on the ground that when a bride is married in the Brāhma form (approved but there less common) her issue belongs to the *gotra* (patrilineal family) of her husband and thus the incestuous nature of the union is negligible; in his view the prohibition applies only where, as was more common, the mother was given in marriage in the Āsura (an unapproved) form with the result that she did not enter the *gotra* of her husband and her issue were of the same *gotra* as their mother's natal *gotra* and thus of her brother's family also. This argument seems weak in view (i) of the fact that it does not avoid the sapiṇḍaship bar, for all children are the *sapiṇḍa-s* of their mothers and hence of their mother's agnates, and (ii) of the predicament in which the castes who married in the Āsura form are left. A not dissimilar step was taken by Devaṇṇabhaṭṭa (c. 1250) to justify the refusal of lawyers in the Tamil country to give to widows the share at a partition to which, according to the *Yājñavalkya-smṛti* (II, 123b) they were entitled: since the Brāhma form was, as it still tends to be,[1] the less common form amongst non-Brahmins in the Tamil country his rule that only those women who were married in the Brāhma form could obtain a share amounted to a virtual emasculation of the right.

A further, but more abstruse, method was that which relied upon the distinction between *vidhi-s*, or injunctions of which several categories were distinguished, and *arthavāda-s*, or allegedly explanatory material. Such a distinction was necessary on account of the theory that no part of the *smṛti* was written in vain. *Vidhi* and *arthavāda* correspond roughly to the Rabbinical categories of *midrash halachah*, which lays down the law, and *midrash haggadah*, which uses the text as merely illustrating, illuminating something else. The criteria for distinguishing these are as yet uncertain, since the practice of the same techniques of *mīmāṃsā* does not yield the same results in different

[1] The Āsura marriage was, in its way, a test for Anglo-Hindu law. Śāstric writers deprecated it, as a sale of the bride. Thus the law could not help to enforce covenants made in connexion with it: but it would not go so far as to declare such marriages void. The law was of interest in connexion with the topic of descent of the property of a woman married in such a form. See in particular *K. Venkata* v. *Lakshmi* (1908) 32 Mad. 185 (F.B.), and *Veerappa* v. *Michael* AIR 1963 S.C. 933 (discussed by S. S. Nigam at (1964) 6 *J.I.L.I.*, no. 4, at pp. 544 ff.).

expert hands. One is left with the conviction, which only future research may shake, that each jurist approached the text from his own standpoint, and that those who were concerned with the practical application of the law did their utmost to expound the texts so that inconvenient or inappropriate rules should be seen as explanatory or subordinate matter. At one time it was believed[1] that a rule of thumb for distinguishing *vidhi* from *arthavāda* lay in the denying of *vidhitva* (the status of a *vidhi*) to any rule which is found expounded in the *smṛti* with accompanying reasons. The presence of reasons was supposed to imply an invitation to the individual to exercise a choice whether he should obey or not. This notion, now happily exploded, was, as their Lordships of the Privy Council remarked, startling, and confuses rather than simplifies the problem.

(2) The *Kalivarjya* theory[2] is a most interesting notion, which rid the law of a number of archaisms (ritual and legal alike), though, one may be permitted to guess, not too soon for influential communities who had already abandoned them. The world's existence being considered as split into four ages, the present being the Kali age, certain items of the civil law were thought of as appropriate to each age. This would account for textual rules which no one who belonged to a respectable caste followed. The commencement of this theory may have been a refusal to accept as binding legal precedents certain apparently immoral acts which the admired gods, heroes and legendary sages indulged in. In traditional language, their strength derived from spiritual merit was so much greater than ours that

[1] V. N. Mandlik's *Hindu Law*, p. 499 followed in *Beni Prasad* v. *Hardai Bibi* (1892) 14 All. 67 (F.B.). In fact words intimating the reason are themselves *arthavāda*, but they do not necessarily lessen the authority of the *vidhi* they accompany: Kāṇe, *H.D.*, III, p. 676, f.n. 1277. The crux is treated with commendable caution by the Privy Council in *Sri Balusu's Case* (above).

[2] For the work of Bhaṭṭāchārya see below, p. 99 n. Kāṇe, *H.D.*, III, pp. 927–68. Derrett, 'The Purāṇas in Vyavahāra portions of mediaeval Smṛti works', *Purāṇa*, 5, No. 1 (1963), 11–30. Robert Lingat in an article in the *Journal Asiatique* of which an English trans. appeared as 'Time and the Dharma (On *Manu* I, 85–6)', *Contrib. Ind. Sociol.*, 6 (1962), pp. 7–16, propounds a view of the Kaliyuga theory which would not merely rescue but in fact strengthen a view of *dharma* as essentially eternal: the moral law does not change from age to age, as the texts literally would seem to suggest. A further analysis of the concepts, especially in the light of the concept of *yuga-s* itself, is desirable.

they could withstand the effects of such lawlessness. But a simpler point of view questioned the relevance of conduct that was good enough for those remote ages as our guide at present. Certain rules inculcated in the *smṛti-s* are agreed on all hands to be obsolete, to be *kali-varjya*, 'to be avoided in the Kali age'. Such a rule is the injunction to appoint a second husband for a widow to raise up seed to her deceased husband. *Niyoga*, as the custom was known, was of great antiquity and was still practised until recently in some parts of Orissa and, perhaps in its original form, in Travancore;[1] it could not be harmonized with the morality taught by Manu, who developed the one-flesh doctrine of marriage, and thus some means of abrogating the *smṛti* rules that referred to it had to be found. Similarly ancient rules of a compassionate nature, such as allowed the remarriage of maidens, were removed by the zeal of more strict ages with the comment that they were 'obsolete in this *yuga* (age)'. Unfortunately the list of *Kali-yuga-varjya-s* was neither long nor elastic and only one writer seems systematically to have attempted to make a collection of archaisms: to all appearances his attempt attracted little support amongst specialists.

(3) Certain not very important rules found in the *smṛti-s* could be embarrassing if held valid without amendment, and this amendment often went beyond the bounds of interpretation. As an example one may take the lists of weights, measures and coins found in the *smṛti-s*. To know the proper fines to be inflicted by the king or his deputy for scheduled offences one must know the weights, measures and coinage referred to there. In the *Mitākṣarā* we find an adjustment of the scale of the *smṛti* (as an antique authority) to the *vyāvahārika*, or current, coinage. In this, as in so many practical contexts, the words of the texts were not allowed to restrict the validity of public acts or necessary institutions. That a text was, unless otherwise stated, illustrative and not exhaustive was a cardinal rule of interpretation, infringed only where a jurist found that to call it exhaustive was necessary to prove his own thesis.

(4) As a last resort certain injunctions found in the *smṛti-s* and incompatible with the demands of contemporary life, if

[1] Sarvādhikāri, *Hindu Law of Inheritance*[2], p. 195. Note also the customs of Krishnanvakas (see 8 Trav. L.R. 51, 61, M. Varkey Ittycheria's *Travancore Case Law, Law of Persons*, 427).

incapable of removal or relegation by interpretation or either of the other methods mentioned above, could be abrogated by a simple condemnation as *loka-vidviṣṭa*, 'intolerable to the public'. The most useful and important half-verse occurs as *Yājñavalkya* I, 156 in the reading adopted by the *Mitākṣarā*, though the text as adopted by his predecessor, Viśvarūpa, is different. Vijñāneśvara quotes it in three places (on Yājñ. I, 109, II, 117, and III, 18). He applies it to render obsolete injunctions to give unequal shares (according to seniority) to sons after the father's death; to sacrifice cows to Mitra and Varuṇa; and to give a learned Brahmin a large bull or a large goat. It is needless to point out that such a maxim emphasized the contact between law and custom. Its capacity for influencing the selection of applicable rules from the source-material of the *śāstra* is far from being exhausted. It runs: *asvargyaṃ loka-vidviṣṭaṃ dharmyam apy, ācaren na tu*, 'One should not practise that which is abhorred by the public, though it be sanctioned in the law, since it leads not to heaven.' Very similar expressions are to be found in the *Manu-smṛti* at II, 57 and IV, 176.[1]

Conflicts between Enforceable Rules

Enough has been said above to make it plain that conflicts within the sphere of enforceable commands were much more readily contemplated by lawyers in touch with practical affairs when the full responsibility rested upon them than the orthodox *śāstrī* of these days feels inclined to admit. Yet the impression would be defective if it ignored the wide scope of conflict which the classical lawyers took for granted and as a rule passed over almost without trace of a comment. Sacred duty and enforceable duties by no means always coincided in the prime of Hindu

[1] *Nirṇaya-sindhu*, III, pt. 1 at p. 206 (Bombay, N.S., 5th edn., 1949) cites the maxim anonymously in the context of marriage of the maternal uncle's daughter, apparently copying Devaṇṇa-bhaṭṭa, *Smṛti-candrikā* (Mysore edn.), I, p. 191. It is of interest that the *Nirṇaya-sindhu* does not cite the maxim where it appears at the commencement of the *Bṛhan-nāradīya-purāṇa* passage on *Kalivarjya-s* (see G. C. S. Śāstrī, *Hindu Law*[3] (Calcutta, 1907), p. 8 where the *purāṇa* is quoted, XXII, 12–16), viz. at III, pt. 1, p. 262. But the defect is made good by Mitra-miśra in the *Vīramitrodaya* (in G. C. Sarkar Śāstrī's edn. and trans., Calcutta, 1879, II, pt. 1, s. 11, p. 61 or at Setlūr's trans., pt. 2, p. 319). See also Kāṇe, *H.D.*, V, 1270, n. 2071.

government; on the contrary three main classes of conflict can be observed.

(i) *Transactions violating an injunction binding in conscience might be valid in law*

The principle laid down in *Sri Balusu's case* was foreshadowed in the famous dictum of Jīmūtavāhana (Dāyabhāga II, 30) that although *smṛti* texts tend to prevent a father's alienating self-acquired immoveable property without his sons' consent, the alienation without such prior consent would be an offence merely in conscience, and not an offence at law–so that the transaction itself is valid; and he comments, 'for a fact cannot be altered by a hundred texts.'[1] Other *smṛti-s* recognize gifts of what is one's own and this is the way the seeming conflict is resolved. The *śāstra* admits that the improper may happen and occasionally legislates for such an eventuality. From Jīmūtavāhana to Jagannātha Tarkapañcānana is not less than seven centuries, nevertheless the latter is found teaching the same sort of doctrine: co-owners who violate the rule about alienating undivided property are liable to correction (he suggests actually punishment), but the transaction as such is not void,[2] embarrassing as it may be to the purchaser when he attempts to come to terms with the family. Similarly, the *śāstra* had always insisted that for a gift to bring about the spiritual merit which was its motive the object given, the donor, and the donee should all be appropriate. Receipt of a gift from an improper donor was an offence for which *prāyaścitta* (penance) was laid down.[3] The question arose whether, since part of the *prāyaścitta* was abandonment of the object given, if the donee failed to give it up and then died, the object was part of the donee's estate, and as such was partible between *dāyāda-s* (virtually, his 'heirs'). The practical answer could only be that the object *was* the property of the donee, and thus was part of the inheritance; any other conclusion would be in the highest degree inconvenient. Vijñāneśvara in the *Mitākṣarā* (I. i, 16) in fact takes the practical

[1] Professor U. C. Sarkar comments that there is a text that nothing is too difficult for a text (so at *Law Review*, 18, 1966, p. 7): but this of course applies entirely to 'unseen' entities. Derret, *Factum Valet*, 7 I.C.L.Q. (1958), 280.

[2] See below, p. 248. [3] Below, p. 142.

view: the gift is effective though the donee himself must perform the penance.

The theme deserves further exploration.[1] Two further illustrations of this important source of conflict come readily to mind: the *śāstra* has always insisted that the intercourse of a Brahmin with a *śūdra* woman (a woman of the fourth caste) was most blameable: Yājñavalkya in fact does not contemplate a marriage between them. How then was it possible for the law to provide for the right of inheritance by sons of such unions? At any rate it is clear that legitimate issue could be born of condemned unions. Again, it is well known that according to the *śāstra* marriages between persons of the same *gotra* were forbidden. We are told, however, that if such a marriage takes place and intercourse has occurred there is no question of nullity of marriage: the parties must perform the appropriate penance, and then live together 'as mother and son' for life.[2] The protection of the woman was evidently the paramount consideration. Occasionally one finds in the *śāstra* prohibitions together with rules indicating what should be done if the prohibitions are ignored. These instances go far to undermine any belief that the injunctions were invariably absolute *per se*, at any rate in the sense in which transactions prohibited by statute may be held unenforceable at common law.

(ii) *Obligations binding in law might not be binding in conscience*

We do not have to look far for examples of these. Medhātithi himself in two places gives illustrations of enforceable laws which have no force in conscience. On Manu I, 21 he speaks of binding rules in the nature of community-edicts (the basis of which we shall investigate elsewhere)[3] such as 'Cattle should not be taken to graze in this locality' and 'This water should not be given for purposes of irrigation of crops to such-and-such a village until we have obtained such-and-such a benefit from that village.' That these should be binding on members of the community by actual or 'social' contract is altogether a different consideration. There cannot, except by a far-fetched interpreta-

[1] Chapter 5 below.

[2] Puruṣottama-paṇḍita, *Gotra-pravara-mañjarī*, ed. J. Brough, para. 2.

[3] Below, pp. 185 f.

tion, be a Vedic authority supposed for such rules as these, and the attempt to hook them, in point of authority, on to an ambiguous verse of Manu is a patent fraud. On another passage of Manu (VII, 13)[1] Medhātithi says that certain orders of the king may not be transgressed. These are issued for the despatch of business and are not inconsistent with the *dharmaśāstra* and (approved) custom; they may be exemplified by 'Everybody should observe today as a public holiday in the city,' 'Everybody should attend the marriage being celebrated at the Minister's house,' 'No cattle shall be slaughtered today by the soldiers,' and 'Public dancing-girls must be entertained by the well-to-do citizens'. Such proclamations bound the subjects by virtue of their political subjection to the king, and he was entitled to enforce that obedience: no question of the rules binding the subjects in conscience could arise. Those rules that *did* bind in conscience did so not because of a psychological predisposition, or a custom, or because of a moral awareness that one owes co-operation to the community or the State. They bound because the sacred scripture in which the individual by definition had faith provided in express words or by necessary intendment that those acts should be done or should be avoided. This is quite a different matter from political obligation to obey the sovereign, of which, naturally, the *dharma-* and *artha-ṣāstra-s* were well aware. There is no suggestion anywhere in either that the king's commands were equivalent in point of obligatory force to an injunction in any of the *śāstra-s* teaching *dharma*, 'righteousness'. It might be righteous to obey the king, or righteousness might require the reverse.

(iii) *Obligations binding in law might be opposed to obligations binding in conscience*

To be a Hindu meant to subscribe to the essential validity of the *śāstra-s*, and to the infallibility of these written materials for discovery of the meaning of the Veda in every possible contingency. Either a rule existed in black and white or by analogy

[1] Discussed by Derrett at 'Bhāruci on the royal regulative power in India', *J.A.O.S.*, 84, no. 4 (1964), 392–5. For Medhātithi's three types of royal order (boycott, grant and legislation) see his comment on Manu IV, 226 and p. 185, n. 5 below.

or otherwise a requisite answer could be provided by the learned. Yet there can be no doubt but that despite the opinion of Medhātithi's commentary, not so far removed from the instances in point of time, rulers, that is to say the kings or their deputies or delegates, *did* legislate from time to time not merely on the indifferent matters mentioned above but also on matters for which the *śāstra* made provision, sometimes not merely so as to contradict expressions in the *smṛti-s* but also those of eminent contemporary jurists. Legislation, which can be investigated elsewhere–for it is relevant to the claim that the Hindu law is a holy law that cannot be tampered with[1]–and will be shown to have been of great variety, dealt with ceremonial matters, with criminal law, civil law (to use modern classifications), and especially fiscal law, on which last the *śāstra* was often very precise. Many examples of caste-legislation, for which no authority other than that of the caste-assembly is quoted, are to be found in the epigraphical collections, and there can be no question but that they were binding on the members of the respective castes, despite the fact that the decision taken might have been plain contrary to the tenor of the *śāstra*. Even groups of castes might unite for the purpose: in mediaeval Mysore we find the so-called 'eighteen castes' decreeing that if a member of any of them died without issue in the male line his entire property was to go to a charity. What is remarkable is not so much the present to the charity as the assumption that the *śāstric* law of descent and distribution of property was of no relative importance.[2]

This account of the conflicts possible in Hindu law before the British period would not be complete without a reference to two

[1] Below, pp. 188 f.

[2] The original passage (at AIR 1953 Journal 61) dissatisfied Mr. (later Chief Justice) M. Anantanārāyanan (see his essay in A. Larson, C. Wilfred Jenks, ed., *Sovereignty within the Law* (New York/London, 1965) at pp. 184 ff., esp. 189–90). His view and that of Prof. U. C. Sarkar generally agree in this, namely that the sovereignty of the ethical-social ideal which was *dharma* is more significant from a comparative standpoint than the instances of kings' and communities' actually having departed from the *śāstra*. In this they may be right, though it is not as significant as has been thought that the instances cited in 1953 (now see pp. 188–90 below) come from mediaeval times only. No one contends that the spirit of the system shifted from the earliest śāstric strata until the beginning of the British period.

conflicts within the system itself which deserve mention, though they differ in kind from those already mentioned. Obligations binding in conscience in the modern Western sense were capable of being unenforceable at law on account of procedural difficulties or of public policy. As an example of the former, we may take rules comparable with the modern rules of limitation of actions,[1] while of the latter some of the most striking examples are the defects regarding time and place, e.g. night time and within doors, which render certain contracts unenforceable. The object there was to minimize fraud, undue influence and the like. There are also the rules concerning illegal or immoral considerations. A good case might be incapable of being proved, as in any other legal system.

Finally, an entire chapter of the *śāstra* (supposedly obsolete today–or perhaps, on the contrary, the only justification in the eyes of the orthodox for their own anomalous proceedings)[2] is devoted to *āpat*, 'time of distress'. It throws light on the character of the injunctions themselves. This is a law of exceptional circumstances. The theory was that restrictions on powers and the seriousness of social misconduct and crimes were automatically modified in a time of distress. This usually meant public distress, such as invasion by the enemy, drought, famine, plague and the like. In such circumstances marriages otherwise improper could be entered into, improper adoptions could be performed, and, most striking of all, the normal precaution against crime and sin might be relaxed. Moreover, as we see from Manu XI, 16–18, which enable a Brahman to steal from a person of lower caste enough to stay his hunger if he has not eaten for three days,[3] even a personal distress, not really qualifying for the relaxations appropriate to *āpad*, which should be a general misfortune, may serve to vary the normal rigour of the law. It must therefore be borne in mind that the interpretation

[1] The reader should be warned that actual limitation as such could not be accepted by the classical śāstric authors: see p. 129 below. It was treated as a problem in evidence.

[2] The limits of the *asvargyaṃ* doctrine (above, p. 90) are evident. The present writer does not recollect its having been adverted to frequently (see above, p. 29): though it was obviously relevant in law-reform debates.

[3] Kāṇe, *H.D.*, III, pp. 932–3. This right was supposedly obsolete in the Kali Age.

of the law was never complete unless the surrounding circumstances of the alleged offender had been taken into account. The full rigour of the *śāstra* unmodified by *āpad-dharma* would seem to most Hindus of today unseasonable, though the courts have never applied that system of modification consciously.

Conclusion

Interpretation, restriction to somewhat rare circumstances or flat abrogation, all these methods have been used from time immemorial to accommodate the written texts to the practical needs of the times. In addition, the political authority has in fact supplemented and contradicted the *dharmaśāstra* where it seemed necessary in the public interest. The academic effort of bringing legislation into alignment with the *śāstra* was contemplated by Medhātithi amongst others. But the method chosen, as we shall see, was to argue that the *śāstra* contemplated only such legislation as its own silences rendered necessary, and there only provided that Vedic authority and valid custom knew nothing to the contrary. The capacity to legislate irrespective of śāstric authority undoubtedly existed, and was utilized in countless precedents before the coming of the British. In these circumstances the suggestion that Hindu law, as left by legislation up to the year 1947, for example, was a 'religious' law and that its amendment would place religion in jeopardy, was a novelty.[1] It was misleading, and also blameworthy, since the means of knowing the true position were available by that time; whereas the equally naïve statement that the *śāstra* mixed up rules of religion and law, a statement current a century earlier and improperly surviving as a result of undue deference to 'authority',[2] could be excused because it was voiced at a time when scholarly research into the question was impracticable. As we have seen religion and law are by no means 'mixed up' in the *śāstra*, which knows a subtle and complex coexistence of forces and sanctions appropriate to its history and its age.

[1] Prof. U. C. Sarkar's disapproval of this passage is voiced at his *Epochs in Hindu Legal History* (Hoshiarpur, 1958), pp. 171 ff., and *Law Review*, 18, no. 1 (1966), p. 7.

[2] E.g. *per* Mahmood, J., at *Binda* v. *Kaunsilia* (1890) 13 All. 126 at p. 138 (the mixing up of religious, civil and criminal rules of law).

4

RELIGION AND THE MAKING OF THE HINDU LAW

Two questions require to be answered: how far has Hindu religion contributed to the style, form and presuppositions of the *śāstra*; and how far has it determined actual rules,[1] which would not present themselves as they do without it? As we saw with the naïve statement that religion and law are 'mixed up' in the *śāstra*, so we find, as stumbling-blocks in our path, propositions confirmed by frequent thoughtless repetition. With all three civilizations, Jewish, Islamic and Hindu, the contention is made, and is made with every show of plausibility, that the rules of law derive from the word of God, from the words of uniquely qualified sages having access to superhuman wisdom, or from the practice of people who must be presumed to have enjoyed guidance of equivalent quality. It is the faith that the rules, and their interpretation, derive from sources hallowed by an occult power, in addition to the obvious quality of age and experience, which justifies individuals in believing that those rules alone *ought* to be followed, whatever convenience there may be in conforming to the lines laid down from time to time by human legislatures and by courts. This belief lies at the back of a phenomenon well known in modern India, the urge to see in the casual conventions of the present some kind of shadow of the ideal life of the ancient law, and to look into the ancient texts and to read into them anticipations of our very different world and its institutions, of which the ancient sages cannot

[1] The substance of the earlier portions of this chapter was published as 'Religion and law in Hindu jurisprudence' at AIR 1954 Journal 79–84. The last section is an abridgement of a lecture delivered in Madras in 1966 and published under the title 'The Role of Dharmaśāstra in Modern Comparative Legal History' at [1966] 1 M.L.J., *J.*, 43–56 (see especially pp. 54–6).

possibly have had any premonitions.[1] But when the *śāstra* was India's jurisprudence, and had the field more or less to itself, what part did religion play in framing it, both in the broad and in detail? It may be convenient to commence with general observations, to investigate the leading examples claimed to prove that Hindu law is a religious law, and after obtaining a startlingly negative result from these, to pass to the question of the conception of the *śāstra* itself, when, by contrast, we shall find a strikingly positive answer, which unexpectedly justifies the traditional outlook.

Hindu Law as a Sacred Law

Modern judges and mediaeval scholars alike point to the Hindu religion as the source of the Hindu law, in so far as the latter has not been amended by statute. The texts (*smṛti-s*) upon which the rules are based do not themselves make a distinction between the obligation to endow a daughter at her marriage and the obligation to bathe after touching one who should not be touched. Both rules are *prima facie* binding on the conscience, though both are not equally enforceable at law.

Though the *smṛti-s* themselves show no sign of making any useful distinction, the *mīmāṃsaka-s* knew the distinction between the *dṛṣṭārtha* injunction and the *adṛṣṭārtha* perhaps as long as two and a half millennia ago. The *Bhaviṣya-purāṇa* is a work of minor juridical interest, and would be regarded as 'late' in comparison with *smṛti-s*. But its author had a shrewd mind and he gives us a little code which bears directly on our problem.

> *dṛṣṭārthā tu smṛtiḥ kācid adṛṣṭārthā tathā 'parā*
> *dṛṣṭādṛṣṭārtha-rūpā 'nyā nyāya-mūlā tathā 'parā.*
> *anuvāda-smṛtis tv anyā śiṣṭair dṛṣṭā tu pañcamī*
> *sarvā etā veda-mūlā dṛṣṭārthāḥ parihṛtya tu.*

Smṛti-s, he says, are of five kinds: those which have a 'seen' purpose (serve a practical object only), those which have an 'unseen' purpose (whose object is not discerned by reason alone), those which partake of both characters, those which are based

[1] The results of this urge are rightly castigated by Dr. N. Subrahmanian in the work cited at p. 63, n. 2 above.

upon reason (i.e. propositions of logic and natural reason), and those which have no specifically injunctive force because they merely repeat a rule laid down in the Veda explicitly. All except the first are 'rooted in the Veda'. The author thus specifically tells us that religion is *not* the root of the rules which are comprised in the *vyavahāra* portions of the *dharmaśāstra*, which are devoted to 'business', litigation, law as we know it.

He goes on to give examples. Amongst 'seen' rules he would place those relating to political science and international relations, which, as it happens, best illustrate a sphere in which flexibility and expediency play a great role, and the supremacy of *dharma*, though asserted by the *śāstrī-s*, is notoriously more honoured in the breach than in the attainment. The 'unseen' rules include those relating to worship and diet. Rules of a mixed character, which *we* should illustrate rather with adoption, he illustrates with the student's (*brahmacārī's*) staff, which has a ritual significance and helps to guard him against dangers. That in a conflict between Vedic texts one may be entitled to choose to follow one of them is a rule of reasoning; and the nature of a repetition needs no illustration, though in fact he does illustrate it by citing Manu's injunctions about abandoning, on retirement, the life of a householder.

These texts of the *purāṇa* are adopted by the twelfth-century jurist Aparārka, and by the seventeenth-century jurist Mitramiśra, and thus are unquestionably standard *dharmaśāstra* material.[1] The great suasive force of the *śāstra*, telling as it does what are the paths towards *dharma*, with its rewards here and hereafter, is no less great in the *dṛṣṭārtha* contexts than in the others. The social norm, the ideal conveyed by the system as a whole, is assuredly there. But the jurists are under no illusions. The extensive rules relating to administration of justice, equally with those referring to politics and international relations, are binding only so far as the individual responsible for the administration chooses, in his discretion, to recognize their force. There is every reason why he should choose to do so; there must be pressing reasons why he should, in any particular case, choose not to do so. But if he acts contrary to a *dṛṣṭārtha* rule he commits no sin so

[1] Aparārka, pp. 626–7; *Vīramitrodaya, Paribhāṣā-prakāśa*, p. 19. Kāṇe, *H.D.*, III, 840–1. B. Bhaṭṭāchārya, *Kalivarjyas*, p. 199. For a reference to *adṛṣṭa* purposes in litigation about twenty years ago, see below, p. 233, n. 1.

long as the general requirements of *dharma* are met and he keeps within his jurisdiction as the *dharmaśāstra* understands it.

In passing we may comment that in the reign of Henry VIII in England, some churchmen argued that canon law was founded in religion and backed by the sanction of divine commandment. They could not see how the details of the ecclesiastical law relating to clerical immunities and sanctuary could be modified by any legislative action on the part of a secular body. Putting the controversy (in which those churchmen lost the day) in Hindu terms, the claim had been that even 'seen' rules (whose objects were rational and prudential) were supported by the sanction attaching to 'unseen' propositions (such as the nature of holy orders) – a confusion which ancient and mediaeval Hindu jurists found no difficulty whatever in avoiding.

Even though these distinctions are not unknown, modern authorities of acknowledged orthodoxy and learning find the basis of all the genuine rules of Hindu law – that is to say rules which do in fact stem from the *śāstra* and are not the result of an Anglo-Indian misunderstanding – in considerations of an unquestionably religious nature. K. V. Rangaswāmī Aiyaṅgār said,[1]

> *Dharmaśāstra* is a comprehensive code to regulate human conduct in accordance with the unalterable scheme of Creation, and to enable everyone to fulfil the purpose of his birth. The whole life of Man, considered both as an individual and as a member of groups (small and large) as well as man's relations to his fellow men, to the rest of animated creation, to superhuman beings, to cosmos, generally and ultimately to God come within the purview of *Dharmaśāstra*. Among the duties that it lays down are both self-regarding and altruistic, those to the living and to the dead, to those who are alive and those who are yet to be born.

This seems, and indeed is, a reflection of the view expressed by the great master, Kumārila-bhaṭṭa, who twelve centuries ago defined *dharma*, which is the subject-matter of the *dharmaśāstra*, as something utterly apart from mundane considerations, something desirable as producing a suprasensible state of bliss which cannot be attained otherwise than by conduct consistent with rules laid down in the *smṛti-s* or otherwise deriving their authority from the Veda, source of all knowledge. He said: 'Such

[1] *Some Aspects of the Hindu View of Life according to Dharmaśāstra* (Baroda, Oriental Institute, 1952), p. 62.

actions as are performed either for the maintenance of the body, or for one's mere pleasure, or for some material gain, are not considered by good people as *dharma*.'[1] Again, when discussing what ultimate authority must be supposed for certain texts and usages for which direct Vedic authority is not clearly available, he held that

> . . . the positive injunction, technically *bhāvanā*, that is inferred, must be that which lays down certain definite actions, sacrifices, charities, offerings, fastings and penances, etc., as leading to specific results, like Heaven and the like, by means of specified processes; and in the case of certain actions of the body, the sense-organs and the mind, that are shunned by certain people, the inference is that of a prohibitive text, pointing out the prohibited action as leading to undesirable results in the shape of Hell and the like.[2]

In fact the unbroken tradition of Hindu legal scholarship has emphasized the concept that the Hindu law concerns itself with eternity and with morality judged against the greater background, and not with material, temporal considerations. 'In the Indian view all conduct rests on a suprasensible basis. This leads to a fusion of religion and morals, which is reflected in the existence of only one word in Sanskrit, viz., *dharma* for both. In modern eyes, in an age in which secularism is upheld as the ideal and religion has long been ignored, such association may appear as an entanglement. The traditional Hindu view is different. Morality, to have effective force, must rest on supramundane sanctions.'[3] So said the greatest interpreter of the *dharmaśāstra* to his contemporaries, Hindu and non-Hindu, young and not-so-young.

But the last quotation serves as a key to the whole approach, and enables us to distinguish between the search for authority (*pramāṇa*) and the search for the source of the rules of law (*vidhi*). Kumārila and his modern co-religionist are primarily concerned with the perennial problem which in Europe gave rise to the evergreen theory of Natural Law and Justice. People are conscious of an ability to detect whether a statutory rule or a particular judicial decision is or is not just, and this consciousness is commonly referred to the alleged existence of a standard

[1] *Tantravārttika* (Jhā's trans.), I, p. 184.

[2] Ibid., pp. 246–7. Kumārila's clear reference to taboos is particularly interesting.

[3] K. V. Rangaswāmī Aiyaṅgār, where cited at p. 100, n. 1 above.

of justice against which every municipal law can be compared, a standard of attainment to which each system of law is perhaps striving in its own way and in its own time. The orthodox solution in ancient India was to refer all disputes with any theoretical content to the crystallized learning of the past, enshrined in the *smṛti-s*, for which Vedic authority could be quoted or inferred. This method was, of course, a religious method since its fundamental assumption was that the Vedic literature, supposedly once all-embracing, was actually and perpetually trustworthy. The assumption was not founded on experience, and the willingness to proceed upon such a hypothesis and to found a system of thought upon it was superstitious. Whether or not this faith was fantastic, it was the only means whereby Hindu thinkers could find a common basis for jurisprudential work. The unorthodox, such as the Buddhists, despised the Vedas and ridiculed their alleged authority, but they nevertheless, so far as we know, followed the Hindu law in so far as it applied to civil disputes and in other respects besides; though the records of the period of Buddhist ascendancy also show that the public were not so wedded to śāstric rules as seems to have been the case in later periods:[1] however that may be, the customary law which is so well reflected in the surviving śāstric literature was not ignored simply because one did not accept the authority of the Veda. Whatever law preceded our Hindu law must therefore have had a basis independently of religion.

Thus, while the authority which justified the application of the law was admittedly religious, the rules themselves could and in fact did persist by virtue of their own merit and not merely by reason of a superstitious sanction attaching to their alleged source. That laws might be binding on those who obeyed them despite the lack of a religious sanction behind them was well known to Hindu jurists from their dealings with the non-Hindu aboriginal peoples of India, with the incompletely Hinduized peoples of remote regions, and with foreigners, Iranians, Central Asians, Burmese and others. Kumārila may say, somewhat spitefully, that Mlecchas 'are believed to be capable of all

[1] N. K. Wāgle, *Society at the time of the Buddha* (Bombay, Popular Prakashan, 1966). The information obtained here from the Pali Canon seems to belong to a few centuries after the time of the Buddha.

actions howsoever abhorrent',[1] yet even they are men! Vijñāneśvara knows that people on the fringe of the Hindu world buy and sell without the aid of śāstric knowledge.[2] Anantarāma, a writer of the eighteenth century,[3] notices that the sons of Yavanas (Muslims?) inherit though no question of spiritual benefit arises amongst them (see below for this concept). A writer, who may be a near contemporary of his, comments on the strange customs of the wicked people of Malabar, amongst whom the sister's son is the heir.[4] But the Hindus had no doubt but that their possession of the knowledge of *dharma* placed them at an advantage over their neighbours, and in most cases it seems they were right.

Having admitted that the Hindu law, like most civilized systems of law, sought for the expression of morality and righteousness, yet drew its formal, scientific authority from a hypothetical body of literature, a holy scripture, we may proceed to a further necessary distinction. It is well known that civil law and religious law were dealt with upon similar terms and often within the covers of the same books. This was inevitable, seeing that the source of all rules and all duties binding upon Hindus was held to be one and the same. From ancient times until legislatures commenced to interfere with the public expression of Hindu religious doctrines (and here we may have in mind the regulations which prohibited sacrifice of children and of suttee, and such statutes as those prohibiting the dedication of dancing girls to temples and interfering with the right of a community to excommunicate its members)[5] the purely ritualistic side of the *dharmaśāstra* was administered by the appropriate bodies in the spirit of the traditional law itself. Until the British supremacy was established, governmental

[1] *Tantravārttika*, cited above, at p. 247.

[2] *Mitākṣarā* (Colebrooke), I, i, 9. Mr. A. S. Naṭarāja Ayyar is proud of this citation as it seems to him to prove that the *śāstrīs* were comparative lawyers: which, with all respect, one may doubt. The *śāstra* was a distinctly inbred science.

[3] In the *Svatvarahasya*, which may not in fact be correctly attributed to Anantarāma (Derrett at *B.S.O.A.S.* 18, pt. 3 (1956), 478–9).

[4] Pāṭṭarācārya, *Dattacandrikā* (of which a copy is available at the Adyar Library (69432) and at the Madras Government Oriental Manuscripts Library (R. 4642a)).

[5] See chapter 13 below.

authorities supervised both the spiritual and the temporal sides of punishment for crime, and the supreme judge exercised at once criminal and ecclesiastical jurisdiction.[1] Even today the religious endowments of the Mysore State are governed from a central organization appertaining to the executive, an arrangement not so foreign in this half-century as it was in British India for a century or so previously. To modern eyes it seems strange that religious questions should be settled by a state official who is not qualified in the religious learning and does not decide issues upon arguments based on the sacred literature. Until this began to happen, nominally with reference only to secular and temporal matters connected with temples and their management, the *dharmaśāstra*, in some cases modified and supplemented by custom, actually ruled in the field. There the religious law was applied untrammelled: while rules from the same books but concerning *temporal* questions depended for their being put into effect upon the attitude of the judicial administrators for the time being.

The Rules of Hindu Law

There remain those instances in the civil law which are pointed to as illustrations of a religious content and a religious source behind the rules actually enforced. They may be taken up from the laws of Marriage, Adoption, Debt and Succession. In every case the rule aims at an object which was objectively worthy of attainment, and the religious argument which supports it is of formal utility but of no substantial value. In other words, the texts served to facilitate legal education and to inculcate the desirability of maintaining the rule, but the rule itself both could and can stand by itself without this adventitious support. In every case the rules are said to be derived from religious doctrine. One must, therefore, carefully distinguish them as a class from topics of the ancient Hindu law such as Ordeals,[2]

[1] Guṇe, *Judicial System of the Marathas* (Poona, Deccan College, 1953), pp. 112–14. In Travancore State even during the British period the ecclesiastical jurisdiction (if we may so call it) properly exercised in caste matters was given full support by the State (Ittycheria, cited above, p. 89, at pp. 32–3).

[2] Sen-Gupta, *Evolution of Ancient Indian Law*, 1st edn. (Calcutta/London, 1953), pp. 61–6. Kāṇe, *H.D.*, III, pp. 358–78.

where in many instances the religion of a party or a witness was utilized as a method of testing his sincerity, or, in default of any means of proof more likely to provide the solution to the dispute, the issue was put squarely before the Deity, who was supposed to answer the question by supernatural means.[1] In the former cases religion served to aid process, while in the latter the court showed its unwillingness to dismiss the plaint for lack of evidence where supernatural evidence might be obtainable: in both types of cases religion did not provide a rule of substantive law.

For the law of Marriage we may take the rules that a woman may not have more than one husband at once; that a girl should be given in marriage as soon as possible after puberty; that a Brahmin may not marry a *śūdra* and that a *śūdra* male may not marry a female of any higher caste; that a man may not marry a *sapiṇḍa*, i.e. a woman related to him within five degrees of the common link, counting inclusively through her mother or his mother, or within seven degrees inclusively through her or his father; and that the wife must remain after marriage faithful to her husband come what may, so that neither divorce nor remarriage are available for her. These rules, except the first, have been abolished by statute, but are still remembered by Hindus as rules of strong suasive authority for social life according to the religious law, even if they are no longer enforceable in the courts, disregarded in litigation, and generally departed from in some sections of society.

An example from the Veda is given by Kumārila of an authority for the rule that a wife may not have two contemporaneous husbands:[2] the text, 'two strings were applied to each (sacrificial) post, hence it is that a man takes many wives, though a woman does not take more than one husband,' is instanced, somewhat sceptically, as an indication of the type of deduction that was then customarily agreed to be allowable from a text designed specifically for a religious purpose. But this is clearly a rule fancifully derived from a quite irrelevant practice (the alleged connexion, conscious or unconscious, between Vedic sacrifices and fertility mimes was not sufficiently near the surface of thought for the relevance to be posited), and Kumārila himself had no confidence in its being genuine authority for

[1] See below, pp. 218–19.

[2] *Tantravārttika,* cited above, p. 211.

the rule in question. It is plain that female monogamy was not the invariable rule until the *śāstra* attained its preeminence in the field, but whether it was a desire to enable every girl to marry or whether it was the change in custom from giving bride-prices to the taking of dowries which actually confirmed the conversion of the respectable public to the orthodox rule, it is perhaps impossible even to conjecture. Marriage, however, implies a relationship of a particularly practical kind and it is submitted that no religious doctrine is needed to justify a development away from polyandry.

Though post-puberty marriages undoubtedly occurred in very ancient times, the developed *dharmaśāstra* condemned the father or other guardian who did not give his daughter or female ward in marriage before puberty as guilty of the murder of potential embryos.[1] This 'justification' of the rule is unquestionably religious, in the orthodox sense, since it is a reason not derivable from experience and observation.[2] But it is plain that the *object* of the rule was two-fold: firstly to encourage the giving in marriage of girls to families requiring potential mothers of sons to till the soil, level the forests, tend the cattle and guard the homestead, and yet not able to offer substantial bride-prices; and secondly to encourage fathers belonging to families which had adopted the custom of giving dowries with their daughters not to keep the latter at home as a means of saving expense. A cynic might add that taboos against marrying non-virgins played their part, and that, although the *śāstra* shows awareness of the unmarried daughter who gives birth to issue in the house of her father, there is an extreme inconvenience in the family's being tied with two generations of infants, thereby subsidizing another family's sexual appetites without responsibility. If daughters are given in marriage at or prior to puberty these inconveniences are totally avoided. The point is not religious (for the taboo referred to is instinctive, not superstitious), but in the highest degree practical. In addition it is by no means impossible that the jurists who adopted this argument had in mind the public policy of restraining marriages *before* puberty in families

[1] Manu IX, 4, 93; Gautama XVIII, 20–3. Kāṇe, *H.D.*, II, pp. 438–47.

[2] Kāṇe, p. 437. Kumārila thought it a sufficient condemnation of the arguments of Buddhists that they were based upon actual experience (*Tantravārttika*, p. 168).

where superfluous daughters, saved by public condemnation, perhaps, of the female infanticide of earlier periods, were simply unproductive mouths. Practice in India tended markedly towards cementing family alliances by betrothals at very early ages, and statutory interference was ultimately required to restrain 'child marriages'. That the father was under no absolute obligation to give his daughter in marriage irrespective of her age or the quality of the prospective bridegroom is placed beyond doubt by Manu IX, 89: 'A maiden, even though she has reached puberty, should rather remain in the house till her death, than that her father should give her to a man devoid of qualities.'

The rules prohibiting union between a Brahmin and a *śūdra* and unions called *pratiloma*, as being against the order of nature,[1] may be said to rest upon religious sanction in that caste distinctions are not based upon material facts but upon theories. They may be compared with the rules of the criminal law which differentiated between penalties appropriate to the caste of the offender and the caste of the injured party.[2] Justification for the caste distinctions is sought in several myths, but the prohibitions here referred to depend obviously upon fear of miscegenation. The social function of the Brahmin community, a specially qualified minority in ancient times, particularly exempted it, so it seemed, from marital relations with women of the *śūdra* caste, which included all the non-Āryan conquered peoples of India and possibly even some Āryans (though this is disputed). *Śūdra-s* might be wealthy and beautiful, but the Brahmin should avoid intercourse with them, which was sinful, however convenient it might seem to be in particular circumstances (e.g. in Kerala in earlier times). The ancient Indians particularly objected to dilution of Āryan blood through unions with these people, who seemed to them to be, as indeed they were, racially distinct types. The appearance of modern *śūdra-s* gives us no clue to this feeling, since it owes much to disregard of the policy through centuries. A general prohibition of inter-caste marriages is admitted to have developed in practice without śāstric sanction, and can be attributed to the gradual hardening of social stratification and the practical discomfort which would arise in the ordinary case from a marriage between members of

[1] Kāṇe, *H.D.*, II, pp. 50–8, 449.

[2] Kāṇe, *H.D.*, III, p. 395.

families of different habits and practices. The rule rests upon prejudices of a fundamental kind by no means confined to India. Hindus have, until very recent times, been more orthodox than their *śāstra*, which inhibited unions between *varṇa-s*, whereas the public forswore unions between castes as such.

A similar prejudice lies at the root of the universal fear of incest. The only room for debate is how far the prohibited degrees should stretch. The sapiṇḍaship bar, referred to above, is only a narrower form of the *sagotra* bar, which prevented the marriage of parties whose *gotra-s*, i.e. whose very patrilineal *names*, happened to coincide. Since in many cases *gotra* names were assumed or held arbitrarily, as in the cases of offspring of *pratiloma* unions, and since even in normal cases the possession of the same *gotra* name could be a genuine indication of descent from a common ancestor of a thousand years or more before, this rule could not in itself be supported by expediency alone. As has been justly remarked, '. . . the prohibition of *sagotra* marriage cannot be rationalized; and those who advocate its removal have to overcome the faith in the superhuman authority which upholds the principle.'[1] However, it is possible to contend that the *sagotra* bar once served to prevent marriage between persons who did belong to the same patrilineal family, but whose exact relationship could not be proved for some reason; while the sapiṇḍaship bar was a real attempt, at a later stage in the development of the law, to define the limits of blood-relationship which would enable families to avoid incestuous unions. Because the limits were much wider than is usual in 'modern' systems it is not necessary to call in religion as the explanation. The concept of incest is bound up with the conception of the extent of the average family dwelling in a single home, and the large joint families of olden days necessitated just such a rule as was in force in Hindu law in India up till 1955; the smaller families of today justify the reduced limits of sapiṇḍaship foisted upon the system by the Indian legislation of that year.[2] The bar to marriage subserves two needs, firstly that of near relations to continue familiarity, irrespective of the puberty of either party, and secondly to look outside the familial

[1] Rangaswāmī Aiyaṇgār, *Some Aspects*, p. 158. One cannot divide a hen, keep one half for laying and cook the other: the *Kukkuṭa-nyāya*.

[2] Hindu Marriage Act, s. 3 (f).

group for sexual satisfaction, instead of overcoming the sexual frigidity, which common upbringing produces, merely in the interests of holding property together. The South Indians on the whole have achieved the latter, that is to say, have for an immensely long period practised cousin marriage and even uncle and niece marriage mainly in order to achieve the solidity of the family group. This others indignantly refused, as we have seen, and the southern jurists' manipulations of the śāstric concept of sapiṇḍaship provoke contempt. At the bottom of this there can be nothing but racial difference.

The old *sapravara* bar, which spins out fantasy still further than the *sagotra* rule, appears to be a yet stronger indication of religious origin of the prohibition, but in fact it seems originally to have been a method of particularizing still more minutely descent from a common male lineal ancestor in view of the fact that sagotraship was recognized not to be an infallible guide. It will be borne in mind that rules of exogamy exist in numerous 'primitive' systems, where no religious justification has been found necessary for inculcating or expounding them.

The faithfulness of a wife to her husband, even after his death, is insisted upon by the *śāstra* and religious penalties are denounced against the faithless.[1] The justification for this apparently obviously desirable rule, so long at least as the husband lives, is sought in the theory that in the course of the marriage ceremonies the wife is taken from her natural family and is made one with her husband, the union being for all purposes, spiritual, physical and practical. This notion is not taken to its logical conclusion in every context, but it is said that as the wife is half her husband's body (*ardhāṅginī*)[2] she survives so as to continue his personality and is never free from her bond to him so as to be available for remarriage. The conclusion which prevents divorce in the orthodox system and which prolongs the husband's dominion after his death seems to be an instance where a theory has got the better of the object which it was designed to serve.

[1] Manu IX, 30. In *Nallaperumal* v. *Neelamma* (1885) 4 Trav. L.R. 1 the Chief Justice declared that it was as much adultery for a widow to remarry as for a wife to be unfaithful to her husband.

[2] Play is made with this notion in case-law. See *Subba Rao* v. *Krishna* AIR 1954 Mad. 227, 228; *Venkatiah* v. *Kalyanamma* AIR 1953 Mys. 92 F.B., at 99. *Chandrasekhara* v. *Kulandaivelu* AIR 1963 S.C. at p. 191.

The union or community of husband and wife is a phenomenon which deserves to be recognized legally in numerous contexts. The virtue of conjugal loyalty is worthy of inculcation by whatever moral and spiritual arguments (the effect of differences upon the emotions being disproportionate to the occasions for them), but hardly needs them in order to acquire legal protection. It is open to question whether the extensions made by the Hindu law are ultimately due to sexual jealousy of a primitive kind or whether they are intended to prevent the passage of property from one family to another by means of second marriages; certainly the remarriage of widows and divorce of wives were both hampered by the theory that marriage was impossible without a transfer of dominion from the natural family to the family of marriage, and since there is in the castes which observe this rule a pronounced prejudice against marrying a woman who has been enjoyed by another, it was probably always in the wife's interest that she should have a completely secure place in the family of her original marriage. We shall not omit to notice that the castes which reprobated or disallowed marriage of widows, or subjected such marriages to an inferior status, were the same castes who did not countenance a woman's inheriting an absolute estate from her husband. The same motive may explain both rules.

In recent years the religious aspect of the law of adoption has had full play, and serious injustice was caused because in the famous and incorrect case of *Anant* v. *Shankar*[1] their Lordships of the Privy Council indicated that, no matter how many years after her husband's death his widow might adopt a son, the latter was entitled to take his place for all practical purposes as a son existing at the time of his adoptive father's death. As a result estates which passed by inheritance in the interval have been divested, with confusion and annoyance such as can easily be imagined. The justification for this has been that the right of a widow to adopt was based upon her duty to provide a son who could offer *piṇḍa-s* and other ceremonial offerings at the periodical commemorative feasts (*śrāddha*) for the benefit of the 'father' and his lineal ancestors. The spiritual happiness of the husband, if he died sonless, was supposed to depend upon the widow's action in adopting, and this consideration was believed to be

[1] AIR 1943 P.C. 196.

paramount, to the extent of overriding the gross inconvenience which its logical effect would create in the matter of property.[1] The act of the widow is admittedly a substitute for a similar act of adoption by her husband himself, and if we examine the matter objectively it is clear that religion has nothing to do with it, except incidentally.

Originally the Hindu law knew thirteen kinds of son. Of these the 'son bought', the 'son abandoned' by his kin, the 'son self-given' and so on are examples. The *dattaka*, or son given by his parents, remains as the chief example of a son recognized by the current law other than a legitimate son of the body, or *aurasa*. This *dattaka* became an institution–to be submitted to modification by the Hindu Adoptions and Maintenance Act of 1956[2]–because of the need to control the devolution of family property. So long as the male line could be extended, as was once the case, and the masculine population of the joint family could be increased by indiscriminate and informal adoptions, the legitimate expectations of wife, widow, daughter, brother and so on (not to speak of the State, which used to take earlier in the order of priority of heirs than it did in recent centuries) would be postponed to numbers of persons whose only title to participate in the family wealth was that they had caught the fancy of the patriarch or even, less tolerably, of some brother or even cousin. Thus the superiority of the genuine son, the *aurasa*, was emphasized, and the other sorts of sons were ranged in order of inferiority after him.[3] They were to be considered as 'substitutes' (*pratinidhi*) in all fields of the family's activities, both spiritual and secular. If they co-existed with *aurasa* sons they were permitted to enjoy the undivided property on equal terms with the latter, but at a partition their inferior entitlement was acknowledged, and their relationship to others than their adoptive parents was sometimes totally denied. An actual 'substitute' for an *aurasa* was of course a son taken by a sonless man under conditions that ensured that the adoptee was as far as possible similar to what an *aurasa* would have been; hence the rule that the *dattaka* must not be a child of a woman whom the adoptive father could not have married. The eldest or only son

[1] Mercifully the Supreme Court limited the principle in *Shrinivas* v. *Narayan* AIR 1954 S.C. 379.

[2] See below, pp. 331, 339.

[3] Kāṇe, *H.D.*, III, pp. 663 ff.

of his natural parents could not be given in adoption, since of course this might create an endless chain of substitutions, the eldest having in Indian eyes (as elsewhere) a special pre-eminence which could not be fully replaced by any substitution. The formalities and refinements were justified by the compensating benefit which the law now allowed to the *dattaka.* The proper precautions having been taken, he was to be treated exactly as an *aurasa,* capable of succeeding not only to his adoptive parents but also to their ancestors and collaterals and even descendants. As a result the Hindu law is approached more nearly by the current English law than by any other system. Greed and jealousy might well have made this substitution impossible in practice had not the *śāstra* availed itself of the theory that a son's chief duty from a religious standpoint was to make the ceremonial offerings to his ancestors, and to provide for their continuation; consequently the father is under a duty to provide himself and his parents with a substitute for a son in case he should die without an *aurasa.* The man's desire to have a son, fully shared by his wife whose own security was threatened if she had none, was objectivized by the theory of the three debts with which every male Hindu is born.[1] The belief that sacrifices with the proper textual recitations could take the boy from his natural family and make him, from an occult point of view and therefore *a fortiori* from a practical point of view, a full member of the adoptive family, was a belief which came to the aid of those who were not satisfied with the earlier śāstric rule that a man was entitled to pretend that for all purposes a brother's son was a son, just as a woman was entitled to pretend that a co-wife's child was her own. This argument silenced opposition, adoptions as *de facto* arrangements were consolidated on a secure foundation, and families were perpetuated without discord. In the Punjab and amongst Jainas adoption in the complete form is known, but without religious significance: in South India the *illatom* form of adoption is really the provision of a man who is called 'adopter' with a son-in-law, and the absence of a religious sanction behind this relationship serves only to emphasize that it is not really an adoption.[2] It was, meanwhile, only in the twentieth century that the religious theory behind *dattaka* adoptions took command in the courts and wrought

[1] See below, p. 113.

[2] Derrett, *I.M.H.L.*, 201, 203.

havoc now happily in the course of being obviated for the future.[1]

The Hindu law of debts has two peculiarities, both of which have in fact a secular origin, though the orthodox would strenuously oppose this interpretation. The first, known as *dāmdupat*, makes it impossible for a creditor to realize interest greater in amount than the principal debt. The rule is now obsolescent.[2] The intention is plainly to strike a compromise between the natural desire of the usurer to lend at the best profit upon the strongest security and the equally natural desire of the borrower to meet his immediate needs upon terms which will not eventually cripple him. The rule devised by the Hindu jurists, which is a survival of a set of rules laying down the permitted multiplication of commodities–*dāmdupat* refers to loans of money[3]–did not hamper usury as such, but made it inevitable that loans should be on a short term, or should be at a small rate of interest.

The second rule, which is frequently alleged by judges to rest solely upon a religious basis, is that known as the Pious Obligation. It is said that the Hindu owes three debts; to the Gods, to the ancestors, and to human beings; by begetting a son he will pay off all three classes of debt. The notion as stated is clearly of a religious origin, except perhaps so far as it relates to the duty to pay debts of a material character, which all systems inevitably provide for. The convenience of civilized life would be seriously diminished if there were no machinery for the recovery of debts, and the Hindu law is no exception in that it provides that all heirs must pay the debts of the deceased. In ancient times, however, a special difficulty arose with regard to the debts of members of the joint family. If the debts were not of a character which the manager of the joint family would be obliged to clear off, the creditor could enforce payment after the debtor's death against the joint-family property upon the basis that the debtor's interest in that property had passed to his sons and sons' sons

[1] See above p. 111, n., 1; below, p. 341.

[2] Derrett, *I.M.H.L.*, 824–9. R. K. Ranade at (1952) 54 Bom. L.R., *J.*, pp. 49–57. Derrett at (1956) 58 Bom. L.R., *J.*, pp. 65–70.

[3] Derrett at *Z. f. vergl. Rechtsw.*, 65, pt. 2 (1963), 172–82. R. S. Sharma, 'Usury in early mediaeval India (A.D. 400–1200)', *C.S.S.H.*, 8, No. 1 (1965), 56–77.

and that the share of the latter must be debited with the amount. The difficulty arose because in the ancient law all property, however acquired, became for most purposes joint-family property until a partition, at which time one who had made acquisitions without the aid of joint funds could, as a rule, keep them as an additional share. The sons and others were held absolutely liable for their ancestor's debts not because of their religious obligation to their progenitor to pay off his three classes of debt, but because they had no separate property of their own, as long as they remained joint, which could be kept distinct from the property or interest which had belonged to their deceased parent or grandparent.[1] Modern modifications have retained part of the old reasoning and have made the sons, sons' sons and sons' sons' sons liable to the extent of their interest in the joint-family property for the debts of the ancestor, though no further.[2] The said ancestor can take advantage of this duty even during his lifetime, not because of any religious obligation of the sons, etc., to pay his debts, but because this has proved a useful indirect means by which creditors, who would otherwise have been cheated of their security, can be partly or wholly paid. True, this rule has not been adopted in all the former native States, though they have come into line since the formation of the Union: but objections to this extension on the ground that the *śāstra* did not provide for it have not been heard. The law of the joint-family disallows certain alienations on the ground that they are unauthorized and against the family's interest; if a father makes such an unauthorized alienation he cannot take advantage of the fact that the alienation is liable to be declared void by the court, if the other members of the joint property-owning body happen to be his sons, etc. It is only reasonable that the weight of the burden of substantiating a father's unauthorized alienation, i.e. giving the alienee value, should fall not on other members of the joint-family but upon his own descendants in the male line who would take his share eventually. These descendants however may escape their liability under the Pious Obligation if they show that the debt was tainted at its inception. The taint is said to deprive the father of

[1] On the radical departure made in the *Shivagunga Case* (1863) 9 M.I.A. 539 see below, p. 424.

[2] See below, p. 427.

the right to expect his sons, etc., to pay his debt: their obligation being based upon religious doctrines, an illegality or immorality in the circumstances in which the debt is incurred is said to vitiate the whole claim. However, a better method of expounding the doctrine is to see in the notion of 'taint' nothing more than a conception of public policy, which formerly extended no further in the case of sons than other heirs. Creditors could not expect the aid of the court in exacting debts which were contracted for illegal or immoral purposes, or which were debts peculiar to the individual and did not attach to his estate. The scope of unenforceability of contracts in the Hindu law resembled to some extent that in other systems. Indeed, in a striking instance, a Hindu judge who, though not an expert in Hindu law, subsequently became Chief Justice of India, applied[1] as a standard of 'immorality' for this purpose a test more nearly akin to those to be applied in English law than those which the jurists of the *śāstra* itself would have contemplated, and that too in a matter closely concerning Hindu family life.[2]

Our final example of a rule of Hindu law which is said to be based upon a religious doctrine is taken from the law of succession to property. It was once generally believed that succession to the property of a male (not a female, nor a male who was a member of a reunited coparcenary) was regulated in accordance with the degree of spiritual benefit which he could obtain from the heir's making his offering to his spirit or on his behalf in the *śrāddha*.[3] Old cases repeat this notion,[4] and the public at one time thought it axiomatic. Where competition was expected heirs used to rush to perform the funeral ceremonies in the hope that if they were not prevented the relatives would be taken to have admitted their right to succeed.[5] Now however it is admitted

[1] *Lakshmanaswami* [1943] Mad. 717.

[2] On the Pious Obligation see Kāṇe, *H.D.*, III, pp. 442–8; Derrett, *I.M.H.L.*, §§. 271, 446, 499, 502–14, 692; R. K. Ranade, (1950) 52 Bom. L.R., *J.*, 1–7; 33–41; (1953) 55 Bom. L.R., *J.*, 94–102; (1961) 63 Bom. L.R., *J.*, 81–4; Derrett, AIR 1960 Journal 2–5.

[3] See D. R. Shāstrī, *Origin and Development of the Rituals of Ancestor Worship in India* (Calcutta, 1963).

[4] *Bhyah Ram* v. *Bhyah Ugur* (1870) 14 Suth. W.R., P.C. 1; 2 Norton 413.

[5] Popular notions to this effect are encountered in remote parts even today. Early examples of the idea are documented at *Doe dem. T. Doss* v. *Ramhurry* (1785) Morton-Montriou 289, 1 Ind. Dec. (Old Ser.) 173, and at

that according to the *Mitākṣarā* and the school of law which takes its name from it, and therefore the juridical theory applicable in the greater part of India, the factor of religious benefit is irrelevant except in order to solve a conflict of claims amongst very remote heirs one of whom is male and one female.[1] According to the *Dāyabhāga*, and the school named after it, which largely applies in Bengal and Assam, spiritual benefit dictates, or is supposed to dictate, the order of succession.[2] In passing it may be noted that a leading authority has quarrelled with the manner in which the Calcutta High Court has applied the doctrine.[3] A close inspection of the Dāyabhāga position on its authorities however suggests that the spiritual-benefit theory was applied with the object of inserting into the list of heirs, which then included only agnates, certain near relations who were cognates. By this means remote agnates were on the whole excluded by comparatively near cognates, and the final effect was to bring near relations through females upon a more nearly equal plane with agnatic kindred. This was most sorely needed, since the existing law of succession excluded large numbers of kindred who had a moral claim on the *propositus*, simply because they did not belong to the patrilineal clan which from the most ancient times had monopolized succession. As a theory in itself 'spiritual benefit' has been shown again and again to be hollow,[4] since the actual *performance* of the duty is not required, for many may perform who do not succeed, and many that succeed do not perform it. Again, artificial distinctions as to the relative quality of the apparently identical offerings themselves depending upon the sex and relationship of the offerer had to be invented by the jurists in order to erect a

Doe dem. Heera v. *Bolakee* (1793) Morton-Montriou 349, 1 Ind. Dec. (Old Ser.) 212.

[1] *Jatindra* v. *Nagendra* AIR 1931 P.C. 268.

[2] See below, p. 442.

[3] Sarvādhikārī, *Hindu Law of Inheritance*[2], pp. 709–10 and footnotes. Mayne, *Hindu Law and Usage*[11], p. 688.

[4] Sarvādhikārī pertinently says, in the work cited above, p. 750: '. . . the real fact of the matter is, the system of inheritance in both the schools is based on affinity only. It cannot be otherwise. The principle of affinity is the natural principle. A system of inheritance based upon any other principle would be unnatural and utterly worthless.' His book, however, is dedicated to explaining the Hindu traditional doctrines seriously.

workable order of preference in the succession.[1] In fact the spiritual-benefit theory is but an example of the notion commonly encountered that property should pass to those who would be grateful to the *propositus* and who can remember him after his death. It serves the more useful purpose of providing an intelligible reason why one relative should be preferred to another. The author of the ingenious theory in its fully-fledged form, Jīmūtavāhana, could not find a more appropriate manner of assessing nearness to the *propositus*.

This review of some of the chief instances of the alleged dependence of rules of Hindu law upon Hindu religion is intended, not to detract from the important part which religion has played in shaping the development of the *śāstra* and making it possible for a coherent and organized body of law to be promulgated, studied and applied to a vast conglomerate people, but to suggest that the actual relationship between religious doctrine and the rules of substantive law is not that of cause and effect, but rather that of form and substance.[2] The teaching of law and its judicial development cannot indeed dispense with formal theories and *a priori* arguments, but it is plain that the law as a living expression of justice can exist, and often does exist, without their aid. Whether the sanction behind the law be the demands of religion or merely those of age and unbroken acceptance, a careful distinction must be maintained between the law's authority and its content. No harm is done if the boundary between the two is allowed to become obscure, provided that, when the rules apparently authorized by the ultimate sanction cease to serve the purpose for which they were intended, there should be no obstacle to their relegation to the legal historian's museum, unsurvived by their formal *rationes*.

The Fundamental Theory of the Hindu Law

Such is the outcome of our investigation whether the claim that rules of Hindu law were based on the Hindu religion could be sustained. Rules that have a religious foundation are, as we shall

[1] Mayne, where cited above, pp. 688–9.

[2] Many of the characteristics of Mitāksharā law are to be traced to 'secular commonsense and secular justice': *per* Raman Nayar, J., at *Mary* v. *Bhasura* [1967] K.L.T. 430, 436.

see in more detail, often neglected, and that without public outcry. Rules which have no such foundation are upheld on the formal ground that they are sanctioned by religion. The liaison between religion and law is not close.

But what if we ask the question, does Hindu religion explain the scope, content, style, outlook and tendency of the *śāstra* as a whole? The result is quite otherwise. The energy needed to settle formulations of law, to bring disparate topics into association with each other, to make a drive, on personal initiative, to put a reasoned and complete system before kings and judges anxious to make their laws and their decisions agree with the dominant, proselytizing culture which was the Hinduism of ancient times, could come only from grand ideas, a comprehensive mind, a genius, not perhaps of a handful of men, but of a small band of intellectuals. It was no ordinary mind that could proceed from an apprehension of general moral ideas to the conviction that instances of usual behaviour embodied and effectuated them: yet many evidently did. Teaching individual rules of law would excite few, enthral fewer: but to teach law as a systematic expression of a cultural vision, of a wisdom that was part and parcel of the Brahmin mission, a source of power already drawn upon for purely religious and often selfish purposes–that might be another matter. The challenge was responded to as never elsewhere. All law and duty could, and must, be taught as part of the Brahmin's role as teacher of the lower castes. The ideal Brahmin, with an ideal and peculiar outlook on life, was the source of knowledge, and the individual conforming to that ideal was entitled to play a role that no other could. Naturally *dharma* was taught as an infinitely vast and cumbersome medley of rules, subordinated to a comprehensive pattern of life and thought. That, when we look at it closely, is religious, superstitious, from top to bottom. Is this *dharmaśāstra* subverted by legislation and incongruous judicial decisions? Hardly–for its intellectual position and claims remain, like its sister disciplines, the Torah of Moses and the Shariat, immutable and immortal, unaffected by the vagaries of judges and the transient preferences of legislatures.

The framework, then, which was exempted from the conclusion that legal rules did not owe their origin to religion, is religious in its entirety. To work out this paradox will be a task of some magnitude, involving a search through many centuries, including our own, and through numerous points of detail. But for the present we must state what that framework was. It was, unexpectedly, very simple, and, as the great mind of that masterly compiler Manu saw it, neat and smooth. It consists of eight propositions, each following directly from the previous. These are not set out in such terms anywhere, but a repeated reading of the sources leaves one in no doubt but that this was the way in which the *śāstra* was developed. Let us take each proposition in turn:

(1) The world depends upon *rain*. Sacrifices to the gods, and especially to the Sun, produce rain. Manu III, 76 is clear as to this.[1]

(2) All beings, including non-believers, require sacrifices to be performed. The teaching contained in the Veda is immortal and it sustains all creatures. The Veda is therefore not merely an obvious cult object and a means of income for those who know it, but also an essential tool for the continuation of the species, and indeed other forms of life which require water. Manu XII, 99 is clear as to this.

(3) Sacrifices can be performed only by Brahmins. When their education is finished they possess the Veda in their memories. They alone have the hereditary gifts and talents for obtaining and retaining sacrificial skills; and they alone have the hereditary gift for undergoing the self-restraint and observances which protect purity, without which sacrificial capacity vanishes.

(4) The Brahmin ideal ethic, with its peculiar un-self-assertive quality, its renunciation, its discipline, its fitness to take upon itself the impurities of others (when accepting gifts and otherwise), must be facilitated and established. Order and good government, the protection of the people, are therefore required. Mixture of castes due to lust or greed, or mere misgovernment must be avoided. Positive patronage through charitable and especially educational endowments is inculcated.

(5) The Brahmin household, protected and endowed, must continue indefinitely qualified for the performance of sacrifices and all the sciences subsidiary to sacrifices (e.g. the *dharmaśāstra* itself). Labour to cultivate the fields, and especially artisans and

[1] Medhātithi on Manu VII, 29; IX, 327. *Maitr. Up.* VI, 37.

merchants to supply Brahmins with their various needs, must reliably perform these functions, or those similar to them. Such avocations must never afford temptation to the Brahmins themselves to compete, as, with their inherited mental powers they very well could (and often did) against the *śāstra*. We have seen that the protection of the people was posited in the Brahmins' professional interests. That required yet another *varṇa*, and Brahmins were not supposed to usurp its (the *rāja's*) functions—if they did they lost their claim to be ideal Brahmins. The rights of property, of the family, and of inheritance must be preserved with scrupulous care, and especially the relative property-entitlement of the various castes: e.g. the king must never take and keep Brahmins' property, for that would invert the order required by nature.[1]

(6) Since all these rights are often doubted in good faith as well as dishonestly, litigation must be contemplated, and rules of law must be established, positive, substantive and adjectival, so that the contentment and efficiency of the ideal Brahmin is secured.

(7) Decisions given in court must be based upon truthful evidence, or evidence which, from a Brahminical point of view, is as good as reliable human evidence. Judgment must be impartial.

(8) To achieve these ends the superstitions of the public may be resorted to. The occult value of behaviour must be explored and established, even from distinct viewpoints. Inconsistencies of philosophy are immaterial, as long as actual beliefs can be tapped. The doctrine of *karma*, which was held as a fact, the notion of transmigration of souls, the theory that wrongdoers suffer in this life and in innumerable future lives, may be utilized. Certainly they cannot be allowed to be questioned. *Dharma* requires that such beliefs shall be exploited in order that those free to act on their own initiative may have a strong sanction against dishonesty and corruption. And if the civil and criminal law does not work efficiently the same sanctions operate to hinder all manner of wrongdoing. As we have seen, penance was as important as punishment, and normally more degrading to the offender and his family.

These are the eight propositions on which the entire *śāstra*

[1] See below, p. 210, n. 6.

rests. It is very natural that prior to the British period no one was heard to deny the validity of the approach, and no competing systems of jurisprudence made themselves felt. The Islamic principles evidently stemmed from sources which were equally committed to drawing upon superstition, and Hinduism suffered no rationalistic attack from that quarter. On the contrary Hindus saw the Muslims as inconveniently powerful, but not culturally dissimilar from themselves in kind. The rationalism and utilitarianism of the Christian rulers of the eighteenth century and after presented a challenge unique in Indian history. But if the *śāstra* was sacred, and its revealed rules were not necessarily so, how could inevitable social and economic development avoid disrupting the *śāstra*, granted that the Veda could neither grow nor change and that practical rulings were supported by ethical sanctions? An example of the work of the jurists will clarify the position.

5

EXPEDIENCY *v.* AUTHORITY: THE RIGHT TO EARN IN ANCIENT INDIA

It is undeniable nowadays[1] that anyone inclined to work should be permitted to earn and to acquire by his earnings the means to keep himself and his immediate dependants.[2] That some theorists object to accumulation beyond this point does not diminish the truth of the contention. A modern society accepts without hesitation that an individual may freely choose (so far as his own prejudices and handicaps permits) the career or way of life which best suits him, without paramount restriction upon his legal or moral capacity to earn, and subject only to such qualifications as employers, for example, will impose upon those whom they propose to engage. We regard as antiquated, if not mediaeval, any system which places artificial impediments in the way of those who wish to take up a particular kind of employment, and the very notion of a monopoly or any unduly onerous restriction upon acquiring a right to earn is hateful to most of us.

Ancient India supplies an especially interesting example of what happens when a social system which presupposes a rigid hereditary occupational classification of the population begins to break down in the face of ever-greater intercourse with foreigners and of ever-expanding opportunities for the enterprising and ambitious. The right to earn had to be established

[1] This chapter corresponds to 'The right to earn in ancient India: a conflict between expediency and authority' which appeared at *J.E.S.H.O.*, 1, pt. 1 (1957), 66–97; save that the Sanskrit text has been omitted as of too little value for the average reader, the draft amended translation has been improved, a correction of Colebrooke has been added and the missing references to the work of A. S. Naṭarāja Ayyar and other less important items have been added.

[2] Cf. *Constitution of India*, Artt. 19 (1), (6) and 41.

upon intellectual as well as practical grounds, and the mental struggles which brought this about are worthy of discussion and documentation. The Hindus of ancient and mediaeval times wanted to earn when the opportunity invited them; their *dharmaśāstra* placed barriers in their way; and, though they succumbed to temptation, they desired to be assured that their acquisitions were really their own; to be told whether they needed to perform some penance to rid themselves of the taint which, many believed, infected them after breaking the ancient code of behaviour; and finally to be satisfied that those to whom their forbidden acquisitions passed would not be affected by the taint, if any, which had attached to the original acquirers.[1] The jurists applied their minds to this problem, and as usual produced results of great subtlety and of course of immense practical importance. We may add that the Hindu scholars were not alone in this, for Jaina as well as Hindu scriptures aimed to control acquisition and dealings with property[2] with markedly similar moral objectives.

This topic has not been ignored by writers in English, and if we refer to Priyanāth Sen,[3] to Kishorī Lāl Sarkar[4] and to Dr. P. V. Kāṇe[5] we do not fail to find substantial material relating to it. They seek to explain how and why Vijñāneśvara decided in this connexion an apparently irrelevant question in an apparently unreasonable way in order to arrive at an answer which anyone would today take quite for granted. Their methods differ considerably, and they are not equally successful. None of them has emphasized the exceptional jurisprudential and practical importance of Vijñāneśvara's work, and it may be that none of them was fully aware of it. To a considerable extent the

[1] One may recollect in passing the Jewish distinction between forbidden objects from which the acquirer must take no profit, and those which, though they may not be enjoyed for their original purpose, may still be employed in some useful manner. The taint affecting the 'hire of a harlot', for example, did not attach to the coins or other objects for which the 'harlot' might exchange it (cf. Mt. xxvi: 6–13, Mk. xiv: 3–9, Lk. vii: 36–8).

[2] Numerous instances occur in R. Williams, *Jaina Yoga* (London, 1963).

[3] *The General Principles of Hindu Jurisprudence* (Calcutta, 1918), pp. 42–6, 53 ff.

[4] *The Mimansa Rules of Interpretation as Applied to Hindu Law* (Calcutta, 1909), pp. 390–4. 'Mimansa' is Sarkar's anomalous spelling of *mīmāṃsā*.

[5] *H.D.*, III, pp. 548–51, with a most learned footnote on p. 550.

neglect there has been repaired by Mr. A. S. Naṭarāja Ayyar in a somewhat obscure journal.[1]

The text was in part translated by H. T. Colebrooke in his *Two Treatises*. His translation, known as the *Mitākṣarā* after the name of the commentary as a whole, was almost immediately adopted as a standard authority in Hindu law by the Anglo-Indian courts, and was, with very few exceptions, the paramount criterion in disputed topics of family law until the year 1956, when its position was undermined by legislation.[2] The prestige of the *Mitākṣarā* somewhat emphasized the unfortunate obscurity of Colebrooke's translation at the very passages where the author, determined to show that there was such a right as we now call the right to earn, leaned heavily upon the authority of an outstanding philosophical writer, and selected *his* approach to the problem as the principal guide to his solution. To this day the actual words of that eminent philosopher, Prabhākara, remain unpublished, and this fact must be the chief excuse for the variety of approaches of previous writers to the original text of the *Mitākṣarā* (which is not very much less difficult in Sanskrit than it appears in Colebrooke's version) and for their comparatively ill success. A rather poor copy of the *Bṛhati*, Prabhākara's sub-commentary on the *Mīmāṃsā-sūtra-s* of Jaimini, was traced recently in the Adyar Library,[3] Mr. Naṭarāja Ayyar incompletely reports another,[4] and it is now possible to attempt to clear up the mystery. But we must begin at the beginning of the story.

Not many centuries after the close of the Vedic period two authorities of enormous subsequent prestige uttered opinions about Property,[5] and in particular about 'lawful' ways of acquiring it. We should not emphasize the relation between their statements and law, for not only was Jaimini not a lawyer, in the sense that jurisprudence was not his special field of study, but Gautama, who certainly fell into the latter category, did not himself contemplate so much strictly legal consequences from a great part of the 'law' which he uttered, as obedience to a moral

[1] 'The Mīmāṃsā View of Property', *Vyav. Nirṇ.*, 4 (1955), pp. 46–64.

[2] See below, pp. 327–8.

[3] Shelf No. 38. B. 6 (4).

[4] Apparently preserved at the Gaṅgānātha Jhā Research Institute.

[5] 'Property' with the capital letter = the abstract right of property; 'property' with the minuscule = an asset.

and social code which he had evolved from his enquiries into behaviour, its variety and its tendencies. This distinction was not however of much moment with mediaeval jurists, who consequently found themselves in the difficulties which we shall briefly review below. Gautama was faced by a group of societies which still nominally respected, and could claim to exemplify, the four-*varṇa* (i.e. four-caste, or better, perhaps, 'four-class') system. This system has been sufficiently studied and no elaboration is required of certain facts, viz. that even in early times the four classes did not correspond to the multitudinous endogamous and occupational sub-divisions of society, each jealously preserving its own customs and traditions and the mysteries of its trade and craft; that the *dharmaśāstra* theory, that this proliferation was due to 'mixture of castes' through inter-caste unions, was itself only a very partial explanation; and that from at least as early as the time of the Buddha the members of the various classes were successfully tempted to encroach upon one another's occupational preserves. Perhaps as early as Gautama himself it was common for Brahmins to earn by methods appropriate to administrators and commercial folk.[1] Doubtless some Brahmins preserved a sense of shame if they were acquiring by 'service', that is to say employment under direction, whether in agriculture or industry–a method traditionally believed appropriate to *śūdra-s*. They also knew that numerous methods of earning a living or doing business were subject to bans in the *dharmaśāstra*,[2] though they may not have observed the restrictions punctiliously. Considerations of prestige as well as greed influenced the public; although it was only concern for the spiritual welfare of a society in danger of losing the services of its hereditary priesthood that concerned Gautama and was to concern Manu and other *smṛti*-writers.

Gautama says:[3]

> An Owner occurs in cases of inheritance, purchase, partition, garnering

[1] As he suggests at VII, 6–7.

[2] Restrictions on sale and even exchange are mentioned at Kāṇe, *H.D.*, II, pp. 108–14, 126–34; IV, p. 116. On castes doing work appropriate to lower castes see II, pp. 120–6. Derrett, 'The development of the concept of Property in India', *Z. f. vergl. Rechtsw.*, 64 (1962), pp. 15 ff., especially at pp. 43 ff. Also *B.S.O.A.S.*, 20 (1957), pp. 203 ff.

[3] X, 39–42, 49. In II, 1 of the Poona edition with Haradatta (1931).

and finding. For the Brahmin acquisition[1] is an additional mode; for the Kṣatriya conquest; for the Vaiśya and the Śūdra wages. For the Vaiśya additional modes are agriculture, trading, tending cattle, and money-lending.

Manu says:[2]

> Seven acquisitions of wealth are consistent with *dharma*: *dāya* [acquisition of joint family property by membership or ancestral property by advancement or inheritance], presents, purchase, conquest, lending at interest, employment in labour, and acceptance from a virtuous person.

Mediaeval commentators expend care on the explanation of the meaning of each of the words used,[3] and although their results differ, they are agreed that it is worth-while to assume that the texts enumerate the methods by which one *may* earn property. In the very next verse Manu tells us that there are ten ways of earning one's livelihood and the list is fairly comprehensive. He does not imply other than that these are the methods that are found to exist, and are stamped with legality, but the commentators say that he means that all ten are available to all Hindus only 'in times of *āpad*'.[4] In other places he inveighs against Brahmins who earn their living in other ways than by accepting gifts from virtuous people (*sat-pratigraha*), teaching the Veda, studying the Veda, performing sacrifices for people, and, by implication, strictly connected activities, and he instructs the disobedient acquirer to abandon the object.[5] Elsewhere we are told that there is 'pure' and 'impure' wealth.[6] Thus at the outset we are in doubt as to whether the texts referred to above tell us what *ought* to be utilized as a method of

[1] Invariably glossed 'acceptance'. [2] X, 115.

[3] L. S. Joshī, *Dharma-kośa, Vyavahāra-kāṇḍa*, I, pt. 2 (Wai, 1938), 1122 ff. G. Jhā, *Hindu Law in its Sources*, II (Allahabad, 1933), pp. 1–6.

[4] See above, p. 95. Manu X, 116 with Medhātithi. Jhā's trans. of this passage (*Manu-smṛti with the Manubhāṣya of Medhātithi, translated* . . . , vol. 5 (Calcutta, 1926), p. 331) is defective–as not infrequently.

[5] I, 88; X, 76 to be compared with III, 64–5, 150–68; also XI, 194 discussed in the *Mitākṣarā* (para. 16 below) and *Madana-ratna-pradīpa*, pp. 325–6.

[6] Kāṇe, *H.D.*, II, p. 130. Lakṣmīdhara, *Kṛtya-kalpataru*, II, *Gṛhastha-kāṇḍa* (ed. K. V. Rangaswāmī Aiyaṅgār, Baroda, 1944), introd., pp. 54, 63, 87–8, and texts there referred to. Lakṣmīdhara, who speaks of *dharmādharma-svatva*, seems to have regarded the texts as absolutely binding in the contexts of religious activity, i.e. the solution of Prabhākara (below) is ignored.

earning; what *was* usually so utilized in the days of the respective authors; or finally what *might legally* be so utilized. And a very great deal depends upon the manner in which we take such texts. If acceptance by a Brahmin from a person who is not virtuous does not give rise to the acceptor's Property a question immediately arises as to what his relationship to that object is, and what his powers are with regard to it. We are reminded that there were prohibitions against accepting from a *Caṇḍāla*; against accepting a ewe and certain other objects; and against accepting anything upon the banks of the Ganges or other rivers.[1] If all these rules are to be taken as strict parallels, does it not follow that the man who acquires against the rules merely sins, but that the acquired object is his, and he can give a good title to someone who may succeed him?[2] However it is by no means certain that they are parallel in this respect.

When Manu says that seven methods of acquisition are 'consistent with *dharma*', the implication is not that others may not be consistent with *dharma* ('righteousness') but may yet be legally valid. The word *dharma* covers civil as well as religious law, as we have seen. If the contention is that Manu allowed acquisition for all practical purposes without restraint, but laid down restrictions for the purpose of increasing the number of actions which led to penance, it must be proved, and there is no proof to this effect. If he had prohibited acquisition except in the ways stated the inference might have been different. Similarly Gautama does not hint that his enumeration is anything other than a careful study of instances of Property-creation, and thus an objective and not merely tendentious pronouncement of law. Property was required for every daily transaction,[3] and even to the ritualist it was essential to know how exactly Property in goods and land *could* be acquired, apart from how it might morally be acquired. Thus, leaving aside the rules relating to *āpad* (which are admittedly exceptional) and the

[1] See p. 125, n. 2 above.

[2] Note *Gautama-dharma-sūtra-pariśiṣṭa* (*Second Praśna*), ed. A. N. Kṛishṇa Aiyaṅgār (Adyar, 1948), X, 15–16: 'From *mlecchas* (foreigners) and the rest a gift of gold (even) amounting to a thousand (pieces) he must not accept. But if he accepts, he must give it to Brahmins.' On the differing viewpoints see Derrett where cited above (*B.S.O.A.S.*, 20).

[3] Nārada II, 39: 'all rituals have their root in assets (*dhana-mūlāḥ kriyāḥ sarvā*)'. This is I, 43 in Jolly's trans. of 1889.

classification into 'pure', 'impure', and 'partly impure' wealth, there was a basis for the assumption by early jurists that Gautama and Manu and others were attempting to give a juristic definition of the sources of Property.

Numerous instances occur,[1] even in unlikely places, of the tradition that the texts of Gautama and Manu placed all restrictions on earning in the category of legal as well as moral fetters, binding upon both the person purporting to acquire and upon the objects in his hands. It was felt that gifts taken improperly from an impure person were hardly distinguishable from objects stolen. Property held without a 'clear-and-pure' title (*śuddhāgama*) was not held in Property at all,[2] but merely possessed *de facto*.[3] One must earn, if at all, according to the custom of one's class, according to the means of acquisition peculiar to that class, according to the means of acquisition open to all Hindus, and finally according to the general requirements of law and morality–and in no other ways. Moral scruples, which may not always have affected a large proportion of the population, but which were none the less acute where they manifested themselves, had no means of being quieted. It is true that the *dharmaśāstra* was in very ancient times equipped with a law of prescription. After a specified number of years of undisputed enjoyment, the true owner being in a position to claim

[1] Vijñāneśvara refers to the view in the paragraphs below. At Yājñ. II, 24 he refers forward to that passage. But at Yājñ. II, 58 he discusses how a pledgee becomes owner of the pledge, the method *not* having been mentioned by Manu or Gautama: his solution is double, that popular recognition justified it, and that the śāstric texts incorporated it inferentially. See also the excellent passage on the same text of Yājñ. at *Smṛti-candrikā* (Mysore edn.), III, pt. 2, pp. 329–31 (popular recognition embraces exchanges). On exchange (not mentioned by Manu or Gautama) see Bharadvāja at *Sarasvatī-vilāsa*, *Vyavahāra-kāṇḍa* (Mysore, 1927), p. 163. Jīmūtavāhana, however, (*Dāyabhāga*, Calcutta, 1930, 19–20; Colebrooke's trans., I, 19) denied that one could acquire by a method not listed in those texts. It is said that Bhāruci and Aparārka had the same view by the author of the *Sarasvatī-vilāsa* at p. 347.

[2] Donors take care to allege that the property they settle on an institution to endow it is 'pure' (cf. Manu V, 106, IV, 170 with Medhātithi): for an example see the Munirabad Stone Inscription (cited below, p. 176, n. 5) where the property is *pitṛ-dhanaṃ*, ancestral and not acquired at all, and *also śukla-dravyaṃ*, 'bright thing'. See also Manu VIII, 201.

[3] Nārada I, 87: the king should punish as a thief the man who possesses without a title even after many hundreds of years.

the property as his own, the possessor might be entitled to resist a suit and give a perfect title to a third party.[1] These very useful texts, had they been treated seriously, would have done much to set at rest the difficulties which are dealt with here. In modern systems moral doubts as to the propriety of methods of acquisition cease with time alone to have any legal relevance. Moreover modern societies enjoy rules with regard to the passing of title in currency and in negotiable instruments, which obviate the need for too close a scrutiny of the way by which a transferor 'comes by' the money or money's worth which he is passing on. But the *śāstrī-s* curiously set about the virtual destruction of their traditional law of prescription.[2] They could not understand how title could be acquired by wrongful means, such as adverse possession. How, they asked, could wrongdoing be a source of title, especially in a system where religion and law were in co-operation? And in consequence they so interpreted the *smṛti-s* which would have given them considerable relief in our present context, that title could only be acquired by prescription in very rare cases where the original owner had actually or virtually relinquished the object. This strange emasculation of otherwise useful texts left the same authors with no escape when they were asked, 'How can my acquisition in gift from a person who is not virtuous become my Property?' And they were obliged to search for a solution elsewhere.

For ancient Indians were by no means solely concerned with moral scruples. The polluting element in an improper acquisition was not so troublesome as the possibility that the property would be recovered even after the lapse of many years, on the ground that it was improperly acquired by the acquirer. Or intended alienees might raise objections on the ground that the original means of acquisition was tainted and there was accordingly no title in the transferor. At a period when gifts of land and gold were the most common means of attempting to earn

[1] Vyāsa I, 84; Viṣṇu V, 186; Yājñ. II, 24; Nārada I, 78.

[2] Compare the treatments at *Mitākṣarā* on Yājñ. II, 24 (trans. Ghārpure, pp. 720–6); Jīmūtavāhana, *Vyavahāra-mātṛkā*, ed. A. Mookerjee, *Memoirs of the As. Soc. of Bengal*, 3, 5 (1912), pp. 277 ff., especially 341–52; and Vācaspati-miśra, *Vyavahāra-cintāmaṇi*, ed. L. Rocher (Ghent, 1956), text pp. 112 ff.; trans. pp. 291 ff. A good summary of the *Mitākṣarā* discussion is given by R. Lingat, *Les sources du droit dans le système traditionnel de l'Inde* (Paris, 1967), pp. 182–6.

spiritual merit, it was of supreme importance that the donee as well as the donor should be satisfied that the asset in question was untainted. Moreover, since the joint-family was in ancient times even more than at present the essential property-acquiring, -managing and -enjoying unit, and the whole family tended to depend upon an undifferentiated mass of property acquired by various members at various occasions, the chaos that would result from too strict an enquiry into the method of acquisition of an item or worse still an item which had been bought out of the proceeds of sale of that item, did not bear contemplating. An authoritative definition of the *possible* (as distinct from *desirable*) sources of Property was thus a desideratum. But it was one which the jurists of the ages subsequent to the composition of the great *smṛti-s* had neither the initiative nor the authority to supply. They could only play with the texts of Gautama and Manu, and make the best of them.

The word *sva-tva* ('own-ness', *proprietas*, Property), is not well described by the lexicographers. Patañjali commenting on Pāṇini said:[1]

> What we call *sva* comes about in four ways: by purchase, by getting, by begging, and by exchange.

Whether this may be justified or not as a laconic attempt at classifying all methods, it is of no real help to us. We remain in the dark, to start with, as to whether one's wife or one's child, or even one's parent is one's Property:[2] for the word *sva* linguistically applies as much to them as to one's cow.

A historically more fruitful way of solving the problem was suggested by Jaimini. His *sūtra-s*, devoted to the evolving of a system of interpretation of Vedic texts dealing with sacrifices, are of quite unparalleled obscurity and ambiguity. Numerous attempts were made in ancient times to make coherent sense of them.[3] The attempt made by Śabara-svāmī led the field, but

[1] *Mahābhāṣya* on Pāṇ. II, 3, 50. Kāṇe's opinion (*H.D.*, III, 550 n. 1027) that the enumeration is only illustrative does not cover all *dharmaśāstra* opinions.

[2] Nīlakaṇṭha, *Vyavahāra-mayūkha*, ed. Kāṇe (Poona, 1926), pp. 92–3. The topic is discussed by Derrett, at *B.S.O.A.S.*, 18 (1956), p. 492, n. 4.

[3] See Jaimini (see *Mīmāṃsā-darśanaṃ Jaimini-Mīmāṃsā-sūtra-pāṭhaḥ*, ed. Kevalānanda-saraswatī, Wai, 1948, p. 80), IV, i, 2. The text which lies at the bottom of the different interpretations is *yasmin prītiḥ puruṣasya tasya*

his commentary on the *Mīmāṃsā-sūtra-s*, though the most famous, did not preclude further critical work in interpretation of this cryptic text. In the fourth chapter Jaimini undertakes to explain the difference between *puruṣārtha* and *kratvartha* (see below), and in the second *adhikaraṇa* of the first *pāda* he mentions *lipsā*, which means 'the desire to acquire', 'acquisitiveness'. This strongly suggests that he was laying down a rule concerning the methods of acquisition prescribed in the *smṛti-s*, which of course had Vedic authority behind them. Not all scholars are agreed that the word *lipsā* was intended to refer to this at all; but Śabara, in his last attempt to construe the passage, accepted this meaning,[1] and expounded, as Jaimini's doctrine, the rule that regulations (inhibitions) concerning acquisition (*arjana-niyama-s*) were *puruṣārtha* and not *kratvartha*; that consequently the *niyama-s* might well produce an unseen (*adṛṣṭa*) result without their affecting in any way transactions of a visible character—from which one may conclude, as his leading commentator, Kumārila-bhaṭṭa, does, that there are not two types of property, one suitable for sacrifices (earned in accordance with the *niyama-s*) and one not suitable for sacrifices, but only one Property in all acquired objects which is none the less Property for the *niyama-s*' (which relate only to the individual) having been ignored. This fits at first sight because a *niyama* is a particular kind of restrictive rule, breach of which, in the ordinary way, leads only to sin in the individual offender, without necessarily leading to a nullity of the transaction. To put it in popular terms, the choice of the word *niyama* to describe

lipsārtha-lakṣaṇā 'vibhaktatvāt. Naṭarāja Ayyar's working trans. is 'what subserves the purposes of man is that upon which follows the happiness of man; and man's purpose is not different from happiness'. The interpretations given by K. L. Sarkar, M. L. Sandal (1923) and N. V. Thadani (1952) are widely different from each other.

[1] *Jaiminīya-sūtra-bhāṣya*, Bibl. Ind. ser., 1873–87, or Ānandāśrama Skt. ser., 1929–34. Gaṅgānātha Jhā's trans. (Baroda, 1933–6) is helpful. See II, pp. 707–16. On the distinction between *puruṣārtha* and *kratvartha* see G. Jhā, *Pūrva-mīmāṃsā in its Sources* (Benares, 1942), p. 292; K. L. Sarkar, where cited above, pp. 52–4. For an instance see Medhātithi on Manu VII, 93. Derrett in *Festschrift Spies* (ed. W. Hoenerbach, Wiesbaden, 1967), p. 36. See also Kāṇe at *A.B.O.R.I.*, 6 (1924), pp. 30–1. The discussion at Kumātila's *Tantravārttika*, trans., II, 1289–1369 (on Jaimini III, iv, 4) is enlightening: the command not to tell lies is *kratvartha* and breach of it is fatal to the sacrifice.

Gautama's and Manu's rules may not be accidental, or coincidental, but may be a sign of conscious awareness of the limitations of the rules themselves. But, however this may be, at first sight this would not appear to help us. Yet it was used by Vijñāneśvara as a lever to shift an encumbrance that was as troublesome to lawyers as to the lay public, and which could not have been shifted by independent creative juristic pronouncement, that is to say, so long as traditional śāstric techniques were to be adhered to.

The Veda insists, rationally, that sacrifices must be performed with *sva*. What sort of things are *sva*, the *Mīmāṃsā* asks in another place? It is settled that only objects over which one has undisputed Ownership can qualify.[1] What if the object is *prima facie* not unsuitable for sacrificial employment, whether as oblation in a Vedic fire, or as *dakṣiṇā* to a priest, or as a gift for *dharma* which is declared to be equal to a sacrifice, but had been acquired contrary to the texts of Gautama, Manu or others? The question might be expected to be answered by Jaimini, and it was quite rational that the chapter on *kratvartha* and *puruṣārtha* should be chosen as the place for the answer. According to Jaimini every injunction of the scriptures has a binding force, but one only–in other words no *vidhi* can enjoin two matters simultaneously. When an injunction relates to a sacrifice it must belong to one or other of two categories, namely either (i) that of those which 'subserve the sacrifice' (*kratvartha*), that is to say, apply within the scope of the ritual itself, so that their purpose and relevance are exhausted when they have been attended to in the ordering of the ritual; or (ii) that of those which 'subserve the individual' (*puruṣārtha*), that is to say, concern the sacrificer, so that their purpose and relevance are exhausted when they have been observed by him as sacrificer, or the equivalent. The possibility that a *vidhi* could be *both* is ruled out by the technique of interpretation itself. The importance of the two categories varies with the context, but on the whole an injunction which is *kratvartha* 'matters' less than does one which is *puruṣārtha* in that a fault or mistake with regard to the ritual vitiates it alone and in many cases jeopardizes the spiritual object for which the ritual is performed, whereas a breach of a *puruṣārtha* rule will

[1] *Taittirīya-saṃhitā* VI, i, 6, 3. Jaimini VI, i, 10–24, 39–40; iii, 21; vii, 5, 7.

affect the happiness of the individual in a variety of situations and is thus a more serious matter. In particular he may have to perform a costly penance. Jaimini's notion, according to Śabara, is that the restrictions upon acquisition are not *kratvartha* because acquisition brings happiness to man, and is thus obviously *puruṣārtha*, and because if acquisition were so bound up with sacrifice (as many contended) that the restrictions relative to sacrifices controlled the nature of Property itself, the result would be that Property could not be used to maintain the individual and, there remaining no sacrificers, there could be no sacrifices: so that the rules would defeat their own object! Kumārila in his *Ṭupṭīkā*[1] puts what is virtually the same point more shortly: if Property exists with a view to sacrifice, Property does not exist for disposal at pleasure, therefore the sacrificer has no Property, of which he can make a relinquishment (*tyāga*). If acquisition subserved sacrifice alone it would be an essential pre-requisite of the sacrifice. No doubt without acquisition antecedently to the sacrifice the sacrifice cannot take place, but is acquisition a part of the ritual, in the same sense as other *kratvartha* actions are, for example the preparation of the *soma* in the *agniṣṭoma* sacrifice? Clearly not, for one can sacrifice with the aid of objects one has acquired without reference to that sacrifice. Finally, the fact that acquisition serves purely secular purposes is clear from practical experience, whereas the contention that the texts of Gautama, etc., are meaningful in all sorts of contexts, religious and secular, is a contention based not upon experience but upon inference. Thus, even though an *adṛṣṭa* ('unseen', 'spiritual') result may be produced by breaking the restrictions or (in an opposite sense) by scrupulously adhering to them–a matter which Śabara does not care to dispute–acquisition itself is found to subserve human purposes, and the rules relating to it must be *puruṣārtha* and not *kratvartha*.

We should now imagine that if the rules were *puruṣārtha* the situation would be worse. Those who take them to be *kratvartha* are at least at liberty to suppose that Property outside the context of the sacrifice is unaffected by the restrictions. But it seems that those who defended the view-point opposite to Jaimini-Śabara's went in fact to the length of asserting that

[1] As reported by Naṭarāja Ayyar (see above).

Property was in existence only for sacrifices,[1] or for doing acts prescribed by the *dharmaśāstra*, and had no existence apart from the religious-and-civil law. This extreme view seems to have done the *kratvartha* case more harm than good. On the other hand if the rules are *puruṣārtha* it would appear that they are intimately connected with human happiness, and the need for watchfulness against a breach of them is greater than ever. But Jaimini is made out to show unconcern with this aspect of the matter. It is up to the individual to interpret the texts as he thinks fit and to perform such penances as are applicable for the breaches he commits. Jaimini is made, in fact, to evade our problem, and to hint that sacrifices, and so meritorious donations, will be valid, notwithstanding the impropriety of the means adopted by the donor to acquire them, and notwithstanding the lack of what to our minds would appear to be a legal and moral qualification for earning the merit. For stolen property is as much outside the qualification laid down by Gautama as property acquired by acceptance from a non-virtuous donor. Other sorts of alienations were ignored.

Moreover we, who are demanding an answer to the question, 'What is the nature of Property, so far as its acquisition is concerned?', have a right to expect the *śāstra* to enlighten us with injunctions relative to that aspect. It is not sufficient to be told that what we have got (no matter how) will be *sva* for the limited purpose of effecting a successful sacrifice. Śabara goes no further into the matter, and, as we shall see, it was left to Prabhākara to take his view to its conclusion. Nevertheless the maxim, 'What I have I hold', may be a fair statement of policy, but hardly of law: as the author of the mediaeval *Smṛti-saṅgraha* emphatically pointed out.

Accordingly we are bound to look with some disfavour upon Bhavanātha's attempt to resolve our problem. Bhavanātha,[2] who as a *mīmāṃsaka* and a follower of Prabhākara certainly accepted the view that the rules restricting acquisition were

[1] Kāṇe, *H.D.*, iii, 609. The view of Bhoja (Dhāreśvara) and the author of the *Smṛti-saṅgraha*. The topic is taken up effectively in the *Smṛti-candrikā* and the *Madana-ratna-pradīpa*. Vijñāneśvara himself quotes with disapproval authorities to the effect that wealth exists for sacrifices (and therefore women are excluded from it) on Yājñ. II, 135–6, Colebrooke II, i, 14, 22–4.

[2] The portion of his *Naya-viveka* so far published does not include the section in which we are interested.

puruṣārtha, put forward in his *Naya-viveka* the view that acquisition as a legal phenomenon was *loka-siddha*, 'secularly established', 'established by the lay public in actual usage'. The right of acquisition not merely historically preceded the formulation of the rules of Gautama and the rest, but deprived those rules of exclusive right to describe it legally. Thus 'birth' might be included as a means of acquisition, though not mentioned here by Gautama or Manu, because the lay public admitted it without dispute (in certain areas).[1] Exchange was another possible method ignored in those particular texts, and acquisition by foreclosure of a mortgage. But we must note that when the same author was discussing the effect of possession upon Property,[2] declaring that possession as such could not give rise to Property, he was prepared to point out that possession was nowhere revealed as a means of acquisition; and thus it is clear that he by no means totally abandoned the *śāstra* as a source of information about acquisition. He merely denied that *svatva* was *śāstraikādhigamya*, 'solely cognizable from the *śāstra*'. Just as usage in speech is recorded in that *śāstra* which dealt with grammar,[3] so usage in business practice was or ought to be recorded in the *dharmaśāstra*, and omissions could be rectified by reference to usage. This latter point was an obvious exaggeration. Much of the *dharmaśāstra* was evidently concerned with what would never enter into practical usage; and we must observe that Gautama's and Manu's texts do *not* belong to sections of the *śāstra* unequivocally dealing with *vyavahāra*, and this is a more potent objection to his otherwise interesting suggestion. Moreover it is clear that popular behaviour, however rarely departed from, can create no more than a social norm,

[1] *Loka-siddhaṃ vārjanañ janmādi*; *ata evānidam-prathama-lokadhī-viṣayatayā sthite nibandhanārthā smṛtir vyākaraṇādi-smṛtivat. Madana-ratna-pradīpa* (where cited). *Smṛti-candrikā* at Dh.K. 1122b–1123a; *Vīramitrodaya*, *Vyavahāra-prakāśa*, p. 420; *Vyavahāra-mayūkha*, p. 89. An example of the usefulness of the doctrine of secular establishment of the concept of Property is the determination, accepted in all writers of the Mitāksharā school, that ownership is obtained by birth alone in the property of male lineal ancestors (see p. 415 below). The text of Gautama which said this (*utpattyaivārthaṃ svāmitvāl labhate*) was not in fact of unimpeachable authenticity.

[2] *Vyavahāra-cintāmaṇi*, sec. 501.

[3] But the grammarian analyses and explains usage, while the jurist attempts to regulate, assimilate, rationalize and innovate. The grammarian is the servant of speech, the jurist is the guardian and preceptor of conduct.

and never a legal definition; since, although the practice of the people may make it necessary to admit the existence of an institution, such as 'right by birth' in ancestral property, this has no closer association with the law than a problem has to its solution. To take an example, popular usage may well permit the transfer of children from parents who want to part with them to people who want to 'adopt' them, but whether the transaction has legal validity or not and what sort of status it creates, if any, is a technical matter involving far more complicated considerations than those which would present themselves to the minds of lay individuals interested in actual instances of so-called adoption. Bhavanātha's opening the door to the supplementation of Gautama and others was at least as dangerous generally as it was helpful in its specific instance.

While the jurists were on the way, not without opposition, towards general agreement that Property was secular, that it was ascertained not exclusively from the śāstric texts, and that it might be acquired validly even in breach of such texts, a solitary voice was raised in protest, but with a strongly constructive suggestion. Treated with ridicule by subsequent authorities, and never again investigated without prejudice, his maxim, though paradoxical in form, contained a profound truth. On the one hand the extremists held that there was no Property outside that which had been acquired in strict accordance with the texts; on the other hand it was urged that, whatever might be the *unseen* force of the texts, Property could be acquired by any sort of acquisition other than one condemned in so many words by a penal text or by popular usage. An anonymous contributor pointed out that *arjanaṃ svatvaṃ nāpādayati*: 'acquisition does not produce Property'.[1] In other words, to him acquisition was one thing and Property was another; the mere act of acquisition, such as theft, did not make the acquirer an Owner. The circumstances in which one may become an Owner were set out by Gautama and others. Property was a technical matter, to be determined from the *śāstra*; but one might well acquire goods, hold them, and enjoy them without necessarily having Property in them (this would explain Manu VIII, 416), and, unless the methods by which one transferred

[1] Quoted also in the *Dāyabhāga*, p. 77 (Colebrooke, II, 67), and Medhātithi on Manu VIII, 416 (trans. IV, pt. 2, p. 434 obscurely).

them to others were found in the texts, one's successors would take no better title. But that defect was not fatal tc most of the purposes for which Property is required. Property was absolutely requisite for the purposes of sacrifice, etc., but could be dispensed with in many other contexts, where a mere possessory title would suffice. What one has acquired need not be one's Property, but it will serve so many practical purposes that it is virtually 'owned'. This brilliant suggestion that *svatva* is not *laukika* ('secular by nature'), but that there can be a *laukikāgama* and a *śāstra-niyatāgama* (a popular title and a śāstrically controlled title), did not appeal to later minds, especially to *mīmāṃsaka-s*, to whom Śabara had virtually prohibited it. To them it was essential that all sacrificial and quasi-sacrificial transfers should be absolutely good in law: so many Brahmin families depended upon them for their livelihood in early centuries. Hence Prabhākara not merely follows and outstrips Śabara in pointing to the soundness of Property in improperly acquired goods or lands, but pours scorn on the clever maxim we have quoted. 'Earning does not produce Property?' he remarks–'What a monstrous self-contradiction!' The solution is dismissed as a contradiction in terms. This became established, and Medhātithi (on Manu VIII, 416 as noticed by Naṭarāja Ayyar but obscured in Jhā's translation) uses the point to prove that slaves and other dependent persons acquire assets, notwithstanding their master's rights, and indeed are recognized by the *smṛti* to have ownership in respect of them.[1]

Following Prabhākara, in a manner and with a motive which will be explained, Vijñāneśvara and his followers,[2] in their

[1] The exact meaning of Prabhākara has been obscured by the construction given to his passage in the *Mitākṣarā* by the authors of the *Subodhinī* (N. Ayyar, p. 57, n. 27) and the *Vīramitrodaya* (p. 421 or sec. 38 in G. C. Sarkar's edn.). We await a critical edition of the *Bṛhati* at the relevant portion.

[2] *Madana-ratna-pradīpa* (pp. 325–6). *Vyavahāra-mayūkha* (pp. 89–92) goes further and suggests that Property is a particular potentiality produced by purchase, etc., a fact known from practical usage and not from the *śāstra*. *Vīramitrodaya* (pp. 415–22, or secc. 12–43 in G. C. Sarkar's edn.). *Smṛti-candrikā*, III, 600–4. *Sarasvatī-vilāsa* (pp. 396–404) in an even more original approach condemns a view of the *Mitākṣarā*. This author takes Property to be *laukika* since it is created by secular acts. The relationship between Owner and Property is *laukika*, like that between father and son (p. 365). A hyperbolical praise of the *Mitākṣarā* for its 'freeing Hindu law from religious fetters' appears at Srinivāsa Ayyangār's edition of Mayne's *Hindu Law* (10th

eagerness to quieten anxiety as to titles, commit themselves to the proposition that the ultimate source of information on the validity of acquisitions is popular recognition: a conclusion which we cannot but deplore,[1] especially when we bear in mind specific instances of the conflict between justice, law and common practice in modern Western behaviour.

We are now in a position to go through Vijñāneśvara's own text, which may be quoted with the present writer's corrections, in Colebrooke's translation. It is the tenth paragraph, in Colebrooke's numbering, which presents the greatest difficulty. Paragraphs 13 and 14 have been omitted here to save space. There Vijñāneśvara recites Gautama's text and asserts that the word 'earned' or 'wages' therein is intended to cover all the classifications of livelihoods known popularly amongst the mixed castes. He also adds an additional argument in support of his viewpoint, which is of no little interest, since it shows that he was aware of our difficulty: he says that Yājñavalkya tells us that a sonless man is succeeded in order by his widow, daughter, daughter's son and so on because, popular recognition being the source of Property, many would seek to succeed simultaneously to the estate. Many readers will comment that this argument is weak, since nothing is more certain than that on the one hand the lay public have notions as to entitlement to be heirs of a deceased person, while on the other, if their notions are confused and self-contradictory in places, the rules to be found in the *śāstra* are no better. In the following passage, which is taken not from the Sanskrit text direct,[2] because that would be of small general interest, but from Colebrooke's old-fashioned and

edn., p. 17, 11th edn., p. 16; also p. 47/44); it is agreed with by N. Ayyar, where cited, p. 62.

[1] Vācaspati-miśra, *Vivāda-cintāmāṇi*, trans. Jhā, p. 61, sec. 249: 'as a matter of fact anything that one has, *in any way*, made absolutely his own (in contrast to joint acquisitions), may be given at his own pleasure', and Manu X, 115 (above, p. 126) is merely illustrative.

[2] Dh.K., pp. 1132–3. Nirṇaya Sāgara Press edition (Bombay, 1909), pp. 197–8. The most useful edition of the text is that by S. S. Setlūr, *The Mitākshară with Viśvarūpa and Commentaries of Subōdhinī and Bālambhaṭṭī* (Vol. I) (Madras, 1912), pp. 592–604, because it is accompanied by the sub-commentaries. Setlūr's translation (*A Complete Collection . . .*) published in Madras in 1911 (see pp. 2–5) keeps close to Colebrooke. J. R. Ghārpure's rendering also keeps close to Colebrooke, who, after all, acquired a unique authority in the courts.

unidiomatic rendering, which we must proceed to correct thereafter, the argument for which we have prepared ourselves will become plain.

Mitākṣarā (Colebrooke: I, i, 7–11, 15–16):

'7. Does property arise from partition? or does partition of pre-existent property take place? Under this (head of discussion) proprietary right is itself necessarily explained: (and the question is) Whether property be deduced from the sacred institutes alone, or from other (and temporal) proof.

'8. (It is alleged, that) the inferring of property from the sacred code alone is right, on account of the text of Gautama; "An owner is by inheritance, purchase, partition, seizure, or finding. Acceptance is for a Brahmana an additional mode; conquest for a Cshatriya; gain for a Vaisya or Sudra." For, if property were deducible from other proof, this text would not be pertinent. So the precept, ("A Brahmana, who seeks to obtain any thing, even by sacrificing or by instructing, from the hand of a man, who had taken what was not given to him, is considered precisely as a thief") which directs the punishment of such as obtain valuables, by officiating at religious rites, or by other similar means, from a wrongdoer who has taken what was not given to him, would be irrelevant if property were temporal. Moreover, were property a worldly matter, one could not say "My property has been wrongfully taken by him"; for it would belong to the taker. Or,[1] (if it be objected that) the property of another was seized by this man, and it therefore does not become the property of the usurper; (the answer is,) then no doubt could exist, whether it appertain to one or to the other, any more than in regard to the species, whether gold, silver, or the like. Therefore property is a result of holy institutes exclusively.

'9. To this the answer is, property is temporal only, for it effects transactions relative to worldly purposes, just as rice or similar substances do: but the consecrated fire and the like, deducible from the sacred institutes, do not give effect to actions relative to secular purposes. (It is asked) does not a consecrated fire effect the boiling of food; and so, of the rest? (The answer is) No; for it is not as such, that the consecrated flame operates the boiling of food; but as a fire perceptible to the senses: and so in

[1] But see below, p. 142.

the other cases. But, here, it is not through its visible form, either gold or the like, that the purchase of a thing is effected, but through property only. That which is not a person's property in a thing, does not give effect to his transfer of it by sale or the like. Besides, the use of property is seen also among inhabitants of barbarous countries, who are unacquainted with the practice directed in the sacred code: for purchase, sale, and similar transactions are remarked among them.[1]

'10. Moreover, such as are conversant with the science of reasoning, deem regulated means of acquisition a matter of popular recognition. In the third clause of the *Lipsā sūtra*, the venerable author has stated the adverse opinion, after (obviating) an objection to it, that, "if restrictions, relative to the acquisition of goods, regard the religious ceremony, there could be no property, since proprietary right is not temporal"; (by showing, that) "the efficacy of acceptance and other modes of acquisition in constituting proprietary right, is a matter of popular recognition". Does it not follow, "if the mode of acquiring the goods concern the religious ceremony, there is no right of property, and consequently no celebration of a sacrifice?" (Answer) "It is a blunder of any one who affirms, that acquisition does not produce a proprietary right; since this is a contradiction in terms." Accordingly, the author, having again acknowledged property to be a popular notion, when he states the demonstrated doctrine, proceeds to explain the purpose of the disquisition in this manner, "Therefore a breach of the restriction affects the person, not the religious ceremony": and the meaning of this passage is thus expounded, "If restrictions, respecting the acquisition of chattels, regard the religious ceremony, its celebration would be perfect, with such property only, as was acquired consistently with those rules; and not so, if performed with wealth obtained by infringing them; and consequently, according to the adverse opinion, the fault would not affect the man, if he deviated from the rule: but, according to the demonstrated conclusion, since the restriction, regarding acquisitions, affects the person, the performance of the religious

[1] But since foreigners know nothing of the *śāstra* it would seem irrelevant to see in their usages any proof that amongst Hindus, who have a *śāstra*, the technical rules regarding the acquisition of Property found in it have no effect so far as practical affairs are concerned.

ceremony is complete, even with property acquired by a breach of the rule; and it is an offence on the part of a man, because he has violated an obligatory rule." It is consequently acknowledged, that even what is gained by infringing restrictions, is property; because, otherwise there would be no completion of a religious ceremony.[1]

'11. It should not be alleged, that even what is obtained by robbery and other nefarious means, would be property. For proprietary right in such instances is not recognized by the world; and it disagrees with received practice.

'12. Thus, since property, obtained by acceptance or any other (sufficient) means, is established to be temporal; the acceptance of alms, as well as other (prescribed) modes for a Brahmana, conquest and similar means for a Cshatriya, husbandry and the like for a Vaisya, and service and the rest for a Sudra, are propounded as restrictions intended for spiritual purposes; and inheritance and other modes are stated as means common to all. "An owner is by inheritance, purchase, partition, seizure or finding."

'15. As for the remark, that, if property were temporal, it could not be said "my property has been taken away by him"; that is not accurate, for a doubt respecting the proprietary right does arise through a doubt concerning the purchase, or other transaction, which is the cause of that right.

'16. The purpose of the preceding disquisition is this. A text expresses "When Brahmanas have acquired wealth by a blameable act, they are cleared by the abandonment of it, with prayer and rigid austerity."[2] Now, if property be deducible only from sacred ordinances, that, which has been obtained by accepting presents from an improper person, or by other means which are reprobated, would not be property, and consequently would not be partible among sons. But if it be a worldly matter,

[1] Medhātithi, Vijñāneśvara's illustrious predecessor, already knew (we do not know his age relative to Prabhākara) that 'rice which is apt for the purposes of man by way of nourishing him is enjoined to be employed in rituals; the acquisition of wealth is not directed to the ritual', and thus links (in his commentary on Manu VI, 89) Śabara on IV, i, 2B (Jhā's trans., p. 713) with our passage. Thus the utilization of the *mīmāṃsā* doctrine antedates the *Mitākṣarā* and if any fulsome praise is due it is owed to Medhātithi, or more probably to a predecessor (other than Bhāruci?).

[2] Cf. Nārada XVIII, 43. Manu XI, 194.

then even what is obtained by such means, is property and may be divided among heirs; and the atonement above-mentioned regards the acquirer only: but sons have the right by inheritance, and therefore no blame attaches to them, since Manu declares "there are seven virtuous means of acquiring property: viz. inheritance etc." '

Before proceeding to comment on this and to give an idiomatic rendering of the difficult para. 10, a small correction is needed. Colebrooke's mastery of juridical Sanskrit was amazing, and he is very seldom detected in error. In para. 8 however he was misled by the Skt. *anyathā*, which besides the usual meaning 'otherwise' bears the meaning 'wrongly'.[1] Therefore, for the passage '. . . and it therefore does not . . . or the like', we should read as follows–and the reader should substitute in his own re-reading of the paragraph: 'Whereas in reality it is not the taker's property because he took the property of another wrongfully (or 'improperly'). Precisely as in the case of the physical appearance of gold, silver, and the like, there should be no doubt whether it is the property of *A* or the property of *B* [for the difference between gold and other metals is not *laukika*, and in our case the *śāstra* might be urged to be the touchstone].' This clarifies the objector's position.

Thus we see that the foundation of the *Mitākṣarā* doctrine on Property, which was later followed substantially by all writers, is Prabhākara's understanding of Jaimini IV, i, 1–3. In order to understand that group of *sūtra-s* it was necessary to establish what was Jaimini's *pūrva-pakṣa*, his lay figure, the *prima facie* case he is about to knock down, and what was his *siddhānta*, 'conclusion'. Prabhākara seems not to have been satisfied as a statement of his author's *pūrva-pakṣa* with the statement alone that if the restrictions were *kratvartha* there would be no Property, because Property would be a non-secular (or impractical) entity; and partly corrected and partly supplemented this by adding (as also

[1] See also Manu VIII, 90. *Anyathā* means 'improperly' at Kātyāyana 546, as explained by the *Mitākṣarā* itself on Yājñ. II, 49. In English as spoken in India the phrase 'He has taken me *otherwise*' implies not merely that the third party has misunderstood but also that he has been offended. 'Otherwise' thus has an idiomatic meaning 'invalidly', as at *Venkalakshmi* v. *Jagannathan* AIR 1963 Mad. 316, 319 col. 1. This usage is a lineal descendant from vernacular usage. Duncan Forbes's *Hindusthānī Dictionary* shows 'inaccurately' as one meaning for *anyathā*.

pūrva-pakṣa) the statement, somewhat oddly phrased, that the fact that Property is achieved by acquisition of goods through acceptance and so on is itself established secularly by the lay public in practical usage. According to Śabara the *pūrva-pakṣa* was merely the statement that acquiring Property subserved the purposes of sacrifice, so that in the conclusion he could establish the opposite, namely that acquisition (he does not in fact say restrictions upon acquisition) served the purposes of the individual. We see that Śabara uses as part of his proof of the conclusion the statement that if Property existed for the purposes of sacrifice there would be no sacrifice, since men would not have the means of livelihood, apart from the question of disposability of what is not one's own, and so would not perform sacrifices (a point which Prabhākara is content to place in the first, and insufficient, part of his *pūrva-pakṣa*), but neglected to go further and deduce from this the inapplicability of the rules to title as such. This is the chief reason why we need not wonder at Vijñāneśvara's choosing to follow Prabhākara,[1] despite the fact that Kumārila, Prabhākara's contemporary, we are told, and a closer adherent of Śabara's interpretation of the *sūtra-s*, had by that time cast Prabhākara into the shade. Further reasons for Vijñāneśvara's reference to Prabhākara are not hard to find. Śabara's admission that the texts have a general *adṛṣṭa* force, which Kumārila accepts, was damaging to the point of view which the *Mitākṣarā* adopts, namely that the rules of the *smṛti-s* are only part of the source on possible methods of acquisition, a source which when complete was binding upon acquirers whether for sacrificial or secular purposes. Moreover Prabhākara was prepared to understand that Jaimini himself in the second *adhikaraṇa* subsumed the absurdity of denying the connexion between acquisition and Property, a connexion which exists only in experience (*laukika-nyāyena*) and not necessarily upon technical authority. This, Prabhākara says, points directly to the conclusion that acquisition is for the purposes of the individual, and *therefore* to the unimportance of breaches of the rules

[1] N. Ayyar, at pp. 63–4 shows that K. L. Sarkar, not having the relevant passage of Kumārila before him, assumed that Vijñāneśvara wished to follow Prabhākara (see p. 395) for a reason which in fact did not operate. These conundrums defeat the specialists no less easily than general readers of the texts.

from the limited standpoint of the sacrificial success, a consideration which is primarily religious but secondarily secular. Śabara is too straightforward and natural; Prabhākara goes out of his way to implant notions in the mind of his author not merely concerning the efficacy of sacrifices (for that would not have been out of place) but especially as to the relative authority of popular and technical legal concepts.

Now in fact Prabhākara nowhere says that *svatva* is *laukika*. On the contrary he says that the authority to earn one's living indirectly comes from the Veda, and is absolutely valid.[1] Is Vijñāneśvara guilty of misrepresenting the source, which he is at such pains to rely upon and which he only quotes in part? It would appear not. For it is true, as he hints, that Prabhākara's conclusion is that acquisition itself is *puruṣārtha* and that breaches of the rules affect the individual and not the sacrifice. The words that he purports to quote are indeed there, and the inference he draws from them is not difficult to support. If acquisition is *puruṣārtha* it seems to follow that Property (the *effect* according to him of acquisition) is also *puruṣārtha*, and thus *laukika*, i.e. indifferent from the point of view of *dharma*, and so freely governable by sources including, but not confined to, the *dharmaśāstra*; while the injunctions concerning acquisition are binding in conscience and breaches thereof lead to penance or alternatively to exclusion from caste. Breaches of popular concepts of acquisition will not be so penalized, unless they are covered by *śāstric* texts such as penalties for theft. In the light of the foregoing a correct translation of para. 10 would appear to be as follows:

'10. Moreover scholars of *mīmāṃsā* believe that Property, the means of acquisition of which are limited, is a concept of a secular character. For example, in the third clause of the *Lipsā sūtra* two interpretations of the *pūrva-pakṣa* (*prima facie* view) are possible. According to the first the proposition is this: "If the *niyamas* (restrictive precepts) regulating the acquisition of assets were directed to the purpose of the sacrifice, Property itself would fail to exist, since Property is a secular concept." Accord-

[1] His words appear to indicate that the *niyama* rules are not void of *adhikāra*, and that *adhikāra* cannot sometimes arise from the Veda and sometimes from another source (i.e. popular usage). The publication of the text in a critical edition is to be awaited.

ing to the second it means "The fact that (technical) means of acquisition, starting from (religious) acceptance, can create Property is itself a secular fact." Prabhākara realized that the first was impossible, and accepted (or propounded) the second. He said, "It is objected that sacrifice itself could not take place, since Property would not exist if the acquisition of assets subserved the purpose of the sacrifice. The nonsensical statement that acquisition does not produce Property is a contradiction in terms." When he comes to the *siddhānta* (conclusion) he admits that Property is a secular concept, and states the object of the discussion: "Consequently breach of the *niyama* affects the individual sacrificer and not the sacrifice itself."

'This is the meaning: the *pūrva-pakṣa* would suggest that if the *niyama-s* relating to the acquisition of assets subserved the purpose of the sacrifice, the sacrifice would be achieved only with objects acquired according to the regulations, but not with the aid of objects acquired by or in breach of a regulation, whereas the individual sacrificer would not be tainted by the fault of breaking the *niyama*. But the conclusion–on the contrary–, relying upon the doctrine that the *niyama-s* relating to acquisition subserve the purposes of the individual himself, is that the sacrifice can be achieved successfully even with the aid of assets which have been acquired in breach of those regulations, while the individual himself is tainted by breach of the regulations. Such a conclusion involves the admission that Property exists in a thing acquired in breach of a *niyama*. Unless this were admitted the achieving of the sacrifice would be prejudiced.'

What is essentially the same point is identified by Naṭarāja Ayyar correctly at *Mitākṣarā* II, i, 23 (not observed accurately by Colebrooke's pandits): the Vedic command to wear gold (*Taitt. Br.* II, ii, 4.6) at sacrificial acts (which Jaimini shows to be *puruṣārtha*) proves that Property must exist apart from sacrifices.

To conclude: the Hindus were sensitive to the discrepancy between the demands of the religious law and the demands of expediency. They were at length prevented from confining the texts entirely to the sphere of religious matters (as a type of black-marketeer might scruple to donate his ill-gotten gains to charity, or a charity might scruple to accept them), and thus from attaining a simple solution, by the doctrine that all portions of the *dharmaśāstra*, both in 'business' sections and in other sections of the sacred law, limited juridical art. The texts of Gautama and others purported to be exhaustive descriptions of the manners of earning open to a Hindu, and this must *prima facie* apply in all contexts of life, or at any rate in contexts where religious merit was at stake. Two alternative solutions presented themselves: either the texts could be inflated by interpretation, so that they might include more than at first sight they appeared to countenance – an expedient which was limited at first by the strictness of the limits placed by the texts themselves between the four classes, and subsequently by the growing rigidity of commentatorial opinion as to the meaning of the texts; or the texts could be held to apply only in sacrificial contexts – but this did not obviate the difficulty, as we have seen, caused by the quasi-sacrificial character of donations of the first social and economic importance, such as to a son-in-law. Consequently the jurists grasped at a straw. *Mīmāṃsā*, which they had been taught to regard as one of their most handy allies, taught that acquisition was itself a secular act, since it produced 'happiness'. From this they jumped to the conclusion that improper acquisitions were improper only in a spiritual sense, and dissociated the spiritual condition of the acquirer from the legal title to the object acquired. Uneasy as many must have felt about this sleight of thought, the consequences were agreeable, and the alleged authority was unimpeachable. And as far as the modern *dharmaśāstrī* is concerned the dispute is at an end.

Postscript

Long after the foregoing study was written a parallel investigation was undertaken into the relationship between *mīmāṃsā* doctrines and the *śāstra* with reference to charitable endowments. As in the previous case, where it was plain that the habits of the people were taken into account – and indeed Vijñāneśvara himself was keen to include customary notions within his concept of *dāya* – so in this case Dr. G.-D. Sontheimer found that the needs of administrators of endowments supported a juridical concept of the ownership of endowed property, which in fact the public who contributed to the endowments would not have accepted.[1] Dr. Sontheimer's study is rounded with parallel

[1] See below, p. 487.

enquiries into the doctrines of various religious schools in addition to the jurists: but the result is the same.[1] The *dharmaśāstra* took up and insisted upon the *mīmāṃsā* doctrine, to the effect that deities do not own, so that the managers of temples and other charities, who in practice exercised great patronage by reason of the wealth at their disposal–not to speak of their personal enjoyment of the facilities the temples themselves afforded–should not have to be accountable on the basis of sacrilege for their appropriations or misappropriations. This motive is nowhere explicitly acknowledged, but Dr. Sontheimer's study leaves the reader in no doubt.[2] We are now in a position to approach the question of what room the *śāstra* itself, irrespective of *mīmāṃsā* pedantry,[3] made for custom and the habits of the people, including sections of the people, for whom the *śāstra* catered.

[1] 'Religious endowments in India; the juristic personality of Hindu deities', *Z. f. vergl. Rechtsw.*, 67, pt. 1 (1964), pp. 45–100.

[2] A third topic seems fit to test the significance of the *mīmāṃsā* as a tool for the use of *dharmaśāstrī-s*, namely the doctrine that the king does not own the land (i.e. the Earth). There is no doubt but that popular belief persisted to the effect that the king was owner or at least co-owner of all the soil of his kingdom, a belief which had (as often) religious as well as practical implications. The *śāstra* prior to the British period and immediately at its commencement agreed. But *mīmāṃsā* taught differently, namely that the king owned only such land as he held privately or was not granted to grantees from him or his predecessors, and the earlier śāstric writers accepted this. See *Vyavahāra-mayūkha*, p. 91. Medhātithi on Manu VIII, 99 (Jhā's trans., VI, pt. 1, 117–18). A. S. Naṭarāja Ayyar, 'The king's right to the soil', *Vyav. Nirn.*, 4(1955), pp. 25–45. See Kāṇe, *H.D.*, II, 865–9; III, 495–6; and Derrett, *Z. f. vergl. Rechtsw.* 64 (1962), p. 94, n. 318. L. Gopal, at *J.E.S.H.O.*, 4, pt. 3 (1961), pp. 240–63 is against a compromise view. The full *mīmāṃsā* position cannot be estimated, however, without a study of Śabara on Jaimini VIII, i, 34; and the practical implications of the divergences of view are not yet sufficiently clear for us to be able to know whether the instance is a true parallel to the pair shown above or not. For the importance of juridical theory see references at D. Rothermund, 'Die historische Analyse des Bodenrechts . . . Indiens', *Jahrbuch des Südasien-Inst., Heidelberg*, 1966, pp. 149 ff., at p. 151.

[3] For the strict *mīmāṃsā* attitude to custom see above, p. 86.

6

CUSTOM AND LAW IN ANCIENT INDIA

On the *śāstra's* provision for recognition of *custom*,[1] misconceptions abound. The relationship between positive law with its scriptural origins and the originally unwritten law which we call 'custom' was subtle and complicated. Although the British and French appreciated the distinction between these two sources of law, and recognized the traditional, legal, priorities to be observed between them in courts of law, no full juridical discussion of the relationship has been published.[2] We need to examine a theory of the relative importance of sources of law, which obviously existed in ancient India, but which, when once consigned to written form, failed as it stood to satisfy authors of *smṛti* material, and was therefore reproduced with commentary of their own. This is evidence of a stage in the composition of *smṛti* material which is virtually unexplored.

The original maxim seems to have been:

dharmaśca vyavahāraśca caritraṃ rājaśāsanaṃ
catṣupād vyavahāro 'yam uttaraḥ pūrvabādhakaḥ–

or something very similar, the meaning of which will have been

[1] This chapter corresponds broadly to 'Law and custom in ancient India: sources and authority', *Revue Intern. des Droits de l'Antiquité*, 3rd series, 9 (1962), pp. 11–32, but that article has been shortened and additional references provided.

[2] The works most worth citing in this connexion are Kāṇe's *H.D.*, which its author repeated in large part in his *Hindu Customs and Modern Law* (Bombay, 1950), and A. S. Altekar, *Sources of Hindu Dharma* (Sholapur, Inst. Pub. Adm., 1953). The out-of-date *Fictions in the Development of the Hindu Texts* by C. Sankararāma Śāstrī (Adyar, 1926) may usefully be consulted at pp. 70 f., 74 f., 132 f., 150, 159. The reader may profitably use R. Lingat, *Sources* (cited above), pt. 2, ch. 2 (*dharma* et coutume) which, without referring to our present article, differs from it in asserting the missionary character of *dharma*, as it gradually confined and refined customary laws.

that (all) litigation rests on four feet (or moves on four feet), as it were, namely *dharma* (righteousness), *vyavahāra* (practice), *caritra* (actual usage in the sense of custom) and *rāja-śāsana* ('royal decree'), and that each later one in this series overruled or put out of court the earlier; so that, for example, one who relied on a previous 'royal decree' would have nothing to fear from an opponent who relied on customary usage. But was this exactly what was implied?

Let us start immediately with the very full text of Kātyāyana (c. A.D. 300), who is comprehensive if not perspicuous.[1] When this has been mastered we may look at the work of the other *smṛti-kāra-s* and test the validity of their contributions.

Kātyāyana says:

> In a dispute where the person guilty of wrongdoing accepts his responsibility for it and where the real owner of the money secures his wealth by the admission of the defendant the decision is by *dharma* itself.

This tells us that the discussion we are about to embark upon presented itself to the *smṛti-kāra-s* as an analysis of the method of deciding lawsuits. The ambiguous word 'method' is used deliberately, for on this it is unfortunately possible to differ from M. Robert Lingat and numerous Indian writers, who have failed to observe that here we have a self-conscious and tendentious debate amongst the *smṛti* writers themselves as to the meaning of an ancient formula which listed the 'methods'. Our present author continues:

> That is said to be *vyavahāra* where, for the purpose of deciding causes, those who are to execute the law rely upon principles derived from *smṛti*.
>
> Whatever a person practises, whether it be in accord with *dharma* or not, is declared to be *caritra* because it is the invariable usage of the country.

This explains what the word *caritra* means in the formula to which we shall return. Much emphasis is to be placed on this verse.

> What a king establishes as *dharma* which is not in conflict with reason[2]

[1] P. V. Kāṇe, ed. and trans., *Kātyāyanasmṛtisāroddhāra or Kātyāyanasmṛti on Vyavahāra* (Bombay, 1933), *vv.* 35–53, 85 (trans., pp. 124–7, 132–it has been varied in points of detail). U. N. Ghoshal, *History of Indian Political Ideas* (Oxford, 1959), pp. 310–11.

[2] On the ambiguity of *nyāya* see Lingat, *Sources*, p. 181, n. 3.

(or equity?) and the *śāstra* or with the outlook of the country is a lawful *rāja-śāsana* (royal decree).

Where a cause is tried by reference to inference and ordeals are excluded, appeal to *dharma* is overruled by *vyavahāra*, but not in other cases.

This warns us that *dharma* as a method of decision had at least two meanings in Kātyāyana's own mind, the first being that noticed in the first of the verses quoted above, where the word means 'righteousness', and the second here, where it means 'unseen justice, divine intervention'. To continue:

He (the king) should not disregard the rules of conduct amongst those who belong to *pratiloma* castes and amongst inhabitants of forts (? including criminal tribes), even if they are repugnant (to *smṛti*).

When the king gives a decision in accordance with that *dharma* (here; 'rule of conduct'), then *vyavahāra* is overruled by *caritra*.

For, as we shall see, the formula is concerned with the relative appropriateness of the various methods of decision *inter se*.

Where kings consider a custom is repugnant to equity (or 'law', 'justice') there the custom is overruled (or 'repealed'?) by the king's command (or 'royal order').

Each succeeding one, when possessed of these characteristics, overrules (the preceding); any other method of exclusion (or overruling) leads to a destruction of *dharma*.

Here, then, we have the 'relative appropriateness' point, in Kātyāyana's formulation. He continues:

If a king decides by his own *fiat* where there is a text (or maxim) on the point it leads him away from heaven, causes ruin to the public, brings danger from the army of the enemy and strikes at the essence of his own longevity.

Therefore a king should decide causes according to the *śāstra*, but in the absence of texts (or maxims) he should administer justice according to the outlook (or 'customs') of the country.

Whatever course of conduct is in use in a country, is of long duration, and is not repugnant to *śruti* (Veda) and *smṛti*, is said to be 'outlook' (or 'custom') of the country.

Between residents of the same country or the same capital or the same hamlet of cowherds and of the same town or village, decision must be by their own conventions, but in disputes between these and others it must be in accord with *dharma-śāstra*.

Conventions settled with the consent of the country, committed to writing and sealed with the royal seal should always be upheld. They should be sedulously preserved as if they were *śāstra*, and the king should decide cases only after consulting them. Conventions arrived at by merchants and reduced to writing must be given effect to and the king should not initiate anything contrary to them.

Whatever had once been decided upon as authorized by the outlook (or 'custom') of the country, and whatever, though not formerly in use, has been laid down in deference to *śruti* and *smṛti*, shall not be departed from subsequently: and what is inconsistent with equity[1] (or 'law', 'justice') must be avoided.

That is called family usage which has come down hereditarily in a family as their rule by way of *dharma*. The king shall preserve it.

These verses sum up, as we may suppose, the correct śāstric position relative to the king's duty to observe and enforce custom. Now we must see what was the background to these statements and how other writers' opinions fit in with them.

The Object of the Investigation

Very extensive investigations of the written law exist–though they are too little exploited in our time–and there is no dearth of records of customary law in many parts of India. The necessity to examine the customary law in order to form a balanced picture of the written law was apparent to Joseph Kohler, whose efforts in that direction ought to be better known than they are.[2] Attempts to place the written texts in a periodical order upon the assumption that customs developed, and that the development is reflected in the texts, have been undertaken from the beginning of this century. Yet what precise part custom played in the development of the written law, what relationships actually prevailed between them in practice, and what processes needed to occur before the law might influence custom, custom might overrule law, and both might be varied by legislation are questions which have been tackled satisfactorily by no one. It is the purpose of this paper to show that the jurists of ancient and mediaeval India were alive to problems that occurred elsewhere amongst their contemporaries, but produced a solution which is in many respects peculiar. The scope of this study does not include the period of European administration, though the question ought not to be studied without reference to work done on the topic after 1800. The period prior to 1800 is treated as 'ancient' since the jurisprudential techniques were

[1] See above, p. 149, n. 2.

[2] *Z. f. vergl. Rechtsw.* 7–10.

traditional and indistinguishable from those in use a millennium earlier.

The doctrine which this paper sets out incidentally to destroy is that law in India was immutable, immemorial custom was transcendent law, and the customs and usages that bound the public were neither open to be influenced by the classical jurists (whose theories were thought to be largely academic) nor amenable to alteration at the option of a political superior. All that is false. There appears to have been no stage at which law was immutable, at which custom was not open to influence from jurists, or to modification or even abrogation at the hands of the ruler. At first sight this seems to be contrary to Indian legal doctrine; an inspection of the facts puts the matter into perspective. Details of the actual customs, and their complex relation with the *śāstra* must await a separate treatment.[1]

History and Vocabulary

In the Vedic period (c. 1500–800 B.C.) the invading Āryans conquered and intermingled with native Dravidians, Kolarians and other peoples. Out of their ancestral cults and the needs of their new environments sprung the literature (*śruti*) attributable to the period and the need to systematize and record it. We now believe that numerous pre-Āryan customs, such as fraternal polyandry,[2] and institutions of law which would have no meaning to nomads, were adopted as a result of intermarriage and a gradual process of colonization and settlement. In the period of the *dharma-sūtra-s*, or earlier mnemonic texts dealing with *dharma*, the essentials of religious and secular duty and many details of legal institutions were recorded. The variations between the prescriptions laid down are supposed to reflect the changed habits of tribes or peoples in different areas, more or less influenced by the indigenous usages or the peculiar exigencies of the political or economic situation. The *dharma-sūtra-s* are believed

[1] See chapter 7 below. It is Bhāruci, the earliest surviving commentator on Manu, who says (on VIII, 41) that *jāti-dharma-s*, the *dharma-s* of 'castes' (as opposed to *varṇa-s*) are eternal, having this quality in common with the *śāstra*. Did it seem so to him?

[2] See the fantastic discussion summarized in P. V. Kāṇe, *H.D.*, II, pp. 554–6 and Roy's trans. of the passage in the *Mahābhārata* there referred to. Altekar, cited above, 42. O. R. Ehrenfels, *Motherright in India* (Oxford, 1941).

to have been compiled between about 800 and 500/400 B.C. Between that period and about A.D. 200 additional works were written to summarize *dharma*, including secular law, which aimed at an educated and adult public, and consequently went into some detail, though with a high degree of subtlety and compression. These were called *dharmaśāstra-s* or *smṛti-s*: they purported to be the remembered wisdom of the race.[1] The extent to which they bound the non-Āryan peoples, such as the Dravidians of the extreme South, is a matter for debate.[2] It appears that orthodox Hindu rulers would have wished to regard the *dharmaśāstra-s* as binding in an ideal sense, and indeed they had no other system of jurisprudence open to them. Upon the *sūtra-s* and the *śāstra-s* or *smṛti-s* commentaries began to be written as early as A.D. 600, and perhaps earlier. All the while 'spurious' editions of early lost juridical writers were being produced, attempting to give in verse the up-to-date and complete law which the commentators were attempting to provide by way of commentary on the 'genuine' texts. The two processes were not completely mutually exclusive, for we find some commentators citing from and relying upon such 'spurious' works as if they were 'genuine'. The period of the commentators was also the period of the great digest-compilers. The *nibandha*, 'digest', had a great vogue, especially with those who wanted authentic texts, and were content to supply applications of their own. Commenting upon *smṛti-s* or editing numerous *smṛti-s* together in the form of a digest were activities which continued until the period of foreign administration, and were even encouraged by European administrators.[3]

The question, 'what is *dharma*?', was the question to be asked with reference to practical problems. The authors of the *smṛti-s* and also their followers, the commentators, were in no doubt but that *dharma* was to be found out from the *dharma-śāstra* ('science of righteousness'), which meant consulting written law, as expounded with the current learning of *śāstrī-s*.[4] The

[1] For *smṛti* as 'memory' see Gautama I, i, 2. Altekar, 11–12. R. C. Hazra at *Our Heritage*, 3 (1955), pp. 221–38.

[2] See below, p. 292. [3] See chapter 8 below.

[4] Kāṇe, *H.D.*, II, p. 969. On the *pariṣad*, or committee of referees, as a source of law see A. S. Naṭarāja Ayyar, *Mīmāṃsā Jurisprudence* (Allahabad, 1952), pp. 63 f. Altekar goes a little far with his 'Council of Elders': pp. 48–54.

authority of the ancient texts could not be replaced by rules of any individual's invention.[1] Yet the texts themselves, in particular the text of Kātyāyana set out above, stated categorically that when one looked for the *dharma* appropriate to a given problem one must often look outside the texts. As we, following Nārada,[2] have already seen, *vyavahāra* ('litigation') stands upon four feet: *dharma* (some would say this means the *śāstra* itself), *vyavahāra* ('business', 'practice'–see below), *caritra* ('custom'), and *rāja-śāsana* ('royal decree'). Each of these derogated from or excluded the prior-mentioned.[3] The view strongly argued for by M. Lingat[4] is that the four 'feet' of *vyavahāra* are means of proof,

[1] Medhātithi on Manu II, 6 (Jhā's trans., I, 1, 204–5).

[2] At J. Jolly's trans. (*Nāradīya Dharmaśāstra . . .*, London, 1876), I, 11, or in the *Sacred Books of the East* series, vol. 33 (*The Minor Law Books . . . Part 1. Nārada. Bṛhaspati*, Oxford, 1889), I, 10. The translation has been criticized, e.g. by Sir S. Varadāchāriar, cited below. Nārada's own explanation of the verse (which we would take seriously but for the self-consciousness of this literature) appears in the next: 'There *dharma* is based on truth; *vyavahāra* on the statements of witnesses; *caritra* (documentary evidence [?]) on declarations reduced to writing; *rājaśāsana* on the pleasure of the king.' Asahāya's commentary says that one proceeds to litigation where the parties do not tell the truth; in litigation documentary evidence is weightier; amongst judgments that given by the king is final and cannot be reopened. But see Nārada himself at p. 156, n. 1 below.

[3] Kātyāyana cited above. Of the two main methods of construing the maxim which lies behind these *smṛti* 'explanations' that which takes the technical terms as relating to means of proof is the one sanctioned (unconvincingly) by mediaeval authors. Classical illustrations of how the scheme worked are given in Kāṇe, *H.D.*, III, pp. 259–62. They are ingenious attempts to make the explanation of Asahāya, for example (see the previous note), rational. But the writer may claim that the *Smṛti-candrikā* passage (Mysore edn., *Vyavahāra-kāṇḍa*, pt. 1, pp. 23–4; cf. Ghārpure's edn., II, p. 11), which Kāṇe paraphrases, entirely supports his view, namely that these are rules regarding sources of law. Kāṇe seems unaware of the inconsistencies of the two methods and (as often) places the śāstric materials in series as if they were harmonious or as if their lack of harmony were of no consequence.

[4] At *Journal Asiatique*, 1962, pp. 489–503. For the earlier literature besides Kāṇe (cited above) see K. V. Raṅgaswāmī Aiyaṅgār, *Introduction to Vyavahārakāṇḍa of (Lakṣmīdhara's) Kṛtyakalpataru* (Baroda, 1958), pp. 6–9; R. K. Chaudhary, 'Conception of law in ancient India', *J. Bih. Res. Soc.*, 33 (1947), pp. 183 f., 189, 192; B. P. Sinha, 'The king in the Kauṭiliyan State', ibid., 40 (1954), pp. 277 f., 282–8; K. V. R. Aiyaṅgār, *Considerations of some Aspects of Ancient Indian Polity*, 2nd edn. (Madras, 1935), pp. 165–70; Vācaspati-miśra, *Vyavahāra-cintāmaṇi*, ed. and trans. Rocher (Ghent, 1956)

or of arrival at a decision. He is supported by certain textual material. The opposite view, which happily has the support of the fresh mind of the late Louis Renou, brought to bear upon the problem in the course of an investigation of Bṛhaspati,[1] is that these four are not means of proof of a litigant's case, but sources of law. This is the view which in our opinion was the original, but which, for a reason as yet withheld from us, later jurists found less than satisfactory. Thus, in *any* litigation, the pleas must rely upon a source of law, but the practical needs of the context will exclude principles of written law which are stated in general terms and which must, according to the general precept,[2] be administered in conformity with *nyāya* or *yukti*, 'natural reason', 'equity'. The usages of business and the course of legal practice, the *summum ius* or *apices iuris*, may have to be set aside where a custom can be proved to be contrary to or inconsistent with the *dharmaśāstra*. Custom itself could not be relied upon where a royal proclamation, or legislation, or administrative order excluded such a plea.

Such would appear to be the effect of the following verses from Bṛhaspati, who is generally supposed to be older than Nārada or Kātyāyana, though this is far from certain:[3]

> By *dharma*, by *vyavahāra*, by *caritra*, by the royal order: the decision of a disputed matter is declared to be of four (possible) kinds.
>
> Where the decision is made by resorting solely to the *śāstra* that is characterized as a *vyavahāra*. By this method alone *dharma* increases.
>
> Where the decision is made by means of the settled practice of the

texts 712–19, trans., pp. 350–2; S. Varadāchāriar, *Hindu Judicial System* (Lucknow, 1946), pp. 125–34; Naṭarāja Ayyar, *Mīm. Jur.* (cited above), 81 ff.; U. C. Sarkār, *Epochs in Hindu Legal History* (Hoshiarpur, 1958), pp. 34 ff., which adds, however, little to Varadāchāriar.

[1] *Études Védiques et Pāṇinéennes*, 11 (1963), p. 7, commenting on Bṛhaspati I, 18. Bṛhaspati, indeed, leaves the matter in little doubt, but it must not be forgotten that he himself is making sense of the same maxim that was before Nārada and Kātyāyana.

[2] Nārada, according to Jolly's trans. of 1876, I, 35, p. 8–the trans. of 1889, I, 40, p. 15 seems less satisfactory. Bṛhaspati, Jolly (1889), I, 24, R. Aiyaṅgār (1941), I, 65; also Jolly II, 13 = Aiyaṅgār I, 116.

[3] The following verses are taken from two passages dealing with virtually the same topic, namely Jolly II, 18, 25–7 = Aiyaṅgār I, 18–21 (Renou, where cited above, pp. 80 ff.) and II, 24 = Aiyaṅgār IX, 7 (also at *Dh.K.* I, 99). The variant readings proclaim the sensitiveness of the profession in this area.

district, applied with logical reasoning, and by virtue of the approval of the citizens (or 'merchants'?), *vyavahāra* is excluded.

However, where the king makes the decision by disregarding the accustomed usage this is 'royal decree'. Through it *caritra* is excluded.

'Royal decree' is that decision which is devoid of authority (i.e. has no text or custom behind it, or (?) is not based upon the evidence or any evidence); another of this kind is well known as that which occurs in a conflict between *śāstra-s* or among the councillors (or between the *śāstra* and the members of the court).

It is evident that even at so early a period the maxim of the four feet of litigation was so well established that there might be some vagueness as to its meaning, for the three authorities differ uncomfortably and unconvincingly.[1] Probably the variations experienced in practice made too rigid a scheme undesirable. Yet we are clear that only royal injunctions, general or particular, could overrule *caritra*, 'custom'.

What sort of custom would qualify as *caritra*? There are long discussions of this question. From the earliest periods *sadācāra*, 'the usages of the good', 'good custom', or *śiṣṭācāra*, which is more or less synonymous, was of prime importance.[2] *Śiṣṭācāra*

[1] With Nārada's main passage on this subject and Kātyāyana and Bṛhaspati it is necessary to take into account the two verses from Nārada's 'miscellaneous' section which, as a whole, is devoted to the reasons, practical and religious, why the royal orders should be obeyed. We may have in mind the *śloka* commencing *rājñām* which is translated by Jolly (1889), XVIII, 23 (p. 217) and that commencing *sthityartham* which is XVIII, 24 (ibid.). See *Dh.K.* I, pt. 1, p. 587. The first may be translated, 'It is in order that, out of fear of the command of kings, the subjects may not swerve from the path, that the "royal decree"–one must know–arises out of litigation.' In other words the 'royal decree', which puts a stop to all debate in litigation (see XVIII, 19: *ājñā tejaḥ pārthivānām*, etc., order [command] is the brilliance [glory, fierce heat] of kings . . .'), occurs, by way of the final judicial sentence, as a source of law and a deterrent, etc. The second means 'For the sake of stability (in the kingdom) the details of customary law (*caritraviṣayāḥ*) are made (*kṛtāḥ*) by kings: people declare that the "royal decree" is superior even to his customs.' In other words here we have an attempt to explain the priority of 'royal decree' over custom (*caritra*) in a slightly different form. Custom can be formed, as well as recorded, by royal intervention and (virtually) legislation. But in litigation the king is not bound finally by any former statement as to, or modifying, any customary law.

[2] Manu I, 108; II, 6; Yājñ. I, 7. Kāṇe, *H.D.*, II, 971–2; III, 826, 875 (where Sir William Jones's celebrated translation of Manu is corrected: but see Hazra, cited below, at pp. 81–5–*ācāra* ought to be followed only if hallowed by *dharma* in *śruti* or *smṛti*). G. Jhā, *Hindu Law in its Sources*, I

was, subject to some qualification, even a source of *dharma* itself where *smṛti* failed.[1] If one followed one's ancestral usages one was more or less certain to be exempt from punishment:[2] but there could be exceptions, to which we refer below. In order that an *ācāra* should be capable of being pleaded in court it must be old, related to a social group or locality (when it may be called *kula-*, *jāti-*, or *deśa-dharma*), followed as a matter of obligation,[3] and not repudiated or abandoned by the party relying upon it. Naturally it could not be relied upon if the opposite party was not assumed to have knowledge of it. Consequently traders, and other communities with special skills and traditions had their own occupational customs,[4] and as often as not their own tribunals before which the customs need not be specially pleaded.[5] Lastly an *ācāra* must not be repugnant to the *śāstra*. This seems like an argument in a circle. The *śāstra* refers in proper circumstances to customs for the solution of disputes, and yet must the customs not be inconsistent with the *śāstra*? The meaning was that the custom should not of its very nature be

(Allahabad, 1930), pp. 33 f. Kauṭilya, *Arthaś.*, III, 7, and Kātyāyana cited by Kāṇe, *H.D.*, III, 566. R. C. Hazra, 'Sources of Dharma', *Our Heritage*, III (1955), at pp. 66–85. See also p. 158 n. 1 *inf.* The notion of *sadācāra* is not extinct. It is mentioned as a source of law by P. B. Gajendragadkar, J., at AIR 1960 S.C. 964, 970, citing Yājñ. I, 7 and 343.

[1] Manu IV, 178 with Medhātithi (Jhā's trans., II, pt. 1, pp. 442–3). The *Mahābhārata* (*Āraṇyaka-parva*, Poona edn., 149, 28–9) ranks *sadācāra* at least equal to the Veda in antiquity and authority! Lingat, *Sources*, pp. 29–31.

[2] So the illustration at Kāṇe, *H.D.*, III, 261.

[3] Bṛhaspati cited in the *Smṛti-candrikā* cited by Kāṇe, *H.D.*, II, 462, n. 1090; Kāṇe, *H.D.*, III, 843–4 and (particularly) 853–4, 876. The *śiṣṭa-s* (*śiṣṭa = gebildetes Mensch*) must follow the *ācāra* under the impression that it is *dharma* and not because it is useful, etc. On the necessary antiquity of an *ācāra* see Kāṇe, III, 970. *Samaya* (n. 4 below) is different: it may well be based upon utility, as any *ad hoc* 'convention'.

[4] Manu VIII, 41; Gautama XI, 21–2; Yājñ. II, 192. Cited by Kāṇe, *H.D.*, III, 857, 859, 860, 884. Nārada, ibid., 882. The king must punish heavily breach of 'conventions' arrived at by communities: Manu VIII, 219–20 with commentaries and Yājñ. II, 187–8 with commentaries. Viś-varūpa takes pains to show that when the king fines offenders, the community and not the treasury takes the fine!

[5] Gaut. XI, 21 and Vasiṣṭha XIX, 7–10 suggest that the king is to judge according to such customs. This does not exclude the jurisdiction of guild courts recognized by Bṛhaspati, cited by Kāṇe, *H.D.*, III, 281. Varadā-chāriar, ss. 27–8.

hostile to the fundamental tenets of the Hindu socio-religious system as expounded in the *śāstra*:[1] thus a custom to allow the younger brother to have intercourse indiscriminately with the elder brother's wife, and a custom allowing the marriage of a girl of a higher caste with a boy of a lower caste would almost certainly be void in kingdoms accepting the authority of the *dharmaśāstra*, i.e. the greater part of historical India, though it is certain that both customs did exist amongst some Indians at different periods. The claim that an ancient family custom is more authoritative than all the *śāstra-s*[2] is late, needlessly frank, and perhaps not properly representative of the position. Uneradicable immoral customs of Kerala, for example, are exceptions that prove the rule.

Acāra and the Śāstra: Custom within and beyond the Written Law

The *śāstra* incorporated numerous customs, inevitably, since it was itself the fruit of customs systematized, compared, and summarily set down.[3] As early as Āpastamba (I, i, 1, with

[1] Jhā, *Hindu Law in its Sources*, I, introd., 33–48, puts the topic in correct perspective. Altekar, 39 ff., is accurate. Ghoshal, pp. 44–5. Kāṇe, *H.D.*, III, 843 ff., 848 ff., 853–5, and Naṭarāja Ayyar, ch. 5, emphasize the *mīmāṃsā*, 'orthodox' angle, exemplified in jurists under the influence of Kumārila, e.g. Medhātithi on Manu IV, 178 (and so Viśvarūpa on Yājñ. II, 191 [187]), and not, of course, absent even in the text of Kātyāyana cited above here. True, such doctrine lasted, as in Jagannātha (Colebrooke's Digest II, iii, 2, text XLIII, p. 379): 'usage alone is no authority unless it be confirmed by construction of express ordinances (i.e. śāstric texts)'. But this is not characteristic of general late mediaeval juridical doctrine. Nor is the technical *mīmāṃsā* attitude to customs, which favours local custom in secular matters but minimizes it in religious contexts: K. L. Sarkar, cited above, p. 123, at pp. 258–9. The Sanskrit for a 'repugnant custom' is *anācāra*. Works devoted to this topic (see *Bhāratīya Vidyā*, 6 (1945), pp. 27 ff.) are all late. See below, p. 159, n. 4. Varāha-mihira is quoted in the *Smṛti-candrikā* as requiring the king to abolish certain customs of loan and attachment for debt (cf. the *Smṛti-candrikā's* position relative to conditional grants, p. 167 below).

[2] *Smṛtiratnākara* or *Mahābhārata* cited by Altekar, p. 43.

[3] Manu says so at I, 107. The fact is recognized by Kāṇe, Sen Gupta and others, also in judicial decisions. The *śāstrī* however, admitting that a non-repugnant custom may be based on a lost *smṛti*, denies that *smṛti* obtains its authority from custom, even if in fact it appears to codify it in places and is explicable only with reference to it.

Haradatta's commentary) *dharma-s* were *sāmayācārika*; *dharma* was that which was approved by Āryas (i.e. *śiṣṭas*). Since the *śāstra* is based on usage, in particular in its practical (*vyavahāra*) chapters,[1] usage may be cited to explain the written law.[2] The customs of Brahmins living in a particular region of northern India were taken as the norm,[3] but numbers of alternative usages, and in particular usages amongst lower castes,[4] were included. The exact method of selection must remain unknown, as numerous customs of early times have disappeared, and others have survived either in attenuated forms, or amongst classes different from those amongst whom they were prevalent when the *smṛti-s* were compiled. The *śāstra* admitted that all, or even most, customs in relation to the ceremony of marriage could not be treated, and only general rules would be given.[5] The *śāstra* made very little attempt to record or to standardize commercial customs, though examples of general commercial usage are to be found.[6] The peculiar customs of specialized trades and communities are referred to, as having a well-known existence, without being represented in detail. The main principles of partnership,[7] for example, are present (very much as are the *pro forma* provisions on the subjects of fines and tolls), but the detailed application to different manifestations of partnership (as to local conditions) is left to individual custom or to juridical development *ad hoc*. That documents must conform to

[1] Compare Nīlakaṇṭha's comparison of law and grammar (p. 135, n. 1 above).

[2] Medhātithi on Manu VIII, 56 (Jhā's trans., IV, pt. 1, p. 76); Nīlakaṇṭha where referred to in the last footnote; Jīmūtavāhana, *Dāyabhāga* (Colebrooke), VI, 1, 54 cited by Kāṇe, *H.D.*, III, 580; Vijñāneśvara, *Mitākṣarā* on Yājñ., II, 119, cited by Kāṇe, 878–9.

[3] Manu II, 17; Yājñ. III, 250 with Viśvarūpa's commentary, cited by Kāṇe, *H.D.*, III, 874. Hazra, where cited, pp. 87–8. The convention was ancient and does not seem to have survived the early mediaeval period.

[4] See p. 160, n. 9 *inf.* Works devoted to the laws and customs of *śūdra-s*: Kāṇe, *H.D.*, I, pp. 640–1.

[5] *Āśvalāyana-gṛhya-sūtra*, I, 7, 1–2, cited by Kāṇe, *H.D.*, II, 527. Women are the actual source of such customs: *Āpastamba-gṛhya-sūtra*, cited ibid.

[6] E.g. 'rescission of sale' conveniently summarized at Vācaspati-miśra's *Vivāda-cintāmaṇi*, trans. G. Jhā (Baroda, 1942), pp. 88 f. Note that 'customary' methods of exacting payment of debt are approved: Bṛhaspati and Kātyāyana cited by Jhā, *Hindu Law in its Sources*, I, 196–7.

[7] *Vivāda-cintāmaṇi*, 49 ff.

local usage is asserted,[1] but questions of draftsmanship are not entered into beyond generalities. Customs relating to land tenure,[2] to tenancies, and the like are given very little space.[3] There is evidence that spurious *smṛti-s* and *purāṇa-s* were written in an attempt to make the *śāstra* complete:[4] but there is also evidence that the texts in question became out of date or repugnant to the general concept of the *śāstra*, and were evicted.[5] The *śāstra* attempted to offer an umbrella, under which various juridical forms could shelter, and in this sense the relation between *ācāra* and the *śāstra* was very like that between the *ius commune* and the *ius scriptum* of the Romano-canonical system. Customs relating to marriage (the celebrated eight 'forms') were incorporated to a limited degree:[6] but the *śāstra* developed tendencies destroying the legal peculiarity of disapproved customary forms, recognizing a public desire for assimilation towards Brahminical norms.[7] Similarly it is well known that in Adoption the customary usages which are reflected in the earliest texts were kept as a matter of form, but the validity of transactions of a customary character was subjected to principles which tended to unify and to reform.[8] The complicated law of succession applied by usage only in the minority of cases.[9]

[1] Nārada at Jolly (1876), IV, 60, p. 31 = (1889) I, 136, p. 76.

[2] Lakṣmīdhara, *Kṛtyakalpataru*, *Vyavahāra-kāṇḍa*, p. 19: an illustration of *deśācāra* (local custom) is the established proportion (of produce) to be paid by way of revenue.

[3] See Derrett, at *B.S.O.A.S.*, 21 (1958), pp. 61–81.

[4] Altekar, p. 19. J. Ganguly, 'Basic authorities utilized in the *smṛti* works of Mithilā', *Our Heritage*, 3, (1955), pp. 255–68.

[5] See n. 3 above.

[6] The discussion by L. Sternbach, *Juridical Studies in Ancient Indian Law, Part I* (Delhi, Motilāl Banarsidāss, 1965), chapter 11, pp. 347 ff. is fundamental, but may usefully be supplemented with the following: J. Gonda, 'Reflections on the Ārṣa and Āsura forms of marriage', *Sarūpa-Bhāratī* (Lakshman Sarūp commemoration volume), pp. 222 ff.; S. Swamikanu, 'The Brāhma and Āsura forms of marriage', 27 Madras Law College Magazine (1953), pp. 22–33; K. V. Venkaṭasubramania Iyer, 'Evolution of the marriage law of the Smṛtis', 15 Madras Law College Magazine (March, 1941), pp. 50–77–the last being the work of a master in all branches of Hindu law.

[7] See the discussion at chapter 11 below.

[8] Derrett at *Z. f. vergl. Rechtsw.*, 60 (1957), pp. 34–90.

[9] The *Smṛtisaṅgraha text* cited in the *Sarasvatī-vilāsa* (Foulkes, 1881), s. 613, p. 122 is more representative of the true situation (see below, p. 208).

Proof of custom would (in the ultimate view) override the written law, and therefore the jurists' task was to perfect the latter and not to expatiate on customary deviations. We may take as a further example the law of usury,[1] and the law of prescription.[2] In both contexts customary rules prevailed. A few found their way into the śāstric texts over the centuries[3]–there to be an embarrassment to the jurists when they became out of date or appeared to be contrary to justice: we have seen that the result was that they were emasculated by interpretation. The law of pre-emption is a further example. Early texts must have retained evidence of rights in favour of relations and neighbours.[4] In the late mediaeval period texts were 'discovered' which explained the institution.[5] A very late text, of very peculiar origin gives various new details, deriving from custom and the author's notion of what was proper.[6] Whether the important institution was finally rehabilitated as a śāstric, as opposed to a customary, institution is still open to doubt: probably it was not. Some custom undoubtedly remained outside the *śāstra* and the question would not, therefore, arise when it should be pleaded in derogation from the book law.

Custom versus *the Śāstra*

In the inferior courts, such as a family or caste tribunal or in a trade or mercantile tribunal, no doubt custom was sufficiently well known to render its comparison with śāstric principles (where appropriate) unnecessary, and reference to the *śāstra* can seldom have been employed. But where a dispute involved persons or communities whose affairs could not be determined

[1] Kāṇe, *H.D.*, III. 417 ff. Derrett, *Z. f. vergl. Rechtsw.*, 64 (1961), at 45–6. R. S. Sharmā, at *C.S.S.H.*, 8, No. 1 (1965), pp. 56–77.

[2] See above, p. 129.

[3] Hence discrepancies such as are shown at Jhā, *Hindu Law in its Sources*, I, 134–6, 144.

[4] Kauṭilya, *Arthaś.*, trans. Kāṅgle, pp. 252–3 (III, 9, 1–9).

[5] *Vyavahāra-nirṇaya*, ed. R. Aiyaṅgār and K. Aiyaṅgār, 355 f. *Sarasvatī-vilāsa* (Mysore edn., 1927), pp. 322 f. On the topic see Derrett at *Univ. Ceylon Rev.*, 19, no. 2 (1961), 105–16; *Adyar Library Bull.*, 25 (1961), 13–27; [1962] Ker. L.T., *J.*, 59–65. On the text of Bṛhaspati on the subject see L. Renou, at *Indo-Iranian Journal*, 6, No. 2 (1962), pp. 97–8.

[6] *Mahānirvāṇatantra* (on which see below, pp. 265–7), XII. 107–12 (Madras, 1929 edn., pp. 390–3).

so simply, as for example where there was a dispute between persons of different castes and different occupations, or between bodies or institutions in different kingdoms, reference to the *śāstra* would be made in the first instance, and to custom if it were pleaded that custom ruled out the book law, or rendered it superfluous.

We may take one actual instance. The *Vaiśya-vaṃśa-sudhākara* records[1] the reference to a committee presided over by the celebrated scholar and writer, Mallinātha, of a dispute between castes claiming to be *vaiśya-s*, and so entitled to privileges accorded to merchants, and other castes which had those privileges and denied that the former were so entitled. This occurred between 1422 and 1466. In effect the committee was to reopen a question that had already been dealt with in a *śāsana* some time before. The final solution to that important caste-dispute was arrived at, apparently, after consideration of actual usage and precedent: but the decisive learning was obtained from the *śāstra* and the literary and other ancillary material explaining the meaning of the *smṛti* texts in question. The castes were found to be *vaiśyas*, their status was indistinguishable from that of their opponents and they were held to be entitled to the privileges they had claimed. Here custom and the *śāstra* were viewed together in a remarkably modern manner, and we have no reason to suppose that similar techniques were not in use much earlier.

The king was traditionally the custodian and also the censor of customs. It was his responsibility (as Kātyāyana has told us) to determine if any were repugnant to the *śāstra* and to cancel or modify customs of proved repugnancy.[2] When it was established

[1] V. Rāghavan, 'The Vaiśyavamśasudhākara . . .', in *A Volume presented to Sir Denison Ross* (Bombay, 1939), pp. 234–40. The episode is mentioned by Kāṇe, *H.D.*, III, p. 252 n.

[2] Manu VIII, 46 with Medhātithi (Jhā's trans., IV, pt. 1, pp. 62–4). Kāṇe, *H.D.*, III, p. 859. Ghoshal, pp. 314–15. The *Milinda-pañha* (III, 30), a work originally in Sanskrit (?) produced in what corresponds to Afghanistan on the extreme north-western borders of India in the second century, shows that a record (*potthakam*) of decrees and rules was then preserved. A reference to consulting such appears at the *Smṛti-candrikā* passage alluded to at p. 154 n. 3 above. Manu VIII, 41 (trans. Jones, relying upon the commentary of Rāghavānanda) is relied on in *Venkataramana* v. *Kasturi* (1916) 40 Mad. 212 F.B., at 222 for the proposition that even in pre-British times evil customs would not be countenanced by the courts.

that the *ācāra* was valid, and not repugnant, a problem often arose as to the manner in which to apply it. There are traces that in ancient times efforts were made to record customs,[1] and to use the records as means of checking upon the correctness of the plaintiff's plea, and the effect of the custom upon his case. The proof of custom therefore lay in written records, either provided for the purpose by royal inquest, or by special muniments, called *śāsana-s*, which set out what the custom was, or provided what it should be. Vijñāneśvara is particular to distinguish (in his commentary on Yājñ. II, 187) conventions (*samaya*), which are as a rule arrived at by corporations or corporate units (*samūha*), and those which the king himself validates or makes law.[2] But that was by no means enough. The implications in the actual case would seldom be covered entirely by any such written records, and the same difficulty would arise when the custom was established by the evidence of witnesses, such as caste-elders, and so forth. Here the skill of the trained jurist came in; and here the *śāstra* took over.

A proved custom would control the topic so far as reason and analogy would allow, and as long as abuses did not undermine the validity of the custom. Where custom failed the principles of the *śāstra* must be resorted to. By what authority? The king decided whether his kingdom was to be governed upon orthodox Hindu principles or not. His decision was guided by the temper and inclination of his people or peoples, who would support a rival claimant to the throne if he offended them in this regard. In nothing were the public so tenacious as of their ancient customs and the social system which they upheld.[3] One who accepted the *śāstra*, either as a hereditary possession, or as a novel import, accepted with it the facility to enforce customs, and also the duty to guide them and to apply them in a manner consistent with the basic principles of the *śāstra*. The authority for using the *śāstra* as the residual system lay, therefore, in the Hinduism or Hinduizing tendencies of the ruler, and ultimately, of the ruled.

[1] See last note. Kātyāyana cited by Varadāchāriar, p. 130. *Arthaś.*, II, 7, 2 cited by Ghoshal, p. 114. Kāṇe, *H.D.*, III, p. 261.

[2] As for example the extent of pasture for a village: Yājñ. II, 166 with *Mitākṣarā* (see Ghārpure's trans.).

[3] Kings must beware of tampering with them: Bṛhaspati and Mitramiśra cited by Altekar, pp. 42–3.

What was the authority behind the *ācarā* itself? Inertia. The maxim *Nil innovandum* could well have been Indian. An ancient custom might be disapproved by Brahmins, and might be confined to small sections of the public. But it was valid custom and those who practised it could not normally be forced to abandon it. When a conqueror came into a conquered land he had the authority to alter customs or laws which he regarded as repugnant to *dharma*,[1] but this merely set up in the new territory a position which existed *ex facie* in his old dominions. The failure of the *śāstra* to embrace and document in detail all current customs was due partly to the impossibility of achieving this;[2] it was also partly due to the missionary and didactic character of the *śāstra* which, while it educated jurists who could function in any area ruled by a Hindu monarch, recognized the possibility of great divergence from its own prescriptions, and of great scope for supplementation in particular chapters. It was thus free to concentrate on the religious and ritual aspects of *dharma*, where it was perfectly possible to be dogmatic without fear of violent economic and social upheavals.

Thus, to sum up, a custom was valid if accepted according to śāstric principles: in derogation from the *śāstra* a valid custom was binding by śāstric authority; but the source of the *śāstra's* authority was the public's acceptance of the postulates of Hinduism, and the source of the custom's factual content and applicability was the public desire not to move from the ways of ancestors. Yet in practice custom was not static, neither was the umbrella provided by the *śāstra* inelastic.

Variation of Customary Law

It might well be argued that just as the *śāstra*, being derived from the teachings of primaeval sages who were in communication with the Self-existent one, is essentially immune from amendment, as for example by legislation,[3] so *ācāra*, though by

[1] *Arthaś.*, XIII, ch. 5. Ghoshal, pp. 114, 131.

[2] Admitted by Maskarī on Gautama I, 1–2, cited by Hazra, where cited, p. 67.

[3] Manu I, 21 with Medhātithi. The conventional view is that the king might make proclamations and regulations furthering *dharma* (e.g. as illustrated by Medhātithi on Manu VII, 13), but not incompatibly with it. For M. Anantanārāyanan's opinion, registering the conventional approach, see

no means so sacred, was, if it was valid, immutable. We know that *smṛti* rules were far from being static. We have seen that *smṛti-kāra-s* themselves rearranged and adjusted their material, and previously it was explained how they and their commentators treated *smṛti* rules as obsolete or inapplicable.[1] Rules which were apparently imperative were treated as merely moral injunctions. The ingenuity of commentators was immense, and alterations were made in the law without varying the text: and if that was not adequate they did not scruple to alter the text itself. There are occasional references to variant readings. Yet the writings of the commentators did not necessarily bind the court. In practice the *smṛti* itself would be relied upon. The various opinions of commentators would be canvassed in a committee of Brahmins convened to settle knotty points of law, which would not happen often unless a good deal of money was at stake. On the other hand customary law would be effectively varied by properly constituted legislative bodies.

This is a delicate issue, about which feeling runs somewhat high. Indian scholars have been wedded to the view that the rulers were subject to the law, and when asked to whom law was subject they are forced to reply 'God'. One may assume this is wishful thinking, and unconsciously entertained for the purpose of making unflattering comparisons with the legal systems of the

above, p. 94. R. Aiyaṅgār, *Rājadharma*, 43–5, 135–6: the same, *Indian Cameralism*, pp. 103–10. Sen-Gupta, *Evolution of Ancient Indian Law*, p. 328. But Aiyaṅgār seems to admit legislative powers at his *Ancient Indian Polity* (cited above), p. 107. Denial of legislative powers occurs at R. C. Majumdār and A. D. Pusalker, edd., *Age of Imperial Unity* (Bombay, 1951), pp. 335–6. A balanced view appears at Ghoshal, pp. 162–3. Medhātithi actually takes the villagers' rights to make regulations (*maryādā*) as divinely ordained. V. P. Varmā, *Studies in Hindu Political Thought . . .* , 2nd edn. (Benaras, 1959), pp. 26, 74, gets out of the difficulty, not by appealing to the idealistic character of the *śāstra* (which pretended to turn a blind eye to occurrences in defiance of itself), but by taking the view that there were few *opportunities* in antiquity for legislation, which, if and when it occurred, was of small consequence. Lingat, *Sources*, p. 253, refuses to allow the term 'législation' to the king's sanctioning popular regulations, because of the individual and limited applicability of these. The French word 'législation' has connotations of universality not possessed by our word 'legislation' (e.g. of the City of London, which has legislative powers). 'Legislation' is used here in the sense of an alteration of law by the State, however limited in scope and application this might be.

[1] Above, pp. 88–90.

West, which was the motive that sent this doctrine on its way.[1] True the śāstric texts, fables, and fantasy sometimes support this notion: it is nice to think that the oriental despot is not a tyrant. But the *śāstra* bound him only in conscience, unless his subjects' discontent with him encouraged invasions from abroad (as Kātyāyana hints frankly). The cause of the difficulty is the failure on the part of scholars adequately to distinguish between the *śāstra* and the law of the courts. We may see some details in another connexion,[2] but the theory may be conveniently explored here. We saw that the *rāja-śāsana* overrode all other sources of law in a judicial dispute. This did not mean that the *śāstra* was changed, even *pro tanto*, by royal decree. It must go its own way entirely in the hands of competent *śāstrī-s* who were alone responsible for it.

The *smṛti-s* do not throw light directly specifically on the question how the king shall make his *śāsana* or decree. What sources should he consult and in what order? Kauṭilya appropriately solves this (III, 1, 43–4): he should consult *dharma* (righteousness), practice, custom (*saṃsthā*), and reason (*nyāya*). He should dispose of the question by reference to custom or usage, by the *dharmaśāstra*, or, in cases where the science of litigation (practical jurisprudence, *vyāvahārikaṃ śāstraṃ*) would be frustrated or obstructed thereby, by reference to righteousness alone. Mere textual law must take second place to a rule of reason where the science (an academic consideration) is contradicted by a rational principle in a point of righteousness (*v.* 45). This is the reason why a properly-founded *rāja-śāsana* takes precedence over *dharma*, etc., when it comes to actual litigation.[3]

[1] Only in very recent years have younger generations been freed from the shadow of foreign rule, so that it is no longer professionally or psychologically necessary for them to prove that India's subjection to foreigners in the eighteenth century was not due to social and political immaturity and incompetence. A plausible explanation why India had no pervasive democratic standards, obviating the suggestion that Indians had always been ruled by tyrants, an explanation which at the same time suggested (as usual) that India had anticipated some long-lived Western political theories, was psychologically attractive: and will take some time to be replaced with something more historical.

[2] See below, pp. 206–11.

[3] *anuśāsaddhi dharmeṇa vyavahāreṇa saṃsthayā*
nyāyena ca caturthena caturantāṃ mahīṃ jayet. 43

What happened when a royal order came directly in confrontation with (*a*) a śāstric rule, or (*b*) an established custom? Instances will clarify the position for us. A front-rank jurist,[1] of remarkable courage, points out that if the king orders Brahmins to present themselves at his palace at the very time when they must be performing their *sandhyā vandana* ('evening worship') the order is void and may be ignored. If the king were to order that gifts should not be given in charity,[2] or that people should not proceed on pilgrimage to holy places, or that priests when performing rituals should or should not use certain formulas or certain implements, his orders would be void. Orders in the two other fields open to him, namely in conformity with the *śāstra*, as for example an order that cattle should not be slaughtered[3]– a class of legislation for which Aśoka is deservedly famous–and in cases when no one could cite an injunction in the *śāstra* one way or another, as for example what should be the extent of pasture in a new settlement, were not open to challenge and therefore must be obeyed subject to royal punishment for disobedience. Where a custom apparently held the field, and it was desired to change it, and the order would come within either of

saṃsthayā dharmaśāstreṇa śāstraṃ va vyāvahārikaṃ
yasminnarthe virudhyeta dharmeṇārthaṃ vinirṇayet. 44
śāstraṃ vipratipadyeta dharme nyāyena kenacit
nyāyas tatra pramāṇaṃ syat tatra pāṭho hi naśyati. 45

Kāṅgle seems to have missed this explanation of his text (*Kauṭilīya Arthaśāstra* III, pp. 222–4). His reading *saṃsthā yā* is less satisfactory.

[1] Devaṇṇa-bhaṭṭa in the *Smṛti-candrikā* at *Vyavahāra-kāṇḍa*, II, p. 525. Up to this point he is copied, by Mitra-miśra in the *Vīramitrodaya* (text, pp. 333–4), and in the *Madana-ratna-pradīpa* (p. 235). Neither author goes past the example given, and Nīlakaṇṭha, who is much obliged to the *Madana-ratna-pradīpa*, thinks it prudent to omit the whole. After quoting Kātyāyana 669 Devaṇṇa continues to say that if the king grants land without allowing mortgage or sale of it his stipulation can, indeed *should*, be ignored: for the 'way of the Veda and the *smṛti-s*' requires (see p. 150 above) that acquired property should be usable at pleasure, and the royal reservations were repugnant.

[2] Unlawful commands by the wicked (legendary) king Vena have a place in juridical theory: *Bhāgavata-purāṇa* IV, 14 cited by R. M. Huntington at *Purāṇa*, 2 (1960), pp. 189–90.

[3] So, for an historical example, we may see *Rājataraṅgiṇī* III, 5, 256. Vijñāneśvara, on Yājñ. II, 186 gives as illustrations of a legitimate *sāmayika dharma* recognized by the *śāstra* orders to provide travellers with food, and not to export horses into enemy territory.

the permitted fields, the custom went down before the royal order: about this there could be no question. An instance would be the late mediaeval instrument[1] whereby a religious institution known as a *maṭha* was converted from being subject to a celibate (or nominally celibate) incumbent to one in which the incumbent was permitted to marry. The competent authority not only passed the necessary orders but, most interestingly, cites as his reasons passages from various scriptures which support the existence of *maṭha-s* of which the head was a married man. Whether married men should be heads of *maṭha-s* was a moot point;[2] the ancient *maṭha-s* were ruled by *sannyāsī-s* who were naturally unmarried, whatever their sexual behaviour in fact. But abuses must be remedied, textual authority was available for the line taken, and, supported by this and by considerations which are tactfully withheld from us, the patron of the *maṭha* (it was presumably he) passed the necessary order.

A *śāsana* embodying a new law, or declaring an old one which had been doubted, was often inscribed on a stone pillar erected at the most important and relevant spot.[3] As to the procedure whereby the *śāsana* was arrived at, there is no evidence that there was any difference between a decision in a dispute which had reached the ruler's court and a decision of a question of policy, as for example whether a grant should be

[1] Inscription from Jambukeśvaram dated in the equivalent of A.D. 1584 (reign of Veṅkaṭa I), published at *A.R.S.I.E.*, 1936–7, no. 135, pp. 91 ff., sec. 79. It is in the form of an order directed to the spiritual head and ten *uḍaiyar* (managers?) from one Ādi-Caṇḍeśvara, a hereditary servant of one Tribhuvanapati. The suspicion remains that the order emanates from a secular authority acting in his capacity as patron of the endowment and purporting to be the mouthpiece of a deity (see below, p. 484). A closer investigation of the text is needed before this can be confirmed. In any event the problem was expected to be solved for all legal purposes by the issue of the order, so that some temporal legality or constitutional validity may be presumed. T. V. Mahāliṅgam at *J.O.R.* (Madras) 25 (1957), 78–9.

[2] The original appointees evidently were not, but the Pāśupata sect had no objection to married *maṭhādhipati-s*: T. V. Mahāliṅgam, 'The Pāśupatas in South India', *J. Ind. Hist.* 27 (1949), pp. 43–53. M. Rājamānikkam, 'Tamil Saiva maṭhas under the Colas (A.D. 900–1300)', in *Essays in Philosophy*, ed. C. T. K. Chari (T. M. P. Mahādevan Volume) (Madras, 1962), pp. 217 ff.

[3] Instances are given below, pp. 189–90.

made, whether custom should be changed, or whether a fair should be set up.

Thus, though it could not be argued that royal decrees could in any way affect the course of development of the *śāstra*,[1] a decision in a dispute could turn upon a royal decree given in some other context, whether in regard to indifferent matters, matters in which the *śāstra* was silent, or in aid of the purposes recognized by the *śāstra*. Not only could custom derogate from the written law, but even when custom was about to be pleaded the opposite party could rely upon a royal decree abrogating or varying custom. Thus for purposes of litigation *śāstra* and *ācāra* were equally vulnerable to modification by royal determination; but apart from litigation the *śāstra* maintained a life of its own, with its appeal to conscience which no royal mandate, no legislation could diminish.

This is important, for, though years have elapsed since the last Hindu kingdom pursued independent rule–in British India at least the period is well beyond living memory–the Hindus retain an ambivalent attitude to legislation which their Muslim compatriots may, or at any rate should not. In 1955–6 the personal laws of the Hindus in India were radically changed, at a time when many vocal opponents of the Hindu Code Bill claimed that the then subsisting law represented the *śāstra* (though it hardly did). The vast project of legislation went through, as many equally radical changes had gone through before. The judicial legislation of the Anglo-Indian period had been tolerated without resentment: and the constitutional parliamentary legislation came to partner and to correct it. Both operated on the citizen in the context of litigation. There the Hindus admitted it without undue animosity or resentment: indeed the signs are that it was welcomed and is being worked like the systems before it. But the *śāstra* and its spirit no one purports to touch. What Parliament does cannot bind the conscience where the religious elements of law are confronted. And this dichotomy is nothing new: it was built into the Hindu

[1] See below, p. 191. The *Śukranītisāra*, which belongs to the first half of the *nineteenth* century (L. Gopal, *B.S.O.A.S.*, 25, pt. 3 (1962), pp. 524–56), matches traditional viewpoints and the needs of the Anglo-Indian world then looming very near to the area for which the author catered (Baroda?) at his I, 292–312; cited by Ghoshal, pp. 499–500.

outlook on law and government, and has a respectable antiquity. The *śāstra* (not altogether blindly) prepared the way for its own relegation to the background of business and practical life, without forfeiting a claim the more securely to bind the private and personal aspects of the individual, which (as we shall see) were always its primary target.

7

LAW AND THE SOCIAL ORDER BEFORE THE MUHAMMADAN CONQUESTS

The Social Scene[1]

The centuries which are best documented are not those about which most has been written from the jurisprudential point of view. Far more has been written about the law and society of the *sūtra-s* and the early *smṛti-s* than about the era of the great commentaries and primary treatises; the well-known works of N. C. Sen-Gupta and S. C. Banerjee illustrate the general position. Yet the meaning, historically, of the *sūtra*-material is far from certain, and if the *smṛti-s* meant what they literally appear to mean, why did the mediaeval commentators so constantly interpret them in other senses? Those early periods remain substantially for the historian, in particular the comparative legal historian, to unfold; we meanwhile can make better use of the secondary materials, so far as legal texts are concerned, and compare them with the practice of the people, so far as this is recorded in inscriptions and other authentic sources. For the historian of Indian society the period between about 800 and 1200 of our era is particularly rich in that the interpretations of the jurists can be related, positively and negatively, to the other evidence, and it is possible, even without the comprehensive and exhaustive researches into the jurists' opinions which still have to be compiled, to assess how far, in general, custom and the classical jurisprudence differed, what

[1] This chapter corresponds to an article of similar title which appeared at *J.E.S.H.O.*, 7, Pt. 1 (1964), pp. 73–120. Since then a considerable number of examples of the points raised have come to hand, and, apart from small adjustments of the text, numerous references have been added in the footnotes.

were the early relations between them, and, consequently, what in reality the jurists were attempting to achieve.[1]

Of the many topics illustrating the gap between the śāstric theory and practice perhaps the most remarkable is the caste-system. The four *varṇa-s* and the mixed castes of the *smṛti-s* are well represented, but different contemporary estimates put the total of castes at 16, 18, 64, 196, and so on.[2] It is not strange, then, that so many centuries before, Megasthenes had found caste-designations differing in number and in functions from the four-fold scheme of the *smṛti-s*. Vaiśyas seldom appear in our sources under that name, but the many subdivisions of the mercantile class would have accepted the description. The original *varṇa*-duty of agriculture seems to have disappeared. Similarly their immediate superiors in status, the Kṣatriyas, are represented more by ruling families and warrior chiefs, the *rājaputra-s* as they are already termed towards the end of our period, than by genuine descendants of the (theoretical) second *varṇa*. The legend of Paraśurāma's destruction of the Kings attested, at any rate, a consciousness that the *varṇa* was represented in historical times by pretenders. The members of the fourth class are no longer servants of the three 'twice-born' classes: they are agriculturalists, often illiterate and thus easily exploited by literate castes,[3] but often wealthy (though not as regularly as the merchants and *some* Brahmins) and, particularly in the South, proud of following the plough.[4] The Vellālas are *śūdra-s*, and the most respectable class in Tamil districts. They

[1] Altekar's *Sources of Hindu Dharma* (cited above, p. 148), will be an excellent introduction for this topic. The author was exceptionally qualified as a historian with a legal training. His teacher's warning is valid for all: '. . . it has not always been recognized that evidence drawn from one period and locality should not be blended with other evidence relating to other times and localities, and discussion has often taken the form of combining stray data from the *smṛti-s* with those drawn from inscriptions widely separated from one another in space and time . . .' (K. A. Nīlakaṇṭa Śāstrī in *Studies in Cōḷa History and Administration*, p. 74).

[2] Alberuni gives 16, Kalhaṇa 64, Ibn Khurdadbeh 7, with 42 sects. We have the '18 *samayas*', and the Valaṅgai and Iḍaṅgai '98' apiece.

[3] See p. 175, n. 2 below on Kāyasthas.

[4] On the early history of *śūdra-s* two important works are R. S. Sharmā, *Śūdras in Ancient India* (Delhi, Motilāl Banarsīdāss, 1958) and W. Ruben, *Über die frühesten Stufen der Entwicklung der altindischen Śūdras* (SB.D.A.W., Berlin, Klasse f. Sp. Lit., und Kunst, 1964, No. 6) (Berlin, Akademie

are hardly 'walking cemeteries',[1] even if some still eat meat. In the North, on the other hand, *śūdra-s* are found in trade. Several *śūdra* families successfully undertook Kṣatriya duties and achieved Kṣatriya status: Raṇadurjaya in the sixth century and the progenitor of the Kākatīyas being well-known examples.[2] The *śūdra-s*' exclusion from Vedic and *smārta* studies seems to have been resented, and this apparently stimulated sects which produced capable imitations of and substitutes for the orthodox scriptures.

An accentuation of the alleged inferiority of *śūdra* cults and occupations followed in an attempt to prevent the confusion of *varṇa-s* which plainly threatened. The *Bṛhannāradīya-purāṇa*, composed between A.D. 750 and 900 according to R. C. Hazra but in any event not many centuries later, despairingly says:[3]

> A man who bows down to *liṅga*[4] or image of Viṣṇu worshipped by a Śūdra has no escape from sin even by performing decades of thousands of penances. Even in dire distress a twice-born man must not take to the profession of Śūdras. If an infatuated twice-born man does so he is looked upon as *caṇḍāla* ('outcaste'). One who after forsaking his own lawful work takes to the work of others is known as a *pāṣaṇḍa* ('heretic'?) and excluded from all *dharma*. He who deviates from *ācāra* enjoined by his own order of life (*āśrama*) is said to be a *patita* ('fallen man'), no matter whether he is given to devotion to Viṣṇu or engaged in meditation on him. Neither visits to holy places nor residence in sacred *tīrthas*, nor performance of various sacrifices saves one who has discarded *ācāra*.

It is possible that this attitude expresses a fear of tantric cults by which even as early as this period men were seeking to bridge the legal and social chasms between the *varṇa-s*, but it is undeniable that the objections were rather to the ability to find a

Verlag, 1965). Chitrā Tiwārī's *Śūdras in Manu* (Delhi, Motilāl Banarsidāss, 1963) is a somewhat emotional essay, showing the contrition of some high-caste Hindus of today about the discrimination against *śūdra-s* with which they find it impossible to be in sympathy.

[1] Yet the term *pāraśava* for the *anulomaja* son of a *śūdra* is actually found in the Tipperah copper-plate, *E.I.* xv, no. 19, p. 301 (at p. 307), of about A.D. 650 (Kāṇe, *H.D.*, II, p. 450).

[2] E.I. xxiii, p. 96. Pratāparudra Kākatīya, though a member of the fourth caste, was a Sanskrit author: I. C. iii, 1936–7, 465 ff. For a *śūdra* district governor see K.I. i, p. 38.

[3] Extracts from the *purāṇa* cited by Hazra, *Studies in the Upapurāṇas* (Calcutta, 1958), I, 324–6.

[4] The symbol of the god Śiva.

common level with 'lower' classes than to the validity of the beliefs and practices of *śūdra-s* as such.

Of the Brahmans it is apparent that they have begun to abandon their *varṇa*-duty. We assume that with the revival of Hindu orthodoxy in the early centuries of our era such Brahmins as were recognized as such must have striven to keep, if only in appearance, the occupational taboos set out in such detail in the *smṛti-s*; the laxities of earlier centuries had come into disrepute. But by now, once again, temptation had proved too strong. Ritual and religious duties and studies are now coupled with literature and miscellaneous sciences. They function by right as ministers, governors, generals, as well as property-owners, particularly in connexion with charities and religious endowments with strong secular implications. However involved in worldly affairs, they carry the formal title, 'endowed with Restraint, Observance, Vedic study, Meditation, Concentration, Silence, Ritual orthodoxy, Muttered prayer, Yogic trance, and Conduct'.[1] There are celebrated instances of Brahmins founding royal dynasties, and, at the other end of the scale, they penetrated the merchants' monopolies, as the *bhaṭṭas* and *bhaṭṭa-putras* found amongst the merchant classes indicate. These other-worldly people were subject to worldly temptations, of which their patrons took notice: thus founders of *agrahāras* laid down that the Brahmins must not find house-room for prostitutes there.[2] Brahmins, sad to say, as soldiers had a special value because anyone who killed them had to perform a penance.[3] There is no evidence that they had yet become cooks. Although the merchants were natural pacifists they had to guard their caravans; they supported paid troops, boasted bellicose titles, and even distinguished themselves as individuals in battle.[4] Thus the confusion of caste-duties feared by the jurists appears to have come about. The picture is

[1] *Yama-niyama-svādhyāya-dhyāna-dhāraṇa-mauṇa-anuṣṭhāna-japa-samādhi-śīla*: Hyd. Arch. S. 8, and *passim* (sometimes the last three are *japa-tapa-samādhi*). For the supposed difference between *yama* and *niyama* see Medhātithi on Manu IV, 204 (below, p. 186). For the thirteen constituents of *śīla* ('conduct') see Kullūka on Manu II, 6, and cf. Yājñ. III, 66.

[2] E.I. xxv, No. 21, p. 199 at p. 218; E.I. xxxii, No. 3, p. 31 at p. 44.

[3] Debated in the *śāstra*, the point was obvious to the public. A.R.E. 1919, st. ins. No. 73 of 1918. K. A. Nīlakaṇṭa Śāstrī, *Cōḷas*, 1st edn., III, 771.

[4] E.I. xxi, p. 9 ff.; A.R.S.I.E. 1935–6, B.K. ins. No. 84.

complicated by the 'mixed castes', some of whom may actually have originated from unusual matings between classes, and are found in our period practising specified professions and trades. Some of them claimed equality even with Brahmins (the Rathakāras are an example),[1] while others, whose status was always a problem, gained prestige as their near-monopolies of various skills advanced them at the expense of the agriculturalist on the one hand and the priest-administrator and warrior on the other. The Kāyasthas best exemplify the capacity of a caste of indeterminate origin and uncertain position in the hierarchy to turn an aptitude to advantage. They became first engrossers of government accountancy posts, with the normal hereditary rights inevitable in a mediaeval society where training, other than in religious studies, is confined to the family, and later, as in the case of twelfth- and thirteenth-century Āndhra, even provincial governors and kings.[2]

But confused as this picture is it was plainly not the 'confusion of castes' which the public at large feared. To them Manu and other primaeval sages taught a fixed order of *varṇa* duties, with discriminations impeding intercourse and in particular intermarriage: this was right, for happiness meant division of function, interdependence of groups, specialization and conglomeration rather than merger and blending. The precise naming of classes mattered less than the stratification itself. The king's duty was to oblige everyone to observe such distinctions.[3] Puruṣottama, minister of Rāmacandra Yādava about A.D. 1310, immediately before the massive incursions of Muslims from the north into the Deccan, claimed to be a student of Veda and *smṛti* and to have given separate courses of conduct to the

[1] E.I., xxxi, p. 3 ff.; A.R.S.I.E. 1938–9, p. 82. A.R.E. 1909, st. ins. No. 479 of 1908. K. A. N. Śāstrī, *Cōḷas*[2], p. 549.

[2] Often appearing as writers (E.I. xxvii, p. 312 ff., e.g.) they later had an involved history. Kāṇe, *H.D.*, II, 75–7. *N.I.A.*, I (1939), pp. 739 ff.

[3] In Gaṇapati's reign 'Dharma increased, the best of the twice-born [Brahmins] rose to prominence, respect and love for elders became manifest and knowledge in the sciences was deep'. So A.R.E. 1911, st. ins. No. 571 of 1910. K. V. Rangaswāmī Aiyaṅgār, *Rājadharma* (p. 23): 'the Indian king was believed to be responsible as much for the correct conduct (*ācāra*) of his subjects . . . as for punishing them when they . . . committed a crime'. The same author's introd. to the *Rājadharma-kāṇḍa* of Lakṣmīdhara's *Kṛtyakalpataru* repeats the point.

various *varṇa-s* and *āśrama-s*, in other words to have administered *varṇāśrama-dharma*, *dharma* in its entirety.[1] The ideal functions laid down in the *śāstra* were looked upon as models, and, so long as change could be justified or explained, movement on the part of larger or smaller groups gradually through the *varṇa* system was not objectionable provided general identification with a particular *varṇa* was always possible.

Untouchability was now defined,[2] though it was elaborated later; the concept of separation of rows of diners where people of different *jāti-s* dined at the same place was attributed to the rule of Manu at IV, 211, if we are to trust Medhātithi, the tenth-century jurist whose information about society in his day is a treasured source.[3] Slavery was a recognized institution, stemming from kidnapping, debt, or crime.[4] Male and female slaves were transferred when the land was sold.[5] The status of *dēvadāsi-s* was regularized – a powerful, wealthy and respectable social group, acting as public and private entertainers although nominally reserved for a god-husband's enjoyment.[6] They and other professional prostitutes were called the 'fifth class',[7] below the well-known four and above the untouchables, because upon that basis any 'clean' male could lawfully have intercourse with them.

The restriction of such facilities to one sect is evidenced in our period, and also the growth of the notion that charities or

[1] E.I. xxv, p. 199 at 213–14.

[2] Medhātithi on Manu X, 54. Kāṇe, *H.D.*, II, 168–75. Hemacandra, *Deśināmamālā*, II, 73; III, 54; *Kīrtikaumudī* IV, 17 cited by A. K. Majumdār, *Chaulukyas of Gujarat* (Bombay, 1956), p. 334. Vijñāneśvara, *Mit.* on Yājñ. III, 30, cites Vyāghrapāda on the distance by which one should avoid a *caṇḍāla*.

[3] Jhā's trans. II, pt. 2, p. 464 is defective here.

[4] Yvonne Bongert, 'Réflexions sur le problème de l'esclavage dans l'Inde ancienne', *B. École Fr. Ex.-Orient*, 51 (1963), pp. 143–94.

[5] Hyd. Arch. S., 5 (1922), p. 11, A.R.I.E. 1959–60, st. ins. No. 483.

[6] Marco Polo and the *Chau Ju-kua*, K. A. N. Śāstrī, *Foreign Notices of South India* . . . (Madras, 1939), pp. 141, 171. L. Sternbach, *Gaṇikā-vṛtta-saṅgraha* (Hoshiarpur, 1953), gives the śāstric and other Sanskrit texts. A.R.I.E. 1949–50, st. ins. No. 365; S.I.I. x, 588; S.I.I. ix, pt. 1, 80, 101; S.I.I. x, 171; A.R.S.I.E. 1939–40 to 1942–3, st. ins. 1940–1, Nos. 29, 160, 176; S.I.I. xx, 74, p. 89; E.I. xxxv, 21, p. 162; Govindasvāmī on Baudh. II, 2. 4, 3. Could they marry: A.R.E. 1913, rep. p. 99?

[7] *Mitākṣarā* on Yājñ. II, 290, following *Skandapurāṇa*. The term is applied also to untouchables.

endowments could be confined to a caste.[1] Instances of charities for the sake of all castes are remarkable,[2] and in contrast with the trend to subordinate activities to caste ambition. Intermarriage between *varṇa-s* persisted in the hypergamous form, with the husband of higher *varṇa*; the hypergamic principle was generally employed within castes as a means of social advancement.[3] 'Good' marriages were a means of 'purifying the *gotra*' and the best proof of a rising status. Hypergamy had its less pleasing sides, besides the inevitable difficulties of the bride in a polygamous household where the first wife was of the same caste as the husband. The curious custom of 'kulinism', whereby a poor husband of higher status earned his living from his numerous brides' dowries, spread towards the end of our period from Mithilā to Bengal.[4] Female infanticide probably commenced now, amongst castes that took inferior daughters-in-law, but could not find a superior caste to whom their own daughters might be given. 'Interdining' seems not to have been prohibited as strongly as in recent times, though a wide disparity between host and guest was certainly deprecated in the case of Brahmins: we have seen how separation of rows was in use. *Mlecchas* (foreigners) were not normally entertained to meals, though they might be on excellent terms with their Indian hosts.[5]

The *śāstra* tells us little or nothing about the customs of *mleccha-s*, forest or hill tribes or other untouchables living on the fringe of Hindu society: the jurisprudence did not grow to include them.[6] No one could claim that Hinduism took root in that quarter. When Kauṭilya observed that *mleccha-s* were not forbidden to sell their offspring, he had in mind Hindus who would like to buy them. Later ages were fastidious and such

[1] M.A.R. 1933, 48 (p. 252). [2] S.I.I. x, 395.

[3] A child takes his mother's caste–for an exception see Medhātithi on Manu I, 2.

[4] *J. Bih. Res. S.*, 33 (1947), pp. 56–7. *Kulīna* means 'noble'. Caste-distinctions amongst Bengali Brahmins were apparent by the fourteenth century. On the abuse known as 'kulinism' see Benoy Ghose, *Iswar Chandra Vidyāsāgara* (Delhi, Ministry of Information and Broadcasting, 1965), pp. 113–18.

[5] Separate accommodation provided for Arabs: *Chau Ju-kua* in K. A. N. Śāstrī, *For. Not.*, p. 147.

[6] See above, p. 103. *Niṣāda-s* alone used 'false' coinage according to Śabara on Jaimini VI, i, 51–2.

information is not offered again. To employ them as policemen was as near as one cared to get to them. Nor does the *śāstra* tell us of the super-caste organizations (other than professional or trade guilds, which are mentioned), such as Valaṅgai and Iḍaṅgai, the 'Right Hand' and 'Left Hand' factions of the Deccan and South India. These wielded great power, and gave solidarity to castes which were struggling to consolidate or to prevent, as the case might be, the gains made by rising artisan and commercial classes during our period. They had their corporate badges and privileges, their procedures for the admission of adherents, and their sanctions against those who flouted their pretensions.[1]

Everyone believed in caste. The diatribes of earlier periods against the institution do not reappear. Jainas were now a caste, though we hear of Brahmin-Jainas just as we hear of Brahmin-Christians in Goa today. The Lingayats advocated intermarriage between castes, but they soon formed an endogamous caste.[2] Sub-castes developed out of differences in location, work, habits and wealth. For the caste-system was regarded as the means of a gentle progress, and without that framework of distinctions progress would be confused or unthinkable. Sectarianism grew rapidly and was used, particularly in South India, for the purpose of differentiating sub-castes. Discovery of a new doctrine diverted the channel of patronage, and might therefore turn out to be more valuable than landed property itself. We hear of Brāhmaṇas, Śiva-Brāhmaṇas, Śrī-Vaiṣṇavas, and so on as if they were different sorts of Brahmins.[3] The *śāstra* itself encouraged 'mixed castes' to improve their status by suitable marriages, suitably repeated in following generations,[4]

[1] A.R.S.I.E. 1943–4, 1944–5, st. ins. No. 276 of 1943–4; A.R.I.E. 1950–1, st. ins. No. 355; A.R.I.E. 1949–50, st. ins. No. 204; A.R.S.I.E. 1936–7, st. ins. No. 31, rep. p. 69; A.R.S.I.E. 1939–40 to 1942–3, st. ins. No. 184 of 1940–1, rep. p. 243; A.R.E. 1913, st. ins. No. 489 of 1912, rep., p. 109. See below, p. 181, n. 4.

[2] M.A.R. 1927, p. 74. Basava advocated intermarriage: Halakatti, *Vacanaśāstrasāra*, I, pp. 376–7, cited by D. Desai, *Mahāmaṇḍaleśvaras under the Chālukyas* (Bombay, 1951), 415.

[3] A.R.E. 1923, par. 33; 1931–2, par. 16; 1910, par. 28; A.R.S.I.E. 1937–8, st. ins., Nos. 320–3; E.I. xxii, p. 207.

[4] *Mitākṣarā* on Yājñ. I, 96, in the light of preceding *śloka-s*. Lingat, in a valuable study of the phenomenon of *jātyutkarṣa* (elevation of caste) at

but it did not enlarge itself to comprehend all the manifestations of social climbing which were well attested in our period.

Ambition could split the Brahmin settlements called *agrahāra-s* (alluded to above), and divided villages, causing animosity which demanded great tact and the intervention of large assemblies representing all interests and all prestige-holding classes. Sudden claims were repressed[1] and individual as opposed to group pretensions were discouraged. Only the *sannyāsī*, who had abandoned the world, was free from the constant supervision of his family, caste, super-caste assembly, and the harsh and over-serious paraphernalia of civilized life.[2] He could do repulsive things if he liked, and his freedom encouraged far more men to become *sannyāsī-s* than the *śāstra* itself permitted.[3]

The ladder of social promotion had several rungs: 'good' marriages, acquisition of property or influential posts, rejection of social contacts with former equals, and imitation of the habits of superiors. In this progress the Brahmins usually led, though there are instances of their declining into the habits of the wealthier *śūdra-s* and having to be sharply recalled to their nominal duties.[4] Because originally the Brahmins were thought to possess supernatural powers, education, disinterestedness and poverty, as well as the fruitful respect which these earned, it was assumed throughout our period that Brahminical ways were to be imitated as far as possible by the Kṣatriyas, those of the Kṣatriyas by the Vaiśyas, and so on, but Brahminical influence

Sources (1967), pp. 58–9, accuses the *śāstra* here of inconsistency (?). Perhaps it was yet another attempt by the *śāstra* to absorb fact.

[1] Regulation covered clothing, ornaments, tufts on the head, sandals, insignia, horses, elephants, umbrellas, upper stories of dwellings, and the right to have them whitewashed. Groups had rights by tradition, see *Tolkāppiyam*, *Poruḷ*, ix, *Marapiyal*, 6181/584: *J.O.R.*, 25 (1957), app., p. 88.

[2] L. Dumont, 'World-renunciation in Indian religions', *Contributions to Indian Sociology*, 4 (1960), pp. 33–62.

[3] Śāstric rules: Kāṇe, *H.D.*, II, pt. 2, ch. 28, esp. pp. 942–5.

[4] A.R.S.I.E. 1943–4, 1944–5, st. ins. No. 4 of 1943–4 (a late example). The king had visitatorial rights over temples and *maṭha-s*, occasionally badly needed: A.R.S.I.E. 1939–40 to 1942–3, p. 244; and see the reference to A.R.E. 1909, st. ins. No. 125 of 1908 at p. 181, n. 6 below; also A.R.E. 1913, st. ins. No. 226 of 1912, and A.R.E. 1918, st. ins. No. 619 of 1917, rep. p. 77.

supported by pervasive propaganda affected all civilized communities. When a group impose a penalty on any who prevent a widow from dying on her husband's funeral pyre[1] they are not furthering (as Rāja Rāmmohun Roy would have had us believe) a barbaric custom for the benefit of interested parties, but are announcing to the world that at some cost they are adhering to better-class habits.[2]

Amongst Brahmins those most respected were the *rājaguru-s*, who corresponded to Chancellors, with wide spiritual and secular powers throughout the kingdom, then in declining order the *maṭhādhipati-s*, 'abbots' or heads of colleges (who were generally celebates),[3] then *sthānapati-s*, managers of temples,[4] whose great riches could be laid out with a fruitful discretion, then the professional and itinerant disputants,[5] the specialists in various sciences, and finally dwellers in *agrahāra-s*. The kings, governors, ministers and those who could give favours naturally chose for appointment the aspiring and successful, and there was every encouragement to 'get ahead'. The hereditary principle did no more clog than facilitate this process. Amongst the Kṣatriyas the actual rulers were naturally the most prestige-worthy; amongst the Vaiśyas the 'great merchants', merchant and banker-princes, flaunting immense riches, and acting as ministers or ambassadors at need; and amongst *śūdra-s* the great donors in charity, the imitators of Brahmin habits, and, upon a somewhat different plane, the very great prestige-earners–those that dedicated their flesh, their heads, or their lives to a deity,[6] to a

[1] A.R.E. 1907, st. ins. No. 156 of 1906.

[2] For an appreciative survey of suttee (*satī*) see U. Ṭhākur, *History oj Suicide in India* (Delhi, 1963), ch. 4.

[3] A.R.E. 1915, st. ins. No. 423; A.R.I.E. 1946–7, st. ins. No. 88; S.I.I. ix, pt. 1, 101, 102; K.I., i, p. 13; E.C. ix Bang. 114–15. See above, p. 168, n. 2.

[4] S.I.I. x, 502; A.R.S.I.E. 1939–40 to 1942–3, st. ins. No. 122 of 1939–40; M.A.R. 1920, para. 77. The term 'shebait' appears as early as 1296 in *J.A.S.B.*, 65 (1896), pp. 229–71. B.A. Saletore, 'The *sthānikas* and their historical importance', *J. Univ. Bombay*, 7, pt. 1 (1938), pp. 29–93.

[5] A.R.S.I.E. 1937–8, st. ins. No. 130; A.R.S.I.E. 1939–40 to 1942–3, st. ins. No. 401 of 1940–1.

[6] S.I.I. xii, 106. A.R.I.E. 1946–7, st. ins. No. 105, rep., p. 3. A.R.S.I.E. 1939–40 to 1942–3, p. 8. Friar Odoric at K. A. N. Śāstrī, *For. Not.* (cited above), pp. 195–7. Attempts to deny suicides under 'Juggernaut', i.e. Puruṣottama at Puri (see Kāṇe, *H.D.*, IV, pp. 698, 701) will convince few.

master,[1] or to a cause or ideal.[2] Gruesome self-slaughter gave the hero's family incalculable promotion, and this was an age when spiritual, intellectual and physical heroism were inculcated and admired amongst all classes.

The law in practice fostered regulated advance by groups. New matrimonial relations were opened not so much individually as by groups. Solidarity was agreed to by castes that had not previously co-operated. Objectionable habits were corporately abandoned.[3] New obligations of a religious and consequently social implication were taken up corporately, and to all these decisions sanctions were attached. The *Agnipurāṇa* pointedly awards heavy fines against those who defy the decision of 'all' when they have consulted the 'public welfare',[4] and the *purāṇa* is repeating a *smṛti* principle.[5] Mistakes, such as a Brahmin's intercourse with a widow,[6] or a love-affair between a low-caste boy and a high-caste girl, could pull down a group, which might be abandoned by its equals unless the 'impurity' were decisively punished. Something like 'public opinion' was recognized as early as Śabara-svāmī.[7] Groups ready to adopt rules of conduct appropriate to formerly superior classes could go to the king and obtain his sanction to their common intention, and the new 'custom' would become law.[8]

[1] M.A.R. 1939, 48; ibid., 1942, 67; ibid., 1943, 33; A.R.S.I.E. 1937–8, st. ins. Nos. 500, 504; ibid., 1939–40 to 1942–3, st. ins. No. 73 of 1941–2; S.I.I. ix, pt. 1, 9; B.K. 1940–1, 1; cf. E.I. xxx, pp. 44–5. A.R.S.I.E. 1939–40 to 1942–3, rep. pp. 285–6.

[2] To get a master a son, or a victory, or to preserve a temple from destruction or pollution, for example. Pictorial representation of a suicide by fire: A.R.S.I.E. 1939–40 to 1942–3, p. 6.

[3] A.R.E. 1913, st. ins. No. 256 of 1912; S.I. Temp. Ins. No. 90 = A.R.E. 1919, st. ins. No. 90 of 1918 (A.D. 1429). K. A. N. Śāstrī, *Cōḷas*², 549. S.I.I. x, 612; A.R.I.E. 1946–7, st. ins. No. 72. A.R.S.I.E. 1926, st. ins. No. 253, rep. para. 36. S.I.I. x, 612 deals with bribery.

[4] Bibl. Ind. edn., cclvi, 39. M. N. Dutt's trans. (1904), p. 931 is unreliable.

[5] Yājñ. II, 188, 191. Mandlik's trans. (1880), p. 230.

[6] A.R.E. 1909, st. ins. No. 125 of 1908 (c. 1291), rep., p. 83. A man brought calamity upon the Brahmin community by bringing a widow from abroad and consorting with her as his wife.

[7] On Jaimini VI, ii, 15, 20; XI, i, 43. See also Medhātithi on Manu IV, 176.

[8] See below, p. 190, n. 3. The king could not refuse to sanction a *jānapada* ('country') proposal on the ground that it was merely *sāmayika* (conventional); he should sanction it for fear of *mātsya-nyāya* (the dreaded 'law of the

Inexpert and unauthorized interference with the complex social co-ordination of the groups forming a village or a district could (as the *śāstra* hints) have serious results. Classes living on the right to perform certain services had a legal right to perform them in the customary manner for the customary payment, however inexpedient influential classes might believe the arrangement to have become. Attempts to rearrange matters without the full assent of all interested parties would hinder the progress of these groups and their competitors and might be checked by the king.[1] The *śāstra* tells us practically nothing of the form which such appeals to the king should adopt, and this extremely important aspect of administration is virtually ignored. Historians who have confined themselves to the Sanskrit texts have gained a misleading impression of social contentment and an absence of ambition.[2] The public in fact accepted the umbrella of the caste theory, but within its shade attempted to rearrange the relative superiorities of actual groups, and these attempts affected numerous considerations which at first sight might appear to be primarily religious or economic.

The Sources of Obligation

By the early centuries of this era the concept of sin had become not only more pervasive than that of crime, but actually

jungle [literally, fish]'): so Bhāruci on Manu VIII, 41 ('Rules relating to grazing of cattle and storing water not having the *śāstra* as their authority . . . And if the king acts contemptuously in respect of conventional compacts (or 'enactments of public bodies') there will be a breach of the established constitution and the Rule of the Fish will prevail.'). At A.R.E. 1919, rep. p. 97, we see the provision that Brahmins shall not till lands with bulls yoked to the plough (i.e. personally): this effectuates śāstric ideas.

[1] A.R.E. 1924, st. ins. No. 69 of 1924. A.R.I.E. 1946–7, st. ins. No. 85. For a typical village see E.I. xxviii, p. 244. Artisans and clerks might be restricted to their own villages: K. A. N. Śāstrī, *Cōḷas*, 2nd edn., p. 511; A.R.E. 1918–19, st. ins. No. 205 of 1919.

[2] K. V. R. Aiyaṅgar, *Indian Cameralism* (Adyar, 1949) and *Aspects of the Social and Political System of Manusmṛti* (Lucknow, 1949). K. A. N. Śāstrī says, 'The problem of "the man versus the State" never arose in a society that is best described as a federation of groups.' Note that Nārada, XV–XVI, 13 (trans., 1876, p. 106; 1889, p. 209) provides that people who are insulted by individuals of lower caste may avenge the insult without approaching the king.

rendered the latter unnecessary. With the growth and complication of societies, the king's power to punish grew alongside his duty to protect from invasion. The ancient tribunals gave or lost much of their jurisdiction to the king, particularly in respect of what we should call (somewhat misleadingly) civil litigation: but the king's criminal jurisdiction, which during our period was exercised in large part by his actual or theoretical delegates[1] (unless circumstances were peculiar, these would normally be the greater land-holders), did not render obsolete the former jurisdictions in respect of sins. Though we are interested primarily in the notion of 'wrong' in a transcendental sense, it is of interest to note, in passing, that when Medhātithi, the great commentator on Manu, comes to deal with the right of the *paterfamilias* to fine his wives who behave indecorously in the matter of drinking in public (Manu IX, 84), he feels obliged to comment that this jurisdiction remains as a matter of usage (as such it is contemplated in Manu IX, 2, where the householder seems to be given independent jurisdiction in minor offences) notwithstanding the fact that the duty to inflict punishment is predominantly that of the king.[2]

The king's prerogative is not absolute. Persons insulted by individuals of lower caste may avenge the insult without approaching the king: so says Nārada,[3] and this is not contradicted. Medhātithi however puts us in his debt by explaining how the Brahmin, whose prerogative it is to declare the sense of the *śāstra*, and the king, whose duty it is to protect the kingdom, divide the task between them.[4] The king, he says, is concerned with the state of the kingdom, but the Brahmin with relieving people's doubts as to rights and duties. The king's concern is to administer punishment: the Brahmin's however is to see that the judgement is correct. This would serve to put the matter in a nutshell.

In our period we may watch the gradual but by no means uniform development of sanctions from mere imprecations or

[1] In his *Rāja-nīti-ratnākara* (ed. K. P. Jayaswāl, pp. 4–5) Caṇḍeśvara says (in the section entitled *rāja-nirūpaṇam*) that a *sakara* (i.e. tributary or subordinate ruler) may or may not have criminal jurisdiction. If it is not conceded to him he will be fined for arbitrarily hearing a case if it is one of 'violence' (*sāhasa*), and in other cases he will be humiliated by the emperor (*saṃrāṭ*); but in neither case will the ruler's decree as such be annulled.

[2] Trans. Jhā, V, p. 71. [3] See p. 182, n. 2. [4] On Manu VIII, 2.

curses (in the form, 'the offender shall be guilty of the five greater sins', and the like), sometimes very elaborate and curious ('the offender's mother shall be covered by an ass', more often 'he shall be born as a worm in ordure for sixty thousand years'),[1] into sanctions of combined curse and threat of punishment, and finally into a sanction of punishment alone.[2] In the last case the holder of the right to punish is specified, and sometimes even the tribunal which would have jurisdiction. Prospective parties in anticipated litigation could create their own forum by agreement.[3] Naturally some misdeeds remained beyond the reach of prophylactics. The girl selling herself into slavery was seriously pictured as agreeing that if she committed suicide under torture she deserved to be reborn as a she-ass (an image throwing an unexpected light on the current Indian view of Indian slavery in pre-British times as a comfortable existence).[4] Meanwhile the nature of sin, and its effects remained unchanged. What would be a sin, however, should not be thought to have received an unchanging answer, for it is clear that views on this subject differed widely.

The *dharmaśāstra*, which has an enormous literature on the difficult subjects of penance and other purifications from sin and its effects (in this and other births), would leave us with the impression that the duty of a Brahmin committee, or in exceptional cases a single Brahmin 'confessor' or referee,[5] began and ended with prescribing a penance, supervising, if necessary, its performance, and certifying fitness to be readmitted to caste privileges. The latter topic is very slightly looked at. Everyone took it for granted, since the very concept of sin, *pātaka*, involved

[1] The ubiquitous formula (cf. Bṛhaspati VI, 23 *bis* at Renou, *Ét. Ved. Pāṇ.*, cited above, p. 155, n. 1, p. 55) is carefully translated in M.A.R. 1945, 21 (tenth cent.) into Kannaḍa, phrase by phrase, in the hope of its being more effective. Kāṇe, II, 1272. M.A.R. 1945, 10 (sin as a deterrent).

[2] A.R.E. 1930, st. ins. No. 175 of 1929–30; A.R.E. 1909, st. ins. No. 363 of 1908; E.I. xx, pp. 52 f., 64 f.; xxiv, pp. 298, 303; xxvi, pp. 127, 232; S.I.I. ix, pt. 1, 378; E.C. vi Tar. 53; xii Tip. 83; ix Nel. 12; K.I. i, p. 9 (= B.K. 1939–40, 4); M.A.R. 1910–11, para. 105; S.I.I. x, 611–2.

[3] *Ins. Pudukkottai St.*, 683. Cf. E.I. xxx, p. 71 f.

[4] *Lekhapaddhati* (Baroda, 1925), pp. 45–7. Majumdār, *Chaulukyas*, pp. 345–9. For the power of an agreement see the first ref. below, p. 216, n. 6.

[5] Kāṇe, *H.D.*, II, pt. 1, pp. 168–9; pt. 2, pp. 971–4. K. A. N. Śāstrī, *Cōḻas*[2], p. 490. Brahmins often received cash penances as their income: K.I. ii, No. 4, p. 11.

exclusion from family and corporate activities until the penance was performed.[1] It does not hint at the immense social pressure which the manipulation of these concepts enabled assemblies, aided by Brahmins, to apply to individuals–about which we know as yet too little. Nor does it hint at what seems to have been a fact, namely that the right to admit to caste privileges was intrinsically subject to political supervision, and that in some areas and periods the caste could expel, but without royal sanction readmission was impossible.

Any community, like a guild, possessed inherent powers of exclusion. This was almost as severe as the death penalty, since only migration to a different country enabled the unfortunate protestant to escape its effects. If the village excommunicated one, the victim could neither obtain services nor use any facility, nor enjoy any intercourse with neighbours.[2] The village assemblies of various types, the district assemblies, religious communities and the governmental power could combine and decree comprehensive penalties for infringement of rules of conduct or prohibitions erected to protect some enterprise.[3] 'He who violates this shall be a traitor to the king, to Śiva, to the community, and to the district.' 'He is far from the land of the living and whoever kills him is a hero.'[4] That the king might issue an order of boycott is expressly recognized in the *dharma-śāstra* itself.[5] The *śāstra* utilized its own distinctions as a rough guide. Negative, prohibitive, injunctions consisted of *yama-s* and *niyama-s*. Brahmin-killing would be an example of the first; earning by forbidden means would be an example of the

[1] Kāṇe, *H.D.*, II, pt. 1, pp. 387 ff.; III, pp. 615–6, 1009; IV, pp. 65 ff., 105 ff. *Lekhap.* (cited above), pp. 53–4: a document attesting an excommunication by relatives, authorizing the punishment of any of them who associated with him, and indicating how he might be reinstated: Majumdār, where cited, p. 350. Penance here anticipates pain hereafter: Śabara on Jaimini III, viii, 9.

[2] Even the name of a reprobate should not be mentioned: Medhātithi on Manu V, 88.

[3] E.g., E.C. iv Gund. 34 (A.D. 1372); ix Nel. 12; E.I. xx, p. 64 ff.

[4] M.A.R. 1943, 14. Cf. E.C. ii, 344. Sanctions (including outlawry) against *nāṭṭudrōhin* (traitor to the country) and *grāmadrōhin* (traitor to his village): A.R.E. 1918, st. ins. No. 92 of 1918. T. V. Mahāliṅgam, *South Indian Polity* (Madras, 1955), 201. A.R.E. 1913, rep. pp. 127–8.

[5] Medhātithi on Manu VII, 13, also IX, 232.

second.[1] One becomes a *patita*, 'fallen from caste', by breach of the former certainly, though whether also by breach of the latter seems not to have been agreed–in one view caste action would be required to achieve this effect. After breaking a *yama* one lost the right to perform the religious acts prescribed for dawn, noon and twilight, and, *a fortiori*, other religious acts of social significance; breach of a *niyama* would not have such drastic effects.[2] Brahmins in practice decided that a particular antisocial act was a sin, imposed upon it in anticipation a penalty appropriate for one who committed subsisting well-known sins, and thus kept in their hands the means to apply the penalty and commute the sentence. Unanimity and conformity were to be insisted upon, at least for appearance's sake, once a public decision had been arrived at, and no one who had not an entire group on his side could flout these group decisions. Touchiness was not uncommon, however, and we hear of migrations, obviously to better prospects and to evade unwelcome restrictions.[3] The way up the social ladder was closely hedged by caste and super-caste sanctions based upon the ultimate threat of excommunication, so that those who climbed with difficulty could not slip down suddenly.

The by-laws of the *agrahāra* of Uttaramerūr are especially interesting as they exclude from the vote in elections to village council committees all members who had been declared enemies of the village or had committed incest *even though they had performed their expiation*, whereas those who had 'fallen' by mere association with sinners might participate after expiation. Those who had eaten forbidden food and taken the ghee expiation were perpetually disqualified, but one may infer that a harder penance might re-enable them to vote. Those who were compelled to ride on asses or had been guilty of forging documents were perpetually disqualified from being elected. The consonance of these drastic provisions with the *dharmaśāstra* is evident.[4]

[1] On the latter see above, p. 131.

[2] Medhātithi on Manu IV, 204 (trans., II, pt. 2, p. 458). For *sandhyopāsana* see Manu II, 69.

[3] A.R.S.I.E. 1936–7, rep. p. 84 (complaint of bribery and loss of prestige). A.R.S.I.E. 1938–9, copper plate no. 3. S.I.I. x, 79. Migrants retained their ancestral usages: Śabara on Jaimini I, iii, 19 (a rule which in principle is observed to this day in the 'personal law').

[4] K. A. Nīlakaṇṭa Śāstrī, *Studies in Coḷa History and Administration* (Madras,

The sins of which the *śāstra* speaks, and which do not include these important *ad hoc* social sins, are treated much as are the sins catalogued in mediaeval western penitentials. Our period saw no fresh examination of the fundamental concepts, and misfortunes, accidental slips and deliberate faults of very different degrees of moral guilt (from the modern viewpoint) are often found classed as equally staining.[1] The sinner was purified, according to the Brahmins' award, by fasting, alms, fines, pilgrimages, drinking cows' urine and the like, and finally propitiation of the community by lavish feasts. It is doubtful whether the castes lower in the social scale were much troubled with sin and penance, and the untouchables must have led an enviably uninhibited existence amongst themselves. An interest in the acquisition of merit and avoidance of rebirth gave universal prestige to Brahmin expositors, tended to spread Brahminical ideas, supported Brahmin teachers in their often difficult task of advising rulers, and encouraged some general unity of outlook throughout the subcontinent.

The right to excommunicate for offences of a purely social or religious character is nowadays called 'caste tyranny'. But in our period it is clear that it was regarded far more as a safeguard for security of livelihood and secular as well as spiritual contentment, more effective in fact that any purely legal procedure. Custom existed for the support, rather than the confinement, of inclinations. It was a great part of *dharma*, 'righteousness', and the rulers that upheld it were themselves upheld.[2]

Customs such as that the feet of a *guru* should be touched in salutation, that the elder brother should be obeyed, and that, for example, the mother's brother's daughter should (or should

1932), pp. 96 ff., pp. 172, 109, 113 respectively for the detail in the order referred to. Nārada, XIV, 11 (trans., 1889, p. 204) says, 'Those who have committed violence (*sāhasa*) of either of the first two degrees are allowed to mix in society, after having been punished, but if a man has committed violence of the highest degree, no one is allowed to speak to him, even when he has received punishment.'

[1] Kāṇe, *H.D.*, IV, chh. 3 and 4. An illustration of prevailing standards: *Moharājaparājaya*, 83: a proclamation that all wrongdoers should be banished, save prostitutes (from whom the king made an income).

[2] Kāṇe, *H.D.*, III, 270, 488, 566, 857, 860–6, 882. Texts quoted in S. Roy, *Customs and Customary Law* . . . , pp. 13–18.

not) be taken in marriage,[1] were perhaps immutable. Customary prices,[2] conditions of tenure of land, rights to services and remunerations therefor, orders of priority of heirship in succession to property, constitutions of guilds and other corporations, tolls, lordships, and so on, were far from being immutable. *Dharma* might be everlasting, but the details of practical law fluctuated, slowly and unevenly, leaving perhaps little surviving documentation, but none the less certainly for that.

We have noticed already[3] the contention that custom and *dharma* were immune from legislation. A comment even in Medhātithi could be construed, if one were hasty, as supporting the permanence of custom. Usage can conclude an issue irrespective of evidence being led.[4] But in fact the reference is to a usage *pro tempore*. Our inscriptional evidence shows India as a patchwork of overlapping or exclusive jurisdictions, comparable with the corporation, borough and manor jurisdictions of mediaeval Europe, with their 'liberties' and 'immunities'. The king in fact created and amended the constitutions of many of these, renewed charters, and raised half-formed commercial or artisan groups to incorporated status with their own courts and decision-making bodies.[5] But the agricultural communities and multi-village caste groups which had functioned before the king emerged as a classical institution retained their exclusive powers, and legislated at their pleasure. It is of no importance whether we call their laws 'regulations' or by-laws, for they were much nearer to the villager, much more real, than the decrees issued at the palace, far away. The local bodies would call upon the king or his deputy to 'authorize' or 'sanction' their decisions only as a precaution against the anticipated insufficiency of their excommunicatory penalties if the laws were invaded by outsiders. Moreover, in a country in which the king reserved the right to appoint all or some of the headmen of the villages it was useful for the latter to have the guidance of laws which his ultimate master had authorized. Written 'conventions' (*samaya*,

[1] See above, pp. 86–7.

[2] A.R.E. 1931–2, st. ins. No. 103, rep., §. 16 S. K. Maity, *Economic Life of Northern India* (Calcutta, 1957), 126.

[3] Above, p. 164.

[4] Medhātithi on Manu VIII, 3.

[5] Vīra Banañjas are an example: E.C. ix Nel. 12; M.A.R. 1911–12, para. 90; 1928, 103, p. 92. For a much smaller corporation reconstituted after an invasion see E.I. xv, pp. 79 ff.

sthiti, vyavasthā)[1] passed by villagers, castes, or guilds for all sorts of local purposes, utilitarian, fiscal, charitable, were contemplated by *smṛti-s* including Manu, Yājñavalkya and Bṛhaspati.[2] The king is enjoined to uphold these, and commentators illustrate the powers of the village or guild to pass these 'by-laws'.[3] The view of Altekar[4] that the 'conventions' were not arrived at by representatives of the castes of the village in village meetings, but were engagements entered into between the individual villager on the one part and the village itself on the other seems to be unnecessary and improbable,[5] and for once Jayaswāl seems to have the best of the controversy. Naturally, in revenue contexts, when the village shared out the responsibility amongst the land-holders and others, individuals took upon themselves engagements: but this–though important–was only a fraction of the scope of *samaya* in village-law. The Brahmins of the village of Lahadapura enacted a *saṃvit* or *sthiti*, which is still to be read in the *sthiti-patra* (bearing a date corresponding to September 5th, 1173) which was drawn up in conformity with Bṛhaspati's injunctions.[6] It provides that plunderers should be slaughtered at sight and their property confiscated, that abettors should be expelled and their houses demolished, and that

[1] The word *saṃvitti-patrakaṃ* ('charter of convention') is used at Bṛhaspati VI, 10 (p. 60; Renou, where cited, p. 54). Medhātithi on Manu VIII, 41. *Vyavasthā* (in the Kannaḍa form *vyavasthe*) is stated to be used at A.R.S.I.E. 1933–4, st. ins. No. 170 (A.D. 994) for 'statute' enacted by King Āhavamalla in favour of the 200 Mahājanas of the *agrahāra*; but on inspection of the text (kindly supplied by the Government Epigraphist for India on March 23rd, 1965) it appears that the word simply refers to the settled draft of a grant agreed to by the Brahmins out of their rights in the city, and thus means no more than 'grant' in this case.

[2] Yājñ. II, 186 with *Mitākṣarā*. Medhātithi on Manu VIII, 41. Variant readings at *Vivādaratnākara*, p. 181, and *Vīramitrodaya*, p. 425 suggest rather agricultural than charitable purposes.

[3] Medhātithi on Manu I, 21; see also Manu VIII, 219. The commentary on the latter by Bhāruci explains that the *saṃvid* of villagers will be upheld by the king who will banish offenders: the by-law being about, for example, pasturing cattle, storing water, repairing temples of deities, and so on. On Manu VIII, 41 see above, p. 157, n. 4.

[4] *State and Government in Ancient India* (Delhi, Motilāl Banarsidāss, 1955, 1962), pp. 149–50.

[5] See Medhātithi and Bhāruci on Manu VIII, 219, also VIII, 41.

[6] See Bṛhaspati cited in p. 157, n. 3 above, also VI, 19 (p. 62) (Renou, p. 55). For the inscription see E.I. xxxii, No. 36, pp. 305–9.

those who offer the guilty parties advice (as we should say, 'counsel and comfort') should be ostracized. Verses apparently authorizing such a punishment are attributed to Bṛhaspati in the noticeably practical-minded Varadarāja's *Vyavahāra-nirṇaya* which belongs to the early thirteenth century.[1]

Apart from such provisions there is no doubt but that, at any rate in South India, the village community had the right to confiscate and sell the lands of inhabitants who defaulted in paying the revenue, and this same sanction was used wherever mischief against the community occurred. Defaulters and murderers were thus treated similarly and the drastic punishment will have been at least as good a deterrent as excommunication.[2]

Sometimes we find the king graciously granting some villages the right of allowing their inhabitants' property to pass, on a death without male issue, to widows; or to a mercantile town the right that property in similar circumstances should not escheat if a brother's son survived.[3] Elsewhere we find the group itself, without mention of any superior, deciding that its habits shall change thenceforward and that any attempt to continue the old practice shall be visited with outlawry.[4] 'Improvement' in customs meant a better distribution of income and a nearer approach to the manners of more prestige-worthy castes, and both led directly to social advancement. The jurisdiction that could make laws, and could, under another name and by another instrument, apply them, could also repeal laws. We have no information whether laws could become obsolete, but it is likely that they could, as for example the laws relating to irrigation in an area where the irrigation system had been irretrievably damaged by warfare.[5] The word 'laws' is properly used of these rules capable of being enforced by penalty, but they can be called 'customary law', not because they were immemorial or immutable, for they were neither, but because they were not 'book laws', the law of the *dharmaśāstra*. No one contends that village assemblies or the king himself could inter-

[1] Ed. K. V. R. Aiyaṅgār and K. Aiyaṅgār, p. 507. Renou, pp. 109–10.

[2] E.I. xxiv, pp. 33 ff. A.R.S.I.E. 1935–6, st. ins. No. 185.

[3] A.R.E. 1919, st. ins. Nos. 429, 538 of 1918, rep., p. 97. E.I. xxx, pp. 163 ff.

[4] See p. 181, n. 3 above. Also S.I.I. x, 221 (succession to a deceased woman's jewels).

[5] Nārada, XI, 21–2 may refer to some such considerations.

fere with 'unseen' matters, with, for example, the *agnihotra* and other aspects of the sacrificial and spiritual life of the castes, using the last expression in its modern sense: within their peculiar sphere the *śāstri-s* totally denied jurisdiction to others.[1] We have already seen Devaṇṇa-bhaṭṭa taking this attitude;[2] Medhātithi had anticipated him. The latter explains in one place how the śāstric rule that debtors must not sell themselves into slavery (Manu VIII, 177) can be set aside by village, district, or royal enactments which come within the category of *dṛṣṭārtha* ('directed to seen objects'), in conformity with Manu VIII, 46: but the latter provision has no application to *adṛṣṭārtha* matters.[3] And this outlook was never challenged until the commencement of Muslim rule in northern India, and the commencement of a certain policy under the Portuguese at Goa, when interference with *adṛṣṭārtha* matters was a matter of pride for some of the conquerors.

The role of the *dharmaśāstra* in the formation of Indian law has been much debated. We see that in our period it was not in force universally, nor even, as a matter of obligation, sectionally, as from caste to caste, or regionally. Perfectly notorious śāstric rules were obviously flouted,[4] both in regard to the ritual law and the more intimate details of the original *varṇa* system on the one hand and in respect of provisions of substantive and adjectival law on the other. The first does not surprise so much as the second. If the *smṛtikāra-s*, for the sake of completeness and with other motives which will be mentioned later, gave details of the customary laws of which they approved relating to matters of 'court law' (*vyavahāra*), they and their

[1] Medhātithi on Manu IV, 178 (trans., p. 442); VII, 13 (trans., p. 280).

[2] Above, p. 167.

[3] See above, pp. 98–9.

[4] E.I. xxvi, p. 155. The reverse is also evidenced, *J.O.R.*, 19 (1952), pp. 219–22. In U. N. Ghoshal's study at *A.B.O.R.I.*, 46 (1965) at pp. 70–1 we are given evidence of Brahmins buying and receiving land for performance of *agnihotra* and the *pañcamahāyajña-s* in the years A.D. 44/34 and 447/8: in perfect accord with strict śāstric theory. There and at pp. 72 and 79 the question of naming arises: Brahmins have, and again do not have, names conforming to the *gṛhyasūtra* rules on the subject. Again, at E.I. xxix, p. 81 the *rākṣasa* marriage is spoken of (cf. Yazdāni, ed., *Early History of the Deccan*, I, p. 252), thus corroborating the *śāstra* (see above, p. 160). But at E.I. xxix, p. 82 we see evidence of females taking kingdoms as heirs, ignoring the spiritual rules about the need of the deceased males to have male heirs, scil. by adoption.

successors would have been expected to take care to depict what was actually in force. It would be misleading to suggest that the *śāstra* never attended to facts, or that the *vyavahāra* portion of the relevant works was based on imagination or pure theorizing. But a marvellous unconcern for some of what must have been obvious legal developments pervades the texts of our period, which include some of the most influential texts of the Hindu law. Such discrepancies in the realms of religion, ritual, and supersensory matters generally could more easily be explained; for the Indian population was as varied a collection of humanity as imagination can conceive, and there was no means of compelling conformity or even general homogeneity of ideas in departments of belief as distinct from those of action. Yet this apparent unreality of the *śāstra* is no accident.

It may be assumed with some confidence that Northern and Eastern Indian customs had been well represented in the *sūtra-s* and *smṛti-s*; and the Brahmin immigrants who settled in the Deccan and the South (sought out because of their provenance from a region where Āryan traditions were supposed to be maintained undefiled) expounded the *śāstra* which was based upon those texts in no less orthodox a manner than their colleagues who remained behind. There was no authority for introducing into the primary sources Southern customs or customs newly developed–though there is (as we have hinted already) some evidence that at one stage interpolations took place which were afterwards ejected[1]–and it followed that the *śāstra* grew more and more out of touch with the actual practice of those to whom the *śāstrī-s* expounded it. But at the same time the desire to imitate Brahmins, or to imitate those who were beginning to imitate Brahmins, gave the *śāstra* a better hearing than it would otherwise have had. The curiously amateurish way in which commentators often guess at the meaning of technical terms in their *smṛti-s* (an odd example is the names of mixed castes at Manu X, 20–3) suggests a well-meant, if feeble, attempt to keep text and usage in touch with each other. The presence of spiritual doctrine and ritual prescriptions alongside court law enabled generalized propositions of law to penetrate under the cover afforded by the much-desired answers to the questions of merit and rebirth. And the atmosphere of the

[1] See above, p. 160, n. 5.

śāstra, with its insistence on a spiritual and moral basis for all rules, and its offer of a consistent and intelligible explanation for obligation of every type, was naturally welcome everywhere. The public were naturally worried by gross variations in usage and ethics.

The *śāstra* was certainly in use during our period, as is proved by the famous case cited by Asahāya,[1] by the instance of the reference to the *śāstra* to determine the status of a particular caste,[2] and, again from the South, the debate whether a daughter's son might succeed to his maternal grandfather's share in a settlement, and if so, upon what terms.[3] Where Brahmins formed the court, where they acted as advisers on points of law,[4] where the topic was obviously dealt with in the *śāstra* and customary law was silent or ambiguous, where parties to a dispute were governed by different customs,[5] and in matters of a technical nature where the *śāstra* supplied learning unobtainable elsewhere, non-śāstric sources would have to be subordinate, and the *dharmaśāstra* was the dominant part of the cultural and technical equipment of the nation. This applies to the South, to orthodox Bengal and to the less orthodox North-West, not to speak of other areas. The *śāstra* was thus well-placed to lead the enquiring mind, and minds were bound to enquire, for, as we have seen, ambitions spurred them on.

There is no evidence that śāstric rules of conduct were enforced upon an unwilling public. The *durācāra-s* or *anācāra-s*, 'anomalous customs', like those of Malabar, which provided a pleasant topic in later periods and must have afforded amusement in our own, were tolerated widely. The jurists attempt to explain this.

They are hardly convincing. The *mīmāṃsaka-s*, as we have seen,[6] contend that only the customs of 'good' men bind the people, while men who practise customs contrary to the Veda cannot be 'good'. The jurists do not go the whole way with them. How could they? They distinguish between congruent

[1] Kāṇe, *H.D.*, III, 289, n. 395.

[2] A.R.E. 1909, st. ins. No. 479 of 1908; cf. ibid., 1925, st. ins. No. 189 of 1925. See above, p. 162.

[3] K. A. N. Śāstrī, *Cōḷas*[2], p. 491.

[4] The title held by *agrahāra* Brahmins at E.C. vii Shik. 178 (*sandigdha-vipuḷa-dharmma-nirṇṇāyakar*) can hardly be a mere formality.

[5] Kātyāyana, cited above, p. 150.

[6] Above, p. 86.

customs and the reverse, and they give interesting illustrations.[1] One obtains an impression that they are staving off the necessity to admit *any* custom as valid (which the *Mahābhārata*, receptacle of all viable opinions and of some that are not viable, already hints) providing that it conformed to the king's general political requirements, and this was the situation which was openly reached in the next period.[2] As for the king, his general obligation to obey the dictates of *dharma*, his alleged 'subjection to law', did not prevent him from altering the law to be applied in his courts or authorizing such a jurisdiction to be exercised by others.

This brings us to the question whether, if the *śāstra* as *śāstra* could not be enforced upon the unwilling, any set of rules could be enforced upon those who did not already admit their validity. The actual situation in mediaeval India has sometimes been misunderstood, and the technical books here as elsewhere fail to enlighten us. The *śāstra* was not like a modern code, and had no obligatory force except in so far as jurisdiction was exercised by those who would naturally guide themselves by it or by actual legal rules that had become incorporated within it. On the other hand we have seen customary law growing and moving with every sign of potent applicability.

It is evident that all legislation required the consent or assent of the persons concerned.[3] To this there is an important exception in respect of the king's prerogatives. His wide criminal powers and powers to control national defence and relations with other kingdoms necessarily gave him scope to order what could not be neglected without fear of severe penalties. The king may prohibit the import or export of commodities, and breach of his order means death.[4] Yet we can see that these

[1] Medhātithi on Manu VIII, 3, 46. Kāṇe, *H.D.*, III, 843 ff., 848 ff., 853–5.

[2] See above, p. 158. U. N. Ghoshal, *History of Indian Political Ideas* (Bombay, 1959), p. 311.

[3] S.I.I. viii, 442 (*Quarterly J. Mythic Soc.*, 46, 1955, pp. 8 ff.) is particularly explicit. Earlier we hear often of 'all the merchants, etc.', 'all the 1,000', 'the nine *nāḍs* (districts)', 'all the Brahmins and subjects', etc. E.g., E.I. xxiv (1942), pp. 29 ff.; S.I.I. ix, pt. 1, 104, 329. Gatherings so constituted also received orders: E.I. xxiii, p. 99.

[4] Medhātithi on Manu IV, 226 (text p. 406, trans., p. 478 (incorrect?)). Nārada, XVIII, 20 ff. Medhātithi classifies royal orders into orders of

powers were not used as an excuse for diminishing the jurisdictions of those communities who reserved the right to control their own local defence and criminal administration. His sanction was required for the imposing of new penalties but this was because in theory all fines belonged to him, and when he disposed of them *in prospectu* he naturally defined, where desirable, what limits should be observed.[1] Again his ownership of land and its produce, his nominal ownership of all property not allowed to his subjects by specific titles and subject to conditions set by custom, by law, or by grant, and excepting also lands dedicated with his or his predecessors' permission to deities,[2] and further his duty to afford protection to the people (a costly undertaking) led to his imposing levies and obligations in respect of property far wider than the land revenue which was the chief source of royal income. And in these two provinces of criminal and military law on the one hand and fiscal and analogous law on the other the subjects' assent was dispensed with as superfluous. In all other contexts consent or assent was absolutely requisite for the validity of decisions, judicial, administrative and legislative.

The methods employed were certainly not democratic. But they give the impression of having been efficient. Just as the younger brother would not speak up in front of his elder brother, the wife in front of her husband, or the pupil in front of his teacher, so the less prestige-worthy would maintain a discreet economy of words before the more important, and only equals would freely discuss problems of common concern. But in the mixed assemblies which were required to decide matters of policy, and in some judicial disputes, representation of all the important castes and interests, government, corporate, spiritual and secular was essential, and no decision was arrived at without full discussion and airing of views. Just as the representatives of the families, castes, interests, regions and so on were chosen by tacit consent, being 'natural leaders', so the ultimate decision was concurred in by all participants without taking a vote.[3] A

boycott (*etasya gṛhe na bhoktavyaṃ*), grants (*asya cāyaṃ prasāda ājñāta*), and legislation (*iyaṃ sthiti rājñā kṛtā*). Literally a *sthiti* (see p. 189 above) means the establishing of something which was previously mobile, i.e. uncertain.

[1] See below, p. 214, n. 4.

[2] On this topic see p. 147, n. 2 above.

[3] K. A. N. Śāstrī, *Cōḷas*[2], pp. 506, 508. Membership was regulated

text which suggests that at a division of opinions that of the majority prevailed, while equality of voices confirmed the better-known position,[1] presupposes an equality of status between members which must have been very rare. The suggestion (not in itself improbable) that commercial partnerships, which might be large, were bound by majority-decision[2] turns out to be without foundation. He who could not persuade was persuaded, and majority decision was normally out of the question. Our inscriptions record the consent of various castes, etc., and the assent even of parties not directly concerned was regularly taken in order to give further notoriety to, and to obviate misunderstandings or evasions of, the decision. Castes which would be affected, but which were excluded from the assembly because of uncleanness, to cite the most obvious reason, would none the less be consulted,[3] and their failure to object would bind them and give validity to the decision. If a man's group had been represented he was bound, and his descendants likewise, until they could harness similar machinery to revoke the decision. Similarly in judicial procedure, even if the losing party had accepted the decision he might reopen the matter if a larger tribunal representing the population more comprehensively might be induced to reverse the decree.[4]

Thus the penetration of śāstric rules into actual legal usage took place as surely through gradual developments from below, as it were, through the free consent or assent of the natural representatives of the interested groups, as through the pronouncements of the *dharmādhyakṣa-s* or *nyāyādhikārī-s* attached to the rulers' courts.[5] The liaison between the two processes is attested by Medhātithi himself (on Manu VIII, 41). It was one

(A.R.E. 1932, st. ins. No. 89 of 1932) and there seems to have been the concept of *quorum*, but mere numbers were irrelevant. Kauṭilya, *Arthaś.*, I, 15, 59 (trans. Kāṅgle, p. 40) authorizes the king to ignore a majority opinion.

[1] *Gobhila-smṛti* (in the Poona *Smṛti-samuccaya*), III, 149.

[2] Kāṇe wrongly cites Bṛhaspati to that effect at *H.D.*, III, 467, n. 806.

[3] In K.I. ii, No. 4, p. 11 or E.C. iv Gund. 32, where consent is not mentioned, it must nevertheless be assumed.

[4] A.R.E. 1913, rep. para. 51; Mahālingam, *S. Indian Polity*, pp. 214–15.

[5] E.I. xv, pp. 80 ff.; E.C. vi Koppa 14. Judicial service involved a minor sin: Medhātithi on Manu XI, 62 (text) = 63 (trans.). Misdeeds of a *vyavahārin* are noticed in E.I. xix, pp. 17 ff.

of the tasks of those functionaries to advise on the enforceability of proved customs. The king's duty could not have been performed otherwise. The legal adviser was enjoined, as that nineteenth-century text, the *Śukranītisāra*,[1] says in complete conformity with much older conceptions, 'to study the moral life obtaining in society in ancient and modern times which have been mentioned in the *śāstra-s*, which are now opposed and which go against the customs of the people, and to advise the king as to which of these are efficacious for this world and the next.'[2]

Jurisprudential Techniques

We are now in a position to appreciate the jurists' task, their facilities and handicaps, their temptations, limitations, successes and failures. Many generations of Indian jurists performed piecemeal a task undertaken successfully by Justinian's editorial committee and thereafter by the glossators and 'post-glossators' of the Roman legal tradition. The absence of a concrete central collection of texts arranged systematically by authority of the state naturally makes their work more difficult to follow, just as it then hampered the public's appreciation of their more detailed endeavours. The great lawyers of the sixteenth and seventeenth centuries could not have been trained without the literature accumulated during our period, and a somewhat close investigation of their predecessors' position is needed before we can fully understand their eminence.

It is to be understood at the outset that the jurists wrote on law only as a portion of Duty. It was the king's duty to apply certain groups of rules, or to recognize certain jurisdictions, or to uphold a particular social order. That part of law which would not normally be applied by the king or under his close supervision was not strictly relevant to this theme, and is therefore for the most part omitted. Legal concepts abstracted from the question of the king's duty as a legal administrator began to interest jurists towards the last two centuries of our period, and many of them took on an independent academic vitality with

[1] On which see p. 169, n. 9 above.
[2] II, 200–3 (noticed at K. V. R. Aiyaṅgār's *Rājadharma*, p. 131). For Medhātithi's discussion see Jhā's trans., IV, pt. 1, pp. 53 ff.

the rebirth of *nyāya*, 'dialectics', in the fourteenth century. But that aspect of juristic writing is beyond our present scope. The king's duty, however, was a specimen of the duties of the *varṇa-s* and of each *āśrama* within each appropriate *varṇa*, and our sources for the most part attempt, not always convincingly, to depict purely legal injunctions as integral parts of a consistent highly complex pattern of *varṇāśrama-dharma*. The most successful of such attempts is that attributed to Manu, but he was perhaps only one of the most eminent of the more legalistic of ancient juridical writers.

If one were to commence legal studies with one of the earliest commentaries, written about the seventh/eighth century A.D., such as Maskarī on the *Gautama-dharma-sūtra*, or Bhavasvāmī on the *Nāradīya-Manu-saṃhitā* (significantly named 'code' of Manu as published by Nārada), or Bhāruci, *alias* Ṛju-vimala, in his *Vivaraṇa* on Manu, one would suspect that the formal sources of the *śāstra* were not in fact its most important sources; and further reading in the next period, commencing with Viśvarūpa's *Bālakrīḍā* ('Child's Play') on the *Yājñavalkya-smṛti* and Medhātithi's great work on Manu, to which we have frequently referred above, would confirm that impression. By the time we reach Jīmūtavāhana's independent treatise on inheritance, the celebrated *Dāyabhāga*, and his younger contemporary Vijñāneśvara's commentary on the *Yājñavalkya-smṛti*, properly entitled *Ṛju-Mitākṣarā* but known to modern lawyers as 'the Mitākshară', we are sure that the traditional sources of the *śāstra* may be basic in a peculiar sense, but they no longer are primary, let alone exhaustive.

The sources of *dharma*, we are told, are the Veda (*śruti*) and *smṛti* (juridical 'memory') and the conduct of those who know[1] the Veda, a corpus overwhelmingly religious in scope and aims. In our period the orthodox accepted the authority of the Vedic literature (including lost parts which served to authorize *smṛti* texts otherwise unsupported),[2] but doubts as to the authority of the *smṛtikāra-s* had to be resolved.[3] Once this was done the process hastened in what appears an undignified way. The word

[1] Haradatta on Gautama I, 1–2; Medhātithi on Manu II, 1.

[2] Kullūka on Manu II, 12; Śabara on Jaimini I, iii, 1–2 (trans., I, 87–91); cf. Medhātithi on Manu VIII, 56 (trans., IV, pt. 1, p. 76).

[3] Medhātithi on Manu I, 1; II, 6 (trans., I, pt. 1, pp. 189–90.

śruti comes to be used for texts other than Vedic texts. Meanwhile propositions found in the Veda are occasionally abrogated on the authority of *smṛti*.[1] *Smṛti* itself, instead of consisting of the quintessence of traditional conduct distilled by the ancient sages who were supposed to be the ancestors of the Brahmins' *gotra-s* and also first hearers of the Veda (whence their authority in theory and practice), became a conglomeration of ancient texts with the current maxims, epigrams, and apothegms which so long served instead of written treatises, and reworkings of all these undertaken so as to keep the basic texts 'up to date'. Towards the beginning of our period rewriting *smṛti* material took place on a large scale. The younger *smṛti-s* of the so-called genuine period had almost certainly been produced to meet the needs of the latest bulk settlements of foreigners in northern and western India and the cultural upheavals due to large settlements of mixed Āryan and pre-Āryan invaders in the Deccan and immigrations into the further South. These, such as the treatises attributed to Bṛhaspati, Nārada, Kātyāyana and others, whose less relative antiquity is proved by their detailed interest in legal niceties, have been placed by some as late as the Gupta period, but this seems hardly credible, and the reasons taken from internal evidence are, like all such evidences, flimsy, because we know that conscious and unconscious adaptation of *smṛti-s* was a continuous process. It served a powerful need and has not stopped at the time of writing. But in our period the so-called spurious *smṛti-s* began to be written, some of which unashamedly state (or appear to state) the cause or the public for which they cater.[2] There followed the later *purāṇa-s*, particularly the Vaiṣṇava *upapurāṇa-s*.[3] Our period saw the redaction of the *Mahābhārata*, with its substantial legal sections in the *Śāntiparva* and *Anuśāsanaparva*, to its final form; but the urge to rewrite *smṛti* material to suit contemporary and sometimes sectarian needs had not exhausted itself by the time British rule commenced, as the curious history of the *Mahānirvāṇa-tantra* shows.[4] All the available sources, of whatever quality and

[1] Ibid.; Kullūka on Manu II, 1.

[2] The *Devala-smṛti* aims to assist readmission to caste of forcible converts to Islam in Sindh.

[3] R. C. Hazra, *Studies* (cited above). See above, p. 88, n. 2.

[4] See below, p. 265.

authenticity, attempt to restate Duty, including many legal details, in a more current form than that to be found in the sources they imitate or plagiarize. The extent to which they were relied upon by first-rank jurists in our period to supplement, or even to contradict, the great *smṛti-s* is only now receiving the attention it deserves.[1] To Vijñāneśvara, for example – and no greater name could be chosen – all ancient vehicles of traditional theories of duty, currently accepted by the learned here or there in India, were legitimate sources of *dharma*.[2]

And it is somewhat alarming that verses are cited in reputable digests on topics of great practical importance in circumstances arguing their relatively recent fabrication.[3] Small wonder, then, that the *Nṛsiṃhaprasāda*[4] actually places *smṛti* and *purāṇa* on a level, allowing a free choice where they contradict each other.[5]

The practice of the learned, of 'good' people, or even of the generality of people, is regularly used not merely to corroborate a controversial *smṛti* rule,[6] but even to select one from among the

[1] R. C. Hazra, *Indian Culture*, 1 (1934–5), pp. 587–614; 3 (1936–7), pp. 477–87; *A.B.O.R.I.*, 26 (1945), pp. 32–88. On the *Kālikā-purāṇa* (eleventh cent. or earlier): Kāṇe, *H.D.*, I, p. 448; Nīlakaṇṭha, *Vyavahāra-mayūkha*, ed. Kāṇe (text, p. 114; notes, pp. 187–8).

[2] In the *Mitākṣarā* (Colebrooke, I, i, 23 and II, i, 22) Gautama is cited from an edition or collection which does not survive. With the former a passage in Medhātithi (on Manu IX, 156) may be compared. There is an untraced citation of Viṣṇu in the *Mitākṣarā* on Yājñ. III, 227 and in Jīmūtavāhana's *Dāyabhāga* (Colebrooke, XI, ii, 23). The fundamental text on the heritable claims of *bandhu-s* (cognates: *Mit.* II, vi, 1) cannot be traced: *Vṛddha*-Śātātapa would be a most dubious source; likewise *Bhṛan-Manu* (ibid., II, vi, 6). All works the titles of which commence with *Vṛddha-* or *Bṛhat-* actually profess to be conflations or inflations and are obviously late. On Yājñ. I, 328 (as Rocher points out at *I.Y.B.I.A.*, 7, 1958, pp. 348–9) Vijñāneśvara imports material from an untraced source, perhaps a lost *nīti-śāstra* work.

[3] Citations of, e.g., Śaunaka arouse suspicion, likewise Bharadvāja (or Bhāradvāja?). Bṛhaspati XIV, 14 (Aiyaṅgār, p. 139) which denies the validity of *post obit* gifts is cited only in the *Vyavahāra-nirṇaya* (p. 298), suspiciously late for so important a text.

[4] Kāṇe, *H.D.*, I, p. 409. The work belongs to the period 1490–1512 and was written under a Muslim ruler.

[5] Further on *purāṇa-s* as a source of law see Kāṇe, *H.D.*, V, chh. 22–4.

[6] *Mitākṣarā* (Colebrooke, I, i, 23).

many frequently conflicting rules of *smṛti*, or to establish a legal rule which *smṛti* fails to supply.[1]

During our period *dharma* moved out of the schools, ceased to be (for Indians) a purely esoteric study, and became, in its moral and ritual aspects, the property of sects and syncretists and in its political and legal aspects that of the public man. There it came at once into contact with its sister science, the *arthaśāstra*. The great *smṛti-s* already incorporated information from an *arthaśāstra* source, though whether from some writers anterior to Kauṭilya must remain open to debate.[2] Kauṭilya was much in use, though a less demanding conspectus of *dharma* and *artha* literature was forming in what was called *nīti*, 'conduct', 'policy', 'propriety'.[3] *Dharma*, after all, was from the very beginning of our period only one of the sources of practical justice, the ruler was exhorted to apply both *dharma* and *artha* considerations in litigation,[4] and we have seen how *vyavahāra*, in the sense of the settled course of judicature, was admitted by the *śāstra* itself to be superior, in a case of a conflict, to pure *dharma* considerations.[5] The practice did not, as we saw, outweigh specific customs, or particular edicts, but these were far too detailed, too localized, and too unstable to find a place in the *nīti-śāstra*, which was not more hospitable to them than the *dharmaśāstra* itself.

Our jurists were concerned to define the standpoint of *dharma*

[1] *Mitākṣarā* (Colebrooke, I, i, ii); *Dāyabhāga* (Coleb., I, i, 12; II, 40; III, ii, 27; VI, i, 53. By the sixteenth century practice may supplant *smṛti: yathā loke dṛṣṭaṃ tathā svīkartavyam* ('We must follow the way of the world'): see *B.S.O.A.S.*, 21 (1958), p. 77.

[2] Derrett at *Z.D.M.G.*, 115 (1965), pp. 134–52. Dieter Schlingloff, 'Arthaśāstra-studien', *Wiener Z.K.S. Ostasiens*, 9 (1965), pp. 1–38.

[3] L. Sternbach, *Cāṇakya-rāja-nīti* (Adyar, 1963). L. Sternbach supposes (*Rajasthan University Studies, Sanskrit & Hindi*, 1965, p. 12 of the offprint) that because Śārṅga-dhara, whose *Paddhati* contains a *rāja-nīti* chapter (c. A.D. 1300–50), quotes no verse from Kauṭilya, though he does quote the *Kāmandakīya*, the former was not known to him.

[4] *Dharma* overrides *artha* where the conflict is direct: *Mitākṣarā* on Yājñ. II, 21. Bṛhaspati I, 111, 113 (Renou, where cited, p. 19). Kāṇe, *H.D.*, III, pp. 8–10. K. V. R. Aiyaṅgār, *Indian Cameralism* (cited above), pp. 47 ff. In *politics* the two are balanced, and if the loss of *artha* would be greater than the gain of *dharma*, *artha* is to be pursued and, if necessary, a penance performed for the breach of *dharma*: Medhātithi on Manu VII, 26 (cf. Manu IV, 176).

[5] See above, p. 149.

itself as the first stage of their duty, and that was sufficiently difficult in view of the discrepancies between the sources. Their aims were, from the later and 'spurious' *smṛti-s* until the end of our period, to interpret traditional statements of law so as to coincide with as many approved customs as possible. It was useless to attempt to cover them in detail. Antique words were retained, and current words were excluded: numbers of technical legal terms familiar at various periods, or current for a time in certain localities, might well have been incorporated, if not in *smṛti-s* at least in the commentaries or the brief notes of the great digests, but they were eschewed as impermanent, for the most part, and local. The umbrella of the *śāstra* was desired to cast the largest possible shadow. The great *smṛtikāra-s* had not been so particular, and the results were instructive: technical terms found there had to be variously interpreted, and were in some cases unintelligible. The history of the word *cāṭa*, 'purveyor', shows that our jurists were right.[1] This has been unfortunate for historians, who find no trace, in what might be thought the proper places, of a description of *nīvi*, 'trust fund',[2] *kuttā* or *guttā*, 'rent',[3] and many other terms that had a long practical life, and who in consequence find it difficult to translate charters which every interested person understood when they were drafted.[4]

But if they avoided such details they tortured their texts,[5]

[1] *B.S.O.A.S.* 21 (1958), pp. 77, 81.

[2] 'Knot of females' lower garments' (*B. Deccan Coll. Res. Inst.*, 8, 1946–7, pp. 162–6); 'inalienable capital fund' (S. K. Maity, where cited, pp. 17, 27); equivalent to the Tamil *mudal keḍāmai* (E.I. xx, p. 53). *Z. f. vergl. Rechtsw.*, 64 (1962), at pp. 68–70.

[3] *B.S.O.A.S.*, 21 (1958), pp. 61 ff. *Z. f. vergl. Rechtsw.*, 64 (1962), at pp. 70–2.

[4] Fiscal terms such as *bhūmicchidra-nyāyena*, perhaps 'trenching the boundary (to plant tell-tale marks)', or 'as if the ground were virgin soil' (?): Maity, pp. 32–41. Then E.I. xxx, pp. 163 ff. is deplorably obscure, crammed as it is with information. Now we have D. C. Sircar's *Indian Epigraphical Glossary* (Delhi, Motilāl Banarsidāss, 1966).

[5] The maxim of *ekavākyatā* required all texts to be unanimous and mutually referable. One method of mutual reference was to assert, under the maxim *daṇḍāpūpa* (*-nyāya*), that if a proposition was stated of one category *a fortiori* all others were comprehended (not excluded!). See *Mitākṣarā* I, ix, 6–11. Inconvenient readings were altered (e.g. *Mitākṣarā* on Yājñ. I, 53; III, 143), and the occurrence of the word *ca*, 'and', enabled additional, unenumerated, items to be inserted by interpretation: e.g.

utilized the doctrines of the *mīmāṃsā* to select one of several apparently unobjectionable alternatives from amongst the confusion of discordant authorities, resurrected *smṛti-s* of dubious origins to condemn *smṛti* rules formerly, they said, good law; artfully distinguished between rules which could and those which could not be ignored in practice; and finally they utilized a most helpful text, which we have already noticed, that allowed public detestation to abrogate a *smṛti* rule—but utilized it, one would think, far too seldom.[1] Successful predecessors amongst the jurists came to be cited as if they were almost as authoritative as the sources themselves.[2] A good jurist cited all authorities, even those opposed to his view, and argued the latter away: but even Vijñāneśvara sometimes failed to perform this duty. The distinction between jurists' propositions were subtle and expressed with a disconcerting brevity. Meticulous accuracy of statement was insisted upon. While early writers accept the possibility that truth may have many faces, and leave the judicial adviser a wide choice of rules all equally authoritative, if mutually incompatible,[3] later authors tend to strive hard to make all sources tell but one tale.

While the *smṛti-s* and their successors in verse form catered for an educated and adult public, the *sūtra-s* had been designed for the aid, so it seems, of law-teachers in academies. Commentaries on *sūtra-s* continued to be produced, as for example

Kullūka on Manu IV, 130; II, 5; *Mitākṣarā* on Yājñ. I, 132, 135; II, 135–6 (p. 221). The word *tathā* could be used for adding whole categories: 'likewise' was not to be used as a term to delimit a category, but as a pointer to further unexpressed items; see below, p. 216, for an example.

[1] See above p. 90, n. 1.

[2] *Mitākṣarā* (Colebrooke, I, vii, 13–14). The *Dāyabhāga* cites Niravadyavidyoddyota (who was he?) as authority for Jīmūtavāhana's peculiar theory: Kāṇe, *H.D.*, I, 323–4.

[3] *Vaikalpike ātmatuṣṭiḥ pramāṇam*: Garga cited by Kullūka on Manu II, 6· Cf. Vyāsa cited in the *Smṛti-candrikā* (Mysore edn., I, p. 17): true *dharma* implies no contradiction but in case of conflict the 'weightier' opinion should be followed. Varadarāja is fond of avoiding a decision (*Vyavahāra-nirṇaya*, pp. 418, 456, 461, 472–3, 476, etc.), but the characteristic is common. The phrase 'others say' does not always introduce the author's own view. The jurist will not exert himself where no practical issue is at stake: *Mitākṣarā* on Yājñ. III, 22 (trans. Naraharayya, p. 48); and many problems in ritual contexts were insoluble: *Mit.* on Yājñ. I, 253–4 (trans. Vidyārṇava, pp. 344–6).

Haradatta's in the twelfth century and Bhavasvāmī on the *Baudhāyana-śrauta-sūtra*, but they were inspired by a desire for the improvement of such esoteric teaching, or for a simple and relatively unembarrassing hook upon which to hang their learning. Commentaries on *smṛti-s* were intended to serve as compendia, as guides for the advanced student, as explanations of their fundamental text for groups which followed them exclusively or mainly,[1] and finally as controversial propositions of law attached to sources, the authority of which would give to the propositions nominally derived from them weight that they might have lacked in any other setting. Alongside the commentaries grew the digest literature, in which law was stated through the sources themselves, with the minimum of comment, but the compiler's service lay in his selection of his material and his interpreting it by skilful juxtaposition. Lakṣmīdhara's *Kṛtyakalpataru* ('The Wishing-Tree of Duty') compiled in the eleventh century, is the best example, serving as a mine for later generations especially in Mithilā, but even much less bulky efforts at digesting, such as Halāyudha's and various other *Smṛtisaṅgraha-s*[2] have failed to find a regular succession of copyists, and the useful digest of Varadarāja survived because it confined itself to law. On the whole the learned public preferred the exhaustive and authoritative exposition of one great *smṛti*. Manu and Yājñavalkya led by a great distance. The *Mitākṣarā* and the gigantic, but not dissimilar, commentary on the same *smṛti* attributed to Aparārka, and the less bulky commentary on Manu by Kullūka in the thirteenth century, met this demand. The conflicts between the digest-commentators at once led to a demand for digests, not of the sources, but of the newer *śāstra* expounded by the various jurists themselves, and, although the great Bhōja's efforts[3] in this direction have perished (perhaps because his views, though logical, were unacceptable to local

[1] Students of Manu: *Hyd. Arch. Ser.*, p. 39 (A.D. 1093). Bhāsa, *Pratimānāṭakam* (*Triv. Skt. Ser.*, No. 42), p. 65. The 'eighteen-fold *dharmaśāstra-s*' were studied at Lokkiguṇḍi: K.I. ii, No. 22, p. 85. A.R.E. 1913, rep. p. 98 (ref. No. 423 of 1906).

[2] *Saṅgraha* or *Smṛtisaṅgraha*: Kāṇe, *H.D.*, I, pp. 239 ff. The frequently cited but anonymous *Caturviṃsati-mata*, ibid., pp. 223 f.; *Ṣaṭtrimśanmata*, ibid., pp. 238 f. There were even other works which purported to give the gist of multifarious *smṛti* texts.

[3] *Mitākṣarā* (Colebrooke), II, i, 8; *B.S.O.A.S.*, 15 (1953), p. 598.

panditry?), his followers, such as Devaṇṇa-bhaṭṭa in the *Smṛti-candrikā*, did magnificent work. A standard work of a later period, the *Dharma-tattva-kalā-nidhi* or *Pṛthvīcandrodaya* attributed to king Pṛthvīcandra, a ruler in North India about the second half of the fifteenth century, serves as an introduction to the bulkier digests of the North, but does not have the juridical richness of the southern productions. The approach, however, enabled fundamental notions to be approached in the abstract, and both the vehicle and the standard were imitated by successors after our period. Little law books were produced plentifully from the twelfth to the fourteenth century: most of them marvels of compression and restatement technique.[1] Not all of them are likely to be printed, and such is the market for such publications that at the time of writing the second part of the *Vyavahāra-prakāśa* of the *Pṛthvīcandrodaya* itself is long overdue from the press. The independent treatise on a particular topic of law, such as Jīmūtavāhana's, was not yet much favoured as a vehicle. Perhaps concentration of such a description lacked prestige-value, though it was amply demanded by the practical situation in India. It may be that efforts of that type soon became obsolete and disappeared, but this is unlikely since such productions flourished in the next period, and have survived in fair numbers.

In all these works a controversialist spirit appears from about the eleventh century onwards. It was only when particular jurists' contributions won wide gratitude that jealousy was aroused. Isolated writers of our period are at times deficient in courtesy, and would have us believe that some interpretations are due to ignorance or stupidity.[2]

Illustrations of Substantive Law

We may now look briefly into some chapters of the medley of the sacred *dharmaśāstra*, customary law, and legislation to obtain a general picture of its character. On the whole the *śāstra* turns a

[1] Nārāyaṇa, pupil of Vijñāneśvara, *Vyavahāra-śiromaṇi: A.O.R.*, 4 (1939–40), pt. 2, Skt. pp. 1–34. Kavikāntasarasvatī, *Viśvādarśa*: text, *J. Univ. Bombay*, 7 (1938), pp. 66–98—but the author's commentary remains unpublished.

[2] *Dāyabhāga* (Colebrooke), I, i; IV, ii, 41; XI, i, 51.

blind eye to the customs of the non-Āryan peoples, in particular non-patrilineal communities, as we have seen.[1] Brahmin specialists in the *śāstra* purported to expound to such castes among them as were fully or partially Brahminized pure Āryan traditions while in fact gradually and unconsciously the latter were contaminated with local biases. Meanwhile the customary law moved towards the *śāstra*, legislation recorded the stages, many a half-way house was tolerated and elsewhere the final adoption of a śāstric rule was triumphantly announced.[2] In the Deccan and the further South these tensions were severe; the same appears to have been the case in the North-West, possibly including Kashmir; while in the North and East the law of the *smṛti-s* appears to have met with the least criticism and the ancient social system to have worked most smoothly. Yet even there, as we shall see, gross deviations from rules found in the *vyavahāra* chapters of *smṛti* were openly tolerated.

Nowhere are the conflicts between the *śāstra* and customs so obvious as in the realm of family law. The *śāstra* nowhere overtly recognizes the high social status and independent capacity of women as known in various parts of the peninsula.[3] The śāstric requirements for a valid marriage–virginity, avoidance of prohibited degrees, compliance with grounds before the supersession of an existing wife–all were neglected by large communities.[4] Smaller but by no means negligible groups allowed polyandry, both in fraternal and other forms. While the *śāstra* now saw the husband as the virtual owner of his wife and children–a view by no means extinct in all parts of India throughout our period[5]–capable of lending his wife to a stranger for purposes of procreation and of selling his daughter in mar-

[1] Above, pp. 102–3, 159. [2] Instances given in n. 3 at p. 181 below.

[3] Reigning queens are found in the Koṅkaṇ and in Orissa (*J.O.R.*, 18 (1950), pp. 49–51) and elsewhere (E.I. xxix, p. 82). Female governors and generals are repeatedly evidenced from the Deccan and a female judge from the far South. Females took gifts for their own purposes and in some communities dealt with property independently.

[4] See chapter 11 below.

[5] *Z. f. vergl. Rechtsw.* 64 (1962) at p. 99. Medhātithi on Manu III, 27, IX, 27, 135. Wives could be given as *dakṣiṇā* (ceremonial present). R. C. Agrawala, *I.H.Q.*, 28 (1952), pp. 327–41. The wife is *urimai*, 'property', at E.I. xxii, p. 53. Self-sale affects some relations and all descendants: *Taḍuttātkoṇḍa-purāṇam, vv.* 51–63: *Cōḷas*[1], I, pp. 257–9; *A.O.R.*, 6 (1942), pp. 83 ff.

riage[1] or for prostitution and his sons into slavery, customs gave the married couple equal rights in the matrimonial property[2] and, especially but by no means exclusively in South India, allowed a wife and a widow to alienate property, even the property inherited from a male owner, without the consent of near agnates of the latter,[3] and restricted the sons' freedom in respect of their deceased father's property while his widow or widows survived.[4] The *śāstra* no longer permitted divorce or nullity.[5] Custom admitted both.[6] Remarriage of widows, anathema to the *śāstra*, regularly occurred.[7] The Āryan rule that the father had an absolute right in the person and property of his son[8] was much diluted, even in the *śāstra*, by the growing rights, under the influence of customs, of the male issue to question dealings with ancestral property otherwise than for family necessity and religious purposes. In practice the South retained its customary concern for the 'rights' of agnates and cognates to supervise dealings with property, and the consent of many relations is regularly taken to a man's transactions though they would hardly be regarded in the *śāstra* as having any substantial claim.[9] Influential śāstric writers, such as Vijñāneśvara,

[1] On the Āsura form see above, p. 87. The sale of daughters is deprecated in so late a work as the *Mahānirvāṇa-tantra*, XI, 84, p. 339.

[2] See below, p. 411, n. 2.

[3] An example of the reverse: E.C. vi Chik. 83. Valuable discussions by D. R. Bhandarkar, E.I. xxii, pp. 98, 100–2, and A. S. Altekar, *Position of Women in Hindu Civilization*², (Benaras, 1956), where inscriptional material is sifted.

[4] See below, p. 412. Joint heirship of sons and widow is indicated in S.I.I. xii, 199 and 224.

[5] See *A.* v. *B.*, cited below, p. 440. But cf. Medhātithi on Manu IX, 203 (where the eunuch's right to marry is asserted), and the *Smṛti-candrikā* (Mysore edn.), I, p. 221 (the remarriage of girls whose marriage has not been consummated was possible only in earlier *yuga-s*, 'ages'): the latter text being put in context in the study of S. K. Tewari, 'Nullity of Marriage in Modern Hindu Law', Thesis, Ph.D., London (unpublished), 1965, pp. 82–3.

[6] *Lekhapaddhati*, p. 52 (divorce deed). The *Mahānirvāṇa-tantra*, XI, 66, p. 334 recognizes divorce.

[7] Hemacandra condemns such unions at *Triṣaṣṭiśalākā-puruṣacaritra*, III, 87–8.

[8] Below, p. 409.

[9] Below, p. 408. E.C. vi Koppa, 53, 54 (early fifteenth cent.); v. Chann., 186, 242; K.I. iii, 6 reflect the śāstric position if the persons mentioned were joint.

ignore an institution as important and pervasive as pre-emption.[1] Of the practice of adoption during our period little is known, for it became popular as an academic topic later, and perhaps was little used, or if used, conveyed minor rights.[2] That *devadāsī-s* recruited partly by adoption we know,[3] but that was a practice for which the *śāstra* made no provision. The *śāstra* said that elder sons were *not* entitled to preferential shares: but in fact they sometimes took them.[4] Inheritance, according to the *śāstra*, went to agnates, and then to cognates (except that in Jīmūtavāhana's view some cognates should be promoted amongst the agnates), with the widow and then the daughter taking immediately after male issue of the *propositus*. The widow's position was controversial, since, on account of her possible remarriage (which the *śāstra* virtually ignores),[5] she might take property from one family to another. Vijñāneśvara plainly served local sympathies well when he allowed the widow to inherit only when her sonless husband was divided and unreunited, a circumstance which was then rare.[6] But inscriptions and other sources make it plain that the śāstric law was little observed, that property was seized by the king or his assignee in the absence of sons, grandsons, or greatgrandsons, and that it was a great favour on the king's part to allow property to pass to śāstric heirs.[7] When the people were inclined

[1] See above, p. 161.

[2] A rare instance, settling a quarrel: A.R.S.I.E. 1939–40 to 1942–3, p. 241.

[3] A.R.S.I.E. 1936–7, st. ins. No. 151: a woman adopts a goddess, endows her with her *strīdhanam*, and celebrates her marriage: this is reminiscent of adoption of daughters amongst *devadāsī-s* and in Kerala.

[4] On the law the *Mitākṣarā* and the *Dāyabhāga* are agreed. In an inscription contemporary with both authors (Munirabad Stone Inscription of Vikramāditya VI, dated the equivalent of A.D. 1088: A.R.I.E. 1959–60, st. ins. No. 483) the land donated is called the *jeṣṭhāṃsada-bhūmi* (*sic*), 'the land of the elder brother's (preferential) share'–and the prevalence of *jyeṣṭhāṃśa* in Northern Indian customs is well known.

[5] See below, p. 235, n. 1.

[6] See below, p. 416. Also *J.R.A.S.*, 1958, pp. 17 ff.

[7] Bṛhaspati cited in *Dāyabhāga* XI, i, 49; *J.B.O.R.S.*, 24 (1938), p. 14; E.I. xx, p. 64; xxv, p. 237; *āputrakaṃ na grāhyaṃ*: E.I. xxx, p. 163 ff. (the property of sonless persons is not to be seized). Kālidāsa, *Śākuntalaṃ*, Act VI. *Moharājaparājaya*, III, 57: Majumdār, *Chaulukyas*, p. 247; cf. M.A.R. 1940, 14; Ibn Batūta in K. A. N. Śāstrī, *For. Not.*, p. 239 (Muslim decedents' privilege); also the problem of Hindus in Goa (reference cited at p. 282, n. 3 below).

to alter their own succession laws or conveyed property subject to the condition that it should pass to heirs other than those recognized by the customary law applicable, they frequently chose a system different from the śāstric.[1] We find a preference for the younger brother, and the inclusion of the son-in-law (who now appears only in Āndhra customary law under the name of *illatom*) and the father-in-law; and we find distinctions such as the *śāstra* never admitted between divided and undivided relations (preserved in modern usage, but not accepted by the courts). What was the outlook of the sacred *śāstra* on such provisions? Fortunately we have a piece of evidence which, though slight, speaks volumes. Kings, and private persons, used to make grants to *agrahāra-s* and otherwise subject to a bar on alienation: there was no point in endowing an *agrahāra* if the inmates sold their shares and drank the proceeds. But the time might come when the managing committee of the *agrahāra*, or the trustees of the temple, or whoever might be in charge of property so dedicated or granted, might *bona fide* wish to re-arrange the capital, and the founder's dynasty might have passed away and the successor royal family might be quite indifferent to such a proceeding. Devaṇṇa-bhaṭṭa, of whom we have already spoken highly, commenting upon a text of Kātyāyana, says that restrictions upon alienation are repugnant to the *śāstra's* definition of Property (which understands the acquirer to have in the object acquired the right of disposal at pleasure) a definition which was required for sacrificial purposes, as we have seen.[2] All such restrictive conditions in grants are repugnant to the *śrauta-smārta-mārga*, the fundamental principles of the sacred legal system, and are therefore void.[3] One looks eagerly in the

[1] E.C. iii Mal. 114; T.N. 21; ix Chann. 73; Nel. 12; Kan. 81; M.A.R. 1920, para. 77; A.R.E. 1919, st. ins. Nos. 429, 538 of 1918; E.C. iv Heg. 88; S.I.I. x, 221. Also p. 210, n. 4 below.

[2] Above, p. 167, n. 1. *Smṛti-candrikā* on Kātyāyana 669: III, 525–6. For the definition of property see above, p. 130, and *Z. f. vergl. Rechtsw.*, 64 (1962), at pp. 113 ff.

[3] For examples of grants subject to restrictions on enjoyment, especially to *agrahāra-s*, see Sirpur (Dt. Raipur) Stone Inscription of Mahāśivagupta (eighth–ninth cent.) *vv.* 31–7; M.A.R. 1916, para. 60, No. 193 of 1916 (inalienable property granted). E.C. xii Chikn. 2, p. 117. A.R.E. 1902, No. 118; 1937–8, No. 512. E.I., xxx, pp. 71 ff. Conditions restrictive of the order of devolution are found in E.I. xxix, pp. 203–7; K.I. iii, No. 13 (sixteenth cent.). Thus grants importing conditions were common. Kauṭilya,

books of Devaṇṇa's successors, to the places where they certainly had his text before them when they themselves wrote: but no trace of the point is to be found, for, evidently, the theory did not win adherents in practice and was best left to sleep where we found it not so long ago. So it is quite possible that *śāstrī-s* objected to those regulations regarding descent of property, but without effect.

The *śūdra's dāsiputra*, the favoured illegitimate son, is usually supposed to have been a pre-Āryan customary heir, retained with reluctance by the *śāstra*:[1] but surviving documents show clearly that in some parts of the South the presumption was against such a person's claims to inherit, as contrasted with maintenance.[2] Varadarāja, whose interest in practical details we have already noticed, cites (wrongly?) no less an authority than Bṛhaspati for the rule that the son of a *twice-born* man by a *śūdra* woman, provided he is the only son, was entitled to take half the estate.[3] Such a proposition, which cuts across the basic rule of the personal law that only the illegitimate son by a *śūdra* woman of a *śūdra* male can in some circumstances take a half of the estate, may indicate that in the South anomalous notions crept at least for a time into the *śāstra* itself. Matriliny in Malabar, though it must have existed, is not well evidenced. But that descent of a male's property through females by preference was an acceptable rule in Malabar is attested by some surviving conveyances.[4] The most striking of all anomalies is the imposition by a Cōḷa king of a death duty upon the estates of male and female Brahmins:[5] the property of Brahmins was 'poison of poisons', and the *śāstra* insisted that it should not pass, by any title, into the king's hands.[6] The Pious Obligation of sons to substantiate their male lineal ancestors' untainted acts in respect

Arthaś., II, 1, 7 (Kāṅgle's trans., p. 63) recognized grants subject to restrictions on alienation. Was Devaṇṇa unaware of this or was he, rather, of the view that the *dharmaśāstra* (in a śāstric work) must prevail?

[1] Kāṇe, *H.D.*, III, pp. 600 ff. Below, p. 408.

[2] Otherwise they would not be specifically provided for: E.C. v Bel. 219; vi Chik. 105; ix Chann. 73; M.A.R. 1933, 48; E.C. i, 59.

[3] At p. 429. Renou, *Ét. Ved. Pāṇ.* (cited above), 11 (1963), p. 123.

[4] E.I. xxix, pp. 203–7; but cf. K.I. iii, pt. 1, No. 13 = B.K. 1939–40, 76.

[5] A.R.S.I.E. 1939–40 to 1942–3, p. 239.

[6] Kāṇe, *H.D.*, III, pp. 190, 228, 384; II, 1273 (text No. 11).

of family properties is attested,[1] and proves that a deep-rooted feeling, never adequately expressed in the *śāstra*, long preceded its efflorescence in Anglo-Hindu law.

It will be recollected that whereas the king was nominally the fount of justice in criminal cases, and other cases brought to him by a complainant, there were jurisdictions of the greatest importance which acknowledged the individual's right to approach the king, if at all, only by way of application for review or in default of justice. To take an example, an inscription speaks of usurpations that took place under a *de facto* régime following upon a foreign invasion, in the course of which members of the village assembly were put under restraint, and the usurper sequestrated lands and disposed of them unlawfully. It was two years before the aggrieved owners could take the matter to the king and obtain restitution.[2] Since, apparently, the authorities of the village were in collusion with the rascals, we are told, in another inscription, that a group of brothers, headed by one who was consorting with a Brahmin widow (the operative complaint?) and engaged in large-scale misappropriations of temple properties of which they were the trustees, were ultimately brought before the king and–we gather–their misdeeds were corrected.[3] Such appeals to the king or his deputy might be difficult indeed, as a characteristic inscription testifies. Some Brahmins acquired lands in a village within the kingdom of Kanauj by methods which were obviously resented, and the inhabitants petitioned the ruler, who was obliged to enquire into the conduct of a public servant. He caused a record of his decision to be erected in a public place bearing the information that the greedy (*lampaṭa*) Brahmins of Suvarṇahala obtained from a named servant of the king a *ku-tāmra* ('false copper-plate grant', not necessarily forged) by fraud, having bribed him (*utkōcaṃ dattvā*), and no reliance should be placed in the said grant and the Brahmins owned no land in the villages in the neighbourhood.[4]

[1] M.A.R. 1911–12, para. 91.

[2] A.R.E. 1909, st. ins. No. 133 of 1908, rep., p. 83, para. 28.

[3] See above, p. 181, n. 6.

[4] E.I. xxxv, No. 5 (A.D. 1169). The guilt of the official exceeded that particularized for the highest punishment in Yājñ. II, 295a. A similar event is referred to in E.I. i, No. 11, p. 73, l. 10 (A.D. 631). On *kūṭa-śāsana* ('false muniment' or 'false order') see Medhātithi on Manu VIII, 148

There was some reluctance on the part of trade and professional guilds and of committees of ritual specialists to permit a dispute of a domestic character to go before the court:[1] they would expel a member rather than allow their secrets to be ventilated in public or their complex law to be expounded before a possibly critical, and to their minds unlearned judge. The power to impose fines on their members is found in their hands from early times.[2] Commercial dealings between a guild-member and a stranger, or ordinary transactions between members of different groups would naturally be suitable for the king's court or that of his appropriate deputy. The *smṛti-s* themselves contain ample material on various types of contract, and it is evident that great freedom of contractual power was available provided the parties were of adequate capacity by their respective customary laws. The jurists however do not elaborate, or complete this branch of *vyavahāra*. An episode well known to modern Hindu law crops up in an inscription dated in the equivalent of 1396: a *mahant* mortgaged *maṭha* lands and these were redeemed in the interest of the *maṭha* by a friend of the next succeeding *mahant*.[3] But the law of mortgage as such is not set out anywhere. It was useless for the jurists to expatiate on bills of exchange or the dozens of types of mortgages when the general principles found in the *smṛti-s* could serve in the king's court, and details of promissory notes[4] and the rest would be out of place in works not likely to be consulted by the tribunals which would actually handle the matters in question. Banking law was not brought up to date. The *śāstra* expatiates on two important topics, which reveal the position. A depositor of a permanent deposit with a trade guild might obtain anything from ½ per cent to 75 per cent on his capital;[5] a short-term deposit might produce less, but we cannot be sure. A money-

(trans., p. 178), also the actual expression used in our inscription explained, at Medhātithi on Manu IX, 232.

[1] Texts at Kāṇe, *H.D.*, III, pp. 283–4. Medhātithi on Manu VIII, 2 (trans., IV, pt. 1, p. 7).

[2] *Agnipurāṇa*, cclvi, 42.

[3] E.I. xxxii (1957–8), No. 29, pp. 229 ff. (A.D. 1396).

[4] K. A. N. Śāstrī, *Cōḷas*[2], p. 599. They may not have been negotiable. A *rāja-huṇḍikā* ('royal promissory note') appears at *Lekhapaddhati*, p. 10.

[5] Derrett, *Hoysaḷas*, p. 231. *Lekhapaddhati*, p. 38, mentions 24 per cent per annum.

lender could count on 200 per cent per annum or more, though the amount would doubtless vary with the status of the borrower and the presence or otherwise of a security: but although it was perfectly legal to torture a debtor to encourage him to be more active, or to disclose his assets,[1] the *śāstra* contents itself with describing the 'just' interest to which a lender was entitled, which turns out in every case to be much less than what we know was obtained.[2] Whereas it is essential for such expanding and enterprising business communities as we know grew in India during our period to have available a law of limitation of actions, the jurists exercised their ingenuity against it, and it seems as if this perverse attitude, to which we have already alluded,[3] was not without backing in public opinion. The persisting rule in India that interest on coin or bullion should not at any one time exceed the principal debt could have been far better expounded in the *śāstra*.[4] The corresponding texts on the maximum amount of interest available on loans of commodities have a forlorn air, as if no usage took them seriously.

On the law of crime we are remarkably well informed. Elaborate studies of *daṇḍa*, the royal prerogative of punishment by force (as opposed to excommunication), appear only after our period, but the theory is well worked out–punishment should fit the crime and be deterrent–and the principal crimes of violence and their analogues, with specimen penalties, and variations in view of the castes of the offender and offended, with distinctions appropriate to the system but foreign, sometimes, to western notions, are described in all the general juridical works.[5] Two principles enunciated by commentators deserve mention: the punishment where the guilty party confesses should be half that prescribed in the *smṛti*; and the penalties stated in the *smṛti* as if they were absolute are really

[1] Abhayatilaka-gaṇi on Hemacandra's *Dvyāśraya* III, 40: Majumdār, *Chaulukyas*, p. 284. Inscriptions refer to temporary asylums, to enable (it seems) debtors to find securities, etc.

[2] Kāṇe, *H.D.*, III, 420 ff. *Z. f. vergl. Rechtsw.* 65, pt. 2 (1963), pp. 172–82.

[3] See above, p. 129. But a plea of long possession might not be final in actual litigation: A.R.E. 1921, st. ins. No. 571 of 1920: *Cōḷas*[2], p. 514.

[4] *Lekhapaddhati*, pp. 34–5. Majumdār, where cited, p. 275. Kāṇe, *H.D.*, III, pp. 423 ff.

[5] Kāṇe, *H.D.*, III, index, 'Crime'.

maxima because the king's duty is to achieve the political purpose which lies behind the *śāstra*, and if this can be achieved with a lesser penalty (and likewise if it cannot be achieved without a heavier penalty) the text may be ignored.[1] It is noteworthy that the *śāstra* aims at the objective punishing of wrongs and seeks to prevent the compounding of offences, or the elimination, as we should say, of the criminal element in favour of the tortious. The judicial administrator is no mere arbitrator but a servant (or even incarnation) of *dharma* or *daṇḍa* personified.[2] Custom allowed some methods of execution, for example, impalement, trampling by elephants, tying to the leg of a buffalo, all harsher than are admitted in the *śāstra*, and the attitude to relative heinousness varied greatly from district to district, probably as the proneness to commit offences varied. Adultery with a widow would be fined in some places but not others; drawing a dagger would be fined more heavily than stabbing in some places; in some, again, a bachelor's fornication with a low-caste female would be punished as heavily as the rape of a virgin.[3] These and many other details of the attitudes of communities, all varying more or less from the śāstric pattern, can be obtained from copies of charters given by the king or his officer to a corporation invested with power to levy, and keep, fines or execute a death sentence without reference to the king.[4] Husbands killed low-caste adulterers *who might otherwise escape trial.*[5] Medhātithi tells us that in his day staring at the king's wife, and spying (a perennial Indian occupation) were, or

[1] Bhāruci on Manu IX, 249 (followed by Medhātithi), 280, 289.

[2] Medhātithi on Manu VIII, 56 (trans., IV, pt. 1, pp. 76–7) is revealing; cf. P. K. Gode, cited below, p. 273, n. 9. Kāṇe's treatment of criminal law appears in *H.D.*, III. An interesting account of the same by an anonymous hand (K. P. Jayaswal?) appears at *Calcutta Weekly Notes*, 15 (1911), pp. xlii ff., li ff., lviii ff., lxvi ff., lxxv ff., lxxxii ff., xcviii ff., cvii ff., cxvi ff., cxxxi ff., cxxxviii ff.

[3] Strict attitudes to seduction and adultery are evidenced at R. Williams, *Jaina Yoga* (London, 1963), pp. 250–1.

[4] E.I. xv, pp. 79 ff.; xx, pp. 64 ff.; xxv, p. 237; xxx, pp. 163 ff., 283 ff.; S.I.I. ix, pt. 1, 77, 102; *Hyd. Arch. Ser.* No. 7, p. 7. S. Lévy, *Le Népal*, III, 1938: the *body* there went to the king (for punishment), the wife and property to the community-grantees (for confiscation). K. A. N. Śāstrī, *For. Not.*, pp. 125–6, 147.

[5] *Mitākṣarā* on Yājñ. II, 286, obviously bending *śāstra* to meet usage.

could be, crimes:[1] if so they were so by royal order, and not by virtue of explicit statement in the *śāstra.*

Civil wrong and crime are difficult to distinguish. The normal procedure was for the defendant tried on the complaint of a subject to suffer a fine, or, perhaps, the most popular penalty, confiscation of all property, with provision for payment of compensation to be paid to the complainant in a suitable case.[2] Thus when *X* rapes *A*'s daughter, or runs away from *A*'s fields after having contracted to work in them, *A* can ask the king to punish *X* and to oblige him to pay *A* compensation. The king or his officer was expected to make good losses due to unpunished thieves,[3] but when villages were granted the rulers could impose upon the grantees the responsibility for robberies committed in them,[4] and thus pass their duty on to the revenue-payer. A village so placed, and indeed others, might make alternative arrangements in the way of insurance with the local banditry (a system that endured in the Tamil country well into the British period). In an accidental killing the slayer might have to pay a penalty to the State, which, in many 'liberties' of South India, turned out to be the village temple, compensation to the victim's relations, and money for a lamp to be burnt in the temple as expiation: needless to say an intentional killing might end with heavier, if similar penalties.[5] Occasional instances are found of reactionary punishments, which stretch beyond not merely what the *śāstra* allows but also what humanity and common sense prescribe. Collective fines are mentioned by Medhātithi, but presumably as instances of what happens, not what should happen – a distinction he is quite capable of making. A king punishing the murderers of his relation confiscated not only the culprits' property, but also that of their relations by blood *and by marriage.*[6] Medhātithi shows that the practice

[1] Medhātithi on Manu VIII, 125.

[2] The principle is disclosed in Manu VIII, 288; IX, 285; Nārada VI, 7–8; XI, 28–31; Bṛh. (Aiy.) XVI, 3–5; XVIII, 3, 4, 7, 9; XXII, 13, 18. When all property is confiscated the workman's tools, and the like, are exempt.

[3] E.I. xv, pp. 77–9.

[4] A.R.I.E., 1959–60, Copper-plate ins. No. 14 (thirteenth cent.).

[5] A.R.E. 1930, st. ins. No. 200 of 1929. Mahāliṅgam, *S. Indian Polity* and K. A. N. Śāstrī's *Cōḷas* and *Pāṇḍyas* afford more examples. The *śāstra* believed that murder could be wiped off by charity: Manu XI, 130.

[6] E.I. xxi, pp. 169–70 (A.D. 988); *Cōḷas*[2], p. 511; cf. E.I. xv, p. 79 ff.

recognized by the *śāstra* was, to our minds, drastic enough;[1] and he recommends in another place that only the offenders and not their close associates should be destroyed.[2] To recover overdue revenue, attachment and auction of property were normal procedures.[3] Where the settlement was, as usual, with groups or societies rather than with individuals, the right to recover from defaulters lay with assessees, who naturally confiscated the shares in question and sold them to raise the amount of the losses. Vendettas appear not to have been unknown, and if a murderer was killed by his victim's avenger his own descendants were entitled to escape a penalty,[4] such as the confiscation of all the culprit's property would naturally have meant to them.

The aggrieved party's chief difficulty was to find a court which would come to a decision. Complaints against government officers could in practice only come before the king, and were sometimes strikingly successful.[5] Lesser persons might refuse to co-operate, and self-help and the various ancient types of distress (compulsion) subsequently known collectively as *dharnā*, were frequently resorted to.[6] Protestations of righteousness, when backed by a willingness to commit suicide or wound oneself severely, might stave off litigation, which was nearly as good as winning a case.[7] Causing a woman to tear her ear-lobe, or driving her to suicide were in some places crimes, and there can be no doubt but that parties traded on a known weakness to give way to vigorous, and apparently desperate protests. There is a śāstric passage on this subject which is little known and deserves attention.[8] In *Yājñavalkya-smṛti* III, 227 there appears the word *tathā* ('likewise'). This gives Vijñāneśvara the opportunity of including amongst mortal sinners those who abet

[1] On Manu VII, 9. [2] On Manu VII, 110 (trans., p. 352).

[3] S.I.I. xii, 199. Kāṇe, III, 495.

[4] A.R.E. 1924, st. ins. Nos. 301–3 of 1923.

[5] S.I.I. ix, pt. 1, 169. On the tact needed in instituting complaints: Medhātithi on Manu VIII, 1. Lingat, *Sources*, p. 280.

[6] A.Ṛ.E. 1912, st ins. No. 512 of 1911 = E.C. ix Cp. 129. For excessive self-help: A.R.E. 1907, rep. p. 77 (concubine's lover stabbed to death). Creditors sent their agents to collect and the latter had to be fed while they waited for payment: A.R.E. 1912, st. ins. No. 512 of 1911; 1913, rep. p. 85.

[7] A.R.S.I.E. 1939–40 to 1942–3, st. ins. No. 162, 1942–3; M.A.R. 1933, 48. At A.R.E. 1907, rep. p. 77, we hear of a woman taking poison to avoid taxes: the official is condemned (!).

[8] *Mitākṣarā* on Yājñ. III, 227 (trans. Naraharayya, pp. 187–92).

crimes in various sorts of abetment. He then cites an unknown pair of verses attributed (falsely?) to Viṣṇu[1] which say that a man must be held to be (as guilty as a) Brahmin-slayer who is the cause of a person's committing suicide due to abuse, beating, or deprivation of the rights of property, likewise when he commits suicide on behalf of a relation, friend, his wife, his dear ones or a field (or perhaps, 'a friend's field'). The commentator adds that this is no less a sin because there are some people who will lose their balance for nothing at all, in which case the person indicated by the suicide has not done anything wrong. It was therefore possible to blackmail an enemy by committing suicide, and doubtless this was a valuable threat in the case of individuals who had nothing but their lives at stake. Medhātithi too throws light on this superstition. One may bring pressure to bear on an alleged wrongdoer by starving oneself, etc. because of the theory that the wrongdoer indirectly caused any harm which the aggrieved party might incur.

In the north of India the śāstric provision of a judge-interlocutor assisted by learned assessors and by qualified *amici curiae* degenerated into a small court of judge and one or more assessors. The readiness of the public in that quarter to acquiesce in the judgements of a single commissioner or government official, a readiness which reflects upon the state of social order, led by the end of our period to the disappearance even of the assessor.[2] Ministers claim to advise their king on points of *śāstra*, and kings would boast of their judging according to it, but this does not prove that courts in fact carried out the detailed requirements of the relevant śāstric sections. Professional counsel were nowhere admitted, doubtless to the advantage of the administration of justice, for 'next friends' were always allowed to assist a party with his personal pleadings:[3] but their exclusion deprived the system of a rule of precedent and of the literature to which their employment would have given rise. In South India government officials lent the judicial assemblies their weight, and attempted to dissuade by threats of displeasure a defeated party, who had (as was regular) accepted

[1] Not traced in the Adyar *Viṣṇu-smṛti* (1964).

[2] Kāṇe, *H.D.*, III, pp. 270 ff. Vācaspati-miśra, *Vyavahāra-cintāmaṇi*, ed. Rocher, gives no information about *sabhya-s*.

[3] Kāṇe, *H.D.*, III, pp. 288 ff.

the decision, from reopening the case before another gathering.[1] But there the most normal constituents of the court were the notables of the district, spiritual and secular, and every effort was made to convene all prestige-worthy elements from as far afield from the affected region as might be.[2] Local knowledge and disinterestedness were both called upon. No doubt the śāstric rule was observed that complainants should give where possible security to prosecute and defendants security to abide by the decision and pay the fine, if any. The śāstric rules can hardly have been in general use, however, to the effect that when the court had decided upon which party lay the burden of proof, that party's witnesses or documents won or lost his case for him without reference to the other party's case. There may have been instances where this would be appropriate. But hardly in a commercial case where, as we are told, the king sat and decided in accordance with the award of a skilled referee,[3] who of course could not administer ordeals and would care little for the book-law on evidence. Ordeals, which were an alternative to 'human evidence' in a gradually diminishing circle of disputes, seem to have been used in such ways, amongst others, that even that party might be subjected to an ordeal, e.g. the accused in a case of embezzlement, upon whom in the natural course of things no *prima facie* burden would lie.[4] Medhātithi says in passing that failures in ordeals were very rare.[5] An instance of the use of them may be cited to show how appeals to religion actually operated. There was a dispute over land[6] and a commission was appointed to settle the matter. The date was 1241. The two parties were apprehended and both made a *pratijñā* (oath?) and made their respective statements. One said he had paid the money to the female and a male and had received possession of the land. The other said he had received no money and had not delivered the parcel in question. The one

[1] Failures: A.R.E. 1922, st. ins. No. 416 of 1921; see above, p. 162, n. 1; cf. the sanction of the *rājaguru* and the *samaya* in M.A.R. 1910–11, para. 105.

[2] E.g. M.A.R. 1915–16, para. 88; A.R.I.E. 1946–7, st. ins. No. 248.

[3] Medhātithi on Manu VIII, 157 (trans., p. 200).

[4] Periodical ordeals for village accountants: *Cōḷas*[2], pp. 510–1. A successful application?: A.R.E. 1907, st. ins. No. 372 of 1906. For doubts about their efficacy see the discussion referred to in the next note.

[5] Medhātithi on Manu VIII, 116 (trans. IV, pt. 1, p. 145).

[6] E.C. viii Sb. 387 (A.D. 1241).

party held the *divya* (object used in the ordeal) before the goddess Kāli of Bandaṇike, while the other stood with his head 'hanging down'. The first then was given his *jaya-patra*, or certificate of having won his case, and the circumstances were carved on stone so that the whole of that little world knew all about it for ever.

The subject is obscure, but we may notice a creditable aspect of the work of the jurists revealed in the contrast between Varadarāja's and Devaṇṇa-bhaṭṭa's treatments of ordeals. The latter declines to treat of the ordeals of water and poison as these had gone out of use (in the regions for which he was catering), whereas his predecessor retained the particulars (and an important successor likewise), presumably supposing that obsolescence in some quarters did not mean obsolescence in all.[1] To return to our topic, the value of a judicial decision would be appraised less from its approximation to abstract justice than from its aptness to please (or displease) both parties, to compromise their conflicting claims, and to prevent their reopening the matter upon some pretext later. Pathetic attempts to bind reluctant parties to such compromises are not uncommon.[2] Bṛhaspati once again is shown as saying openly what must have been the usual practice: 'Where *dharma* is doubtful and the *vyavahāra* is before the king an accord (*sandhi*) must be made, as between two heated irons.'[3] The mental image of two angry litigants, whose rights are unclear, being forced to come to an agreement or compromise by a king hammering them like a smith hammering red-hot iron is certainly forceful. When the irons cool they cannot again be separated provided they have been hit hard enough. What was wanted was not only a compromise, but one that stayed binding upon those who were brought to agree to it.

The law relating to evidence and ordeals becomes elaborate after our period. Documents are already much more than memoranda of oral transactions, and legal draftsmanship is already an established art.[4] Much that is found in the *śāstra*

[1] Introduction to the *Vyavahāra-nirṇaya* of Varadarāja (ed. K. V. R. Aiyaṅgār), pp. lxix–lxx.

[2] E.C. v Chann. 170.

[3] III, 46 (Aiyaṅgār, p. 43) (Renou, where cited, p. 41).

[4] Both the *Lekhapaddhati* and the *Lokaprakāśa* are old precedent-books,

must have been near the practice of the people: e.g., that prestige-worthy witnesses are better than others, and that only when the witnesses fail to tally, and their worthiness is equal, should the court follow the majority of them.[1] We know that notorious 'sinners' (in local terms) could not act as sureties[2] and it is very likely that they could not act as witnesses. Witnesses were sometimes sworn, according to śāstric recommendation. An oath consisted of placing the hand on the head of the witness's son, wife, etc., and invoking evil.[3] The long history of objections to oath-taking has still to be worked out and we are left with an impression that the complaint was largely social in origin. Oaths seem not to have been taken to confirm contracts.[4] The *śāstra's* failure to distinguish cogency from admissibility in evidence is disappointing, though judges must have been aware of it; and the appearance in a charter of different penalties for a crime according to whether it is evidenced directly or circumstantially or otherwise has a distinctly amateurish air,[5] not unknown, though usually deplored, in other civilizations. The judge's discretion to vary the penalty according to the caste of the offender is explicitly stated in one charter,[6] but may be read into all śāstric laws of criminal sentence and penance. Failure to obey the court's order led to death if the court was that of the king or of one of his assignee's of criminal jurisdiction, or to excommunication if it were the court of a community. We hear little of imprisonments and enslavements (though both existed), but much of fines.

Sources by no means hostile to political arrangements of their day inform us that professional judges or regular members of courts (perhaps in towns in particular) were corruptible.[7] Certainly to take a present from each side was not inconsistent

brought 'up-to-date' by subsequent editing: cf. an actual deed of mortgage of A.D. 1212: E.I. xxv, pp. 1 ff.

[1] Manu VIII, 73; Yājñ. II, 78; Nārada I, 229–30.

[2] Marco Polo in *For. Not.*, p. 169.

[3] Medhātithi on Manu VIII, 110 (cf. Manu VIII, 114).

[4] Kalhaṇa, *Rājataraṅgiṇī* provides an example of an oath over a quartered goat. The *Arthaśāstra* curiously recommends hearty oaths to seal treaties (the breaking of which it recommends under certain circumstances).

[5] E.I. xxv, p. 237.

[6] E.I. xx, 64 f.; cf. Kāṇe, *H.D.*, III, p. 395.

[7] *Mattavilāsa-prahasaṇam*, 33: Mīnākshī, *Administration and Social Life under the Pallavas* (Madras, 1938), p. 58. Medhātithi on Manu VIII, 45.

with judicial integrity: it gave them an interest in their work. Medhātithi speaks also of witnesses taking bribes to tell lies.[1] Perhaps for this reason merchants in particular were keen to have their own courts, and at any rate in the South jurisdictions multiplied. These courts appeared to have consisted of a large, fluctuating, and representative (though not elective) membership, and will have given just decisions–just, that is to say, according to local notions of justice. The expenses and uncertainties of litigation in the king's court, of which Medhātithi does not fail to take note,[2] would be avoided.

Conclusions

The system described was groping for unity. The *śāstra* was preaching cultural and jurisprudential harmony if not homogeneity. Gradually anomalous customs began to give way.[3] Processes started in the fourth and fifth centuries are beginning to bear fruit in the twentieth. But substantial success was achieved even during our limited period. Meat-eating and spirit-drinking became unfashionable and eventually objectionable, widow-marriage and divorce became rare in respectable classes, vicarious procreation of children and promiscuous adoptions of sons were looked down upon, many humane and intelligent doctrines percolated through hostile layers of custom and prejudice. 'Hinduization' progressed upon legal as well as religious fronts. But the hard core of convenience stood out against theory, and to this day some ancient customary elements have succeeded in defying śāstric pronouncements–even those which were never compromised by dilution and customary material. Witnesses are not more truthful than they were a thousand years ago. 'Religious' suicides are now rare, oaths to

[1] On Manu IV, 170.

[2] On Manu VII, 12. The gross miscarriage of justice, lack of judicial independence, and superficial attention to *smṛti-s* demonstrated in so celebrated a drama as the *Mṛcchakaṭikā* gives the reader no very exalted idea of the judicial process in contemporary times. H. S. Ursekar, 'Court scene in Mṛcchakaṭikā', *Velankar Commemoration Volume* (1965), pp. 180–9.

[3] Lingat (*Sources*, p. 227) compares the influence of Roman law during the Middle Ages upon the French customs of the regions principally governed by customary law. In either case the 'written law' had a delimiting effect upon custom.

maintain unity in spite of king and country are unheard of, but the right to be a *sannyāsī* though one is a *śūdra*, to marry a widow, and to reject a spouse who is impotent or insane, have reasserted themselves in spite of all the pressure of orthodox opinion based upon the *śāstra* and its teachings.[1]

The unity of the *śāstra* itself was threatened during our period, and before it ended different schools of law appeared.[2] These were not the distinct schools known to Islamic tradition, but they were sufficiently unlike in the interpretation of a few basic texts that reconciliation, often attempted, proved impossible. The state of public order especially in the Deccan and further South[3] was often so poor, the need for tranquillity so dominant, that the practical giving of justice often took second place to political considerations; the Brahmins themselves knew that this could be cured only by empires, they advised acquisitive war, and worsened the symptoms they hoped to alleviate.[4] In view of the way in which officials disregarded what we nowadays call the rule of law, even in good times,[5] and the peculiar prevalence of dacoits, who often shared the plunder with prestige-worthy persons and official partners in crime,[6] it is astonishing that the *śāstra* impressed itself so widely as it did. But it never had time to rethink its basic propositions, no breathing-space to consider the position of the individual as against the community to which he belonged. It could hardly have been satisfactory that he *could* persuade his uncle to oppose a project or a proposed sentence in the local assembly. The fantastic stories of the Hindu king at whose gate hung a bell-chain which could be pulled by any aggrieved person,[7] the king who would decapitate his own son rather than leave a cow unavenged, indicates the longings of

[1] See below, chapter 12.

[2] An early recognition of the 'southern school': *Mitākṣarā* on Yājñ. I, 256 (trans. Vidyārṇava, p. 353). The *Mit.* took *sapiṇḍa* to mean 'blood relation' (*piṇḍa* = body), the *Dāyabhāga* to mean 'sharer in whole offerings to ancestors in the *śrāddha*' (*piṇḍa* = rice-ball), and the laws of marriage and inheritance became irreconcilably divided.

[3] Foreign visitors found good order in the North, by contrast: *For. Not.*, p. 124.

[4] *I.Y.B.I.A.*, 7 (1958), pp. 361–87 = *Rec. Soc. J. Bodin* 14 (1962), pp. 143–77.

[5] M.A.R. 1939, 35. [6] A.R.E. 1910, st. ins. No. 315 of 1909.

[7] H. C. Raychaudhuri, *I.C.*, 7 (1940), pp. 1–2.

a people pinched by pressures from so many directions that only he who could himself bring pressure to bear upon all (except perhaps the Brahmins) could seem to offer relief. The critic of the established order, the innovator, was not encouraged: for him there were few alternatives–*sannyāsa*, migration, or the life of an outlaw. Progress meant group progress, and conformity was a condition of progressing in step with and under the protection of one's group.

These aspects of life depict the Indian's distance from his European contemporary. The latter was more free from communal pressure, and (as yet) of royal power. Royal jurisdictions were gradually absorbing and displacing local jurisdictions, until one secular law would apply throughout the country. In India this could not be dreamt of until the coming of European (not the Islamic) supremacy. Again, the European subject owed allegiance to two authorities, each supreme in its own sphere although the spiritual affected, often with success, to control the secular. It is debatable whether this was to the subject's advantage, but when the inevitable clash between secular and spiritual jurisdictions came the latter had eventually to give way. In India the Brahmins' poverty kept their *varṇa*, for all the vices of some individuals,[1] in high prestige, and since they sought influence without control, and their *śāstra-s* were (taken as a whole) recommendatory, or at most directory, rather than mandatory, their lack of a hierarchy and a judicial system distinct from those under the State's ultimate control was no handicap to their system, but an advantage. The *dharmaśāstra* was gradually embraced, of their own free will, by those who had not been brought up in its traditions, and rulers boasted of their personal adherence to its tenets and of their application where possible of its principles. A Gaṅga king 'lived in accordance with the *smṛti-s* for a hundred years'.[2] A Cōḷa king claims to be the 'restorer of the race of Manu', the mythical but ideal line, to which many claimed to belong who desired a reputation for hereditary orthodoxy. Thus the severance of law from 'right' which gave a severe shock to the conscience of Europe during the Reformation, from which we never recovered, did not take place in India.

[1] E.C. iv Gund. 32, 33; Hemacandra, *Triṣaṣṭiś.-p. -c.*, III, 86 f.
[2] Cf. M.A.R. 1944, 15; E.C. iv Gund. 34.

Sanātana-dharma, the *aram* of the Tamils and their *seṅkol* (the straight sceptre), *nyāya* (justice or equity) and similar terms were vaguely apprehended, but not impractical. The subject knew that every decision demanded the consideration of more than abstract principles of law. No problem presented sharp blacks and whites. A truly final decision was founded upon as many proper considerations, taking the long view, as the wisdom of the judges could embrace. 'Liberty', 'equality', 'democracy' were all unknown to him. What was wanted was meticulous attention to the minute adjustments of a prestige society–larger shares for the great, smaller for the humble; security for the rich, squalor (though hardly callous oppression) for the poor: as it was, as, one believed, it always had been, and as it ought to be. To keep the *status quo* was an object in itself. But religion supported this outlook. In future lives one's attention to the *ācāra* of this life would be rewarded, and promotion in the caste-scale from *carmakāra* (tanner) to a *kulīna* Brahmin was a legitimate aspiration. Even in this very life one's group might soon be less poor if one obeyed the injunctions of the *śāstra* and fulfilled voluntarily works and vows which religion recommended and endorsed–less squalid, less fearful, less degraded and disregarded, more worthy, and thus more likely to inherit the fruit of the patient effort of generations or at least to commence a store for one's descendants. A thousand years ago the promise of a 'socialist pattern of society' based upon adult suffrage would have dismayed all alike. It is difficult to imagine who would have been more offended, the *dharmaśāstrī* or the untouchable.

8

THE BRITISH AS PATRONS OF THE ŚĀSTRA

The administration of Hindu law by the British[1] is a complex story with two distinct sides. We deal with the first in this paper.[2] Granted that the seventeenth-century English and Scots (not to speak of Welsh) adventurers who came to do business and later to fight, make money, govern and to die in India came with an outlook on law which was not our own, how was it that they were more sympathetic than we can be to the religious laws of 'Moors' and of 'Heathen' ('Gentios', 'Gentoos' = Hindus)? Were they all sentimental antiquarians like Sir William Jones? We, who profess to show every consideration for the religious susceptibilities of subject peoples, have in fact done nothing to preserve and expand their learning and their religious literature. They, who had strong ideas about superstition and especially about superstition linked to the State, set about finding out in detail what these laws were, so far as they could, with resources in the way of dictionaries and handbooks infinitely small compared with our own: and they went further; they stimulated the native scholars to give of their best and tell their own tale in a fashion intelligible to and useful for Europeans. The Europeans of the eighteenth and early

[1] This chapter corresponds closely to 'Sanskrit legal treatises compiled at the instance of the British', *Z. f. vergl. Rechtsw.*, 63 (1961), pp. 72–117, but the particulars of the *Vyavahāra-mālā* (Malayālam text) and of the *Mahānirvāṇa-tantra*, notes of additional works suspected to have been produced in the British period, and some additional references have been added. The writer is obliged to Pandit K. Parameśvara Aithāl for bibliographical help at the Adyar Library, January 1966. The additional details about Jagannātha formed the scope of a lecture delivered at the Sorbonne, École Pratique des Hautes Études, 1963.

[2] Other aspects are dealt with in chapter 9 below.

nineteenth centuries, and particularly the British, played a sympathetic part in the revival of Hindu learning. What use they proceeded to make of it is very much a part of our story, and characteristically complicated: but that is reserved for the next chapter. That they came to the Hindus not as teachers but as pupils and even colleagues should be of lasting significance, especially in respect of Indians' own notions of the standing of their native sciences—which in view of the normal nature of Indian self-awareness must be important.

Not that the first contacts were propitious. The extremely popular satirical poet, Venkaṭādhvarin *alias* Venkaṭārya, who must have lived towards the end of the seventeenth century, speaks of the *Hūṇas* (i.e. Huns) of the region around the shrine of Pārthasārathi, that is to say at Cannapaṭṭaṇa (Madras).[1] The two characters of his tale are Gāndharvas who go on an air-borne tour through India exchanging comments on the various regions and the vices or, less frequently, the virtues of the inhabitants. One of them, Kṛśānu, takes a somewhat acid view of what he finds, whereas his companion, Viśvāvasu, tends to look on the bright side. The whole composition repays study as a social document of the end of the Vijayanagara period, compiled from the point of view of a Telugu-speaking (Āndhra) Brahmin. But we are interested in what is said of the inhabitants of Madras, evidently at a period when the British administration was finding its feet. Kṛśānu admits that the region has its virtue, but 'there is a great defect here, because of our proximity to a particular city which is crammed with a disagreeable folk who are mostly Hūṇas, who have not the slightest use for the virtues with which the locality is endowed. In the whole world it would be difficult to find people more utterly base than the *Hūṇas*!'

The *Hūṇas* are devoid of compassion; they do not count the community of

[1] *Viśvaguṇādarśa* or *Viśvaguṇādarśa-campū*, verses 262–4 (in the Bombay editions of 1889 and 1899 and in the Vidyābhavan Sanskrit Series edn., ed. Surendra Nāth Shāstrī [Benares, 1963] which has the Sanskrit commentary *Padārtha-candrikā* and a Hindi version), corresponding to verses 268–71 in the Kannaḍa script edition of 1887. The work has been published several times in the Telugu and Grantha scripts and was translated into Kannaḍa in 1912. The English translation by Kāveli Venkaṭa Rāmaswāmī (*Viswaguna Darsana or Mirror of Mundane Qualities* . . . Calcutta, 1825) lacks polish and accuracy (as A. C. Burnell noted in his *Tentative List of Books . . . Portuguese* . . . [Mangalore, 1880], p. 131). For our passage see pp. 77–8.

Brahmins worth as much as a straw [need one say more?] – the faults of those people beggar description, for they do not even purify themselves.

The state of things is truly dreadful!

> Wealth is given to *Hūṇas* and others who abandon all trace of purity, while distress is the portion of the well brought-up; lordship over the earth is given to the stupid, and utmost beggary to the intelligent; beauty [i.e. a fair skin] is given to women belonging to low-born folk while high-born dames are plain: Creator! thou hast been at great pains – O evil fate! – but what fruit hast thou gained thereby?

The last of the series of complaints shows the author's playfulness, but Viśvāvasu's answer is very revealing: 'Observe, even amongst *them* good qualities are to be found!:

> 'Never do they seize the flow of others' wealth unlawfully. They tell no untruths. They create a marvellous object. They themselves inflict punishment upon their offenders in accordance with law. Now you must accept that there are virtues even in the *Hūṇas*, who are sinks of iniquity.'[1]

The ability of the British to import manufactured goods, and indeed the skill of Europeans generally in clock-making and the like would go far to endear them to a nation like the Indian. Their conscientious difficulties about inexcusable looting and appropriation of their heathen neighbours' goods (at any rate in the period under discussion) was bound to draw approval, even if the abstention from deceit cast an indirect criticism on the contemporary state of South Indian politics and society. But what really interested the Hindu observer was the incredible ability to inflict penalties, to administer justice, to one's own immediate associates, irrespective of their influence and without fear of their resentment. Justice without fear or favour was evidently a foreign characteristic, a British quality recognized by even so hostile a critic as the learned author. What really hurt was that such ingenious and law-observing people should not patronize Brahmins and indigenous scholarship and should not observe the lavatory and other taboos of their high-caste

1 *prasahya na haranty amī para-dhanaugham anyāyato*
vadanti na mṛṣāvaco viracayanti vastv adbhutaṃ
yathā-vidhi kṛtāgasāṃ vidadhati svayaṃ daṇḍanaṃ
guṇān avaguṇākareṣv api gṛhāna hūṇeṣv amūn. 264

The first translator into English says (with his tongue in his cheek?) that the *Hūṇas* were the (White) Huns who devasted northern India in ancient times. Burnell says, with equal certainty and plausibility, that these unpleasant people are the Portuguese (!)

neighbours. As to the latter the strangers were never converted: as to the former they mended their ways.

The reference to the British is deliberate. There is no evidence, as yet, that the Portuguese, the Dutch (for example in Cochin), or (with few and very late exceptions) French rulers patronized Indian writers to the extent of encouraging them to prepare treatises for the foreign governments' use.[1] All these nations are known to have preferred, in general, the application of their own laws to the natives of eastern territories which they came to rule; though this generalization must not be allowed to suggest either that they were identically disposed, or that none of them actively fostered the investigation of Indian customs and the means to apply them in proper cases in practice. In fact the Dutch and Portuguese are known to have compiled some customaries, one of which actually led to the codification of the law of the Tamils of Jaffna.[2] But the British actively furthered the production of Indian law treatises by Indian jurists, and the reasons must be studied in detail. There is also the extraordinary case of a spontaneous production with a large legal content, the *Mahānirvāṇa-tantra* (now regarded as a great religious treatise by Bengali and other enthusiasts for the tantric religion), which could not have been produced without the stimulus of Anglo-Indian legal uncertainties at a very early period; this tribute of religion to law deserves a brief notice.[3]

[1] G. Orianne, in his *Traité Original des Successions* (Paris, 1844) relies substantially on the *Mitākṣarā* and the *Dattaka-candrikā* (on which see below), which could not have happened without native assistance. F. E. Sicé, *Législation Hindoue publiée sous le Titre de Vyavahāra-Sāra-Saṅgraha, ou Abrégé substantiel du Droit* (Pondicherry, 1857, also Paris, 1858) was a translation from a Tamil summary of the *Smṛti-candrikā* made by M. Kandaswāmī Pulavar and printed in Madras in 1826. The work of translation had been begun by M. Petit d'Auterive in 1847.

[2] On the *Forál* of Mexia for the Old Conquests of Goa (1526) see Derrett, 'Hindu law in Goa . . .', *Z. f. vergl. Rechtsw.*, 67, pt. 2 (1965), 203 ff. The Portuguese also prepared a *Forál* of the Kingdom of Jafanapatam (Jaffna) in 1645. The Dutch prepared the Tesavaḷamai (see below, p. 406) for the Tamils of Jaffna (completed in 1706).

[3] J. Mossel, 'Het Chormandels Heidens Regt von de Geslagten Wellale en Chittij', i.e. the law of the Coromandel Hindus belonging to the castes of Vellāla and Chetty, is a valuable commentary on the law administered to Hindus in Negapatam by the Dutch about the year 1737 or later. This last is still unpublished. India Office Library, Mackenzie Collection, Pr. 55, 10,

The British as Patrons of the Śāstra

The Dharmaśāstra in 1765

When the East India Company acquired the *divānī* (i.e. became the Diwan) of the Mughal Emperor in respect of the provinces of Bengal, Bihar and Orissa the fundamental law, as the conditions of the appointment show, was Islamic law. The Islamic law however explicitly recognized the jurisdiction of Hindu referees and arbitrators to settle disputes amongst Hindus according to their own laws and customs, reserving to itself exclusive jurisdiction in matters of crime and the constitutional and fiscal administration.[1] Where Muslims occupied the seats of power, disputes between Hindus which were brought before them were often remitted to Brahmin jurists for an opinion, upon which the parties were compelled to compose their differences. By far the greater part of litigation was never brought before Muslim officials, but was settled by recourse to traditional methods of resolving disputes, which differed according to the caste, the status in society, and the locality of the parties. Into these details, as yet little explored, we cannot enter. But it is certain that amongst Hindus the *dharmaśāstra* held very high prestige, served as the only indigenous system of jurisprudence, and supplied actual rules of law in a wide variety of contexts, especially (in Northern and Eastern India) in matters of inheritance. The native professors of the *śāstra* were therefore consulted on such matters as were indisputably within their province,[2] and it was usual for the parties to obey the decision,

pp. 471–511; ibid., Mack. Coll., Class XIV, 10 (f), fos. 82–93 (English trans.). The Dutch materials on Malabar law from Cochin have still to be traced and published.

[1] Sir G. Rankin, *Background to Indian Law* (Cambridge, 1946), pp. 3 ff. Sir T. E. Colebrooke, *Miscellaneous Essays of H. T. Colebrooke with a Life of the Author* (London, 1873), I, p. 96.

[2] The continuation of the system into the time of Warren Hastings is to be seen in actual *vyavasthā-s* (opinions) of *pariṣad-s* of Brahmins at Benares published in S. Sen and U. Mishra, *Sanskrit Documents* (Allahabad, 1951). There was nothing to prevent a Muslim governor deciding (of course on Hindu advice) a case on the tenure of a high Hindu religious office. Particulars of an instance occurring in 1674 (a decision of one Abdul Hussain Saheb) is published at *Dept. of Archaeology, Annual Report on Indian Epigraphy* (cited below as *A.R.I.E.*) *for 1949–50* (Calcutta, 1956), Copper-plate no. 59.

provided that it was not open to doubt whether the report was biased in favour of one party. There appears to have been by 1765 a slender establishment for the maintenance of such scholarship, by way of charitable endowments at Benares, in Mithilā and elsewhere, and by way of posts in princely households.

The professors of the *śāstra*, in view of their Vedic learning, were entitled to be called *paṇḍita*, 'Pundit' or 'pandit'. Being all Brahmins, and dependent on charity or some hereditary income by way of endowment, they were neither wealthy nor independent. Other Brahmins of course might be both, sometimes to their undoing. Pandits were to be found all over India, but they were not very numerous, the depth of learning was uneven, and the extent to which they were consulted in litigation varied considerably. In the very South a powerful opinion was voiced early in the British period that though the *śāstra* ought to be consulted, few of the inhabitants knew anything about it.[1] However, these pandits actively contributed to the maintenance and extension of learning in their science. They copied ancient and mediaeval manuscripts, added their own commentaries, and wrote their own digests and specialized treatises. Vast masses of these works have survived, and yet we can be sure that the remains are only a fragment of what was originally available. Learning was encouraged by frequent migrations for study and discussion; colloquia, debates and lectures gave a lively air to a somewhat esoteric science; and pre-eminence in knowledge of *dharmaśāstra* was highly regarded. Much of the basic textual material was committed to memory. The composite picture in the professors' minds was made up from technical śāstric material, from epics and legends, and from other treatises of relatively late date (such as *purāṇa-s*, spurious *smṛti-s*, *āgama-s*, and *tantra-s*) which, although they would not have satisfied the modern historian, played then a valid part in expounding Hinduism as it was lived, learnt, and understood.[2]

The eighteenth century was not a particularly brilliant cen-

[1] In particular a series of works by J. H. Nelson, referred to below at p. 292. For Mayne's reply see (1887) 3 *L.Q.R.* 446. Lingat, *Sources*, pp. 158–162.

[2] Note the pandit's reliance on the *Mahānirvāṇa-tantra* in the pre-emption case as reported by W. H. Macnaghten (see below, p. 289, n. 3).

tury in the history of *dharmaśāstra.* Works of importance in the popularization of the law were, however, published before the arrival of the British,[1] and there had been no interruption in the progress of scholarship since the seventeenth century when numerous outstanding works of learning had been produced. The two major trends were firstly the assimilation of the learning of the great logicians of Bengal, who had established themselves as the intellectual masters of the North and East of India and had turned their attention to some legal problems; the second was the gradual admission into the *dharmaśāstra* of customs and usages that had developed under the influence of the Muslim rule,[2] or had achieved a new prominence with the growth of importance in the peoples or groups which employed them, itself possibly a result of the Islamic supremacy in political life. Both these trends are visible, but they had by no means markedly altered the character of śāstric learning by the time the British arrived on the scene. When the East India Company stepped into the shoes of the Muslim emperor's deputies in Eastern India it found a flourishing, but not assertive or brilliant tradition of śāstric learning available both for intellectual exercise and for the direction of the Hindu public.

The Dilemma of the British Administration

The story of Warren Hastings' disappointment at the results of native administration of justice has been told many times.[3] When disorder increased to the point of breakdown of administration new orders were issued, and responsibility for justice was

[1] Śrī-Kṛṣṇa Tarkālaṅkāra and several juridically-minded Mahārājas of Tanjore antedated British influence. Kṛpārāma's *Navyadharmapradīpa* (below, p. 273) seems to stand on the border, about the very commencement of the British period. The date of the anonymous *Śvaśrū-snuṣā-dhana-saṃvāda* must be *c.* 1800.

[2] W. H. Macnaghten reports in his *Principles and Precedents of Hindu Law* II (Calcutta, 1828), pp. 272–3, replies of pandits in the slavery case which showed their awareness that the *śāstra* must move with the times. They admitted that what was not inconsistent with the *śāstra* might well be good law.

[3] B. B. Misra, *Central Administration of the East India Company, 1773–1834* (Manchester, 1959). M. P. Jain, *Outlines of Indian Legal History*[2] (Bombay, Tripathi, 1966), chapters 6 and 7.

placed in the hands of European officials. None of these had had a legal training, and it was long before some of the recruits of the East India Company's service specialized in law, read English and Roman legal treatises, and fitted themselves for the task of being Judges. But even if the first Judges in the district and provincial appellate courts had been professional lawyers it is certain that they could not have coped effectively with the flood of petitions and complaints brought to them by a public aware of the possibilities of the new system in their schemes to harass their 'enemies'.

All the British courts were believed to be like those that had functioned in Calcutta. They had combined a readiness and sureness of execution and attachment with a willingness to consult native expert opinion in technical matters, and they had been very popular.[1] As soon as it was evident that the power of the new rulers was at the disposal of a successful litigant, and that to be successful it was only necessary to make a case which the native assistants of the Judges certified to be good, the breakdown of the system was imminent. A flood of cases arose, and accusations of corruption and inefficiency against the native assistants multiplied.

That the European Judges must remain at their posts, and that appeals from their courts should pass to a hierarchy of appellate courts seemed absolutely certain. But the public must have confidence in the quality of the justice administered, and the responsibility for propounding it must be shared between the sources of law, and the law-enforcers: hence the very peculiar provisions of Warren Hastings' *Plan* of 1772[2]–closely connected with the *Plan* of March 28th, 1780, which became the Administration of Justice Regulation of April 11th, 1780. The outstanding features of the scheme were (i) the responsibility of the *śāstrī-s* for the law they reported, and for the sentence depending therefrom; and (ii) the necessity to consult

[1] The Preamble to the Charter of the Mayor's Courts (1726) recited what was evidently a fact, namely that the English courts offered remedies which native courts could not offer.

[2] *Plan for the Administration of Justice Extracted from the Proceedings of the Committee of Circuit* (Cossimbazar) *15 Aug., 1772* being pp. 13–15 of *Extract of a Letter from the Governor and Council at Fort William to the Court of Directors, 3 Nov. 1772*. Forrest, *Warren Hastings*, II, App. B, p. 290.

these professors on *listed subjects only*. The list has a considerable curiosity value. We have already seen how wide the *śāstra* was and how well-stocked, especially in procedural matters.

'Inheritance, marriage, caste, and other religious usages or institutions' were to be administered to Hindus according to the laws of the 'Shaster'. Why these topics and not others? Two forces were evidently at work, the influence of the local jurists on the Company's representatives, and the predispositions or prejudices of the latter. As far as the former were concerned, Hastings had obviously been advised that in all questions of caste-breaking, religious institutions, and those topics of the *śāstra* which were founded upon 'unseen' motives (and therefore would not submit to argument, as, for example, the criminal law would had it been in force locally) the laws of the Hindus must be ascertained from the sacred śāstric texts and the learning enshrined therein.[1] It would be essential to consult pandits to discover what the appropriate rule was. Hastings and his colleagues were, of course, predisposed to see the division of topics of law in terms of the contemporary English division. All matters of marriage and divorce, and all questions of testaments and distribution of goods (the doctrine that the English law of real property *might* have been introduced into Calcutta–it was not–had not then been mooted), all matters of religious worship and discipline, excommunication and so forth were within the exclusive jurisdiction of the Bishops' courts, and the law was ecclesiastical law. So the pandits' distinction between 'unseen' and 'seen' will have coincided with the Englishman's notions of the scopes, respectively, of the 'courts christian' and 'courts temporal'. This comparison is made clearer by some phrases used casually by contemporaries, and by the fact that when Parliament contemplated the setting up of the Supreme Court, as a King's court, at Calcutta the jurisdiction of that court was to include the entire law of inheritance, including testamentary matters, and the whole of contract and 'dealing between party and party', for that court had a 'law' and an 'equity' side, and rules of equity could be applied in any litigation. The Supreme

[1] On the virtue of 'unseen' (*adṛṣṭa*) purposes behind rules see *Madhavrao* v. *Raghavendrarao* [1946] Bom. 375, where Kāṇe referred to his *H.D.*, II, pt. 1, p. 437. The case is strongly criticized by A. S. Naṭarāja Ayyar, *Mīmāṃsā Jurisprudence* (Allahabad, 1952), pp. 11–14.

Court therefore, though applying Hindu law in this much wider jurisdiction, did so as a combined temporal and spiritual court.[1]

But to return to the Company's courts: in all *other* topics of law not specifically governed by Company's Regulations–and these were many–the former law applicable to the inhabitants, whether śāstric or customary, would be applied. But although it might be desirable to consult the pandit, especially if the parties required it, it would not be obligatory to do so in those cases, and the report of the court pandit would not necessarily be the ground of decision and the pandit would not be under the obligation of signing the decree. The comparison with the English position is worth recalling. When a question of legitimacy, for example, arose in a common-law court, which could not be solved without reference to the ecclesiastical law, the common-law judge sent a letter of request to the court of the Ordinary (the Bishop) for a certificate as to the law applicable to the facts. When this certificate arrived the common-law judge was bound by it and proceeded with his judgement on the basis of this step in ascertaining the rights. When the Anglo-Indian judges sent, as they subsequently constantly did, for 'opinions' (*vyavasthā*) on Hindu law from the pandits, and acted upon these certificates without bothering to see whether they agreed with others given by the same persons in the like circumstances, they were imitating the practice of the King's Bench or the Common Pleas. This was of a piece with the error perpetuated by Sir William Jones, that Brahmins were 'priests'. Very few Brahmins were priests, and there were priests who were not

[1] In 1838 the Parsi Panchayat of Bombay solicited a formal mandate from the Legislative Council. But the Judges of the Supreme Court at Bombay reported unfavourably. 'But we conceive the inevitable consequence would be, that, unless they had a lawyer as an assessor, which probably they would by no means desire, the Parsi community would be greatly harassed by collision between that Court and the Supreme Court.' Writs of *mandamus* and prohibition would be sued for in the latter. 'From the Reformation to the eighteenth century, in the course of which period most of the chief questions have been settled, our books are full of collisions of this kind between the spiritual and temporal courts in England. But it is manifest that they would be more frequent and more harassing here.' D. F. Karaka, *History of the Parsis* (1884), I, pp. 238–9. Had Hindu panchayats been invested with legal jurisdiction such collisions would have been certain: as it was, no court has ever issued a prohibition against a panchayat's process or a *mandamus* to compel it to perform any function.

Brahmins: and similarly pandits were not Bishops' Officials, or anything of the kind. They were however jurisconsults, which had quite another implication.

Hastings was right in leaving a certain vagueness with respect to non-listed topics, since the operation of custom could not be foreseen, as we have already come to understand. There cannot be any doubt but that Hastings knew that in Hindu courts, those of the Marāṭhas and of the small princes of Bengal and Bihar, pandits were consulted on all manner of questions, and their opinions often led to attempts at reform by the *rājā-s*, who were the proper authorities to undertake such steps.[1] The learning of the pandits available to or paid by the Company was therefore to be had for the asking: but one could not lay down in advance the exact scope for this outside the listed topics. No steps were taken to collect evidence of local or caste custom, and this is sometimes regarded as a mistake. Perhaps something should be said on the Company's side: the peasants of the regions in question may have cared little enough for the *śāstra*; but they were made to pay for having harboured great traditions of śāstric learning.

It is further to be observed that the system envisaged by Warren Hastings automatically left out of view the principle of *stare decisis*, for until the major jurisdictions of the ecclesiastical courts were abolished in England in the middle of the nineteenth century there was no principle whereby previous decisions bound the judges of those courts. The advocates relied upon principles enshrined in learned books by authors emanating from various regions and periods–exactly (it seemed) as was the case with the pandits. Thus at first Hastings and his colleagues were not concerned at discrepancies between the reports of pandits in different courts, or discrepancies between the reports of the same pandits on similar matters. After all, the *śāstra* being a complicated system, and the opinion of the great 'doctors' differing frequently, even within the major schools, there was ample room for honest disagreement and a change or growth of opinion. The pandits, having a sense of responsibility, would be likely to mould their answers to suit the needs of the

[1] *Proceedings of the Legislative Council of India* for Saturday, November 17th, 1855 (a Rāja attempted to persuade his pandits to give a *vyavasthā* permitting widow-remarriage).

situation, and they might take into account the effect which the decision would have. Tolerance of this somewhat fluid state of affairs was hindered by the existence of the Supreme Court at Calcutta, in which of course *stare decisis* would tend to be the rule and English practitioners functioned, and the relationship which developed between it and the Sadr Diwani Adalat there from the time of Sir Elijah Impey, the first Chief Justice.[1]

The King's court was intended to administer English law and operate as a control over the proceedings of the Company's servants. The unhappy story of the relationship between the Judges and the Council of the Presidency has been told before and need not be more than referred to here. The Hindu inhabitants of Calcutta desired to litigate in this court, and when its jurisdiction was revised in 1781, the laws and usages of Hindus were enacted by Parliament to be applicable in 'inheritance and succession to land rent and goods and all matters of contract and dealing between party and party'. The Supreme Court was thus authorized to decide matters such as had previously been litigated in the former Mayor's Court, consulting the Hindu law and deciding cases in Hindu law as if they had been cases before the King's Bench or Chancery.

After the Supreme Court had been functioning for a short while it became evident that in such contexts the Hindu law would have to be discovered as each case arose, and, copying the arrangement in the Company's courts, pandits were appointed to the Supreme Court itself (February 3rd, 1777).[2] The result, confirmed, as to the Company's courts, by the 'Cornwallis Code' (as the Regulations of 1793 are known), was that pandits were attached to the district courts, to the provincial courts, to the Sadr Diwani Adalat in Calcutta (except for the early period when its difficulties with the Supreme Court did not permit it to function at all) and to the Supreme Court itself. It was evident to Impey and his successors there that as

[1] On whom see J. F. Stephen, *The Story of Nuncomar and the Impeachment of Sir Elijah Impey* (London, 1885); B. N. Pandey, *The Introduction of English Law into India* (London, 1967); also Derrett, at *English Historical Review*, 1960, pp. 223 ff.

[2] Impey's *Speech delivered by him at the Bar of the House of Commons* (London, 1788), Appendix, pp. 53 f. F. W. Macnaghten's work (see below) frequently demonstrates the Supreme Court's availing itself of the facility of calling upon the pandits of the Sanskrit College for additional help.

the decisions given on the reports of the pandits were decisions of an English court the principle of *stare decisis* could not be totally excluded. The practice of the Sadr Diwani Adalat, as the Company's chief court of appeal in the Presidency, would naturally tend to draw the provincial courts together, and regard for precedent began very gradually to be felt in the *mufassil* as well as in Calcutta. This gradually brought into the administration of Hindu law an entirely new feature, highly embarrassing to the pandits.

The Search for Certainty

Sir William Jones arrived in Calcutta at a time when the prestige of the Supreme Court needed to be restored, and harmonious relations with the Company re-established. As a Judge of that court Jones received every co-operation from Warren Hastings, and it is obvious that his scheme to make the Hindu and Islamic laws known to the European Judges, and thus capable of steady and consistent administration throughout British India, was highly approved by the Company. Hastings had already made considerable strides in the desired direction, and these must be described before Jones's conduct is considered.

Hastings, knowing that pandits would be required for many more courts than had existed and functioned with their assistance before the *Plan* of 1772, had taken up the question of furthering śāstric education. Part of his plan materialized in the establishment of the Sanskrit College at Benares, the traditional centre of Brahminical learning,[1] and this was extended by the foundation of the Sanskrit College at Calcutta. Both these establishments in time produced experts in the *śāstra*, and their professors were consulted regularly in the course of litigation.

In the training of pandits for the Company's service an essential ingredient must have been an agreed bibliography of leading textbooks. We are fortunate in having a list of the works used at Calcutta from 1821 to 1837 (at the earliest).[2] These

[1] G. Nicholls, *Sketch of the Rise and Progress of the Benares Pathsala or Sanskrit College* (Allahabad, 1907); V. A. Narain, *Jonathan Duncan and Varanasi* (Calcutta, 1959).

[2] Alexander Duff, *New Era of the English Language and English Literature in India* (Edinburgh, 1837), p. 9. In 1829 a Hindu who studied in the Sanskrit

were Manu, the Mitāksharā, the *Dāyabhāga*, the *Dāya-krama-(saṅgraha)*, the *Dāya-tattva*, the *Dattaka-candrikā*, the *Dattaka-mīmāṃsā*, the *Vivāda-cintāmaṇi*, the *Tithi-tattva*, the *Śuddhi-tattva*, and the *Prāyaścitta-tattva*. If the list in the 1780's resembled it, as it may well have done, it is significant that Maithila as well as Bengali works were to be studied there, and this helps to account for the readiness with which the pandits could report the law according to the predominant school of Benares and Mithilā or according to the local, the Bengali school. Southern works are not represented here. The fourteen books which were taught at the Benares College are not specified for us. Apart from the differences between Bengal and Mithilā there were also different views from the South to be contended with–if not frequently in practice at least in theory. Some means had to be found whereby interim decisions might be come to as to what rules ought to be applied under the new régime. The obvious course was to summon a 'synod' of the most learned and respected jurists, as if it were a kind of convocation, to induce them to compile a digest similar in form to the digests compiled in more or less recent times for emperors and kings in not altogether dissimilar circumstances, and to give to the result an

College, Calcutta could become 'judge-pandit' to a District Judge if he completed a ten years' course, passed the Law Committee's examination and thus qualified for the Certificate: Benoy Ghose, *Iswar Chandra Vidyāsāgara* (cited above), pp. 18, 31–2. Vidyāsāgara obtained a prize of Rs. 25 for proficiency in the Company's laws. In 1850 he recommended that Raghunandana's works (the 28 *Tattvas*), excluding the specifically legal portions, should be discontinued as prescribed books at the College, being useful only to priests. Srīschandra, who was a lecturer at the College, became 'judge-pandit' at Murshidabad (p. 94). The title 'judge-pandit' derived from the fact that between 1805 (see Reg. XV of that year) and 1831 (see Reg. V of that year) all native Law Officers of the District Court were *ex officio* Sadar Ameens (vested with jurisdiction over civil cases up to a pecuniary limit). As these native professors allowed their conscientious scruples to interfere with the administration of the Company's Laws (which, *inter alia*, permitted a Muslim to charge or take interest on a loan) from 1831 only those Law Officers were appointed Sadar Ameens who were found fit to hold that post. They were paid fixed salaries of Rs. 100 per mensem from May 1st, 1824 in addition to their salaries as Law Officers; from 1831 they drew Rs. 250 in their judicial capacities, after passing the examination and being selected for appointment. This information is derived from Chittaranjan Sinha, *The Evolution of the Structure of Civil Judiciary in Bengal, 1800–31*, Thesis, Ph.D. London (unpublished), 1967, pp. 37, 83, 99.

authority which those pre-British compilations had never had. No one could foresee whether the pandits who did not form the 'synod' would accord to its efforts the respect which they accorded to the previously authoritative literature; would they abandon their eclectic and empirical methods? But if the Company required that the proposed digest should be followed wherever possible, the advantages of certainty and uniformity might be gained. Moreover, since the Company paid the court pandits there was no reason to doubt but that they would follow the authority they were given, and if any hesitated, others would take their places.[1] Moreover, it had been rumoured that certain pandits had been issuing *vyavasthā-s* which agreed with the wishes of the wealthier party to the dispute in question. If the law were digested by an authoritative and independent committee, it would not only be easier to learn and to refer to than the extensive and vague literature normally consulted, but would also render corruption difficult to hide.

In May 1773 eleven pandits, including some persons of known eminence in their profession, commenced their labours at Calcutta, finishing a digest to Hastings's specifications in February 1775.[2] The work was called *Vivādārṇava-setu*, or 'bridge across the ocean of litigation', and it acquired soon afterwards the alternative title *Vivādārṇava-bhañjana*, 'breakwater to the ocean of litigation',[3] implying thereby that the certainty now for the first time offered to litigants in the Company's territories would put some check upon the appalling flood of cases which inundated the courts. In its Sanskrit form it was multiplied and

[1] Pandits' willingness to use the material is evidenced in the notes to the Appendix below. Anantarāma in his *Vivāda-candrikā* (India Office Library Ms. at fo. 19 b) bears witness to the authority of the work of a committee such as this was. For the tergiversations at Tanjore see below, p. 241, n. 4.

[2] The date is mistaken at Kāṇe, *H.D.*, I, pp. 465, 622. Three of the same pandits, Bāṇeśvara, Kṛpārāma and Sītārāma were already in Calcutta in April 1773, for on the 6th or 7th they were asked a highly important question in fiscal and constitutional law, returning their answer, which has an interestingly academic air in contrast to that of the treasury-officials' on the same subject, on the 27th: India Office Library Mss. (Rec.), *Home Misc. Ser.* 124, pp. 73–4 (Letter of P. Francis, dated March 12th, 1776).

[3] These are not two works as stated by Aufrecht, Jolly, and Kāṇe. Dr. P. K. Gode supplied the writer with extracts from Ms. No. 364 of 1875–6 at the Bhandarkar O.R. Institute, Poona in 1955 (*B.S.O.A.S.*, 18 (1956), p. 478, n. 8).

distributed. But this was only the first phase of the operation. In order that the honesty of the pandits should be beyond reproach, it was intended that an English translation should be available to the Judges. Therefore it was translated immediately into Persian, notwithstanding the losses that the process must necessarily involve, and this was translated into English by N. B. Halhed. Hastings wrote home to Lord Mansfield[1] to ask approval for his idea of applying native laws from books, for example from this product. In March 1775 this translation, prefaced with a long and interesting dissertation on the cultural background of the work, was sent by Hastings to London, where it was printed, under the title *A Code of Gentoo Laws, or, Ordinations of the Pundits*, in 1776, reprinted in 1777 and 1781. It was translated at once into French by Robinet and into German by Raspe,[2] and these translations, published in 1778, form, together with the English original, the source of interest in Europe in the laws of the Hindus. It maintained, despite Sir William Jones's disparagement, a more practical air than his own *Manu*, published long afterwards, could ever aspire to. The Sanskrit original is available in manuscript in the India Office Library. Another contemporary copy was carried eventually to Mahārāja Ranjit Singh of the Punjab, who intended to govern his own kingdom according to its principles; from him or his successor it was obtained by the Venkaṭeśvara Press in Bombay, where it was printed in 1888. No copy can be traced in Bombay today. There may be one available in Calcutta. There is certainly one at Adyar. The rarity of the original text (of which no copy exists in Europe) in comparison with the frequency with which we may come across copies of the English translation of the Persian version tells it own tale.

The topics upon which the *Vivādārṇava-setu* was compiled show what Hastings believed would be needed by the courts in the *mufassil*: Debt, Inheritance, Civil Procedure, Deposits, Sale of a Stranger's Property, Partnership, Gift, Slavery, Master and

[1] G. R. Gleig, *Memoirs of Warren Hastings* (London, 1841), I, pp. 399 ff., at p. 400. The letter is important for this critical phase of Indian legal history.

[2] [J. B. R. Robinet] *Code des lois des Gentoux, ou Réglemens des Brames, traduit de l'Anglois* (Paris, 1778). R. E. Raspe, *Gesetzbuch der Gentoo's, oder Sammlung der Gesetze der Pundits, nach einer persianischen Übersetzung des in der Schanscrit-Sprache geschriebenen Originales. Aus dem Engl.* (Hamburg, 1778).

Servant, Rent and Hire, Sale, Boundaries, Shares in the Cultivation of Lands, Cities and Towns and Fines for Damaging Crops, Defamation, Assault, Theft, Violence, Adultery, Duties of Women, Miscellaneous Rules (including gaming, finding lost property, sales-tax, adoption). The order of appearance of the chapters, and the relative weight given to each does not correspond with anything known to the usual śāstric works, and it is evident that the committee was working to a list of topics supplied by Hastings or his immediate adviser. Unfortunately the order lacks logic as well as completeness, and the general appearance, though neatly digested for a Sanskrit legal work, is repellent to a lawyer trained in the common law. The work however was not ill received. References to it are sufficient. The Board at Murshidabad relied upon the Code in 1779,[1] Sir William Jones relies upon it in a judgement in 1788,[2] and we find it relied upon as late as 1791,[3] besides numerous other occasions.[4] It failed to deflect pandits from their normal sources of information, and merely added another to their many reference works. Sir William Jones's disparaging comments[5] were

[1] *Factory Records* (India Office Library Mss.), Murshidabad 16 (May 3rd, 1779): they rely on *Gentoo Code* II, 1, ss. 7–8, p. 30.

[2] *Kistnochurn* v. *Ramnarain,* Morton-Montriou, 297 = 1 Indian Decisions, Old Ser., 178. Jones cites the *Code,* II, s. 12 and gives his own trans. of the original Sanskrit also his own trans. of Manu.

[3] *Isana Chandra's Case,* Morton-Montriou, xvi = 1 I.D., OS, 399.

[4] Of great political importance was the question of the legality of the adoption of the boy Serfoji, later Mahārāja of Tanjore and much addicted to legal studies. In 1787 twelve pandits there declared that the adoption of an only son and one over 5 years of age was void (Sir Archibald Campbell in Council, Madras, April 6th, 1787: Madras Military Consultations, vol. 119, p. 15). The influential missionary C. Swartz changed his own opinion after reading 'the translation of the Hindu laws which was published in Bengal' (W. Hickey, *Tanjore Mahratta Principality,* Madras 1874, p. 95). The pandits repented, policy having changed, and the adoption was recognized (Sir Charles Oakeley and Council to the Court of Directors, Madras, May 2nd, 1793: Political Despatches to England, vol. 2, pp. 206–10; Lord Hobart in Council, Madras, July 1st, 1796: Military Consultations, vol. 208, pp. 2719–2770; the Directors approve the restoration of Serfoji: Lord Clive and Council, Madras, October 15th, 1798: Political Despatches to England, vol. 4, pp. 200–8). The references are owed to a research scholar in Madras.

[5] Sir J. Shore (Lord Teignmouth), *Memoirs of the Life, Writings and Correspondence of Sir William Jones* (London, 1804), pp. 276–7, 294. He calls it 'as far as it goes a very excellent work', ibid., p. 309. He painstakingly

formulated long before he had become acquainted personally with the manner in which law-books were compiled in Sanskrit, and it may be that his judgement is unfair. The orientalist speaks of the Persian version as 'a loose, injudicious, epitome of the original Sanskrit, in which abstract many essential passages are omitted, though several notes of little consequence are interpolated from a vain idea of elucidating, or improving, the text'. There is evidence that even as late as 1792 authorities in India sympathetic to Hindu culture (of whom Jonathan Duncan was the best example) and likewise authorities in England somewhat earlier (such as J. Lind in his report used by H. Dundas but probably made to Thurlow or Lord Mansfield in 1779 or 1780) regarded the 'Gentoo Code' as an authentic and reliable source of Hindu law for practical purposes. Duncan wanted it to be consulted in Malabar, recently taken from Tipoo Sultan, and Lind follows Impey in wishing it to be consulted in the Supreme Court in Calcutta.[1]

Our first example, therefore, of a Sanskrit legal treatise compiled at the instance of the British turned out to be, from the practical point of view, a somewhat qualified success. The appointment of special pandits to the Supreme Court's service, which we saw happened in 1777, emphasized that that court and its Bar were unable to perform their functions in Hindu law matters with that Code's aid alone.

Jones arrived eight years after the presentation of the Code to the East India Company. He determined to provide in its place some sources which should be usable by European Judges,

corrects the translation at Sir T. Strange, *Hindu Law* (London, 1830), II, p. 251. Colebrooke disparages the *Code* in his Preface to his translation of Jagannātha's work (see below) by copying Jones's letter to Lord Cornwallis of March 19th, 1788; but he speaks less disrespectfully of it in 1796 (T. E. Colebrooke, cited above, at I, p. 84) only regretting its conciseness.

[1] J. Duncan, *Observations on the Administration of Justice as applicable to Malabar* (a report completed October 14th, 1793 and printed in 77 unnumbered pages in vol. iii of *Reports of a Joint Commission from Bengal and Bombay appointed to Inspect into the State and Condition of the Province of Malabar in the year 1792 and 1793* . . . (Bombay, N.D., 1794?), ss. xix, xxix ff., xxxvii, lxxvii f.). India Office Library Mss. (Rec.), *Home Misc. Ser.*, 339, p. 172. For the abortive scheme concocted by Impey and members of the Council at Calcutta in 1776 with an intended Act of Parliament, see *C.S.S.H.*, 4, no. 1 (1961), pp. 51–2 and B. N. Pandey, *The Introduction of English Law into India* (cited above), pp. 123–7.

comparable with Justinian's *Corpus Juris*. But this would be a vast task. Meanwhile the Supreme Court's work had to go on, and the pandits continued to perform their function. Jones was very soon impressed with their opportunities for corruption. It seemed to him that if they favoured one side in a case they could pull out from the ocean of the *śāstra* any authority that might be needed to support it.[1] Even when the questions were put to the pandits in abstract terms they could easily discover which dispute was in question. They were often examined in private by a Master of the court, but the parties were at liberty to file opinions opposed to those returned by the court pandits, and it later became quite usual for large numbers of pandits to be ranged on either side.[2] The court then had to make up its mind upon principles of Hindu law, of which it had not yet assumed judicial knowledge (this came in 1864), but which it must affect to understand unless the process of discovering the law were to be frustrated by the differences between the pandits. It is now thought that Jones's, and subsequently the Macnaghtens' and Strange's suspicions of the pandits were exaggerated;[3] but it is certain that the pandits could mislead the court, did in some instances favour the interests of their own caste,[4] and might produce anomalous *vyavasthā-s* without adequate supporting authority. Treated as witnesses on a foreign system of

[1] 'It would be absurd and unjust to pass an indiscriminate censure on so considerable a body of men; but my experience justifies me in declaring, that I could not with an easy conscience, concur in a decision, merely on the written opinion of native lawyers, in any cause in which they could have the remotest interest in misleading the Court...' This letter of Jones's is gleefully quoted in Sir F. W. Macnaghten's extraordinary Preface to his *Considerations on the Hindoo Law as it is Current in Bengal* (Serampore, 1824), pp. x–xi.

[2] F. W. Macnaghten, Appendix. *Rutcheputty* (1839) 2 M.I.A. 133, 138; *Bhugwandeen* (1867) 11 M.I.A. 487, 504, 509.

[3] J. B. Norton, Preface to *A Selection of Leading Cases on the Hindu Law of Inheritance*, pt. 2 (Madras, 1871), p. v: 'We have abolished the Pundits, and ourselves kicked down one of the ladders by which we have climbed; for time was, when there was scarcely another source of law open to us to consult. We can now run alone, or so flatter ourselves; and are out of leading-strings. Still I think hard measure has, on the whole, been dealt out to those old Hindu lawyers; and I am glad to find that they are more mercifully dealt with by the Privy Council, than by some of the Courts and authorities in India.'

[4] Strange, cited above, II, p. 300.

law in the Supreme Court, they were often questioned about the authorities upon which they relied, and it was desirable that the Judge should be able to make up his own mind as to whether the opinion of the pandits was founded upon adequate and relevant materials. Naturally it was desirable that the texts of adequacy and relevance should be as far as possible Hindu in character and not English. And this led inevitably to a demand for further and better particulars about the Hindu law. The ignorance of the English Judges at that time was complete, notwithstanding Halhed's book, and Jones–who was probably more tolerant of oriental piety and its manifestations–set about the task of remedying it.

From 1783 to 1788 Jones worked on Islamic and Hindu laws. He was instructed in the latter by pandits, who apparently delighted in their task. He got to know the pandits' mentality well and their pleasure in having him for a pupil was equalled by his determination that the British should administer to their people the best śāstric law that could be discovered. In 1784 or 1785 we find him writing,[1]

> Will you have the goodness to ask Mahesa pundit, whether the university of Tyrhoot is still supported, and confers degrees in Hindu law; one of our pundits is dead, and we have thoughts of requesting recommendations from the universities of Hindustan, particularly from Benares, and Tyrhoot, if it exists; so that the new pundit may be universally approved, and the Hindus may be convinced, that we decide on their law from the best information we can procure.

There is no question here but that the law was not unwritten custom, but only the śāstric law. And we note that he is looking for a Maithila (or as we should now say a 'Mitāksharā') pandit, for presumably the Supreme Court kept one Maithila and one Gauḍa (Bengali) pandit to report on the law relative to the two schools, where either might be appropriate. In 1785 he is in the centre of Brahmin intellectual life in Bengal, Nadiya, and studies the legal texts in Sanskrit, 'for', he says, 'I can no longer bear to be at the mercy of our pandits, who deal out Hindu law as they please, and make it at reasonable rates, when they cannot find it ready made.'[2]

[1] Shore, cited above, p. 254.

[2] Ibid., p. 264. Because of suspicion lower courts sought further expositions from the law officers of the higher courts. For an instance in 1794 see Bengal S.D.A. Proceedings, India Office Library (Rec.), Range 152, vol. 44, no. 10.

By 1788 the need for a Code was clear in his mind and, as this must be financed by the Company, he applied to Lord Cornwallis.[1] The European Judges must, in his opinion, be furnished with sufficient means of checking what the pandits reported. If necessary it should be possible to confront them with the Code, and require them to report in accordance with it. Taking Halhed's work as the basis for comparison, he approved it so far as it went, but showed that its treatment of contracts was too succinct and superficial (we have already seen why this was). Cornwallis and his successor approved and forwarded the enterprise. The urgency of the need was emphasized by the fact that in 1789 Jones detected a forgery.[2] Hindus were objecting to taking oaths when giving evidence in open court, and, in particular, to taking oaths on Ganges water. A Brahmin then compiled a treatise to show that swearing on Ganges water was prohibited. Had the forgery been undetected no doubt other productions would have increased the number of texts pandits might cite, and indeed it was easy to compile legal texts, and to interpolate elements into old works, which could not be distinguished from the original by any but an expert with a great library at his disposal.

From 1788 to 1793, indeed until his premature death in 1794, Jones was actively engaged in supervising the compilation of the Digest. He planned it, selected the principal author and his collaborators (in so far as he might), prescribed the arrangement, and specified what materials were to be used. The result, Jagannātha Tarkapañcānana's *Vivāda-bhaṅgārṇava*, or 'Ocean of resolutions of disputes', playfully referring to Halhed's 'Gentoo Code's' original title, was a success. It was completed

By Reg. II of 1798, s. 4, it was provided that where the judges doubted the accuracy of the opinion of their law officers because of an objection of the parties founded upon other law opinions exhibited by them or from reference to known books of Hindu law, they might obtain a further exposition from the law officers of the superior courts. W. H. Macnaghten gives an instance of ten pandits giving a corrupt opinion due to bribes: *Reports of Cases determined in the S.D.A.*, new edn., I (Calcutta, 1827), p. 40 (a case of 1801 relating to matters of 1793–5). Zillur Rahman, 'The Evolution of Civil Procedure in Bengal, 1772–1806', Thesis, Ph.D., London [unpublished], 1967. The bribing of a pandit was suspected in *Nundram* v. *Kashee Pandee* (1822) 3 Sel. Rep., 232; referred to at (1869) 3 Beng. L.R. 41.

[1] The letter has been cited above. Shore, pp. 306–12.

[2] Shore, pp. 325–6.

shortly after Jones's death, and the task of translating it fell to his natural successor, H. T. Colebrooke, about whom something must be said here. But before speaking of him and his work it is necessary to see how Jagannātha came to be chosen and why he produced the work as he did.

Since the law administered both in the Company's courts and in the Supreme Court was that of the twin schools of Mithilā and Bengal (corresponding to the modern 'Mitakshara' and 'Dāyabhāga' schools) it was necessary to have two digests, one to be applied to the litigants of each school. Jones's first attempt to obtain information was from Mithilā, and a concise Code, giving the law in a short and compact form, traditionally suited to students and (it was supposed) equally to European enquirers, appeared from the pen of Sarvoru Śarmā Trivedi in 1789 entitled *Vivāda-sārārṇava*, 'Ocean of all disputes'. This work, of which a copy is to be found in the India Office Library, formerly in Colebrooke's collection, was neither translated nor published: for then the enterprise entrusted to Jagannātha was expected to improve upon it.[1] Jagannātha was certainly conversant with every school of law and with the literature of every quarter. He tried to gather conflicting interpretations on every point at which the schools disagreed within the scope allotted to him, and carefully showed where the Maithilas and Gauḍas differed. Thus his digest rendered the work of Sarvoru Śarmā superfluous. However his assistants, most of whom were his pupils, were Bengalis, and were by tradition attached to the Bengal school. A preponderance of ideas properly belonging to that school was therefore to be expected, and it is certain that when Jagannātha's work was sent for here and there throughout British India Bengal biases were given additional support. Hence it is normally considered to be an authoritative work in the Bengal school, although in fact its plan was intended to incorporate Maithila notions as well as Bengali. The choice of author was appropriate since Jagannātha was not only a living encyclopaedia of law but also amongst the senior Hindu scholars then alive.[2] Whatever he wrote was bound to command respect,

[1] For an instance where it is known to have been used see below, p. 271, n. 2.

[2] Jagannātha was born in or about 1695–7: Kāṇe, *H.D.*, I, p. 466; J. Harington, *Elementary Analysis*, I (Calcutta, 1805), p. 182.

but his method was likely to be that approved by his own teachers and colleagues as in use before the British period; subject, that is to say, to his willingness to answer questions set for him by the British employers–a point to which we must return. The application of the techniques of *mīmāṃsā*, so puzzling to foreigners when encountered in a bare and unannotated translation, and of *nyāya* (logic), and the constant attempt to give every possible interpretation of the basic texts their due scope, resulted in a puzzle of exceeding complexity, and could only disappoint a reader who wanted to find out the rule of decision with the minimum of labour. Unwilling to stigmatize an intellectually respectable opinion as wrong, the author tactfully, and characteristically, states the less approved interpretation first, and follows with those which he approves. Sometimes a choice is not possible, and the responsibility for choice is thrown back upon the Judge, who is asked to decide whichever way appeals to him in the circumstances.

A careful examination of Jagannātha's work reveals something to which his translator does not refer, though it deserved mention. Jagannātha has some peculiar views, and harbours peculiar opinions for which no parallel can be found. His attitude to custom and usage is odd: it may be submitted that he accepts judicial practice as law, almost *communis error facit ius.*[1] From where could such a notion have come? Obviously some English lawyer has been consulting with him, putting questions to him, guiding him as to where Hindu learning must somehow be forthcoming. Similarly his comments on a wide range of topics reveal intercourse with a western mind. Apart from the *Mahānirvāṇa-tantra*, to which we shall return, this is unique. He reveals his being influenced in his discussions of assignment of debts,[2] the status of 'kings',[3] fraudulent litigation,[4] fraudulent practices,[5] the court's power to appoint guardians,[6] land-revenue settlements,[7] attachments of land and chattels and execution-sales in satisfaction of a decree for debt,[8] 'marksmen',[9] fraud and remedies therefor,[10] fraudulent and mistaken transfers

[1] I, pp. 69–70 (Madras, two-volume edition of 1864–5).

[2] I, 65. His concept of the status and role of the advocate in litigation (as a surety) is particularly interesting: I, 169, 172.

[3] I, 420. [4] I, 441. [5] I, 203. [6] II, 266, 576. [7] I, 308.

[8] I, 305–6, 316–17. [9] I, 442. [10] I, 404, 455.

contrasted,[1] also *bona vacantia* and voidable titles,[2] illegal contracts and restitution,[3] also the procedure to discover frauds in partition-accounts.[4] He may have heard of testaments, a possible rationalization of which seems to occur.[5] For our purposes it is particularly interesting that Jagannātha's opinions on the powers of the manager of a joint-family[6] and the powers of an undivided coparcener to alienate his share in the family property[7] (topics much in evidence in Anglo-Hindu law) go well beyond the scope of pre-existing Hindu textbooks and betray the conversation of an equity lawyer. The attempted rationalization of Chancery notions in terms of Hindu law texts is fascinating, and was fruitful in terms of the modern Hindu law, then in its birth-pangs. The śāstric law was hostile to fraud (*chala*) but the implementation of this hostility awaited such care.

The Digest consists of a continuous running treatment of Inheritance and Contracts, these being the topics prescribed for administration, as we have seen, in the Supreme Court. The *smṛti-s* appear in the course of the treatment as it proceeds. In the translation which Colebrooke completed in 1797 these *smṛti-s* were printed in large type and numbered, and the surrounding matter was printed as if it were a commentary upon them. This misleading method of presentation is largely responsible for the impression which many readers have gained of Jagannātha, that he was verbose, devious, inconclusive and self-contradictory.[8]

Colebrooke's qualifications for making the translation have remained unrivalled. A comparison of the translation with the original text, which is preserved in the India Office Library, and remains unpublished, shows the translator's competence.[9] All

[1] I, 227. [2] I, 456. [3] I, 457. [4] II, 489.
[5] II, 237. [6] I, 196, 203. [7] I, 154, 303–4, 402–5.

[8] Colebrooke attacks Jagannātha: T. E. Colebrooke, cited above, p. 224; Strange, cited above, II, pp. 175–6; the Preface to the *Two Treatises on the Hindu Law of Inheritance* (see below). Sir F. W. Macnaghten makes fun of Jagannātha constantly in his Preface, though he refers to him with respect in the body of his work.

[9] The doubts cast upon his skill by the late K. V. Veṅkaṭasubramania Iyer relate to a few very restricted instances, and the instance given above (p. 142) can hardly be regarded as significant, given the vast area of law Colebrooke effectually handled.

his life he pursued Sanskritic studies far beyond law. By 1794 he was able to publish a paper giving material taken direct from Sanskrit legal texts.[1] Between 1786 and 1791 he had been taking advantage of the same sort of technical assistance as that available to Jones, and he was able to speak to his pandits in Sanskrit as well as Persian, and to dispute on topics of law as well as any pandit. The virtues of learning 'the hard way' are borne out in his success. He came to India at the age of eighteen and his mind had received no confirmed preoccupation with Western cultural materials.

Colebrooke, however, differed somewhat from Jones in his estimate of the value of the scheme set out for Jagannātha. Colebrooke knew better than Jones that no production, even that of a committee, could by any governmental authorization oust the textbooks and treatises which formed the existing śāstric learning. The pandits would be glad to cite Jagannātha, as they did more eagerly than he had expected or welcomed.[2] But from such a work they would not find conclusive answers to all the questions put to them by the courts, nor be able to instruct the European Judges in the technique by which they were themselves bound. Jagannātha recorded the state the *śāstra* had reached, stimulated, as it were, by questions from some attorney or barrister. He aimed to do no more. This is where the misunderstanding lay. Modern Islamic and Jewish scholars will admit at once that even an orthodox scholar cannot fix the *fiqh* or the *halachah* for all time. Even Maimonides did not put an end to Jewish legal scholarship. Likewise Jagannātha would have rejected as comical the notion that he had preserved the *śāstra*, as it were, in cold storage.

To Jones, persuaded that Hindu law was immemorially old, if not as old as the beginning of the Kali age (!), and that it was possible to fix it at any given moment without doing it any harm, it seemed quite practical to cause a book to be written from which the lawyers of the new age could cite as they would cite the *Corpus Juris* or 'Coke upon Littleton'. Jones's attitude is exemplified by the extraordinary episode of his pandit and

[1] 'On the duties of a faithful Hindu widow': T. E. Colebrooke, cited above, II (*Essays*, vol. 1), chapter 3.

[2] Strange, cited above, II, pp. 175–6.

Halhed's *Code*. In a letter dated May 6th, 1786 to Sir J. Macpherson he said,[1]

> One point I have already attained; I made the pundit of our court read and correct a copy of Halhed's book in the original Sanscrit, and I then obliged him to attest it as good law, so that he never now can give corrupt opinions, without certain detection.

It is obvious that Jones believed that the conscientious opinions of the *śāstrī-s* could be made to assume a fixed form,[2] from which neither they nor their successors would be able to deviate. The absurdity of asking any lawyer to certify the correctness of any book, even one of his own composition, did not apparently strike him. The need for certainty took precedence over the comfort of the science of jurisprudence. The *dharmaśāstra* as a living and responsible science in matters which might come before a court of law died when the courts assumed judicial knowledge of the system in 1864, but the death-sickness commenced with Jones's quaint act of 1786. Colebrooke was not so naïve. Jones's translation of the *Manu-smṛti*, destined to have more effect on oriental studies in the West than it ever had on the administration of law in India, was a project of which he could hardly disapprove, but which he cannot have believed useful for the purpose in question. No translation of any *smṛti*, even that of Manu, could enable the courts to administer to the Hindus the 'law of the Shaster' or their 'law and usages'. In the same way no single text could do duty for an able pandit's learning if honestly applied.

Colebrooke therefore set about the task of supplementing Jagannātha's *Vivāda-bhaṅgārṇava* with work in English and Sanskrit which would, he hoped, both make Hindu law more certain, uniform and accurate, and at the same time open the whole subject to European judges, and so make them independent of their 'Hindu Law Officers'.

Translators, Critics and Patrons

Jagannātha was difficult for Europeans to follow. A shorter work crystallizing the rules and eliminating the *mīmāṃsā* reason-

[1] Shore, cited above, pp. 276–7; 294.

[2] Yet the *Vivādārṇava-setu* itself (*Gentoo Code*, 1777 edn., p. 282) says that the peasants are bound to obey the *śāstra* as expounded by pandits, and that pandits who do not expound what the *śāstra* says are to be fined.

ings was needed. The efforts of commentators should be capable of being distinguished from their sources. The work must be by an authority of eminence. Two pandits of the Benares school were approached successfully, the aged Bālam Bhaṭṭa and the Maithila pandit Citrapati.[1] The latter completed his work in 1803–4, rather long after Colebrooke's service at Mirzapur (1795–9), while the former disappointed his patron by supplying material only by fits and starts, and then copying quantities from a seventeenth-century work which he obviously thought was too good to improve upon. Neither Citrapati's nor Bālam Bhaṭṭa's efforts were translated or published, and the patronage was wasted. Colebrooke in a somewhat peevish manuscript note to the material received from Bālam comments that he might be obliged to undertake a śāstric digest himself, arranged upon principles which the European lawyer could understand and consisting of rules which the native jurist could accept. He did in fact proceed far upon this project.[2] From quite early on however it was evident to him that his results might be received with scepticism. As an English pandit his determinations of controversial matters might convince neither the native population nor the European judge. Yet during 1800 to 1815, when he returned to England, we hear repeatedly of the progress of his project, and his hopes of publishing the result. Meanwhile he had been appointed to judicial office in the Sadr Diwani

[1] Govinda Dās, introd., Bālaṃ-bhaṭṭa, *Vyavahāra-Bālaṃbhaṭṭi* (Benares, 1914), pp. 46 f.

[2] India Office Library. Eggeling's Cat. of Skt. Mss., no. 1507, p. 458 (margin of the *Dharmaśāstra-saṅgraha*): '1st May, 1800. The first sheets were received from Bāla Sarma Payagunda on this date.–This is little else but the Viramitrodaya revised. As it is a scarce book and very little known, Bālasarma and his pupil Menudeva did not suspect I could detect the plagiarism. But as Mitra Mirsa's work is far better than the Payagunda is capable of producing himself, there is no reason to regret this imposition. I shall nevertheless pay him the promised reward and continue his monthly establishment until the work be completed and the reward be delivered to him. After the experience I have had, that no Pandit is capable (or adapted by his habits of thinking) to compile a digest in the form I require, I must now seriously set about compiling it myself. I shall take the arrangement of this compilation for the basis; because the public have, no doubt, more confidence in the Pandits than in me. 3rd May, 1800. H.C.' References to the abortive Supplementary Digest are made in various letters, in T. E. Colebrooke, cited above, I, pp. 137–8, 140, 209, 212, 219, 225, 226. See also ibid., pp. 275–6.

Adalat, and this kept him very busy. He maintained a correspondence with other persons interested in Hindu law, and regularly commented on pandits' opinions from the Madras Presidency.[1] He prepared an English translation of the *Mitākṣarā* (inheritance portion) and the *Dāyabhāga*, with a valuable introduction to both, in order that the judges might have the means of learning at first hand how the basic principles of the two schools of Hindu law were originally formulated.[2] Before he left India, and indeed for some time after it was his translation of Jagannātha that was in demand and was repeatedly cited;[3] thirty years later the reverse happened: few consulted Jagannātha and regular reference was made to the other work. The change of climate influenced his decision not to publish his Supplementary Digest. An effort was made to provide a Digest of the Law of Contract, but this contained more civil law than Hindu law, and was very little used.[4] A general lack of interest in further publication supervened and from the last decade of his life (1827–37) until the 1860's no further research was done into the textual bases of the *dharmaśāstra*.

Meanwhile the process initiated in the 1790's was bearing fruit. The various pandits in the earlier days were appointed without examination and apparently upon the basis of prestige, which would in any case be very difficult to determine.[5] Pandits

[1] Strange, cited above, vol. II. He was prepared to give Strange an opinion as to whether the *Smṛti-candrikā* or the *Parāśara-Mādhavīya* was the better work (neither were cited in Bengal).

[2] The *Two Treatises* (cited above, p. 248, n. 8) was first published in Calcutta in 1810, and subsequently often reprinted. The Preface to it was reprinted in Cowell's first volume of the *Essays* (T. E. Colebrooke, cited above).

[3] T. E. Colebrooke, cited above, I, p. 277.

[4] *Treatise on Obligations and Contracts*, vol. I (all published) (London, 1818). Cited as an authority on Civil Law in (1855) 11 S.D.A. Rep. (Beng.), 553, 554–5. Cited as an authority on Hindu law in W. H. Macnaghten, *P. and P. of Hindu Law*, II, 279 n., 283 n., 285 n. Also in *Doe d. Kullammal* (1862) 1 M.H.C.R. 85, 88; *Virasami* (1863) 1 M.H.C.R. 375, 379; *Dantuluri* (1865) 2 M.H.C.R. 360, 361. T. E. Colebrooke, cited above, I, pp. 279–280, 315, refers to the work.

[5] H. H. Wilson's review of Sir F. W. Macnaghten's book in *Quarterly Oriental Magazine*, III (1825), pp. 171 f., reprinted in Wilson's *Works*, V (1865), pp. 1 ff. For the succeeding period see Kalikinkar Datta, 'Some judicial appointments', *J. Bih. Res. Soc.* 33 (1947), pp. 193–7, discussing a Resolution of 1825 and Regulation XI of 1826. See p. 237, n. 2, above.

of the Supreme Court were at one time a byword for inefficiency. Because they were likely to be consulted by clients and because the appointments were sufficiently well paid there seems to have been some competition for the posts. The same must have been the case in the subordinate courts as in Calcutta itself. As soon as it became known that Colebrooke was looking out for treatises on the subjects usually handled in the courts, that he was not only collecting old works but interested in new ones, two sorts of treatise began to appear and to be offered to him. When he commissioned work he paid for it out of the Company's funds, and doubtless when these works were offered to him he returned a suitable present. The traditional interest in controversial legal work was stimulated, and treatises appeared which merely continued the line of older works such as had been reviewed by Jagannātha. At the same time a relatively new type of production appeared, which concentrated on the rules and eschewed discussion. Through either sort of work prestige could be gained, and the offer to government through Colebrooke could result in prospects of a lucrative appointment as well as immediate reward. An otherwise inexplicable plethora of works on Civil Litigation, Inheritance and Adoption began to appear, which apparently did not abate until about 1830.

Some of the pandits holding high appointments were authors and their works have survived. On the whole they are much more concise than Jagannātha, but appear more narrowly traditional. The printing of such work hardly commenced before 1826.[1] In that year Pītāmbara Siddhāntavāgīśa's *Dāya-kaumudī* appeared with the commentary of one Rāmanātha Gosvāmī. The Calcutta press was soon busy with other similar work. Lakṣmīnārāyaṇa Sarasvatī, himself a pandit and the son of Gadādhara Tarkavāgīśa who was a pandit of the Sanskrit College at Calcutta in 1824, invested in the printing of Raghunandana's *Dāyatattva* and Śrīkṛṣṇa's *Dāya-krama-saṅgraha* in 1828 and in their master's, Jīmūtavāhana's, *Dāyabhāga* in 1829 (an order of priority which is enlightening, for it seems that then it was believed, correctly, that the pupils were more important than their master). Lakṣmīnārāyaṇa's own work–for it seems

[1] According to Burnell (*Ordinances of Manu*, London 1884, p. lxii, n. 5) Colebrooke's protégé 'Bābu Rām' published a bad edition of Manu in Calcutta, 1813, which apparently was available to Bühler.

that he was the Lakṣmīnārāyaṇa Nyāyālaṅkāra who wrote the semi-popular *Vyavasthāratnamālā*, or 'Garland of Jewels of Legal Opinions' on inheritance and adoption–was published in 1830.[1] Rāmajaya Tarkālaṅkāra Bhaṭṭācārya, the son of Mṛtyuñjaya, Supreme Court pandit c. 1818–21, and himself Supreme Court pandit in succession to his father, wrote a *Dāya-kaumudī*, 'A Clear Light on *Dāya*', a *Dattaka-kaumudī*, and a *Dāna-kaumudī*, elucidating respectively inheritance, adoption and gifts. The first was published in Calcutta in 1827, the second at the same time, while the last, plainly because of its inferior practical importance, apparently remains unpublished. Concise and up to date, the works deserved to be used. It appears however that they were seldom relied upon, though an instance of reliance upon a citation in the *Dāya-kaumudī* as late as 1868 may be referred to.[2] There are many works that cannot be ascribed to this period with certainty, but in the Appendix to this chapter appears a list of the authors and works which may in all probability relate to Colebrooke's time or that which immediately followed it. The special cases of the Malayālam *Vyavahāra-mālā* and the *Mahānirvāṇa-tantra* to which we have already alluded must be treated separately.

One may wonder why 1826–9 were critical years in the publication of modern śāstric literature. After that date a long gap intervened until in 1863 pandit Bharatcandra Śiromaṇi published the *Dāyabhāga* with all the important commentaries. The truth seems to be that the group that appeared between those years were in answer not so much to the needs of court pandits or the students of the Sanskrit College, who were virtually the only people who could use them, as to the impression created amongst the judges and the public at large by the publication of Sir Francis W. Macnaghten's *Considerations* in 1824, and, to a much more limited extent, by Sir Thomas

[1] In Bengali with Skt. citations. British requirements were met. Definitions and propositions are arranged in logical sequence. Question, Answer, and Authority appear regularly in that order. This service to Bengalis other than *śāstris* anticipates the work of Nandakumāra Kaviratna Bhaṭṭācārya, whose *Vyavasthā-sarvasva* in Bengali appeared in 1858, and that of Śyāmacaraṇa Vidyābhūṣaṇa Śarmā. The latter falls outside the scope of this essay. The present writer has not seen a copy of the *Mitākṣarā* said to have been published by Lakṣmīnārāyaṇa Nyāyālaṅkāra in 1829.

[2] *Jijoyiamba* (1868) 3 M.H.C.R. 424 at 451.

Strange's *Elements* in 1825. If this is so the pandits' answer was full of dignity. Such publications best refuted the damaging calumnies cast upon them and their learning by Macnaghten, and reassured Europeans against the doubts which even so well-meaning a writer as Strange could not fail to arouse. Not that these works necessarily appeared without European aid. They appeared more or less simultaneously with W. H. Macnaghten's first issues of the *Sadr Diwani Adalat Reports* (1827), and the two volumes of his *Principles and Precedents of Hindu Law* (1828–9). Yet the fact remains that the works of European authors were of far more practical use than even the excellent printed copies of genuine Sanskrit śāstric works. The courts used less and less the recent miscellaneous works and relied more and more upon the ancient works which had been translated. The pandit as a professor of a living science was rejected for the more or less fossilized treatises which would head the pandits' lists of references.

This tendency was encouraged by features of panditry to which we have already referred. There was no knowing whether the pandit's references were genuine or not. Attempts to collect Sanskrit manuscripts were going ahead. The pace of search, copying and collection increased from the beginning of the third quarter of the nineteenth century, but in the vital period which we are considering practically no good library existed under European control except Colebrooke's, and that went to England in 1815. The doubts regarding the origins of the *Dattaka-candrikā* were symptomatic. It is accepted without question by Bengali pandits that the *D.-c.*, which attributes itself in most copies to an otherwise unknown Kubera, was the work of Raghumaṇi, a well-known pandit of the 1790 period, teacher of Raghurāma Śiromaṇi, whom we find as a pandit of the Supreme Court in the 1820's and in 1818 as a referee in some litigation, the author of the *Siddhānta-nirṇaya* and the *Dāyabhāgārtha-dīpikā-padyāvalī*. Other works of Raghumaṇi besides the *D.-c.* have not been traced, and so it is impossible to check the assertion. A verse at the end is said to reveal Raghumaṇi's authorship.[1] It is

[1] G. C. Sarkār Śāstrī, *Hindu Law*, 3rd edn. (Calcutta, 1907), p. 30; the same, *Hindu Law of Adoption* (Calcutta, 1891), pp. 122–6. Kāṇe, *H.D.*, I, p. 557, is guarded. W. H. Macnaghten's silence is interesting; both he and his father treat the work seriously.

alleged that he foisted this text upon the courts when an authority was needed to prove a particular point. That forgeries did occur to win available rewards is certain.[1] But there is no proof that it was widespread or that persons as highly placed as Raghumaṇi would stoop to it. H. C. Sutherland has been blamed for having chosen the *D.-c.* and the *Dattaka-mīmāṃsā*, as if they were taken at random from a wide selection of texts on adoption, in order to make his translations of original works on that subject. The truth may be that the *Dattaka-candrikā* was so highly regarded on its merits that any question regarding its authorship could be neglected. Two recent editors of the text take it as genuine, though nothing is known of the author, and the present writer is inclined to think that the rumours in Calcutta were false. The Calcutta High Court acknowledged the work's authenticity[2] in 1917 and the Supreme Court of India has not reopened the question when opportunity to do so presented itself. The episode however illustrates the suspicion with which recent works were regarded even from the time of Sir William Jones and W. H. Macnaghten, and explains in part why great efforts were made to obtain works of antiquity. The same point of view was shared by Rāja Rāmmohun Roy, who himself was conscious of forgeries interfering with the intellectual atmosphere when social and religious questions came to be debated.[3]

Colebrooke's *Two Treatises* was followed by P. M. Wynch's translation of the *Dāya-krama-saṅgraha* (1818), Sutherland's version of the two selected works on adoption mentioned above (1821, reprinted in 1825) and, in far-off Bombay Presidency, Borradaile's translation of the *Vyavahāra-mayūkha* (1827, the first of a line of versions of that important work). None of these translations, for long the only books available to the courts besides Jagannātha, Colebrooke's *Two Treatises* and Jones's *Manu*, was up to the standard of Colebrooke's work; and the correctness of the translations, as well as the standing and authority of the works themselves generally and in parti-

[1] D. C. Bhaṭṭāchāryya, 'The Śrāddhasāgara of Kullūka Bhaṭṭa (a Spurious Work)', *I.H.Q.*, 27 (1951), pp. 109 ff.

[2] *Asita Mohan* AIR 1917 Cal. 292.

[3] Writing in 1830 (*Abstract of the Arguments . . .*) in J. C. Ghose, *English Works of Raja Rammohun Roy*, II (Calcutta, 1901), p. 191, footnote.

cular localities, have often been the subject of debate in the courts.

No such work was done in South India until the time of A. C. Burnell. The Madras judges had the aid of pandits whose learning was not equal to the standards usual in Mithilā and Bengal. That the Company had really attempted to know what the Hindu religion taught in law as in other spheres is proved by a manuscript of a Telugu translation of the *Mitākṣarā* now to be seen at the School of Oriental and African Studies and dated 1695.[1] A copy of the *Smṛti-candrikā* written in Telugu script is to be seen in the Madras High Court library.[2] *Exempla* of Jagannātha's digest in Telugu script are to be seen in Madras and Mysore, thus proving that the British patronage of that author had its effect in the far-off peninsula. More interesting, perhaps, is the fine *devanāgarī* copy of the fifth (*dāyabhāga*) chapter of Jagannātha's digest to be seen at the Kerala High Court Library (Ernakulam).[3] It is written on paper watermarked with the date 1867 and the copy itself is dated *saṃvat* 1925, i.e. 1868. The previous history of this apparently out-of-the-way copy is unknown, but it was not in the Cochin High Court Library in 1949, though Cochin would have been a reasonable place to find it in view of the Hukumnāma of 987 M.E., i.e. 1812, on which we shall have more to relate in another place.[4] The study of Bengal works in Kerala is proved by a further curious find. At the Tripunithura Grantha Library (seven miles from Cochin) there is a palm-leaf[5] in a fine clear Malayālam

[1] Accession No. 12904. The book contains a Telugu version of the *Daivajña-kaṇṭhābharaṇa* (on cosmogony), the *Sūrya-siddhānta* (astrology), the *Śaiva-siddhānta* (religion), and lastly the *vyavahāra-kāṇḍa* of the *Mitākṣarā*. One wonders how this came to Britain, as it must have been intended to belong to the Library of the Mayor's Court, Madras. The colophon explains that it was made for the *mahārāja-vartaka-śiromaṇi* (Chief Merchant of the Great King) 'Inggilisu Yistriye-yilu'. Enquiries of Telugu-speakers, a search through Sir C. Fawcett's *First Century of British Justice in India* (Oxford, 1934), in *Factory Records, Fort St. George*, vol. 10, and at the India Office Records, Commonwealth Office, have failed to clarify who or what these words mean. Whoever he was, the colophon tells us that he 'was curious to know about *dharmas* of Telugu people at Channapatna (Madras)'.

[2] Vol. 1290. It came into the possession of Sir T. Strange, who gave it to Sir J. H. Newbolt, September 17th, 1816 when he handed over his office as Chief Justice of the Supreme Court (Madras) to the latter.

[3] No. 8366. [4] See below, p. 263. [5] No. 683.

script containing the *Vyavahāra-tattva* and the *Dāyabhāga-smṛti-tattva* by Raghunandana, followed by the *Dāyādhikāra-krama-saṅgraha* of Śrī-Kṛṣṇa. These works certainly were copied in Kerala during the earlier years of the British period, for the first-named work would be of no interest once civil procedure had commenced upon its Anglo-Indian path and the Kerala Mahārājas had imitated British practice in this respect; while the study of Bengal texts in any part of Kerala prior to the British period is most improbable. As we shall see, even South Indian legal texts were by no means commonly known there.

Even in Madras, long before Burnell came in 1860, it was essential to know what the *śāstra* was and said. The Recorder's Court and later the Supreme Court repeatedly sent outside Madras for information. The judges obviously did not treat the *vyavasthā-s* of their pandits with entire confidence. In one instance it is clear that the replies of the pandits of the Supreme Court were far from satisfying, and the judge turned to Tanjore.[1] The Mahārājas of that state through several generations attempted to be model rulers on the orthodox pattern, and not only kept many pandits at their court engaged in legal research and the compilation of treatises, but actually engaged themselves in the work of codification under the supervision and with the assistance of these pandits. Questions were therefore sometimes sent through the Company's Resident with the Mahārāja to his pandits, with good success.[2] The surviving manuscripts at Tanjore attest the great interest of the pandits there in *dharma-śāstra*. Tanjore was an oasis. There was some activity in the *śāstra* in Kerala, possibly at Trivandrum and Cochin, but we have little information about it.

The man who knew the position in South India best was F. W. Ellis, who, arriving in India in 1798, soon acquainted himself with the languages of the South and also learnt Sanskrit. His career was unhappily cut short by accidental poisoning in 1819. What he has left indicates a very thorough

[1] Strange, *Hindu Law*, II, pp. 182 f. Cf. the contemptuous attitude which Holloway, J., (on whom see *RabelsZ.*, 24, pt. 4 [1959], pp. 670–82) took towards the texts obtained from the Tanjore Library in *Collector of Madura* (1864) 2 M.H.C.R. 206 at 222. The Privy Council's censures on the attitude then shown towards pandits were well merited.

[2] Strange, II, pp. 188 f. Misprints unfortunately obscure the names of the texts on which they relied.

acquaintance with Sanskrit legal texts and the state of the *śāstra* in South India.[1] In his view the *śāstra* must be applied according to the texts most approved by South Indian jurists, and traces of well-known customs to be found in such works must be respected, notwithstanding the fact that some authorities upon which other, or even the majority of, respectable śāstric commentaries depend would deny the customs legality.[2] There were some differences of viewpoint between Ellis and Colebrooke. Ellis seems to have had a bias against Brahmins. He certainly had sympathy with non-Brahmin castes which had attained education and culture without Brahminical guidance. As far as publication was concerned, his interest was to see Sanskrit legal authorities translated into the regional languages and so made available to the people who were in future to be governed by them. It is almost certainly to Ellis we owe the Tamil translation of the Malayālam *Vyavahāra-mālā* (which he knew as *Vyavahāra-samudram*). He seems never to have been able to translate the whole of it into English:[3] but then, at that date, an English version was of much less use than a Tamil one (designed for use in Tamil-speaking districts in Malabar and for use at the centre of law in the Presidency, the Sadr Court at Madras itself).

Though the compilations and studies at Tanjore attracted little attention it is certain that the British period saw a revival of interest in the *śāstra* throughout South India. The contributions which the British inspired were few, individual and curious.

A *tour de force* was the *Dāya-daśaślokī* of an otherwise unknown Śrīdhara or Lakṣmīdhara. The work, a marvel of brevity, bears the alternative name *Vyavahāra-daśaślokī*. The pair of names is of

[1] Many of Ellis's manuscripts, including those used by Sir T. Strange, are lost. Some contributions of his are published in *Asiatic Journal*, 7 (1819), pp. 644–6; 8 (1819), pp. 17–23; others, through the instrumentality of Sir Alexander Johnston (who was greatly interested in customary law in South India and Ceylon), at *Law Magazine* (London), 9 (1833), pp. 217–24. Ellis's work on the Malayālam *Vyavahāra-mālā* (*-samudram*) will be mentioned below. Likewise his treatise on Mirāsī right was published belatedly by C. P. Brown (*Three Treatises . . .*, Madras, 1852).

[2] Strange, II, p. 192.

[3] He dealt with it in an article on the Malayālam language, published by W. Elliot at *Indian Antiquary*, 7 (1878), pp. 275–87. For Ellis's work in general see *Indian Antiquary*, 4 (1875), pp. 220–1. The present writer owes this capital reference to Dr. K. Kunjunni Rāja.

some interest as it tells us that a Decad on Inheritance (*dāya*) was for some purposes more or less the same thing as a Decad on Law. This speaks of the British period, though Śrīdhara is totally unknown. The work spread through Madras Presidency and is available in Mysore and Kerala. The commentary on it, short and crisp, was made by one Durgayya, *alias* Siṃhasvāmī, *alias* Nṛsiṃhamuṇi, son of Vāsudeva, daughter's son of Nārāyaṇa, a *vandī*, or 'minstrel', of the god Raṅgarāja–an extremely unlikely person to engage in Sanskrit juridical work. The commentary is called *Dāyadaśaślokī-vyākhyā* and provides what Colebrooke was looking for, though that Colebrooke himself ever heard of Śrīdhara or Durgayya, or that they heard of him, is very unlikely. The commentary could be treated as a treatise in its own right, supporting the stanzas and explaining them, or, if the reader were not capable of profiting from it, could simply be discarded. The general notion of summarizing information in a limited number of verses was a commonplace, and here an Indian literary form subserves an Anglo-Indian need. The date can be settled, so far as the commentary is concerned, within some margin, by the fact that it contains rules which could only have been known to a pandit working through *Bengali* material.[1] In the ordinary way, before Jagannātha, such a development would have been virtually impossible, or at any rate in the immediate pre-British centuries. Thus the commentary which almost invariably accompanies the text belongs to post-1795. Durgayya must have been a member of one of the despised class of temple-Brahmins, dedicated to the service of the deity. Two suggestions about his caste have appeared: one that he was an Arayar from Seringapatam in Mysore or Srirangam near Trichinopoly; another that he was a Telugu Vaishṇava of the community styled Sāttānis. He wrote a work called *Duṣkaramālā* with a commentary consisting of a hymn to Viṣṇu illustrating rhetorical devices. He would never have written a legal treatise had he not been encouraged to do so by special circumstances. Just as the magistrate, as Ellis put it, had according to the *śāstra* a discretion to settle many questions of procedure according to equity and the needs of the case, so he could decide upon what authorities it would be most proper to rely. The individual pandit (as we have seen) was under a

[1] See *Z. f. vergl. Rechtsw.*, 61 (1959), pp. 1 f., at pp. 2–3.

conscientious obligation to report the law as he understood it from the sources which he regarded as appropriate; but the judge was under the contrary obligation of not enforcing the law as reported unless it accorded with what he felt appropriate in the circumstances. Thus, strictly according to Hindu theory as understood in Madras, the government would have been entitled to authorize the application of Durgayya's work in any court in the Presidency. We have no evidence that it did so. In view of the failure by Ellis and Strange to refer to Durgayya or even to Śrīdhara the completed work may be dated provisionally c. 1825.

When A. C. Burnell[1] came to India he was struck by the inadequacy of the textual material at the disposal of the Judges, of whom he was one. Although a hardening of the case-law had taken place since the 1830's it seemed still possible that a return to the *śāstra* might take place in several connexions, and Burnell set himself to produce material in English and Sanskrit which would enable the High Court at Madras to administer pure Hindu law. He was impressed by the *Dāya-daśaślokī* and published a translation of the text,[2] but not of the commentary, which remains to be edited and translated–yet another indication of the monumental lack of interest in this science. He paid some attention to another mysterious South Indian work of apparently recent and unexplained origin. This was the *Vyavahāra-mālā* which we shall call the Sanskrit *Vyavahāra-mālā*. It is evidently associated with Kerala, and copies with a Malayālam commentary–almost certainly the original publication–were collected by Colin Mackenzie and by Burnell; many are still to be seen in Trivandrum, not to speak of Madras. It consists of verses and commentary, and claims to have been written at the command of 'the king'. The verses are taken from standard authors, and it appears to be a traditional digest: it covers practical litigation including the topics which would normally be found in older treatises on *vyavahāra*, such as the *Vyavahāra-mayūkha*. It is concise. The edition in *devanāgarī* script of 1943 presents it in 97 pages. The edition of 1100 M.E., i.e. 1925, by Ullūr S. Parameśvara Iyer, containing the Malayālam comentary, is

[1] He was a 'Writer' in 1860 and became District and Sessions Judge in S. Canara in 1877.

[2] At Mangalore (S. Canara) in 1875.

a bulky publication. There is a version with a Tamil commentary, which may have been made for use in Pālghāt, but which, more probably, was intended in case the work acquired authority in the East Coast districts. Burnell was interested in the Sanskrit *Vyavahāra-mālā* and also in Varadarāja's work[1] to which we have often referred. In error it was supposed that the former was in some way connected with the latter. If we compare the texts on identical topics we see at once that they are quite unassociated. A slight indication of date is provided by the certain fact that the very curious Malayālam *Vyavahāra-mālā* was inspired as to title and as to some of its contents by the Sanskrit work of the same name.

Though the Malayālam *Vyavahāra-mālā*, known to Ellis and some others as *Vyavahāra-samudram* (due to a variant reading of the first verse?) says nothing about the British, it seems certain that it was written to provide a book-law for the Malayālam-speaking inhabitants of Malabar at a time when they returned to relative self-government after the East India Company acquired the Malabar District from Tipu Sultān. The enquiries of the British commissioners took place in 1792–3.[2] The Malayālam law-book was available in 1800.[3] Its style is very hard, and it seems to have been an experiment in versifying law and custom in a *maṇipravāla*, mixing local and (sometimes ungrammatical) Sanskrit words. There is a considerable *śāstric* element, but the bulk of the work concerns contracts and customs relating to Malabar, or at any rate to Kerala at large.[4] Aspects of the language identify the author as belonging to Malabar itself. There is no likelihood that such a work would have been written but for the presence of the British rulers and their notions of how local law should be found out and administered. And the

[1] He published a translation of a portion from Mangalore in 1872 under the title *The Law of Partition and Succession from the MS. Sanskrit Text of Varadaraja's . . .*

[2] See p. 242, n. 1 above.

[3] Major Walker, *Report upon the Tenures and Forms of Transfer of Land in Malabar, 20 July 1801* (Calicut, Malabar Government Press, 1862). In handwriting of the early nineteenth century is a manuscript of this work in the Madras High Court Library (Vol. 2691) which is dated (wrongly?) 1879.

[4] We await a critical text of the work at the hands of Vidwān A. D. Hariśarmā of Ernakulam.

attempt to give the whole system, including maxims of wisdom, legal procedure, land-tenure and rent questions, was evidently based upon the theory that if local laws could be made out the rulers would have them applied. And so in fact it turned out, by and large, in Malabar, more than in any other district of the Madras Presidency, though we cannot attribute this decisively to the law-book itself. The model, to some extent at least, was the Sanskrit *Vyavahāra-mālā* which would naturally have little appeal to a people not much given to respecting pure śāstric rules. Thus the Sanskrit work in question was almost certainly in existence by 1800. But it need not have been compiled much earlier than that. Direct approaches to Cochin and Travancore became common during the period following 1791, when the Company's boundaries with these states were enlarged, and political interests, in opposition to Tipu, coincided. It is very likely that the Sanskrit work was compiled not merely in imitation of British patronage in Bengal (of which perhaps not very much was known), but in response to a request for a South Indian law-digest. It must have been known that repositories of Sanskrit learning existed in Travancore, for example, as rich as, if not richer than what could be found at Tanjore–indeed Tanjore pandits would have confirmed this themselves. And meanwhile the resources of Mysore, a country also well provided with śāstric learning, were cut off due to hostile relations between that state and the British. If efforts were made to introduce the Sanskrit *Vyavahāra-mālā* into the East Coast they failed, as the better-established works, such as the *Smṛti-candrikā* and the *Sarasvatī-vilāsa*, gave, for those who could understand them, more than sufficient information with local nuances. Strange makes no reference to this work and we can take it as certain that by 1830 or so it was forgotten, except in Kerala. It may well have been used in Cochin and Travancore, under the system prevailing in those states. Legislation in Cochin in 1812[1] required that the Hindu law and custom should be the fundamental law of the state, and works dealing with all aspects of the system must have been required there more frequently than in contemporary Madras.

[1] Pandiyat Sankara Menon, *Cochin and her Courts of Law* (Ernakulam, 1937), pp. 101–2. *Malabar Law Quarterly*, 1 (1907), p. 6. A. Madhavan, 'Evolution of the Judicial System in Kerala', *Kerala L. J., J.*, 1963, pp. 14–18.

Less shadowy is the provenance of the curious publication of V. Vāsudeva Parabrahma Śāstrī entitled *Vyavahāra-darpaṇa* ('Mirror of Litigation') or *Jān Phraiyar Ṭāmas Bhūpāliyam.* Because it has been misdescribed by the late K. V. Raṅgaswāmī Aiyaṅgār[1] it deserves more than passing reference. This appeared in the Telugu script in Madras in 1851. Dedicated to John Fryer Thomas, whose 'realm' is referred to in the alternative title, it is an original treatise on Hindu law, divided into three sections (called *bimbas* or 'circles', *scilicet* of the 'realm') on Debt, Inheritance and Adoption respectively, and based on the mediaeval works authoritative in Madras, the *Mitākṣarā*, the *Smṛti-candrikā*, and so on. The larger portion of the work is in Sanskrit in Telugu characters, followed by summaries in the Telugu language. Because of the script and language it is virtually unusable by living specialists in the *śāstra*. However it is evident that Thomas patronized the author, largely because he was prepared as some others in the Presidency and indeed at Pondicherry had been prepared before him, to make Sanskritic learning available to the general public. The scope of the work including as it does Debt (which by implication includes Contract), proves what was formerly only suspected from the earlier work of Sir Thomas Strange, namely that the Hindu Law of Contract was administered in the East India Company's courts as well as in the Supreme Court at Madras down to as late as 1851.[2] Thomas was an apt person to be a patron. His career embraced a long judicial service and he had more than a trifling knowledge of Sanskrit. In 1851 he was a Member of Council at Madras and combined in his own person the Chief Judge of the Sadr Diwani Adalat and of the Sadr Faujdari Adalat (a court of short life): he was therefore virtually the Company's Chief Justice in Madras, and a fit person to receive the dedication in question.[3] There is no evidence that the

[1] At p. xi of his edition of the *Vyavahāra-nirṇaya*. It is not a mere condensation of that treatise.

[2] It was applied in the Small Causes Court in Madras as late as 1868 (*Vembakum Somayajee* (1868) 4 M.H.C.R. 176) and presumably until the passing of the Indian Contract Act, 1872.

[3] He was Sanskrit Examiner to the College at Madras in 1819. Sir T. Strange was under obligation to him for information on Hindu law, as is evident from the Preface to the first edition of Strange's work dated Bath, August 1825, at p. xxvi of the 1830 edition of the same.

Vyavahāra-darpaṇa was widely used. But the existence in the Madras Government Oriental Manuscripts Library of a separate copy of the Inheritance *bimba* in Malayālam script[1] proves that some attempt was made to introduce it into the western coast.

The Mahānirvāṇa-Tantra

We have followed the patronage of Sanskrit and other juridical writers from the beginnings of the British period in Bengal until the mid-nineteenth century, through all which period the courts were developing the rules of what is called 'Hindu law', and gradually and unevenly laying down the lines of the personal law of the Hindus which so grossly caricatures the *śāstra*. How exactly this caricature came about–a story important in itself, for otherwise we cannot understand contemporary Indians' ideas about their inherited laws–is a story for another chapter. At the very commencement of the story a most curious literary production appeared, which deserves separate treatment, since, though it was inspired by the foreign government, it was not directly the result of British patronage or instigation.

The *Mahānirvāṇa-tantra* purports to be a sacred book, and it is immensely popular, especially amongst Bengalis. The tantric religion, which is a variant of Hinduism, is there depicted in a comprehensive and elaborate form reminiscent of older and better-authenticated tantric works. Some respectability is induced into tantric theory and ritual, and the book would have a considerable claim to be the holy book of a reformed and missionary tantrism, if not actually of a reformed and missionary Hinduism. Though a religious book, it was actually used as a law book,[2] in view of its lengthy and scattered legal portions,

[1] Ms. B. 274. A copy is in the S.O.A.S. Library, London, accession No. 9118.

[2] The undated story is told by Macnaghten at his *Principles and Precedents of Moohummudan Law* ... (Calcutta, 1825), pp. xvii–xix. Macnaghten comments on the 'interminable and troubled ocean of Hindoo jurisprudence', and advises compulsory restriction of citation to 'works of notorious authority'. This in effect was done. The *Mahānirvāṇa-tantra* was not cited by the pandits in any of the numerous opinions published in the *Dharma-śāstrīya-vyavasthā-saṅgraha* (Allahabad, 1957) and belonging to the years 1824–36. The book is referred to at *Bhupati Nath* (1909) 37 Cal. 128, 137, 157.

but it has recently been rejected as an authority by the Supreme Court of India on the ground of its not being a specifically legal text.[1] Its author and date are unknown. Rāmmohun Roy was of the view that it was as authoritative, for his purposes, as the Upanishads, the *smṛti-s* and the *purāṇa-s.* It is odd to see him citing this bogus work as if it were scripture. But it was a work of genius and preached numerous notions favourable to the most advanced school of Hinduism of the day. Widow remarriage, abolition of suttee, abolition of slavery, intercaste marriage: all these were consistent with the religion here taught. The adepts at the doctrine were expected to engage in religious rituals in which all castes, including Muslims and by implication even Christians, could join. Consecrated food was to be eaten and even wine drunk by all initiated persons, whatever their origins. A form of marriage, called Śaiva marriage, with sacramental undertones, would enable unions of a matrimonial nature to occur which the *śāstra* forbade. By means of this easily-joined religious sect, had the author succeeded in his aim, not only all Hindus, but all Indians, could have joined in a religious brotherhood with a personal law transcending all personal laws.[2] The self-consciousness and self-suspicion of the religious Bengali of the early British period could be totally by-passed, if he became a *kaula* and adopted the tantric religion. The members of the sect were under the orders of the god Śiva, who, in this simulated conversation with the goddess Pārvatī, laid down the duties for the *kaulas.* These duties cover a much wider scope than the *śāstra.* There is a great deal of law of a practical nature, e.g. pre-emption, nuisances, breach of contract, highway robbery, and so on. Details are given of incestuous unions, and of the order of descent and distribution of property such as never occur in genuine śāstric works. The basic theory is that members of this 'new' religion, which would have been only a revived and spiritualized tantrism,[3] would claim to be governed

[1] *Shri Audh Behari Singh* [1955] S.C.R. 70, 74.

[2] The detailed references to the various passages of the *tantra* are given by the present writer in an extensive study of the work and its psychological background, 'A juridical fabrication of early British India: the Mahānirvāṇa-tantra', *Z. f. vergl. Rechtsw.*, 69, pt. 2 (1968), pp. 138–181.

[3] It may be emphasized that the religion of the book, for all its polytheistic shape, professes to lead to knowledge of the one Brahma (XIV, 123–5, 203, 211), and thus is fundamentally a monotheistic treatise, in the

by the laws set out in this sacred book. Thereupon they would be able to take advantage of a reformed and reinforced and comprehensive Hindu law, much better adapted to the needs of English judicial enquirers than the śāstric libraries then existing. The style was simplicity itself, and many of the Sanskrit terms are literally translated from English. If one looks again closely throughout the legal portions numerous rules are really Hindu versions of well-known rules of English law. Thus it is clear that the author, a religious thinker of exceptional stature, had access to someone who was himself acquainted with English law-books and legal thinking. English advocates in Calcutta had of course their Bengali clerks, and it is just conceivable that one acquired the necessary knowledge by this period. The work, in view of its expectations as to the jurisdiction of the courts and the style and probable complexion of the legal system under British government, cannot have been written later than 1785 or earlier than 1775. During this period no one doubted but that the key to legal administration was the religion of the parties, or at any rate of the defendant: and of this theory the author made the utmost use. Unfortunately for him and his remarkable book, the authorities became suspicious of recent and obscure texts and the generation of W. H. Macnaghten discouraged the pandits' reliance upon any that came into that class.

Conclusion

Scholarship both in India and in Europe was much retarded by the failure to produce adequate texts and translations, and an antiquarian interest in *smṛti-s* filled the niche which a comparative interest in the mediaeval and modern jurists should have occupied. Too great a concentration on *smṛti-s* followed, together with an inordinate interest in purely philological questions, which did nothing to advance the cause of purity in Indian legal-historical tradition. The British fellow-workers with the pandits were concerned with administration from day to day, and the philological background of the basic texts, and even the basic texts themselves, had only a very indirect bearing

characteristic Hindu fashion, according to which belief in or worship of many 'gods' does not preclude belief in One God.

on that. Europe did nothing to help India at that vital stage. What were the results, then, of that fruitful early period of British and Indian co-operation?

Although the materials require a far closer survey than they have obtained certain propositions may be put forward for further consideration.

(1) The jurists who were the authors of the works commissioned or inspired by British officials were glad to supply advice to the new 'monarch', the East India Company, just as if it had been a Hindu king.

(2) They quickly grasped the idea that a law would be administered: a 'new *śāstra*', bearing a real relationship to the ancient system, not standing utterly aloof from it as the Islamic system of the previous rulers had done, and yet growing upon and out of it in some way that could only be grasped if English lawyers and their ideas were studied. The most emphatic example of this was the *Mahānirvāṇa-tantra*, which failed as a law-book but has survived with acclaim as a book of religion.

(3) They were able to assimilate some of the constitutional changes, and Jagannātha at least was able to adjust the law he was codifying to some of the developments initiated by the British administration itself. Flexibility was not entirely lacking.

(4) Their ability to digest, and to state propositions of law, was greater than their ability to understand the precise requirements of a British court, and in particular that the European would find it difficult to arrive at practical conclusions by way of traditional Hindu reasoning and flexible Hindu administrative procedure.

(5) Knowing that different parts of India favoured different schools of law (though whether they envisaged 'sub-schools' is doubtful), and that one law could seldom be posited for all Hindus, they could not see that a definite solution to a legal problem was of more value in Anglo-Indian practice than the hypothetical correct solution at which they, as professors of law, were aiming.

(6) Finally, they were divided on the question whether a 'modern' work should attempt to *report* or to *reconcile* the divergent views of the schools. The progress of British administration did not allow time, in which agreement might be reached on this question. As a result works juxtaposing *Mitākṣarā* and

Dāyabhāga viewpoints exist, contrary to pre-British usage; and works amalgamating and compromising the divergent traditions in a manner reminiscent of the sixteenth century, but hardly consistent with the position as established by the middle of the eighteenth century, when the schism between Bengal and the rest of India had been accepted as incurable.

The works produced during c. 1772–1851 had little practical influence, being used somewhat unevenly by pandits. Their function after 1864 was minimal. Closer work on them is needed before we can be sure why this was so. But if the whole process of restating Hindu law came to be abandoned, the responsibility must be laid in part at the pandits' door: what the British really required was hardly within the pandits' power to supply; had they been beyond suspicion they would have continued to be treated as experts, and it is just conceivable that under British pressure a working compromise between the two very different jurisprudential techniques might have arisen not too far from *stare decisis*. In the course of this it would have emerged that the Hindu religion was consistent with far more flexibility and far more novelty than the British observers of the period of Rāmmohun Roy and later could have believed. As it was, the British administrators insisted upon clarity, certainty and finality in terms foreign to Hindu tradition, and if the pandit was true to his *śāstra* he could not at the same time substitute the new attempts at legislation for his own old authorities. Perhaps the attempts were doomed to failure.

Appendix

The following two lists are given subject to correction. A closer study of the works and their contents may reveal that some were produced during the British period but not directly under the influence of foreign stimulus. Such discoveries must await further research.

I. Works attributable to British influence or patronage

Title	*Author*	*Date*	*Published or translated*
Dattaka-kaumudī	Rāmajaya	c. 1827	Pub. 1827[1]
Dāna-kaumudī	Rāmajaya	c. 1827[2]	
Dāya-kaumudī	Rāmajaya	c. 1827	Pub. 1827[3]
Dāyabhāgārtha-dīpikā-padyāvalī	Raghurāma	c. 1800[4]	
Dāyabhāga-vinirṇaya	Kāma-deva	c. 1825[5]	
Dāya-daśaślokī savyākhyā	Durgayya	c. 1825	Trans. (text only), 1875[6]
Dāyādhikāri-krama	Lakṣmīnārāyaṇa	c. 1829(?)[7]	
Dharmaśāstra-saṅgraha	Bālam-bhaṭṭa	1801–3[8]	
Mahānirvāṇa-tantra	*unknown*	c. 1775–85	Pub. 1876–;[9] Trans. 1892, 1913
Vivāda-candrikā	Anantarāma	c. 1790[10]	

[1] The *author* is referred to frequently by Sir F. W. Macnaghten. The *work* is referred to by W. H. Macnaghten, *P. and P. of Hindu Law*, II, p. 200. Kāṇe, *H.D.*, I, p. 557. It is referred to in at least one *vyavasthā* in the *Dharmaśāstrīya-vyavasthā-saṅgraha* (above: 1824–36 being the outside years). A copy in *grantha* script is available in the Madras G. O. Mss. Lib. (R. 4669) proving again the spread of even minor works from Bengal in the British period.

[2] Kāne, I, p. 559.

[3] W. H. Macnaghten, where cited, II, 138.

[4] The author was a pupil of Raghumaṇi, pandit of Colebrooke. Rājendralāl Mitra's *Notices* (hereafter 'N'), new series, I, p. 174. Kāṇe, I, p. 561.

[5] W. H. Macnaghten, II, 135. Eggerling's Cat. of Skt. Mss. in the India Office Library, 1525. Hṛiṣikeśa Śāstrī and S. C. Gui, *Descr. Cat. of Skt. Mss. in the Library of the Calcutta Sanskrit College* (hereafter 'Cal.S.C.'), 161. Kāṇe I, p. 561 under D.b.-nirṇaya.

[6] Text: Keith's Continuation of Eggerling's Catalogue, 5516. P. P. S. Śāstrī's *Descriptive Catalogue of Skt. Mss. in the Tanjore Mahārāja Serfoji's Sarasvatī Mahāl Library*, Tanjore (hereafter 'T'), 18884–5. With the commentary it is available Keith 5517; Madras G. O. Mss. Lib., R. 1806 (also R. 612 b); T. 18886–8; at the Adyar Library (73477, 68282); of three copies at Mysore only one has the commentary; also Travancore Univ. Mss. Library, 7841. Kāṇe, I, p. 560. A copy of text and commentary is available at the S.O.A.S. Library, London.

[7] Kāṇe, I, p. 561.

[8] Eggerling, 1507. Incomplete. See above, p. 251, n. 2.

[9] For bibliographical information see *Z. f. vergl. Rechtsw.*, 69, pt. 2 (1968), 138 ff., where the only commentary is referred to.

[10] Aufrecht, *Catalogus Catalogorum*, 519. *New Catalogus Catalogorum* (Madras), p. 138. Eggerling, 1530. W. H. Macnaghten II, 139, 140. The author was the son of Rāmacaraṇa Nyāyālaṅkāra.

Title	*Author*	*Date*	*Published or translated*
Vivāda-bhaṅgārṇava	Jagannātha	1792–4	Trans. 1796–7[1]
Vivāda-sārārṇava	Sarvoru Śarmā	1789[2]	
Vivādārṇava-setu, -bhaṅga	Bāṇeśvara, etc.	1773–5	Trans. 1774–5 Pub. 1888[3]
Vyavasthā-ratna-mālā	Lakṣmīnārāyaṇa	c. 1829	Pub. 1830[4]
Vyavahāra-darpaṇa	V. Parabrahma	c. 1850	Pub. 1851[5]
Vyavahāra-mālā (Skt.)	*unknown*	c. 1792	Pub. 1925, 1943[6]
Vyavahāra-mālā, -samudram (Mal.)	*unknown*	c. 1795[7]	
(Vyavahāra-) Siddh-ānta-pīyūsā	Citrapati	1803–4[8]	
Siddhānta-nirṇaya	Raghurāma	c. 1800[9]	

[1] Above, pp. 245–8. W. H. Macnaghten, I, pp. xxii. Referred to by pandits, ibid., I, 89 (1807); II, 177 (1810), 295 (1817), 213 (1820), 48 (1823), 184 (1824), 271–2 (1825), 95 (1826), 98 (1827), 45, 113–14, and 223 (undated); also F. W. Macnaghten (cited above), App., pp. li, lii, lv (c. 1818–23), pp. 114, 117, 130, 138, 148, 403. Amongst copies in Telugu script see Keith, 5502. Aufrecht, 580. Kāṇe, I, p. 622. The *vyavasthā-s* printed in the *Dharmaśāstrīya-vyavasthā-saṅgraha* (see above p. 265, n. 2) refer to this work frequently.

[2] Aufrecht 580. Madras G. O. Mss. Lib., *Desc. Cat. Skt. Mss.*, VI, no. 3203. Adyar 8.I.9 (note these S. Indian references for a minor British work). Referred to by pandits in No. 18 of 1814 at 1 Sel. Decrees (Madras) 104, cited at (1864) 2 M.H.C.R. 213. Kāṇe, I, p. 622. It is of interest that it does *not* appear to have been cited by the Bengali pandits in the *vyavasthā-s* printed in the *Dharmaś.-vyav.-saṅgraha* (above).

[3] Aufrecht, 580. Eggerling, 1506. W. H. Macnaghten, I, pp. xxii, 48; II, pp. 135, 138, 139, 141. Referred to by pandits ibid., II, 177 (1810), 280 (1822), 184 (1824), 95 and 212 (1826), and 45, 70–1 (undated); also in F. W. Macnaghten, App., p. lv (c. 1818–23); also frequently in the *Dharmaś. -vyav.-saṅgraha* (above). Kāṇe, I, p. 622. See above, pp. 239 ff.

[4] Aufrecht, 616. See above, p. 254, n. 1. [5] See above, p. 264.

[6] See above, p. 261. Eggerling, 1504. Keith 5507–9 (all three collected by Mackenzie and datable in the 'eighteenth century' or c. 1800, c. 1810). Madras G. O. Mss. Libr., R. 1850, 2441. With Malayālam commentary: ibid., 15, 943; Keith 5506 (dated 1810). The Poona edition was based on mss. in private hands in Kerala. There are seven mss. in Malayālam script in the University Mss. Library at Trivandrum, and one ms. with the same Malayālam commentary is at Tripunithura, No. 1295. Kāṇe, I, p. 630. See above, p. 263.

[7] See above, p. 262.

[8] Eggerling, 1508–10. Cal.S.C., 142. Kāṇe, I, p. 631. Two copies in Mithilā (Nos. 356, 356A, 411) are noted in K. P. Jayaswāl and A. P. Śāstrī, *Desc. Cat. of Mss. in Mithila*, I (Patna, 1927), at pp. 397, 486.

[9] Aufrecht, 719. See above, p. 270, n. 4.

II. Works possibly written in response to British request or encouragement

Title	*Author*
Aprajā-strīdhanādhikāra[1]	
Avibhakta-dhana-viṣaya[2]	
Avibhakta-bhrātṛ-putra-vibhāga[3]	
Asagotra-putra-parigraha-parīkṣā[4]	
Jīvatpitṛka-vibhāga-vyavasthā-sārasaṅgraha	Madhusūdana[5]
Datta-candrikā	Paṭṭarācārya[6]
Datta-ratnākara	Dharmarājādhvarī[7]
Dattaka-candrikā	Kubera-bhaṭṭa[8]
Dattaka-darpaṇa	Dvaipāyana[9]
Dattaka-mīmāṃsā	Sudhākara[10]
Dattakolāhala	Raṅganātha[11]
Dāyabhāga-tīkā (?)	Kṛṣṇa-kānta Śarma[12]
Dāyabhāga-siddhānta	Balabhadra Tarka-vāgīśa[13]
Dāya-sarvasvaṃ[14]	

[1] T. 19, 024. [2] T. 19, 033.

[3] Madras G. O. Mss. Lib., C. 1430, of which there is a copy in the S.O.A.S. Library.

[4] Asiatic Society of Calcutta. Microfilmed, India Office Library, Reel 366.

[5] Madras G. O. Mss. Libr., R. 2529. Written in Lahore towards the middle of the nineteenth century? Cf. Aufrecht, 617: *Vyavahāra Sāroddhāra.*

[6] Adyar, 69432. Madras G. O. Mss. Library, R. 4642 a.

[7] Adyar, 70298. Madras G. O. Mss. Libr., D. 3167. Available also at Mysore.

[8] Aufrecht, 243. See above, p. 256. Macnaghten refers to it, where cited, I, p. xxiii and *passim.* Kāṇe, I, p. 557. Sutherland's 'mistake' in attributing it to Devānda, *alias* Devaṇṇa-bhaṭṭa is at last explained by the appearance of a copy actually ascribed to 'Devaṇḍa-bhaṭṭa' (No. 185 in Jayaswāl and Śāstrī's *Catalogue*), if the particulars are to be trusted. The Adyar palm-leaf ms., 75808, has the attribution to Kubera-paṇḍita. The script is *grantha* and its age indicates it may have been written between 1800 and 1850.

[9] Adyar, 2109. Telugu script. Also available at Mysore and in the Madras G. O. Mss. Library.

[10] Adyar 73925. Telugu script. *Upajātī* metre. 91 verses. Not noticed by Kāṇe.

[11] Madras G. O. Mss. Library, R. 6852. Available at Mysore. Adyar, 2107, in Devanāgarī script, 7 folios, 200 granthas. He refers to the *Varadarājīya*, as well as the *Candrikā, Datta-ratnākara* and *Datta-mahodadhi*; and therefore may well be a southerner. He refers to Jagannātha at fol. 5a, line 10. He may be a late nineteenth-century author.

[12] First published in 1866. Kāṇe, I, p. 560.

[13] Eggerling, 1529. Kāṇe, I, p. 560.

[14] Asiatic Society, Calcutta, G. 3951. Microfilmed, Indıan Office Library, Reel 366. Not in Kāṇe.

Title	*Author*
Devara-suta-sapatnī-sutā-dhana-vivāda[1]	
Navya-dharma-pradīpa	Kṛpārāma[2]
Mitākṣarā-tīkā	Bālam-bhaṭṭa[3]
Vibhaktāvibhakta-nirṇaya[4]	
Vivāda-vyavahāra	Gopāla Siddhānta-vāgīśā[5]
Vyavasthā-saṅkṣepa	Gaṇeśa-bhaṭṭa[6]
Vyavasthā-saṅgraha	Maheśa[7]
Vyavasthā-setu	Iśvara-candra Śarmā[8]
Vyavahāra-vidhānaṃ[9]	
Vyavahāra-sāra-saṅgraha	Nārāyaṇa Siddhānta-vāgīśa[10]
Vyavahāra-sāra-saṅgraha	Rāmanātha[11]
Vyavahārāloka	Gopāla Siddhānta-vāgīśa[12]
Śvaśrū-snuṣā-dhana-saṃvāda[13]	
Strīdhana-nirṇaya[14]	
Strīdhana-vibhāga-viṣaya[15]	
Smṛti-sarvasvaṃ	Nārāyaṇa[16]
Smṛti-sāra-vyavasthā	Vidyāratna Smārta-bhaṭṭācārya (?)[17]

[1] T. 19,006. An interesting question in the descent of *strīdhanam*.

[2] Pupil of Jayarāma. One of the compilers of the *Vivādārṇava-setu*. N (n.s.), II, p. 92. Kāṇe, I, p. 571.

[3] Aufrecht, 454–5. See above, p. 251. Kāṇe, I, pp. 456 f.

[4] T. 19, 002.

[5] Kāṇe, I, p. 662.

[6] Kāṇe, I, pp. 629, 692. Called also *Dāyabhāga-vyavasthā-saṅkṣepa*: Cal. S.C. 162.

[7] Kāṇe, I, p. 722. Asiatic Soc., Calcutta, G. 3484. Microfilmed: India Office Library, Reel 366. Maheśa was the name of a pandit employed c. 1784–5 (see above, p. 244).

[8] Kāṇe, I, p. 629. A copy dated 1819–20 is recorded: cf. Aufrecht 617.

[9] T. 19, 001 D. It is a revised version of Vimalabodha's commentary on a portion of the Śāntiparva of the Mahābhārata. See P. K. Gode, *Studies in Indian Literary History*, I, pp. 212–4; also Derrett, *B.S.O.A.S.*, 15 (1953), pp. 598 f.

[10] Aufrecht, 617. Eggerling, 1495. Adyar 11.F.18. Cf. Cal.S.C. 120. N, iii, p. 126–7. Various names are given in Kāṇe, I, pp. 631, 708.

[11] N (n.s.), III, pp. 191–2. Kāṇe, I, p. 631.

[12] Cf. Aufrecht, 617. Kāṇe, I, p. 631.

[13] T. 19,0003–5. Kāṇe, III, p. 706, n. 1351. Almost certainly by the author of *Devara-suta-sapatnī-sutā. dh. v.* (above).

[14] T. 19, 021.

[15] T. 19, 025 (a collection of citations from older *nibandha-s*).

[16] Eggerling, 1487. Note observation in Kāṇe, I, p. 673.

[17] Eggerling, 1498. Kāṇe, I, p. 673.

9

THE ADMINISTRATION OF HINDU LAW BY THE BRITISH

We have seen that the knowledge that the British were bound to administer a 'new' *śāstra*,[1] the traditional book-law in a new guise, and would introduce deliberately or accidentally concepts drawn from their own legal background, had several effects on the Hindu scholarly public.[2] We have tentatively concluded that they, for all their remarkable adaptability, were not fit to supply the newcomers with an Indian law which could be applied without difficulty or doubt. Between 1772 and 1947, when India became independent, attitudes towards the indigenous laws developed and acquired their present peculiar form. It is not English, and it is not the attitude of the *śāstrī-s*. How it came about requires a recognition of the status of the legal decision as a maker of ideals. When this has been grasped we shall be half-way to understanding the colour of the subject, though its content can only be made out from a detailed examination, which should certainly be attempted. We should look once again at the picture of custom and law, of usage and jurisprudence, of legal endeavour and rough-and-ready 'palm-tree' justice, and ask whether the British administration made a difference, and if so what and how. We know that English administrators were sincerely anxious to find out what native laws were. Now we must see what success they made of applying them.

The Historical Background

Europeans acquiring territories in India were obliged by the

[1] This chapter is based on an article of the same name which appeared at *C.S.S.H.*, 4, No. 1 (1961), pp. 10–52. It has been shortened somewhat. Some references have been omitted and others added.

[2] Chapter 8 above.

constitutional law of the kingdom or empires within which their *zamīndārī-s*[1] lay, to administer justice to the natives within their jurisdictions in a fashion generally agreeable to the natives themselves. The East India Company in fact appointed one of their servants to be *zamīndār* in Calcutta and to preside over the 'Court of Cutchery' which decided suits between natives. J. Z. Holwell, who held the post between 1752 and 1757, claims to have had much success (as the Company admitted) without introducing violent innovations.[2] The Portuguese, though recognizing no Indian territorial sovereign in Goa, seem not to have differed in their attitude markedly from that of the British in Bombay and Madras.[3] The newcomers took advantage of existing rights in revenue matters. In criminal matters they were torn between a desire to leave the natives to solve their own problems and a fear that unredressed complaints might endanger the peace, and so the trade and other activities which explained the Europeans' presence in Asia.

It was early recognized that Muslims claimed to be governed by rules derivable from the *Koran* and textbooks written by the 'doctors' of the Shariat (*sharī'a*), while the Hindus recognized, at the least, the general claims of the *śāstra*. But it was evident that these sources of law were consulted to extents varying with the topic, the locality, the efficiency of the court, the notoriety or otherwise of a custom *prima facie* applicable, and with the caste of the party or parties concerned. The integrity of the official judges varied enormously, from the type of the Unjust Judge of the parable (Luke xviii. 2–6) to even less satisfactory types. The Europeans themselves were, at this period, less scandalized by this state of affairs than were their successors of the mid-nineteenth century, for conditions in India and in Europe were then more comparable than later. There was a natural reluctance to assume the position and responsibilities of the persons who in fact resolved disputes between natives, and a consequent lack of interest in the formal sources of law which

[1] *Zamīndārī* = 'tract of land constituting the possessions of a Zamīndār'; *zamīndār* = 'occupant of land entitled to collect the revenues therefrom for Government'.

[2] Holwell, *India Tracts*, 3rd edn. (London, 1774), pp. 175–6, 178, 203, 228, 252.

[3] For the British see Sir C. Fawcett, *First Century of British Justice in India* (London, 1934).

these functionaries might consult in their discretion. Natives might be ousted from their traditional methods of settling disputes by the intrigues of individuals whom the Company trusted–as happened at Madras, where misinformed British legislators cut off the jurisdiction of the Company's court and the natives were driven to various shifts to enable their causes to be decided there indirectly.[1] On the other hand native princes might differ as to the advisability of administering English law in India; in 1642 the Nayak requested the Madras Council to execute native murderers after the English fashion, but in 1770 the Nawab of Arcot resented his servants being tried by English law.[2]

When Britain, in the person of the East India Company, accepted the *divānī* of the Eastern Provinces that reluctance had to be abandoned. The result of an attempt at the former method led to chaos. The actual power had to 'stand forth' and displace the nominal authorities behind whom they had hoped to hide, and administer justice directly. By British statute the Company's courts became subject to the appellate jurisdiction of the Privy Council in London (at first not effective), and the Company steadily appointed better qualified men to judicial posts. By the time the Company's courts were merged with the Queen's courts the standard of Company's justice was little inferior to that administered by the courts set up under Royal Charter, staffed by appointees of the Crown, and served largely by members of the English Bar.

The structure of the judicial system by 1861 may briefly be described as a group of mutually independent superior appellate courts, viz. the High Courts of Calcutta, Bombay and Madras, subject only to the Privy Council, each at the top of a pyramid of inferior courts in the districts, themselves hearing appeals from courts of first instance which were situated in some of the towns, apart from such limited original jurisdictions as they themselves might have. While the most humble of these series of courts were staffed by Indians, the higher were presided over by junior British officials, until one reached the seniormost of the latter, who remained in the District Courts if they could not

[1] India Office Library Mss. (Records), Home Miscellaneous Series, vol. 372, p. 261; vol. 414, pp. 244–51; vol. 427, pp. 111 ff.

[2] Home Misc. Ser., vol. 427, pp. 2 ff., ibid., pp. 59–68.

attain a seat in the High Court. Outside the High Courts the practitioners were Indians, none of whom learnt the English legal system in England, and, what is more significant, none of whom could have become professionally qualified in the Islamic or Hindu classical systems, for the careers are incompatible.[1] They started their careers as mere 'pleaders', and acquired proficiency in the somewhat rough-and-ready atmosphere of the juniormost courts which preceded the British system in some areas.[2] The best practitioners were soon siphoned off into the higher courts, for litigation was always remunerative and brains found their own level at the High Court Bar as soon as native practitioners could cope with its procedure. The intellectual gap between judgements delivered in the High Courts, where some judges were English barristers of standing, and the country *vakīls* who were supposed to advise their clients according to them was, and to a large extent remains, marked.

While this judicial hierarchy was developing, a striking dichotomy emerged between the court law and the popular law, the interacting components we have already observed for a somewhat earlier period. It is not clear whether a precise counterpart has developed elsewhere. Its emergence is an important part of this story.

The situation prevailing when foreign rulers assumed their respective judicial responsibilities was, for all its faults, empirical. In no case did theory impose some juridical technique which had not emerged from the needs and history of the relevant group. In a relatively small area might be found several native types of decision-making and decision-enforcement, all satisfactory within the given limits, none suitable for

[1] See Judges mentioned below, pp. 304–5. V. N. Mandlik, J. C. Ghose, G. C. Sarkār Śāstrī, P. V. Kāṇe, J. R. Ghārpure, and K. V. Venkaṭasubramania Iyer were both practitioners and authorities in *śāstra*: all made great marks on the literature as well as in the cases. But how few these are when seen against the hundreds of thousands of advocates, and against the ever-dwindling numbers of *śāstrī-s*! In our own day śāstric knowledge and skill in handling cases has been possessed by A. S. Naṭarāja Ayyar and by U. C. Sarkar, but a glance at their works shows how ill the oil and water mix. The latter's work may be conveniently compared with that of Paras Diwan (an expert in Anglo-Indian law) in successive issues of *Law Review* (Punjab Univ.).

[2] See C. R. Baynes, *A Plea for the Madras Judges* (Madras, 1853).

sudden transference into other spheres, and hardly any conformable to British presuppositions about judicial administration. The types may be roughly categorized as (1) tribal government, where the circle of pressures would be narrow and influence from outside slight, as in cases resembling that of Santals today; (2) amongst agriculturalists a hierarchy of political governors, who could take administrative action to solve problems which family, sub-caste, village or district leaders could not solve–a situation in which approaches to litigation would occur chiefly where pressures were nearly equal, and delinquents could not be controlled, unanimity being more important than abstract justice;[1] (3) in better organized societies, in towns particularly, the *panchayat*, or *ad hoc* committee of castes, functioned, staffed by members identified by a kind of natural selection; the higher the standing of the parties the greater likelihood that the *śāstra* would be consulted and applied; while (4) Brahmin sub-castes would be directly served in their disputes by *śāstrī-s*, and the *śāstra* would more frequently be consulted. Throughout, however, the principle was the same: no litigation until social pressures had been tried and exhausted. Excommunication was available and operated well in some areas and for some offences. The state was called in to cope with robbery and killing and serious mayhem. Powerful groups could defy the law, and public indignation against them found no machinery wherewith to express itself. The 'king' was at all times necessary to keep the social balance, and one who could manage to achieve this by force of personality, wealth, or arms, had a good claim to be, in the locality, 'king'.

The Hindu system gave everyone his place in every possible contingency; individuality was not prized, disobedience was anathema; functions were fixed by the caste system; and sources of pressure (outside the wild and barely Hinduized tribes) were many. Where the Muslims had succeeded to Hindu rulers they took over a going concern; they authorized the natural leaders to continue their previous functions; they respected fundamental customs; they even admitted Brahmins to be the proper authorities to determine certain disputes; and they tolerated the

[1] Anthropologists are agreed on the criteria of 'justice' in traditional circles today. E.g., A. Mayer, *Caste and Kinship in Central India* (London, 1960), p. 126 and elsewhere.

indigenous system so long as it did not conflict with their own.[1] The Islamic law of crimes, and their law of evidence in the criminal and possibly also in other courts, were in force where Muslims ruled, but otherwise there was no question of administering Islamic law as such to non-Muslims. In Bengal and Madras the Hindus were used to living under two systems simultaneously, both administered under the authority or with the sufferance of the ruler, and this must have gone a long way towards preparing them to accept a third.

British Presuppositions

British administration early attracted Indian litigants. The Portuguese, Dutch, French and Danish, so far as we know, did not have quite the same experience. The 'success' of the British was misunderstood and led to puzzling decisions on the part of the relevant authorities. The secret of the flood of Indian cases to the early British courts, such as the Mayors' Courts, lay in the immediacy and violence of the remedies offered: needless to say the Supreme Court at Calcutta gave an even more dramatic impression of this sort. The chances of losing a good case were high,[2] but if one won, the prizes were larger than would be available under the native system. Following the commercial class, others were attracted to enlist the aid of this new instrument of applying pressure. The British supposed that Indian litigants would elsewhere suffer from corruption or prejudice. It did not strike them at once that the Indian could take advantage within the British jurisdiction of rules of law which did not exist outside it. He could not only get his decrees executed, without relative delay or appeal, to the great discomfiture of the opposite party, but he would be able to gain legal advantages of which the native legal system knew nothing. In those very early days the English law was enforced in 'country' disputes provided the parties submitted to the jurisdiction, and since only English attorneys then knew the English law the party who

[1] Sarkar, *Epochs*, pp. 209 ff., gives a more faithful picture than that suggested by material cited by Sir G. C. Rankin, *Background to Indian Law* (Cambridge, 1946), pp. 3–6.

[2] On the irregularities of the 'Black Court' see T. K. Mukherji, 'Aldermen and attorneys . . .', *I.H.Q.*, 26 (1950), pp. 51–6.

submitted to the summons must frequently have been shocked at the system which he had obliged himself to obey: but as the communities in question found the gains greater than the losses a speedy adjustment to the situation took place. Where what was virtually an English court, set up under an English charter, dealt with a case between natives, English remedies and English law were inevitable. It was feared that the English law must rule even in Company's courts which existed purely for native use: this could be avoided by extensive recourse to 'arbitration', which might, it was fortunately believed, let in the native laws indirectly. In spite of themselves the Company were found administering justice along lines acceptable to the natives but under the cloak of the English legal system.[1]

The acquisition of Bengal, Bihar and Orissa posed the problem in an acute form. Indians who might never wish to submit to a British jurisdiction were forced to do so because the British Company was *divān* of the Emperor. The questions were what form the jurisdiction should take, and what law or laws should be administered.

We have already noticed that other European powers had possessions in India. The choice which lay before the Company and later before Parliament was between following the system in use in the Portuguese possessions, or that in use in the Dutch and French possessions, on the one hand, or striking out for an improvement on both. The problem was complicated by the fact that the litigating public in the Presidency towns differed from that in the *mufassil* (the 'balance', i.e. the greater part, of the area). Its dealings with the European traders were regulated by English law and in certain of its private affairs it was accustomed to utilize the facilities of the British courts.

The French Revolution had not yet occurred. All Europe was accustomed to a confusion of local laws, to the general prestige of the Roman law, and to the practical application of much of the Roman law in the still active ecclesiastical courts. We have

[1] Their problem is well demonstrated in Madras by John Browne's opinion of 1738 (Home Misc. Ser. 427, pp. 27–8), the heart-searching of the Choultry Court in 1774 (Home Misc. Ser. 427, pp. 91–2, where an excellent picture of the current native methods of administration is given), and the general question of jurisdiction to set up courts in the Northern Sirkars (ibid., pp. 71–174, an opinion of Russell's of 1785).

seen what a parallel there was between the dual system of Europe and in particular England and the scheme envisaged by Warren Hastings in 1772.[1] In ancient periods ecclesiastical courts in Europe claimed jurisdiction in conscience in civil and criminal matters when the state courts did not conform to the doctrines of the Church.[2] The sanction of excommunication there relied upon was early identified with the right of castes to excommunicate their members. *Panchayats* might have been left entirely alone to continue their functions alongside the foreign courts, which could have confined themselves to disputes between natives and foreigners, and to constitutional and criminal matters. The superstitious fear which the caste Hindus had of excommunication (especially in Bengal) or of anathema at the hands of tribunals including a Brahmin, and the helplessness of a defeated litigant or delinquent who would not accept the decision of a tribunal entitled to apply a complete boycott, impressed Europeans with the notion that this system hardly required civil or criminal penalties in the western sense, and that it was grounded in immemorial usage and unalterable custom, interpreted in the last resort by 'priests' (as they thought) learned in the *śāstra*. It seemed as if a system of 'Roman' law were alive in a system of 'Canon' law, in which the public believed, and which had long since won a position at the expense of the secular power. The question whether the *śāstra* was really in use at the beginning of the British period is conclusively settled by the publication of various documents which are *jaya-patra-s* ('certificates of victory') issued in the eighteenth and nineteenth centuries in circumstances suggesting scrupulous adherence to the *śāstra* on the part of the courts that issued them.[3]

The Portuguese had in fact left all judicial administration to the Hindus themselves. They took it for granted that converts would be subject to Portuguese law and would litigate in Portuguese courts and not in Christian 'caste tribunals'.[4] Ecclesiastics

[1] Above, pp. 233–4.

[2] See for example the canons attributed to St. Patrick in J. T. McNeill and H. M. Gamer, *Mediaeval Handbooks of Penance* (New York, 1938, 1965), pp. 78–9 (canon 21).

[3] Kāṇe, *H.D.*, III, 381 provides all the references. See above, p. 229, n. 2.

[4] Judges for 'all Christians', provided for in 1584, were not actually appointed till May 20th, 1682.

pointed out that a Christian king could not permit subjects to obey customs in conflict with Natural law, and as a result of a Provincial Council certain propositions were formulated which subsequently became law, by which Hindus were amenable to the Portuguese courts for violent crimes, polygamy, concubinage and usury.[1] But well into the modern period Portuguese Hindus were governed by the Hindu law substantially as administered under the sixteenth-century pre-Portuguese Muslim rule.[2] Hindus tended to negotiate with their rulers to obtain amendments favourable to them, and one controversy illustrates the atmosphere. The *Forál* of Alfonso Mexia of 1526 mentioned the then established rule that in default of *male* heir the property of a decedent passed to the Treasury. After 1691 the Hindus succeeded in persuading their Portuguese king to decree that the law of Portugal should apply to descent and distribution of Hindus' estates, with the motive of preventing property passing by escheat to the state. They asked for too much, for they really did not want daughters to share equally with sons, and this indirect effect was in fact felt as a great inconvenience. During the eighteenth century repeated attempts were made to reinstate the old customary rule that sons excluded daughters, but the Portuguese, after prolonged investigations, would have none of it, and the Portuguese law of inheritance remained at any rate for the Old Conquests of Goa, until in 1880 the remaining chapters of Hindu law were abolished in favour of the Portuguese system.[3]

The French on the other hand, seem to have admitted Hindus to their courts at their option and administered to them French law, whilst at the same time they were forced to interfere in serious caste disputes, and to settle according to native custom matters which the natives would not assume the initiative to settle for themselves. This meant taking the advice of native leaders, or caste heads, and thence developed a system which later (1827) came to maturity, of a standing consultative com-

[1] *O Primeiro Concilio Prouinçial Celebrato em Goa no Anno do 1567* (Goa, 1567), Decc. xi, xii. For the literature see *Z. f. vergl. Rechtsw.*, 67, pt. 2 (1965), pp. 203 ff.

[2] A. E. d'Almeida Azevedo, *As Communidades de Goa* (Lisbon, 1890). Lingu Roguvir Dolvy, *Decreto de 16 de Dez. de 1680* . . . (Bastora, 1916).

[3] The story is set out at length in the article cited at n. 1 above.

mittee of Indian jurisprudence, as it was termed. This seems to have worked extremely well.[1] The French enforced the decisions arrived at entirely by native authorities. These took opinions from various castes, consulted the *śāstra* where they felt so inclined, and disposed of the matter by taking into account considerations they deemed appropriate, giving as many and as detailed reasons as they felt desirable. A form of giving reasons later became established as French officials took more and more interest in the process, and it is possible to follow the development of this quasi-customary law. As did the British, the French kept revenue, excise and criminal law entirely in their hands, together with other topics that were essential to the good government of the settlements, and would not offend the susceptibilities of the native inhabitants.

The Portuguese method was what, roughly speaking, the British attempted. Criminal justice broke down. British judges were essential. They tried to keep the peace and to satisfy litigants. Actual determination was really in the hands of native officials who could alone understand the disputes, many of which would never have arisen as litigation prior to the British period. Warren Hastings came to the conclusion that the confusion meant nothing but corruption, and he may largely have been right. He first thought that well-qualified or chosen arbitrators should dispose of disputes, and the judges should give force to their awards. By 1769 the British had no intention of

[1] The bibliography on Franco-Hindu law is: G. Orianne, *Traité Original des Successions* . . . (Paris, 1844); E. Gibelin, *Études sur le Droit Civil des Hindous* . . . (Pondicherry, 1846–7); C. Boscheron-des-Portes, *Aperçu historique et analytique du droit hindou suivi d'une notice sur le régime judiciare et administratif des établissements français dans l'Inde* (Paris, 1855); F. N. Laude, *Manuel de Droit Indou* . . . (Pondicherry, 1856); the same, *Manuel de Droit Indou applicable* . . . (Pondicherry, 1869); the same, *Établissements français de l'Inde. Recueil de Législation* (Paris, 1869); A. Eysette, *Jurisprudence et Doctrine de la Cour d'Appel de Pondichéry* . . . (Pondicherry, 1877–9); L. Sorg, *Introduction à l'étude du Droit Hindou* (Pondicherry, 1897); the same, *Avis du Comité consultatif de Jurisprudence indienne* (Pondicherry, 1897); the same, *Traité théorique et pratique du Droit Hindou* (Pondicherry, 1897); the same, *L'état présent du Droit Hindu* (Tribune des Colonies, 1896); J. Sanner, *Droit civil applicable aux Hindous dans les établissements français de l'Inde* (Pondicherry, 1916–17); M. J. Gnanou, *Étude sur la condition juridique de la femme mariée Hindoue dans les établissements Français de l'Inde* (Aix-en-Provence, 1923); Gnanou Diagou, *Principes du Droit Hindou* (Pondicherry, 1929–32).

accepting more knowledge or interest in Hindu or Muslim customs or laws than was essential for performing the functions which had devolved on them.[1] The natives were to govern themselves, provided that the government should retain all the advantages of any authority or jurisdiction which the Company had inherited. So elaborate a method as the later French system was impracticable in vast territories inhabited by a more miscellaneous population. Another method, operated by the Dutch, was repellent in one respect.[2] Our material on the Dutch administration is scanty but significant. Anthony Pavilioen, Commander of Jaffna in Ceylon, left in his Memoir for his successor in 1665 the remark 'the natives are governed according to the customs of the country if these are clear and reasonable, otherwise according to our laws', and this must have been the approach in India also. Where the litigants were governed by a clear native rule of custom the Dutch applied it; but the Dutch applied the Roman-Dutch law where the decision would involve an institution unknown to native custom, or custom was silent, or the customary rule was hostile to the prejudices of the rulers. In Ceylon, Sinhalese law relating to prohibited degrees for marriage was modified by a *Placaat* of May 28th, 1773,[3] and the Indian possessions must have been ruled by similar methods. The result was that, although native susceptibilities were respected to a considerable degree, Dutch courts were predominantly European courts, and bore a close resemblance to the Supreme Courts in the British Presidency Towns. Had this been followed in the *mufassil* it would have meant that parts of the very peculiar English law, hardly suited to the

[1] Instructions to 'Supravisors', August 16th, 1769, quoted W. A. Montriou, *Hindu Will of Bengal* (Calcutta, 1870), p. lvii.

[2] See above, p. 228, n. 3. In Chinsura Roman-Dutch law seems to have been applied to Hindus: *Luckunchunder*, 1 Boulnois, cited in argument at 8 M.I.A. 78.

[3] H. F. Mutukisna, *The Tésavaḷamai* (Colombo, 1862), p. 712. It is true that the Anglo-Indian legal system did little to protect the workers employed by the indigo-planters (one of the few real blots on the history of Anglo-Indian law), but it is impossible to find a counterpart to the stern and barbarous measures taken by law to prevent cultivators from plucking up their coffee plants in Ceylon, measures compatible with the Dutch concept of justice and equity: see S. Thananjayarājasingham, 'A phonological and morphological study of a Tamil plakkaat', *Tamil Culture* 11, no. 2 (1964), pp. 173 ff. The *Placaat* is dated 1727.

Presidency Towns themselves, would have been imposed upon an entire nation without its consent and without a rational precedent. What had emerged, then, by 1772, was a system by which European overseers authorized, at their discretion, the decision made and enforced by native officials of government who administered whatever law struck them as suitable in the circumstances.

Efforts to uphold ancient methods, such as the caste *panchayats*' sentences, must fail in this atmosphere. Only in remote regions where the officials and 'arbitrators' of the new government were unknown, was the previous system still in use. Movement backwards was impossible, and in moving forwards a choice existed. Decisions should be given *ad hoc* by the natural leaders, or some fundamental and stable system should be sought, which might be applied as a matter of rule. British prejudices, developed in an atmosphere where local customs were construed with extreme strictness, where franchises were preserved only with much legalism, and where the supremacy of the king's courts over all inferior tribunals was being established, were decidedly against haphazard methods. Precedent, and the certainty that the law would not depend upon the personality of judges, but upon the skill of advocates and the court's learning, were the pillars of the English system. The British were opposed to self-help in destraint for debt, to excessive rates of interest, and to allegedly unreasonable elements of the previous system, naturally fit to be disallowed.[1] The native system had always admired abstract justice from afar, but it applied only on levels where more pressing considerations were absent. That all men should be equal before the law was an attractive proposition only where the defendant was a government official.[2] The British judicial system, with its disregard for social distinctions, its dependence upon pleadings and

[1] On interest and self-help the Plans (see above, p. 232, n. 1) and Jonathan Duncan's Regulations for Malabar (above, p. 242, n. 1) agree. On caste and crime see citation from records of the Nizāmat Adālat (the criminal court deriving from the grant of the *nizāmat* from the Moghul emperor) for October 9th, 1794 in Home Misc. Ser., vol. 420, p. 365 (stealing cows from butchers allegedly lawful), and (1857) 13 S.D.A. Rep. 402 (lower castes should be glad to be beaten).

[2] Views and citations in O'Malley, *Modern India and the West* (London, 1941), pp. 59, 370, 632.

evidence, its failure to take into account questions which, although distinct from the issues, were actually part of the same complaint in the eyes of the parties, and its harsh and rapid methods of execution–taking no account of the native genius for delay and contempt for the decisive–caused consternation.[1] A flood of plaints and petitions occurred, and actual and potential defendants, guilty and innocent alike, were known to migrate into territories administered by native rulers until the abnormal times should end.

Indian Reactions

Litigation soon became just another weapon of policy.[2] Merely to summon a defendant was enough to cause him expense. The *vakīls* (agents) who soon became available to represent clients ousted the parties themselves who had formerly appeared in person or through relations or well-placed patrons. The latter acted gratuitously, but the former required to be paid and learnt how to protract litigation. Direct contact between the judge and litigant occurred in the earliest period only. The *panchayats*, on the other hand, were at a disadvantage. They had retained their effectiveness in Hindu states and in many Muslim-ruled states; but in Bengal, Bihar and Orissa the attraction to the courts was so strong that eventually they emerged with only a fraction of their power.[3] An excommunicated man could get well-paid employment with the foreign government, and he could even bring a suit against those who had excommunicated him. At the height of the agitation against the missionaries and their very qualified success in Calcutta and its environs the

[1] This was the real horror in the execution of Nandakumar. For the general attitude of Elphinstone see below, p. 292. The story in O'Malley, where cited, p. 625 ('the *adālat* is coming') makes sense in this context.

[2] Cf. the modern study by B. Cohn, 'Some notes on law and change in North India', *Economic Development and Cultural Change*, 8, pt. 1 (1959), pp. 79–93. See below, p. 364, n. 1.

[3] The *panchayat* is by no means an extinct institution even in fields not covered by the relatively recent Panchayat Raj legislation (with its statutory *panchaiti adālats*). In *Mokka* v. *Ammakutti* (1927) 51 Mad. 8, 13 we are told of the council of twenty-four Pattikars with their head called Nattamakkar. In *Loganathan* v. *Ponnuswami* AIR 1964 Mad. 327, 328, col. 2 we see how the *panchayat's* award was followed by litigation by the successful party.

orthodox Hindu leaders were unable to use the weapon of excommunication effectively, although public opinion as a whole was rather on their side than that of the missionaries–for employment and trade, upon which Calcutta was based, cared nothing for this weapon.[1]

Caste tribunals functioned in spiritual matters which the courts left alone. A Bengali who killed a cow, in the same period to which we referred above, would no doubt be forced to undergo grievous penances.[2] Their standards were often out of tune with those presupposed in the courts. A man might be excommunicated for doing something which the courts allowed was good.[3] In parts of India which came later under British rule the dichotomy of standards was more marked. The judicial administration became eventually, despite expert advice, more or less homogeneous throughout British India, and the natives even of western India had to respect the newfangled and the ancient system simultaneously, even when they were incompatible. We shall see, in another connexion, how the courts themselves might defer to the caste's opinion,[4] but this was not the general pattern. The court-law had its sphere; the caste-law was independent of it to a very great extent.[5] Though it could not effectively transfer land or create a status which the court alone had jurisdiction to recognize, it might still, if the caste were well-knit and active, be as inhibiting and pervasive as the court-law; and indeed in many spheres (disregarding the not unimportant religious sphere which was largely its own) it reached levels of obedience far more directly than any decree of

[1] See work cited at p. 83, n. 2 above.

[2] Nirad C. Chaudhuri, *The Autobiography of an Unknown Indian* (Bombay, Jaico, 1964), pp. 453 ff. The author's sarcasm does not disprove the complete continuity of the ideas to which he testifies.

[3] *Kshiteesh* [1937] 2 Cal. 221; *Madhavaro* [1946] Bom. 375, 415. *Sambhu* (1876) 1 Bom. 347 (see *Keshav* (1915) 39 Bom. 538 and Kāṇe, *Hindu Customs and Modern Law*, p. 66). Now, if a husband is outcasted this will not serve as a ground why an order of restitution of conjugal rights should not be decreed against his wife: *Mohan* v. *Smt. Shanti* AIR 1964 All. 21.

[4] See below, p. 359.

[5] *Soobba* (1870) 6 M.H.C.R. 40. Members of a caste attempting to prevent a fellow member from worshipping in a temple may be restrained by injunction: the civil right justifies the interference with a caste in a matter of religion: *Anandrav* (1883) 7 Bom. 323. See O'Malley, cited above, pp. 370, 633.

the State court. Indians learnt, however, how to litigate on British lines. Dedicated men spent their entire lives mastering the art. Some specialized in handling such litigation at the district level, others at the High Courts. From them developed the class of lawyers with the occasional jurist, which played a very great part in achieving Independence and modifying the country's legal system. The intellectual domicile of this class provides a problem which many have attempted to solve, and which is beyond our present scope; but it may be remarked that the failure of the lawyers to stand up to the often less well-equipped political bosses of the post-Independence period may not be so much the result of adult franchise as of the cessation in the public sphere of the totally fictional standards at handling which the lawyers were the only adepts prior to Independence. When the Old India sought to reassert itself those who were dedicated to knowing the machinery of British India continued to assume what was not relevant to the same extent as before, and thrust aside with commendable impatience the foggy, 'oriental' principles which still adhered to the grass-roots of the culture. The conversation was no longer with the British, for whom law was part of their common language, nor with others in the hearing of the British, but with the politicians whose language the lawyer-class had long since taught itself not to speak.

Sources of Law

The scheme of 1772 has already been outlined.[1] In the view of K. V. Venkaṭasubramania Iyer, Hastings misunderstood what function the *śāstra* had, when he made it the sole source of law: this is not quite certain, but the fact that the doubt can arise is significant. Instead of using the native referees as sources of customary law, as he might well have done, and in a special case was later done,[2] Hastings had directed that reference

[1] Above, pp. 232 f.

[2] Reg. I. of 1796 (M. N. Gupta, *Analytical Survey of Bengal Regulations* . . . [Calcutta, 1943], p. 103): Rajamahal tribes. The pre-British method of investigation is illustrated at *Madho* (1837) 1 M.I.A. 351; and early British methods in *Luximon* 2 Knapp 60, 1 Norton 169.

should be made only as to what the *śāstra* provided. The order was that 'the laws of the Koran with respect to Mohamedans and those of the Shaster with respect to the Gentoos shall invariably be adhered to'. The same scheme, with the addition of 'succession' as a topic, was enacted in the Administration of Justice Regulation, July 5th, 1781, s. 93. Impey advised introducing in secs. 60 and 93 a provision of enormous significance. Since the sources of law for the *mufassil* had never been established beyond the extremely vague provision for Islamic law in the Divānī Grant itself, and since the Supreme Court had been passing judgement on the validity of the Company's servants' acts in their judicial capacity, it was necessary to introduce a residual source of law for all cases and contexts in which the two personal laws could not apply in terms of the Regulation. In such cases judges were to act according to Justice, Equity and Good Conscience, which was certainly *not* intended for the multiplication of reference to English law, whatever may have been the effect of this step.[1]

There was no intention to exclude from the Company's courts the two indigenous systems in non-listed topics. It was later surmised that the supersession of these laws in those topics was intended, but this seems not to have been the case.[2] Strange ignorance about the systems and the way they were used had perpetuated misconceptions. Pandits *might* be consulted in the non-listed topics, but the practice, as the English judges became more confident, was for them to assess the equity of the rules applied outside the listed subjects; where they were satisfied that the customary rule was inappropriate or insufficient, the matter was not referred to the *śāstrī* (who was relieved of responsibility in such cases), but dealt with out of hand.[3]

So in the *mufassil*, and their chief appellate court, the Sadr Divānī Adālat at Calcutta and in the Supreme Court, the

[1] The origin and scope of this maxim is investigated in Derrett, 'Justice, Equity and Good Conscience', in J. N. D. Anderson, ed., *Changing Law in Developing Countries* (London, Allen & Unwin, 1963), pp. 114–53. Now see also *Superintendent* v. *Corp. of Calcutta*, AIR 1967 S.C. 997.

[2] Rankin, pp. 5 ff., 19 ff.

[3] Rankin, p. 25. The reply given by the Sadr Divānī Adālat to Macnaghten's enquiry about pre-emption amongst Hindus shows that pandits might be consulted on non-listed matters (*P. & P. of Moohummudan Law* . . ., pp. xvii–xix, referred to at p. 230, n. 2 above).

indigenous laws occupied a large place.[1] The law was to be found out from the professors, and not by reference, for example, to a jury or any equivalent.

Meanwhile the ruler's responsibilities with regard to caste matters were by no means abandoned. The Company retained the right to superintend the administration of temples,[2] and the management of places of pilgrimage.[3] But in course of time a definite disinclination to interfere in matters of Hindu religion emerged, and even a distaste for cases involving claims to dignities and honours of a religious character and claims relating to ceremonies in idol worship 'for the benefit merely of the few who profit by them'.[4] There was a definite withdrawal from responsibility. Castes, who had from the remote past looked to the 'king' to keep the balance, were left to manage their own affairs; their decisions were, if otherwise unobjectionable, treated as valid, but they were not supported by state power. The rulers dissociated themselves from any mechanism tending either to maintain or to modify the existing caste structure.[5] Jurisdiction

[1] In the Supreme Court there was at one time difficulty in admitting that the ecclesiastical side could undertake administration of Hindus' estates, but the convenience of a positive answer could not be ignored for long: see (1776) Morton 1; (1838) ibid., 22; (1867) 1 B.L.R., O.C., 24.

[2] Called in S. India the *melkoyma* right. Madras Reg. VII of 1817 defined the duties, divested by Government in 1842: *Venkateśa* (1872) 7 M.H.C.R. 77. O'Malley, p. 591 for the offering to the goddess Kālī in gratitude for the defeat of Napoleon, and other curious evidence of the governmental association with the religion of the majority of the inhabitants.

[3] O'Malley, p. 591; also 3 Harrington's *Elementary Analysis*, 207 ff.

[4] In 1788 a project whereby the British should administer punishment to Hindus and Muslims for religious offences was turned down on Sir William Jones's advice: letter of February 7th to Shore, Shore, where cited, p. 315; and cf. the problems (1809) on which Ellis (see above, p. 258) expressed an opinion restrictive of the court's jurisdiction at 2 Strange, *Hindu Law*, pp. 261–4, 266–8. *Subbaraya* (1905) 28 Mad. 23. *Sangapa* (1878) 2 Bom. 475–6. *Stríman Saḍagópá* (1863) 1 M.H.C.R. 301, 308.

[5] *Gadigeya* (1910) 34 Bom. 455. L. T. Kikani, *Caste in Courts* . . . (Rajkot, 1912), p. 28. *Sivappachari* (1862) 1 M.H.C.R. 50. The near-śāstric division into 4 castes (*varṇa-s*) was maintained, and attempts to improve caste status blocked: *Manickam* (1934) 66 M.L.J. 543; *Manipuzha* AIR 1955 Mad. 579; *Adugula* [1956] An.W.R. 314; *V. V. Giri* AIR 1959 S.C. 1318. Caste attitudes conflicting with English juristic presuppositions might be ignored: (1857) 13 S.D.A. (Cal.), 402; *Keyake* (1868) 3 M.H.C.R. 380, 381. Caste privileges as such were recognized: *Srinivasa* (1869) 4 M.H.C.R. 349; *Narasimma* (1871) 6 M.H.C.R. 449; *Paigi* (1886) 8 All. 78; *Rani* (1930) 34

to supervise castes was very early forbidden in Bombay Presidency; elsewhere the 'law' laid down in caste tribunals was never enquired into unless some civil and proprietary right was alleged to have been violated. Any caste decision which was within the caste rules and arrived at without violating a rule of natural justice was immune from review.[1] Belief that the caste was some sort of private association within the State upon an analogy with an English club was responsible for this considerable deviation from the pre-British position.[2]

C.W.N. 648. On the right of worship see p. 454, n. 3 also *Narayan* (1872) 9 B.H.C.R. 413. Prior to Independence, and indeed until the adoption of the Constitution in 1950 the courts recognized caste rules and supported claims based upon caste exclusiveness provided they related to religious contexts; but, unless there was a clear custom to the contrary, caste exclusionary practices were not upheld in regard to 'secular' public facilities. For details see the original and full treatment in M. Galanter, 'The religious aspects of caste', in D. E. Smith, *South Asian Politics and Religion* (cited above, p. 32, n. 1), at pp. 282–6.

[1] Kikani, cited above. *Nathu* (1902) 26 Bom. 174; *Vallabha* (1889) 12 Mad. 495; *Gobind* (1917) 44 I.A. 192. In *Jagannath* (1894) 21 Cal. 463 the court purported to limit the right to continue an excommunication. Bombay statutes have modified the right to excommunicate (see below, p. 473) and have removed the *purohit's* right to damages if another priest is employed for the customary rituals.

[2] Inter-caste relations were then more important than individual litigation. For the modern outlook see *Vallabha* and *Nathu* cited above; also *Rama* (1928) 51 Mad. 68. *Ganpati* (1894) 17 Mad. 222; *Namboory* (1845) 3 M.I.A. 359; *Stríman* (1863) 1 M.H.C.R. 301; (1869) 11 W.R. 457; but cf. *Srinivasa* and *Narasimma* (above) and *Appaya* (1899) 23 Bom. 122; *Venkatachalapati* (1889) 13 Mad. 293. On caste autonomy see M. Galanter, where cited, pp. 286–9. Galanter cites, appositely, at p. 284, *Michael Pillai* v. *Barthe* AIR 1917 Mad. 431, where the court refused to grant an injunction to require the bishop to re-erect a wall of separation between Roman Catholic Pillais and Mudalis on the one hand and fellow worshippers of low caste on the other. The ground was that, being Christians, and having ceased to be Hindus the plaintiffs could not claim recognition of caste-distinctions including untouchability. This is a rare instance of a court interfering, on grounds of religion, with what were obviously (though regrettably) customary caste notions, and that too in a religious context. Caste-consciousness between Roman Catholics caused unedifying conflicts such as are incidentally related in the ensuing litigation in *R.C. Bishop of Trichinopoly* v. *Amirthaswami* [1944] Mad. 785.

Abrogation and Selection of Rules of Hindu Law

Let us turn for purposes of comparison to Ceylon. When the British assumed judicial administration in the Kandyan Provinces they found that the indigenous system afforded not one book to guide them. The Chiefs acted as assessors, with the Judicial Commissioner or Government Agent as judge. After the law had been declared in instances over a period, British authors restated the Kandyan law in legal principles.[1] Sufficient knowledge had been accumulated for recourse to native assistance to be dispensed with by the time administration had been centralized in Colombo. The divergencies between Anglo-Ceylon practice and that which had prevailed in the Kandyan kingdom prior to 1815 were similar to those noticed in India. But no complaint was made, for the method adopted to ascertain the law was nearly foolproof. In Bengal, unfortunately, Hastings and his contemporaries, in particular Colebrooke, Jones and their successors, were gravely misled. Hindus had succumbed unwillingly to Muslim criminal administration;[2] and the vocal Brahmin jurists explained that the Hindu law was wide enough to cover all problems. Non-Brahmins will have admitted that the Brahmins were the expounders of law, and that the Hindu religion required obedience to the *śāstra* which Brahmins alone knew. The *śāstra* itself admitted customary deviations subject to rules of its own, and in religious contexts the *śāstra* was paramount. All *śāstrī-s* would assert that the *śāstra* was a single science and applicable in theory to all Hindus everywhere so long as they could be recognized as Hindus. This was, as we have seen, the outlook followed in 1772. It was nearly a century before the mistake was generally recognized,[3] but in the meanwhile Mountstuart Elphinstone, taking over the administration of newly acquired territories in Western India,

[1] Hayley, cited below, p. 406 n. 2.

[2] Preface to Halhed's *Gentoo Code* (p. 240 above), at p. lxxiv of the 1777 edn.

[3] *Kattama* (1870) 6 M.H.C.R. 310, 341 ('grotesque absurdity') (cf. *Viswanatha* (1925) 48 Mad. 944, 947–8). For the collection of works by J. H. Nelson, especially his *View of the Hindu law as Administered by the High Court . . . at Madras* (Madras, 1877) see Derrett, 'J. H. Nelson . . .', in *Historians of India, Pakistan and Ceylon* (London, 1961), ed. C. H. Philips. Above, p. 230, n. 1.

insisted that not only the Company's normal judiciary but also its methods of applying the personal laws should be kept out, and he was to some extent successful.[1] Yet even in Bombay, the *śāstra* under the British made advances over custom, despite explicit protection of the latter; and custom has been forced to struggle against what might be called Anglo-śāstric law.[2]

The Hindu law of evidence survived but was overshadowed by the corresponding Islamic law, which was gradually amended and curtailed until abolished with the enactment of the Indian Evidence Act.[3] There being little discrepancy between the Hindu law and the English on the subject,[4] the disappearance of the former was barely noticed. The Hindu law of crime survived in western India until superseded by local Regulations which paved the way for the Indian Penal Code. The Hindu law of contract and trusts did not disappear so quickly. The latter has been referred to respectfully in relatively recent times,[5] and the former, referred to surprisingly often even outside the Supreme Courts' jurisdictions, survived until British

[1] Rankin, pp. 14 ff. K. Ballhatchet, *Social Policy and Social Change in Western India 1817–1830* (London, 1957). 1 Knapp 320–1. *Mokuddims* (1845) 3 M.I.A. 383. *Nusserwanjee* (1855) 6 M.I.A. 134, 158–9. *Regulations Passed by the Governor in Council in Bombay from . . . 1799 to 1816* (London, 1822), pp. 8, 20, 21, 34, 46, 58, 59, 72, 250, 251. Jonathan Duncan's *Observations* (cited above, p. 242, n. 1). He believed that pandits would assist in checking upon reports of custom.

[2] Pandits could be hostile: *Sumrun* (1814) 2 S.D.A. (Cal.) 147; cf. Ellis at 2 Strange, H.L., 353. Yet the validity of customs was referred to them: *Ramgunga* (1809) 1 S.D.A. (Cal.) 362. 'Hindu law' attacked custom in *Karsan* (1864) 2 B.H.C.R. 124; *Duttnarain* (1799) 1 S.D.A. (Cal.) 27; *Bhyroochund*, ibid., 36; *Narasammal* (1863) 1 M.H.C.R. 420; *Tayumana* (1862), ibid., 51; *Upoma* (1888) 15 Cal. 708, 710; *Tukarambhat* (1898) 23 Bom. 454, 457; *Chidambaram* AIR 1953 Mad. 492; *Subramaniam* AIR 1955 Mad. 144; cf. *Serumah* (1871) 15 W.R. 47, 49 P.C. The situation in the United Provinces (now Uttar Pradesh) is illustrated by cases overruled in *Muhammed* (1912) 17 C.W.N. 97 (P.C.). Rankin. p. 6.

[3] Act I of 1872.

[4] But see Strange's comments to Colebrooke on the discrepancy and its solution (1812) at 2 Strange, H.L., 143.

[5] *Kahandas* (1881) 5 Bom. 154, 161, 170, 173–4. West, J., said that English law 'embraces and effectuates the Hindu law' of trusts. *Venkatachella* (1869) 4 M.H.C.R. 460. *Krishnaramani* (1869) 4 B.L.R., O.C. 231. *Tagore* (1872) I.A. Sup. Vo. 47, also 4 B.L.R. 401–2, 416 (in the High Court). Also *per* Markby, J., in *Krisharamani* (1869) 4 B.L.R., O.C. 244 f. The Hindu law of charitable trusts retains its Hindu roots.

Indian legislation.[1] The Indian Contract Act,[2] like the Indian Trusts Act (1882), took the place of much less developed and less uniform rules, which had had to be supplemented by English law. Parts of the Hindu law of contract survive, precariously in the case of *dāmdupat*,[3] and tenaciously in the law of the Pious Obligation.[4] In Hindu testamentary law another fragment exists.[5] Even apart from the surprising references to the Hindu law beyond the listed topics, references to Hindu constitutional law are not unknown.[6]

The topics which were retained in practice were retained out of a conscious regard for Hindu prejudices. It was believed that the British had legislative power to abolish any Hindu customs,[7] and the omission to eliminate Hindu family law was thought

[1] H. T. Colebrooke on Obligations (see above, p. 252, n. 4) preserves Hindu rules at pp. 7, 25, 26, 28, 45, 58, 138. Instances of citation of Hindu rules: *Rajunder* (1839) 2 M.I.A. 181, 202–3, 204; *Ramloll* (1848) 4 M.I.A. 339, 349; *Doolubdass* (1850) 5 M.I.A. 109, 119, 127; *Alvar* (1862) 1 M.H.C.R. 9; *Doe d. Kullamal* (1862), ibid., 85, 89; *Pitchakutti* (1863), ibid., 153, 157; *Kadarbacha* (1863), ibid., 150; *Çrinivasammal* (1864) 2 M.H.C.R. 37; *V. Somayagee* (1868) 4 M.H.C.R. 176, 179; *Rajah Suraneni* (1869) 13 M.I.A. 113, 136; *Lalubhai* (1877) 2 Bom. 300; *Waman* (1879) 4 Bom. 126, 152 f.; *Saunadanappa* (1907) 31 Bom. 354. Hindu law merchant considered: *Davlatram* (1869) 6 B.H.C.R. 24; *Megraj* (1870) 7 B.H.C.R. 137; *Kedarmal* (1908) 33 Bom. 364. Onus of proof of Hindu law lay on the party relying on it: *Maharaja* (1844) 3 M.I.A. 261, 273. In an insurance case a contract in English form was said to raise a presumption of English law: *Haridas* (1875) 12 B.H.C.R. 23. Hindu pre-emptions were held governed by Islamic law (see above, p. 161, n. 5): *Gordhandas* (1869) 6 B.H.C.R. 263. The *Pakka Adatiya* agency (which is a traditional contractual relationship) is still very much alive (see, e.g. *T. G. Lakshmi* AIR 1965 A.P. 136), but its historical origins are unknown. In *Daroga* (1936) 16 Pat. 45 the Hindu law was taken into account even when the law of limitation would have suggested otherwise.

[2] Act IV of 1872. Note also the Specific Relief Act, 1877; Transfer of Property Act, 1882; Indian Sale of Goods Act, 1930; Indian Partnership Act, 1932.

[3] See above, p. 113.

[4] See above, p. 113, and below p. 427.

[5] B. C. Law, *Law of Gift*, 2nd edn. (Calcutta, 1926), pp. 51 ff. Derrett, *I.M.H.L.*, §§. 735–6.

[6] *Sec. of State* (1868) 5 B.H.C.R. 23, 48–9 (debts to the king). Note also *Pitambar* (1871) 8 B.H.C.R., A.C.J., 185, 189 (boundary disputes); *Kashiram* (1870) 7 B.H.C.R., A.C.J., 17 (defamation).

[7] *Kojahs and Memons' Case* (1847) Perry 110, 122.

meritorious.[1] Certain Charters (of 1798, 1800 and 1862) required the courts to administer the native systems 'by such laws and usages as the same would have been determined by, if the suit had been brought and the action commenced in a native court'. Since it was never possible to determine judicially exactly how this would have been done, this requirement was never treated very seriously. Suttee (*satī*) was a somewhat unusual case. Its late abolition in British India was odd, for the removal of several characteristic usages such as ritual murders, sacrifices of children, religious blackmail,[2] and the like could be carried through expeditiously and without causing rebellions.[3] Even primogeniture, a harmless custom (one would think), was abolished within certain limits by a Bengal Regulation.[4] The tardy elimination of female infanticide, which, if not admitted as good by the *śāstra*, was certainly tolerated by the Hindu religion, is a near parallel with suttee. In the long battle to mitigate and perhaps even to abolish the indigenous laws relating to slavery various legislative steps were taken which interfered with the native legal system. A Regulation of May 17th, 1774, prohibited the buying or selling of slaves not already in slavery, and any *Kazi* who granted a deed for such a sale after a certain date should lose his own appointment. In 1798 the Company enacted that Hindu and Muslim slaves should have the benefit of their respective religious laws irrespective of the religions of their masters:[5] and this was a period when it was supposed that the native laws could grow towards the abolition or severe limitation of slavery–one of the institutions of Hindu law which the author of the *Mahānirvāṇa-tantra* wanted to eliminate.[6] A process of abrogation of rules thought unfit to be allowed or

[1] Perry, where cited, p. iv. Harrington, where cited, vol. I, pp. 178–9, 341, 343, 344 suggested useful regulation or reformation.

[2] See above, p. 216.

[3] B. B. Misra, where cited (p. 231, n. 3 above); Ballhatchet (cited above); Rankin (cited above). Early sources are apparent from Harrington (cited above) and in M. N. Gupta, *Analytical Survey* (cited above, p. 288, n. 2).

[4] XI of 1793; X of 1800. *Rajah* (1841) 2 M.I.A. 441.

[5] Beng. Rev. Consult., L.S. No. 213, May 17th, 1774. Minute of J. H. Harrington, November 21st, 1798, referred to in Bengal Crim. Jud. Consult., No. 14 dated December 26th, 1826. These references are owed to Dr. A. K. Chattopadhyay.

[6] VIII, 140 (opposition to traffic in slaves).

enforced, and of selection of rules fit to be enforced went on throughout the last decades of the eighteenth and the whole of the nineteenth century, but, as usual with the British, in no systematic or coherent manner.[1]

Until their final dismissal in 1864 the *śāstrī-s* continued to report the sense of the *śāstra* in answer to questions put to them. Discrepancies were observed;[2] the *śāstra* was a potential source of uncertainty; the personal standing of pandits did not always put them above pleasing parties and they were suspected of corruption.[3] *Vyavasthā-s* began to be collected and digested, and the rules that emerged began to be scrutinized.[4] Some seemed

[1] The abolition of disqualification from inheritance, taking a share at partition, etc., on the ground of conversion from Hinduism (Bengal Reg. V of 1831; Act XXI of 1850) was unfavourably received by opponents of Europeanization: H. H. Wilson, ed., W. H. Macnaghten's *Principles of Hindu and Mohammadan Law*, 2nd edn. (London-Edinburgh, 1862), p. xii. Miscellaneous examples: *Jugget* (1871) 14 M.I.A. 289, 303 and *Heeralal* AIR 1955 N.U.C. 1624 (dedication to idols, and adoptions do not require state consent); *Prannath* (1801) 1 S.D.A. (Cal.) 60 (confinement to extort revenue); *Kalachund* (1809) ibid., 374, *Behoree* (1816) 2 S.D.A. (Cal.) 210, cases of 1844–5 referred to at 1 M.H.C.R. 353, *Ramasawmy* (1863) 9 M.I.A. 344, and Reg. XXVII of 1793 (monopolies); *Cossinaut* (1819) 2 Morley 198, 201, 203, *Koshul* (1811) 1 S.D.A. (Cal.) 448, *Luximon* 2 Knapp 60, 63–4 (rules of partition); *Lakshman* (1880) 7 I.A. 181, 195 (Mitākesharā interest not disposable by will–see p. 338 below); *Visalatchi* (1870) 5 M.H.C.R. 150 (ancestral property recovered); *Venkatachella* (1869) 4 M.H.C.R. 460–1 (supersession fee); *Sri Sunkur* (1843) 3 M.I.A. 198, 211, 239 (privileges); *Teeluck* (1864) 1 W.R. 209, cf. H. S. Gour, *Hindu Code*, 4th edn., p. 61 (renouncing the world and property)–all obsolete. For further examples see below, p. 297, n. 1.

[2] See above, p. 243. Conflicts could be serious: *Rungama* (1846) 4 M.I.A. 1, 55–67; *Bhugwandeen* (1867) 11 M.I.A. 487, 500–5. Early British authorities insisted that certainty was essential, accuracy less important.

[3] See above, p. 243. Pandits did sometimes mislead the court: *Sheonauth* (1814) 2 S.D.A. (Cal.) 137; *Tara* (1864) 7 Sel. Rep. (Cal.) 273; *Rathinasabapathi* AIR 1929 Mad. 545, 549. See the careful and detailed comment of Edge, C. J., in *Bhagwan* (1895) 17 All. 294 (F.B.) at pp. 365–7. The court was capable of misquestioning and misunderstanding the reply: *Goureepershaud* (1814) 2 S.D.A. (Cal.) 175. Pandits disliked displeasing patrons; they were used to appear and file opinions on behalf of parties; they contradicted official court referees; they assembled in great numbers on either side; and even in the clearest case they preferred to be tactful where possible: *Rutcheputty* (1839) 2 M.I.A. 133, 138; *Namboory* (1845) 3 M.I.A. 359, 365; *Bhugwandeen* (cited above).

[4] The court might consult pandits and check their reply with reference to

uncertain;[1] some impracticable to administer for another reason;[2] some, like the rule that the administrator must recoup the owner of stolen goods if the thief is not caught, were inconvenient and Hastings and his successors had no intention of recognizing them; some rules were intended to be only morally and not also legally binding;[3] and some were plainly obsolete.[4] Mistakes were made in some cases and corrected later.[5] The

decided cases: *Raja* (1816) 2 S.D.A. (Cal.) 217. Colebrooke, Ellis, and much later G. Bühler (in West and Bühler's *Digest of the Hindu Law* . . . 3rd edn., Bombay, 1884) repeatedly commented on *vyavasthā-s* and compared them. H. H. Wilson and Shāmāchurn Sirkar continued the work of W. H. Macnaghten in this respect. Pandits formed their opinions to a pattern and kept copies (one result of which is the *Dharmaśāstrīya-vyavasthā-saṅgraha* (1957), cited above, p. 265, n. 2).

[1] *Narasimharav* (1865) 2 B.H.C.R. 61. *Nanomi* (1885) 13 Cal. 21 (P.C.). *Lachman* (1896) 19 All. 26. *Ladu* (1925) 4 Pat. 478, 482. *Masit* (1926) 53 I.A. 204. Rules lacking definition often slid away.

[2] On disqualification see 2 Norton's L.C. 440–1; *Choondoor* (1858) Mad. Sad. Rep. 118; *Coll. of Masulipatam* (1860) 8 M.I.A. 501. *Coll. of Trichy* (1874) 1 I.A. 282, 293. Contra: *Chalakonda* (1864) 2 M.H.C.R. 56, 75 (prostitution legitimate).

[3] See above, pp. 78–9. Also *Kandasami* (1896) 19 Mad. 6, *Kasubai* AIR 1955 Nag .210, 213; *Deivanai* AIR 1954 Mad. 657; *Dubey* AIR 1951 All. 530; *Deoki* AIR 1958 A.P. 693; *Muniammal* AIR 1955 Mad. 571; *Anilabala* AIR 1955 N.U.C. 811. Customary rules may equally be distinguished: *Kunwar* (1935) 62 I.A. 180, 195.

[4] *Kayarohana* (1915) 38 Mad. 250, 254; *Venkata* (1903) 26 Mad. 133; *Bharmappa* AIR 1922 Bom. 173; *Chalakonda* (1864) 2 M.H.C.R. 56, 60; *S. Namasevayam* (1869) 4 M.H.C.R. 339. *Ganga* (1875) 1 All. 46 F.B. *Vedanayaga* (1904) 27 Mad. 591, 598. *Paili* (1120/1944) 36 Cochin 300 (F.B.). *G. Narsi* [1964] 1 An.W.R. 261, 263 and *Dudh Nath* AIR 1966 All. 315 F.B. though recent examples only follow the established tradition. In the first an attempt to rely upon a śāstric rule (adoption) led to the comment that 'we have advanced and developed modern social and ethical standards and outlook'. In the second the literal text of the *Mitākṣarā* (I, i, 28–9) was rejected because 'Hindu law as administered in this country is not as given in the original text but as declared by courts of law' and *Amrit* AIR 1960 S.C. 964 (below, p. 312, n. 1) is cited. See also below, p. 300, n. 4.

[5] Corrected errors: *Doe d. Narrayen* (1849) Perry 133, 137–8; *Apaji* (1891) 16 Bom. 29 (cf. 5 All. 430 F.B. and below, p. 430); *Soundararajan* 39 Mad. 159 (F.B.) (cf. (1915) 35 Mad. 47 (F.B.), AIR 1953 Mad. 240); *Rahmed* (1859) 1 Norton 12 (cf. 18 Cal. 264, AIR 1950 Mys. 26); *Sinammal* (1885) 8 Mad. 169; Anon. (1837) Morton 22; *Raja* (1834) 2 Knapp 219; *Sootrugun*, ibid., 287, 290; *Soorjomonee* (1873) 12 B.L.R. 304, 314. Uncorrected: *Kerutnaraeen* (1806) 1 S.D.A. (Cal.) 213; *Moniram* (1880) 7 I.A. 115; *P. Valloo* (1877) 4 I.A. 109; *Aravamudha* [1952] 1 M.L.J. 251; *Gopi* AIR 1954 Or. 117;

clear course of enquiring what rules were in force amongst the natives before the British period seemed too cumbersome and impractical, and with every succeeding year less likely to bear fruit. The texts alone had been selected as the guide, and their defects started out when this unexpected weight was placed upon them. English tests eliminated many rules and sheer ignorance caused others not to be consulted.[1]

The British method of deducing the law from the European textwriter's idea of what the pandits meant, coupled with whatever might be deduced from the translations of a few prominent Sanskrit legal texts, and put cheek-by-jowl with decided cases (which might not correctly reproduce the traditions in the locality) enabled the law to be deduced in a most artificial and remote manner, the despair of scholars able to read the Sanskrit original authorities. H. H. Wilson, Th. Goldstücker and A. C. Burnell could not speak too contemptuously of the 'hybrid monstrosity' that emerged, or of the 'able demonstrations that the moon is made of green cheese'.[2] Yet this was the law that was defended by patriots against the codification proposals of 1941, 1947 and 1951! When newly translated texts became available the court could be shy of consulting them.[3] The

Khetramani (1868) 2 B.L.R., A.C. 15, 33, 36; *Jagannath* (1868) 1 B.L.R., A.C., 114; *Raghbir* AIR 1943 P.C. 7; *Akku* [1945] Bom. 216 F.B. (which though disapproved by Kāṇe and N. Chandrasekhara Ayyar, the last editor of Mayne's *Hindu Law*, is approved in *A. Raja* AIR 1965 S.C. 1970); *Shamsing* (1901) 25 Bom. 551 (cf. Mysore Act XV of 1938, s. 2, illus. f.).

[1] For a striking example see Kāṇe, *H.D.*, III, p. 461, n. 788. Better acquaintance with śāstric material does not prevent glaring mistakes under modern conditions: see [1959] 2 M.L.J., J. 19–21.

[2] Burnell, *Ordinances of Manu* (London, 1884), p. xlv: extraordinarily outspoken.

[3] P. C. Tagore's trans. of the *Vivāda-cintāmaṇi* (1865) and Kristnaswamy Iyer's trans. of part of the *Smṛti-candrikā* (1867) were widely used, beyond Mithilā and Madras (e.g. 5 All. 509 F.B.; 17 Bom. 303; 41 Bom. 618; cf. 5 I.A. 40, 46). Other nineteenth-century translations were not so well used; but there are exceptions. In *Muthukaruppa* (1914) 39 Mad. 298, 301–2 a wide range of śāstric material was seen in order to evade a rule found in the *Smṛti-candrikā*. This gave a very rare opportunity for use of Sītārāma Sāstrī's translations of the *Madana-pārijāta* (Madras, 1899) and the *Vivāda-ratnākara* (Madras, 1898), both so far as they deal with inheritance, and both reprinted by Setlūr in his *Complete Collection of Hindu Law Books on Inheritance* (Madras, 1911). It is a matter of astonishment that the *Arthaśāstra* of Kauṭilya, which became available relatively recently, has been cited in

authority given early to certain texts precluded the introduction of equally valuable works except upon a lower level, if at all.[1] The pandits' *vyavasthā-s* were at times despised if they disagreed with a European writer's statements;[2] the different parts of India were artificially divided, so that some texts might be consulted in each, and where they differed it was dangerous to consult one in another's Presidency (a scheme that repeatedly broke down).[3] Only recently, in an important family question, the Kerala High Court declared itself bound by the *Mitākṣarā* unmodified by later South Indian developments, irrespective of what Madras had been ruling for a century or so.[4] Sometimes the *smṛti* was taken as a standard, and the commentators ignored,[5] while at others the commentators were supposed the

judgements (not being a legal work as such): *Venkatalakshmammal* AIR 1960 Mad. 270, 272; see also ibid., pp. 501, 505.

[1] *Surayya* AIR 1941 Mad. 618. *Himoti* AIR 1945 Nag. 71, 72.

[2] *Myna* (1861) 8 M.I.A. 400, 422, 424; *Coll. of Masul.* (1861) ibid., 529, 552; *Thakoorain* (1867) 11 M.I.A. 386, 392, 404. Their function misunderstood, but their opinion upheld: *Coll. of Madura* (1868) 12 M.I.A. 397, 439; *Rakhmabai* (1868) 5 B.H.C.R. 181. Opinion rejected for 'want of authority': *Chuoturya* (1857) 7 M.I.A. 18, 51; *Inderun* (1869) 13 M.I.A. 141. Contradicted: *Kalgavda* (1909) 33 Bom. 669.

[3] *Sabitri* AIR 1933 Pat. 306, 370, 395. *Sambhu* (1926) 54 Cal. 171. Govinda Dās, *Introd.* to Bālambhaṭṭa (1914). Instances of citation of books outside their provinces are many and praiseworthy, though uncharacteristic: *Gajadhar* (1932) 54 All. 698; cf. *Ramcharan* (1916) 38 All. 416. Also *Kayarohana* (1915) 38 Mad. 250; *Velayutha* AIR 1942 Mad. 219.

[4] *Saraswathi* [1965] K.L.T. 141, discussed at [1965] K.L.T., *J.*, 36 ff.

[5] *Thakoor* (1866) 11 M.I.A. 139; *Bachiraju* (1865) 2 M.H.C.R. 402; *Ramalakshmi* (1872) 14 M.I.A. 570. S. S. Setlūr, *Complete Collection* (Madras, 1911), pp. xv–xvi, protests. Kāṇe, *Kātyāyana-* (cited above, p. 149, n. 1), p. 306 n., protests against *Natha* AIR 1931 Bom. 89 where *smṛti-s* were followed against the authority of the *Vyavahāra-mayūkha*. Strange modern examples: *Kamani* AIR 1946 Pat. 316, 322 (*smṛti* overrides the *Mitākṣarā* itself); *Kastoori* AIR 1960 All. 446, 449. In *Soundararajan* (1915) 39 Mad. 159 (F.B.) at pp. 181–2 Sadasiva Ayyar, J., propounds the 'legal history' of the period: 'The older and purer Hindu Law was altered by the Mitakshara . . . it is now almost a truism with careful students of the Shastras that the older and purer sources of Hindu Law are more in consonance with the needs of a progressing and progressive society than the rules introduced by the glosses of mediaeval commentators on those texts (the glosses very often being far-fetched and even distorting the texts). Such new rules were made according to the temporary exigencies of the times and places . . . The consequent degradation of the Hindu Law by the mediaeval commentators . . . is being gradually got rid of through the development of the law by the several

only valid authorities, whatever the *smṛti* might appear to say literally.[1] At times the commentators themselves were followed if local usage supported them;[2] at others the local usage could be presumed.[3] In all cases, once the line of decisions had been established, the court was reluctant to depart from it even when it was shown that the *dharmaśāstra*, treated historically, went the other way.[4] The outlook is well demonstrated by part of the judgement of Innes, J., in *Muttu Vaduganadha Tevar* v. *Dora*

decisions of the Privy Council and the older and purer Hindu Law is being gradually brought back.'

[1] The correct view: *Coll. of Madura* (1864) 2 M.H.C.R. 206, 227; the same, (1868) 12 M.I.A. 397, 436; *Salemma* (1897) 21 Mad. 100; cf. the opposite technique in *Dhondappa* AIR 1949 Nag. 206. *Sambasivan* (1921) 44 Mad. 704, 712.

[2] *Coll. of Madura* 12 M.I.A. 397, 436. *Venkatachalapati* (see below). *Bai* (1897) 22 Bom. 973. *Appaji* (1930) 54 Bom. 564, 595, 602. *Yashvantrav* (1888) 12 Bom. 26 *per* Nanabhai Haridas, J. In *Mouji* (1911) 38 I.A. 122 the P.C. held, 'where this form of marriage is shown to be obsolete among the members of a caste, the Courts are not bound to recognize it in deference to ancient texts.'

[3] *Bhagwan* (1899) 26 I.A. 153 (above, p. 80). Enough to show that the usage had not died out: *Kamani* (above). Commentaries incorporated custom (cf. *per* Sadāsiva Ayyar, J., p. 299 *supra*): *Sri Balusu* (1899) 26 I.A. 113 (above, p. 78 f.); *Chandika* (1902) 29 I.A. 70; *Muthukaruppa* (1916) 39 Mad. 298, 301 (above, p. 298, n. 3); *Atmaram* (1935) 62 I.A. 139. *Kasubai* [1955] Nag. 281, 308 (F.B.). Usage can supplement texts: *Lallubhai* (1880) 7 I.A. 212; *Vallabhdas* (1901) 25 Bom. 281, 286.

[4] *Vallinayagam* (1863) 1 M.H.C.R. 326, 340; *Thakoorain* (1867) 11 M.I.A. 386, 403; *Rao Kurun* (1871) 14 M.I.A. 187, 196; *Narayana* (1930) 53 Mad. 1 (F.B.); *Chockalingam* [1943] Mad. 603, 613 P.C.; *Madhavrao* [1946] Bom. 375, 423 (above, p. 287, n. 3). An excellent example would be *Nagendramma* AIR 1954 Mad. 713 scathingly treated at *Kasubai* (above). In *Arunachala* AIR 1953 Mad. 550 we are told that old case law must not be sought to be disturbed by research into antiquities of texts and verses. *Vedachala* (1921) 48 I.A. at p. 358: 'It is hardly possible for their Lordships to pronounce an opinion on the authenticity of the passage condemned in such strong terms by a Hindu judge. They can only observe that it appears to have been accepted by a series of commentators and by eminent Hindu judges in the British Indian Courts. Any doubt at this stage as to its character or authority will . . . lead only to perplexity and confusion.' We cannot go back to the texts (whatever their sanctity): *Lakshminarasamma* [1950] Mad. 1084 cited at *Ranganatha* [1961] 1 M.L.J. 404, 408. Speculations about the *śāstra* must be discouraged: Hegde, J., at AIR 1960 Mys. 299, 302–3. But the *śāstra* alone is cited, construed, and applied at *Padmanabhan* [1967] K.L.T. 555, and the *śāstra* alone was relied on (by analogy) at *Guruswami* [1950] Mad. 665, 675–678.

Singha Tevar which was decided on January 31st, 1879 in the Madras High Court.[1] The question was what was a *rānī's* tenure of an estate she had inherited.

> The Hindu law on the subject which the Court should endeavour to ascertain is the existing living law which is to be sought not merely in ancient treatises and commentaries, but in the consciousness of the people and the practice of everyday life. From the commencement of the British administration the Courts have made it their business to ascertain the alterations to which in the course of ages the ancient law has been subjected, and for this purpose the Judges have from time to time consulted text-books and commentaries and the opinions of learned Hindus and eminent Englishmen who have made the subject of Hindu law a special study; and unless we are willing at the suggestion of recent writers to ignore the principle of *stare decisis*, we shall not be prepared to introduce doubt and uncertainty into titles by treating every question of Hindu law hitherto decided as *res integra*, nor to confine ourselves to the consideration of obscure and conflicting texts, the binding authority of many of which has become obsolete; still less to yield to the prevalent spirit[2] of depreciation of the labours of our predecessors and the long course of decisions on questions of Hindu law which tend to show what the law has been in modern times and still is.

Stare decisis was, however, seldom blindly insisted upon, and reconsideration of rules is frequently met in reports as late as the 1930's. A particularly critical moment was the creation of the High Courts in 1861, when the rules of the Sadr Courts or the Supreme Courts, which found themselves merged into one institution, could be discarded or modified. Nevertheless it is evident that learning in Anglo-Hindu law did not keep pace with historical research into the *dharmaśāstra*, perhaps because certainty of titles was more important than the satisfaction of the somewhat erratic academics of the period. Antiquarianism had obvious dangers, as witness *Venkatachalapati* v. *Subbarayadu*,[3] decided in the Madras High Court about ten years after the case quoted from above. In this case the district *munsif* had held that a plaintiff who had been excluded from the inner shrine of a temple, because of his excommunication for his marriage to a widow, was entitled to damages against those who had excluded him, to a declaration that he was entitled to enter the inner shrine, and to an injunction restraining them from excluding

[1] 3 Mad. 309, 310.
[2] Referring to Nelson's views (above, p. 292, n. 3).
[3] (1889) 13 Mad. 293.

him. The district *munsif* had come to this conclusion after investigating the *śāstra*, and customs to the contrary he held void.[1] The High Court could not accept this position: after pointing out that the Veda, *smṛti*, and *ācāra* were sources of *dharma*, Muttuswāmī Ayyar, J. (perhaps the most famous of the many famous Indian judges on the Madras High Court bench) said,[2]

> This conventional rule of interpretation is acknowledged by all. But under the teaching of Sankara another conventional rule came to be adopted together with it by commentators of authority who consolidated the diverse law-sources into a consistent system of law. They considered that all the recognized law-sources were inspired writings, and that if properly understood, they were capable of being reconciled, and attached great weight in connexion with their interpretation to usage approved by learned and pious men. Thus a latitude of interpretation was introduced by them and their exposition of law which was at times wide both of the conventional rule first mentioned and of the rules of doctrinal interpretation, was in many cases readily adopted by the people as authoritative, and as a guide to their caste practice in consequence of the great respect which they had for their authority as men of learning and piety. After the practice of the people continued for some time, it reacted on the mode in which commentators reconciled the original law sources with each other, and gave to what was originally a mere juristic thought the force of a rule of law. Whilst this accounts for the belief of the general community that what they practice is consistent with the original law-sources as authoritatively interpreted and adopted for many generations, it suggests also a stand-point from which a reformer who desires to revive some practice of ancient times as being salutary may act. He may treat the authoritative commentaries as misinterpreting the original law-sources, and ignore the juristic thought which they contain as a legitimate factor in the development of Hindu law. The District Munsif apparently confounds the functions of the judiciary with those of the reformer. In administering Hindu law the former has only to see what is the Hindu law as received and practised by the Hindu community in general with the conviction that it is law, and to declare and enforce it when it is ascertained. It is not for him to go beyond, to resolve the Hindu law as received by the people into its historical factors, to see how far its historical development has diverged from the logical or philosophical development in the light of modern civilization, and to reconstruct a system of Hindu law which the people ought to have received and followed as consistent with their *śāstras* . .

[1] Cf. *Venkataramana* (1916) 40 Mad. 212 (F.B.), 222 (cited at p. 162, n. 2 above).

[2] At p. 302. It is important to realize that this point of view represents the 'correct' tradition of administration of Hindu law as contrasted with the later opinion evinced by Sadāsiva Ayyar, J., at p. 299, n. 5 above.

A disquisition into the several law-sources, such as *śruti*, *smṛiti*, and *mahāpurāṇas*, and custom, is of a judicial value only for the purpose of elucidation and of tracing the consciousness of generations that have passed away that what is practised was law. If such disquisition leads them to a period when the law and usage were otherwise, such discovery should tend only to enable them to trace the origin and development of the law and usage as they since came to prevail. It is not permitted to the judiciary to push the disquisition beyond these legitimate limits . . . It must always be remembered that the Hindu law, which the Courts are bound to administer, is the law as received by the Hindu community and not as it stood either in the vedic or *smṛiti* period of their history, and that no other conception of Hindu law to be administered by the Courts is either judicial or rational. If it were otherwise, the Courts might have to force upon the Hindu community of this century the several portions of obsolete Hindu law which existed at some former times and have since fallen into disuse . . . (and the learned Judge instances *niyoga*[1]).

The textbooks, which might have been expected to offer fundamental help here, trimmed their treatment to accommodate the case-law,[2] and lawyers trained in the subject were content to dabble in as much of the Sanskrit learning as related directly to the law administered in the courts.[3] The reformers of 1955–6 were educated in the period 1900–25, when *dharmaśāstra* learning was at a low ebb, and when what was left of Sanskrit sources in Hindu law was being fastened upon chiefly as proof of the survival of Hindu culture through the period of Western political, economic and cultural supremacy; so that the resulting reforms reflect rather the neglect than the pursuit of the *śāstra*.

[1] See above, p. 89.

[2] Contrast Jhā (note his bitter comments at *Hindu Law in its Sources*, II, 1933, Preface, p. *v*) with Mayne, Mulla, Rāghavāchāriar, Gupte, Gour, and even Kāṇe, whose concentration on topics relevant to Anglo-Hindu law was as natural as it is marked. It is gratifying to see the handsome tribute to Jhā at *Ram Khelawan* AIR 1950 Pat. 194, 28 Pat. 1008 (cited by Naṭarāja Ayyar, *Mīmāṃsā Jurisprudence*, p. 3), but Jhā was after all a Bihar man. His *Hindu Law in its Sources* was used in *Kunwar Rajendra* [1952] 2 All. 681, 688; but these citations are rare.

[3] At no time since 1864 have practitioners attempted to administer Hindu law in the spirit of the *śāstra*; i.e. the natural checks and balances of the system have been ignored while the leading maxims and principles deduced from them have been learnt up parrot-fashion. It would, however, be unfair not to remark on the very wide Sanskrit sources used in *Srinivasa* v. *Sheshacharlu* [1942] Mad. 42, 53–5, and on the quotation of the *Skanda-purāṇa* in *Chandra* v. *Jnanendra* (1923) 27 C.W.N. 1033–such instances, though rare, demonstrate skill and ingenuity in action.

Yet British judges and their Hindu and Muslim colleagues handled the Hindu law with ultra-sensitive care. The diffidence of the Privy Council in contexts which had a connexion with what western jurists termed 'religion' is remarkable.[1] They have maintained a critical approach to Indian High Court judgements on appeal, together with a reluctance to differ from established courses of decision, especially where these are founded upon the judgements of eminent Hindu judges.[2] This latter stems not from the supposed learning of Hindu judges, but from their likelihood to know what would be acceptable to the Hindu community. For, with outstanding exceptions such as Justices Muttuswāmī Ayyar, Chaṇḍāvarkar,[3] Telang, A. Mookerjee,[4] D. N. Mitter and B. K. Mukherjea, Hindu judges have

[1] *Ramtonoo* (1829) 1 Knapp 245, 247; *Rungama* (1846) 4 M.I.A. 1, 97–8; *Bhyah* (1870) 13 M.I.A. 373, 390. The religious origin of law in India was overemphasized: *Skinner* (1871) 14 M.I.A. 309, 323; *Sec. of State* (1868) 1 B.L.R., O.C. 87, 100–1. Govind Das, cited above, quoted with approval G. C. Sarkar Śāstrī's work on Adoption, p. 84: 'The greatest impediment in the way of Hindu jurisprudence was offered by the theory of its divine origin, which stamped a stationary character upon it.'

[2] The following appeared in vol. I of C. S. Ramakrishna [Aiyar's] *Hindu Law Journal*, bearing the dates May 1918 to June 1919 (p. 129): 'The Law enunciated by their Lordships of the Privy Council to-day is nothing less than the law of peace, harmony and love, which was the basis of the original law of Manu and it is the same Manu whose law is embodied in the words "justice, equity, and good conscience" that inspires their Lordships of the Privy Council to lay down principles of Hindu law for the guidance and well being of the numerous classes that inhabit this holy land of ours. Inspired by the highest and noblest considerations of equity, justice and good conscience, their Lordships of the Privy Council have laid down the principles of Hindu law in several of their invaluable judgements, principles that are quite in consonance with the basic principles of the Hindu religion and law and that conduce to the growth of the Hindu Jurisprudence in a way which is consistent with the aspirations and changing conditions and environments of the Hindu people.' The author, who emanated from Coimbatore District, seems to have had a fanciful notion of what 'justice, equity and good conscience' was (and is) (see above, p. 289); but his apparent satisfaction with the Privy Council was (and is) widely shared.

[3] *Chunilal* (1909) 33 Bom. 433, *Jagannatha* (1910) 34 Bom. 553, *Dayaldas*, ibid., 385 (F.B.), and *Tukaram* (1911) 36 Bom. 339 (F.B.) show unparalleled erudition. Did he go too far in *Tara* (1907) 31 Bom. 495?

[4] Brilliant in all he touched, his Sanskritic learning is shown in an edition of a work by Jīmūtavāhana, and in, e.g. *Bhupati* (1909) 37 Cal. 129 (F.B.) and *Manohar* AIR 1932 Cal. 791. At *Hindu Law Journal*, 6, pt. 5 (Dec. 1923), p. 99 appears the following remark, 'Since the establishment of the British

been undistinguished for learning in *dharmaśāstra*. For, although a Hindu judge might investigate the *śāstra* as a hobby (amongst living examples the former Justices P. B. Gajendragadkar, S. Varadāchāriar and T. L. Veṅkaṭarāma Iyer are prominent), śāstric training and the busy practice which is the essential prerequisite of promotion to the High Court are quite incompatible. Occasionally judges, including Hindu judges, have denounced rules of Hindu law as inappropriate to modern times,[1] but once a rule found a place in a textbook or had been confirmed by a court it was usually proof against all but legislation. Judges in East Africa may prove more independent, and judicial amendments are threatened there.

The basic faults of the system are these: firstly the great chasm between custom and law remained; and secondly the English system of piecemeal manufacture of law proved costly and embarrassing. Left to itself custom has no doubt gradually tended to yield to the 'personal law', i.e. the Anglo-Hindu law.[2] The process is undocumented and bears no relation to castes' anachronistic self-Brahminization.[3] The public adjusts itself slowly and unevenly to the court-law. Custom has had to be proved specifically in derogation from the personal law.[4] Proof can be difficult, although the courts do not insist upon all the

Courts in India, no Judge, Indian or English, has written judgements like Sir Asutosh Mookerjee', a comment which remains true. Sir Ashutosh turned his judgement on every issue, however small, into a miniature Ph.D. thesis.

[1] *Srinivasa* (1921) 44 Mad. 801, *Subramania* (1927) 51 Mad. 361 (F.B.), 365, 367; *Udhao* [1946] Nag. 425.

[2] *Rajah* (1872) 19 W.R. 8 P.C., *Gigi* AIR 1956 Ass. 100, *Ujagar* AIR 1959 S.C. 1041: cf. *Kunji* AIR 1954 T.C. 371, *Karthayini* AIR 1957 Ker. 27, where the residual law fills gaps.

[3] Mayer, where cited. McKim Marriott, ed., *Village India* (*American Anthropological Association Memoir*, No. 83, 1955). See above, p. 190.

[4] *Coll. of Madura* (1868) 12 M.I.A. 397, 436, *Nirodhini* AIR 1945 Cal. 213, *Seetha* AIR 1939 Mad. 564, *Venkata* AIR 1953 Mad. 571, *T. Saraswathi* AIR 1953 S.C. 201. For a good recent example see *Mst. Maro* AIR 1966 H.P. 22. After the Constitution (*Maniram* AIR 1962 M.P. 275; *Bhau Ram* AIR 1962 S.C. 1476; *Sant Ram* AIR 1965 S.C. 314) and after codification of Hindu law (*P. Latchamma* AIR 1961 A.P. 55) numerous customs, even if satisfactorily proved, will be cut down. Custom can sometimes be taken into account in *penal* law, to mitigate an offence and abate a sentence: *Garab* AIR 1927 Nag. 279 (Gond wrongful confinements and rapes amount to 'rude proposals of marriage').

criteria known to English law when taking evidence of Indian customs.[1]

The unhistorical distinction between a 'Hindu' and a non-Hindu, for the purposes of application of the Hindu law produces anomalies[2] to which delicate subject we must return,[3] custom is to be proved by instances of usage, but there have been exceptions, where custom has perhaps been relied on too readily.[4] Some customs accepted by courts resemble usages that found a place in the *śāstra* and were excised thence a thousand years ago,[5] others that are known to prevail correspond to what the court-law was half a century or more ago,[6] and if the usage corresponds to the śāstric law as opposed to the court-law the court may or may not accord it validity, depending upon the context.[7] The vitality of ancient customary ideas was vindicated in the Hindu Code, which reintroduced rules consistent with lower-caste custom.[8]

The fundamental and obvious rule of the Roman Digest,[9] that no pronouncement should be made without reviewing the whole of the law, is often ignored. Particular decisions relate to particular issues, and reference has seldom been made to aspects of the law which at once strike the jurist, but which are not

[1] *Kojahs* (1847) Perry 110, 120–1, *Ramalakshmi* (1872) 14 M.I.A. 570, 585, *Hurpurshad* (1876) 3 I.A. 259, 285. Customs relating to family succession, succession to *mutts*, commercial usage, divorce, and adoption have often been proved. Failures: *Padmavati* AIR 1951 Or. 248; *Nanu* AIR 1957 T.C. 289; *Mathura* (1880) 4 Bom. 545; *Balusami* AIR 1957 Mad. 97; *Vallabhalalji* (1961) 64 Bom. L.R. 433 (S.C.).

[2] *Dashrath* AIR 1951 Nag. 343, *Rafail* AIR 1957 Pat. 70. For the problem see above, pp. 45 f.

[3] In chapter 17 below.

[4] *Madhavrao* [1946] Bom. 375. Frequent proof has established the custom: *Rama* (1918) 45 I.A. 148, *Gopalachariar* AIR 1955 Mad. 559, *Ujagar* AIR 1959 S.C. 1041. Custom of user or non-user improperly relied on: *Mayna* (1864) 2 M.H.C.R. 196, 201–2; 8 M.I.A. 400, 423; *Apaji* (1891) 16 Bom. 29, *Krishna* (1908) 12 C.W.N. 453.

[5] *Niyoga* (above, p. 89, n. 1); polyandry in Kerala and Assam; the special share of the eldest son (above, p. 208), partition 'by mothers' (or *patnī-bhāga*).

[6] Mayer, where cited, p. 245 provides an instance relative to adoption.

[7] *Nilmadhub* (1869) 13 M.I.A. 85, 100. *K. Subbaya* AIR 1958 An.P. 479. In *Chandrasekhara* AIR 1963 S.C. 185 the *sapiṇḍa-s*' objections, which the court brusquely rejected, coincided with unprovable custom and tradition.

[8] See chapter 11 below.

[9] Dig. I, 3, 24.

immediately relevant in the sense familiar to Anglo-American lawyers. This breeds litigation,[1] and makes law teaching painful. Anomalies abound,[2] and the constant divergencies of the High Courts,[3] deprive the system of dignity, for they involve the possibility that lines of decision in any individual High Court may be overruled by the Supreme Court, without our being able to foretell which will be overruled. At one stage judicial legislation amplifies the law; at another judges hope the legislature will be forced to intervene.[4] But because there is no close contact between the *śāstra* and the public, nor between them and their Anglo-Hindu system (where this still operates), nor between the nation and the legislature (where experts in the system have been prominent and even experts in the *śāstra* have made their mark), there has existed no atmosphere such as enabled the Common law (in which piecemeal law-making is endemic) to function smoothly and grow harmoniously.

Distortion of Rules

The *smṛti-s* were enlivened by commentators who introduced customary elements into their exposition.[5] To them the law was a whole, each chapter explaining and being explained by others. The Government of India neglected to publish texts, to

[1] Derrett at AIR 1960 Journal, pp. 71 ff., also ibid., p. 97; AIR 1961 Journal, 10–11.

[2] *Ramchandra* (1958) 60 Bom. L.R. 82, 84. *Bhagwantrao* [1938] Nag. 255, 264.

[3] Cf. *Martand* AIR 1939 Bom. 305 (F.B.) with *Babarao* AIR 1956 Nag. 98. *Manabai* AIR 1954 Nag. 284 (cf. *Ram* AIR 1951 M.B. 96). In Madras recently a last-minute attempt to bridge the gap between Madras and Bombay authorities on the heritable rights of cognates failed: *Kaliammal* v. *Muthu Pillai* AIR 1966 Mad. 118.

[4] 'Piece-meal legislation is no doubt not desirable but so long as the generality of the followers of Hindu law, even in the same province, are not willing to have it ascertained by a commission and codified according to the recommendations of that commission, piece-meal legislation is the only course open to the Legislature:' *Soundararajan* (1915) 39 Mad. 159, 183 *per* Sadāsiva Ayyar, J. 'The duty of the court is . . . to give effect to the letter of the rule and not its spirit:' *Lilavatibai* [1948] Bom. 301. The legislature must cope: *Sharad Chandra* AIR 1944 Nag. 266 (F.B.). *Amrit* AIR 1960 S.C. 964, 970.

[5] See above, p. 161, n. 5. See also Kāṇe's criticisms of *Chandika* (1901) 29 I.A. 70 at *H.D.*, III, p. 729, n. 1408.

procure translations, and to record customs; similarly it viewed with indifference the possibility that segments of Hindu law could be distorted by severance from the body to which they belonged. English procedural methods altered much substantive law, curtailing some rights and amplifying others.[1] Some rules intended for a limited purpose were developed to create rights beyond the contemplation of the original framers, while others were so cut down as to be scarcely recognizable.[2] Distortion occurred through supplementation (see next section), both in substantive and adjectival law. Numbers of Hindu rules were silently and even accidentally abolished by the latter process.[3] Occasionally rights were created under the general law of India which diminished the importance of similar, or connected, rights under the personal law.[4]

Throughout the period prior to codification the court took care to add as little as possible, either by analogy or by inference, from the known authoritative rules.[5] From the beginning

[1] Observed in *Ruckmaboye* (1851–2) 5 M.I.A. 234, 263. See above, p. 296, n. 1. *Deen* (1877) 4 I.A. 247 (below, p. 418); *Suraj* (1879) 6 I.A. 88 (below, p. 311). Cf. *Bhuwanee* (1847) 7 Sel. Rep. (Cal.) 429, and the limits observed in *Bebee Muttra* (1832) Morton 191, 210. The distinction between 'void' and 'voidable', which pervades the Anglo-Hindu system, was probably unknown to the *śāstra*.

[2] Adoption and the Pious Obligation grew surprisingly. Guardianship in marriage, the powers of alienation, and dependants' rights of maintenance out of property seem to have been attenuated.

[3] Statutes directing Courts of Wards, or laying down the devolution of *tālukdārī-s* and other tenures; the presumption of death (a question of evidence); the law of adverse possession; the law relating to the form of dispositions, and construction of documents with reference to the calendar: illustrations of abrogation. Custom can suffer likewise: *Mudara* AIR 1935 Mad. 33. We should not lose sight of the Married Women's Property Act, 1874, s. 6 (1) (which interferes with the law of succession). The Act was recently extended to Buddhists.

[4] The illegitimate daughter's rights (of an emergency nature but none the less often resorted to) under the Criminal Procedure Code (Derrett, *I.M.H.L.*, §. 35: see also *Mascreen* [1956] Mad. 834; Derrett at (1960) 62 Bom. L.R., *J.*, 22–3) have hid the fact that her personal law gave her no right to maintenance against her putative father. The Arya Marriage Act and the Special Marriage Act no doubt did much to delay the development of lawful inter-caste marriages between Hindus.

[5] *Bhyah* (1870) 13 M.I.A. 373, 390. Yet judicial legislation by analogy is found: *Lallubhai* (1881) 5 Bom. 110, 7 I.A. 212; *Ramasami* (1894) 17 Mad. 422; *Uma* [1942] 1 Cal. 299; *Akshay* (1908) 35 Cal. 721; *Athilinga* [1945]

British judges were alive to the need not to allow analogies from any foreign system (especially the English) to warp their judgement.[1] Protestations that English law is inapplicable abound, and some characteristic English distinctions were rigorously excluded as incompatible with the Hindu system.[2] At the same time the mere statement of Hindu rules in English legal terminology has tended to fashion the effect which the rules have been given;[3] and although it is constantly noticed that such unconscious influence must be avoided the suspicion that Anglo-Hindu law draws something from English legal classification is confirmed by a comparison with the Franco-Hindu rules that have grown from the same śāstric sources under the influence of the French system.[4] This is not to suggest that the French did not distort Hindu law and custom by introducing categories and analogies from French law: complaints that such tampering took place in certain chapters (especially the joint-family and succession) seem to be well founded.

Despite the claims of the Bombay High Court to have a 'school' of its own, and thus to evade Privy Council decisions on appeal from elsewhere,[5] the influence of that court has been pervasive. Even *obiter dicta* in its Advices have had more weight

Mad. 297 (on which see Derrett at (1965) 67 Bom. L.R., *J.*, pp. 167 ff., at 172–4); *Rambhau* AIR 1946 Nag. 206; *Raghavamma* AIR 1964 S.C. 136. The uneasy relationship between textual law and case-law is illustrated in *Sivagami* AIR 1956 Mad. 323 (F.B.).

[1] *Kashinath* (1826) in Montriou, *Hindu Will of Bengal*, p. 106; *Doe d. Dorabji* (1848) Perry 498, 501–2; *Bhubon Moyee* (1865) 10 M.I.A. 279, 308; *Bhyah* (above). On Roman influence see Derrett at *RabelsZ.* 24 (1959), pp. 657–85 and compare Chandavarkar, J.'s, denunciation of a tendency to 'romanize' Hindu law at *Kalgavda* (1909) 33 Bom. 669. Muhammadan law should not be resorted to (!): *Zuburdust* (1866) N.W.P., F. B. Rulings (Agra, 1867), 77.

[2] *Varden* (1862) 9 M.I.A. 303; *Jotindra* (1872) 9 B.L.R. 377, 393, 401 P.C.; *Kenchava* (1924) 51 I.A. 368.

[3] The use of English terms was unavoidable: *Sadanund* (1863) 1 Marshall, 317; *Jamiyatram* (1864) 2 B.H.C.R. 11; 46 I.A. 72, 84. Compare *Sarubai* [1943] Bom. 314, 317 (criticized at (1958) 61 Bom. L.R., *J.*, p. 627 at p. 631).

[4] Gnanou Diagou, cited above, pp. 98 ff., 106 ff. The divergences of Franco-Hindu from Anglo-Hindu law are noted by Sorg (see above, p. 283, n. 1). For example, the death of a *communiste* (i.e. coparcener) dissolves the coparcenary.

[5] *Gandhi* (1900) 24 Bom. 192; *Bhau* (1925) 50 Bom. 204; *Shankar* (1926) 51 Bom. 194; *Appaji* (1930) 54 Bom. 564 (F.B.).

attached to them in India than would have been expected in New Zealand or Canada.[1] The remoteness of the Privy Council, despite the presence of ex-High Court Judges, Indian judges and others on the Board, has, however, contributed to judicial caution where the Indian Supreme Court of today can, if it wishes, be less conservative,[2] but there were mistakes which a court in closer contact with the people might have avoided.[3]

A literal and obstinate adherence to śāstric rules, misunderstanding their original purport, has at times produced situations inconsistent with the traditional Hindu background;[4] the result

[1] *Lajwanti* AIR 1924 P.C. 121 (cf. *Kirpal* [1957] 21 S.C.J. 438; *Tilakdhari* AIR 1963 Pat. 356; Derrett at AIR 1955 J., pp. 10–19; *Gunderao* AIR 1955 Hyd. 3 [F.B.]); *Krishnamurthi* (1927) 54 I.A. 248 (cf. [1960] 23 S.C.J., *J.*, 43 ff.); *Suraj* (1879) 6 I.A. 88, 106; *Sat* AIR 1925 P.C. 18, 22; *Udmiram* AIR 1956 Nag. 76 (cf. *Lakshmanaswami* AIR 1943 Mad. 292); *Narain* (1917) 44 I.A. 163 (cf. *Madan* (1931) 53 All. 21); *G. Anantapadmanabhaswami* (1933) 60 I.A. 167, 174; *Sukumar* AIR 1956 Cal. 308.

[2] *Coll. of Masulip.* (1860) 8 M.I.A. 500, 524; *Lakshman* (1880) 7 I.A. 181, 195; *Vellaiyappa* (1931) 58 I.A. 402; *Akhara* AIR 1945 P.C. 1. The Privy Council's care does not invalidate the complaints of Govinda Das or Setlūr. In the case of *Guramma* v. *Mallappa* AIR 1964 S.C. 510 (discussed by Derrett at [1964] 66 Bom. L.R., *J.*, 129, AIR 1965 Journal 34–7, [1966] 68 Bom. L.R., *J.*, 41–2) the Indian Supreme Court disregarded textual law and reinterpreted the *śāstra* along with customary law and judicial decisions in a manner of which the Privy Council would have been incapable.

[3] Mistakes corrected: *Thakoorain* (1867) 11 M.I.A. 386 (cf. 2 B.L.R. 28, 6 M.H.C.R. 278); *Rai* (1884) 11 I.A. 164 (cf. 1 M.H.C.R. 77); *Venkayamma* (1902) 29 I.A. 156 (cf. *Muhammad* (1937) 64 I.A. 250; [1950] Mad. 1084); *Girdharee* (1874) 1 I.A. 321 (cf. *Ponnappa* (1881) 4 Mad. 1); *Sahu* (1917) 44 I.A. 126, 131 (cf. *Brij* AIR 1924 P.C. 50; *Abdul* AIR 1954 Mad. 961 F.B.); *Naragunty* (1861) 9 M.I.A. 66; *Rani Sartaj* (1887–8) 15 I.A. 51; *Rama* (1918) 45 I.A. 148; *Baijnath* (1921) 48 I.A. 195; *Coll. of Gorakhpur* (1934) 61 I.A. 286 (cf. Madras Act 1 of 1914; AIR 1949 Bom. 391; AIR 1952 S.C. 29); *Anant* (1943) 70 I.A. 232 (cf. *Shrinivas* AIR 1954 S.C. 379; below, p. 341). Uncorrected: *Rao* (1898) 25 I.A. 54; *Sheo* (1903) 30 I.A. 202; *Jatindra* (1931) 58 I.A. 372. The following are of questionable correctness: *Gadadhur* (1940) 67 I.A. 129; *Nataraja* (1949) 77 I.A. 33.

[4] Instances occur in the law of adoption, and in the following topics: the divided coparcener's disentitlement to marriage expenses; the idiot's former right to marry; the limitations on a female's rights at a partition; the after-born or adopted son's right to reopen a partition in some cases but not others; the right of the separated son to share in property passing from his father. Examples of the narrow approach are *Jinnappa* (1934) 59 Bom. 459 (overruled by the Supreme Court in *Guramma* AIR 1964 S.C. 510; see above, n. 2); *Gulabrao* [1952] Nag. 591.

is that the Anglo-Hindu system is occasionally more orthodox than the *śāstra*; or where the words have not been distorted the spirit has been abandoned. Instances of this are not, however, so numerous as those of supplementation and blending with English rules.

Supplementation by Imported Rules

A rapid growth occurred in enterprise and extensive changes in the social outlook of the classes most likely to profit from it. The ancient ways no longer satisfied those who envied the more individualistic ways of their rulers. Questions were asked of the pandits which their sources could not answer, and their successors, authors of textbooks, were expected to suggest how new facilities could be obtained on the basis of old rules. New legal institutions, such as English-type negotiable instruments, were expected to supplant the traditional customary law, or like Insolvency were expected to be engrafted upon Hindu institutions.[1] There were doubts how far importations such as the latter penetrated into the structure of the system. Where the texts provided no explicit indication of the way in which a right was to be worked out, or how a particular disposition should be construed, English rules filled the gap.[2] This happened frequently even without conscious reference to Justice, Equity and Good Conscience, the residual source of law, since, to take as an example testamentary bequests[3] or the alienation of undivided interests in coparcenary property,[4] the Judges were not aware that in applying English Common law or Equity they were doing anything else but expounding the Hindu law on the point. So many rules of English law seemed to be merely rules of universal law.[5] The present judiciary are under

[1] *Narayana* AIR 1937 Mad. 182; *Natarajan* AIR 1943 Mad. 246; *Venkatarayudu* (1934) 58 Mad. 126; *Hanumantha* [1947] Mad. 44; *Honna* AIR 1949 Mad. 165.

[2] The equity of redemption was imported into Hindu conditional sales: *Ramji* (1864) 1 B.H.C.R. 199; *Venkata* (1863) 1 M.H.C.R. 461; *Pattabhiramier* (1870) 13 M.I.A. 560, 568, 571–2; *Thumbasawmy* (1875) 2 I.A. 24, 250 f.; *Ramasami* (1881) 4 Mad. 179 F.B.

[3] See above, p. 290, n. 1.

[4] *Suraj* (1879) 6 I.A. 88, 102, Derrett at [1966] K.L.T., *J.*, pp. 29–49.

[5] *Coll. of Masulipatam* (1860) 8 M.I.A. 500, 524–5; *Ranee* (1864) 10 M.I.A. 123, 145; *Lopez* (1870) 13 M.I.A. 467, 473; *Sheo* (1872) 4 I.R. 910, 917–18; *Nandi* (1888) 16 I.A. 44, 47.

the impression that the contribution of Justice, Equity and Good Conscience has transformed the śāstric law to such an extent that the texts as such have lost their authority.[1] A complete list of the debts owed by the Anglo-Hindu law to English law would be extremely lengthy.[2] Yet in hardly a single case are the judges not discovering the Hindu law through the imported rule. Sometimes doubt arises as to whether the importation has taken place, as in the topic of Guardianship, which is almost entirely English in character;[3] but normally it is assumed, rightly, that without the importation the Hindu institution could not have been applied effectively or without unjust results. Refusals to apply an English rule as such have been common.[4]

English law is sometimes consulted under Justice, Equity and Good Conscience, so long as it is not unsuited to Indian conditions.[5] Since the Hindu system is said to be equipped with its own system of interpretation[6] and since the judges attempt to fill gaps from Hindu legal sources where possible,[7] there would appear to be no unbounded scope for English rules. But in fact

[1] *Dudh Nath* and *Amrit* cited at p. 297, n. 4 above.

[2] Instances: *Mulraz* (1838) 2 M.I.A. 54; *Maharajah* (1877) 4 I.A. 228, 245; *Padman* AIR 1915 P.C. 111; *Hunooman* (1856) 6 M.I.A. 393 (see below, p. 426); *Venkayya* [1942] Mad. 24; *Gujrath* [1943] Bom. 423; *Kochu* [1959] S.C.R. 63; *Sridevi* AIR 1960 Ker. 1.

[3] *The King* (1814) 2 Strange N.C. 251; *Sriramulu* AIR 1949 F.C. 218; *Besant* (1914) 41 I.A. 314; *Kakumanu* AIR 1958 S.C. 1042. Laude, *Recueil* (cited above, p. 283, n. 1), p. 26 shows that the French applied French law in such matters.

[4] *Gopeekrist* (1854) 6 M.I.A. 53, 75–9; *Adv. Gen.* (1863) 9 M.I.A. 387, 426–8; *Chedambara* (1874) 1 I.A. 241, 264; *Khwaja* (1910) 37 I.A. 152, 159.

[5] *Degumburee* (1868) 9 W.R. 230, 232; *Rajah* (1879) 6 I.A. 145, 159; *Waghela* (1887) 14 I.A. 89; *T. Saraswathi* AIR 1953 S.C. 201. The topic is treated at length by Derrett cited above, p. 289, n. 1, also at (1962) 64 Bom. L.R., *J.*, pp. 129–38, 145–52. Sir Asutosh Mookerjee in a speech delivered at Benares Hindu University, August 4th, 1923 (reprinted from the Calcutta Law Journal in *Hindu Law Journal*, 6 pt. 5 (1923), pp. 45 ff., esp. 50–1) gives a short critique of the function of Justice, Equity and Good Conscience, and advises students (in the manner of Gargantua's letter to Pantagruel: Rabelais, II, *Pantagruel*, ch. 8) to study Coke, Blackstone, Kent, Burge, and the principles of Roman law (!).

[6] *Ramchandra* AIR 1914 P.C. 1, 5; *Kalgavda* (1909) 33 Bom. 669, 680. But the *śāstra* could not anticipate all our quandaries: *Shivprasad* AIR 1949 Bom. 408, 410. *Raghavamma* AIR 1964 S.C. 136, 151 (village polity).

[7] *Martand* AIR 1939 Bom. 305 F.B.; *Jagarnath* (1934) 57 All. 85, 100, 107; *Krishna* [1939] 2 M.L.J. 423, 434; *Natha* AIR 1931 Bom. 89.

the search for local rules has not been laborious, and both Common law and English statute law have been resorted to.[1] At times the general Hindu law has been used to assist with the application of customary law,[2] and customs have even thrown light on what the personal law ought to be:[3] but the contribution of imported law has been far more prominent than either of these indigenous sources. The resulting patchwork effect should be recognized for what it is.

'*Obsolescence*' *and* Stare Decisis

Strictly traditional and also progressive elements have been represented amongst the Indian judiciary. P. B. Gajendragadkar, formerly a Judge of the Bombay High Court, then a Judge and Chief Justice of the Supreme Court, later Vice-Chancellor of the University of Bombay, actively forwarded the codification of Hindu law both on, and off the Bench. Reviewing the case-law, however, a consistent pattern cannot be made out. It is dangerous to suggest that any śāstric rule is obsolete.[4] The *śāstra* is still a source of law by statute, except where repealed.[5] 'Advanced' groups of Hindus have procured this repeal by stages in certain sectors.[6] After the formative period, however, embarrassing pieces of genuine śāstric law, not represented in the textbooks, have on occasions been declared 'obsolete', as not confirmed by usage.[7] 'Usage', however, might turn out to be a

[1] *Sec. of State* AIR 1937 Nag. 354, 367–8; cf. *Cheriya* AIR 1955 T.C. 255 F.B.

[2] *Maktul* AIR 1958 S.C. 918.

[3] See the *vyavasthā* at 2 Macn., P. & P., 101 (about 1817). References to Steele in *Rungama* (1846) 4 M.I.A. 1, 100; *Kayarohana* (1915) 38 Mad. 250, 254; cf. *Krishna* (1908) 12 C.W.N. 453. Cf. the reference to caste recognition in *Muthusami* (below, p. 358) and *Kaura* AIR 1943 All. 310.

[4] *Vallabhram* (1867) 4 B.H.C.R., A.C., 135. *Rajani* (1920) 48 Cal. 643 F.B. (cf. 43 Mad. 4, 45 Mad. 949); *Sambasivam* (1921) 44 Mad. 704; *Surendra* [1944] 1 Cal. 139 (cf. 24 C.W.N. 601, 610 [P.C.]). *Natha* AIR 1931 Bom. 89. For *G. Narsi* [1964] 1 An.W.R. 261 see above, p. 297, n. 4.

[5] *Sadananda* AIR 1950 Cal. 179. *Anukul* [1939] 1 Cal. 592, 601. Abhorrent or unpleasing rules adverted to: AIR 1950 F.C. 142, 177–8; [1942] Mad. 807, 827 (F.B.); AIR 1958 An.P. 693.

[6] The Bombay Hindu Heirs Relief Act, 1866 is an early example of the piecemeal reform referred to below at pp. 327 f.

[7] Above, p. 297, n. 4. Also *Chockalingam* [1943] Mad. 603 P.C. *K. Malla* AIR 1956 An. 237; *Perumal* AIR 1955 Mad. 382; *Subbanna* AIR 1945 Mad. 142 F.B. *Vedanayaga* (1904) 27 Mad. 591, 598.

creation of the courts themselves without reference to practice independent of court-law (which would be speculative). *Stare decisis* will support wrong precedents.[1] Even well-known usages of former times have sometimes been declared obsolete, and their śāstric representatives with them.[2] Castes outgrowing certain practices have sometimes managed to prevent them by legislation, of which the impractical Dowry Prohibition Act, 1961, is the most striking example;[3] and their influence can be traced in the law reports, which from time to time refer to the current spirit of the community (*sic*).

When a new rule has to be made it is questionable whether attempts to effectuate the 'spirit of the community' are more correct than strict application of principles derivable from older authorities.[4] But where an old rule is to be applied to new facts, room for such adjustment seems desirable.[5] The 'orthodox' who can read the *śāstra* without an Anglo-Hindu gloss have, it need hardly be added, no use for either result. The *śāstra* lives on in its own small sphere (amongst scholars, priests, genealogists and the like). Some believe that it has an important moral mission yet. The reformers who carried through codification cannot accept this, for their work largely prolongs the direction taken by the Anglo-Hindu law of which they had become tired.

A need to keep the law up to date is obvious in the case of communities who cannot exclude their members from the courts by caste-rules backed up by the threat of excommunication.[6]

[1] *Jagubhai* (1925) 49 Bom. 282; *Gurunath* AIR 1955 S.C. 206; *Venkanna* AIR 1951 Bom. 57; *Ramji* (1959) 62 Bom. L.R. 322, 335; *Maktul* (above); *Amrit* AIR 1960 S.C. 964. See also *Firm* AIR 1960 M.P. 56, 58, col. 1. *Lalu Jela* AIR 1962 Guj. 250. Limitations of the doctrine: *Mohammad* [1947] All. 520 (F.B.).

[2] *Advyapa* (1879) 4 Bom. 104; *Jagarnath* (1937) 57 All. 85, 104; *Venkata* AIR 1955 An. 31; *Deivanai* AIR 1954 Mad. 657 criticizing 3 All. 738.

[3] Derrett, *I.M.H.L.*, §§. 217–18 and pp. 607–10.

[4] *Shantabai* (1958) 61 Bom. L.R. 627; *Madaswami* 1947 Tr. L.R. 822. In *Madhavrao* [1946] Bom. 375, 428 a new ideology of Hindu society was used to limit the application of an existing rule.

[5] *Venkata* AIR 1954 Mad. 222, 226; *Govinda* AIR 1958 Mad. 510; *Jaggamma* AIR 1958 An.P. 582; *Comm. of I.-T.* AIR 1949 Nag. 128, 129. 'The modern trend of decisions is to take a more liberal view . . .': *Martand* AIR 1939 Bom. 305 (F.B.). Cf. *Bankey* (1931) 53 All. 868 (F.B.).

[6] On the abolition of excommunication in some areas see below, p. 473. The Vāgrī community of Gujarat prohibited its members from approaching

When statutes amended the law the courts had a choice between deciding analogous cases in conformity with the new law or refusing (and thus was obviously more correct) to extend the spirit of the statute beyond the scope given to it by the legislature. There have been instances of both approaches,[1] and more recently the statute-reformed system has attracted to itself its unreformed predecessor, as Judges are easily persuaded that the law always must have been what the legislature says it is[2]–but this is an intellectual exercise that few Judges would feel inclined openly to imitate.

Conclusion: the Place of 'Hindu Law' in India

It is confidently asserted that the British period kept suppressed a dynamic element in Hindu society, so that the personal law of the Hindus was fossilized.[3] One could equally well say that the codification which took place in 1955–6, the culmination of the

the courts: *Pūrna* (Navsari), October 1949, pp. 101–4. Where a complete code of caste rules is provided, free access to courts would frustrate it.

[1] *Bhimabai* AIR 1956 Nag. 231; *Sivathwaja* AIR 1949 Mad. 779. *Venkataramayya* [1953] 1 M.L.J. 508; *Kirpal* AIR 1951 All. 508; *Thirumaleshwara* AIR 1953 Mad. 132.

[2] *Kastoori* v. *Chiranji* AIR 1960 All. 446.

[3] See below, p. 318. Mr. J. Nehru said on May 21st, 1954 in the Lok Sabha that the coming of the British to India had suppressed a dynamic element in Hindu society and made it unchangeable except by legislation. See the same point of view expressed by Gurudass Banerjee, *Marriage and Stridhan*[5], pp. 7–8. U. C. Sarkar holds that, on the contrary, the British rule gave the Hindu law a definite direction not always in keeping with its orthodox genius (cited above, p. 3). Kāṇe called for codification in 1924–5 not because the system had become too rigid, but because of the shilly-shallying of the courts: *J.B.B.R.A.S.*, 6 (1925), pp. 34–9, cf. his *H.D.*, III, pp. 820–3. For other allegations against the British administration see below, p. 403, n. 1. Professor S. Venkaṭarāman, an expert, says, much more cogently, 'Till 1864 it could have been said in regard to Hindu law that no voice was heard unless it came from the tomb. Thereafter it proved to be a living and growing system showing an amazing adaptability to modern conditions. This was mainly due to the impact of English law on the Hindu law. The main effect of English law is to be seen in the secularization of the law of marriage. . . .': 'Influence of Common Law and Equity on the Personal Law of the Hindus', *Rev. del Inst. de Der. Comp.* (Barcelona), 8–9 (1957), p. 178.

period of reform and attempted reform which started for practical purposes in 1928 or even in 1920[1] did even more to fossilize the system.[2] A statute obviously pegs the law down much more firmly than case-law can. Thus the public was not worried about the effects of fossilization: what had bothered people was the distance between the personal law and the system by which they wanted to live. But the psychological reasons leading up to the partial destruction of the Anglo-Hindu law in India must be treated elsewhere. It is the state of that system and its causes which concern us now.

The choices made and confirmed in 1772 and 1781 are responsible for this system. Hastings and his contemporaries cannot seriously be blamed. Other choices could hardly have been made, in view of the ignorance of the population, the apparent absence of effective means of ascertaining custom, and the grave danger that the entire administration would collapse under multiple sources of corruption.

Major changes took place on account of this start, most of them beneficial. The law became, for all its many anomalies, more certain and much more uniform. Changes in Hindu usages, for which neither *śāstra* nor customs as usually understood could have made room, were accommodated. The massive introduction of English law or English-type law on other fronts, which excited hardly any criticism, has been harmonized with the existing personal laws. If natural growth was to be looked for, from where would it have come? The pandits were confined to reporting the rulings of long-dead authors. The *śāstra* as an academic discipline retained some moral but little legal authority amongst the castes at large. The artificial revival of interest in India's cultural heritage from the last quarter of the nineteenth century stimulated a romantic interest in Manu; and it is from there that the continuing interest in the *śāstra* comes which we find in some cultured classes. The interest is reflected in some legal contexts outside Hindu law. This is intriguing in its way,[3] but beyond our present study. Public opinion had no

[1] Gaṅgānātha Jhā, *Hindu Law in its Sources* (cited above, p. 126), I, *preface*.

[2] See report of opinion of the late Sir C. P. Rāmaswāmī Iyer at [1966] 1 M.L.J., *J.*, p. 43, n. 1.

[3] *State of Bombay* (1957) 59 Bom. L.R. 945, 969 (gambling); *Gherulal*

organ of expression. If the government had backed the customary law instead of the *śāstra* literally hundreds of different systems of customary law would have emerged, like the scores of instances of the *riwāj-i-ām* of the Punjab. An old-fashioned method was practicable on the happy-go-lucky basis known in several 'backward' native States before 1948;[1] but it was not the goal of the reformers in 1955–6.

In 1864 judicial knowledge of Hindu law was assumed.[2] If this had been refused, and the system had been treated as a foreign law (to be proved in evidence), growth would have been continuous. But the apparent unreliability of the pandits indirectly obviated this possibility. Even otherwise, pandits' powers of 'text-torturing' were not boundless. To introduce divorce on western-type grounds, and inheritance of shares by daughters along with sons was impossible for them–yet this, it is evident,[3] was the sort of growth the reformers wanted. To find authority for such modifications they had to dig much deeper into their cultural heritage than the legal authorities operative amongst Brahminized castes in the pre-British period.

It might be argued that in the French territories, where neither *stare decisis* nor a doctrinaire reverence for texts was to be found, the position must have been healthier. The Consultative Committee could contradict itself without causing a scandal. The area of general law available to Hindus was wider[4] than the very small *lex loci* in matters of private law available to Indians in British India. Yet, for all the differences, Franco-Hindu law and Anglo-Hindu law were sufficiently alike for Anglo-Hindu authorities to be commonly cited in Franco-Hindu law textbooks,[5] and for very occasional French decisions to be cited in

(1959) 22 S.C.J. 878 (wagering contracts); *M. H. Quareshi* AIR 1958 S.C. 731 (cow-protection); *V. V. Giri* AIR 1959 S.C. 1318, 1330–1 (elections).

[1] Strange, 1 N.C. 136; *Bhaeechund* (1836) 1 M.I.A. 155, 172; *Jewa-jee* (1842) 3 M.I.A. 138, 153; *Jesa* AIR 1958 Raj. 186.

[2] But courts consulted pandits as late as 1873 (*Moniram* 7 I.A. 115, 117). Note the Privy Council's animadversions at *Masjid* (1940) 44 C.W.N. 957, 964, referring to *Aziz* (1925) 47 All. 823, 835.

[3] See below, p. 336.

[4] Indians might subject themselves to French civil law (arrêté, Jan. 6th, 1819); arrêt du 16 Jan. 1852 (*Cour de Cassation*).

[5] See works listed at p. 283, n. 1 above.

British Indian courts.[1] The former native States which possessed regular judiciaries likewise differed from Anglo-Hindu law in about the same measure as the French courts (though not necessarily on the identical topics), but the divergencies were small, and in the direction of the traditional and 'old-fashioned'. So, far from showing how Hindu law could progress away from British influence, they have showed the reverse; and every one of these special rules has been abolished to conform to the general Anglo-Hindu pattern,[2] and finally to the modern Hindu legal pattern.

If Hindu law 'stagnated' under the British, Islamic law died. After numerous adjustments during the formative period, and the elimination of criminal law and evidence and absorption of contract and civil wrongs, the texts were found to supply ascertainable rules to meet most situations, and case-law is much less important than in the Hindu system. Enactments modifying Islamic law have, by comparison, been trifling; and since there is little impetus to reform Islamic law in India it would appear that the method adopted to ascertain and apply it was agreeable to the Muslim public–but on that topic there remains more to be said.[3] The method accorded in fact exactly with that adopted with reference to Hindu law, except that the British could not stimulate Muslim jurists to write for them in the early days as Hindus had done.

A comparison with Ceylon is instructive. A desire to reform Kandyan law and Tesavaḷamai (Tamil customary law in Jaffna)[4] has been manifested. The latter was administered with the aid of a code prepared under the Dutch; the former, as explained above, is basically customary law. The judges have done little to modernize or develop either system, though the residual Roman-Dutch law has filled some gaps. Amendments have proceeded through legislation.[5] No one suggests that the

[1] For example, *Coll. of Madura* 12 M.I.A. 397, 439.

[2] For particulars see *C.S.S.H.*, 4, No. 1 (1961), p. 49, n. 190. For a recent refusal to accept Madras notions of *marumakkattayam* law in Kerala see article in [1966] K.L.T. cited below at p. 418, n. 1.

[3] See below, p. 538.

[4] Sir W. Ivor Jennings and Justice H. W. Tambiah, *Dominion of Ceylon* (London, 1952); H. W. Tambiah, *Laws and Customs of the Tamils of Jaffna* (Colombo, 1950).

[5] Reported and discussed in the works cited in the last note.

British 'retarded' or 'fossilized' the laws of Ceylon. In Burma, where the texts of the so-called Buddhist law presented intractable problems of interpretation in the field of family law, the simplifications and adjustments made by British judges were accepted without resentment or even question.[1] The court, no doubt, consulted contemporary customary behaviour, and the size and homogeneity of Burmese Buddhist society may have helped. In any case the era of the old academic jurists seems never to have been regretted.

Where a system of law, apparently confined within the margins of written texts, comes to be administered by a foreign power, the people naturally expect it to be administered in the spirit of the compilers. When the relationship between textual law and non-textual customs (which are recognized as valid in the texts) is in debate, some choice has to be made and some decision taken. It is not clear what conclusion is to be drawn from the public's acquiescence in that decision. When they change, they feel that the law administered to them is antiquated and 'rigid'. It is open to them either to admit that innovation is necessary and that this may mean the importation of foreign rules, or to accuse the judiciary of failing to interpret the sources with appropriate elasticity. The latter course is attractive when one is committed to (i) proclaiming one's own advance from the position one's ancestors occupied when foreign power commenced; and (ii) asserting that the same textual system and its cultural *corpus* anticipated all the advances–the current social position correctly expressing the spirit of the ancient past.

If Hindu law had been forcibly codified in 1858 it appears that there would have been no objections, except from the cautious (not to say timid) and sentimental administrators who in fact refused the responsibility when the project was mooted. So long as no legislature properly represented the population, legislation must needs be rare and cautious, especially when the governing

[1] O. H. Mootham, *Burmese Buddhist Law* (Oxford University Press, Bombay, 1939). Social developments render much of the textual law obsolete (*Maung Thein* [1935] 13 Ran. 412); textual law binds if it expresses a legal and not merely a moral duty (*Mi Thit* 1883, S.J., 197, 199); case-law supplements and defines, as well as selects, *dhammathat* rules; and statute abrogates them.

power is wedded to the notions (i) that the religions of the inhabitants must at all costs be respected and (ii) that the personal laws were 'religious'.[1] After 1930 Hindus became alive to their opportunity to amend their personal law at their pleasure. They moved with caution and undid none of the previous legislation. Nothing done in 1955–6 suggested that in so far as the British amended, modified, abrogated or supplemented the law their administration had been mischievous or misdirected. Some of the rules which appear in the 'Hindu Code' do not carry the law any further forward than it had gone by case-law alone. As we have seen, the gap between popular standards and usages and the court-law prevents our answering as we might otherwise do, namely that the law as it had developed had moulded the people themselves. In fact the portion of the law which suffered severe modification during the British period, that relating to the Joint Family,[2] remains to the time of writing this chapter untouched in important respects. So much for the charge that the system was fossilized: what then was codification expected to achieve? And what relation does that enterprise have to the tradition that family law is part and parcel of the religion of those whose personal law it is? These are complicated questions which must be tackled in our next chapter.

[1] When, in 1837, the question was mooted whether the remarriage of widows should be permitted by a facultative statute–a proposal to which numerous learned as well as 'advanced' Hindus gave their assent–the (European) Registrars of all the Sadr Courts agreed that a statute allowing remarriage of Hindu widows would greatly offend native sentiment and would violate the Government's pledge to respect native faiths and customs. See Benoy Ghose, *Iswar Chandra Vidyāsāgar* (cited above), p. 78. It is of great interest that although enlightened Hindu sentiment was behind that statute (passed in 1856) even now, a century afterwards, the permission granted by it is rarely utilized and the religious prejudice against remarriage of widows has not diminished.

[2] See chapter 12 below.

10

THE CODIFICATION OF HINDU LAW

Whatever the reformers achieved in 1955–6[1] they did not go back on the achievements of the Hindu law during the British period; they did not return to the *śāstra*. They claimed that progress had been too slow and that the reforms they initiated ought to have been brought in long before. They did not seek the support of religion, and they rejected the aid of those who claimed that Hindu scriptures, rightly interpreted, really foresaw such amendments as they were proposing.[2] The claims were more or less fantastic, and the reformers proceeded largely upon the basis of common sense and the general demands of society: indeed the Anglo-Hindu law had little obvious sense, and no one could have constructed such a system *de novo* on any rational basis. Nevertheless, although Art. 44 of the Constitution distinctly anticipates the time when there will be a single civil code for all citizens of India,[3] the 'Hindu Code', as we can call the statutes of 1955–6 (which describe themselves, somewhat misleadingly, as codifying as well as amending Acts), is only a half-way house to this end, and is still part of a system of personal law applicable to people principally on the grounds of their religion. We are left

[1] This chapter is based on an article entitled 'Statutory amendments of the personal law of Hindus since Indian Independence' which appeared as a Report in the *Rapports généraux au Ve Congrès international de droit comparé*, Bruxelles, 4–9 août 1958 (Brussels, Établissements Émile Bruylant, 1960) at pp. 101–24. The text has been brought up to date and the bibliography transferred to the general bibliographical note of this book.

[2] Works such as B. N. Chobe, *Principles of Dharmshastr* (Hyderabad, 1951) have fallen into oblivion.

[3] A directive principle of state policy. 'The State shall endeavour to secure for the citizens a uniform civil code throughout the territory of India.' Basu, *Commentary on the Constitution of India*[4], I, pp. 315–16.

in this indefinite interim period with the anomalous situation, in which, by reason of their religion or supposed religion, nearly four hundred million Indians have applied to them, whether they like it or not, a system of law which has certain roots in the Anglo-Hindu system, certain roots in the shiftless cosmopolitanism of vocal and influential elements of the Indian population, certain roots in rather questionable academic propositions about law, but has little to do with Hinduism by any possible definition of that term.

Muslims in India have as much need, from an academic and a practical viewpoint, to have their personal law (or rather laws) reformed, and perhaps codified:[1] but the movement towards that end, skilfully led by able people, cannot 'get off the ground'. The steam which made the Hindu Code Bill project into a great news item for India throughout about fifteen years was apparently played out by the end of 1956, and few now seem really interested in that class of law reform. Even the excellent attempt at reform of Islamic law in Pakistan has not evoked a response in India, and various excuses are given why the matter cannot be tackled. The reasons for this have to be conjectured for they cannot be determined by the simple process of listening to what people say. Indians frequently, especially Indian politicians and other public figures, say what is appropriate at the time; deep self-examination is a luxury which can be enjoyed but rarely, and if there is an audience even that will be controlled self-exhibition. One is thus left to conjecture motives from actions which are admitted to have been intended – and this produces, in our case, intriguing results. It links modern India with her remote past. That may satisfy many scholars, if not the persons chiefly concerned who, if I know them, will vigorously repudiate it as an example of a disclosure more ill-mannered than inaccurate.

The fantasy-life of the Indian public figure is to be taken as seriously as his real life, and those who are accustomed to dealing with him on the first level must beware of the effects of calling up the second. To mix these two manners of approach is likely to produce uncomfortable results, and it is natural that those who are accustomed to move in the field of Asian studies in reliance upon the co-operation of Asians will try to avoid

[1] See chapter 15 below.

offending them by not drawing attention to anything which they themselves would wish to keep unspoken. At present it is the fashion for Hindus to be upholders of Hinduism in certain safe connexions and in public: because of the nature of Hinduism, which we have already discussed, it is not expected of them that this attitude should reflect their real life or their personal opinions. Those who strenuously advocated reform of Hindu law did not, in our submission, have any interest in Hindu law as such: they had other, simple and obvious interests, and once these were successfully served the question of further law reform could be shelved indefinitely. The two things everyone cares about seriously are marriage and inheritance and these two topics received a thorough overhaul. They were overhauled not in the direction of coming closer to Hinduism in any sense which any Hindu religious teacher could imagine, but in a direction subserving the personal interests of a class of Hindus, in fact a class which had given to Hinduism a relatively new flavour, pioneers in the modification of a culture.

This is not to suggest that they imagined that they were foisting upon the remainder of the public something for which they alone had any use: they believed that sooner or later the remainder, the submerged six-sevenths of the iceberg, would share their outlook and their needs. They were leaders and were giving to others as well as to themselves benefits which, in their view, had been withheld from them by the foreign government. And in this there was a grain of truth: the passionate Hinduism of the fighter for political freedom took its colour from his struggle. Whatever compatriots might think of inconsistencies of approach the British would not treat seriously claims for an overhaul of the religious law from the same quarter that was relying upon the religion's inner strength for their own emotional support. The reforms of Hindu law during the British period were half-hearted, a comment which could not be made after 1947. Meanwhile the major reform of the Islamic law, the Shariat Act as it is usually called, was reactionary and tended entirely to the consolidation and unification of that community in terms of its personal law.[1]

It is time to review what the codification achieved, without undue stress upon technical detail, and then to suggest why and

[1] See below, pp. 520–2.

within what limitations the Hindus of twelve years ago took it upon themselves to do what they did, why they did no more, and where the reforms have left them. What follows, up to sec. IV, is based on a report to the Fifth International Congress of Comparative Law (Brussels, 1958), made with the aid of an able and stimulating critique of the Code by the highly talented M. Anantanārāyanan, I.C.S., then Director of Legal Studies at the Law College, Madras, and afterwards a Judge, and later Chief Justice, of the Madras High Court.

Introduction

Mr. Anantanārāyanan drew attention to the fact that the new Code (for this convenient name, though not quite accurate, may appropriately be used) was in a sense a culmination of modifications which had been made, either by judges or by the legislatures, during the British period and immediately thereafter. He emphasized however the marked manner in which the Code 'repudiates in an implied or explicit manner the values and ethos of the ancient background'. He pointed out that, 'there are not wanting Indians, some of them men of intellectual eminence, who lament the passing away of the old order, which, according to them, was admirably designed to fulfil the needs of individual men and women in a socially dynamic environment', and added that these voices were always in a minority–a question to which it will be desirable to return. In Mr. Anantanārāyanan's view the 'irrational elements' of religion, 'social ethics derived from religion, and commandments born of faith in unseen powers have been completely eliminated from the *corpus* of Hindu law'. There can be no doubt but that this view is very widely held, and, if it is true, it raises questions of grave importance. The same reporter asserts (what cannot be denied) that the population of India is predominantly rural, and adds that it is conservative and filled with faith in the revealed nature of Hindu religion and ethics. The implication, that the enactments were directly opposed to profound sentiments among the electorate, was irresistible, and questions as to the desirability and the eventual success of the Code cannot be evaded in such a study as the present. Mr. Anantanārāyanan notes that Hindus are now virtually forced to execute wills in cases where formerly intestacy was usual, and expresses the gravest misgivings as to the propriety of extending to women in general the freedom of disposition of property which was formerly reserved in large measure for men. To his mind this reform in particular should have been preceded by education fitting women for their future responsibilities. Yet in his conclusion he expressed feelings of resignation, as he admits that change of some kind was inevitable, that the direction was to some extent foreseeable, and that political, or as he prefers to say, 'progressive', considerations have taken a priority that was–though we admit it with regret –their due. This reaction was in every respect typical of the reactions of enlightened Indian opinion amongst classes that have shared in the tradition of their ancient culture, have loved the classics (whether in Sanskrit or a regional language), filled as they are with a pervasive ethical and social message,[1] and have also received a training in the techniques imported from the West–the techniques that have ultimately led to the conflicts suggested in that report. A critique of the Code must take account of what it evidently aimed to do, and of the results, with special reference to the signs of haste and the lack of detailed care which the presence amongst the reformers of some highly competent lawyers, like Sir B. N. Rau and Dr. Ambedkar, ought to have obviated. The actual authors of our Code keep silence while legal writers and others have drawn attention frequently to actual or supposed faults in the Acts. It is left to those who have to work the Code to make known their difficulties and their disappointments.

An important statute in 1962 (Act 45 of that year) amended the Hindu Adoptions and Maintenance Act, 1956, so as to facilitate the adoption of orphans, and in so doing made the first wide breach in the requirement of religious qualification, though it did so in passing. This amendment was of a kind that

[1] It would be impossible to recommend a more relevant work than V. S. Śrīnivāsa Śāstrī's *Lectures on the Rāmāyaṇa* (Madras, Sanskrit Academy, 1949). Valuable information may be culled from F. S. Growse's *Rāmāyaṇa of Tulsi Dās* (Allahabad, Ram Narain Lal, 1937). D. P. Vora's *Evolution of Morals in the Epics* (*Mahābhārata and Rāmāyaṇa*) (Bombay, Popular Book Depot, 1959) was a doctoral thesis in sociology. Benjamin Khan's *Concept of Dharma in Valmiki Ramayana* (Delhi, Munshi Ram Manohar Lal, 1965) gives useful detail, but appears to lack depth.

remedied a defect in the original draft, and showed that Parliament was responsive to comments from the public. A number of Bills were introduced in the Lok Sabha in 1958 with the intention of amending the Code so as more effectively to carry out the broad intention of Parliament, with especial reference to marriage and divorce. But these Bills lapsed, and further amendment of the law of divorce, which is called for in numerous directions, remains problematical in 1967. In the view of the present writer very substantial and thorough revision of the Code is called for. The same opinion was voiced by Sir S. Varadāchāriar (*The Hindu* newspaper, Madras, February 23rd, 1958) though he tactfully speaks of 'a few ambiguities and omissions'. The passing of years has not removed doubts but rather added to them.[1] None of these comments must for a moment obscure the magnitude of the achievement effected in codifying the former system and amending it comprehensively. Kenya and Uganda have paid a tribute to India in using her Hindu Marriage Act as a model for their own Ordinances on the same subject,[2] and it is only a matter of time before they introduce Succession Ordinances for Hindus based ultimately on the Hindu Succession Act. Pakistan, Burma and Malaysia have yet to tackle the question. Sooner or later though, the antiquated Anglo-Hindu system must be reformed and India's lead is bound to be recognized. The world has appreciated India's momentous experiment, which for width of scope and boldness of innovation can be compared only with the *Code Napoléon*. The point of making criticisms here is to show that the reforms were part of a process which can be explained only against the long history of religion, law and the State in India: the Code is not a child of this century alone, in spite of appearances to the contrary.

[1] Numerous detailed criticisms of the Code appeared in vol. 5 of the *Jaipur Law Journal* (1965), which is devoted to the teaching of Hindu law. An anonymous writer in *Lawyer* (Provincial Bar Federation Journal, Madras) for November 1965, at pp. 184–99, draws attention to flaws in an article entitled 'Lacunae, conflicts, anomalies and defects of modern socialistic Hindu laws'. The (unnecessary) use of the word 'socialistic' is significant.

[2] See below, p. 357.

The Codification of Hindu Law

Antecedents of the Hindu Code

Attempts to reform Hindu law so as to enable it to meet the needs of modern life commenced during the British period.[1] Those however which were successful in British India were much less remarkable than those enacted in Native States under enlightened rulers. The piecemeal reforms in British India, such as the Caste Disabilities Removal Act, 1850, the Hindu Widows' Remarriage Act, 1856, the Hindu Inheritance (Removal of Disabilities) Act, 1928, the Hindu Law of Inheritance (Amendment) Act, 1929, the Hindu Gains of Learning Act, 1930, the celebrated but unfortunately drafted Hindu Women's Rights to Property Act, 1937, and the Hindu Married Women's Right to Separate Residence and Maintenance Act, 1946, were all departures from the *śāstra* and were intended to give relief to those who were not content to abide by the ancient law; but they were timid and unco-ordinated attempts to deal with a problem of wide implications; and, outside British India, Mysore and Baroda had, by 1937, enacted general and comprehensive amendments of the Hindu law which served as stimuli, though not models, for similar attempts elsewhere. The desirability and feasibility of codification was reported as early as 1941, but the war and later the problems of the unification of independent India postponed the project until 1951. A storm of objections, and a temporary failure of political nerve, wrecked the original Hindu Code Bill. The temper of the first regularly elected Parliament of all India was tested by the Special Marriage Bill, which was to apply to all Indians, whatever their religion. The success of that measure in 1954[2] led directly to the

[1] Mahāmahopādhyāya Dr. Sir Gaṅganātha Jhā was in favour of comprehensive reform, and he laboured to enable future reformers to know what they would be reforming. A little known contribution to the subject is the set of six lectures given at the Bhandarkar Oriental Research Institute (Poona) in 1933 by Mahāmahopadhyāya Śrīdhara Śāstrī Vedāntavāgīśa. These were in Sanskrit. P. V. Kāṇe gave a winding-up lecture and R. R. Kāle gave a concluding lecture recommending a reform similar to that which took place in 1937. The lectures were called *Dharmśāstra-vyākhyāna-mālā* and lectures nos. 4, 5 and 6 are printed at *A.B.O.R.I.* 15 (1933/4) at pp. 31–63 of the Skt. section.

[2] It is surprising to note that by the Special Marriage (Amendment) Act, Act No. 32 of 1963, Parliament de-codified the general law, to the extent that marriages may be valid if performed under this statute although they

introduction of the Hindu Marriage and Divorce Bill, which has some distantly similar features in it. When this became law as the Hindu Marriage Act, 1955 (Act No. 25 of 1955), it was felt that the cause was as good as won, and the remaining Acts followed in quick succession: the Hindu Succession Act, Act No. 30 of 1956; the Hindu Minority and Guardianship Act, Act No. 32 of 1956; and finally the Hindu Adoptions and Maintenance Act, Act No. 78 of 1956. The Hindu Joint Family Bill was stillborn. A large number of books purporting to expound the meaning of these Acts has been published,[1] and case-law is accumulating, with the usual appearance of conflicting decisions, as a kind of commentary on the Code. The Supreme Court has dealt successfully and suggestively with problems in matrimonial causes and on the new absolute estate for women even in property possessed by them prior to the coming into force of the Hindu Succession Act, but this amounts to a mere fraction of the scope covered by the statutes, so that considerable uncertainty remains, and is likely to remain for some time.

The chief reason for the Code's unsatisfactory features is that the drafting was shared successively by the Hindu Law Committee under Sir B. N. Rau, a subsequent Committee of a totally different composition, Select Committees convened to report on each Bill and including only occasionally a member highly skilled in Hindu law matters, draftsmen normally occupied in

are within the prohibited degrees, provided that a custom governing at least one of the parties permits of a marriage between them; and 'custom' is specially defined for the purpose of the Act as a 'rule which the State Government may, by notification in the Official Gazette, specify in this behalf as applicable to members of that tribe, community, group or family.' The State Government is bidden not to make such a notification unless it is satisfied that the rule has been continuously and uniformly observed for a long time, that it is certain and not unreasonable nor opposed to public policy, and that, if a family custom, it has not been discontinued. The oddity of this statute and its provisions needs no underlining, and imagination cannot conceive how it came to be passed, except to satisfy some influential individuals. One may conjecture some cause as bizarre as the results, e.g. a family in which one member changed his or her religion, and members including this member wished to marry whilst within the customary degrees for marriage in the caste, but by reason of the change of religion they were unable to marry at Hindu law.

[1] For a bibliography see General Bibliographical Note at pp. 569–70 below.

drafting statutes on every conceivable topic, and finally by members of Parliament when the Bills were actually before the Houses and when it was politically desirable that they should be passed with the minimum of delay. The inconsistencies of tone and unevenness of quality displayed by the Acts is thus not at all surprising. It is much more remarkable that they came to be passed at all.

Objects and Overt Reasons behind the Code

It is not to be assumed that the members of Parliament were united in this context, any more than were their constituents. But amongst them the educated and 'enlightened' Hindus, who fill most of the judicial and administrative posts in the country and are well represented at the Bar, whose society engages the admiration and emulation of wealthy contractors and others (whose backgrounds may be mixed but whose wealth stems ultimately from the State), form the compact core of the Congress Party which was at that time pledged to secure reform of the Hindu law. Obscurantist and ultra-orthodox elements in this, the then major party, existed, and indeed were needed to give it 'tone', but they were there in a minority, whereas the 'advanced' Hindus, whose economic, social, and political ambitions conflict significantly with traditional Hinduism, were dominant. It was doubtful whether they would retain their hold in the next Parliament (unnecessary doubts, as it turned out), and hence arose the haste to codify the Hindu law.

If this dominant group represented its own attitude to life effectively it did not pretend to represent the views of the typical Indian, who regards the progress of his personal law with apprehension and, in certain respects, with horror. But it believed that the reforms were in the best interests of the nation, and as the villager is accustomed to paternalistic government, and has a general belief in the 'Socialist Pattern of Society' which Mr. Nehru's government had vigorously forwarded, there is every likelihood that the clock will not be put back. The villager is used to being told that he is ignorant and does not know what is best for him. The critics of the Code are for the most part amongst would-be reformers whose views did not achieve adequate notice at the critical time. The time for all criticisms to come together will therefore be when the promised Indian Civil Code is being hammered out.

(*i*) *The desire for unity and certainty*

The Congress Party, in its pre-Independence manoeuvres, established the theory that all 'Hindus' form one community. In the sphere of religion this was more than questionable, but in the field of law it was patently false. Not only had several 'schools' of Hindu law developed from the ancient texts and the judicial interpretation of their rules, but various High Courts interpreted the law differently. Customs at variance with the book-law were widespread and irreconcilably diverse, yet they were in some parts of India predominant, and in the rest of India were enormously important. The special position of the Native States referred to above, went to complicate the position when India was unified; while in some States a large proportion of the population consists of 'Scheduled Tribes' whose claim to be 'Hindus' was none the less thin for the eagerness of politicians to claim their allegiance to the Hindu standard. At one time it was seriously proposed to abolish customs entirely, and to submit all persons not Muslims, Christians, Parsis or Jews, to a single unvarying Code. At present the diversity of rule has been eliminated and the customs of all Hindus abolished except for certain limited survivals, and except for an anomalous and probably accidental omission to legislate for Punjab family law in an important respect.[1] Customs enabling Hindus to marry within the prohibited degrees have been saved, and married persons and boys over fifteen may be adopted where this was customary. Customary divorces, many of which are virtually by mutual consent, have been similarly retained;[2] in the law of succession slight concessions have been made to matrilineal communities of Kerala, whose customs, deviating markedly from those of the rest of India, are otherwise threatened with extinction. As for the Scheduled Tribes, these have been exempted temporarily from the Code, but this concession appeared upon the scene comparatively shortly before the enactments took place.

Since unity amongst Hindus is the first step to unity amongst

[1] See below, p. 345. [2] See below, p. 357.

Indians,[1] it is not surprising that the definition of 'Hindu' is as wide as possible. No religious test is in fact applicable except in a negative manner: an atheist is very likely to be a 'Hindu' for the purposes of the Code, but the matter is not free from doubt, despite the latest pronouncement of the Supreme Court.[2] Difference of caste which used to provide sharp differences, in purely legal terms, between Hindus has been almost completely eliminated. With a very limited exception a marriage between persons of different castes (only the four *varṇa-s* having been recognized as caste-divisions during the British period) was void until 1949 (Act No. 21 of that year) and this reform is continued in the Hindu Marriage Act (hereafter referred to as *HMA*), s. 5 and s. 29 (1). Formerly the illegitimate sons of the most numerous *varṇa*, the *śūdra-s*, were entitled to inherit half the share which each would have taken had he been legitimate, and in certain circumstances to even larger benefits out of the estate, provided their mothers were in the exclusive keeping of their fathers at the time of conception. This privilege (which strikes the 'advanced' Hindu as anomalous) is removed by implication in s. 8 of the Hindu Succession Act (hereafter referred to as *HSA*). The validity of an adoption might turn on the performance or otherwise of certain ceremonies, which in the case of *śūdra-s* were unnecessary. The requirements of the Hindu Adoptions and Maintenance Act, 1956 (hereafter cited as *HAMA*), s. 11, remove this anomaly. The adopted son of a *śūdra* might share equally with a legitimate son, according to some High Courts, whereas adopted sons in the higher castes were confined to a one-fourth share. Adoptions taking place after the *HAMA* came into force will in every case place the adoptee on an equal footing with a subsequently born legitimate child–if we except the question of entitlement to joint-family property–and, more strikingly, adoptions may be made for the first time from castes other than that of the adoptive parent.

[1] It is of interest to observe that India's predicament and its results did not stand alone. In Africa the desire for political unity within the newly independent territories has given rise to visionary and hasty enterprises, painful to the jurists who observe them. A. N. Allott, 'The future of African law', in H. and L. Kuper, edd., *African Law: Adaptation and Development* (University of California Press, Berkeley and Los Angeles, 1965), at p. 225.

[2] See above, p. 49.

After marriages between castes were generally validated, certain ancient rules giving preferences to issue of higher caste in succession to the father, and to issue of the husband by a wife of a higher caste in the Bengal school, were accidentally revived, and these have been eliminated by the scheme of the *HSA*.

Reference to caste may still have to be made if questions arise as to whether a *śūdra* had validly abandoned the world, and so caused succession to open to his estate (according to a portion of the former law apparently saved by the 'overriding effect' section of the *HSA*); or whether a non-*śūdra* (i.e. 'twice-born') could validly be adopted after the age of fifteen but before marriage: previously considerations of caste made the answers negative. However, but for these possible exceptions, a clean sweep has been made of caste as a consideration of importance in private law, and this reform, it is hoped, may encourage abandonment of *caste* as a factor in other sectors of law where discrimination is accepted as an interim public policy.[1]

The desire for unity expressed itself in another way. On the one hand opportunities were offered in the Special Marriage Act, 1954, for Hindus to make 'special marriages', i.e. civil marriages, at the cost of severance from their joint families if any, and with the consequence that succession to their estates and those of their issue would be governed by the Indian Succession Act, 1925, and not by the Hindu law. It was felt that the ranks of those who so married–a group of Hindus roughly corresponding to the most emancipated of the 'advanced' and reforming classes–had a claim to recruits for every class; and that statute offers to those married at Hindu law the chance to register their marriages under the Act with retrospective effect, so as immediately to entitle them to relief under that Act (which contemplates divorce by mutual consent) at the cost of virtual exclusion from their community so far as the application of law is concerned. On the other hand the penalties for changing one's religion, not from Sikh to Jaina, or from Hindu to Sikh, or from Hindu to Buddhist (for these are not distinguished) but from Hindu to Christian, are many and varied. The spouse may obtain a divorce; children of the convert cannot inherit from the latter's relations; the convert is disqualified from being

[1] See above, p. 65.

the guardian of his own child;[1] he cannot give or take in adoption, nor prevent his wife from giving his child away in adoption or from taking a child in adoption; and he loses not merely all rights of maintenance which the Hindu law would otherwise give him but even alimony obtained in divorce proceedings. The 'secular' state thus seems to take away with one hand the virtue of the apparently liberal reliefs offered with the other. The explanation for the discrepancy is that the system is a personal law and that only those who belong to the religious community can take advantage of it. But it remains odd that a system which has no roots in Hinduism, and which does not claim to be a religious legal system as such, should contemplate such drastic effects in cases where persons formerly subject to it by being Hindus cease to be Hindus by conversion to another religion, not accepted as a 'Hindu' religion for the purpose of the application of these statutes. Finally the reforms carried out for the benefit of the Hindu community were considered precisely in that light, and that Hindu law has *not* been reformed which applied as a matter of custom in those parts of India, or with regard to that class or classes of property, in respect of which Muslims retained it instead of their religious law.[2]

(*ii*) *The desire for equality of the sexes*

The influence of Western standards and the expansion of opportunities for Indian women was nowhere more violent than in contexts where tradition obliged the female to remain subservient to the male. The orthodox regret the 'Code' more keenly for its having attempted to put the sexes on a level–indeed now it turns out that more property will devolve on females than upon males; it was characteristically with the intention of equalizing them that Parliament departed most radically from the ancient law. Divorce was unknown until the advanced States of Bombay and Madras introduced it in 1947 and 1949 respectively (that is to say if we neglect the castes where customary divorces were normal–castes which were despised by the

[1] The orthodox legal position, that a natural guardian does not forfeit merely by change of religion, though in a particular case it may be better for the child's upbringing in the father's religion that he should be consigned to the *custody* of a relation (such as an uncle) who remains of that religion, is retained in Pakistan: *Mst. Ghulam Fatima* v. *Chanoomal* P.L.D. 1967 Kar. 569.

[2] See below, p. 522.

others for the very freedom which they enjoyed). Nullity for impotence, for example, was beginning to make its reappearance about the time of Independence after a millennium's hibernation; but nullity for insanity was still a doubted remedy when the *HMA* was passed. The *śāstra* regarded marriage as a rite of consecration (*saṃskāra*) too holy to be undone. Now the wife is well protected: she can obtain separate residence and maintenance (under the *HAMA*), judicial separation, nullity, or divorce (all under the *HMA*), whensoever her marriage took place; on the other hand she can rest assured that if her husband purports to exercise his ancient right of remarriage during her lifetime and without a previous divorce, the second marriage will be void and the issue illegitimate. Whereas judicial separation is now available for a single act of adultery, living in adultery is a ground for divorce, and living with a polygamously-married 'wife' is living in adultery.[1]

The grounds for divorce are many, and some of them have a specially Indian flavour; one of the Bills of 1958 sought to add to their number adultery *simpliciter*, cruelty, and desertion for three years. It went further and sought to enable Hindus who have been estranged for two years or more to obtain a divorce by mutual consent. Uttar Pradesh State has gone so far as to introduce cruelty (Uttar Pradesh Act 13 of 1962), and went some distance towards meeting the needs of those whose *consortium* had broken down. Now by Act 44 of 1964 Parliament itself has amended s. 13 of the *HMA* and introduced as a new ground for divorce either the failure of the couple to resume cohabitation for two or more years after the passing of a decree for judicial separation, or a failure of restitution of conjugal rights for the same period after a decree for restitution had been passed. The novelty in this was that the *HMA* originally allowed divorce on such grounds only to the spouse who was successful in obtaining the decrees in question, which was unrealistic. It might be asked why desertion is not a ground for divorce: it is possible that it may not be added, when it is open to the deserted spouse to obtain a decree for restitution, and where this is not complied with for two years the marriage can be dissolved now at the petition of either party. Restitution will not be decreed, of course, in any case where the respondent is

[1] *Gitabai* v. *Fattoo* AIR 1966 M.P. 130.

not in desertion in the eyes of the law. Divorce by mutual consent–which belongs to the sphere of customary marriage-law and to marriages under the Special Marriage Act–is not likely to be introduced into the *HMA* by way of amendment.

The emancipation of women has gone far, and the husband himself is not always in a worse position. In providing that the costs of litigation and interim maintenance may be ordered against the respondent, Parliament has given the husband rights against the property of his wife in case he is the petitioner –a striking instance of equality when it is observed that the husband is not a dependant of his deceased wife under the *HAMA*.

Formerly a mother might not act as guardian in the presence of the deceased father's testamentary guardian; and her power to appoint such a guardian was defective. These anomalies were cured by the Hindu Minority and Guardianship Act, 1956 (hereafter cited as *HMGA*), s. 9. Formerly a Hindu might adopt without consulting his wife, and could give her son away in adoption without taking her consent; she for her part was in some places unable to adopt without his actual consent. These disabilities were taken away by *HAMA*, s. 7 and 8. The last section now enables her to do what was possible previously only in a minute part of India, namely to adopt to herself (instead of to her deceased husband). A female had not been capable of adoption, except in restricted Malabar customs, for at least two millennia, when the *HAMA* restored the right by ss. 10 and 11. Illegitimate daughters had no rights of maintenance at the civil law until the *HAMA* made her a maintainee of her living father, and a dependant on his estate after his death, while her right to inherit from her mother, and perhaps from her mother's kin (a point depending upon the correct interpretation of the obscure *HSA*, s. 3 (1) (j)), is established in the *HSA*.

Formerly sons and normally widows excluded daughters in succession to males, and if daughters normally excluded sons in succession to females in the predominant school of Hindu law this was hardly a consolation as the amounts in question were seldom comparable. Females generally were either excluded from succession entirely or came ridiculously low in the order of heirs. In Madras, for example, the sister was 466th in order until 1929, when she was advanced to the 13th place, after the father's father. Male agnatic heirs had an ancient preference and apart from some special exceptions in the Bengal school (Dāyabhāga) cognates, if they were females, either did not inherit or came very low, and if they were males were postponed to agnates within fourteen inclusive degrees of ascent and fourteen of descent. When women did inherit, whether from a male or a female, the estate in their hands was not freely alienable, but must descend to the next heir of the person from whom it had descended, diminished only so far as was requisite for the female owner's limited physical and spiritual needs and for the spiritual needs of the deceased owner. Mr. Anantanārāyanan pointed out that this disability, which automatically affects the value of the property subject to this limitation, was really intended not so much for the protection of the reversioners as for the security of the young, ignorant and helpless females themselves. No doubt both motives operated. Agnatic preference remains in the order in which general classes of heirs, and even some sub-classes, are set out in the *HSA*, but where females and males actually compete no distinction between them is retained. In order to soften the blow there are provisions giving male heirs a right of pre-emption over their female competitors' shares, and preventing a female heir from intruding her husband into the family dwelling. It is widely expected that this increase in the daughter's rights will lead to quarrels between brothers and sisters unless the latter not only take the dependant attitude which is traditional but also prevent their relations by marriage from attempting to exercise these rights on their behalf. There is some fear that the same pattern of conflicting interests may emerge as actually happened in the undignified squabbles in Goa in the eighteenth century.[1] However that may be, all female heirs may now inherit whether or not they are chaste at the time when the succession opens, a departure from the ancient religious law varying with the degree to which the courts in the British period had maintained the original rule: *HSA*, s. 28.

The foregoing remarks apply to widows, but their position deserves a special comment. Before 1937 the widow succeeded, if custom allowed, only in the absence of male issue (up to and

[1] See above, p. 282.

including the son's son's son). By that year it was felt that the traditional status of the Hindu widow was outgrown, and she was substituted, subject to the limited estate, for her husband in the ownership of his interest in Mitāksharā joint-family property, which is the most important category of property in India as a whole, and she was for the first time permitted to share equally with a son in the deceased's separate and self-acquired property. The Act of 1937 did not apply to every kind of property, several States refused to extend its application to agricultural land, and doubts long remained as to its meaning. On the whole however it might be urged that the method adopted tended in principle towards an English rather than any other solution of the problem of the spouse's rights. In the *HSA* a curious step was taken along quite a different path. As Mr. G. K. Dabke has pointed out,[1] the widow now shares on equal terms with son, daughter, issue of predeceased son or daughter and widow of predeceased son, not to mention the mother of the *propositus*, with the result that her participation in the estate is much reduced. Tradition, and the growing familiarity with the working of the Act of 1937, have alike been flouted. It may be urged that an absolute estate in a portion is worth as much as a limited estate in a larger fund, but this is a doubtful justification and would be true only in some cases. The attempt to place the sexes upon an equal footing has nearly succeeded, however, though a comparison of the order of descent of a male's and that of a female's property reveals substantial differences, which may be accounted for by reference to the pre-existing law. By contrast, women, who were generally free from obligation to maintain others, have now, under the *HAMA*, been made liable very nearly coextensively with males.

But by far the most dramatic step towards equalizing the status of men and women was the abolition of plural marriages, which were formerly open only to men, and which the religion sanctioned subject to conditions which in fact the Hindu law in British India had ignored. A Hindu could run away from his wife[2] and marry again validly, without his first wife having any

[1] At (1958) 60 Bom. L.R., *J.*, 8 ff. See also his remarks at (1957) 59 Bom. L.R., *J.*, 132 ff.

[2] Or indeed stay at home and set up a plural household (with or without the first wife's consent).

hope of freedom. It would have been possible to limit the husband's right of remarriage to cases where the wife was afflicted with an incurable disease or had not borne any child within ten years or so of marriage, or where she had lost caste. Such indeed were the provisions of a statute of limited application, the Madras Nambudri Act, No. 21 of 1933 (repealed by s. 8 of the Madras Act 6 of 1949). But this did not appeal to Parliament, which abolished polygamy by declaring marriages taking place during the subsistence of a previous marriage to be bigamy within the meaning of the Penal Code.

(*iii*) *Desire to eliminate restrictive and antique rules*

The 'reformers' are large earners and are jealous of the keenness of their agnates, who might claim as members of the same joint-family at Mitāksharā law, to share their property to the partial or total exclusion of their own spouse, daughter, cognatic relations or friends. Formerly a man had little say in the use to which his earnings were put unless he separated from his family. In Kerala such separations were difficult until relatively recent times; in the regular Hindu law they were in theory easy, but were hampered by sentimental considerations. The Act of 1930 helped, but was little used in practice except where families were estranged. As a result there was a powerful desire, deplored by Mr. Anantanārāyanan amongst others, to destroy the legal joint-family. After much discussion it was decided to make the undivided interest pass by succession, testamentary or intestate, in the hope that when the joint-family property had been split up after a few deaths the old 'coparcenary' would disappear. Unfortunately the *HSA*, which sought to bring this about by s. 6, omitted to destroy the ancient 'birth-right' with the result, which one of the abortive Bills of 1958 sought to cure, that joint-families between father and son will continue to exist, even after the father has taken the property from his own father by succession.[1] The general effect of this change, however, will be to abolish the restrictions on the disposition of family property which formerly gave rise to so much litigation. Just as a woman may now dispose of her inherited property freely, so the 'manager

[1] See below, p. 422. That the birthright subsists here is doubted by Mr. G. K. Dabke at (1966) 68 Bom. L.R., *J.*, 113–15. *Ghasiram* v. *Commr. of Gift Tax* AIR 1967 A. & N. 48 decided against the birthright (*per incuriam*?).

of the joint-family' will now tend to disappear. In another respect, however, a restriction has been imposed which was not present before. A minor Hindu's property can no longer be alienated, even for his benefit, without the consent of the Court, and this innovation by the *HMGA*, attempting to assimilate the position of Hindu minors to that of Christian minors, may well prove a great inconvenience.

The desire to make property freely transferable was matched by a desire to abolish rules that smacked of antiquity. An orphan can now be adopted (*HAMA*, s. 9), and an illegitimate child, though strangely not by his own mother, though the amendment of 1962 allowed those who are guardians of abandoned children and those whose parentage is unknown to take such children in adoption with the court's consent. An illegitimate daughter is now entitled to maintenance. The archaic rules allowing a boy of fourteen to adopt, and a young widow to adopt a married man as heir to her husband are abolished. A concubine can no longer claim lifelong maintenance from her paramour's estate, whatever rights she may retain, in special circumstances, out of his interest in joint-family property. In Bengal and Assam until the *HSA* was passed a man or woman could be excluded from succession or partition on the ground of his being blind from birth or deaf and dumb, of being an idiot, or of being affected by virulent leprosy, in addition to unchastity in the case of female claimants. There was something very archaic about the rule which enabled a father to pile up debts which his sons were obliged to pay out of their interests in joint-family property, provided that they could not prove that he incurred them in pursuit of illegality and vice to the knowledge of the lender (where the debt was a borrowing and not a tortious liability). This, which we have encountered under the name Pious Obligation, fades as the extent of property held in the Mitāksharā coparcenary tenure dwindles.

But it is not certain that all restrictive and antique rules have gone. The woman who has been declared absolute owner of all classes of property may still have to take her husband's consent before she parts with some categories of it. The manager of a temple is, as before, subject to restrictions in dealing with the deity's property. And the general overhaul of the Hindu law has concentrated on removing 'abuses' of a notorious character rather than constructing a coherent and up-to-date system. Thus one cannot adopt a son if one has one already, nor a daughter if one has a daughter or a son's daughter. This is plainly archaic, and in the second case has no authority even in the former law. That the state should take the property only after all blood relations have been eliminated seems odd in a country where folk generally keep in fairly lively touch with relations of considerable remoteness, with the result that proof of the total absence of kindred will in many cases be impossible. Yet the present rule stems from tradition, Parliament omitting to notice that formerly five degrees was the limit for heritable cognates.

The Code in its Present Form

(*i*) *Will it be a success?*

Since the Code replaces to a considerable extent the previous system, leaving it in force in marginal or transitional contexts, or in fields, such as religious endowments, where comprehensive legislation is expected to cover the ground adequately, one naturally supposes that the new law is more certain, uniform, consistent, rational and more in keeping with the public's needs than that which it replaced. Professor S. Venkaṭarāman, a prolific writer on Hindu law problems, voices a common reaction when he says that the Code is a bold social experiment, and when he comments on the *HAMA* in terms hardly of appreciation, but of doubt as to whether any Hindu henceforward will care to adopt a child. There seems to be no doubt but that Hindu religious forms and the law that purported to depend on Hindu religious beliefs supported each other. The removal of the religious sanction behind adoption as set forth in the *HAMA* is said to have led to two opposite phenomena: (*a*) adoptions carried out as if no statute had been passed, in the hope that all who took part in them would support the effects, come what may; and (*b*) a decline in religious practice and observance, and with it the dissuetude of the institutions formerly connected with them. The fact that a śāstric adoption, fit to provide for the *śrāddha* of the sonless adopter or of the deceased husband of the adopting widow, can still be performed with full spiritual efficacy now within the framework laid down by the statute, does not serve to keep the religious doctrine at the front of the mind as it was before, when the collateral effects (which were in practice more prized), such as the adopted child's right to recover his adoptive father's estate from all and sundry, have been denied in so many words by that statute. In some communities the two trends, of religious observance and of legal modernity, will be observed together, and the possessors of the late adoptive father's property will themselves instigate the adoption or voluntarily hand over the estate. The power to do this has not been taken away by statute; but the onus is on the conscience and sincerity of the parties, whereas previously the law so provided that all religious requirements (within the limitations set by the inaccuracy of the Anglo-Hindu system) were met, because the best and the traditional motives were imputed as a matter of course to the prime movers of the adoption.

Other writers left us with the impression that it is all very well to legislate in New Delhi, but that when the Act of 1930 has hardly been absorbed by the villagers, let alone that of 1937, it is unfair to expect them, without ample explanation of what that Code means, to react in the way that the townsfolk are already beginning to do. For no one can deny that the departures from the old law are so many and so grave that for many years the total absence of a transitional stage will catch the majority unawares. The Code puts much business into the hands of the Bar, instead of diminishing litigation: it tends to diminish uncertainty, but the certainty which has been achieved will bring with it strife and perplexity which the law itself, perhaps by developing the Family Arrangement, must strive to mitigate. For some time to come the villager will find the new system less homely, more hazardous, and more expensive.

Had the Code been a response to a general demand amongst the less vocal majority the clack of clarity, uniformity, consistency and rational principle which carping critics might find in it would have been tolerable. A slow progress from the known to the unknown, building little by little upon experience, produces awkward and illogical laws, but subjects the public to less risk. In India theory got the upper hand of the Hindu law, but it was theory almost uncontrolled by experience. That the Code is in operation no one can deny, and the spread of popular 'guides' throughout the country must have acquainted many with its broad outlines. But in order to see whether it is a success in other, and perhaps more important senses we shall have to enquire into its faults of matter and manner.

(*ii*) *Some uncertainties*

It is hardly satisfactory that s. 5 of the *HMA* should have left it uncertain whether or not marriage between children is voidable; whether Hindus and Christians may marry at Hindu law as by custom in many places they actually did; or that the *HAMA* should not say whether the Christian married to a Hindu before the Code can still claim maintenance from him;[1] or that doubt should remain whether some persons entitled to be maintained prior to the *HAMA* were disentitled as from the commencement of the Act; whether a girl can marry under age if there is no guardian as listed in the *HMA*; whether persons of indeterminate sex (who may be many in so vast a population) are succeeded under the *HSA* by heirs there listed; whether tenants under State tenancy legislation are succeeded under that statute or under some other statutory provisions;[2] whether illegitimate children are related, for example, to their mothers' fathers for purposes of succession; whether a legacy of a share of no particular size will exonerate the estate from the claims of a dependant; whether a legatee is an 'heir' in the same connexion; whether the husband's heirs who are supposed to take what a woman inherited from her husband or father-in-law are the heirs of her first or any subsequent husband; whether testamentary contracts will be binding upon the estate so as to displace the rights of dependants; whether illegitimate parents are

[1] Hindus and Christians marry at Hindu religious ceremonies by custom in certain classes and areas. The priest no doubt risks prosecution, for the Indian Christian Marriage Act purported to prevent such marriages: *In re Kolandaivelu* (1917) 40 Mad. 1030 (F.B.), deplored at 1917 M.W.N. clxxxiv–v. But the validity of the marriage is not affected. *Rajammal* v. *Mariyammal* AIR 1954 Mys. 38. The ruling to the effect that there could not be a valid marriage between a Christian and a Hindu celebrated according to Hindu rites in *Swapna* v. *Basanta* AIR 1955 Cal. 533 is not founded on careful investigation of authorities and may be *per incuriam*. See *Dubey* v. *Dubey* AIR 1951 All. 529, where expressions of opinion tend in the opposite direction.

[2] At the time of writing there is a conflict between *Gopi* v. *Bhagwani* AIR 1964 Punj. 272 and *Indubai* v. *Vyankati* (1965) 67 Bom. L.R. 612, as to the meaning of *HSA*, s. 4. (2). Tenancies may be governed by widely differing laws. See *Suraj* v. *Ram* [1965] All. L.J. 665.

entitled to maintenance under *HAMA*, s. 21 (why not?); and so on. Intermediate between an apparent uncertainty and an unfortunate slip is the instance in *HSA*, s. 6, where we are told that in certain circumstances an interest in a Mitāksharā joint-family property will pass by survivorship to the surviving members of the coparcenary, and widows who have taken an interest under the Act of 1937 (and these are numerous)[1] are apparently excluded because they are not coparceners. Prior to the passing of the *HSA* a difference of opinion arose between the High Courts as to the extent of joint-family property that could be alienated by an undivided coparcener. That doubt has not been settled, but a new one has been created along similar lines by the Act: where a coparcener dies the interest passes by succession in most cases; this is equivalent to the share he would take if a partition of the property had taken place immediately before his death; the rule apparently brings in the previous law relating to partitions, according to which in some parts of India some females, in other other females, and others still no females at all are entitled to shares at a partition; and the result is a confusion and a divergence of method of partition and succession between the various States.[2] We are still uncertain whether when a man dies leaving a son and a son's son and a widow his death actually divides the son from the son's son: apparently not, but the reasoning of a recent judicial construction of the statute leaves the matter in the air.

(*iii*) *Anomalies*

We have just seen an anomaly accidentally left as a result of blending the old law of partition with the new law of succession. Uncertainties are probably more troublesome than anomalies. These however are quite numerous. They include the following rules. Grandparents are not entitled to maintenance as dependants, although parents are (*HAMA*, s. 21); uterine half-brothers and -sisters are excluded except as cognates (?), yet uterine second cousins share equally with full second cousins to the exclusion of second cousins by consanguine half-blood

[1] See below, pp. 418–19.

[2] *Rangubai* v. *Laxman* (1966) 68 Bom. L.R. 74 is discussed by Derrett at (1966) 68 Bom. L.R., *J.*, 45 ff., and by Mrs. S. Manohar at the same place, pp. 60–2.

(*HSA*, ss. 3 (1) (e), 18, Schedule); a woman's property *inherited* (whatever that means) from her parents passes by a special mode of descent, but gifts do not (*HSA*, s. 15 (2));[1] a woman's great-grandchild is so remote an heir as seldom to be capable of succession (*HSA*, s. 15 (1) (a)); in succession to a male his predeceased son's issue take by representation, but his predeceased daughter's surviving issue alone take the property (*HSA*, s. 10, Rule 4 (ii)); a female heir may claim partition of a dwelling-house where there are two or more male co-heirs, but not if there is one only (*HSA*, s. 23, if literally interpreted), and only certain female heirs are liable to this disadvantage; if the father's widow remarries she can inherit her step-son's estate notwithstanding her remarriage, but a predeceased son's widow or a brother's widow is excluded for her remarriage (*HSA*, s. 24); a widow is a dependant of her deceased husband's estate, but not a widower of his deceased wife's (*HAMA*, s. 21); and although many State marriage and divorce statutes are repealed by *HMA*, s. 30, the important Hindu Code of Baroda, whose provisions conflict with those of the *HMA* in many respects, has not been repealed, with the result that so much of the former as is not overridden by s. 4 of the latter, will continue to be in force in Baroda, a not inconsiderable portion of the State of Gujarat.

(*iv*) *Slips*

Evidently we have noticed slips in passing up to this point. The curiosity to look for slips in these statutes is not confined to the practitioner who has to negotiate them, but arises also in the historian, who takes note of them when he enquires why the measures were put through with such speed in the shape in which they have appeared.

The legislature noticed at least one slip immediately and another shortly afterwards. *HSA*, s. 30 (2) was repealed by *HAMA*, s. 29; and *HMA*, s. 10 (1) (d) was corrected by s. 2 of Act 73 of 1956. Other slips have not escaped notice. Mr. S. Easwara Iyer in his Bill No. 45 of 1958, cl. 4, drew attention (fruitlessly) to the fact that adopted children are overlooked in the *HSA*. This was due to the mechanical splitting of the Hindu Code Bill into parts. Haste in redrafting is evident from the superfluous words in *HSA*, s. 17. Property is purported to be

[1] *Ayi* v. *Subramania* AIR 1966 Mad. 369.

given to the heirs of living persons by the unfortunate words of s. 15 (2) of the same statute. The need to repeal s. 2 of the Hindu Widows' Remarriage Act, 1856, was overlooked.[1] The Courts have yet to cope adequately with the extraordinary terms of *HMA*, s. 16, which, by the inclusion of superfluous words (copied from the correct s. 26 of the Special Marriage Act, 1954), appears to suggest that the issue of void marriages might be legitimate.[2] The *HMA* in a unique section provides (s. 9 (2)) that in answer to a petition for restitution of conjugal rights nothing shall be pleaded which shall not be a ground for judicial separation or for nullity of marriage or for divorce. Doubts have been expressed as to the purpose of this, and the best view is that it is a slip.[3] In *HMGA*, s. 7, the guardianship of an adopted son is provided for, but by inadvertence not that of an adopted daughter. Both in the *HAMA* and the *HSA* it is evident that Parliament did not have Punjab customary law in its view.[4]

(*v*) *Novel elements*

The opportunity afforded by codification naturally enabled Parliament to draw upon experience garnered from all over the world. Unfortunately there has been little boldness, for the reformers' motives were chiefly negative in character, and what has appeared has not pleased all critics. The introduction of divorce by consent to those who register their marriages under the Act of 1954 gives alarm to many, while it encourages others to demand the same facility without the need for such registration. The *HMA* indirectly introduces into some parts of India

[1] See K. Venkaṭasubramanian at [1965] 1 M.L.J., *J.*, 15–16.

[2] Dr. P. W. Rege comments on this at *Jaipur L.J.*, 5 (1965), pp. 46 ff. and Mr. G. K. Dabke had commented on the same at (1956) 58 Bom. L.R., *J.*, 148 ff. Obiter dicta at *Gowri* v. *Thulasi* AIR 1962 Mad. 510, 512, and *Smt. Chandra Mohini* v. *Avinash* AIR 1967 S.C. 581.

[3] See below, pp. 371 ff.

[4] S.6 of the *HSA* does not deal with interests in ancestral property at Punjab customary law, but only Mitāksharā law: therefore a proprietor of such an interest cannot dispose of it by will by virtue of the statute (*Kaur* v. *Jaggar* AIR 1961 Punj. 489). The meaning of 'coparcenary property' was entirely at large in the context of customary law, and it was necessary to determine *quoad* a daughter-in-law's rights to maintenance whether 'coparcenary property' included 'ancestral property' (*Gurdip* v. *Ghamand* AIR 1965 Punj. 238 (F.B.)).

for the first time large chapters of English matrimonial law. The Act has many features in common with the English Act of 1950. But it has equally striking differences (there are no decrees *nisi* and no co-respondents),[1] and there appears to have been both an incomplete digesting of the development of English divorce law since 1937, and an absence of principle in amalgamating Hindu and western notions. In the *HAMA* it appears that even testamentary dispositions may be reduced by dependants if they act quickly and prevent the alienation of the estate by the heirs: if so there has been a blending of the Indian position regarding the entitlement of heirs and the position in many Commonwealth countries where dependants may apply to the personal representative for maintenance notwithstanding the provisions of the will and/or (in some jurisdictions) the intestate law. Whether the result will work well has yet to be seen. In the *HAMA*, s. 9, the Indian courts are given for the first time jurisdiction to order adoptions, and doubtless the law applicable here will have to be imported from England or America. The new orders of descent and distribution in the *HSA* depart violently from the *śāstra*, but they show little logic, and are a compromise between traditional and western rules. The result must be an enormous increase in wills, to the satisfaction of the Bar. The same statute introduces a novelty for Hindus, namely pre-emption in relation to shares in estates of deceased persons: the law on this subject will be available in connexion with pre-emption customary in other contexts in India. Following a non-Indian custom Parliament has introduced a rule prohibiting the Slayer's Bounty (s. 25) and a *Commorientes* rule[2] (s. 21). Both appear to be improvements on the English rules, since in the former case the murderer is disqualified from taking even property in furtherance of the succession to which he committed the murder, and in the latter case the addition of a few words avoids an anomaly that appeared in England. But in both

[1] Whether co-respondents figure in Indian matrimonial proceedings depends on the High Court Rules, which differ from State to State. In the Punjab it is felt that public policy negatives the citing of co-respondents: *Smt. Sarla* v. *Smt. Shankuntala* AIR 1966 Punj. 337. In Uttar Pradesh it is required.

[2] Concerning rights arising when persons die in an uncertain order of priority, as for example in a common calamity, and if the order were known property might pass from one to the other or through the other.

contexts more imagination could profitably have been used. In short the work betrays the fact that no such thorough comparative study of family laws was made before codification as might have been thought desirable; and this is strange, since when the Constitution was framed no pains were spared.

The Reasons for Codification?

The partial codification which we call for convenience the Hindu Code was advocated, and resisted, with great heat over a long period. The battle was joined in earnest as soon as India became independent. The Hindu Code Bill of the 1941 period had aimed at much less radical reforms, most of them merely simplifying the law, making it more uniform and up to date. It was cautious and conservative. What finally emerged was the result already described, to which neither of these epithets could be applied. The machinery was worked by steam which, as we have seen, somehow blew away, so that no impetus for further reform remains, except amongst jurists who cannot catch the legislators' or the public's ear. How did it all happen? The answer is very simple, as was suggested above.

One of the objections to British rule was that it provided India with a ruling caste (Europeans) into and between which the native population could not by any kind of emulation percolate. The instinct of the non-Brahmin classes, especially those with money, was to imitate as many of the Europeans' ways as they could without being outcasted, and sometimes even to cross that barrier. The search for prestige was naturally to imitate the prestige-bearing caste, namely the rulers and their associates. The Indian faculty for imitation and adjustment without losing their identity had as full play under the British as it had had in very remote times and in more recent times under the Muslims. Indians became poets in English as they had previously been poets in Persian and Urdu. Hindus mastered English law, for all its intricacies, as they had previously mastered the workings of the Mughal administrative system and revenue. Indians became members of the English Bar and of the I.C.S., and percolated where they could–but this did not take them to the very top, to which colour (to their disgust) and provenance proved an insuperable bar. Brahmins were in a peculiar difficulty in that if they were true to their inherited prestige they could not seek this adventitious prestige. One could not eat beef and drink whisky and pretend still to be a Brahmin and hope to be worshipped by non-Brahmins as a human divinity. But within the limits set by this situation, seeing that the respect of the many below was of more value than the speculative regard of the few above, even Brahmins adjusted themselves to a cosmopolitan attitude to life, developing the well-known mental dexterity whereby a man talked and thought one kind of life in the office and another at home, worshipped the gods at home and edited a 'modern' newspaper for his daily bread.

The non-Brahmins were true to basic Hindu principles, eschewing widow remarriage and even meat-eating, and glorying in the cultural heritage of their country, because amongst Hindus high caste was identified with subservience to Brahminical ethics. At the same time the veneer of observances which centuries of imitation of Brahmins had fixed upon them was gradually detached by the influence of Europeans, whom they found it on the whole easier to mix with and to imitate in fact or in imagination either by watching them, or reading about their 'goings-on' in newspapers and novels. Independence found India with an emerging partly-westernized class of well-to-do people, which was to all intents and purposes a caste. But parallel to them, existed another caste whether of Brahmins, Rajputs or others that was neither fully westernized nor fully entitled to the respect and imitation of the remainder of the population. As soon as the Europeans had ceased to be the fountainhead of money and power–as soon, that is to say, as they had turned from rulers into guests–the prestige holders were this double emergent caste of Indians which received all the strings of power. Now the essential factors of a caste are that it should be endogamous within the larger unit and exogamous within the sub-unit, and that it should be self-supporting in respect of opportunities, mutual aid, and absorption and retention of power. The Hindus who were at the top of the power ladder wanted to intermarry with Muslims similarly placed, not to mention Hindus of equal influence but lower caste. The antiquated personal law prevented the formation of a true ruling caste, an administrator-élite, a successor reservoir to the prestige abandoned by the British, in the following ways: firstly it prevented marriage between even remote relations of the same caste, let alone members of different sub-castes; next, because the marriage of daughters was founded upon the theory of the sacrament, marriage being indissoluble and unavoidable (in both the senses of that word), the father of a girl had a social duty to effect his daughter's marriage. The offer of a dowry on his part and the acceptance of the highest possible offer on the part of the father of the boy prevented not merely the free choice of partners in marriage but tended to give relations and persons with whom the family already had matrimonial connexions an unfair claim upon a man who was a social climber. These grievous handicaps were objected to because they hindered the advanced classes from getting together and knitting their common interests in the traditional manner. Marriage has always been a dynastic matter, and people near the top wanted to ensure in the Indian fashion that they and their children stayed there: yet their colleagues in this laudable endeavour were people who did not speak their house language, not to broach the question of sharing a common caste or marriage-market. Hence the old marriage laws, and the dowry system were anathema. The reasons actually put forward for the abolition of these were of course much more intellectual ones.

Europeans did not have dowries; they had love marriages and divorces. The lurid aspect of European life, especially in the East, did not deter Indians from envying the West its matrimonial freedom. This is extraordinary, for along with the demand for reform of the Hindu law we heard much of the depravity of the West. Moreover, if marriage is to remain a dynastic affair it is difficult to see how the introduction of divorce into respectable society could be advantageous. Yet once again the answer is simple: marriage arranged between persons of different backgrounds who share nothing but money and access to power, marriage arranged not upon the mere promise of a dowry but upon considerations into which the education and personality of the bride, her ability to travel and so on enter quite as prominently, must be an institution as flexible as that known in the West. A wife who lives happily in her husband's home and does her duty, as is still expected of her, inherits at his death, whether or not he has children by a previous wife, and whether or not he leaves other near dependants besides herself. The law of inheritance accordingly has to be mended so that expectation at the death of the ascendant takes the place of 'advancement' at the time of the marriage. The inheritance is her reward for faithful housekeeping. But if the husband and/or the wife, belonging as we suppose they do to a partially cosmopolitanized class and sharing the tastes and prejudices and to some extent the standards of their western contemporaries, go astray, behave with cruelty, or give other causes of complaint which people in respectable society cannot be expected to have contracted to suffer, then matrimonial relief must be available. The new system presupposes small families, in which in-laws are not conspicuous. Such a presupposition fits the ruling class and those who now imitate it. If your 'in-laws' are in fact people with whom you can converse only in English and whose closest common interests are their days at Columbia or Moscow, the question of their sharing a house with you must be remote. And the joint-family which propped up many an unhappy young wife against the neglect, indifference, or sheer barbarity of her husband is not there for the fashionable modern bride to lean upon.

Thus the real reasons which propelled Hindus into the 'Hindu Code age' were not in any sense religious any more than they were anti-religious. They had to do with the formation of a new nameless caste, the caste of the 'haves', who naturally have the instincts of all previous castes. And a thoroughly reasonable programme it was. The aid of the lawyers was taken at the right moment, but when the lawyers' energy flagged (too much of it at the time was taken up with the demands of the nascent Constitution) the men and women who ruled India supplied all that was needed. Their opponents, the 'orthodox', were people who did not need to contemplate intercaste marriage and suspected the motives of those who did. Religion was attempted to be used as a means of preventing what influential society wanted, and it might have succeeded had not the previous custodians of the Hindu law made out of it, *bona fide*, so appalling a system, from which anyone would have been glad to escape who cared for his country's prestige.[1]

[1] Detailed handling of the Anglo-Hindu system is to be found in Derrett, *Hindu Law, Past and Present* (Calcutta, 1957).

Now it is necessary for us to turn and see what results are beginning to emerge from the Code, since those who fought for it have bequeathed it to the nation. We shall do well to take up the topic of marriage, where, if anywhere, the religious arguments (against divorce) would be expected to have weight and so religion would show itself in practice. It is in marriage more than anywhere else in a legal system that the spirit of the religion can be expected to be influential. Have Hindus rejected divorce, and the other matrimonial reliefs? Have those who have had recourse to them been unorthodox people, people with no claim to being true Hindus? Or is it the case that here, as in other chapters, religion does not enter into it, and the law subserves purposes beneath the surface?

II

ASPECTS OF MATRIMONIAL CAUSES UNDER THE HINDU CODE

It is beyond doubt[1] that some parts of India find those sections of the *HMA* that provide for matrimonial relief useful. The great number of cases from the Punjab might suggest that an area not remarkable for Hindu orthodoxy and already very tolerant of customary divorces and the remarriage of women was an obvious area to avail itself of the provisions of the Act. One would assume that information from such an area would not be typical of India. But abundant use of the statute is evidenced from other areas and amongst castes about which the same allegations could hardly be made. Research carried out two years before the Act was passed showed that a provision of nullity and divorce did not accord with the aspirations of the majority of the lower, more rustic and less educated sections of the community.[2] Not by coincidence those provisions, and others too, fail to accord with traditional Hinduism, which still has a hold on the sentiments and often the usages of a substantial proportion of the population. Given the diverse attitudes of Hindus on this important subject, it is no small matter that a statutory régime which is foreign at any rate in origin has been imposed upon so vast a number of the inhabitants of Asia.

Is the régime being used, after all, in the spirit of the Code as written? Will its application intensify the clash between the Old and the New India? Would the situation alarm India's many

[1] This is a version of 'Aspects of Matrimonial Causes in Modern Hindu Law' which appeared at *Revue du sud-est asiatique*, 1964, no. 3, pp. 203–41. It has been augmented and brought up to date with the inclusion of later references, and the footnotes have been shortened.

[2] B. Kuppuswamy, *A Study of Opinion Regarding Marriage and Divorce* (Bombay, Asia Publishing House, 1957).

foreign well-wishers? These questions may be approached through the reported decisions of the Indian High Courts and the Supreme Court. The latter, however, has yet to pronounce on many of the intricate legal problems involved, and its policy, as we shall see (at *Conclusion* below) is still in a formative stage.

As with much Indian litigation, the true significance of the disputes seldom emerges clearly on the face of the record, still less in the reported judgements. The case of *M.* v. *S.*,[1] to which we shall return, is a remarkable exception. One might naturally suppose that the adoption by independent India of a divorce law for Hindus similar to what is normal in countries of the common-law tradition was merely a further, and perhaps more agreeable, example of India's modernizing tendencies, and a further (and perhaps gratifying) piece of evidence that Hindus were not so 'backward' as some other 'underdeveloped' peoples or communities. It needs hardly more than a survey of recent case-law to realize that this would miss the truth. The cases are by no means evidence that India is being modernized by this method. They are not to be read, however, in a straightforward comparison with their English or American counterparts. On the contrary it may be argued that this aspect of the 'education' of Hindus in India is one more only partly realistic piece of subservience to the ambitions and sentiments of the governing classes, with whom other educated classes sympathize only to a limited extent. Is it not, after all, one more instance where law is not what it seems, and where the technical apparatus of Anglo-Indian jurisprudence is called upon at long range to aid operations for which, indeed, jurisprudence as we understand it was not designed?

Rustic spouses can pose puzzles for Judges having English decisions as their guides. In *Smt. Umri Bai* v. *Chittar*[2] the wife was suspected of misbehaviour after five years or more of marriage, she went to her father, was falsely charged by her husband with immorality, and when she petitioned for judicial separation the latter craftily agreed to take her back. To the court, Shiv Dayal, J., it was evident that the husband had been cruel, and he might be more so. He might cut off her nose! The

[1] [1963] K.L.T. 315.

[2] AIR 1966 M.P. 205.

husband's behaviour was cruelty whether there would be an English precedent for it or not.

> . . . the Courts should be extremely careful while seeking assistance and guidance from English decisions, or even Indian decisions based on other laws . . . and should not follow them blindly, particularly while dealing with persons whose manners, customs and mode of life may be different from those of the parties concerned in those decisions.

If the distance between Parliament and the public is great, that between the judiciary and the remainder of the public may be no less significant. As we shall see, the judges are still influenced by the now traditional Anglo-Indian 'Victorian' attitude to women. This stemmed from the British period, some of whose fancies left an enduring mark upon at least the upper levels of consciousness of western-educated Indians a generation or so ago. A judge who would never allow his wife to be seen by a male other than a blood-relation, and who would be incredulous if his wife or unmarried daughter attempted to enter into an important transaction without his advice, consent and participation, will nevertheless speak from the bench of women in general in terms reminiscent of the Victorian poets and those novelists who depict the 'chivalry' of an earlier time, and will apply to his fellow-countrymen, whether educated, western-educated, or uneducated, standards of an 'enlightened', 'progressive' age, an age, needless to say, which has yet to 'arrive' so far as the bulk of the Hindu community is concerned–though it may arrive the sooner for these judicial statements. One instance will serve. In *Kusum Lata* v. *Kamta Prasad*,[1] a dispute between Hindu spouses, the judge, a Muslim (M. H. Beg, J.), was grieved to find that the wife-petitioner's case had been mishandled in the court below. The lower court held that the wife's complaints against her husband were frivolous (as they evidently were by 'country' standards), and mocked her for her manner of formulating her grievances. This was in keeping with the traditional outlook namely that a wife must adjust herself to her husband and take his oddities or unsympathetic behaviour in good part. One must recollect that the court below had the opportunity of seeing and questioning the parties, which makes a great deal of difference. But the learned judge in the High

[1] AIR 1965 All. 280. See especially pp. 285–6.

Court exposed an inadequacy in this approach to the wife's complaints. He insisted that in the modern set-up the court must show sympathy for both parties, and he proceeded to put forward a conception of cruelty highly favourable to an Indian wife's situation and, though not out of keeping with Anglo-American ideas, relatively novel for India. No one could be more chivalrous to an Indian lady than this Muslim judge, and once the notion spreads it cannot but have a disturbing effect on marriage in India, which is still, for the vast majority of people, not only the most important event in life, but also more of a dynastic and social, not to say even economic proposition than an emotional union between two individuals.

Apart from this intriguing aspect of Indian national 'education', the cases, for all their obliquity, give occasional rare glimpses of the 'Old' India at work.[1] The manner in which such cases are handled and evidence is taken, and from remarks dropped often, it seems, unconscious of their significance, the dreadful incongruity of the new law with the mentality of many of the people stands revealed. The quaintness of many of the cases is thus evidence of a powerful kind. But we must not make the mistake of supposing that India stands still here or elsewhere, and the follies of the 1950's may not necessarily endure into the 1970's.

[1] Cases in criminal law are equally revealing. In *Sakhu* v. *State* [1951] Nag. 508 the wife stabbed her husband to death when he with some friends broke into her father's house to 'abduct' her (i.e. take her home). She was held to have exercised her right of 'private defence'. In *Kanwal Ram* v. *H.P. Administration* AIR 1966 S.C. 614 the husband was prosecuted for bigamy, and admitted that he had sexual intercourse with the second wife, claiming that his marriage to her took place only after his earlier marriage had been dissolved (pleas of customary divorces which cannot be traced are not infrequent: see *Mohd. Ikram* v. *State of U.P.* AIR 1964 S.C. 1625, 1631; *Edamma* v. *Hussainappa* AIR 1965 A.P. 455): but the court held that as an essential ceremony was omitted the accused could not be convicted (see the complaints by Sri M. B. Mujumdar at (1966) 68 Bom. L.R., *J.*, 57 ff.). In *Parbia Ram* v. *Smt. Thopli* AIR 1966 H.P. 20 the husband applied for restitution but the wife argued that an essential ceremony was omitted (*arti* of the bridegroom), and restitution was refused! Why was the *arti*, a trifling ceremony, omitted? Or (if this is the correct question) why did witnesses depose that it was omitted? In *Khageswar* v. *Aduti* AIR 1967 Or. 80 corroboration of the wife's plea that her husband was impotent was discovered in the wife's complaint that the sorcerer employed to cure the husband's impotence had outraged her modesty.

It might be argued that the scheme enacted in the Hindu Marriage Act was not novel. Restitution of conjugal rights was already an old remedy in British India.[1] Baroda State was, under its Mahārāja Gaekwaḍ, introduced to a reformed matrimonial system for Hindus as early as the 1930's. In 1947 Bombay enacted a statute introducing judicial separation and divorce,[2] an innovation necessitated by the prohibition of polygamy in the same State.[3] Madras followed suit with somewhat similar legislation in 1949.[4] A few other States introduced similar legislation upon the eve of the codification by Parliament in 1955.[5] But it is to be noted that in the State of Mysore, which, like Baroda, was outside British India, but enjoyed a liberal and enlightened rule combined with a substantial cultural, educational and administrative association with British India, no move towards the introduction of judicial separation and divorce for Hindus has been recorded. Since Mysore had enjoyed, well before independence, statutory reforms of Hindu law in the fields of the joint-family and succession, more comprehensive and radical than any British India had attempted, this omission is significant. Moreover, relatively little use has been made of the Bombay and Madras statutes, a fact of great significance since those states included the highly westernized cities of Bombay and Madras, traditionally the domiciles of rootless, mobile people, outcasts and rebels, the normal sources, one would think, of matrimonial instability. Whether extensive use was made of the Baroda legislation has not yet appeared: but it is notorious that many of the Mahārāja's subjects belonged to castes in which divorce by custom, and even by consent, was valid. This unexpected feature of the Indian scene, which might give rise to misunderstandings, requires discussion from two standpoints.

The introduction of a general divorce law to Hindus, for whom divorce has been, or at least theoretically, abhorrent, was

[1] *Hur Sookha* v. *Poorun* (1867) Rep. HCJ, NWP (Agra, 1867), 115.

[2] Bombay Hindu Divorce Act, 1947.

[3] Bombay Prevention of Hindu Bigamous Marriages Act, 1946.

[4] Madras Hindu (Bigamy Prevention and Divorce) Act, 1949.

[5] Saurashtra Prevention of Hindu Bigamous Marriages Act, 1950; Saurashtra Hindu Divorce Act, 1952 (see *Dave Kantilal* v. *Bai Indumati* AIR 1956 Sau. 115, where the wife was an imbecile and the husband was evading his liability to pay maintenance).

justified during the Hindu Code Bill agitation by, amongst other reasons, the allegation that 80 per cent of Hindus (if we include the Scheduled Castes and Tribes) enjoyed the right by custom to have their marriages dissolved by the decision (by consent) of an *ad hoc panchayat* of caste elders. The force of the argument was somewhat lessened when it was discovered that Parliament intended to offer to *all* Hindus a western-type divorce law, leaving unaffected (as necessity seemed to indicate) the jurisdiction (now concurrent) of *panchayats*, however informal, to grant divorce in castes where the custom is in force.[1] This was by no means the course which the 'educational' theory would have indicated: for in Kenya and Uganda, the Ordinances[2] give with one hand rights of judicial separation and judicial divorce, and with the other abolish the jurisdiction, or alleged jurisdiction, of *panchayats* to give matrimonial relief within the scope contemplated by the Ordinances themselves. Had the intention been to regulate the granting of divorces throughout India, surely the jurisdiction of *panchayats* would have been regulated;[3] and in those castes where such a custom of divorce did not exist it was at least plausible to argue that public opinion there had long been against its availability. The objection to the introduction of judicial divorce remained valid, therefore, notwithstanding the presence of divorce by caste custom amongst the allegedly 80 per cent of the 'Hindu' population.

The situation was complicated by the fact that in some castes separation by agreement existed (and still exists) whereby the husband 'dismissed' or 'released' the wife with a bill of divorcement, without the necessity to face a caste tribunal, or even to consult the elders (frequently called simply *panchayat*) who may in all castes unofficially act in an attempt to reconcile families and spouses who are involved in some matrimonial dispute. In many cases where the husband is prosecuted for bigamy he enters a defence that his marriage was terminated by a

[1] *HMA*, s. 29 (2).

[2] Kenya Hindu Marriage and Divorce Ordinance, 1960; Uganda Hindu Marriage and Divorce Ordinance, 1961. On these see Derrett at *Amer. J. of Comp. Law*, 11 (1962), 396–403, also Derrett, *I.M.H.L.*, ch. 11.

[3] K. M. Kapadia, *The Hindu Marriage and Divorce Bill (A Critical Study)* (Bombay, Popular Book Depot, 1953), suggested this at pp. 12–13.

customary divorce,[1] but these cases will not be those where by merely handing the wife a *tyāg-patra* or *farkhat* ('deed of release') the husband may put an end at will to a matrimonial situation which does not suit him.[2] They will presumably be cases where the consent of the spouses gave the caste tribunal the authority to declare them divorced. The higher the caste the less acceptable would any of these methods be, and, as we shall see, they were in any case an extreme step.

The custom of a caste with reference to marriage has always enjoyed a special privilege. In other contexts the book-law, in its Anglo-Hindu form, would rule unless a valid custom could be proved to the contrary, and indeed even in the context of marriage we know that the invention of new ceremonies was not countenanced by the courts. But in general the opinion of Sir James FitzJames Stephen expressed on January 27th, 1872, is regarded as correct, when he found difficulty in rejecting as valid a custom as to marriage which was of recent origin. In *Muthusami* v. *Masilamani* Saṅkaran Nair, J., made it plain that if the caste accept a marriage as valid, the courts would not interfere to hold the marriage void; whereas if the parties neglect the caste rules and marry under the shelter of the book law the court will uphold the marriage though the parties be excommunicated:[3]

[1] See p. 355, n. 1 above.

[2] *Rahi* v. *Govinda* (1875) 1 Bom. 97, 114, 116. *Reg.* v. *Sambhu* (1876) 1 Bom. 350. *Empress* v. *Umi* (1882) 6 Bom. 126; *P. Jina Magan* v. *Bai Jethi* [1941] Bom. 535; *Manglabai* v. *Deorao* AIR 1962 M.P. 193. Note that *natra* 'marriage' after such a divorce may be construed by the courts as a mere concubinage: *Laxmansingh* v. *Kesharbai* AIR 1966 M.P. 166. Yet a careful consideration of bigamy within the context of modern Indian law has revealed that the bigamously married Hindu woman lies in a legal no-man's land, so that she cannot claim any of the advantages to which a concubine was entitled under the old law: *Narayanaswami* v. *Padmanabhan* AIR 1966 Mad. 394. Whether she has a moral right sufficient to support a family arrangement in her favour remains to be determined (probably she has).

[3] (1909) 33 Mad. 342, 354–5. *Dhedu Sheoram* v. *Mst. Malhanbai* AIR 1966 M.P. 252. The *panchayat* excommunicated the wife for adultery, because she was carrying a child who must have been conceived at a time when by custom her husband should not have had access to her. But because the husband was living in the same house during the period the Court held that the child was his and there were no grounds for divorce under the *HMA*, s. 13. It would be difficult to find a better example of the contrast between caste rules and State law.

'The legal rules put forward by the sacred writers are primarily intended only for those who accept in theory the religious belief, the religious, social and moral obligations which form the foundation of that system. On the others it is binding only by adoption, and though it will be presumed that as Hindus they are governed by that system of law, circumstances may exist to throw the burden of proof on the party asserting that they have adopted any specific rule of Hindu law . . . Where therefore the religious and legal consciousness of a community recognizes the validity of a certain marriage, it follows that it cannot be discarded on account of its repugnance to that system of law.

'Whether the marriage is valid or not, according to the caste rules, it is for the caste itself to decide. So far as ancient history and modern usage go, marriage questions have always been settled by the caste itself and the validity of a marriage between the members of a caste who recognize it as binding has not been questioned by outsiders though the caste itself may be lowered in their estimation when such marriages are repugnant to their notions of morality . . .

'It does not follow that a marriage opposed to the usages of the communities and not recognized by them would be invalid. A marriage whatever else it is, i.e. a sacrament, an institution, is undoubtedly a contract entered into for consideration with correlative rights and duties. The Civil Courts Act only requires that so far as Hindus are concerned its validity must rest upon Hindu law, i.e. as explained above the law of the Dharma Shastras as distinguished from caste rules or the caste law. If it is not recognized by the caste or caste rules, the parties may cease to belong to the castes whose usages they have violated and who would therefore expel them. There is nothing to prevent a man from giving up his caste or community . . .'

Thus although in other contexts proof of custom would exclude the book-law, here the Hindus have virtually had a choice, under the Anglo-Hindu system, between their custom and the Hindu law itself, the courts being willing to recognize either source of law indifferently.[1]

The objections to divorce were not entirely unheeded by Parliament itself. The grounds now provided for judicial divorce throughout India do not include cruelty, nor adultery *simpliciter*. Where judicial separation has been decreed, or a decree of restitution remains unsatisfied, the spouses can proceed to divorce two years after the decree in question: so that wider grounds, with a compulsory waiting period superadded, will

[1] It is a strange feature of Indian law that while a caste may determine what capacity a man has to marry, its *panchayat* has no jurisdiction to *annul* a marriage!

serve for a divorce.[1] Parliament, though pressed from some quarters to do so, was evidently not prepared to go to all desirable lengths in providing divorce for all Hindus, a contention entirely supported by the fact that in 1954, hardly eight months before our statute was passed, the same Parliament had enacted the Special Marriage Act, under which divorce was made available for cruelty and for adultery, amongst other grounds, and a divorce may be obtained (after certain specified delays) upon any or no grounds, provided the couple are determined upon a divorce from each other. That Act governs the matrimonial disputes of all Indians married under it or its predecessor,[2] and also any Hindu couples not married under either of them but choosing to register their existing marriages under the Act of 1954. Parliament evidently thought that what was desirable for such rather rare birds was not proper for other Hindus.

A powerful plea against a divorce law for Hindus was made by Mr. A. N. Mukherjee, a District and Sessions Judge, as late as 1964, when the Hindu divorce law had already got into its stride.[3] He uncharitably pointed out that those best acquainted with the English divorce law had denounced it, and were advocating some retreat from it (how, no one can suggest!): so that while India was busy imitating the West the West itself had reason and experience enough to be doubtful of its earlier wisdom. But he does not go on to suggest that the right of divorce amongst the 80 per cent should be taken away by statute–and this is really the point, once the principle of attempting to unify the personal law of Hindus has been accepted. Even more recently he has argued from his experience of matrimonial causes that the pursuit of relief is often unjust. He says, 'I tried a matrimonial suit where the husband, a

[1] *HMA* s. 13 as amended by the Hindu Marriage Amendment Act, 1964, which introduced sub-section (1A) after the former sub-section 1, which was itself amended.

[2] Namely the Special Marriage Act of 1872, intended originally for Brahmos, who were Hindus who deviated from many then characteristic Hindu beliefs and yet wished to marry within their own sect or at any rate without conversion to Christianity or Islam (the previous alternatives as the law then stood).

[3] *Law Quarterly* (J. of the Indian Law Inst., W. Bengal State Unit), 1 No. 4, pp. 321–5.

medical practitioner, wanted to divorce his graduate wife on the ground that she was (a) lunatic and unchaste. The case was a protracted one. Respectable relations of the husband tried to support him. But the wife was neither lunatic nor unchaste as the evidence disclosed.' He finds the recent amendment of the Hindu Marriage Act, whereby either spouse can obtain a divorce if cohabitation is not resumed for two years after a decree for separation or for restitution, most unhappy as it encourages husbands virtually to obtain divorces as a prize for their own wrongdoing.[1]

Granted that Hindu statutory divorce law bears signs of compromise, of tinkering with the western model to make it conform to some degree with traditional upper-class Hindu antipathy to divorce, what is the situation prevailing amongst those castes in which divorce is available by custom? A word must be interjected about the not unimportant State of Kerala, in which, by statute, various castes enjoy the privilege of divorce by mutual consent embodied in a decree of the court,[2] or judicial divorce upon grounds, the latter being for the most part lenient and even including 'incompatibility of tempera-

[1] *Law Quarterly*, 3 No. 2 (1966), pp. 81–7. In a telling article entitled 'Matrimonial cruelty in Hindu law', [1966] 2 S.C.J., *J.*, 105–12, Ramesh Chandra quotes expressions of judicial opinion in *Umri Bai* v. *Chittar* AIR 1966 M.P. 205 to the effect that spouses must bear and forbear and stop allowing foolish advisers to add fuel to the flames. In an article appreciative of the Hindu Marriage Act (at *Law Quarterly*, 3 No. 2, pp. 96 ff.) Madhuri Ghose asks for patience and insight in its administration and perspective in its criticism. The Madras Provincial Bar Federation considered in October 1963 amongst other matters the marriage and divorce laws. K. Rājah Iyer reported that husbands of childless wives are taking 'concubines' as virtual second wives. He disapproved of restitution and judicial separation in practice. D. Krishnamūrthi Iyer, who approves of the sacramental nature of marriage, asked for divorce by consent to be introduced for Hindus. T. Ramappa contended that a single act of adultery should be a ground for divorce. M. Anantanārāyanan summed up: the tension between the *saṃskāra* and contractual elements in marriage had not been resolved. *Proceedings of the Seminar*, ed. T. V. Viśwanātha Aiyar (Madras, Prov. Bar Fed., 1964), pp. 18–64.

[2] If, as sometimes happens, they dispense with the formalities (e.g. a registered instrument where the relevant statute calls for this) they may find themselves still married and their children by others illegitimate, perhaps many years afterwards: *Nangu Amma* v. *Appi Parameswaran* AIR 1966 Ker. 41 (F.B.).

ment'. These castes have a wholly or partially matrilineal and polyandrous background, in which at one time marriage as known in Hinduism hardly figured. The 'education' of the castes in question proceeded largely by imitation and emulation spontaneously, signalized by the statutes. These people may take advantage of the Hindu Marriage Act if they wish;[1] but this right to obtain divorces under the local statutes has been carefully preserved to them.[2] Unlike the situation which may be called the 'Kerala situation', elsewhere in India certain castes in all regions, and all castes in a few regions, are able (as we have seen) to solve all matrimonial problems by agreement, with the aid of the intervention of elders or 'respectable persons', the exercise of pressure by relatives on both sides, and finally the procedure (by consent) before the *panchayat*.[3] Brahmins everywhere (so far as is known) despise this sort of activity as barely Hindu; and all 'respectable' castes have dropped, or purport to have dropped, all trace of this custom. Amongst them the independence of women was so little valued that there could be no approximation, even in theory, to the 'progressive' approach characteristic of the leading classes of Indian society, without the heavy hammer of legislation. Men's dissatisfaction with their wives could be solved by their taking additional wives (now an unpopular practice except amongst farmers and the village notables of the South); but women's dissatisfaction found vent in tragedies, an abandoned home, or suicide. Society, true to the spirit of the ancient texts of Manu's fifth book,[4] made a virtue of wifely submission, and pawned humanity for respectability. To make a western-type divorce law available to such classes must be, at first sight, to equate them with the masses from which they seem to have climbed, and the moral pressure against a spouse's availing himself or herself of the new laws will be tremendous. Meanwhile the castes which retain the custom of divorce by *panchayat's* decision remain without effective supervision, at any rate until litigation, very late in the day, takes the parties' affairs before a regular court.

[1] *Chellappan Nair* v. *Madhavi Amma* AIR 1961 Ker. 311 (F.B.).

[2] *HMA*, s. 29 (2).

[3] *Keshav* v. *Bai Gandi* (1915) 39 Bom. 538.

[4] R. M. Das, *Women in Manu and his Seven Commentators* (Varanasi, Kanchana Publications, 1962) is a specimen of the 'Victorian' approach to the subject.

What goes on before such *panchayats* can only very rarely be glimpsed. In *Smt. Pemanbai* v. *Channoolal*[1] there was a matrimonial dispute between members of a caste known as Patwas. Before the *panchayat* both the spouses gave their consent, and they were divorced. For reasons which are not clear the regular court was approached for a declaration that the marriage still subsisted. Perhaps the husband had married again, and since the right to have more than one wife had been taken away by the statute of 1955 even in the case of a member of such a caste, the wife may have wanted to obtain better terms upon the footing that her marriage had not been dissolved. She alleged that she was only fourteen or fifteen years of age when she consented to the divorce. It is possible that no one knew her real age. Her case was that her consent to so important a question as her divorce could not be valid at an age when she could not have bound herself legally by a contract. The judge held (1) that she had sufficient understanding to give her consent, and (2) as the husband did not allege that in such cases caste custom did *not* permit a divorce to be granted, her consent was competent. It was argued on her behalf that the general Hindu law would not regard a girl of fifteen years of age as having sufficient discretion to consent to her own divorce–a submission that might have been sustained had it been adequately considered; but it was held that it was useless to speak of an age of discretion according to the general law, for divorce was unknown to the general law (i.e. the unamended personal law). This somewhat surprising decision should not, perhaps, be cited as an authority; but it illustrates how divorce is granted amongst the lower castes, and how loath the regular court is to interfere with the *panchayat's* jurisdiction. The latter can virtually make its own law and procedure, provided that it does not violate the requirements of natural justice. In *Kishenlal* v. *Mst. Prabhu*[2] the Rajasthan High Court insisted on strict proof of the *panchayat's* jurisdiction, and of its compliance with natural justice. Otherwise the alleged custom would be unreasonable and opposed to public policy. It is not yet clear whether this judgement represents a new trend.

The new law, therefore, of judicial separation, restitution, nullity and divorce gives to some a set of remedies which, as

[1] AIR 1963 M.P. 57. [2] AIR 1963 Raj. 95. The caste were Mehtas.

such, they do not require; and to other classes a set which they have long pretended respectable society ought not to want. How has this law been used? Is it possible to contend that it has been used by the people, whether they had customary divorces or not, as a means of bringing pressure to bear upon those who refuse or delay what is claimed to be due, and that matrimonial causes are being used, like others of the Anglo-Indian legal weapons, in the contests for gain, prestige and the like? If this is proved it will be no novelty in itself, but it will be a somewhat extreme symptom of a well-known, deplorable phenomenon.[1] The present writer recently (1965) asked a practitioner of the Madras High Court whether such suits or petitions were being used for indirect purposes, and his answer was that they were not so often as they used to be. Madras may be reforming itself. Can it also be contended that in the administration of this new chapter of law the judiciary are weaving through the fabric of Indian life strands which are incongruous and inassimilable with the remainder, potential irritants, so that ultimately either Hindu society must change, or the law itself must develop so as to cease to be recognizably comparable with its English and American counterparts? If this also is proved we have a phenomenon of interest to comparative lawyers. The advantages of the common law system (taken in its widest sense) are meeting a searching test in southern Asia.

The case-law on *divorce* so far is not especially interesting, though we are well aware that in some castes it is the relations

[1] G. V. Narasimham, at [1962] 2 Sup. C.J., *J.*, 74, draws attention to the possibility that separated or estranged wives may withhold their consent to their husbands' adopting a child merely as a form of harassment: this is the way the wind blows. In order to achieve harassment it is, of course, not necessary that one's suit should have any merit. In Bombay, we are told (by Messrs. Bhat and Jogal, AIR 1967 Journal 73), 21,000 cases are pending in the City Civil Court and other courts are not much better placed. It takes four years or more for a civil suit to be decided (at first instance) and final disposal may take twenty years. 'By the time the case is over, the affected parties are financially ruined, psychologically broken, and physically shattered.' But the litigious plaintiffs have the best of it. 'The litigant' (i.e. especially the defendant) 'is made to visit the courts literally fifty times. The number of visits to the lawyer is anybody's guess. Some courts in Bombay are more crowded than the third-class compartments of the local trains'–a breathtaking comparison.

that manoeuvre the divorces[1] and not the spouses alone. The courts apply English precedents, with the aid of earlier constructions and applications of the Indian Divorce Act,[2] which did not apply to Hindus unless they had married under the old Special Marriage Act. But the law of restitution and judicial separation, and that of nullity satisfy the requirements of the present study. In order to explain these fields it will be necessary to review the background of Hindu marriages, without which the case-law will hardly be intelligible. But at the outset the reader must be warned that no generalization will be entirely satisfactory in a country of India's infinite diversity.

Nine marriages out of ten are (except amongst the very poorest classes) arranged marriages, in which the opinions of the spouses are barely consulted. Young men, experienced in the world and technology, perhaps graduates of several, including foreign, universities, tell their fathers, 'I shall be very happy with any choice you make for me', and, what is more surprising, leave it to their parents to determine the time of the wedding, which suits the family's convenience and pocket, and not by any means necessarily theirs. The spouses generally meet for the first time at the ceremony, whereafter they are put together, if not on the first night, at any rate within the first few days of the actual wedding, or, where the parties were then too young, the ceremony marking the bride's final transfer to her husband's home.[3] Young men married off immediately before their departure for study in Europe or America have no difficulty in passing themselves off as unmarried men, and not infrequently genuinely believe themselves so to be. It is not common for couples to show joy at their weddings. In the usual photograph the bridegroom wears a dejected expression. Marriages are not consummated as the result of mutual attraction, let alone affection, but of the abnormally heightened sexual anticipation which results from the enforced separation of the sexes coupled with an idealized romanticism which is fostered by literature, motion pictures and

[1] As in *Keshav* (above).

[2] A statute of 1869 desperately in need of revision.

[3] Tradition nominally provided that couples should sleep together *in chastity* for three nights after the ceremony: A. Mahādeva Śāstry, *Vedic Law of Marriage or the Emancipation of Women* (Madras, V. Rāmaswāmy Śāstrulu & Sons, 1918, reissued in (?) 1945), being lectures delivered in 1907 and 1916 and discussions arising therefrom.

patterns of conversation amongst age-mates. Cases of purely nervous, though happily temporary, impotence are by no means uncommon, with the dreadful emotional tensions to which this would be likely to give rise.[1] The Court's pontifications on the various kinds of impotence make horrid reading against this background. Couples not so afflicted may yet be dissatisfied with their first sexual experience and love grows, as best it can, within the rigid pattern of etiquette within the joint-family, under the eyes of stern parents, and as the result of sharing the ups and downs of life. The rich and the fashionable evade this by insisting that the young couple have their own flat: but that does not, in a society used to centuries of joint-living, ensure that a man and a woman make, all at once, an efficient team. The bride is supposed to fulfil herself in marriage, and in presenting her husband and his ancestors with a male heir. Even in families where *śrāddha-s* have fallen out of use and the ancestors are forgotten, a couple's social situation and personal happiness are transformed when, after perhaps three or four daughters, a son is safely born to the family. The privilege of being the mother of a son does not depend upon knowledge of antiquated texts. It is a reality of Indian, and particularly Hindu life, take it from what source you will. This privilege outweighs, or is supposed to outweigh, any indifference or slights or even assault from her husband, and is certainly commonly taken to be an ample consideration for her tolerating her mother-in-law's stern discipline, and the insolence of her elder sisters-in-law or her husband's sisters.[2] The treatment of married women is related to the attitude towards separation and divorce. 'Respectable' classes are often unfeeling towards young brides, once the formal present-giving is over. They can afford to be. They take them

[1] A sad instance is fully documented in *Lalithamma* v. *Kannan* AIR 1966 Mys. 178 (discussed below).

[2] The psychology of young motherhood and family etiquette are discussed by Bimalendu Gupta in Baidya N. Varma, ed., *Contemporary India* (London, Asia Publishing House, 1964), at pp. 187 ff. Upbringing in an Indian home can have results conforming to patterns, some of which are discussed in the well-documented article of M. K. Dhillon, 'Causes of delinquency in India', *Law Review*, 18 No. 1 (1966), pp. 137–62. Some very shrewd remarks on the position of the daughter-in-law are made by T. Madan in his *Family and Kinship* (London, A.P.H., 1965). He is the first to attribute her plight to inadequacies on the part of *males*.

in marriage as young as possible, in order to break them in to the family's ways, and weigh them and their dowries together. Marriages in such classes are dynastic alliances, arranged preponderantly for purposes of finance and prestige, and divorce is of course unthinkable. It is only in the numerically insignificant superficially westernized classes that dowries are not expected, legacies *via* women can be expected, and divorce is contemplated as a possibility.

In the classes where divorce is easy by caste custom the freedom accorded to women is naturally higher; these are also castes in which widows and divorced women may (from a social point of view) freely be married. In classes standing in a midway position there are customarily intermediate types of marriage, the first and senior wife being married as a virgin, accompanied by a dowry (or what passes in these days for a dowry, since dowries *eo nomine* are prohibited), and second or junior wives taken either from somewhat lower classes, or, as divorcees or widows, from classes of equal status but in an inferior 'form', such as the well-known *pat* or *karewa* marriages.[1] In all castes the wife is ideally subordinate to her husband in all questions; sexual infidelity on her part is heavily frowned upon and occurs nowadays, if at all, under very unusual circumstances.[2] If it occurs it is usually as a result of the temptation brought by unnatural segregation of the sexes or unrealistic romanticism and a desire for adventure. An unfaithful wife can rarely run away with or to her paramour (though this is not unheard-of), and unfaithfulness occurs (if at all) more often casually and evanescently, or as incest within the family circle.[3] Consequently if an unfaithful wife is detected she is not normally abandoned; she lives on in the family under a cloud until she is forgiven. For a man to divorce his wife for adultery would cause

[1] This often involves a bargain between the first husband's relatives and her second husband: *Ude* v. *Mst. Rajo* AIR 1966 Punj. 329.

[2] Social sharks are still an anomaly: see the interesting cases of *Bipinchandra* v. *Prabhavati* AIR 1957 S.C. 176 and *K. M. Nanavati* v. *State of Maharashtra* [1962] 2 S.C.J. 347.

[3] Lower-caste attitudes to incest are rarely elicited, but the Vāgrīs of Gujarat not so long ago enacted as a caste by-law that adultery by a father-in-law should incur a fine of Rs. 125, by an elder brother-in-law Rs. 100, but by a younger brother-in-law Rs. 40. The source of the money in each case might well be the same; it is the family's loss which counts.

the whole family to lose face. Except in the lower castes irregularities would be swallowed, rather than allowed to disrupt multiple and often reciprocal ties between families–so much more depends upon a marriage than the mere convenience of the spouses.

A fact of not less importance must be added. For sentimental company, and indeed for emotional satisfaction, Hindu males do not look exclusively to their wives, or indeed necessarily to women. The days when a Hindu found a public woman more entertaining, exciting and companionable than his wife can be said to be past for practical purposes: 'high moral tone' has succeeded in taking over from the pre-British *mores*. But that their wives can be good friends to them dawns upon many Hindu husbands somewhat late in the day.[1] They and their wives and their friends and their friends' wives seldom form a social circle, except amongst the westernized élite, where there is no embarrassment in conversing on any objective matter and where the ladies' forthright opinions, founded on a well-educated experience of the world, would have left their grandparents' womenfolk speechless with amazement or indignation. Even in the present writer's lifetime the intimate friends of the sons of the family, not actually brought up in the household, would not expect to have conversations with their mother in any sort of comfort. The phrase 'She does not come out' is no doubt used now less as a term of commendation than as a sign of being behind the times; but for the majority of the population the old ideas are still good breeding, and jealousy between the genders bites to the bone. For those who do not know India it may be worthwhile to remark that even in 1966 a man would stand up on an exceedingly uncomfortable country bus for a matter of some hours rather than occupy an empty seat next to some lady, and the custom is so strong that 'ladies' seats' will not normally be occupied by men; and fathers and daughters, brothers and sisters will sit apart. The modern fashion, however, which

[1] Indian novels in English throw light on Indian attitudes. See in particular R. K. Narayan, *Mr. Sampath* (London, Eyre and Spottiswoode, 1949), Bhabani Bhattacharya, *Music for Mohini* (New York, Crown, 1952), and R. P. Jhabvala, *To Whom She Will* (London, Allen & Unwin; Toronto, Nelson, 1955). M. E. Derrett, *The Modern Indian Novel in English* (Brussels, Institut de Sociologie, 1966).

allows husband and wife to sit together in public places grows apace: a concession to modernity. To produce a photograph of a woman with a man other than her husband is to offer proof, according to local notions, of her living in adultery with him.[1] These points must be borne in mind while studying the working of the Hindu Marriage Act in practice.[2]

A difference of opinion which emerged between the Allahabad High Court and the Supreme Court is enlightening. The former is in closer touch with local ideas, the latter with cosmopolitan notions. In *Smt. Chandra Mohini Srivastava* v. *Avinash*[3] the wife was divorced because the co-respondent had written her (unasked) 'improper letters'. The Supreme Court could not agree that these letters were evidence of an illicit relationship.

Unsatisfactory relations between husband and wife and between a wife and her husband's relatives by no means always produce in the husband the sort of emotional tension which in other countries leads to threats of separation or actual separations, or tends directly or indirectly to divorce. In regions where manners are less inhibited and characters more open–amongst these the Punjab stands out notably–husbands see no harm in giving their wives a sound beating, a proceeding believed to be good for the morale of all concerned. That a Sikh or Jat wife should complain of being beaten by her husband would seem at first either quaint or in bad taste: though it would be another matter if she complained of being beaten by her father-in-law.

We are now in a position to look into some restitution, separation and nullity cases. Unlike the position in England and America restitution can be desired for its own sake, for the loss

[1] For example take evidence tendered in *Pattayee* v. *Manickam* AIR 1967 Mad. 254.

[2] In *Subbarama Reddiar* v. *Saraswathi* [1966] 2 M.L.J. 263 we read that the unwritten taboos and rules of social morality in 'this' country and particularly in village areas must necessarily be taken into account. If an unrelated person is found alone with a young wife after midnight in her bedroom in actual physical juxtaposition, unless there is some explanation forthcoming for this, which is compatible with an innocent interpretation, the only inference that a court of law can draw must be that the two were committing an act of adultery together. In this case the wife's relations contended on her behalf that penetration had not taken place: they contended in vain (an attempt at adultery cannot be proved to rebut the inference that adultery has taken place). But far more innocent behaviour than this may be suspect.

[3] AIR 1967 S.C. 581, on appeal from AIR 1964 All. 486.

of money, jobs, or prestige can be worse than cohabitation with an irritating spouse; judicial separation, likewise, can be of real value to both parties. This has been contradicted,[1] on the footing that judicial separation was an unnecessary import, and that circumstances which justify separation would justify divorce even amongst Hindus; but it is to be noted that in *A. Annamalai Mudaliar* v. *Perumayee Ammal*[2] the Madras High Court reviewed the parallel remedies, separate residence and maintenance under the *HAMA* and judicial separation, and commented that these lesser remedies are appropriate to cases where the wife does not want divorce or, wanting it, would for any reason be unable to obtain it. To women in castes where divorced or widowed women are not customarily taken in marriage the remedy of divorce may be altogether too drastic: to husbands the prospect of a second or subsequent marriage may not be realistic in view of the financial outlay customarily associated with weddings, and one must remember that, to many Hindu males, to have been married is traditionally much more important than to live with a wife.[3] Nullity is important in a society where divorce might be ardently desired at too early a stage in the matrimonial life, and when no possible grounds can be found for a dissolution.[4]

In all discussions it must be borne in mind that all respectable Indian groups, particularly Hindu castes, regard matrimonial disputes as eminently distasteful, but that once litigation is afoot they have no hesitation in attributing any sort of motive to the opposite party.

In *Gurdial Kaur* v. *Mukand Singh*[5] the court decreed the husband's petition for restitution of conjugal rights. The wife

[1] By Krishna Bahadur at *Jaipur L.J.*, 5 (1965), at pp. 125–6. See also p. 361, n. 1 above.

[2] AIR 1965 Mad. 139.

[3] The *dharmaśāstra* emphasizes that a husband must 'approach' his wife at least once in every menstrual period (immediately after the cessation of the menstrual flow). It is Hindu belief that a woman is *entitled* to intercourse. A Hindu who has begotten a son is advised to beget another since a man with only one son is virtually son-less (the first might be lost). These ideas speak for themselves. On fantasies connected with marriage see G. Morris Carstairs, *The Twice-born* (London, 1957). See above, p. 65, n. 1.

[4] As evidently in *Jayaraj* v. *Mary* AIR 1967 Mad. 242 (F.B.).

[5] AIR 1967 Punj. 235.

had refused to return home. Her relations pretended the husband was a total stranger to them and that he masqueraded as her husband *because he hoped thereby to inherit her mother's property*. We note incidentally that the personal law does not recognize a son-in-law as a female's heir (but that did not deter these hardy liars). When the wife's mother was asked why she had not arranged her daughter's marriage until the advanced age of twenty-five, she replied that a pandit had told her that if her daughter married before that age she would become a widow. When cross-examined the girl's uncle knew nothing of this story. No other explanation of the wife's behaviour was ever forthcoming.

Restitution of Conjugal Rights

The *HMA* provides, by s. 9 (1):

> When either the husband or the wife has, without reasonable excuse, withdrawn from the society of the other, the aggrieved party may apply, by petition to the district court, for restitution of conjugal rights and the court, on being satisfied of the truth of the statements made in such petition and that there is no legal ground why the application should not be granted, may decree restitution of conjugal rights accordingly.

To this there appears the curious reservation, by s. 9 (2):

> Nothing shall be pleaded in answer to a petition for restitution of conjugal rights which shall not be a ground for judicial separation or for nullity of marriage or for divorce.

These words represent a formulation of the English divorce law as it was before the Matrimonial Causes Act of 1884 (47 & 48 Vict., c. 68) and find a counterpart in s. 33 of the Indian Divorce Act, 1869. Parallels are still to be found in the Commonwealth generally. It is no more than an encumbrance in a statute where divorce may be obtained for far more substantive offences than were contemplated at the time of the English statute in question, and its presence proved the absence of the requisite comparative legal skill when the Hindu Marriage and Divorce Bill was being drafted and went through its committee stages. Nevertheless one of the first tasks for the Indian judge has been to determine what meaning, if any, is to be attached to this subsection. The *prima facie* view (incredible as it is) has found expression, that a spouse could not file any defence which was not one of the statutory grounds for judicial separation (e.g. desertion for two years, cruelty), or for nullity (e.g. impotence, idiocy or lunacy), or for divorce (e.g. living in adultery, ceasing to be a Hindu by conversion to another religion).

In *Rukman Kanta* v. *Faquir Chand*,[1] a Punjab case, Shamsher Bahadur, J., held that a plea of desertion raised by the wife in answer to a petition for restitution could not be entertained when desertion was not shown to have lasted for the statutory period of two years required as a ground for judicial separation (s. 10 (1) (*a*)). As we shall see, this case may not be good law, but the circumstances have an interest in themselves. The marriage took place in 1952, the husband being a head constable in the police, a relatively poorly-paid occupation. In 1954 he was about to be accused of embezzlement to the tune of Rs. 1,300 (£65), unless he deposited that amount. He approached his father-in-law and brother-in-law through his wife, in vain. He raised the money elsewhere, but was convicted and fined. Embittered by his father-in-law's refusal, he raised funds by selling ornaments he had himself given his wife at their wedding. Marital life was discontinued for a year or so after he sent his wife to her family for the money; she later rejoined him but they parted when he eventually obtained another employment. He filed an application for restitution alleging that his wife would not reconcile herself to his humble circumstances (an allegation, one would incline to suppose, rather in her favour than his), and she entered a defence on the grounds that he treated her cruelly, unsympathetically, and offensively. Our first introduction to common-form pleading is true to the type. She (i.e. her father's pleader on her behalf) alleged that the husband 'filthily abused and mercilessly beat her during the period she lived with him and never cared for her when she fell ill'. According to her he was addicted to gambling and drinking and was a reckless spendthrift(!). She further alleged that he was always trying to extort money from her father (!) on some pretext or other. She claimed that he severed all connexions with her and her parents by letter when he failed to obtain the money, and she had been deserted by him when in September 1954 he gave her a receipt for her jewels (!). In early 1956, she admitted, he asked for

[1] AIR 1960 Punj. 493.

forgiveness, but during her short stay with him he was 'cruel, callous and mercenary'; he kept on pressing for money and gave her a beating, and then in June 1956 turned her out. The question was whether she had withdrawn herself without reasonable excuse. The trial judge thought not. Plainly in his view the woman was simply a pawn in the game between her family and her husband. In the wife's appeal it was contended that she has suffered cruelty and desertion, grounds for judicial separation under s. 10 (1) of the *HMA*. The learned judge held that even if the letter sent by the husband were to be construed as desertion (which was not the case, since it was a letter couched in terms of irony expressing his disappointment at their deserting *him* in his hour of need), the mode of living in 1956 constituted desertion. But, since the application was filed in 1957, the facts alleged in respect of the wife's leaving in 1956 could not support desertion lasting the requisite two-year period. The charges of cruelty were dismissed as merely 'normal incidents in conjugal life', or 'the ordinary wear and tear of married life'. The Judge said, 'I am not unmindful of the ever-broadening concept of cruelty, but I cannot persuade myself that the wife's allegations . . . can individually or collectively be regarded as legal cruelty.' We noticed that if the application for restitution had been rejected, the effect would have been to strengthen the hands of the parents of wives in cases where the usual manoeuvring which happens when families fall out had not actually developed into a genuine *personal* breach between the spouses themselves.

It must be borne in mind throughout that the father-in-law usually keeps on as good terms as are possible with his son-in-law, for the latter (as cat's paw for his family in many cases) can blackmail the former by threatening to maltreat his wife: and there comes a point where a father-in-law must be firm in his refusals. How delicately the two families handle this situation can be determined by whether they threaten litigation, or commence litigation for the lowest relevant form of relief, or rather go all out at once for divorce. The latter course would naturally be appropriate where, as is reported to have happened, the cruelty was not by the husband, but by his family, who imprisoned the girl and fed her on bread and water and beat her occasionally, in order to extort the remainder of what they apparently alleged was the promised 'dowry': *Shyamsundar* v.

Shantamani.[1] *Manglabai* v. *Deorao Gulabrao*[2] was a suit for divorce brought by the wife who claimed that her husband and his father beat her. It was alleged on her behalf that they attempted to persuade her to urge her mother to give her (the mother's) house to the husband, and she suffered ill-treatment in the course of this. The court held that these allegations were mere afterthoughts. By this stage every reader must have realized that whereas in matrimonial disputes as western countries know them the Judge obtains a sympathetic view of the case of one party, in India, though the tendency to sympathize with one spouse is evident, and indeed inherent in the nature of the proceedings, the evidence and pleadings would demand an investigation of the entire background to the dispute in its familial setting, out of which sympathy, if any, ought to emerge, not for one or other of the spouses, but for one or other of the families involved. And this inherent contradiction in matrimonial causes in India may seem to present a real danger for the hopes of the modern reforms as such.

To revert to s. 9 (2), it is now established that it is to be read subject to the words of the previous subsection, namely 'without reasonable excuse', and '...no legal ground why the application should not be granted', so that the scope of the respondent's defence is not more important than the virtue of the petitioner's case. Moreover, we must take into account the important provision of s. 23 (1) (*e*) of the same statute: 'In any proceeding under this Act, whether defended or not, if the court is satisfied that– . . . (*e*) there is no other legal ground why relief should not be granted, then and in such a case but not otherwise, the court shall decree such relief accordingly.'

The result of reading these provisions together is that restitution may be refused if the court is satisfied that the respondent's defences show that the 'withdrawal' was not without reasonable excuse, or that there is a legal ground why the application should not be granted, even though the behaviour, condition, or conduct complained of would not amount to a ground for substantive relief.

In *Mst. Gurdev Kaur* v. *Sarwan Singh*,[3] another Punjab case, the wife appealed against a decree for restitution which had been granted to her husband. The marriage took place some fifteen

[1] AIR 1962 Or. 50. [2] AIR 1962 M.P. 193. [3] AIR 1959 Punj. 162.

years before. Two and a half years prior to the filing of the petition the appellant lost the sight of one eye, which she attributed to one of the beatings she alleged she had suffered. She alleged that even in the presence of mediators (*panchayat*, as they are called in the judgement) her husband slapped her. Her mother applied to a magistrate for a search warrant under s. 100 of the Code of Criminal Procedure, 1898, on the ground that she was being kept under illegal confinement. When she was produced before the magistrate she alleged that her husband maltreated her and forced her to have intercourse with his own brother, and let other persons (unnamed) loose upon her. The magistrate consigned her to the care of her mother. In the trial court the issue framed was whether she had been treated with cruelty within the meaning of s. 10 (1) (*b*), so as to have a defence to her husband's application. The Judge held that such cruelty had *not* been established. The charges regarding the eye injury and the allegation regarding her husband's brother were found to have no substantial foundation. But the appellate judge, A. N. Grover, J., was impressed by the magistrate's issuing the warrant, and his action when the wife was produced before him. The mother's act corroborated the wife's contentions. This proved cruelty 'in the broader and general sense'. After reviewing the older English law on the subject similar with our s. 9 (2) the judge pointed out the need to read all the relevant provisions of our Act together, so that he was able to refuse the decree for restitution because he had found a reasonable excuse for the wife to leave her husband. 'The test', he said, 'as to what constitutes reasonable cause would vary with the circumstances of each case. It will have to be applied in the changed social conditions as they obtain today and not with the rigid background of the tenets of the old texts of Manu or other Hindu lawgivers.' And he referred to decisions under the Hindu Married Women's Right to Separate Residence and Maintenance Act, 1946, a statute now repealed, but replaced by the similar s. 18 of the *HAMA*.[1] His Lordship pertinently pointed out that if a wife were found entitled to separate residence and maintenance under that statutory provision, having a justifiable cause for living separate, that right 'cannot be defeated by the husband subsequently filing a suit for restitution under s. 9 of

[1] Derrett, *I.M.H.L.*, §§. 263–8.

the Hindu Marriage Act and by showing that the wife cannot establish any of the grounds covered by s. 10, 12 and 13 of the said Act'. These words were needed because of the practice, which is not less than thirty years old,[1] of filing such petitions with the sole motive of delaying execution decrees for maintenance. In *Sirigiri* v. *S. Rushingamma*[2] the suit filed by the husband for judicial separation or divorce was inspired by his anxiety to avoid paying his wife the maintenance to which she was entitled. The learned judge in our case seems to have held that the illegal confinement was *res judicata* and that this alone constituted a reasonable excuse for the wife to withdraw herself from her husband's society. But we are left with the apprehension that the actual circumstances of the matrimonial dispute were never before the court, and the suspicion that, as often happens, no effort was made to proceed beyond the pleadings and the evidence which, if it is a weakness, is one inherent in the adversary system which ex-British India (as contrasted with ex-French or ex-Portuguese India) has inherited.

The same approach to s. 9 (2) was taken in *Gurcharan Singh* v. *Smt. Waryam Kaur*[3] and also in *Smt. Putul Devi* v. *Gopi Mandal*,[4] where the Patna High Court wisely follows the Punjab. It was most unfortunate, perhaps unaccountable, that none of these cases was cited in *P. Annapurnamma* v. *Appa Rao*,[5] where the Andhra Pradesh High Court held, incorrectly, that mild leprosy in the husband was no defence to his petition for restitution because it was not within the defences contemplated literally in s. 9 (2). But the example was within the category of the old maxim, that 'hard cases make bad law'. The Allahabad High Court more recently, in *Jagdish Lal* v. *Smt. Shyama*,[6] refused to decree restitution where the husband could be shown to have been impotent from the marriage but not right up to the time of the suit, and where, therefore, the wife had no defence which would have entitled her to a decree for nullity, etc., on the ground that to construe subsection (2) of the section as a bar to

[1] *Mt. Kishan* v. *Mangal* AIR 1935 All. 927; *Venkatapathi* v. *Puttamma* AIR 1936 Mad. 609; *Ude* v. *Mt. Daulat* AIR 1935 Lah. 386. See p. 377 below.

[2] AIR 1963 A.P. 323.

[3] AIR 1960 Punj. 422.

[4] AIR 1963 Pat. 93.

[5] AIR 1963 A.P. 312, criticized at (1964) 66 Bom. L.R., *J.*, p. 137 ff.

[6] AIR 1966 All. 150, at p. 155.

the consideration by the court of any other save those referred to therein would render the other conditions laid down in sub-section (1) entirely nugatory. With respect, this must be taken as an accurate exposition of the law.

Each of these cases throws light upon the manner in which restitution is needed and used, and the contexts in which litigation of this sort commences. *Gurcharan Singh's case* is typical. The parties were married in 1954, they became estranged, and a son was born to them in 1957. Shortly afterwards the wife applied for maintenance under s. 488 of the Criminal Procedure Code, which enables a magistrate to order the maintenance of his spouse and minor children by a man liable to maintain them and neglecting to do so.[1] The day after the application was filed the husband sent a lawyer's letter asking his wife to come and live with him. Over three months later he filed the restitution petition, alleging an unreasonable withdrawal about three years earlier, but a final accrual of his cause of action when she finally refused to return home. She alleged that she had been ill-treated by her husband and his relatives, and that her father and 'respectable persons' had brought her away because of this cruelty. The petitioner, she said, had falsely accused her of adultery, and had taken no steps to bring her home, except for process before the *panchayat* which she claimed was not *bona fide*. His petition was simply a 'counterblast' to her maintenance proceedings (as would seem to be the case). The trial court held that the petitioner had been guilty of delay in bringing the petition; that he was guilty of desertion; that the petition was not *bona fide* since he did not really want his wife back and had

[1] 'If any person having sufficient means neglects or refuses to maintain his wife or his legitimate or illegitimate child unable to maintain itself, the District Magistrate . . . may . . . order such person to make a monthly allowance . . . not exceeding fifty rupees . . . and to pay the same to such person as the Magistrate from time to time directs . . .

'If any person so ordered wilfully neglects to comply with the order any such Magistrate may . . . issue a warrant for levying the amount . . . and may sentence such person . . . to imprisonment . . . provided that, if such person offers to maintain his wife on condition of her living with him, and she refuses to live with him, such Magistrate may consider any grounds of refusal stated by her, and may make an order under this section notwithstanding such offer, if he is satisfied that there is just ground for so doing . . .' The last provision is of course the ancestor of the practice of countering maintenance applications with suits for restitution.

never enquired about the birth of his son; moreover he doubted the paternity of the child, which imputed immorality to his wife. The petition was rejected. On appeal to the High Court (I. D. Dua, J.) the respondent succeeded again. Even up to December 1958 the respondent had not been paid anything by way of maintenance, though an order under s. 488 had been passed in her favour for Rs. 15 (15/-) a month. The High Court had then ordered payment of fixed sums in respect of her maintenance and towards the expenses of the proceedings. The order was not obeyed, and its execution was ultimately ordered when the wife prayed that the appeal should be dismissed for the appellant's contumacy. The appellant in any case absconded in order to avoid execution, his counsel at the Bar declaring ignorance of his client's whereabouts. The learned Judge adverts to the fact that the wife's allegations of physical cruelty were not convincingly proved, no medical evidence was called, and no satisfactory corroboration shown: moreover it is the law that isolated acts of assault do not necessarily amount to cruelty. But he adds, 'It is fully established on the record that, ever since the lady was taken away by her father, when she was in the family way, the husband has not cared either to send maintenance to her or even to take interest in his wife or even in the child; he did not keep in touch even with the birth of the child.' Consequently the husband was not entitled to his decree. His Lordship added remarks on the cruelty issue, which evidently would have gone against her on the footing of her allegations that her husband and his relations ill-treated her:

> . . . whether or not isolated acts of violence amount to cruelty normally depends on the facts and circumstances of each case and the modern tendency of the society is at least to treat with disapproval acts of violence or assault towards women. New rules of social behaviour and conduct must, therefore, be recognized by the courts in determining what would amount to cruelty in the present set-up, and I would be disinclined to dismiss lightly the so-called isolated acts of violence and assault as not amounting to cruelty, if the victims of such assaults resent and take exception to them.

In *Smt. Putul Devi* v. *Gopi Mandal*[1] the facts are somewhat obscure and must be disentangled from the judgement. The husband once again was the applicant for restitution, to which

[1] AIR 1963 Pat. 93.

the defence was cruelty. The origins of the quarrel between the husband and his brother and their wives' family are not disclosed: but it is evident that it had embraced both families. Two sisters were married to two brothers, and both returned, or were taken back, to their parents' home. In an effort to recover them, or to break the deadlock, the husbands launched a prosecution against their father-in-law under s. 498 of the Penal Code,[1] alleging that he had enticed his daughter away for immoral purposes and with the intention of giving her in marriage to some third party (unnamed). It appears that in the caste in question termination of marriage *de facto* and remarriage of divorced or separated women was at least open to contemplation. The allegation that the parents, after arranging one marriage, are scheming to arrange another is not so uncommon: it was made far away in Madras not long afterwards in a divorce case instituted by the husband, who accused his wife of multiple uncorroborated adulteries: the wife alleged that the suit was brought by the husband merely because the wife refused to agree to an arrangement which would have enabled this remarriage to take place, which the trial judge actually believed.[2] In the *Putul Devi* litigation the father was ultimately acquitted, and there being no other ground upon which the return of the wife to her husband could be legally objected to, it was alleged that her husband's launching of the prosecution was cruelty to her! How far she was personally involved in this struggle nowhere appears. The learned judge opined that it was impossible to order restitution: the father and his supporters won that round at the expense, at least for the time being, of the couple's chances of matrimonial happiness. His reasons were curious. Even though the prosecution proved to be unsuccessful, in that the father was acquitted, the nature and grounds of the prosecution were such as openly to disgrace the wife, imputing to her unfaithfulness to her husband in that her father was (with her consent?) arranging another marriage or profiting from her immorality. These suspicions and imputations, though fictitious and imaginary and purely for the purposes of harassment, would be (in his view) distressing to the wife, and so cruelty. In

[1] Enticing or taking away a married woman with intent that she may have illicit intercourse.

[2] *Bikram Singh* v. *Sudarsan Singh* AIR 1961 All. 150.

view of the attitude prevailing in India with regard to chastity and the importance of matrimonial relations no wife could be ordered home whose husband was prepared openly to suggest that someone else was relying upon her being unfaithful (irrespective of actual caste usages). Moreover, when she did return home she could expect bad treatment, having been a pawn in a game played by her husband's enemies: a lurking apprehension of her husband taking revenge upon her was to be expected (no evidence on this point had, however, been led). Consequently she had withdrawn with a reasonable excuse–a conclusion which by no means, it is submitted, follows from the facts so far as these are ascertainable.

Our remaining authorities on restitution, while they do not substantially add to the picture of an incompletely mastered technique of solving matrimonial disputes, illustrate graphically the Indian context of such litigation, and support the argument that recourse to the court can occur as an aspect of interfamilial bargaining as much as in a genuine attempt to heal matrimonial grievances, as these are understood in the West. *Teja Singh* v. *Sarjit Kaur*[1] is a further example of the type illustrated by *Gurcharan Singh* (above). The husband applied for restitution. The couple had been married some twelve years and they lived together as husband and wife for about three years. The latter left, according to her husband, of her own accord but she had subsequently obtained an order for maintenance under s. 488 of the Code of Criminal Procedure. The wife resisted the application on the ground that she had been ill-treated by her husband at the instance of his brother's wife. She alleged that he had beaten her, failed to comply with a request from her father and 'respectables of the village' that he should take her back, and had neglected her for more than six years, whereupon she had been compelled to have resort to s. 488. She contended (as usual) that his application was simply to avoid liability to pay the maintenance fixed by the court, which amounted to Rs. 30 (30/-) a month. The court ultimately decided that the husband had not written to his wife nor maintained her for six or seven years, and had thus neglected her. His witnesses were disbelieved. These alleged, amongst other suggestions which the trial court rejected, that the wife left home as a 'hot-headed young

[1] AIR 1962 Punj. 195.

woman' because she suspected that her husband was carrying on with his sister-in-law. It emerged that the husband *had* been living with his sister-in-law for the same period as that during which he had neglected his wife, and this hardly helped his case. In view of the unnecessary and improper delay in instituting the proceedings they were dismissed, for the applicant's intention was simply further to delay the payment of maintenance which the magistrate had ordered.

In *Tulsa* v. *Pannalal Natha Koli*[1] the husband-petitioner once again made accusations against his wife's family as well as against his wife. He made out that she requested him to escort her home, and then refused to return. He admitted that he used to beat her occasionally, and specified his grounds, namely (1) her getting up at 7 a.m. instead of 6, and (2) wearing clothes other than those he wanted her to wear. He complained that he had to go to recover her from her parents eight or nine times. The learned Judges, Shib Dayal and P. R. Sharma, JJ., considered whether, in view of the admitted beatings, she had withdrawn without 'reasonable excuse', as was argued. Whether or not the actual beatings amounted to cruelty, if she had a reasonable excuse she could resist the petition. The first-named judge spoke as follows:

> As a devoted wife it was no doubt Tulsa's duty to get up before her husband was to leave for his work, but if she did not, the husband was not entitled to beat her. Likewise, as the dutiful wife, she should have respected the wishes of her husband as to the particular clothes to be put on (on) a particular occasion. But if she did not, again, the husband had no right to beat her. The husband cannot be heard to retort that the wife should also bear his irritating idiosyncrasies when he beats her. Everyone has certain whims in his ways of life, but no husband has the right, irrespective of the community to which he belongs, to do physical violence to his wife. And if he does, she has every right to resent . . .

It was held that she had left with a reasonable excuse, that her husband had not made any attempt at reconciliation or amends, and that she was justified in living separately within the meaning of s. 18 (2) of the *HAMA*, and that the petition must be dismissed.

A case supporting our suspicions is *Smt. Mango* v. *Prem Chand*,[2] where the wife was evidently the victim of a plot hatched by her

[1] AIR 1963 M.P. 5.

[2] AIR 1962 All. 447.

father-in-law. The parties lived as husband and wife for a few days, after which the husband alleged that her uncle fetched her away and that her parents refused to allow her to return. She alleged that her husband was impotent, of weak intellect, and had (within the very few days available) treated her with cruelty and deserted her. She also alleged that her father-in-law intended to rape her. The trial judge disbelieved her and made the order for restitution. On appeal Mithan Lal, J., set aside the order. Both husband and wife were heard in open court in an attempt to effect a reconciliation. This seems to have been an ill-chosen device on the part of the husband's pleader, for the husband's true mental level was revealed. Though not actually an idiot, he lacked ordinary intellect. His evidence was shown to have been a fully tutored statement. But to his statement on deposition, 'My father teases me and my wife', which he followed by weeping, the court gave full credence. His father would not let him give food to his wife, and, according to his own explanation, kept him and his wife like dogs (which in an Asian environment does *not* mean like pets). He ultimately denied that he filed any suit against his wife (i.e. the petition was filed in his name by his father). The court was impressed by his account of how his statement had been tutored. It was found that (whether or not he was also impotent) the husband was under the thumb of his father and that the intentions of the father appeared 'not to be above board'. The husband was a mere tool of his father. He was not, said the judge, fit to keep a wife. The cruelty of the *father-in-law* was held to have been proved, also that the husband wanted the wife to be 'available to others'. A further example of a restitution case in which the defence was cruelty not of the husband himself but of his parents (a defence which was not believed) is *Tayawwa* v. *Chinnappa*,[1] where, as is frequent in India, refuge was taken in procedural technicalities when an acceptable judgement could not be obtained on the merits.[2]

[1] AIR 1962 Mys. 130.

[2] The guilty, but neglected wife's pleadings in *V. Varadarajulu* v. *Baby Ammal* AIR 1965 Mad. 29 are interesting though the learned judge (wrongly?) believed them. She alleged that her husband was of weak intellect; his parents wanted him to marry someone else; his father tried to get her consent to this and on her refusal brought this action based on allegations of successive adulteries.

But the shoe may well be on the other foot. Perhaps one of the more curious of the recent cases is *Smt. Sau. Shakuntalabai* v. *Baburao Daduji.*[1] There the husband-petitioner was working at the time of the litigation in Bombay as a mechanic, while his young wife was staying at Indore in the house of her aunt, who was attached to her and acted *in loco parentis* to her. She appeared to declare that the matrimonial home was established by the couple at her aunt's house, and that he refused to come and live there with her. He alleged that he had repeatedly urged her to come and live with him in Bombay, but she had refused and the court (Newaskar and Krishnan, JJ.) believed him. The wife's case was obviously a tissue of lies. In fact the husband, whose earning capacity would always be low, was married to his wife at the instigation of the aunts of the couple, each of whom belonged to a well-to-do family, and at the time of the marriage lived on good terms with each other. The wife's aunt intended to endow the wife, who came to live with her after the two aunts had fallen out and it was impossible for the couple to reside with the husband's aunt. The wife's aunt disapproved of the wife receiving money from any hands but her own, and so the husband was forced to send remittances and presents to her through friends, behind the aunt's back. In due course the husband thought of approaching the wife's aunt for money to invest in a 'machinery establishment'. But by this time the aunt had formed the impression that he was a good-for-nothing, and refused to help. While in Bombay he got into some trouble, to get out of which he had to fall into debt to the aunt, and at the trial the aunt's lawyer produced this as evidence of his 'depravity' in a manner, as the Court says, 'that is nothing short of nauseating'. After the husband insisted on his wife and children coming to Bombay, and the aunt and his wife under the aunt's influence had refused, the husband took away the baby in arms to his own aunt's house, hoping to force the wife to follow. The learned judge says, 'The younger child was a problem, and after waiting for a few hours, the husband sent it back to the obviously triumphant satisfaction of the wife and (her) aunt. It is this anecdote which has been described as an act of hard-hearted cruelty (on the husband's part).' The allegations against the husband included gross brutality in that his

[1] AIR 1963 M.P. 10.

pregnant wife was supposed to have been pushed, dragged, or thrown down stairs. A comical feature of the three versions of the story put forward in evidence is that the picture painted by the aunt, which is itself a shade worse than that given by the wife, is shown in much darker hue by the aunt's woman servant. The whole incident was a figment of the women's imagination. The court held that it was fantastic to suggest that the couple had a matrimonial home in Indore, and rejected the wife's appeal against the decree of restitution given by the lower court. His Lordship said,

> In the social conditions that prevail in India, the oppressor is quite often the husband; but that is not invariably so. The present case is one where an overbearing aunt and her protégé, the wife, are the oppressors and the husband, a poor but obviously self-respecting mechanic, is the victim.

The remaining cases in restitution are either of a purely technical interest or throw little additional light on our problem. A typically Indian defence to a petition for restitution is the allegation that the husband had married again. In *Mst. Deepo* v. *Kehar Singh*[1] the wife's defence included the allegations that she had been beaten and turned out, and that she had filed an application for maintenance to which the present petition was a counterblast, and finally that she was after all the second wife, as the petitioner had already one wife living with him. The trial judge granted the decree. The wife appealed. For the husband it was argued that the wife had known full well that he was already married when she married him (prior to the coming into force of the *HMA*), and that she could not use this as a defence to the petition now. The court held that, whether or not she could actually obtain a divorce on this ground (see s. 13 (2) (*i*) of the Act), the ground itself, which was present, was within the contemplation in any event of s. 9 (2), which we have already discussed. Consequently restitution would be refused. One may compare the case of *A. Annamalai Mudaliar* (above), in which the wife petitioned for separate maintenance on the ground that the husband had another wife living with him. The court show that they were satisfied that if the husband chose to abandon the other wife he could still obtain a decree for restitu-

[1] AIR 1962 Punj. 183.

tion against this wife, because a lawfully twice-married man may have an option with which he shall live and the court will effectuate this. There is no conflict between these cases from different parts of India.

We may now proceed to see whether a similar pattern emerges from cases founded on other provisions of the *HMA*: if we are right in our contention it should be exemplified from any chapter of the new law.

Judicial Separation

It will not be necessary to detail the facts in cases of judicial separation to the same length. We are interested in a tendency and that is soon detected.

The provisions of the Act of 1955 are as follows:

> s. 10 (1) Either party to a marriage, whether solemnized before or after the commencement of this Act, may present a petition to the district court praying for a decree for judicial separation on the ground that the other party–
>
> (*a*) has deserted the petitioner . . .
>
> (*b*) has treated the petitioner with such cruelty . . .
>
> (*c*) has, for a period of not less than one year . . . been suffering from a virulent form of leprosy . . .
>
> (*d*) has . . . been suffering from venereal disease . . .
>
> (*e*) has been continuously of unsound mind for . . . two years . . .
>
> (*f*) has, after the solemnization of the marriage, had sexual intercourse with any person other than his or her spouse . . .
>
> (2) Where a decree for judicial separation has been passed, it shall no longer be obligatory for the petitioner to cohabit with the respondent, but the court may . . . rescind the decree . . .

It is of practical importance to note that a petition for divorce can give rise to relief by way of judicial separation if the grounds admit of the latter but not of the former, even if judicial separation is not in terms petitioned for.[1]

In *Mst. Mato* v. *Sadhu*[2] the wife petitioned on the grounds of desertion, cruelty and adultery, alleging that she had to leave her husband's home because of his persistent refusal of intercourse and that she had been leading a life of promiscuous adultery (with unnamed men) as a result of his conduct. The

[1] *Bhagwan Singh* v. *Amar Kaur* AIR 1962 Punj. 144.

[2] AIR 1961 Punj. 152.

court (Shamsher Bahadur, J.) pointed out that matrimonial relief can normally be given to a petitioner who comes to the court with clean hands, a rule established in India since 1923 at the latest. Her allegations, moreover, conflicted with her case that she was deserted. Another court might have taken another view of the effect of a persistent refusal of intercourse, but an Indian court could naturally draw the proper inference from her admitted life of adultery, that she had not been deserted by her husband, but *vice versa*. The crux of the case, in which the wife accused her husband of adultery with his own sister-in-law, appears in the learned judge's penultimate paragraph:

> (The petitioner's father) has exposed the case of the petitioner in its stark reality. He stated that the marriage of his daughter Mato to Sadhu was performed as a part of an exchange transaction; his own son was married to the cousin of Sadhu. (This son) having died, his wife left the house and accordingly (the father) brought back his own daughter from the house of Sadhu. In face of this statement it is difficult to sustain either desertion or cruelty as set up by the petitioner.

Of course, the pleadings were drawn up by the petitioner's father's pleader, and the woman herself had little initiative in the affair.

Pleadings are not always inept. Bombay, which has had somewhat longer experience of 'separation' than other parts of the country, provides an example of acumen. In *Shantaram* v. *Hirabai*[1] the *husband* commenced proceedings for judicial separation, alleging cruelty and desertion. In fact he was refusing, in what the court called a 'blameworthy fashion', to support his wife, his children, and even his aged mother. As soon as the wife entered her defence, the husband asked permission to withdraw his petition. He seems to have done this in order to avoid liability for maintenance, which could be contended for if a *decree* were actually granted under the Act.[2] He likewise seems to have hoped that *res judicata* would operate to hinder the wife's own efforts to obtain maintenance (no doubt wrongly). The ruse seems to have succeeded; the wife could not even pay for counsel, who appeared and then left the court before argument.

[1] AIR 1962 Bom. 27.

[2] *HMA*, s. 25 (1): 'at the time of passing any decree or at any time subsequent thereto . . .'

A genuine petition for separation by a husband is considered in *Sm. Kako* v. *Ajit*[1] where the wife's desertion of her husband not long after their marriage had been consummated was proved. As usual, she alleged that he beat her; but the true reason for her leaving the home may lie in the fact that she was about twelve years older than her husband.

The case of *Mst. Bhagwanti* v. *Sadhu Ram*[2] is another window onto the Indian scene. The appellate court ultimately rejected the husband's petition for judicial separation against his wife in the following circumstances. The husband had two wives and in 1950 fell out with one, to whom he had been married fifteen years. In 1950 and 1953 this wife's claims for maintenance under s. 488 C.P.C. were compromised, on the latter occasion one-third of his land and one room in his house (only) being given to her. In 1957 he petitioned for divorce or judicial separation on the grounds of adultery and desertion. He said that he was unable to trace the adulterer. As an afterthought he added in evidence the name of a person from whom his wife, now driven to carry on a milk-trade, rented an apartment. The wife herself was no chicken; the alleged adulterer had about nine children and a number of grandchildren. The trial court somehow found the wife to have been in desertion, since it was she that started to live separately (!). In support of the allegations the husband's counsel urged that she was actually a prostitute. The apartment however was no more than sixty feet from the husband's house, and her brother's schoolgirl daughters had been staying with her while this immorality was supposed to have been going on. The Judge (I. D. Dua, J.) concluded that the real (or perhaps sole) object of the petition was to enable the husband to avoid complying with the later of the two compromises (possibly at the instigation of the first wife?).

A straightforward case of cruelty to the wife appears in *Smt. Kaushalya* v. *Wisakhi Ram*,[3] where the husband's defence lay partly in denials, partly in the petitioner's not having taken her alleged injuries to the doctor, and partly in the usual claims of her having deserted him, whereupon he had filed the usual restitution petition (to forestall an action for maintenance). The details of the cruelty would astound a non-Indian, but the main

[1] AIR 1960 Punj. 328.
[2] AIR 1961 Punj. 181.
[3] AIR 1961 Punj. 521.

interest in the case lies in a part of the judgement (of I. D. Dua, J.):

> Women in such circumstances as those of the appellant in our society normally submit themselves to their husbands, and unless a climax is reached, they usually do not take the desperate step of going to a police station to lodge a report; the poor financial condition of such women and lack of proper understanding on their part would also stand in their way of securing a proper medical certificate . . . Besides even if the injuries on the person of Smt. Kaushalya are considered not to be so serious as to call for their treatment by a medical practitioner, if she has actually been ill-treated as deposed by her, that treatment must be held to amount to cruelty according to the standards of all civilized societies . . . the approach of the court below appears to me to be inconsistent with the public policy clearly discernible in the recent legislative measures whereby attempts have been made to raise the social status of women in this Republic. New rules of social behaviour and conduct in respect of the status of women in the Indian society of today must, in my view, be recognized and kept in the forefront while determining what would really amount to cruelty under the Hindu Marriage Act.

In contrast to the lower court's indifference to that wife's sufferings we find an equally genuine (and, one would think, expected) Indian reaction in *Smt. Kamla* v. *Amar Nath.*[1] Whether or not it is the law that a false accusation of unchastity must be cruelty to the wife, as here stated, as opined in a case between Muslims under the Dissolution of Muslim Marriages Act, 1939, and as confirmed in *Kusum* v. *Kamta Prasad*,[2] in *Kamla's case* it was held that of all the allegations (sale of ornaments, beating, drunkenness, etc.) the crucial one was that he had commenced a criminal proceeding under s. 498 of the Penal Code (see p. 379 above). The wife deposed that the false suggestions against her chastity greatly shocked her and had affected her reputation. The learned Chief Justice (J. N. Wazir) said:

> False accusations of unchastity made by the husband may cause the wife great mental suffering which may be much severer than bodily pain caused by some beating. Such accusations certainly would amount to cruelty in the eye of law. In *Sm. Pancho* v. *Ram Prasad*, AIR 1956 All. 41, it has been held that a husband prone to make adverse statements against the chasity of (his) wife *to meet the exigencies of the situation* (emphasis added), cannot be said to be a husband who has taken a kindly attitude towards the wife. (The) conception of legal cruelty undergoes changes according to the changes and advancement of social concept(s) and standards of living.

[1] AIR 1961 J. & K. 33.

[2] AIR 1965 All. 280.

It comes as a shock to some husbands' pleaders to realize that the genuine Indian horror of imputations of unchastity may overcome in practice the equally genuine Indian habit of using all practicable legal means (whatever their nature) to achieve a particular object.[1] In one case in which the husband had used various allegations against his wife the court actually complimented him on not having accused her of adultery (*Narayan* v. *Smt. Prabhadevi*),[2] a mark of restraint which entitled him to the sympathy of the court.

Consistently with the general outlook, if a wife's suit for separation is progressing well, it is usual for the husband's pleader to introduce an offer by the husband to take her back, and the same ruse is adopted even at the inevitable appeal stage, in the hope that the amount of maintenance will thereby be reduced. Courts are alive to this manner of proceeding.

Our final example of separation cases is valuable, not so much because of the glimpse it gives of the quaint situations which can develop in India, but because it is a splendid example of the preference for judicial separation over divorce. In *Sayal* v. *Smt. Sarla*[3] the spouses had married in 1948 and had two children. They fell out and in 1951 the wife administered a poison prescribed by some *yogi* as a love-potion. The husband developed various symptoms terminating in a complete breakdown of his health. The wife, greatly troubled, confessed. They had lived apart since 1953. The husband alleged that he had a reasonable apprehension that she might do the same sort of thing again! It was argued for the wife that the husband had cohabited with her for about three years after the poison had been administered, but this was (properly) rejected on the ground that during that period he had not become aware of the full effects of her 'treatment'. That he did not want a divorce is probably *not* to be attributed to vindictiveness on his part.

Nullity

The provisions of the Act of 1955 relative to nullity of marriage are lengthy, and it is not requisite to set them out here *in*

[1] In *P. Venkatramayya* v. *P. Mahalakshmamma* [1966] 1 An.W.R. 346 it was observed that such allegations are not *per se* cruelty.

[2] AIR 1964 M.P. 28.

[3] AIR 1961 Punj. 125.

extenso. There are two types of proceeding, one to obtain a declaration that an allegedly void marriage is null and void, and one to obtain the annulling of a voidable marriage. Within that former come the grounds of previous marriage, prohibited relationship or prohibited kinship (sapiṇḍaship); within the latter some (see s. 12) impotence, idiocy or lunacy at the time of the marriage, consent or consent of the guardian as the case may be, obtained by force or fraud, and, subject to special limitations, the wife's pregnancy by another at the time of the marriage.

The advantages of petitioning for nullity are that a marriage can be brought speedily to an end, and the wife's alimony (*dum casta*: see s. 25 (3)) is likely to commence at a low rate, and must cease altogether when a further match (if possible) is arranged for her. Nullity, as contrasted with divorce, enables the dynastic bargainings to be scrapped and started afresh, though it must be recognized that the parents of a girl whose marriage has been annulled will not be in as strong a position to bargain as they were when they made the first match for her. But note that nullity involves the returning of all the gifts or consideration that may have passed (though some litigants may not know this), since the marriage has failed altogether. And moreover, nullity for impotence has the great advantage to the Indian mind of removing the chief obstacle to a woman's re-betrothal, namely her having been 'enjoyed' (as the phrase goes) before.

There are instances where nullity may be granted on the ground of impotence a very long time after the marriage. In *A.* v. *B.*[1] the husband gave the wife large presents. She waited until there could be no chance that her action would prejudice the marriages of her brothers' and sisters' daughters and then filed her petition. The court condoned her delay 'because of Indian conditions'.

Not that the usefulness of nullity was as widely appreciated formerly as it might now be. In *Lalithamma* v. *Kannan*[2] the husband, who wanted to live and work in Madras State, failed to obtain intercourse with his wife and after some time left her in the care of her father who had wanted the couple to live with him in Mysore, and not long afterwards in 1948 married a second wife. When the first wife sued for divorce and alimony

[1] AIR 1967 Punj. 152.

[2] See above, p. 366, n. 1.

the husband, who had done nothing to improve his marriage with her but had equally not sought nullity, sought to prove that she had refused intercourse because of hysteria, drug-taking and disease. The court held that the wife 'was a victim of what may well be described as excessive pride and self-opinionated conduct of her father and her husband'. She therefore remained a married woman (unable to lead a normal life) with an empty right to maintenance out of her husband's earnings until she took the step of suing for divorce on the ground of his second marriage. Nullity at an early stage would have freed her for a normal life. But this did not suit the husband while, with less cost, he could exercise his then right of marrying again.

All these points give grounds for anxiety. It is not uncommon for spouses to hate each other at sight, a difficulty overcome for the time being on a physical basis, later smoothened out under the influence of the traditional obligation upon a wife to adjust herself to her husband and his family. If there is the slightest ground for the wife to suspect that her husband is impotent, even though shyness or repugnance might be a sufficient explanation for his not being able to consummate the marriage within a few days, she can fasten upon this, and actually prevent success thereafter. A rush to court three days or so after the marriage would make little sense against a non-Indian background, but may be intelligible (though hardly excusable) under Indian conditions. Since marriage is often a means whereby the bridegroom finances his schemes and even his entire career, the bride's family regard themselves as entitled to a *quid pro quo*. Formerly settlement-day could be postponed by various shifts, but now, if the bridegroom shows signs of refusing to sign the undertakings or otherwise carry out his part of the bargain, the bride's parents can hang a nullity petition round his neck, and nullity for impotence fits all the requirements. Further, spouses who feel that their marriage is an insult to both, since each is in love (actually or in imagination) with someone else, may agree that 'impotence' gives the way out. All that is essential is that the bride shall not be pregnant, though, as we shall see, even that does not render their scheme utterly impracticable. The law leaves a loop-hole, extremely rarely used in England yet apparently fascinating to the Indian legal public. The rule concerning a man who is normal physically, but unable to consummate marriage with a particular girl, a case of impotence *quoad hanc*, casts no slurs in effect upon either spouse. One of such pleas had a strongly collusive air about it, so that it was delayed for several years by judicial doubts,[1] but in *Jagdish* v. *Smt. Shyama*[2] the wife-petitioner was certified by her doctor to be still a virgin, while the husband's doctor certified that he was potent. The conflict of evidence was complete but the *quoad hanc* doctrine showed the way out. The learned Judge said both witnesses were to be believed, for though the husband might be as potent as the next man he was impotent as far as his wife was concerned, and so the decree was pronounced. Unless some way can be found to control this the remedy can get out of hand. *Jagdish Kumar* v. *Smt. Sita*[3] shows how Indian unfamiliarity with the procedure, indelicacy and downright lack of good feeling may make a tragedy out of a couple's initial discomforts. A genuine case of impotence with sad social overtones appears in *Venkateswararao* v. *Nagamani*.[4]

The peculiar purposes for which nullity petitions on the ground of impotence can be used are illustrated perfectly by *M.* v. *S.*[5] A wife is not impotent where the aperture, though tight, can be eased by operation. The husband, without accepting the reports on the success of the operation performed on his wife, persisted in urging that she was impotent and that the marriage was a proper one to be annulled. The court was satisfied that after the operation the wife was not incapable of intercourse, and that the husband had not been willing to consummate the marriage after the operation–this did not help his petition. The wife alleged that the petition had been filed on account of her husband's avaricious nature. He insisted on getting more jewellery and other articles from her family than were given him at the time of the marriage. The court found

[1] *Arun* v. *Sudhanshu* AIR 1962 Or. 65 S.B. The decree of nullity was confirmed when suspicions of collusion were removed: *Arun* v. *Sudhanshu* AIR 1966 Or. 224 S.B.

[2] AIR 1966 All. 150.

[3] AIR 1963 Punj. 114. In *Khageswar* v. *Aduti* AIR 1967 Or. 80 the husband was examined in the presence of counsel for both sides (!) but the doctor was not even called as a witness.

[4] AIR 1962 A.P. 151. The bridegroom said that he was afraid to visit his parents-in-law's home in case his father-in-law gave him a beating.

[5] [1963] K.L.T. 315.

that her allegation was true. In dismissing the petition the court thus prevented one of the husband's schemes for extorting money from his 'in-laws'–the whole affair had no bearing on the personal relationship between the spouses.

An alternative method of avoiding a marriage is to claim that the parties did not consent, or that their apparent consent was no real consent since it was obtained by force or fraud, whether of them or of their guardians. If this approach works it allows a marriage to be broken up, though there are no grounds for divorce or separation, some time after it is consummated. Unfortunately the law is in chaos, with the result that there must be many infructuous suits. There is substantial doubt about the need for and role of consent in Hindu marriages (consent is required by law only under the Special Marriage Act) though obtaining consent by fraud is a ground for nullity under s. 12 (1) (*c*) of the *HMA*, and a criminal offence; and in view of the 'modernization' of Hindu matrimonial law there is every fear that law developed in connexion with Indian Christian marriages and 'special marriages' under the Act of 1954 and its predecessor will percolate into the Hindu law. The extraordinary case of *Shireen* v. *Taylor*,[1] strange in its law rather than its facts, shows that in India where a spouse had no intention to marry as contrasted with going through the marriage ceremony and cohabiting, the marriage may be annulled on that ground alone, proof of his intention being obtainable from his deserting the other party shortly after the wedding and making no attempt to maintain her as his wife. If this rule were exploited by Hindu couples any husband who developed 'cold feet' (as often happens) and stays away long enough can claim that he never intended to marry the girl, who was his father's choice, etc., and nullity could hardly be refused even though intercourse had taken place, which would be a tragedy indeed under prevailing Hindu social conditions. Attempts to avoid marriages on the grounds that the spouses were too young, or that their guardians in marriage were too young, have been made, but have so far failed: minority alone cannot affect the consent or capacity to act as guardian for this purpose (the relevant maxim being *factum valet*): *Mt. Kalawati* v. *Devi Ram.*[2]

[1] AIR 1952 Punj. 277.

[2] AIR 1961 H.P. 1, followed in *Smt. Naumi* v. *Narotam* AIR 1963 H.P. 15.

The special instance of fraud offered as a ground for nullity in s. 12 (1) (*d*), that the respondent was pregnant by some person other than the petitioner, deserves treatment before the cases on fraud or force, because of its apparent encouragement to spouses to break up their marriage even if intercourse has taken place and a child is to be born. Since conception may occur immediately after the marriage, and the child will be born before the conclusion of the statutory period of limitation for such actions, fantastic suspicions and collusive agreements have equally good scope. In *P. S. Sivaguru* v. *Saroja*[1] it was held that the husband must affirmatively prove that the child was not his, as well as the other conditions laid down by the statute, namely that he was ignorant of the facts alleged, etc. An apparently genuine resort to the statute was unsuccessful, because of a procedural defect, in *Savlaram* v. *Yeshodabai*,[2] but because the judgement concentrates upon that defect we cannot judge whether the husband might not in fact have been the father of the child which his wife had been carrying for three months when he married her.

A decision which is probably not legally correct attempts to establish the position that fraud concerning the bridegroom's caste and social status will serve to annul the marriage. The circumstances very plainly show that the grievance developed long after the marriage, as there are unexplained delays in presenting the petition and traces of family intrigues are plain even from the facts recited in the judgement. In *Bimla* v. *Shankerlal*[3] the father of the bridegroom concealed the fact that the latter was not a legitimate son of the same caste with himself, and this concealment was aggravated by the representations continued at the very ceremony itself. The court held that the consent of the bride herself and her guardians was vitiated by this concealment. Frauds of such a character are particularly likely in India, especially when betrothals are effected by mail and as a result of newspaper advertisements followed up by an exchange of photographs. An attempt to avoid a marriage on the ground of fraudulent concealment of tuberculosis failed (perhaps fortunately for Indian law?) in *Anath* v. *Sm. Lajjabati*,[4]

[1] AIR 1960 Mad. 216.
[2] AIR 1962 Bom. 190.
[3] AIR 1959 M.P. 8 discussed and criticized at (1959) 61 Bom. L.R., *J.*, p. 82–7.
[4] AIR 1959 Cal. 778.

where it was held that consent at the time of the marriage was the material consent, and that concealments practised up to the time of the ceremony were not significant, a ruling which is not perhaps entirely beyond criticism. Authoritative constructions of the Indian Divorce Act showed that concealment of a disease was not the type of fraud which would go to the root of consent to marry. But we may wonder rather what circumstances could lead to such a petition for nullity (the once-tubercular girl had recovered by the time of her marriage, and appears not to have been a menace, or an expense, to anyone). Perhaps the most curious feature of nullity law in India is that petitions on the ground of force are almost unheard of. That spouses are sometimes overawed into marriages, even led through the ceremony and deprived for the purpose of any independent volition, is notorious. Only in *B. Ankamma* v. *B. Bamanappa*[1] was it held that the bridegroom's hands were forced. But it can be assumed to be good law that even in that case had they slept together after the ceremony the decree could not have been granted.

Two recent cases illustrate the way in which the jurisdiction of the court comes to be invoked, and recall a vague echo of the old conceptions of the *saṃskāra* and what might be a fraud upon it–a consideration conspicuously absent from our discussions so far. In *Harbhajan* v. *Smt. Brij Balab*[2] it was said that marriage is still a sacrament and cannot be avoided for fraud as defined under the Contract Act. The sanctity of marriage would be imperilled by such a view. Here there was a representation that the bride was a virgin and of good conduct, her family concealing the fact that she had given birth to a child prior to the marriage–or so it seemed on the pleadings and the evidence. But the case was suspect. The wife in her defence to the petition for nullity took the line that the case against her was fabricated, because her husband and his father were greedy, trying to extort money by this means from her father. Their demands

[1] AIR 1937 Mad. 332.

[2] AIR 1964 Punj. 359. This case was referred to in *Surjit Kumar* v. *Raj Kumari* AIR 1967 Punj. 172, where English authorities were followed (wrongly?) to the effect that it is not 'fraud' as understood in the law of nullity when the relations of the girl who has been unchaste observe that she is 'good' to the bridegroom who then fails to make independent enquiries.

were unreasonable and they harassed her and she and her father resisted this harassment, whence the petition, which indeed was filed a year exactly after the alleged 'fraud' was discovered. The District Judge thought her admission of an illegitimate birth was forged and that the husband was forced into this unpleasant position by his parents. The happy couple had been victimized by the parents. The District Judge dismissed the petition. On appeal by the husband the High Court (P. C. Pandit, J.) held that even if the facts did support fraud, a marriage could not be annulled merely because of representations relating to past conduct.

In *Kunta* v. *Siri Ram*[1] the girl, according to the boy, was pregnant by him and lived with her mother and brothers. The boy abducted her and had a marriage ceremony performed with doubtful rituals by suspect persons in the absence of relations. The boy petitioned for restitution, and the girl countered with a petition for nullity on the ground of force and fraud. She claimed that her pregnancy was due to someone else and that she had been abducted and forced to undergo a mock marriage ceremony. The court censured the authorities who had lent themselves to the ceremony, and had no difficulty in annulling the so-called marriage, since no voluntary intercourse had taken place between the parties which might have neutralized the effect of early coercive and fraudulent acts. The suggestion that the ceremony constituted a sacrament was not given the slightest attention, in view of the whole proceeding having been bogus.

Conclusion

The potentialities of nullity, separation and restitution suits give at least one observer ground for wondering whether the *HMA* has actually done for the classes ready for reform what they expected would be achieved by it. It may be urged that in the case of restitution the uses to which the procedure was put were already known and there was no novelty, no upheaval: but it can equally well be urged that this put Parliament on enquiry, whether the remainder of the Bill, so far as it offered matrimonial relief, was well-conceived. Humanitarian motives,

[1] AIR 1963 Punj. 235.

widespread as they undoubtedly are, are all very well (see Tek Chand, J.'s, remarks in *Munishwar* v. *Smt. Indra*[1] about the State's paramount interest in preserving the integrity of marriage as an institution) but have the new opportunities for litigation achieved or furthered predominantly *humanitarian* ends?

This is a risk which is involved in the determination to use law as a means of social change. The present writer would not urge that law should not be so used, but rather that the urge to copy western models can indirectly work in a fashion not contemplated by the reformers. The answer would seem to be an investigation into the way in which litigation as such is used to solve family problems: an investigation on a broad front might have suggested in this instance that there is something to be said for the method now introduced into Pakistan, under which matrimonial problems are ventilated in the first instance before local committees which need not investigate judicially and which are not bound by any strict rules of evidence.[2] But that particular expedient has yet to be tried in the fire of experience.

Meanwhile, undoubtedly, the conflict between the New India and the Old makes any such decision very difficult. The new matrimonial régime fits the needs of the New India. It is assumed that the Old India will eventually catch up, and accommodate itself to the legal machinery: an odd notion, but not altogether unnatural. Meanwhile the clash goes deep into the foundations of the administration of the new law. The case of *Lachman* v. *Meena*[3] illustrates this perfectly. After a very lengthy litigation the problem was aired in the Supreme Court on appeal from the Bombay High Court. The majority of the

[1] AIR 1963 Punj. 449, 456. The theory of the indissolubility of marriage which properly belongs to the *saṃskāra* tradition on the subject was uncompromisingly asserted in relation to marriages solemnized under the Special Marriage Act (which contemplates primarily civil marriages, possibly between persons of different faiths, including Muslims, for whom marriage is not basically a religious, but a contractual, institution) in *M. P. Shreevastava* v. *Mrs. Veena* AIR 1965 Punj. 54. There I. D. Dua, J., spoke of the social duty of spouses to discipline into compatibility their differences of temperament. They must not exaggerate or let loose their passions, frivolous dislikes and abnormal impulses.

[2] Muslim Family Laws Ordinance, 1961. See below, p. 533.

[3] AIR 1964 S.C. 40.

judges believed that the wife had deserted her husband without just cause, and that the husband was not in the wrong in not perpetually exhorting his wife to return home to him. The formal requirements of the English law were applied to the pathetic Indian facts, and the husband was awarded his decree of judicial separation when he had in fact been living separate from his wife for several years and had no desire to live with her again. This was to be the first step towards his divorce from her. The minority of the Supreme Court, Subba Rao, J., who began, in several Supreme Court cases, to take a novel view of the Hindu law, had quite another conception of the problem. To him the behaviour of the wife was a flight from the tyranny of her parents-in-law, with whom her husband eventually sided in the foolish, weak, compliant attitude well known amongst husbands who live with their parents under the old joint-family system. The irrational hostility of the mother-in-law and sisters-in-law, founded in many cases (as in this one) on the 'modern' ways of the more cosmopolitan family from which the bride had come, led, as it so often leads, to hardship. Thus when the husband fails to protect his wife against his own relations the wife is justified, says Subba Rao, J., in running to her own folk for protection. Thus she did not desert her husband (because she had reasonable cause for absenting herself), and the husband's petition should have been rejected. Moreover, the husband's attitude in commencing the proceedings only went to show that, under his parents' influence, he really desired to terminate the marriage and was in a sense a party to his wife's absence from the matrimonial home.

Thus the majority of the Supreme Court view the facts of the familiar Indian situation as if they were the facts of an English family, so that facts and law appeared to be of a kind, suitable to be fitted to each other. The dissenting judge, on the other hand, saw the Old India at work and believed that the facts of Old India could be read along with the law of the New India. Time will tell which approach will gain favour.[1] In the mean-

[1] Facts of 'Old' India are certainly capable of being read with the Anglo-Indian law and the current Indian legal scene. See *Trilochan Singh* v. *Director, Small Industries Service Institute, Madras* AIR 1963 Mad. 68 (the student who wrote two love letters was guilty of a criminal trespass), and *Zafar Ahmad* v. *State* AIR 1963 All. 105, where a boy of sixteen doing a little

while the question remains whether the habits of Indian families will alter to take account of the new matrimonial reliefs and matrimonial practice. One may be forgiven for doubting whether there is strong ground for expecting that they will, at any rate in the near future.[1]

'Eve-teasing' (as it is called) was held guilty of an 'obscene act' (s. 294 of the Penal Code) and sent down for three months' rigorous imprisonment. In other words Indian judges are quite capable of construing statutes which do not primarily or explicitly cater for an Asian environment as if they did so cater.

[1] Since this chapter was written Miss P. K. Virdi in a detailed and perceptive study ('The grounds for divorce in Hindu and English law: a comparative study', Thesis, Ph.D., London [unpublished], 1966) showed that terms of art belonging to English matrimonial causes are bound to be applied literally, but with different and at times the opposite effect, in India. Chief Justice Anantanārāyanan, meanwhile, in *Subbarama Reddiar* v. *Saraswathi* [1966] 2 M.L.J. 263 (cited above), at p. 266, warns us that English cases are very useful as a resort for basic principles, but they should not be used further: '. . . there is no sphere in which it is more unsafe to draw generalizations from the facts of judicial precedents in quite different countries such as India and England, than the sphere of social relationships and morals . . .' For doubts about the correctness of relying on English precedents in Indian 'fraud' cases see p. 395, n. 2 above.

12

A HISTORY OF THE JURIDICAL FRAMEWORK OF THE JOINT HINDU FAMILY

While the law of marriage[1] has suffered both the nominal and actual amendments which we have observed, the law of the joint-family, the core of the Hindu personal law and its most difficult–to newcomers its least comprehensible–part remains (despite pleas from lawyers) uncodified. It is more than unlikely that this is out of deference to religion. True, as we shall see, the śāstric juridical scaffolding of the joint-family remains (as it was in Medhātithi's time)[2] the theory of subordination of property to rituals, many of which were intended for the supersensory benefit of the living family and the deceased ancestors. But there is less evidence in life than in the books to support the reality of these important theories, and it is improbable that they have placed a *conscious* brake upon the legislatures, a brake which could not be applied in the realm of the root of the family, marriage.

In the detailed account which appears below there is evidence of seeming neglect for traditional, including religious values–but if one looks closely one sees that the changes tend to keep the institution in being rather than to demolish it.

[1] This chapter corresponds closely to an article with a similar title which appeared at *Contributions to Indian Sociology*, No. 6 (1962), pp. 17–47. Certain ideas expressed there had already appeared in *The Economic Weekly* (Bombay), February 13th, 1960. For an informed Hindu view see B. N. Sampath, 'The joint Hindu family: retrospect and prospect', *Banaras Law J.* I, 1 (1965), pp. 33–77.

[2] A boy takes the householder's estate when he has learnt the Veda (for his livelihood?) and received his share of the ancestral property from his father. If he has not obtained a fire (for sacrifices) at his marriage he takes his 'share' of the ancestral fire: Medh. on Manu III, 3, 122, 212.

In the study of the joint-family and its rôle in determining the development of personality and character and its function in contemporary Indian society, the fundamental texts of traditional Indian jurisprudence have played practically no part; the popular notions of what happened when the *śāstra* merged or dissolved into its contemporary representative, Anglo-Hindu law, have on the whole been accepted at their face value. The impression that the joint-family is 'breaking up', or 'breaking down', is very general: and it would seem axiomatic that to understand an institution which is manifestly undergoing change we need not investigate texts written between about two thousand and three hundred years ago, nor puzzle over the Anglo-Indian case-law which is described by those who know the *śāstra* in opprobrious terms.[1] In any case the approaches of the lawyer and the sociologist differ, and co-operation between them has not proved to be as easy as many think it ought to be. This article is devoted to showing how far the śāstric texts and related material available to historians provide a background against which the observed facts of Hindu family life may be seen in perspective. The deductions of sociologists have been of immense help in reconstructing the meaning of innumerable śāstric and historical non-śāstric sources, for modern attitudes very often repeat those of mediaeval, if not ancient, India. It is possible that a sociologist's reading of legal materials may have some effect on Indian sociology.

At the outset, the limitations of the survey which follows must be acknowledged. The history of Marumakkattayam and related matrilineal family-systems in Kerala (so soon to disappear) is outside our present scope. We have seen that Kerala customs were known to at least one orthodox jurist,[2] and it is possible that other śāstric writers, even earlier, contemplated relationships which would arise when men governed by what we now call 'Hindu law' formed ties with women governed by Marumakkattayam.[3] But, interesting as would be an attempt to reconstruct this contact, speculation would play too great a part

[1] E.g. opinions cited by A. C. Burnell, *Ordinances of Manu* (London, Kegan Paul, etc., 1891), p. xlv.

[2] See above, p. 103.

[3] Derrett, 'Kamalākara on Illegitimates', (1956) 58 Bom. L.R., *J.*, pp. 177 ff.

and it would diminish the value of our main discussion. Other customary family-systems which have not obtained recognition within the *śāstra* are likewise ignored here. Marriage and adoption are very much parts of family law, but they naturally appear here only in passing. We shall by choice be confined in principle to the joint-family as a legal institution in itself.

When we want to know the law relating to the joint-family we must ask ourselves certain preliminary questions: are we thinking of the *śāstra*, of Anglo-Hindu law (AHL),[1] of customary laws, or of Modern Hindu law (MHL)? To historians of legal exposition the older books on AHL are of interest, but they can be misleading to non-lawyers, and they should not be cited. We must remember that just as textbooks relating to the AHL get out of date, so works dealing with the earliest period of the *śāstra*, and works on the MHL also–even after a decade since codification–can be unreliable: in both cases because speculation plays a great part. On the first there is a scarcity of reliable and three-dimensional material, and what there is may be interpreted variously; while the Acts and their related statutes are as yet only vaguely understood, for the courts have not construed more than a fraction of them.[2]

The relationships between the *śāstra*, the AHL, and the MHL, and of both the latter with customary law, have been the subject of debate. In a subject where what would elsewhere be known as 'fundamental research' has hardly begun, and where the workers are few and apt to be easily satisfied with provisional hypotheses (not being subjected to constant criticism and the invigorating experience of interrogation and competition) it is not surprising that the enquiring sociologist may be disappointed by a conflict of opinions regarding a relatively limited amount of material, the authority of which is accepted by all, each asserted with the unashamed positiveness characteristic of the lawyer. There is, after all, no substitute for personal inspection of the sources, and in this paper the references are selected

[1] The expression 'Anglo-Hindu law', objected to by Professors S. S. Nigam and A. T. Markose, but approved by former Justice T. L. Venkaṭarāma Iyer (*B.S.O.A.S.*, 29, pt. 1 (1966), 172) and by Mr. M. R. Vakil (67 Bom. L.R., *J.*, 160), was used as long ago as 1922 by a learned writer whose article (43 M.L.J., *J.*, 29–36) is entitled 'A century of Anglo-Hindu law and its sequel'.

[2] See above, pp. 352–3.

to enable any reader to check the curious history of the joint-family in Indian law for himself.

On the whole one accepts the following propositions, upon which it is not desirable to expand here: (i) the authors of śāstric treatises were comparative jurists, wrote carefully and deliberately, and adjusted their authoritative sources by interpretation, selection, and otherwise, so that they might serve the needs of communities whose actual customs were within their contemplation in each case respectively; (ii) the AHL endeavoured to apply the works of these authors, so far as practicable, given the form, staffing, and policies of the tribunals, to the situations that became subjects of litigation, situations which included some of those contemplated by the śāstric authors, but also many others that were themselves the products of the European period and of the Anglo-Indian legal system; (iii) under the impression (possibly only partially justifiable) that the Hindu law had stagnated during the British period,[1] Parliament enacted the statutes comprising the greater part of the MHL, and in so doing discarded much that had been achieved, added much that was new, and pruned and redesigned the system so as to satisfy a wider scope of the Hindu public than had formerly exercised any influence upon earlier stages of the system.[2] The impression that the AHL undermined, and for practical purposes destroyed, the joint Hindu family (as lawyers always call it) is very commonly ventilated.[3] We shall see whether there is any truth in it when the materials are viewed historically. The provisions of MHL will here be seen as a sequel to the AHL, though other aspects of MHL have interest for sociologists which we have tentatively sketched above.[4]

[1] V. Rāmaswāmi, 'Hindu law and English judges', AIR 1960 J. 82–92. But compare Derrett at *J.A.O.S.* 81 (1961), 251 ff. The accusation is repeated by P. B. Gajendragadkar in his Foreword to P. V. Deolalkar's *Hindu Marriage Act, 1955* (Nasik, the Author, 1959) and from the bench in *Amrit* v. *Doshi* AIR 1960 S.C. 964. See also his remarks at G. S. Sharma's *Secularism: its Implications for Law and Life in India* (cited above), p. 2 (British regard for custom and the need to prove any custom conclusively hampered the growth of custom such as would reflect the dictates of social conscience). Yet see above, p. 315, n. 3.

[2] See chapter 10 above.

[3] For example by Viśwanātha Śāstrī, J., at AIR 1952 Mad. 439, col. 2.

[4] At pp. 371 ff.

It is a fact that the *śāstra-s* catered for Āryans and non-Āryans, though with differing efficiency in different parts of India at different epochs. The assumption that the Āryans at a *very* remote period preserved homogeneous customs different from non-Āryan Indians', and that the *śāstra-s* emanated from sources influenced by Āryan tradition, is consistent with what we know of the history of the growing *śāstra* after 'pure' Āryan laws had apparently vanished from practice. The *śāstra* itself makes a distinction between Āryan and non-Āryan, and although the concept is not exclusively racial the connotations to the historian are still decidedly so.[1]

During the period when *smṛti-s* were being compiled it seems that some slight attempts were made at accommodation between Āryan tradition, which formed the core of the *śāstra-s* as set out in Vedic and the earliest *smṛti* texts, and the surviving non-Āryan usages of peoples who had joined the 'orthodox' fold and were accepted as caste Hindus. To this extent elements were introduced into the basic śāstric authorities which were inconsistent with the traditional Āryan way of life, and it appears that some were eventually excluded or became obsolete as the predominant tone of the *śāstra-s* prevailed, and the distinction between śāstric and non-śāstric customs emerged. Later (though still prehistorically) non-Āryan races seem to have become ritually and otherwise partially aryanized: the umbrella had therefore to be widened. The *smṛti-s* were interpreted by generations of writers. They seldom explain the feat which they are achieving, but from their techniques and (more significantly) their results we gather what they were about. In this way

[1] *Ārya* had a cultural connotation even in the time of the Buddhist scriptures. The Āryan-Dravidian dichotomy used by philologists is not serviceable to sociologists, who doubt whether language or supposed linguistic affiliations have any correlation with culture, let alone race. The historiography of ancient Indian law has not yet been able to do without this, or a similar, dichotomy. That there were cultures which stemmed from a pre-Āryan origin or origins can be taken as certain; to such communities Āryan habits were *brought*. The theory that jurisprudence as we have it started amongst Āryans, or, if you prefer, sub-Āryans, cannot be discarded so long as it is useful; and while there is evidence that non-Āryan ways had their uses for Āryans or sub-Āryans, there is little room for doubt that the non-Āryans deliberately acquired or pretended to acquire attitudes and habits from the others. Quite why and how they did so remains to be established.

non-Āryan attitudes to the family have survived in the curiously warped manner in which certain leading *śāstrī-s* of mediaeval times handled the *smṛti-s*. And again during the British period, and from evidence from French India and Ceylon, we find traces of what some important non-Āryan types of family were like. Since most well-to-do communities even in remote parts of India have been emulating brahminical traits so far as these could be imitated in externals (a process that has evidently been going on for centuries) there are few communities now governed by 'Hindu law' who are not touched in many places by traditional practices either conforming to, or intelligible in terms of, śāstric concepts. For this reason no pure non-Āryan family-systems have come to light within the chosen periphery of this discussion. The evidence supports a guess as to what non-Āryan families were like when Āryan tradition first offered itself to them for imitation, and our story is bound to start in that conjectural atmosphere.

Despite this element of conjecture, we rapidly enter the realm of texts, where the conflicts between different conceptions of the family make themselves very plain. The AHL accepted the hardly completed situation as if it were final, and applied the law as laid down by the most prominent commentators. Attempts to exempt families from the case-law were only successful if customs could be proved in derogation from the general personal law, as a result of which position the AHL applied to far more families than had been subject formerly to the śāstric family law. Many different types of family were hypothetically squeezed into one juridical mould, but the resilience of the people has been so remarkable that on the whole they have adjusted their affairs, so that they have been more of an embarrassment to judges and academic jurists than the law has been to them. Parliament assumed that this situation was to be taken as formally stabilized, and the MHL proceeds upon that basis in a new direction.

To describe the legal history of the joint-family we must answer certain questions. Who are the members of the family? Which of them have interests in its property, what sort of interests are there, and how are these interests distributed amongst the members? How is property acquired by the members, and in what ways are acquisition and management related to the membership? What, in particular, is the result of death, departure in adoption, marriage, renunciation of the world and severance (or partition)? How is the property managed, by whom, and in what circumstances may it be alienated (i.e. given, mortgaged, or sold)? To draw all the threads together we may finally consider the present function of the joint-family, and its probable future.

Membership of the Family

The non-Āryan family (i.e. the family unrepresented in the earlier and even in certain later *smṛti-s*) evidently was typically a 'natural' or 'nuclear' family consisting of husband and wife, their unmarried daughters and their unmarried sons, except where, for special reasons, the eldest, the youngest, or any other son stayed with his own wife and children in the original home in order to look after his parents and their farm with the prospect of inheriting it on his parents' decease.[1] Daughters, like the sons, went away on their marriages in order to form new households with their husbands. Where all the children were married and had left the home a widowed mother might choose to live with one of her sons, but on this aspect of family life we have no information. As the remarriage of widows was not frowned upon and divorce was tolerated, a young childless widow or divorcee would have little difficulty in finding another husband, though he might be of lower social status than that of her first. The evidence that non-Āryans practised polygamy and polyandry is strong, and that some peoples actually practised both seems likely:[2] but it is impossible to predicate of all

[1] A non-Āryan system of advancing sons is to be seen in the Tesavaḷamai (currently spelt Thesawalamai), which is printed as an appendix to H. W. Tambiah's *Laws and Customs of the Tamils of Jaffna* (Colombo, Times of Ceylon, 1950). T. Srī Rāmanāthan, 'Origin and sources of the law of Thesawalamai', *Ceylon L. Soc. J.*, 7, no. 4 (1962), pp. ci–civ surmises that Roman-Dutch law is the residual law where the customary law is silent, and to that extent his article seems defective, but otherwise it provides a welcome view of the history of the system.

[2] The writer's suggestion that the Pāṇḍyas of Madura were polyandrous and polygamous provoked indignation–but it may not be false. The evidence on Kandyan customs is relevant. The primary source is still F. A. Hayley, *Treatise on the Laws and Customs of the Sinhalese* (Colombo, 1923). On

non-Āryans that polyandry was usual, just as it is difficult to reconcile polygamy with what we know of very early Tamil matrimonial and sentimental notions.[1] However, it is not impossible to reconcile polyandry with a stage of family life at which separation of sons takes place upon their marriage, but poverty prevents the marriages of all sons as soon as they are mature.[2] Polygamy, likewise, may have been normal in families in which many females were needed to do the hard work, or in royal or princely families for which polygamy may have served special political purposes and received special sanctions. But these are guesses. So also is the highly plausible suggestion[3] that non-Āryans lived in exogamic tribal society, which possessed the characteristic of caste (*jāti*) long before the Āryan *varṇa* made its appearance.

The non-Āryan family, for all its 'natural' scope, was not necessarily rigidly confined to parents and unmarried children. The family that had one or more daughters and no sons, and needed a substitute for a son to manage the estate, seems to have adopted the device of taking a son-in-law (or perhaps more than one?) into the house, and there giving him a status similar to that of a son, subject to his good behaviour.[4] Naturally relatively poor boys would welcome such a proposition. Moreover, the non-Āryans obviously thought extremely highly of all blood-relationships, and of relationship by marriage–a characteristic

the relationship between Kandyan law (which is the remnant of Sinhalese law) and the ancient Hindu law see Derrett, 'The origins of the laws of the Kandyans', *Univ. of Ceylon Rev.* 14 (1956), pp. 105–50.

[1] In 'Patterns of early Tamil marriages', *Tamil Culture*, 11, no. 4 (1964), pp. 329–38, M. E. Manickavasagom finds four types of marriage: the romantic, that effectuated with a bride-price, where the groom is picked after a contest, where a second marriage is contracted during the lifetime of the first wife for the sake of issue (all of which leave parallel traits in contemporary culture) and marriages associated with bull-catching or equivalent feats of heroism.

[2] This was the reason for polyandry in the Kandyan Provinces and apparently in parts of Kerala. The *śāstra* preserves (in the texts of joint performance of sacrifices in the household fire: L. S. Joshī, ed., *Dharma-kośa, Vyavahāra-kāṇḍa*, Wai, 1938, p. 1128) traces of a situation where younger unmarried brothers shared the elder brother's fire–and his marriage?

[3] By N. Subrahmanian in his *Hindu Tripod* (1965). Dr. Subrahmanian is a specialist in the history of the earliest Tamil societies and their literature.

[4] On the *illatom* son-in-law see Rāghavāchāriar, *Hindu Law*[5], §. 176, Derrett, *I.M.H.L.*, §§. 201, 203.

linking them somewhat tenuously with Africa and distinguishing them plainly from their Āryan counterparts. We shall not go so far as to say that the parents-in-law, or even sons-in-law actually had a right to be maintained (i.e. in the śāstric phrase to be 'fed and clothed'); but that they were on close affectionate terms and were believed to have some indefinable right in the property of the couple seems evident.[1] Relations on the father's and also on the mother's side were considered close, in about equal measure, though there is the inevitable accompaniment of virilocal living that the husband's parents must have been looked to more often than the wife's for material assistance, but we cannot stress this. Slaves and concubines were no doubt usually to be found in the well-to-do family, and the fact of birth was sufficient to give the sons of 'female slaves' a status only slightly inferior to that of *aurasa*, or legitimate sons of the body by the wife.[2]

The Āryan family differed by reason of rigid patriliny, and the steady growth of joint living. There is evidence of Āryan copying of the non-Āryan habits of polyandry amongst brothers, and the 'son-in-law in the house',[3] now known as *ghar-jamāī*.[4] There is ample evidence of partition, or separation at marriage and of the advancement of sons at marriage or later,[5] so that the family home would by no means always shelter all the sons and their wives. But in time, perhaps as a result of a narrowing scope of opportunities, sons married and stayed at home, and the joint-family became the rule rather than the exception. Divorce became unseemly, polygamy frequent, and the common father of many children by more than one wife was their master as well

[1] Such relations could be heirs in the mediaeval Deccan: E.C. III, Tirum.-Nars. 21; IX Nel. 12; cf. M.A.R. 1910–11, §. 105.

[2] On the high status of the *dāsiputra* in the Deccan see inscriptions cited above, p. 210. See also Viśvarūpa cited by Kāṇe, *H.D.*, III, p. 602, n. 1138.

[3] The father of the *putrikā-putra*, or son of a daughter designated to supply an heir for her father, has obviously a special place in the father's household. Manu IX, 135.

[4] Rattigan, *Digest of Civil Law for the Punjab*[13], pp. 430, 456; S. Roy, *Customs and Customary Law in British India* (Calcutta, 1911), p. 477.

[5] Shares by way of advancement of sons: Āpastamba II, 10, 14; Gautama XXVIII (see Bühler's trans., S.B.E., vol. 2); and other texts printed in *Dh. K.* 1158–74. As late as Aparārka it was emphasized that sons were fit to take shares when they were married or marriageable.

as head.[1] The ranks of the sons were swelled with adopted sons of various categories, some of whom were little better than servants.[2] Freemen and slaves were capable of being incorporated into the outer rim, as it were, of the family circle; their needs, and those of their children, being the responsibility of the head of the family. The family became monolithic in form, though varied in personnel. The head was trustee, in a non-technical sense, for a host of dependants of various qualities. His and his sons' concubines were members of the family for purposes of maintenance, and frequently lived in the same building with the male members' wives. The illegitimate children were likewise members of the family, but their status was much lower, and their expectations more humble than those of their counterparts in the non-Āryan family. The circle was not widened by the addition of 'in-laws'. Relations with families into which one had given daughters and from whom one had taken daughters were formal. Widowed daughters had by no means so great a claim upon the head of the family as his widowed daughters-in-law. The former had legally left their family of birth, acquiring a new identity at their marriages, but as blood is thicker than water they were exceptionally allowed to visit, or even reside with, their near blood relations if life was not comfortable for them with their families of marriage. It is of interest to note that in communities which practised marriage by purchase (the so-called *Āsura* form) the total incorporation of the wife into the family of her marriage was not contemplated by public opinion, as is reflected in the *śāstra*, which omits to say (what may well have been the case in earlier periods) that on her husband's death she could be transferred by her blood-relations to another husband, by reason of their residual rights in, and on behalf of, a daughter of the family. If this is correct it is small wonder that the *śāstra* praises the *Brāhma* form of marriage in which the family of the bride totally and completely part with all rights in respect of her, and her marriage is (as Kauṭilya says) indissoluble, and, if sentiment and superstition kept company, did not end even with her husband's death.

[1] While the father lives the sons have no independence and, according to an ancient maxim embedded in Manu, no property: VIII, 416.

[2] Derrett, 'Adoption in Hindu law', *Z. f. vergl. Rechtsw.* 60 (1957), pp. 34–90.

The *śāstra*, by the age of the commentators, attempted to propound the law for both sorts of family simultaneously. The *gharjamāī*, however, was ignored, as such, but he was fancied to be intended by the husband of the Āryan *putrikā-putra*, the daughter who served as a son, herself a feature of both non-Āryan and the less 'pure' Āryan families. The *śāstra* emphasized the patrilineal nature of family-ties, and it is only in non-legal or occasional, less authoritative, texts that the importance of relationships with relations by marriage and maternal relations is noticed.[1] The manner in which substitute sons might enter the family, and the rights which they acquired are elaborately discussed, and various developments are to be seen. The special position of the illegitimate son is recognized in a curious way: the non-Āryan provision for the son of the continuous concubine is continued, but only in favour of *śūdra-s*, and the texts give no sign of recognizing that this is an adaptation of a pre-Āryan, non-śāstric rule.[2]

The degree of membership of the family on the part of concubines and female slaves is open to debate. Various categories of women were recognized as members of the family, and their rights were assured so long as they were not merely temporarily attached.[3] The *śāstra* was barely aware of the fact that daughters did not invariably marry and go out of the family,[4] and ignored the position of the widowed daughter; but it was highly aware of the various circumstances in which women, married or single, could come into more or less permanent relationship with a member of the family. Polyandry at this stage of development of the law disappeared practically

[1] Medhātithi on Manu XI, 62 (Jhā's trans., V, p. 390) shows that a destitute *maternal* uncle should be maintained. The nineteenth-century *Śukranītisāra* mentions that certain relations by marriage are to be maintained (III, 249–50, cf. Manu II, 130; III, 119, 148), and this must stem from a Hindu, not a foreign, source.

[2] Yājñavalkya II, 133–4. Kāṇe, *H.D.*, III, p. 601 ff.

[3] Classes of unchaste women are categorized: *Mitākṣarā* on Yājñ. II, 119; Kāṇe, *H.D.*, III, p. 815. *Akku* v. *Ganesh* [1945] Bom. 216 (F.B.). The *Brahmavaivarta-purāṇa*, *prakṛti-khaṇḍa*, ch. 28 (cited at *Ram Pergash* v. *Mst Dahan* [1923] 3 Pat. 172) lists seven categories of married women: *pativratā* (no. 1) is plainly the wife approved by the *śāstra*; *kulatā* (no. 2) apparently remains in the family; nos. 3–7 are various kinds of promiscuous women, no. 7 being supposed to have had more than eight 'husbands'!

[4] Citations given at AIR 1957 Mad. 330.

without trace: but signs of successive marriages of the mother of the family (though strictly anathema to the *śāstra* in the chapter concerning marriage) are not wanting.[1]

Interests in Joint-Family Property

The word 'interest' has a technical sense in AHL but for the present we shall use it in a more general sense. The non-Āryan families, it seems, allowed only the married pair interests in the property of the marriage,[2] which came from husband and wife or their subsequently-acquired property. There is no reason to suppose that their children had more than a right to be maintained until their marriages, and a right at their parents' discretion to a share by way of advancement at that point. If the father died their future shares apparently became hypothetically distinct rights in a half of the estate, the other half belonging to the surviving spouse.[3] There is evidence that the immovable property belonging to the couple was regarded *by their issue* as peculiarly intended for the enjoyment of future generations, and in order to prevent the father, who was the manager of the estate, from alienating it improperly they had a right of protest.

[1] Manu IX, 191 can be interpreted in terms of polyandry, but none of the commentators does so. The *Vivādaratnākara* of Caṇḍeśvara (p. 543) commenting upon Yājñ. II, 120 (*Dh. K.*, p. 1200), Maskarī on Gautama XXVIII, 25 (ibid., p. 1466) and Nandapaṇḍita's *Vaijayantī* on Viṣṇu (I, p. 294: the passage cited from Jolly's report of it in *Narayan* v. *Laxman* (1927) 51 Bom. 784 at p. 793) distinctly envisage uterine half-blood, which the *śāstra* (and, curiously, even the HSA) ignore for purposes of inheritance.

[2] The text *daṃpatyor madhyagaṃ dhanaṃ* which appears in works emanating from Bengal and is discussed in *Sabitri* v. *Savi* AIR 1933 Pat. 306, 390, 395 (and dealt with at *Z. f. vergl. Rechtsw.* 64 (1962), pp. 62–4: see p. 415, n. 3) is intelligible in terms of Tesavaḻamai. The Mitākṣarā at I, iv, 2 (Colebrooke) betrays (with the phrase 'or mother') the S. Indian persistence of the idea. The origin of the community of goods between Syrian Christians in Kerala is not known. The AHL ignored this topic.

[3] Tesavaḻamai and Kandyan law. Under the latter the widow has a life-estate in the whole immovable property. In movables she takes a right equal to that of a child. The conflicting evidence of Kandyan law suggests that even in immovable property the widow can opt for a share. The Kandyan rules show a stronger similarity to usages (sub-Āryan) evidenced in the *śāstra* than they do to the known Dravidian customs, but the subject is complex. H. Bechert at *Paideuma* 7 (1960), pp. 179 ff. would not relate Kandyan customary law to an Āryan source.

That all relatives were 'interested' in the property belonging to each other is clear,[1] and everyone was a potential heir to his relations, and so entitled to a general interest in the prosperity of his nearest kin: but this did not amount to a right of maintenance, still less of interdiction of improper (e.g. improvident) expenditure.

It is evident that so long as the sons remained undivided, in the sense that after their father's death they had not married, or if they had married had not set up separate homes, the acquisitions made as a result of the cultivation or investment of the undivided property (which they would eventually take in distinct shares) would belong to them jointly. It might be very difficult to determine what particular acquisitions were derived from the joint nucleus, and what from windfalls, or individual unaided enterprise. Naturally rules developed which excluded at a partition property which could be traced to what is now known as *bona fide* self-acquisition, e.g. a gift (other than a ceremonial gift) from a friend. As for the rest, so long as the brothers remained undivided they had a fractional interest in the acquisitions made after the father's death corresponding in proportion to the fractional shares themselves.

In the non-Āryan family, then, the wife was interested in the joint estate to an extent which secured her maintenance, and a half-share of the corpus on divorce or her husband's death.[2] The daughters were interested to the extent of maintenance and their marriage-portion, which was afterwards known as *strīdhanam.*[3] The sons were interested to the extent of maintenance and their shares after the father's death, or advancements amounting to shares on their marriages during his lifetime.

[1] This background to Mitāksharā law is well brought out by I. S. Pawate, *Dāyavibhāga: or the Individualization of Communal Property and the Communalization of Individual Property in the Mitakshara law* (Dharwad, 1945).

[2] See p. 411 n. 3 above. In non-śāstric systems divorce and the husband's death appear to have had similar effects.

[3] This use of the word *strīdhanam* (as opposed to its regular use as 'paraphernalia') survives in those few śāstric texts which speak of a man acquiring (impartible) property by way of *strīdhanam* (i.e. his wife's dowry). South Indian inscriptions invariably mean by the word *this* category: it is viewed as property subject to the husband's control and not as a species of females' separate estate (as normally in the *śāstra* and AHL). The Tamil *cītanam* corresponds to this non-Āryan *strīdhanam.*

Beyond these, and the customary right of protesting if the father alienated immovable property without corresponding benefit to the entire family, no further 'interests' can be detected other than those of maintenance in the cases of members of the family entitled to be maintained, e.g. illegitimate sons and permanent concubines.

The typical Āryan family knew only 'interests' amounting to the right to a dowry, where customary, and to maintenance. There is no trace in the earlier texts of a right of interdiction on the part of sons, still less a right to demand a share of the ancestral estate. The father was master of all the estate, movable and immovable, and because this might work hardship where he had come under the influence of a young, junior wife, it was provided that he *ought* not to make alienations of the entire property,[1] with the implication that if the welfare of the family could be provided for otherwise, even so drastic an alienation (prompted by religious mania or otherwise) would be valid.[2] The duty of sons to support or make good obligations undertaken by their fathers was apparently early established, and even as early as the thirteenth century it was understood that this obligation prevented them from questioning alienations.[3]

The mediaeval writers stood apart into two camps, of which we have taken notice already. Those in Bengal (the so-called Dāyabhāga school) contended that the absolute discretion of the father, governed only by moral considerations, was free of interference by wife or sons. The sons' rights, or 'interests', in the property arose merely on the father's renunciation, exclusion from caste, or death.[4] At that time they came into the ancestral (i.e. patrilineally descended) and self-acquired property of the father for undivided shares of fixed proportion. Since their legal interests did not arise previously there was no

[1] Derrett, 'Prohibition and Nullity', *B.S.O.A.S.* 20 (1957), p. 205, n. 11 and the following discussion.

[2] Jīmūtavāhana, *Dāyabhāga* II, ii, 24 (Colebrooke). The first two chapters of this work are interesting as a fight to justify intrinsically Āryan traditions against texts developed under sub-Āryan or even non-Āryan influences centuries before.

[3] Litigation reported in M.A.R. 1911–12, §. 91 (A.D. 1255), cited above at p. 211.

[4] *Dāyabhāga*, chh. 1 and 2 (cited above).

question either of preventing alienations by the father of ancestral property, of demanding any particular shares in it at any time, or of claiming any right to manage or direct the family's affairs during the father's lifetime. There was nothing to prevent the Āryan laws relating to inheritance applying with equal validity to the share taken at a partition of a deceased father's property and to the self-acquisitions of a brother. Acquisitions made with the aid of undivided wealth would be joint property, as explained in reference to the non-Āryan family. The mother had a *moral* right to delay partition[1] (as in non-Āryan families) but the sons could, if they wished, separate the property over her head, provided they gave her a share equal to that of a son and so secured her maintenance and residence.[2]

The other school, known as the Mitāksharā school,[3] took a much more complicated line. The Āryan texts relating to inheritance were preserved, subject to small adjustments by way of interpretation which do not concern us here; the texts relating to the shares of mothers and wives of the father were also preserved unaffected. But the mutual interests of relations, the more than imaginary expectations of sons, and the social and economic importance of inherited land, especially in the case of Brahmins and dominant castes that received lands as a subsidy for learning and reward for loyalty, altered the picture of the family to such an extent that while the ancient sages would not have recognized it, the Dravidian types of family would fit into it, though with much careful definition of ancient Sanskrit terms. First *strīdhanam*, instead of being the wife's interest in the joint property of the spouses, became the separate property of the wife–a purely Āryan notion, we may be sure–separate from the claims of all but the husband, and available to him

[1] Ibid., III, i, 1–14. This is ignored in AHL under the maxim *factum valet* (see above, p. 91), of which Jīmūtavāhana himself would probably have approved.

[2] Rāghavāchāriar, §. 354. The fight to exclude mothers from an actual share (rather than maintenance) is seen as early as Haradatta's commentary on Gautama XXVIII, 1 (*Dh.K.*, 1144–5). H. was a southern author. It is not necessary to assume that southern śāstric hostility to mothers' shares at a partition reflect Dravidian usage: they may reflect dyed-in-the-wool southern orthodoxy.

[3] For the *Mitākṣarā* itself (A.D. c. 1125) see above, p. 124, and Kāṇe, *H.D.*, I, sec. 70.

only in a family emergency.[1] A highly interesting body of law developed in mediaeval India as to the meaning of the ancient classifications and cross-classifications of *strīdhanam* developed in an Āryan juridical context.[2] Secondly, the wife's interest in the family property was redefined as practical, and as religious,[3] but not amounting at any time to a right to a share greater than she might take *at a partition* between her husband and his sons, or between her sons or grandsons. The possibility of divorce and remarriage was ignored. Such things happened, no doubt, but they were no part of *dharma*. The sons, instead of having a practical interest in the estate which they would eventually share, and which, if it was ancestral, was considered the natural provision for their own futures and their sisters' marriages,[4] became joint owners with their father in anything which he had inherited from *his* father, and the natural accretions to this.[5] As a result, they could demand a partition of ancestral assets, and could insist upon equal shares with the father; and this was a useful threat to hinder his alienating ancestral property except for religious purposes, benefit of the family, or a pressing necessity.[6] The movables were within the father's special control still, even if they were ancestral,[7] and his privilege to make 'gifts of affection' to his daughters, sisters, and even sons, was not questioned.[8] Thirdly, because the separation of sons from each other at their marriages could not be assumed; and because in

[1] Rāghavāchāriar, §§. 468–89. P. W. Rege. 'The Law of Strīdhana . . .', Thesis, Ph.D., London (unpublished), 1960.

[2] Rege (above). For a rapid survey see *Kātyāyana-smṛti-sāroddhāra*, ed. and trans. P. V. Kāṇe (Bombay, 1933). *vv.* 894–916.

[3] The *daṃpatyor* text was whittled away. Derrett at *B.S.O.A.S.* 18 (1956), p. 490, n. 4. Earlier references than Śūlapāṇi have been found since 1956, e.g. in Śabara-svāmī and in Viśvarūpa, who was undoubtedly a southern author. Kullūka (on Manu IX, 45) cites *daṃpatyor aikyaṃ* from the *Vājasaneya-brāhmaṇa*.

[4] *Mitākṣarā* I, vii, 5–14 correctly shows the brothers as trustees for their sisters, laying down a proportionate share for unmarried sisters: this was ignored at AHL (see *Guramma* v. *Mallappa* AIR 1964 S.C. 510, above, p. 310, n. 2). The fixed share is not always the most favourable arrangement for the unmarried daughter, and the MHL has, rightly, not departed from the AHL position, whilst giving the daughter an intestate share along with her brother as a matter of course.

[5] *Mit.* I, xi, 23, 27; I, v, 5.

[6] *Mit.* I, i, 27–9.

[7] *Mit.* I, i, 24–7.

[8] See last note; Rāghavāchāriar, §§. 378–9; Mayne, §. 370.

respect of valuable family assets partition might not be practical (e.g. pensions), the theory was developed that while during the lifetime of the father the sons had a right of interdiction in respect of ancestral property, and so were owners with him of the *sādhāraṇam*, or joint-family estate, the death of any one of them did not convey any particular share of ownership to anyone else, but those who remained owned the whole as before, but with a higher presumptive share, i.e. the share available to each at partition (if he lived so long). The list of heirs according to the ancient law was manipulated by the fourth amendment, which was that since a son dying before partition was only a *co-owner* and not a full owner of a defined share, on his death the interest in the joint property did not pass by succession at all, but remained with those who were co-owners previously. Thus the widow, daughter, daughter's son, mother and father, who would take separated property, if any, in that order, could not participate in the undivided interest;[1] and indeed even if a son had separated he could reunite by agreement,[2] and so cut out his future widow and his daughter who had in the meanwhile expected to inherit. Instances are not wanting in Punjab customary law[3] where the undivided interest passes on death (or did until certain modifications were made by the *HSA* in 1956) to the widow and other heirs exactly as if it were separate property; so that it is possible to observe that the *Mitākṣarā's* manipulations must have had dominant customs behind them, able to override the literal text of the *smṛti* in fact, though not in appearance.

The AHL called the process whereby the interest did *not* pass by succession 'survivorship',[4] and the undivided owners 'co-parceners'.[5] The ownership was not full ownership, because of the

[1] *Mit.* II, i, 39.

[2] *Mit.* II, ix.

[3] In Kerala also families governed by *makkattāyam* (patrilineal descent) may not recognize the Mitāksharā distinctions. An example of the opposite to what is stated of the Punjab is to be found amongst Thīyas. The separate property may pass to brothers and not to the widow: *Rarichan* v. *Perachi* (1892) 15 Mad. 281.

[4] *Lakshminarasamma* v. *Rama* [1950] Mad. 1084. Rāghavāchāriar, §. 266. Goldstücker, *On the Deficiencies in the Present Administration of Hindu Law* (London, 1871), deplored this importation from English law. Burnell agreed, and see the first case cited at p. 426, n. 2 below.

[5] With a new sense. Rāghavāchāriar, §§. 234–9.

rights of maintenance attached to the joint property. The interest of a living coparcener was seen as something that could not be defined before partition, fluctuating hypothetically until then with births and deaths.[1] The right of partition was admitted to be absolute in Mitāksharā law; and the right of interdiction, transmuted into a right to 'avoid' (i.e. to sue to set aside) alienations within the period allowed by the law of limitation, attached to all joint-family property whatever its nature,[2] while, on the other hand, the self-acquired immovables of the father were held to be equally freely alienable by him with his self-acquired movables.[3] The law was thus somewhat 'tidied-up', but in defiance of the original text. The wife had no interest in the property, though her right to maintenance could be protected by applying for the creation of a charge over some or all of it for that purpose.[4] Daughters could sue for their marriage expenses,[5] and sons for their maintenance if they had been excluded from joint possession and enjoyment of the joint estate.[6] The sons' right to question improper alienations by their father was much weakened by the rule that private untainted debts of the father would have to be paid out of sons' interests, so that at one or two removes the alienation could convey away their interests without any security that they would benefit.[7] Non-managing coparceners and their immediate families could not be completely protected against their ancestors' follies.

Nor was the coparcener allowed to hide behind his joint status in order to defeat creditors. The undivided interest might

[1] Rāghavāchāriar, §. 236.

[2] Partition: Rāghavāchāriar, §. 343; Derrett, *I.M.H.L.*, §§. 512–25; avoidance of alienations: Rāghavāchāriar, §§. 283, 291; Derrett, *I.M.H.L.*, §§. 437 ff., 473.

[3] *Rao Balwant Singh* v. *Rani Kishori* (1898) 25 I.A. 54, a case accepted without hesitation in India, though technically wrong.

[4] Rāghavāchāriar §§. 208, 226; Derrett, *I.M.H.L.*, §§. 400–1 *Ambika* AIR 1956 Pat. 293 illustrates modern difficulties. *Muthalammal* v. *Veeraraghavalu* [1952] 2 M.L.J. 344.

[5] *Alagammai* v. *Veerappa* AIR 1956 Mad. 428 was a suit by an orphaned girl against her paternal uncles.

[6] Rāghavāchāriar, §. 216; Derrett, *I.M.H.L.*, §. 410.

[7] *Brij Narain* v. *Mangal Prasad* (1924) 51 I.A. 129. The topic is discussed above at pp. 113–14.

be sold by the court to satisfy private creditors,[1] while in South India it might be alienated on the coparcener's own initiative.[2] The alienee who had given value was allowed to step into his alienor's shoes and work out his rights by a suit for general partition,[3] in which all joint-family debts and assets would be marshalled. The law of insolvency has allowed the interest to vest in the Receiver for the benefit of creditors,[4] and the deaths of coparceners other than the insolvent would operate for the benefit of the latter's creditors.[5] However, neither alienations nor insolvencies nor attachments (i.e. processes whereby property of a defendant is restrained from transfer pending adjudication of the plaintiff's claim) affect the status of the coparcener,[6] and when he does separate in interest he may take a share in after-acquired, or in the remaining assets.

For Income Tax purposes special rules apply.[7] Wealth-tax has to be paid by joint-families as if they were groups of individuals owning property,[8] though it is evident that no existing group can actually exhaust all the rights against the joint-family property. A joint-family may own a business in which the coparceners take interests by birth if they are governed by Mitāksharā law: such firms are only superficially like partnerships, and their character has on the whole not been tampered with in the course of litigation, since analogies from the law of partnership have seldom been allowed to influence it.[9]

The Hindu Women's Rights to Property Act, 1937 (now repealed), introduced a new element: the widow was made

[1] Rāghavāchāriar, §. 289. *Deendyal* v. *Jugdeep* (1877) 4 I.A. 247. For a discussion of the law behind this see Derrett at [1966] K.L.T., *J.*, 29–49.

[2] Rāghavāchāriar, §. 289; Derrett, *I.M.H.L.*, §. 461. *Suraj Bunsi* v. *Sheo Persad* (1878) 6 I.A. 88. See last note.

[3] *Peramanayakam* v. *Sivaraman* AIR 1952 Mad. 419 (F.B.).

[4] Rāghavāchāriar, §. 318. Derrett, *I.M.H.L.*, §. 489.

[5] *Hanumantha Gowd* v. *Off. Rec., Bellary* [1947] Mad. 44.

[6] *Sheonandan* v. *Ugrah* AIR 1960 Pat. 66.

[7] See below, p. 428, n. 3. Moreover in *T.S. Srinivasan* v. *Comm., I.T., Madras* AIR 1966 S.C. 984 it was decided that an unborn person cannot be an 'assessee', so that the doctrine that a Hindu undivided family comes into existence when a son is conceived cannot fit into the scheme of the Income Tax Act.

[8] *Mahavirprasad* v. *M. S. Yagnik* AIR 1960 Bom. 191. Derrett at (1960) 62 Bom. L.R., *J.*, 25; [1962] K.L.T., *J.*, 18–21; [1966] K.L.T., *J.*, 71–3.

[9] Rāghavāchāriar, §. 285; Derrett, *I.M.H.L.*, §. 453.

owner of her deceased husband's undivided interest. If she died without separating it passed by survivorship to those who would have been her husband's coparceners if he had died when she died.[1] This interruption of survivorship in favour of the widow was a great novelty. It is true that in some mediaeval communities widows might inherit both the undivided interest and the separate property, in the absence of male issue,[2] but actual competition between widow and sons, etc., was unknown. The Act of 1937 however provided that the widow should take these statutory benefits similarly with any estate which widows took until 1956 in any inherited property, i.e. subject to the restriction that she could alienate the corpus to the prejudice of the previous male holder's next heirs only for necessity or the benefit of the estate or for the spiritual welfare of her husband (if he were the last male holder).[3] This provided some security that the property would not find its way into another family by the widow's remarriage. Thus the structure of the joint-family was hardly interfered with. If the widow chose to separate, naturally a fraction of the property would be lost to the sons, but if she spent, when separate, little more than she would have spent when joint, the loss would not be considerable. It would depend upon the coparceners whether it was open to the widow to choose a path which would work out cheaper for all of them.[4]

A big step was taken when the Estate Duty Act was passed in 1953. In order to prevent coparceners from merging (as they legally might without formality) all their separate estates with the coparcenary property before their deaths, and so dying

[1] R. L. Chaudhary, *Hindu Woman's Right to Property, Past and Present* (Calcutta, K. L. Mukhopadhyay, 1961). Derrett, *I.M.H.L.*, §. 416.

[2] A.R.E. 1919, Nos. 429 and 538 of 1918. The customs of Jainas to our own day. For a general discussion see A. S. Altekar, *Position of Women in Hindu Civilization*² (Benares, 1956).

[3] Rāghavāchāriar, §. 527; Derrett, *I.M.H.L.*, §§. 683 ff.

[4] An important discovery was made in *Manicka* v. *Arunachala* AIR 1965 Mad. 1 (F.B.) (see Derrett at [1965] 1 M.L.J., *J.*, pp. 13–15, also [1965] 67 Bom. L.R., *J.*, 35–41), whereby it appeared that the widow's rights were less than those of her coparcener husband, in that her share could never grow to amount to more than one-half of the estate. She could never take by survivorship from the last coparcener or a widow similarly placed with herself. This discovery (happily?) confirmed the profession in their supposition that the widow had *not* become a substitute in law for her deceased husband.

without estates assessable to estate duty, the Act provided that even the undivided interest should be liable for duty, upon the basis that the deceased fictionally owned the amount of joint-family property which would have come to him had he demanded partition immediately before his death.[1] The effect of this immediately was no more than to lessen the total joint-family funds in a new way. But it was realized that this was the way in which to regulate the law of succession so that rights of inheritance might be substituted for rights of maintenance in certain favoured cases. One of the favoured persons was the widow herself. When the *HSA* introduced (as we have seen) several close relations as simultaneous heirs for a man's separate property, the principle alluded to above made it imperative that the same law should apply to his interest in joint-family property at Mitāksharā law. (By oversight Punjab customary variations of this were ignored.)[2] Therefore it was provided that the interest, which was not to pass by survivorship, should be that interest which the deceased would have realized had there been an actual partition of the property immediately prior to his death. The effect of this when read with Supreme Court decisions on another part of the same statute, and with the Mitāksharā law enabling wives to take shares at a partition (a rule that survives in Maharashtra, Kerala and Northern India), was the unexpected one, that the widow would share as a wife, and then share again as a co-heiress, in both guises for an absolute estate. This goes so contrary to Hindu sentiment, and a firm trend at AHL, that voices have been raised against this interpretation of the statute.[3]

The right of maintenance was not legally an 'interest' in the technical sense. If one lived jointly the cost of maintenance was much less than if one lived separately: therefore joint-families tended to be large except where enterprise or the possibility of employment, or the needs of the business or businesses drove people from the family home for long periods or even permanently. The law took no account whatever of these developments, concentrating upon the *right* of maintenance. Those who had the right but lived away must work out that right, by suit if necessary, and if they had to live separately the manager of the

[1] Estate Duty Act, 1953, s. 7 (1), s. 39 (1).

[2] See above, p. 345. [3] See above, p. 343.

family would have to pay the difference out of the common chest. A highly curious development of AHL was the division of rights of maintenance into 'legal' and 'moral' rights. A person legally entitled to maintenance, such as an illegitimate son, could live in the family home, or if the others would not have him, they must pay for him to live elsewhere. But a widowed daughter and a widowed daughter-in-law had a moral claim *only* to be maintained by the father or father-in-law respectively, which they could for the first time enforce at law after his death against his heirs (and, some held, his legatees). Purporting to derive from the *śāstra*, this rule seems thoroughly un-śāstric. MHL has allowed the widowed daughter-in-law, if not able to support herself from the estates of nearer kindred or by allowances from her own children, to claim maintenance in rare cases from her father-in-law or his estate at law. But the 'interest' of the widowed daughter remains in the no-man's-land of the AHL rule. In a sense the MHL has strengthened the joint-family bond, rather than loosened it,[1] in so far as it has not confirmed property rights formerly accorded to those whose status in the family depended only on sentiment.

Maintenance was generally thought of as the opposite of independence, for in practice suits for a higher rate of maintenance were rare and unseemly. Thus, the inevitable step, now that separate living was more usual in the case of widowed daughters, daughters-in-law, and so on, was to separate from the persons who could claim nothing but maintenance those who were thought fit for promotion to the class of sharers. So some members of the family, who had previously been entitled to maintenance or the somewhat restricted rights given by the Act of 1937, were made first-class heirs, and the coparcenary interest itself was made capable of passing by succession.[2] Testamentary disposition of the interest was introduced, in order that the coparcener might decide for himself in what proportions his near relations and others might share his

[1] Compare the position at Rāghavāchāriar, §§. 223–5 with the provisions of *HAMA*, s. 19. The limitation imposed in s. 19 (2), which goes behind recent AHL decisions, is odd. As a result of s. 6 of the *HSA* there will be few widowed daughters-in-law who have no share in their husbands' estates, and so will be entitled to claim maintenance from their fathers-in-law.

[2] *HSA*, s. 6.

undivided interest as well as his separate property.[1] The extent of the undivided interest was to be assessed as we have seen. The results of this, in addition to that already feared, are that much of the coparcenary property goes outside the joint-family (e.g. to married daughters), and that sons taking as heirs hold in two capacities: as statutory owners of fixed shares in the interest of their father, and owners by Mitāksharā birthright of their own interests. The *HSA* did not, however, abolish the birthright as such, but provided that when the undivided interest passed by succession both it and any separate property that might so pass should be taken by sons as tenants-in-common (i.e. co-owners owning fixed, unfluctuating fractions of undivided property).[2] The effect of this was to keep sons separate from each other in respect of an important item of the former joint-family estate; but their residual jointness in other respects, and their jointness in respect even of this property, each with his own male issue, was not affected.[3]

Acquisitions

There need be no doubt but that the notion that three generations of descendants owned *in some sense* the acquisitions of their common ancestors in the male line was older than the *Mitākṣarā*.[4] But the provisions about self-acquisitions and property impartible on that account were embedded in the *śāstra* from a very early period, and we are certain that the conflict between basic joint ownership between coparceners, which is evidenced from the mediaeval period, and the separate claims of individuals who wanted to benefit their immediate relations rather than those of their collaterals was no new importation by the Āryans.[5]

[1] The same statute, s. 6 read with s. 30. The statement frequently heard that the Mitāksharā coparcener can in any case dispose of his interest by will is incorrect.

[2] *HSA*, s. 19 (b).

[3] For doubts, see reference at p. 338, n. 1, above.

[4] The notion of living on ancestral property is as old as the Veda: *Ṛgveda* I, 5, 20, 9 (*Dh.K.*, 1158). The topic of adverse possession illustrates the identity of title of father and son. See Medhātithi on Manu VIII, 148 (Jhā's trans., IV (i), 177), 149 (ibid., 183), 185 (ibid., 235); IX, 209 (Jhā, V, 173); and *Mit.* on Yājñ. II, 6.

[5] From Sāyaṇa on the *Taittirīya-saṃhitā* II, vi, 1, 6 (*Dh.K.*, 1161) and on the *Aitareya-āraṇyaka* II, i, 8 (*Dh.K.*, 1163) we see the actual practice of

The mediaeval śāstric writers differed as to the items that might be kept separate at a partition: but if no partition took place for generations we are entitled to assume that even gifts from friends became eventually joint-family property. The *Mitākṣarā* in fact took an extreme view, that only slender categories of earning could be impartible and so reserved for the acquirer alone.[1] The AHL, which has not been modified except by the Hindu Gains of Learning Act, 1930, provides that all acquisitions with the use of joint-family property are joint-family property,[2] even if they are acquired by a sole surviving coparcener (i.e. a former coparcener left sole 'owner' by the deaths of his coparceners),[3] unless they are wages, salary, or other income due to learning, or any kind of training whether or not imparted at the family's expense.[4] The result of the development is that very important classes of earning are not by nature joint-family property, and mere generosity shown by the earner to his relations cannot amount to a renunciation on his part of a separate interest in them[5] (though, as we have seen, he can merge his own property with the joint stock if he wants to).[6]

The greatest alteration made by the AHL in this chapter was the early determination to treat self-acquisitions as property separate by nature, whether or not the acquirer lived or died separate. By a most curious misunderstanding the Anglo-Indian courts had arrived at a position that self-acquisitions might be given away or bequeathed without the consent of coparceners,[7] so that such acquisitions constituted what was virtually a distinct estate. It was a small step from this to determine that if a coparcener died his undivided interest passed to his surviving

coparceners to enjoy each other's acquisitions without leave. In Vācaspatimiśra's *Vyavahāra-cintāmaṇi* (Ghent, 1956), trans., pp. 192, 210–1 we have incidental proof that acquisitions during jointness were presumed joint-family property. Derrett at [1956] S.C.J., *J.*, 103–11.

[1] I. iv.

[2] *Comm. I.T.* v. *Kalu Babu* AIR 1959 S.C. 1289; *Smt. Parbati* v. *Sarangdhar* AIR 1960 S.C. 403; *M./S. Piyare Lal* v. *Commr. I.-T.* AIR 1960 S.C. 997. Derrett, *I.M.H.L.*, §. 547.

[3] *Sivaramakrishnan* v. *Kaveri* AIR 1955 Mad. 705.

[4] The statute of 1930. *Ramakrishna* v. *Vishnumoorthi* AIR 1957 Mad. 86.

[5] *Rukn ul Mulk* v. *R. Vishwanathan* AIR 1950 Mys. 33; *Pratap Kishore* v. *Gyanendranath* AIR 1951 Or. 313, 319.

[6] *R. Subramania Iyer* v. *Commr. I.-T.* AIR 1955 Mad. 623.

[7] On the early history of wills in Madras see Mayne, §. 740.

coparceners (such as his brothers and nephews) but his self-acquisitions (e.g. a *zamīndārī* conferred by Government) went to his widow or daughter by succession, as if he had borne at the time of his death two characters in respect of the two sorts of property.[1] As a result much property which would have fallen into the joint stock, by reason of the deaths unseparated of persons who had acquired without detriment to the joint estate, began to pass, from early in the British period, to heirs by will or on intestacy. This gravely diminished the importance of the joint estate in the everyday life of the joint-family, though the law relating to the family was unaffected by the development. In Kerala, where until recently partition was very rare, the self-acquisitions of a member of a joint-family governed by customary law fell automatically to his family, or at least to his branch within it, if he died without disposing of it elsewhere.

Management and Alienation

We have seen that the 'Āryan' law attempted to restrain the father from alienating the whole ancestral and joint-family estate while he had dependants, but that this restraint operated only in the moral sphere. A son might theoretically take legal action against his father for an alienation in defiance of the ban, but, though this remained true even in Bengal under the Dāyabhāga system,[2] the general impropriety of sons litigating with their fathers must have given fathers much liberty in practice. The non-Āryans, we have seen, considered the ancestral estate joint property of father and sons, and we have seen how that notion developed in the *Mitākṣarā* and in the dominant AHL joint-family system that derives from it. The *śāstra* did indeed view questions of management and alienation from the point of view of the necessities of the family's circumstances, but upon the footing that the manager was responsible for the members' maintenance: but this was in the chapter relating to

[1] *Katama Nachiar* v. *Rajah of Shivagunga* (1863) 9 M.I.A. 539. Joint acquisitions, even without the nucleus of ancestral property, may be held to be joint property between coparceners who have earned them: Derrett, *I.M.H.L.*, §. 547.

[2] Jīmūtavāhana, *Vyavahāra-mātṛkā.* Vācaspati-miśra, *Vyavahāra-cintāmaṇi* at (trans.), p. 362.

debts.[1] Elsewhere the predominant question, viewing the matter from the angle of inheritance or rather *dāya,* was 'what powers of alienation has the father?' It is assumed that as long as he is not disqualified by senility or depravity, etc., the common ancestor will be the manager. His rights to manage stem, according to the *Mitākṣarā,* simply from his being the family's representative and the chief, or predominant, owner amongst owners, for he has not only *svāmyam* (ownership) but also *svātantryam* (independence), which latter no one else has during his life.[2] After his death, naturally, the question of a partition becomes more practical, and the elder brother who is presumed at AHL to be the manager,[3] has not the same dominance over his collaterals, for his presence does not diminish their *svātantryam.* Nevertheless, by ancient custom the younger brother while joint with the elder brother was not fully competent in law to alienate the family property,[4] and he could do so only in an emergency when the manager was incapable of acting.[5]

The Mitāksharā law on the powers of the manager has not been followed perfectly in a number of respects. Firstly, the author intended that when the last coparcener died the different customs of different castes should determine how the family property should be managed for the benefit of the dependants. While one coparcener lived all the rest of the family were dependent upon him in virtue of his being the custodian of the estate; after his death various expedients might be adopted to see that the females and other claimants were satisfied appropriately. The text itself leaving this embarrassing *lacuna,* courts

[1] See Derrett, 'May a Hindu woman be the manager of a joint family at Mitakshara law?', (1966) 68 Bom. L.R., *J.*, 1–11.

[2] The *smṛti-s* upon which the *Dāyabhāga* leans heavily insist upon the absence of *svātantryam* amongst sons while their parents live, and the voluntary nature of younger brothers' submission to their elder brothers. *Svāmyam* and *svātantryam* are discussed in *Baba* v. *Timma* (1883) 7 Mad. 357 (F.B.) (a father, while unseparated, has no power except for purposes warranted by special texts to alienate gratuitously to a stranger his undivided share in the ancestral estate movable or immovable).

[3] *J. Sreerama* v. *N. Krishnavenamma* [1956] An.W.R. 565.

[4] *Vyavahāra-contāmaṇi* (trans.), pp. 364–7. Kauṭilya, *Arthaśāstra* III, 1, 12 (Kāṅgle's trans., p. 221). Medhātithi on Manu VIII, 197–8 (Jhā's trans. IV (i), pp. 245–6).

[5] With the previous note's references cf. *Mit.* I, i, 29. *Gour Chandra* v. *Garib* AIR 1957 Or. 212.

in British India decided that the joint-family property should pass as if it were the separate estate of the last male holder.[1] This in practice favoured the widow of the last male member to die. In courts outside British India some held that the estate must go to the widows of the deceased coparceners in equal shares, or as a joint estate, so that the senior widows would not only not lose, but actually have a predominant say in the management.[2]

Further the actual text provides that even in the case of legal necessity and positive benefit to the family, or for the purposes of religious benefit which the family needed (e.g. marriage of a granddaughter, endowment for worship of ancestors, pilgrimages for widows), the major members of the coparcenary were not bound without their consent, while only minor members and members whose consent could not be obtained or ought to be disregarded would be bound by the manager's independent action.[3] This rule was preserved for long in Mysore State and perhaps elsewhere,[4] but in British India the doctrine of the rights of the *bona fide* purchaser for value (the favoured child of Equity, whom the law protected against outraged beneficiaries of a trust)[5] so redefined the rights of non-alienating coparceners that distinctions between major and minor coparceners, etc., became otiose. This has largely increased the powers of the manager, but has been offset by the better provision for upsetting alienations which were neither for the benefit of the family nor for the payment of an antecedent untainted debt of the ancestor. We have already noticed the novel development

[1] *Peddamuttu* v. *Appu Rau* (1864) 2 Mad. H.C.R. 117.

[2] *Ramal* v. *Ammani* (1887) 5 Trav. L.R. 45 (F.B.). See (1960) S.C.J., *J.*, 49, and [1965] K.L.T., *J.*, 39. The senior of the widows would act as manager of the family: *Dacshinamoorthy* v. *Narayanan* (1935) 51 Tr.L.R. 150, 153. The *Śvaśrū-snuṣā-dhana-saṃvāda* argued that mother-in-law and daughter-in-law should share the estate–an abortive suggestion (p. 273, n. 13 above).

[3] *Mit.* I, i, 29.

[4] *Nanjundegowda* v. *Rangegowda* AIR 1953 Mys. 138. Old British Indian decisions (*Muthoora* v. *Bootun* [1870] 13 W.R. (CR) 30, *Upooroop Tewary* v. *Bandhjee* [1881] 6 Cal. 749) which were faithful to the spirit of the text have ceased to be the law (*Ponnappa* v. *Pappuvayyangar* [1881] 4 Mad. 1, 18; cf. also *Miller* v. *Runga Nath* [1885] 12 Cal. 389, 399) as noticed at Mayne, §. 358; but the latter apparently inspired a misleading dictum in the Supreme Court (note the warning at Derrett, [1965] 67 Bom. L.R., *J.*, 96–8).

[5] *Hunooman Persaud* v. *Mst. Babooee* (1856) 6 M.I.A. 393.

whereby, under the Pious Obligation, sons and other male issue are disenabled from impugning certain alienations by their ancestor.[1] In many courts outside British India the ancient doctrine, that the father's debts would bind the sons' interests only after his death, continued for long in force.[2] The desperate controversies between the High Courts on the issue of 'antecedency' (i.e. whether any alienation by mortgage will bind the sons' interests *ipso facto*) do not affect the question from our present point of view, and the question whether the Supreme Court has silently put them to rest (which will agitate the High Courts themselves) can be passed over as mere evidence of the confused state of the uncodified law.[3]

Lastly, in defiance of Mitāksharā theory, as we have seen, individual coparceners have been allowed since the earliest British period in South India only to alienate their undivided interests for value.[4] The alienee is given an equity against the entire joint-family estate, and he may step into the shoes of his alienor in a suit for general partition.[5] If an individual object is alienated the alienee has no absolute claim to it, and must wait and see whether the court in partition proceedings considers it equitable for him to be put into possession of it.[6] Since what is to be transferred is no more than the presumptive share of the alienor in the net distributable assets of the family it follows that demands for maintenance and other charges on the family's resources may reduce the actual share available unexpectedly.[7] In Dāyabhāga law no such difficulties exist, as the coparcener can sell or mortgage his share, and the alienee may bring a suit for partition of the fraction. The right to alienate coparcenary property was always denied by the *śāstra*, and up to the beginning of the British period it was believed that to alienate a share of undivided joint-family property was an offence even at

[1] See above, pp. 115, 417.

[2] *Hutcha* v. *Dyavamma* AIR 1954 Mys. 93 (F.B.).

[3] *Virdhachalam* v. *Chaldean Syrian Bank* AIR 1964 S.C. 1425. A decision in the Supreme Court has put an end to doubt where the father accepts personal liability–the sons are bound: *Faqir Chand* v. *Sardarni* AIR 1967 S.C. 727.

[4] See the article referred to at p. 418 n. 1 above.

[5] See *ibid.*, n. 3 above.

[6] *Jagdish Pandey* v. *Rameshwar* AIR 1960 Pat. 54. Derrett, *I.M.H.L.*, §. 500.

[7] *Kokila* v. *K. M. Rajabather* AIR 1957 Mad. 470, 472.

Dāyabhāga law,[1] and that the penalties applicable could be avoided only by showing the consent of the other co-owners. Perhaps partly as a result of Jagannātha's suggestions the basic doctrine of the coparcener's ownership of his share prior to partition, when seen in the light of the common law attitude to dissolution of a partnership in a *forum* in which both common law and equity were administered, has been allowed to dominate in this field during the British period. The development in South India (Mitāksharā school) was based in practice on a refusal to allow the coparcener to hide behind his jointness. It was very useful for the coparcener to employ his interest in undivided property without having the nuisance and embarrassment of a partition merely because the father or elder brother refused to sanction the transaction: and in theory the sale-price or mortgage-amount was joint-family property and the alienor's act caused no total loss, for his appropriation by these means could be debited to him at a partition between himself and his coparceners.

The Hindu Women's Rights to Property Act, 1937, led to the widow's being admitted in some Provinces to be manager in default of a coparcener,[2] and she could alienate her statutory interest in South India as if she were a coparcener, and according to some Judges, even in some parts of India where her husband himself could not have alienated his undivided interest: but these questions, trammelled with the inconvenient consequences of the limited estate which the statute gave her in such property, have come to an end with the passing of the *HSA*, which, as we have seen, enlarged her estate into an absolute tenure.

The manager has now the duty of coping with the income-tax status of his family. He can show the joint members of the coparcenary as separated for assessing the income of certain items of joint-family property.[3] He can, as many do, actually separate his sons from himself at their majority (usually eighteen)

[1] For Jagannātha's views (above, p. 248) see Derrett, 'Alienations at Hindu law . . .', [1957] S.C.J., *J.*, 93–4.

[2] *Radha* v. *Commr. I.-T.* AIR 1950 Mad. 538.

[3] *Charandas* v. *Commr. I.-T.*, (1960) 62 Bom. L.R. 663 (S.C.). Derrett, at (1961) 63 Bom. L.R., *J.*, 17 ff. *Joint Family of Udayan* v. *Commr. of I.-T., Gujarat* AIR 1967 S.C. 762 illustrates the special effects of joint or separate status for the purpose of assessment.

or sooner, and thereby avoid a proportion of the income-tax liability which would fall upon the pair of them had the property been joint. He can as guardian of his minor separated son, or merely with the consent of his major separated son, loan his son's share to himself at interest, with consequent income-tax advantages. But this does not mean that the two do not continue to live exactly as if they were joint, the sentimental and social conditions of family life being entirely unaffected by these financial arrangements of which the law takes adequate notice.[1] Other burdens fall on the manager. He must pay the Estate Duty when a coparcener dies. He must provide accounts for relations who have inherited undivided interests, or even shares in such, under the *HSA*. He must make up his mind whether to continue businesses for the sake of their preservation from the time of partition until the asset is liquidated or assigned undivided to a member or members.[2] He will also act in the capacity of manager of the family, agent for the legatees or heirs of joint-family interests or fractions thereof, and in many cases partner in partnerships with strangers in which he represents the joint-family interests.[3] It need hardly be said that his duties are more complicated than in śāstric times. In addition he is liable at partition for any frauds or misappropriations and also any amounts which are proved to have come into his hands, but for the non-application of which according to AHL he is unable to give a satisfactory explanation.[4] Where the maintenance of a member of the family has been threatened by an alienation which cannot be proved to have been made to meet joint-family debts the manager may be called upon to account personally for so much of the property alienated as would have been sufficient to provide the maintenance.[5] Otherwise the

[1] Where a father obtains a consent decree for partition against his son, and then seeks assessment as a separated member of the family, while the two continue to live together as a joint family, he risks being assessed as if he had escaped assessment during the relevant year: *I.-T. Officer, Lucknow* v. *Bachu Lal Kapoor* [1967] 1 S.C.W.R. 14.

[2] Rāghavāchāriar, p. 310; Derrett, *I.M.H.L.*, §§. 454–60.

[3] *Ram Kumar* v. *Commr. I.-T.* AIR 1953 All. 150.

[4] *L. Bappu Ayyar* v. *Renganayaki* AIR 1955 Mad. 394. *K. V. Narayanaswami* v. *K. V. Ramakrishna* AIR 1965 S.C. 289, 295.

[5] *Chunilal* v. *Bai Saraswati* AIR 1943 Bom. 393. *Muniammal* v. *Ranganatha* AIR 1955 Mad. 571.

maintained relative's only hope, besides obtaining a charge (above), is to demand maintenance from the alienee, and this is not available where the latter has taken for value and without notice of the claim of the relative in question.[1] This further instance of the blend of śāstric law and equity in AHL illustrates how the juridical structure of the joint-family altered during the British period.

During śāstric times a family were known to be joint from the fact that no transactions took place between members. Now a joint family may *pay* a *kartā* for his services, and the opposite extreme has been reached.[2]

Leaving the Joint-Family

Ancient custom amongst the Āryans prevented the sons' separation without the father's leave, and this remains a rule in the Punjab. In Mahārāshtra to this day a son may not partition the joint-family property with his father against the latter's will if he is joint with his own collaterals[3]–a rule, perhaps based upon a misunderstanding of law coupled with an incomplete apprehension of local usage, which has been eroded by a curious decision in Gujarat which, if it achieves anything, tells us that in that commercially-developed area separations of sons without their fathers' consent are not frowned upon.[4] Otherwise the *Mitākṣarā's* notion that a son may force his father to divide equally with him the property of the deceased grandfather, unpopular amongst successors of the *Mitākṣarā* itself,[5] has made great progress in AHL. Partition is free. The same naturally attaches to the interests of widows under the Act of 1937 and *a fortiori* under the Act of 1956. Yet the notion of separating from

[1] *Dattatraya* v. *Tulsabai* [1943] Bom. 646, construing Transfer of Property Act, s. 39 (see Mulla on the Transfer of Property Act, 1882[5], 1966, *ad loc.*). The MHL does not depart from the position: see *HAMA*, s. 28.

[2] *M./S. Jugal* v. *Commr. I.-T., U.P.* AIR 1967 S.C. 495.

[3] *Apaji* v. *Ramchandra* (1892) 16 Bom. 29 (F.B.)

[4] *Jaswantlal* v. *Nichhabhai* AIR 1964 Guj. 283.

[5] Unless this writer is mistaken neither the *Smṛti-candrikā* nor the *Vyavahāra-mayūkha* (see, e.g., Setlūr's *Collection*) confirms the sons' right to demand partition against the father's will. The latter at VI, 4–6 deals with the father's deposition on grounds of vice or senility.

the father seems objectionable even in the South.[1] In practice great use is made of the quite ancient scheme whereby the father 'advanced' his sons by transferring a share to each, and separated them from himself and from each other at times agreeable to himself. A father may be induced to give the son a slice of the ancestral property, to set him up in life, and also a slice of his self-acquired property (for in practice the distinction is not observed between father and son with such nicety as the law would allow): in respect of the latter he is under no obligation to observe equality between the sons.[2] The ancient rules allowing sons different shares according to their mother's status or the number of sons *per* mother,[3] having long been obsolete; equally so the rules allowing the eldest son a large extra share, and a gradation of shares for younger sons.[4] They belong to a stage of development of enterprise which is not even remembered. Unfortunately, whatever might be the position at śāstric law, the separated son would be totally excluded from *all* property, which would pass by succession *or* survivorship to any joint son.[5] Thus to give a son a share and send him off was to adeem any rights he might have in future, somewhat similarly with the daughter's position, for her dowry was in lieu of a share in the paternal estate. The rule has been continued in the MHL in the case of a son who separates *himself*.[6] All surviving oddities of Hindu succession law are now supposed to be capable of adjustment in individual cases by testament. By giving a son away in adoption a parent could thereby put an immediate end to all his rights in the family of his birth. The *disqualified* son[7] cannot initiate a partition of family property.

Non-coparceners, and those who have no statutory interest in

[1] Demanding partition was a sin: Medhātithi on Manu IX, 209 (Jhā's trans. V, p. 173). One who separated against his father's wishes could not attend *śrāddha-s* and was thus virtually ostracized. But the legal right was there.

[2] Rāghavāchāriar, §. 331.

[3] Some ancient rules survived until 1956 in the Punjab and elsewhere. Gautama XXVIII, 17 (*Dh.K.*, 1234), Bṛhaspati (*Dh.K.*, 1237) followed by Vyāsa are the root texts surviving in the *dharmaśāstra*. A form of partition in which, when mothers share with their sons, each mother shares equally with each of her own sons as against the sons by a co-wife is still in force at Dāyabhāga, but not at Mitāksharā law: B. Sivarāmayya at AIR 1963 Journal 67–8.

[4] *Mit.* I, ii, 13 ff.

[5] See above, p. 422, n. 5.

[6] *HSA*, s. 6, expl. 2.

[7] Rāghavāchāriar, §. 353; Derrett, *I.M.H.L.*, §. 409.

the joint-family property have a right of maintenance, and no further: consequently they have a right to live apart, and to obtain a decree for maintenance if they cannot be induced to live together with the manager. But there is no means by which their connexion with and drain upon family finances can be severed, equal to the coparcener's severance and partition. In practice such relatives are often offered a settlement or agreement, which, if carefully drawn, will bind them not to ask for more or claim an increase in the rate: but the terms of the *HAMA* have been held to enable even a binding agreement to be broken in order to afford such a relative a higher rate.[1]

In view of the developments of the manager's powers to allot shares of joint-family property coparceners and others it is more usual to live separate than to sever. In severance there is the chance of losing a windfall by cutting oneself off from the benefit of survivorship. True this benefit is much lessened by the operation of *HSA*, s. 6, whereby one who is survived by his *mother*, *wife*, or even *daughter* has as his heir either a legatee of his, or whichever close relatives in the first class of the schedule to that statute are available to take his property on intestacy (including his undivided joint-family interest) in shares absolutely. But this fact will not have penetrated so deep as to disturb the usual reluctance to separate where this can be avoided. True, even separated brothers will support each other more faithfully than brothers in other civilizations do in the ordinary way, but the psychological damage done by severance is worth avoiding. Thus the appearance of several small joint-families or even several small nuclear families, often masks a large family which is joint in law but has numerous sundered branches. The Income-tax law operates favourably to partitions, but, as we have seen, does not force a complete partition upon members who can make convenient arrangements retaining their residual jointness. Even after partition of status coparceners and their dependants often continue to live together, giving a deceptive appearance of the opposite kind. There is at AHL no obligation upon separated members to partition 'by metes and bounds' at any particular time.[2]

[1] *HAMA*, s. 25. Derrett, *I.M.H.L.*, §. 665, also *Seshi* v. *Thaiyu* AIR 1964 Mad. 217.

[2] *Martand* v. *Radhabai* AIR 1931 Bom. 97. Rāghavāchāriar, §§. 329, 336.

The Function of the Joint-Family in the Future

The MHL appears to have dealt a great blow to the family. We have noticed its interference with survivorship, much more severe and pervasive than that initiated in the Act of 1937. All other (including the much older) modifications of the family law are thought to have undermined its essential characteristics. On the one hand the public, seeing the dwindling of the extended family under the pressure of later marriages, education for women, and growing individualism (as well as the growth of enough means to enable people to live out of several pots instead of one), believe that the joint-family as an institution is as good as dying; on the other hand the law, indifferent apparently to the social and religious sanctions still attaching to the family as an extended social unit, eats away at the juridical framework. But is the common conclusion justified?

A special instance of deceptive appearances is provided in the customs of some South Indian castes. There it is usual, as before the *Mitākṣarā* came their way, for brothers to live together after their marriages and to manage their affairs separately, but, where they overlap, through a manager, usually their senior member. The costs of the individual branches are debited in cashbooks, and when it comes to an eventual partition the shares are debited with the past expenses. Alternatively the acquisitions of the branches are set off against the expenditure of these branches.[1] These arrangements are looked upon as modifications intended to encourage enterprise; in fact they seem to be survivals of the juridical position before Mitāksharā law was generally enforced. Because those who owned shares in the estate chose to live jointly it did not follow that the needs of each should be at the charge of all. The same anomalous habits prevail in such castes even between a married son and his father. The AHL says that they are joint, because no partition has taken place: the actual usage treats them as separate for some purposes. Yet the law of survivorship has not been taken away and the joint ownership of father and son is not doubted. In many castes the shadow of a partition hangs over the family's

[1] Derrett, 'The Supreme Court and acquisition of joint-family property', (1960) 62 Bom. L.R., *J.*, 57 ff.; to which add *Chidambaram* v. *Subramanian* AIR 1953 Mad. 492 (to n. 33 on p. 63).

arrangements far more than in others, and curiously more in South India than in the North.

All the burdens placed on the structure of the joint-family seem to be the result of a desire to retain the father-son relationship as the pivot or axis of the family, despite the development of taxation and the modern commercial expedients to which the actual movements of the organism have had to adjust themselves. The functional (not consensual) solidarity of father and son in the face of their joint religious and social obligations seems to be the core of the joint-family. Its psychological traces are noted variously in the *śāstra*, which tells us that in the son who 'pays his debts', the father is actually re-born (not so in the daughter).[1] The religious symbolism clothes a deep belief, far older than history, let alone legal history. The son saves his father from hell, the sight of the son's face gives the father not merely sentimental delight (as anywhere else) but also supersensory, 'unseen', satisfaction, and likewise to his ancestors long since dead. Upon the need to get a 'good' son is founded the elaborate religious law relative to marriage which, as we have seen, guided and to a large extent successfully moulded the customary notions about unions between the genders. Bad marriages make bad offspring: bad in a supersensory, if no other sense. These are unquestionably religious notions, and to disentangle the rational and sentimental from the religious elements in the beliefs relative to the birth of a son, and especially the first son, is a profitless exercise for our purpose. The law–surely not by coincidence?–has left that hard axis of the family alone, while it has pruned the periphery savagely.

The intrusion of females as owners of coparcenary assets will probably not alter the basic character of the institution of the family. In the majority of cases the legal rights will not be exercised, or will be exercised subject to restraints–for some of which the *HSA* realistically makes provision. Where the remarriage of widows and divorcees is already normal no extra strain

[1] Kāṇe, *H.D.*, II (i), 428–9, 560–1. The magical ceremony in which a father, anticipating his death, transfers his powers and attributes to his son, so that the latter absorbs (as it were) his personality totally, with legal effects, is a relict of the Vedic age (Bṛh. Up. I, 5) passed over in śāstric law. *Śaṅkhāyana-āraṇyaka* V, 15 (cf. *Kauṣitaki-upaniṣad* II, 10): I. S. Pawate, *Res Nullius* (Dharwad, 1938), 185 ff.; G.-D. Sontheimer, 'The Concept of Dāya: a comparative study', Dissertation (Acad. Postgr. Dipl., Law), London (unpublished), 1962, pp. 36–7.

will be placed on the habits of the family: and in general it appears that though the corpus of family property is reduced the nature of the institution remains much the same. So long as the father and his sons regard themselves as jointly and successively responsible for the maintenance of members of the family, the joint-family will remain, and the MHL has not taken away its juridical framework. That the religious conception has not been enfringed tells rather for the discrimination (if only unconscious) of the reformers. And that relates to the place of religion in Indian law, to which we are about to come.

The fact that some members may now have independent means will not necessarily alter the situation, as indeed the possession of a share does not automatically free the joint estate from the duty to maintain. If a share is spent or lost it is not impossible that the dependant may still sue for bare maintenance.

It is argued that where all the brothers may be earning separate salaries in different places, unlike the old-fashioned agricultural and mercantile classes, the function of the joint-family has ceased at least as far as they are concerned. But whatever the relationship between the brothers, who, even if they actually separate, retain as long as they live the right to reunite, it is the position within the branch that matters. As soon as a son is born the story starts again. Legal reforms can cut down the amount of property available, and free members from the restraints which the previous law had fastened upon them with its rigorous logic; but to stop the formation of new joint-families as soon as an old one is split far more drastic legislation will be needed than has hitherto been devised, and such a task, if not beyond the competence, may well be beyond the desire of the legislatures as well as the courts of India.[1] It will be observed that by 'joint-family' the present writer, as lawyers do in

[1] In *B. Balaiah* v. *C. Lachaiah* AIR 1965 A.P. 435 the question was of construction of s. 10 (3) (a) (iii) of the Andhra Pradesh Buildings (Lease, Rent and Eviction) Control Act, 1960. A tenant may be evicted if the owner-applicant 'requires it for a purpose of a business which he is carrying on or which he *bona fide* proposes to commence'. A father-manager, who wanted his undivided son to carry on his business in the building, applied for eviction of the tenant. To this it was objected that the word 'he' did not include the owner's *son*. The learned judge held that 'he' included his son. In construing such statutes social and religious customs must be borne in mind: '. . . the necessity of realizing that the family in India whether joint or separate is the social unit of Indian civilization and it is greater public importance to keep it together' (*sic*).

general, means the unit which holds property in common or which can hold property in common in the peculiar joint-family tenure – not the houseful of relations which the expression 'joint-family' usually conjures up for the Indian layman.

It is also argued that the law imposes at present a notion of jointness, and, by means of out-of-date presumptions, keeps alive an institution which, if Hindus could accept the logical implications of their increased separate living and increasing impatience of restraint by elders, would have died a natural death. No doubt a knowledge of the law as it is administered affects the behaviour of those who normally come within the scope of litigation; though against this it must be remembered that law has never penetrated as deeply into the consciousness and preoccupations of the majority of Hindus as did their pre-British customs. Yet law can neither give nor take away the fundamental sense of mutual belonging, even of the *ideal* mutual belonging, which exists respectively in the male lineal descendants of a common male ancestor and their wives and unmarried daughters. Mutual belonging, mutual responsibility, reinforced and expressed in terms of ancestral lands and privileges and ancestral religious rites and shrines, and the common unquestioning *ideal* obedience to the senior, most prestige-worthy representative of the lineage, still make what the author of the *Mitākṣarā* would call 'unseparatedness' (as we say 'jointness') the rule rather than the exception: and the louder people clamour that 'the joint-family is breaking up' the clearer they make what seems to be the fact, namely that the strains this adaptable institution now takes are heavy – but not yet too heavy for it.[1]

[1] A convenient, if somewhat pedestrian, documentation of the well-known features of joint-family life is included in Aileen D. Ross's *Hindu Family in its Urban Setting* (University of Toronto Press, 1961), ch. 1 of which broaches questions touched upon in this chapter. Irawati Karve's 'The family in India', in Baidya N. Varma, ed., *Contemporary India* (London, Asia Publishing House, 1964), pp. 47–58, admirably summarizes the current classes of family, and shows how joint-families, as usually understood, are disappearing leaving the joint-family psychology intact. For a comparative view of Equity in the realm of Indian joint-family law see now Derrett, 'Fiduciary principles, the African family, and Hindu law', (1966) 15 *I.C.L.Q.* 1205–16. The present writer has not seen I. P. Desai's *Some Aspects of Family in Mahuva: a Sociological Study of Jointness in a Small Town* (Bombay, 1964).

13

RELIGION IN MODERN INDIAN LAW

Religion and law[1] come into contact in many spheres of Indian law but it is not convenient to tackle all of them together. The major questions raised by religious and charitable endowments, both public and private, must be reserved for the next chapter. A natural tendency would be to seek for a common characteristic within or behind all the points of contact and to illustrate it from any or all of these. As before, the seeker for a simple and straightforward formula of description is frustrated, and we are once again in the convolutions of all Indian phenomena. It is not satisfactory to put it down to India's size, age and diversity, as if that were any excuse. The answer to the conundrum, as usual, must be that convolution and discrepancy are the natural qualities of the Indian scene, and that the balance of contradictions in fact makes the life: it did so through the centuries, and it still does. Let us take our topics as they arise, and reserve the conclusion until the end of the next chapter.

Decisory Oaths: the Past Undisturbed

It is traditional in India to recognize a dispute's quality by the presence or absence of the willingness to compromise. Apart from litigation conducted on what might be called a cosmopolitan footing, as might arise anywhere in the world, there are

[1] This chapter traverses ground covered in part briefly at (1959) 61 Bom. L.R., *J.*, pp. 17–23; in the same volume at p. 38; at (1958) 8 *I.C.L.Q.*, 221–4; the same, vol. 10 (1961), pp. 914–16; the same, vol. 12 (1963), pp. 693–7; and in lectures given at the convention of the Association of Asian Studies, Philadelphia, 1963 and at the University of Chicago, Spring 1963, brought up to date with recent references and with an outlook wider than was possible on those occasions.

instances which do not amount to mere harassment and feuding, but which represent a failure of two individuals or families to find a new point of balance. In certain of these cases a compromise could be worked out, but arriving at it is postponed or hindered because the right or truth of some issue is unknown. In the vast majority of Indian disputes the facts are well known: they are only disputed for the fun or hazard of litigation which is entered into for speculation, revenge, or caprice; similarly any doubts about the law that there may be could easily be waived if the parties felt it was in their interest to come to terms and save the heavy lawyers' fees and court fees. But the odd case arises where the actual truth is unknown. If one party suspects that the other knows it, but cannot prove it, and is willing to allow the opprobrium to rest upon the other party if the latter is willing to pledge his credit, the dispute can be settled judicially by recourse to an ordeal. Ordeals we have already come across in Indian legal history.[1] Though rare they still exist in practice. The party who undertakes to be bound by the other's oath may allow him to take this oath, whereupon the case is decided against him.[2] No movement exists to remove this archaism from the Indian law, for of course it is up to litigants whether they consider the taking of an oath by their opposite parties to be a sufficient consideration in the general framework of their dealings to justify this course; they must decide whether it is worth while to enter into litigation in the first place when the case is so ill prepared.

Thus we have at least one instance where the contact between religion and law stays unaffected by social, political and indeed intellectual movements of all kinds.

The Personal Laws: Interference with Religion?

The contention that the personal laws are bound up with religion raises its head frequently. Dr. Luthera specifically charges the Indian legislatures with interfering with religion in the course of reform of the Hindu law.[3] The Constitution does not in fact prevent this, if indeed it has happened, and it would

[1] See above, p. 218.

[2] Indian Oaths Act, 1873, ss. 8–10. *Indar* v. *Jagmohan* (1927) 54 I.A. 301.

[3] *The Concept of the Secular State and India* (Calcutta, 1964), pp. 96–7.

be odd if it did. The whole course of Indian legal history, as we have seen, evinces a tendency to manipulate the sources of law. The systems of which the present personal laws are remnants have been vigorously truncated and surreptitiously modified without any outcry from those who now feel that their religion has been endangered.[1] The agitation about the Privy Council's decision, long ago, not to recognize illusory Muslim *wakfs* (an altogether sensible and practical decision from which Indian courts have by no means resiled),[2] took on a form which suggested that the religion of Islam was not sufficiently attended to by their Lordships, and the Indian legislature of the time did what it could to set the law straight.[3] Similarly the ancient rule that non-Muslims cannot make dedications to a Muslim charity or make gifts which will be valid in the eyes of the Islamic law[4]– a rule which admitted non-reciprocity between the religious legal systems in India–has been quietly dropped by a Parliamentary amendment without fuss.[5] The public's response to interference with the personal laws is uncertain and generally feeble, as would be likely when the theory that the laws are based on religion is so insecurely based, and when the public lives so remotely from the technicalities of the law applied to it. Thus it would have been very strange if the Constitution had introduced restraints upon the legislatures' capacity to legislate

[1] See above, pp. 293–4.

[2] *Fazlul Rabbi* v. *State of W. Bengal* AIR 1965 S.C. 1722: see below, n. 3.

[3] Mussalman Wakf Validating Act, 1913. See below. *Faqir* v. *Mus. Abda* [1952] 2 All. 806; *Thakur* v. *Thakur* AIR 1962 S.C. 1722. The Act of 1913 was given retrospective effect by the Mussalman Wakf Validating Act, 32 of 1930. These acts were judicially applied in Cochin as 'more in conformity with modern concepts': *Off. Receiver* v. *Kassim Moosa Sait* [1966] K.L.T. 985, 990 (justice, equity and good conscience).

[4] *Mst. Mundaria* v. *Rai Shyam* AIR 1963 Pat. 98 and references there given.

[5] S. 66C was inserted into the Muslim Wakfs Act, 1954 by the [central] Wakf (Amendment) Act, 34 of 1964: 'Notwithstanding anything contained in this Act where any moveable or immoveable property has been given or donated by any person not professing Islam for the support of a wakf being– (*a*) mosque, idgah, imāmbāra, dargah, khāngah or a maqbāra; (*b*) a Muslim graveyard; (*c*) a choultry or a musafarkhāna, then such property should be deemed to be comprised in that wakf and be dealt with in the same manner as the wakf in which it is so comprised.' *Syed Edulla* v. *Madras State of Wakf Board* [1966] 1 M.L.J. 17. An attempt at a similar amendment was made by the abortive Madras Act 19 of 1961 which did not obtain the President's assent.

in matters of religion or appertaining thereto, restraints which had not been recognized by the previous Government.

We have already discussed the question of the rôle which religion played in Hindu law.[1] It may be possible to argue that its rôle in Islamic law is different – a point to be pursued later.[2] The case can however be presented that, whether or not the Hindu religion determined the content of any of the chapters of the Hindu law even before the British, French and other foreign governments assumed responsibility to administer it (a contention we have disputed in an earlier chapter), the reform of the Hindu law which was the first step towards the Indian Civil Code interfered with Hindu religious beliefs and practices. If some sections believe this, and we can be sure from Dr. Luthera's thesis that some do, the point is worth investigation independently of the validity (if any) of the common constitutional and the less common historical justifications that can be offered.

No one will doubt but that the *śāstra* utilized and inculcated religious doctrines in the core of its family law.[3] The family law which was applied to Hindus in South Asia in 1955 was based on the *śāstra* and claimed not to have departed from it substantially in spirit except to the extent provided for in two provincial statutes. The case in defence of those statutes may rest with the case in defence of the central statute of 1955. The religious doctrines were not only accepted and relied upon, as in the celebrated case of *A.* v. *B.*,[4] in which nullity for impotence was declared part and parcel of the Anglo-Hindu law, but formed the logical skeleton of the otherwise appallingly complicated and antiquated system itself. Teachers of Hindu law in the law colleges of undivided India had for more than a half-century relied on these doctrines as 'principles' which, though often apparently strange to their students, made it possible to tolerate and learn an otherwise archaic-seeming and thorny subject. Fortunately we can recapitulate these principles, which have already come to our attention, in an unexpectedly short space.

In the orthodox view of things every male child was born in debt to his ancestors (irrespective of the other debts),[5] a debt

[1] See above, pp. 117–19. [2] See below, pp. 535 f. [3] See above, p. 120.

[4] (1952) 54 Bom. L.R. 725 = [1953] Bom. 487. The entire judgement is redolent of religious concepts.

[5] Kāṇe, *H.D.*, II, pp. 270, 560; III, pp. 415–17.

which he must pay by providing a male child, or better still not less than two male children to carry on the obligations of the line. This is the father-son axis of which we have already treated.[1] The family revolves around it, and it is the pivot of Hindu society, as society has no other pivot than the axis of each and every Hindu family. Since the son should be encouraged to beget a male child or better still not less than two male children, his marriage must therefore be arranged to a suitable mate. Adequate male children able to satisfy the ancestors are not to be obtained merely by secular, observed, conduct, such as intercourse as such.[2] Intercourse must take place in circumstances proper for the purpose, accompanied (actually or fictionally) with the appropriate sacraments. The sacraments cannot be performed on a non-virgin,[3] and naturally a girl suspected or even capable of being a non-virgin is from religious as well as social standpoints decidedly less acceptable. If the wife does not bear a son the husband is justified in marrying again, for the purpose of obtaining male issue. In the absence of male issue from wives he should adopt in the form of adoption admitted by the *śāstra* to provide a substitute for an *aurasa* son.[4] Equipped with a son the householder may perform ceremonies of religious value; accompanied by his wife he performs other daily and occasional ceremonies.[5] The ancestors will not be pleased and various evils will befall the family if the ceremonies are not conducted, and especially the ceremonies in worship of the ancestors themselves. The existence of the son guarantees the performance of *śrāddha-s*, which were at one time thought essential for agricultural prosperity. Since the worship of images plays a part in family religious life, it is natural that there should

[1] At pp. 433 ff. above.

[2] Basic matrimonial theory is expressed by Manu at II, 28; III, 28, 31–45, 37–42, 137–8; IX, 161.

[3] Derrett, 'The "Discussion of Marriage" by Gadādhara', *Adyar Library Bulletin*, 1963, pp. 171, 199. Kāṇe, *H.D.*, II, pp. 438–46. The rule applies to Brahmins and was adopted by some non-Brahmins in imitation of them.

[4] Derrett at *Zeits. f. vergl. Rechtsw.* 60 (1957), pp. 34–90. Kāṇe, *H.D.*, III, ch. 28. Golāpchandra Sarkar Śāstrī, *The Hindu Law of Adoption* (Calcutta, 1891).

[5] Kāṇe, *H.D.*, II, pp. 428–9; V, p. 1287. The main purposes of marriage are two: the wife enables a man to perform religious rites, and is the mother of a son or sons who were supposed to save a man from hell. See, e.g., Manu IX, 28; Yājñavalkya I, 78.

be a shrine either in the house or in an adjacent temple or in some place easily accessible to the family. The wife alone can perform worship as her husband's deputy. The family's property has a tacit charge upon it for performance of all religious rituals in addition to the other tacit charges for maintenance of dependants and hospitality. The manager of the family is the *kartā*,[1] the person responsible for religious worship of all kinds.

The Hindu Marriage Act, 1955, has made it possible for Hindus to marry women who do not speak their language, let alone share their religious background. The children born of such unions are incapable according to the *śāstra* of giving adequate spiritual benefit to ancestors. The total impossibility of spiritual benefit from these 'illegitimate' offspring is not asserted in the śāstric literature,[2] and this is a point we must watch. Moreover, in ancient history, kings used to marry women from various regions and peoples who virtually brought their gods with them, and a polytheistic outlook on religion found no incongruities in that. Yet the Hinduism of 1955 backed up by the Hindu law of that period found inter-caste marriages an abomination.[3] The worship of the household deities could lapse. The Hindu Succession Act, 1956, had, amongst other novel effects, the result of sending the property away from the relation next best qualified to attend to the duties of religion. The person through whom or by whom the *śrāddha* of the deceased male or his lineal ancestors could most efficaciously be performed,[4] who was often the preferential heir at Anglo-Hindu law until the amending statute of 1929[5] slightly varied the systematic scheme, is now passed over and the property is more often than not fragmented amongst many heirs. The son remains liable under the *śāstra* to perform the *śrāddha*, for the

[1] Literally 'performer'. The term is not found in śāstric works, but is accepted at AHL. Kāṇe, *H.D.*, III, p. 592.

[2] See references at Derrett, 'Illegitimates . . . ,' *J.A.O.S.*, 81 (1961), p. 255, n. 18; nn. 32–5; 58 Bom. L.R., *J.*, pp. 184–6.

[3] Kāṇe, *H.D.*, II, pp. 447–52 (historical development). References in AHL are discussed in *Smt. Kastoori* v. *Chiranji* AIR 1960 All. 446.

[4] For the theories see R. Sarvādhikāri, *Principles of the Hindu Law of Inheritance*[2], (Madras, 1922). See also an article, 'Sapindaship and religious efficacy' at (1959) 61 Bom. L.R., *J.*, pp. 177 ff.

[5] The Hindu Law of Inheritance (Amendment) Act, 2 of 1929. Derrett, *I.M.H.L.*, p. 624.

religious obligations[1] have not ceased because the property has been taken by the statute and placed elsewhere. The work of Parliament might be classed by the *śāstrī-s* along with the evils done by 'thieves and the king', to which people merely have to adjust themselves. The sacred law goes on notwithstanding.

An effect of the Hindu Succession Act is to weaken the family's beliefs in their religious observances. It is left virtually to the eccentricities and fantasies of males or to the faith and orthodoxy of females. The Hindu Adoptions and Maintenance Act, 1956, enables widows to adopt without thereby making, as before, a posthumous heir for their deceased husbands: even if they comply with the *śāstra*–which they need not in order to comply with the statute–the same statute takes the property specifically out of the adopted child's hands.[2] Adoption of daughters[3] will give no spiritual benefit to anyone. Sons may be adopted whose qualifications are such that they can never give spiritual benefit.[4] And what seems worse, males who despair of sons and previously used to be able to adopt virtually on their deathbeds, are prevented by the statute from making a legal adoption if they are under the prescribed age.[5] To return to marriage: there is now nothing to prevent a Hindu lad from marrying a widow, a divorcee, a prostitute, of any or no caste, and if society shuns him for his act he can claim that the weight of 'enlightened opinion' is behind him in utilizing his new freedom.

Very little challenge has been brought to this way of proceeding. True, castes can excommunicate (outside Maharashtra and Gujarat) anyone they choose[6]–provided they abide by the caste rules and observe natural justice–and to that extent a social group which wishes to observe the *śāstra*, or, if they know it better, the Anglo-Hindu legal complex as it existed before the Hindu Code, may enforce obedience. But so far as the law of the land is concerned it really seems to have dealt religion a blow, and has all the prestige of the government and the 'New'

[1] One who takes the property is liable to perform the *śrāddha* if nearer kindred are not available. Kāṇe, *H.D.*, III, pp. 734–5.

[2] *HAMA*, s. 12 (c). Derrett, *I.M.H.L.*, p. 601.

[3] *HAMA*, ss. 10, 11. Derrett, where cited, pp. 599, 600.

[4] Patently such sons as are contemplated by *HAMA*, ss. 9 (4), 11 (vi).

[5] *HAMA*, s. 7. For the previous law see Derrett, *I.M.H.L.*, §. 142.

[6] See below, p. 473, n. 1. See also above, p. 314, and p. 358, n. 3.

India behind it. Recent complaints in the Haryana Legislative Assembly, to the effect that the HSA has struck at the core of Hindu family ethics, are symptomatic of a general (but impotent) feeling.

The courts' answer to the challenge that has been made is curious, and somewhat misleading, but not nevertheless wrong, either logically or historically, as will be contended later. In *State of Bombay* v. *Narasu Appa Mali*[1] the Bombay statute was attacked as unconstitutional, being in violation of the fundamental right guaranteed by the Constitution which is conveniently, but misleadingly called 'Freedom of Religion'. The statute had imposed a penalty upon a subject for contracting a bigamous marriage,[2] and it was further contended that this was discrimination against Hindus (for Muslims were still permitted the dubious privilege of polygamy) in violation of Art. 14 of the Constitution, irrespectively of its violation of the Article in support of religion. The very interesting arguments and judgements must be abbreviated. The result was a foregone conclusion in view of the actual terms of the Constitution which may be set out here:[3]

> *Art. 25* (1) Subject to public order, morality and health and to the other provisions of this Part, all persons are equally entitled to freedom of conscience and the right freely to profess, practise and propagate religion.
>
> (2) Nothing in this article shall affect the operation of any existing law or prevent the State from making any law–
>
> (*a*) regulating or restricting any economic, financial, political or other secular activity which may be associated with religious practice;
>
> (*b*) providing for social welfare and reform or the throwing open of Hindu religious institutions of a public character to all classes and sections of Hindus.
>
> *Explanation I.* The wearing and carrying of *kirpāns*[4] shall be deemed to be included in the profession of the Sikh religion.
>
> *Explanation II.* In sub-clause (*b*) of clause (2), the reference to Hindus shall be construed as including a reference to persons professing the Sikh, Jaina or Buddhist religion, and the reference to Hindu religious institutions shall be construed accordingly.

From this it was evident that 'social welfare and reform' could operate as a justification for any attack upon profession, prac-

[1] (1951) 53 Bom. L.R. 779 = [1951] Bom. 775. Luthera, cited above, p. 83.

[2] See above, p. 356.

[3] D. D. Basu, *Commentary*, 4th edn., II, p. 143.

[4] Literally, 'swords'.

tice and propagation of any religion.[1] That particular bench of the Bombay High Court could not be expected to hold that statutes prohibiting bigamy were not passed in the interests of 'social welfare and reform', and it is very doubtful whether any bench in any High Court could take such a view. In *Srinivasa* v. *Saraswathi*[2] the Madras High Court took the same line as the Bombay High Court in a case which was of virtually the same complexion. The argument that statutes punishing bigamous marriages and facilitating marriage between castes, abolishing age-old bars to marriage, and removing the ancient distinctions between classes of heirs were not in fact incidents of 'social welfare and reform', but were a partisan scheme intended for the social advancement of a particular layer or set of layers of a dominant wealthy class of Hindu society was never raised, and could not be raised so long as there was a chance that anyone seized of this problem could sympathize with the aspirations of this class and hope to join it. Modernization, westernization, and the removal of archaic features in the personal law were aims to which everyone with a claim to be patriotic found himself pledged.

The shoe pinched in individual cases. Polygamous marriages do in fact take place (sometimes masked by nominal divorces of the first spouse), and the courts can wink at them by the interesting and perfectly legal device of refusing to recognize the second marriage as a properly solemnized marriage, irrespective of the apparent intentions of the parties to the ceremony![3] The man who can get society on his side may be pinched more adequately by the prejudices of his employer. The Government of the Uttar Pradesh, as some other State governments and the armed forces, laid down in its government servants' rules (Rule 27) that no servant of the State should contract a bigamous marriage even if his personal law for the time being permitted such marriages.[4] In *Ram Prasad* v. *The State of Uttar*

[1] Luthera, cited above, p. 113. [2] AIR 1952 Mad. 193.

[3] See above, p. 355. *Kanwal* v. *H. P. Administration* AIR 1966 S.C. 614.

[4] Compare, for example, the situation of school-teachers under the Kerala Education Rules, 1959, as amended up to 1965 (see [1965] K.L.T., Kerala Rules and Notifications, p. 42): 'cl. 63. *Bigamous Marriages:*—(i) No teacher who has a wife living shall contract another marriage without first obtaining the permission of the Government, notwithstanding that such subsequent marriage is permissible under personal law for the time being applicable to

Pradesh[1] an engineer in the Public Works Department married in 1934 and had four children amongst whom no son survived. Under the alleged impression that he could not attain salvation without a son he sought his wife's permission to remarry. She at first agreed, but when he prepared to marry again, the Chief Engineer, at the instigation of the wife, refused him permission to marry without the permission of the State Government. He applied for a writ of mandamus commanding the State of Uttar Pradesh to dispose of his application in accordance with the *śāstra*, and not the provisions of the *HMA*, which, in so far as they would inhibit his remarriage, were in violation of his constitutional right to profess and practise his religion. His religion obliged him to marry again in the hope of obtaining a son. Rule 27 of the Uttar Pradesh Government Servants' Conduct Rules was therefore in conflict with his religion. But the court had the Madras and Bombay cases before them, the same distinction which was made there was made here more effectively, and the point is more distinctly observed in *Ram Prasad's case* than in the earlier cases. The State's acts were valid.

All three cases link with *Lakshmindra's case*, to which we shall return in the next chapter.[2] Granted that the Constitution, by Art. 25 (2) (*b*) gives full permission to the State to amend the personal law of the Hindus and others, the conflict with religion which is posited above remains an embarrassment which the judges do not relish. It was not necessary in any of these cases to refer to that conflict for the decision of the dispute. But since the plaintiffs or applicants relied heavily on the grievance that their freedom of religion had been infringed, it was not unnatural to enquire whether, after all, religion had been interfered with. The Constitution allowed the legislature to amend the personal laws in the interests of 'social welfare and reform', and the Article started from the assumption that it might be alleged that such interests would clash with the right 'freely to profess and practise' religion. But were such allegations justified? Their Lordships in Bombay say,[3] 'It is rather difficult to accept the proposition that polygamy is an integral part of (the) Hindu

him. (ii) No woman teacher shall marry any person who has a wife living without first obtaining the permission of the Government.'

[1] AIR 1957 All. 411. [2] AIR 1954 S.C. 282; see below, p. 494.

[3] Quoted at AIR 1957 All. 411, 413 col. 2.

religion.' In other words the courts can determine what is an integral part of religion and what is not. The word 'essential' is now in familiar use for this purpose. As we shall see there is a context in which the religious *community* is allowed freedom to determine what is 'essential' to its belief and practice, but the individual has no freedom to determine what is essential to his religion, for if it were otherwise and if the law gave any protection to religion as determined on this basis the State's power to protect and direct would be at an end. Therefore the courts can discard as non-essentials anything which is not proved to *their* satisfaction – and they are not religious leaders or in any relevant fashion qualified in such matters – to be essential, with the result that it would have no constitutional protection. The Constitution does not say 'freely to profess, practise and propagate *the essentials of* religion', but this is how it is construed.

Polygamy was a social result of a belief which was expressed in religious as well as other terms. The Bombay High Court could not accept that the legal condemnation of polygamy amounted to an attack on the essentials of Hinduism. That the State had an alternative, namely to forbid bigamous marriages not permitted by a board set up with jurisdiction to enquire into the circumstances of each case and to permit remarriage in circumstances where the *śāstra* itself would have recommended it, was not discussed, and the legislature's wisdom in simply penalizing all bigamists was accepted as justified. Similarly in *Ram Prasad's case* the Allahabad High Court say,[1] 'Under the circumstances it cannot be said that it is obligatory as an integral part of a Hindu religion to marry in the presence of the first wife if from the first wife a Hindu has no male child.' For after all it was open to him to adopt. This must be emphasized. A way out known to the *śāstra* lay ready to hand, and therefore he could not claim that his religious freedoms were infringed. The same argument was raised successfully in the Cow-slaughter cases to which we shall come presently.[2] To the present writer's mind the argument, though it comes from the mouth of people hardly qualified to express any opinion on such highly delicate matters, is historically and logically right.

The Hindu in India, whose religious law has been amended, and whose performance of religious duties has been hampered,

[1] At the same place.

[2] Below at pp. 471–2.

or at least not facilitated, is not left without alternatives at least *known* to the *śāstra*, or to any recognizable religious sectarian belief which is not sought to be put into practice in such a way as to offend against public order, morality and health. Thus those who believe that salvation is obtained by religious suicide can validly be prevented from committing suicide in the interests of public order, morality and health. This can be done without the dominant society's fearing that it has trampled upon the Hindu religion which sanctions or at least acknowledges such notions, because an alternative exists which the religion countenances. It seems precisely because the wearing of *kirpāns* by Sikhs is unequivocal and has no alternative that Expl. I to the article refers explicitly to this custom.

Protection of Religion

The protection of religious belief, in the limited freedom of conscience guaranteed by Art. 25 (above), requires little comment. Attacks on people's beliefs, as such, are rare in India, and, as we have said, even Muslim and Christian teachers whose religions both authorize and require them to spread their creeds, operate at a much lower key in India and do not in practice set out to obtain adherents on any large scale. Proselytizing is rare and attacks on other religious in point of *belief* still rarer. However the protection afforded to religion by the Indian Penal Code is occasionally called for and deserves mention. While s. 298 protects the feelings of individuals, ss. 295 and 295A protect the religion of a class or classes.

S. 295. Whoever destroys, damages or defiles any place of worship, or any object held sacred by any class of persons with the intention of thereby insulting the religion of any class of persons or with the knowledge that any class of persons is likely to consider such destruction, damage or defilement as an insult to their religion, shall be punished with imprisonment of either description for a term which may extend to two years, or with fine, or with both.

S. 295A. Whoever, with deliberate and malicious intention of outraging the religious feelings of any class of citizens of India, by words, either spoken or written, or by visible representations, insults or attempts to insult the religion or the religious beliefs of that class, shall be punished with imprisonment of either description for a term which may extend to two years, or with fine, or with both.

Many offences *prima facie* punishable under s. 295 or s. 295A are really not about religion as we understand it, but are directed to communal or simply financial ends – personal religious antagonisms seldom enter into the affair.[1] The classic case is that of *Sheo Shankar* v. *Emperor*.[2] It gives, it is true, a view of the law's attitude to religion which is out of date; but it is plainly a communal case. Ahirs, who were *śūdra-s*, assumed the sacred thread reserved for (twice-born) initiates. Brahmins forcibly tore it off. This was held by English judges not to have been an offence under either section. 'Where persons observing the *same* religion broke the thread of someone whom they regarded as an upstart wearing something which he was not entitled to wear, it cannot be supposed that either the victim of assault would be likely to consider that act an insult to his religion or the assailant could be considered to have the knowledge that he was likely so to do.'

There is no doubt but that the intimate connexion between religion and caste or community has in the past encouraged attacks on communities by way of attacks on their religion or religious practices. These sections are therefore intended rather for the keeping of the peace than for the protection of religion as such, but this last object cannot be said not to be served by them. The majority can no more insult the religions of the minorities than the latter can set out to outrage the religious feelings of the majority. This is a feature of India which goes far to justify its claim to be a secular state in the sense that there is no preference for the religion of the majority of the inhabitants. Three cases illustrate how this protection works. In *S. Veerabadran Chettiar* v. *E. N. Ramaswami Naicker*[3] an object held sacred by many Hindus, namely a clay image of the god Gaṇeśa, was publicly destroyed as part of some political campaign, possibly with the object of opening the eyes of the masses (?).[4] Local

[1] *Saidullah Khan* v. *State of Bhopal* AIR 1955 Bhopal 23, *Public Prosecutor* v. *P. Ramaswami* AIR 1964 Mad. 258, and *Ahmad* v. *The State* AIR 1967 Raj. 190 were communally inspired. *Gulab* v. *State* AIR 1955 N.U.C. 9 was probably communal.

[2] AIR 1940 Oudh 348.

[3] [1959] 22 S.C.J. 1.

[4] See R. L. Hardgrave, *The Dravidian Movement* (Bombay, Popular Prakashan, 1965), the same, 'Religion, politics, and the DMK', in D. E. Smith, ed., *South Asian Politics and Religion* (cited above), ch. 10.

judiciary, unable to ignore, it would seem, political overtones, acquitted the offender on the ground that the image was not consecrated and so was not an idol in the śāstric sense, that it was no more holy than a picture in a print-shop or a 'doll' in a souvenir stall. The Supreme Court wrathfully denied that reference to the *śāstra* was appropriate: the object broken was held sacred by people, and that was all there was to it. The guilt of the image-breaker was established. This reference to people's actual beliefs, without reference to book-learning, is significant–but it must be remembered that the context is communal peace and harmony and the ancient traditional ideal balance of the groups. Had it been a religious exercise in which a religious teacher had broken an image to prove that religion (that is to say the Hindu religion) did not need images, and without the intention of insulting a religion, a conviction under s. 295 of the Indian Penal Code would have been unlikely.[1] The purpose of our image-breaker was avowedly political. In a case in Assam where Muslims killed a cow in full view of protesting Hindus the offenders were convicted not under s. 295 but under s. 298,[2] although there was an authority to the effect that cow-slaughter in a place where Hindus may see it was not an offence within the Penal Code,[3] because their act was an insult to the Hindus and undertaken with that object. The cow is a sacred animal within the protection of the section.

It was argued in *Ramji Lal Modi* v. *State of Uttar Pradesh*[4] that s. 295A was invalid in view of the Constitution's protection of

[1] In *Chakra* v. *Balakrushna* AIR 1963 Or. 23 Brahmins in *sabhā* (panchayat) fixed the dates for animal sacrifices. Because of a cattle epidemic the villagers wanted to offer sacrifices on another date. The Brahmins refused as this would infringe their custom. Other Brahmins were fetched, the villagers offered their sacrifice and blood was poured on the deities. The Brahmins prosecuted the offenders. Held: a civil right may have been infringed but the motive was to propitiate the deities and not to wound the feelings of the Brahmins.

[2] 'Whoever, with the deliberate intention of wounding the religious feelings of *any person* . . . places any object in the sight of that person, shall be punished . . .' (emphasis added). *Kitab* v. *Santi* AIR 1965 Trip. 22. Compare *Imam Ali* (1887) 10 All. 150 F.B.; *Ali Muhammad* (1917) P.R., No. 10 of 1918 (F.B.).

[3] *Sheikh Amjad* v. *King-Emperor* (1942) 21 Pat. 315. Exhibiting cow's flesh has been held to be an offence within s. 298: *Rahman* (1893) 13 A.W.N. 144.

[4] AIR 1957 S.C. 620 = [1957] S.C.R. 860.

religious profession and practice and the guarantee in Art. 19 (1) (*b*) that all citizens should have the right to freedom of speech and expression. But Art. 19 (2) enables the State to make laws relating to libel, slander, etc., or any matter which offends against decency or morality or which undermines the security of, or tends to overthrow, the State. This substantial abridgement of the freedom of speech and expression naturally protects s. 295A, which was enacted, as we have said, not specifically for the benefit of religious belief or propagation of religion but for the good order and peace of society which would be disturbed by attacks on the religion of a class.

Religious worship that takes place in an 'assembly' is protected from disturbance by s. 296 of the Penal Code, trespass in any place of worship, etc., is penalized by s. 297, and (as we have seen) utterances, gestures, etc., with the intention of wounding religious feelings are penalized by s. 298.

The Constitution, as we have seen, does not start with the assumption that religion may freely be practised, or that beliefs which are religious deserve protection against the state. Like many of the Constitution's articles Art. 25 sets out a fashionable proposition subject to so many qualifications and restrictions that the reader wonders whether the so-called 'fundamental right' was worth asserting in the first place. Art. 25 even *commences* with the restrictions in favour of public order, morality and health. Naturally it is left to the legislature to determine what subserves public order, morality and health. These public policies not being sufficiently specific to cover programmes to which the Congress Party was committed, specific reservations, as we have seen, were introduced to cover intended regulation of political or other secular activities associated with religious practice–for the so-called Founding Fathers intended to clip the wings of the wealthy Religious Endowments, to whom we shall return–and to cover legislation intended to throw open Hindu religious institutions of a public character to all classes and sections of Hindus.

We have already noticed in passing the Madras and Bombay statutes prohibiting the dedication of *devadāsī-s*.[1] The notion that

[1] Madras Devadasis (Prevention of Dedication) Act, 31 of 1947; Madras Devadasis (Prevention of Dedication) (Andhra Amendment) Act, 19 of 1956; Bombay Devadasis Protection Act, 10 of 1934; Bombay Devadasis

merit is gained by donating a daughter to an idol (a practice that bears a generic resemblance to a girl's being professed as a nun in Christendom) is obviously religious. The subsequent lives of these women did not disturb the Hindu conscience for more centuries than can be counted.[1] The notion that the *devadāsī* should actually be allowed to marry a human being (her previous prostitution being a by-product of the status of *devadāsī* at which no Hindu seems to have been revolted until missionary-inspired education made Hindus self-conscious about it), is abominable to religious sentiment, quite as abominable as nuns being released from their vows and entering into human marriage. The British period had not ended, however, before legislation, which is on the whole successful, freed existing *devadāsī-s* from their status and prohibited the dedication of any more of them. Lands that had been set aside by pious people for their maintenance were enfranchized and passed back into the market. Anyone who attempted to challenge these statutes would at once be answered with the words 'morality and health', on the footing that modern Hindu morality (i.e. the morality of the educated upper and middle classes)[2] cannot countenance temple prostitution. To this no practical reply seems feasible. One can *believe* that *devadāsī-s* were pleasing to the idols they served, but one cannot follow up one's belief in practice–for, after all, other ways of pleasing the Lord are available besides dedicating one's daughter to Him.

We have also noticed the curious Madras statute[3] which forbids the sacrifice of animals and birds. Neither Bengal nor Orissa is yet ripe for such a statute, though there would seem to be room for it if upper and middle class religion has its way with religious people there as it has had with religious Madrassis.

Protection (Extension) Act, 1957, 34 of 1958. See remarks of Sinha, C.J., quoted below, p. 481, n. 1.

[1] Marco Polo in K. A. Nīlakanta Śāstrī, *Foreign Notices* (cited above, p. 176), p. 171. Kāṇe, *H.D.*, II, pp. 903 ff.

[2] The 'high moral tone' approach to the old-fashioned family is seen in *P. Lakshmanaswami* v. *Raghavacharyulu* AIR 1943 Mad. 292. The learned judge was not particularly experienced in Hindu law cases, and speaks as a Hindu of his period.

[3] Madras Animals and Birds Sacrifices Prohibition Act, 32 of 1950, amended by Act 22 of 1957. *Cf.* Dumont (cited at p. 572 below), pp. 293–4.

The fact that Mysore has not followed Madras's example is also significant. The doctrine alluded to in the 'Objects and Reasons', that such sacrifices are not a part of true Hinduism (i.e. Vedic Hinduism, not the Hinduism of the mass of the common people), is not nor can even be superior to, or conclusively contradictory of any Hindu belief, because Hinduism cannot by its very nature have a creed. But it served as an excuse for the furtherance of a particular programme of religious reform, and it is interesting to speculate how the statute would be defended if it were attacked under Art. 25. Since public order, morality (in its cosmopolitan sense), health, social welfare and reform are not in question, those who would support the statute must fall back on regulation or restriction of an economic or secular activity associated with religious practice; but they will find it hard to persuade a court that a religious sacrifice is a secular activity. Fortunately the problem has not arisen, and it is doubtful whether it will arise.

Our remaining topics are the thorny questions known as Temple Entry and the abolition of Untouchability. The statutory reforms in the first case are multiple and remain so.[1] The reforms in the second case have been largely codified in the central statute, the Untouchability (Offences) Act, 1955.[2] In order to carry out these reforms wholesale attacks had to be made by the State upon the consciences of vast numbers of Hindus, or so it would appear. Dr. Luthera is right in detecting that a state which acts so cannot call itself a secular state on a pattern known to the United States, for example. In this approach to India, Professor Donald Smith and Dr. Luthera are

[1] The statutes are listed in the Schedule to the Untouchability (Offences) Act, 22 of 1955. See n. 2 below. Also Bombay Hindu Places of Public Worship (Entry Authorization) Act, 31 of 1956.

[2] Discussed by M. Galanter at (1964) 6 *J.I.L.I.*, pp. 185 ff., and R. V. Kelkar at *Vyav. Nirṇ.* 5 (1956), pp. 127–44. The latter says, 'Let us wait and see how the Act works. If the Act is strictly implemented, it may perhaps be hard to bear the rigour of it. Much depends on the good sense of those who are to administer the Act. Sometimes it is likely to be used as a cloak for mischief. Sometimes its implementation is likely to be neglected due to fear of public displeasure. The insufficiency of the existing provisions may perhaps be felt and become apparent in due course of time.' Foot-dragging in the enforcement of the Act is evidenced in *Benudhar* v. *State* [1962] Cut. 256; compare *State* v. *Kanu* (1955) 57 Bom. L.R. 524.

virtually agreed.[1] It can hardly be a secular state which has as one of its admitted aims a programme to which the accepted and acknowledged religious authorities of the majority of the inhabitants (not merely a minority) are determinedly opposed.

The objections to the entry into a temple of persons of such low caste that they were previously excluded from the entire temple, and to the entry into the temple's inner parts of persons who were previously confined to the outer regions of the temple, are of the simplest description.[2] The idol is naturally a holy object, and would have no value in worship if it were polluted. At a time when it was universally believed (not excluding the untouchables themselves) that a Brahmin would be rendered impure by proximity to an untouchable it was obvious that no idol could be allowed to be approached by an untouchable. The managers of the temple have as their duty the regulation of worship of the idol, as a facility for the public or for the section of the public which has patronage rights in respect of the temple. The priests have as their duties the actual worship which they perform and the regulation of worship by individual worshippers. The status of a worshipper is a valuable status with social and sometimes financial implications.[3] If the idol were allowed to be polluted by any means, including the approach of an untouchable, the trustees would have failed in their duty.[4] The enterprise, which, as we shall see, has its financial side, would have collapsed until such time as the idol could be cleansed and rededicated or installed, an expensive and troublesome business.

Some castes had become so exclusive that although their temple was a public temple the priests were customarily authorized to exclude even Brahmins from the holy of holies, unless they belonged to the sect of the founder or founders. Śrī-Vaiṣṇavas often act as cooks for Śaivite Brahmins in these days, as Brahmins may well eat food prepared by Brahmins; but since they do not take exactly the same ritual precautions as the Śaivites, and the same deficiency occurs where a Śrī-Vaiṣṇava

[1] D. E. Smith, *India as a Secular State* (Princeton University Press, 1963), ch. x. Luthera, cited above, p. 108.

[2] The social aspect of 'purity': Dumont, index. 'Intouchables'.

[3] *Venkatachalapati* v. *Subbarayadu* (1889) 13 Mad. 293.

[4] See p. 469 below.

family takes a Śaivite cook, the individuals are liable to suspicion of pollution, and it is not safe to eat with them, certainly if one is to present oneself without elaborate purifications before the ancestral idol. The idea that the idol has no objection to be visited and worshipped by *any* Hindu, whatever his religion or irrespective of whether he has any religion or none, is an idea that can lodge only in the brain of the managers, who are appointed by law or custom. Their religious belief naturally enters into this. Now the legislatures have in effect changed their minds for them whether they like it or not, and so have changed the idols' minds too.[1] The results are various, but the principle is the same throughout. Attempts were made to compromise, by allowing low caste Hindus to come nearer within the temple than had been possible before but still withholding them from sight of the idol. Attempts were made to distinguish the religions, so that a low caste *Hindu* might not enter a *Jaina* temple–until this anomaly was cured by statute.[2] But in general the case is that any Hindu, who is a Hindu by definition of law, whether or not he is clean (i.e. ritually clean) can present

[1] The will of the idol is expressed through its guardian: *Pramatha* v. *Pradyumna* (1925) 52 I.A. 245, cited in B. K. Mukherjea, *Hindu Law of Religious and Charitable Trust*², (Calcutta, 1962), p. 226. Indian law regards the idol as the embodiment or symbol of the religious purpose of the worshipper, not as the deity itself–but these subtleties invite confusion. *Atmaram* v. *King-Emperor* AIR 1924 Nag. 121 illustrates the previous situation. On Sept. 17th, 1922 thirteen Mahars entered the enclosure of an idol worshipped by Kunbis, slaughtered a goat there, sprinkled its blood on the idol, put *shendūr* (red lead) on the image and adorned it with flowers. They were held rightly convicted of an offence under s. 295 of the Penal Code.

[2] Compare the wording of s. 3 (1) of the Madras Temple Entry Authorization Act, 5 of 1947 (amended by Act 11 of 1952) with the sense of Bombay Hindu Places of Public Worship (Entry Authorization) Act, 21 of 1956 (to be read with Act 36 of 1958), which has the effect of nullifying the law as decided in *Bhaichand* v. *State of Bombay* (1951) 54 Bom. L.R. 69 that the Bombay Harijan Temple Entry Act, 1947 did not do away (for this purpose) with the distinction between Hindus and Jainas. *Bhaichand* was however followed in *State* v. *Puranchand* AIR 1958 M.P. 352 (Indore) and *State of Kerala* v. *Venkiteswara* AIR 1961 Ker. 55. The Kerala Hindu Places of Public Worship (Authorization of Entry) Act, 7 of 1965, not only unifies the law in Kerala, repealing the Acts formerly in force on this subject in the Travancore-Cochin and Malabar areas of the State, but also nullifies the conservative effect of the last decision. All Hindus as defined in the statute may enter all 'places of public worship' dedicated to or for the benefit of or used generally by Hindus or any section or class thereof.

himself before the idol and offer worship, or for that matter merely decline to make any worship, as of right, and those who would prevent him may be punished. Managers and priests who cannot accept this position, and who do not grasp that the idol, by Act of the State Legislature, no longer objects to the presence of śāstrically impure people, simply vacate the temple and leave it and its properties to their fates. But of course they can set up a private idol and worship the same god there. What they have lost is their social and financial monopoly–which was one purpose of the enterprise of reform. Numerous Hindus believe that the Almighty is not more present in one image than another, and that even worship of images is unnecessary for salvation: but they would not contend that their doctrine should be enforced at the expense of other more ancient and continuous Hindu beliefs to the contrary, since to have such a view would be tantamount to leaving Hinduism itself. Thus no Hindu supposes that Temple Entry, which is now an established fact, is a victory for a particular Hindu doctrine, nor that the public in acquiescing in it have changed their beliefs. But what is accepted is that the exclusive use of a public temple by a caste or castes to the disparagement of lower castes should cease, since the claim on the part of lower castes to worship *that* idol in *that* temple is a legitimate expression of disbelief in caste exclusiveness with its social implications, support of which disbelief the development of the nation has made inevitable.

Untouchability is only another side of the same picture. The discrimination against untouchables makes little sense in a nation committed to the doctrine that Harijans must 'come up', and to that end for the time being discriminates against other communities so as to put a stop to the educational and social backwardness of the former untouchables.[1] The practice of untouchability which included (i) confining untouchables to their own public facilities in the way of paths, wells, shops, etc., and (ii) outcasting or otherwise socially punishing caste-fellows for associating with untouchables or neglecting the discrimination against them, is penalized in the central statute which takes the place of local statutes to similar ends. One may *believe*

[1] N. Rādhākrishnan, 'Units of social, economic and educational backwardness: caste and individual', 7 *J.I.L.I.* (1965), 262 ff.; Marc Galanter, 3 *J.I.L.I.* (1961), 39 ff.

that untouchables have the power to render a caste Hindu polluted and ritually unclean, but if one says so in a manner penalized in the statute one risks punishment.[1] And to apply social penalties to those who do not practise untouchability is also a punishable offence.[2] What is the result? Those who believe in caste, in caste purity and in the need to avoid pollution must make a society for themselves within their own walls, and forgo the daily life in which untouchables now neglect to do what formerly was second nature to them, namely take care of the religious susceptibilities of their higher-caste compatriots. Here again religion has suffered a blow. Or so it seems.

Religious Bequests

To test the modern Indian law from another standpoint we should see whether the Hindu religion, which has been under fire in connexions we have just examined, has withstood modern tendencies in a somewhat conservative area of law that is less often looked to by our political scientists. Appeal to the religion of the people did not save any of the institutions or practices which have gone under in recent years. The people believed that *devadāsī-s* were an age-old institution of a religious significance and the rare survival of analogous institutions in country districts shows that they still have a rôle to play. The educated and 'advanced' Hindu turns up his nose at this 'survival'. The people likewise certainly believed in caste, if we can judge by the tenacity of the institution in contexts that really matter. They were not so concerned about its religious overtones, and those great concessions to egalitarianism were made. But where promotions and contracts and the like are in question, caste curiously often rears its head. It would be odd if it did not, since no adequate supercaste mutual-support society has yet become a fact. Would it be true to say that the people's religious beliefs are no longer recognized in Indian law?

[1] Act 22 of 1955, s. 7 (1) (*c*): 'Whoever . . . by words, either spoken or written, or by signs or by visible representations or otherwise, incites or encourages any person or class of persons or the public generally to practise 'untouchability' in any form whatsoever; shall be punishable with imprisonment . . .'

[2] The same statute, s. 7 (2) (ii).

Once again contrary and conflicting evidence is available. Indian law recognizes popular religious beliefs provided that these are not merely superstitious, and provided also that the traditional, book-religion supports them. What if the book-religion does not? Their beliefs may be protected by the sections of the Penal Code referred to above, but the court will not countenance them for the purpose of creating or furthering a charitable trust such as the law must protect. Instead of taking evidence of what the group in question believe, and being guided solely by that evidence, the court takes judicial knowledge of the Hindu religion, and decides whether a belief is religious or not, or whether it is merely superstitious. This distinction reflects the impact of foreign notions, for the distinction between religion and superstition is foreign to Hinduism; but it does not follow that it is un-Hindu for all that, if we take the broad view of the history of Hindu religious behaviour which these confused stories demand of us.

In *Saraswathi Ammal* v. *Rajagopal Ammal*[1] the Supreme Court was faced with an attempt to create a perpetuity of a curious kind, but evidently, as events have since shown,[2] not unthinkable and perhaps even fashionable in a small community. The settlor wanted himself to be buried (an unusual practice for Hindus other than *sannyāsī-s*) and to have worship conducted at his *samādhī*.[3] The court decided that the religious object was not consistent with Hinduism, being unheard of in books of authority. Jagannādhadās, J., said,[4]

> To the extent ... that any purpose is claimed to be a valid one for perpetual dedication on the ground of religious merit though lacking in public benefit, it must be shown to have a shastraic basis so far as Hindus are concerned. No doubt since then other religious practices and beliefs may have grown up and obtained recognition from certain classes, as constituting purposes conducive to religious merit. If such beliefs are to be accepted by (the) Court as being sufficient for valid perpetual dedication of property therefor without the element of actual or presumed public benefit, it must at least be shown that they have obtained wide recognition

[1] AIR 1953 S.C. 491.

[2] The facts in *Ravanna* v. *Vana* AIR 1962 Mad. 500 = [1962] Mad. 974 reveal that the practice was not unusual. The case is instructive on the Hindu law of charities.

[3] 'Tomb', 'place of burial', not 'place of cremation' here.

[4] At p. 495.

and constitute the religious practice of a substantial and large class of persons. That is a question which does not arise for direct decision in this case. But it cannot be maintained that the belief in this behalf of one or more individuals is sufficient to enable them to make a valid settlement permanently tying up property. The heads of religious purposes determined by belief in acquisition of religious merit cannot be allowed to be widely enlarged consistently with public policy and needs of modern society.

Prior to that case, in *Kunhamutty* v. *Ahmad Musaliar*[1] the Madras High Court had held that to create a valid trust for religious purposes there must be a charitable object, and a dedication for the purpose of reciting the Koran over a private person's tomb did not create a valid *wakf*. It must be recollected that the definition of charity in India includes religion, so that what is a religious purpose or object must be charitable at law.[2] But the sanctity of tombs in popular Islam did not affect the court's decision. In *Draiviasundaram* v. *Subramania*[3] the same High Court had held, following *Kunhamutty's case*, that the direction that money should be spent on the building of a *samādhī* and its maintenance did not constitute a charitable endowment. A dedication to an existing foundation may well be valid, whatever the circumstances attending the original foundation, but a dedication for worship at a *samādhī*, a type of worship having a hold on the sentiments of unorthodox or uninstructed Hindus, will be void: so says the Bombay High Court in the case of *Rangrao Bhagwan* v. *Gopal Pundlik*.[4]

From the extreme positions that the legislature can dictate on questions of public worship and that the courts can limit the bounds of 'religion' in an alleged charitable bequest some small but significant retreats are to be observed, and in so far as these show the courts' sensitiveness to these questions the wind obviously blows in the right direction.

In *Chhotatal Lallubhai* v. *Charity Commissioner, Bombay*[5] some monies held apparently subject to charitable trusts had accumulated. The learned Judges took the view that whatever the motive of the founder of the charity many of the objects were not religious, and no such trusts had been created. It is sufficient

[1] AIR 1935 Mad. 29.
[2] *S. M. N. Thangaswami* v. *Commr. I.-T., Madras* AIR 1966 Mad. 103.
[3] AIR 1945 Mad. 217.
[4] (1957) 60 Bom. L.R. 675, 677.
[5] (1957) 59 Bom. L.R. 349.

to quote a few words from the judgement of Shah, J., which show their Lordships' attitude:[1]

> We do not think that the other bequests can be regarded as religious. A bequest to Panjrapole,[2] i.e. a home meant for maimed, aged and deformed animals, can by no stretch of imagination be regarded as a religious bequest. Similarly, a bequest for practising kindness to all forms of life cannot, in our judgement, be regarded as a religious bequest; and a bequest for providing food to pilgrims visiting temples or providing clothes to Jain male and female Sādhus and Sādhvis cannot also be regarded as a bequest for religious purposes.

This extremely negative attitude towards the charitable understanding of a member of a well-to-do and notoriously charitable and religious community, who was bound to have had spiritual advice before he made the disposition in question, did not entirely meet with the approval of the Supreme Court when the case came before them on appeal. We must notice that the Bombay High Court's judgement was delivered in 1956 and the Supreme Court's judgement was delivered in 1965, by which time the large question of the 'secular state' and the rôle of law as an apparent hindrance to religion had been abundantly discussed. The judgement of the Supreme Court, which is of wider interest than the issue (which was a question of the applicability of the doctrine of *cy près*), is published under the heading *Shah Chhotalal Lallubhai* v. *The Charity Commissioner, Bombay*.[3] In the event various directions in the scheme framed by the court below were regarded as objectionable and were set aside, because the basic principles of the law relating to trusts had been lost sight of. But meanwhile the lower court's attitude to the allegedly religious bequests was disapproved of. It is true that the question of the accuracy with which the various bequests could be said to be religious was not settled finally in the absence of satisfactory pleadings and evidence, but the fact that these were impliedly held desirable was itself a step forward. Their Lordships (through the mouth of Bachawat, J.) speak of these matters as follows:[4]

> One Jhaverchand Dahyabhai Shah died in 1916, leaving a will dated August 6th, 1915 . . . He professed the Jain religion, and believed in the tenets of the Swetambar Murti Pujak sect of Jains. By cl. (7) of the will, he

[1] At p. 353.
[2] Usually *pinjarapāl*.
[3] (1965) 67 Bom. L.R. 432 (S.C.).
[4] At pp. 432–3.

directed his executors to spend out of the earnings of his shop every year during the lifetime of his niece ... the amounts mentioned below on the following religious objects:

(1) Rs. 100 for feeding cattle with grass, fodder, oil cakes, in the Broach Pinjrapole.

(2) Rs. 100 for *Jiva-dayā Khata* (fund for kindness to animals).

(3) Rs. 25 for offering flowers for the worship of Lord Rikabdev in the Jain temple at Vejalpore, Broach.

(4) Rs. 200 for providing food to *Shrāvak* pilgrims at the Shatroonjaya Hill at Palitana.

(5) Rs. 50 for providing food to pilgrims at Mount Girnar.

(6) Rs. 50 for providing food to pilgrims at Mount Abu.

(7) Rs. 250 for providing cereals, clothes, etc., to *Shrāvaks* and *Shrāvikās*.

(8) Rs. 100 for providing cloth to Jain *Sādhus* and *Sādhavīs*.

(9) Rs. 200 for education and food of Hindu orphans.

(10) Rs. 200 for Jain *Gyān Khata* (fund for imparting knowledge).

(11) Rs. 100 for feeding *Shrāvaks* and *Shrāvikās* who have observed fast.

(12) Rs. 300 for giving food, cloth, etc., to the blind, lame and crippled members of the Hindu Community.

In addition, he also directed his executors to give a *Swāmivatsal* feast or meal consisting of *methi-dal* and *ladhus* made of sugar to the members of his caste at 15 specified villages and towns in the Broach and Surat Districts every year on the occasion of the sacred festival of *Pajusan* ...

His Lordship proceeds to explain how the litigation commenced, as a result of the registration of the trust under the Bombay Public Trusts Act, 1950, and the difficulties caused by the accumulation of the unexpended income of the trust. The powers of the court to apply trust funds for purposes other than those laid down by the settlor were given by this statute.

The High Court held that the Court could on an application under s. 55 of the Act deviate from the directions of the settlor, even if the purpose of the trust has not failed, where the Court finds that it is inexpedient, impracticable, undesirable, unnecessary or improper in the public interest to abide by his directions, but the Court could exercise this power only in respect of funds of a public trust which was not a trust for religious purposes. The High Court held that none of the purposes mentioned in cl. (7) of the will except the one mentioned in item 3 of the clause could be regarded as religious, that the object of providing funds for annual *Swāmivatsal* feasts was charitable and not religious, and that the Court was therefore competent to entertain the application under s. 55. The High Court further held that providing a feast to the members of the caste even on the occasion of a religious festival or on days which may be regarded as holy is not expedient, desirable, necessary or proper in the public interest, and the directions of the District Judge with regard to the distribution of the funds should not be interfered with ...

But the respondents made out no case for a diversion of the trust funds.

> The giving and taking of the *Swāmivatsal* feast on the occasion of the holy festival of Pajusan, if not a religious act, is a meritorious act prescribed by the scriptures of Swetambar Murti Pujak Jains. The wider public interest does not require that this special charity for a section of the Jain public should be subverted and overthrown. In the wider public interest also, it is expedient, practicable, desirable and proper to respect the sentiments and interests of this section of the Jain public and to give effect to this charity . . .
>
> . . . The question whether or not objects mentioned in cl. (7) of the will are religious objects is not raised in the pleadings. No issues were framed and no evidence was led on this point by either party. What are religious purposes must be decided according to the tenets and religious beliefs of the Murti Pujak Swetambara sect of Jains, to which the testator belonged. It is difficult to decide the point in the absence of relevant pleadings, issues and evidence. The High Court too lightly brushed aside this finding. Chapter IX of the Report of the Hindu Religious Endowments Commission (1960–2) contains an interesting discussion of Jain endowments. Paragraphs 7 to 11 of Chap. IX of the Report refers to seven types of religious funds specifically recognized by the Jain scriptures concerning (1) *Jeena Bimba*, (2) *Jeena Chaitya*, (3) *Gyān Fund*, (4) *Sādhu*, (5) *Sādhvi*, (6) *Shrāvak*, and (7) *Shrāvikā*. The Jains recognize numerous other endowments or funds for general or specific purposes, the corpus or interest of which is to be utilized as per the donor's intentions. The question whether the several objects of the trust including the giving of a *Swāmivatsal* feast are religious in their character must be left open for future decision . . .
>
> . . . The savings of the income spendable during these years [during which the feasts could not be given owing to rationing] should be applied suitably for carrying out the same object in future. The balance savings, if any, should be devoted towards increasing the amounts spendable for the other objects of the trust . . .

Though the Supreme Court refer, similarly to their reference in *Saraswathi Ammal's case*,[1] to scriptures, there is no doubt but that they did *not* intend to depart from their previous ruling in the important case of *Ratilal Panachand Gandhi* v. *State of Bombay*.[2]

In that case petitioners had assailed the constitutional validity of the Bombay Public Trusts Act, 1950 which at that time made provision for the registration and superintendence and administration of public trusts including public religious trusts.[3] It was

[1] Above, p. 458, n. 4. [2] (1954) 56 Bom. L.R. 1184 (S.C.).

[3] The provisions of the statutes are sufficiently extracted and considered in the case in the Bombay High Court (below).

contended that the powers which might be exercised under the Act as it then stood would infringe the rights guaranteed under Arts. 25 and 26 of the Constitution. When the case was before the Bombay High Court a negative line was taken towards the constitutional freedom of religion, of which the Supreme Court heartily disapproved; and in order to understand what the Supreme Court meant by freedom of religion, with special reference to Art. 25, it will be necessary to repeat certain portions of the judgements in the court below as well as in the Supreme Court. It will then be evident that the Supreme Court have a much wider view of the fundamental right, and a more realistic, as well as more traditionally Indian, view of what religion is and how its nature and content should be determined. This is after all likely, since Bombay, as a modern and cosmopolitan city, full of its own function as the gateway to India from the West in much more than a geographical and mercantile sense, might have been expected to try to run before India could walk.

Chief Justice Chagla spoke as follows, *not* (it must be repeated) representing the correct position:[1]

> It may be said that both Arts. 25 and 26 deal with religious freedom, but as I shall presently point out religious freedom as contemplated by our Constitution is not an unrestricted freedom. The religious freedom which has been safeguarded by the Constitution is religious freedom which must be envisaged in the context of a secular State. It is not every aspect of religion that has been safeguarded, nor has the Constitution provided that every religious activity cannot be interfered with. 'Religion' as used in Arts. 25 and 26 must be construed in its strict and etymological sense. Religion is that which binds a man with his Creator, but Mr. Somayya on behalf of his client says that as far as Jains are concerned they do not believe in a Creator and that distinction would not apply to the Jains. But even where you have a religion which does not believe in a Creator, every religion must believe in a conscience and it must believe in ethical and moral precepts. Therefore, whatever binds a man to his own conscience and whatever moral and ethical principles regulate the lives of men, that alone can constitute religion as understood in the Constitution. A religion may have many secular activities, it may have secular aspects, but these secular activities and aspects do not constitute religion as understood by the Constitution. There are religions which bring under their own cloak every human activity. There is nothing which a man can do, whether in the way of clothes or food or drink, which is not considered a religious activity. But it would be absurd to suggest that a Constitution for a

[1] *Ratilal* v. *State* (1952) 55 Bom. L.R. 86 at p. 96.

secular State ever intended that every human and mundane activity was to be protected under the guise of religion, and it is therefore in interpreting religion in that strict sense that we must approach Arts. 25 and 26.

Mr. Chagla is of course a Muslim, though a Muslim of a minority community amongst Muslims, and this (apart from his unfortunate attention to an etymological [Roman] definition of the word) may have contributed unconsciously towards his view of religion–for Islam as a religion is notoriously simpler and more direct than, for example, Hinduism or even Christianity. Absolutely obligatory beliefs and therefore acts are much fewer. Moreover, in 1952, when this case was before the Bombay High Court, the theory that India was a secular state was sufficiently alive for it to be assumed that that theory was a means of interpreting the Constitution, whereas we now know that in order to determine what kind of state India is we must see what the Constitution says and how the courts apply its provisions and the provisions of statutes which are constitutionally valid. In the same case Mr. Justice Shah, whose narrow view of 'religion' in the religious bequest case we have already studied above, said,[1]

> In the very nature of things it would be extremely difficult if not impossible to define the expression 'religion' or 'matters of religion'. Essentially religion is a matter of personal faith and belief, of personal relation of an individual with what he regards as his Maker or his Creator or the higher agency which he believes regulates the existence of sentient beings and the forces of the Universe. Again, in view of the fact that there is not one religion but there are numerous religions and different persons residing within this country and within this State profess different religious faiths which seek to identify religion with what may in substance be mere facets of religion, it would be difficult to devise a definition which would be regarded as applicable to all religions or matters of religion. To one class of persons mere dogma or beliefs or doctrines may be predominant in the matter of religion; to others rituals or ceremonies may be a predominant facet of religion; and to another class of persons a code of conduct or a mode of life may constitute religion. It may be that even to different persons professing the same religious faith these aspects of religion may have varying significance . . . It may not be possible to devise a precise definition of universal application as to what is religion or what are matters of religion, but that is far from saying that it is not possible to state with reasonable certainty the limits within which the Constitution conferred a right freely to profess religion . . . The right . . . which is conferred by Art. 25 is not an absolute or unfettered right of freedom of

[1] In the same report at pp. 107–8.

professing or practising or propagating religion, but it is subject to legislation by the State limiting or regulating any activity, economic, financial, political or secular associated with religious practice. Similarly, that right is also subject to the social welfare and reform legislation of the State. There, Art 25 while conferring a right upon the citizens and others freely to profess, practise and propagate their religion does not confer upon the citizens and others an unfettered right to carry on economic, financial, political or secular activities associated with religious practices, nor does it prevent the State from passing any legislation for purposes of social welfare and reform, even though such legislation might directly or indirectly be inconsistent with the religious beliefs of some of the religious denominations . . . The right of management again is of the denomination or section thereof and is limited to matters of religion, or, in other words, to matters of religious faith and to matters of religious belief . . .

The distinction attempted here between matters of faith or belief and matters affecting property is one which appeals to those who have been brought up under the influence of the religions current in the West, and does not correspond to categories native to India. It is no wonder that the Supreme Court put the matter straight, and incidentally made it clear that the ultimate test of what is religious, though within the court's jurisdiction, is to be applied to materials furnished by the community or sect itself: the court does not force any religious group to express its beliefs in a form predetermined by the law. Their Lordships say:

What sub-cl. (*a*) of cl. (2) of Art. 25 contemplates is not State regulation of the religious practices as such which are protected unless they run counter to public health or morality, but of activities which are really of an economic, commercial or political character though they are associated with religious practices . . .[1]

. . . This means that the State can regulate the administration of trust properties by means of laws validly enacted; but here again it should be remembered that under Art. 26 (*d*), it is the religious denomination itself which has been given the right to administer its property in accordance with any law which the State may validly impose. A law, which takes away the right of administration altogether from the religious denomination and vests it in any other or secular authority, would amount to violation of the right which is guaranteed by Art. 26 (*d*) of the Constitution.

The moot point for consideration, therefore, is where is the line to be drawn between what are matters of religion and what are not? Our Constitution-makers have made no attempt to define what 'religion' is and it is certainly not possible to frame an exhaustive definition of the

[1] (1954) 56 Bom. L.R. 1184, 1189.

word 'religion' which would be applicable to all classes of persons. As has been indicated in the Madras case referred to above,[1] the definition given by Fields J. in the American case of *Davis* v. *Beason*[2] does not seem to us adequate or precise . . .[3]

It may be noted that 'religion' is not necessarily theistic and in fact there are well-known religions in India like Buddhism and Jainism which do not believe in the existence of God or of any Intelligent First Causes. A religion undoubtedly has its basis in a system of beliefs and doctrines which are regarded by those who profess that religion to be conducive to their spiritual well being, but it would not be correct to say, as seems to have been suggested by one of the learned Judges of the Bombay High Court, that matters of religion are nothing but matters of religious faith and religious belief. A religion is not merely an opinion, doctrine or belief. It has outward expression in acts as well . . .[4]

Religious practices or performances of acts in pursuance of religious belief are as much a part of religion as faith or belief in particular doctrines. Thus, if the tenets of the Jain or the Parsi religion lay down that certain rites and ceremonies are to be performed at certain times and in a particular manner, it cannot be said that these are secular activities partaking of (a) commercial or economic character simply because they involve expenditure of money or employment of priests or the use of marketable commodities.[5] No outside authority has any right to say that these are not essential parts of religion and it is not open to the secular

[1] *Lakshmindra's case.* [2] (1890) 133 U.S. 333, 33 Law. ed., 637.
[3] At 56 Bom. L.R., p. 1190. [4] At the same place.
[5] We see with satisfaction the terms of the Kerala Rice (Service at Functions) Restriction Order, 1958, s. 5: 'Nothing in this Order shall apply to the service, distribution, providing for consumption or preparation for consumption of any prohibited eatable as Prasadam (*prasāda*) or as part of a recognized religious ceremony, provided the quantity so served, distributed, provided for consumption or prepared for consumption does not exceed 2 tolas per head.' Whether the Rajasthan statute restricting the consumption of food at a *mṛtyu bhoj* ('death feast') interferes with a religious ceremony must remain for the present doubtful. In the 'Objects and Reasons' it is said (see, for Rajasthan Act 1 of 1960, [1960] *Current Indian Statutes*, Raj., p. 20), 'In several parts of the State big feasts are arranged on the occasion of or in connexion with the demise of persons. Such feasts sometimes also take the form of distribution of prepared or unprepared food to the relatives of the deceased. Such feasts, though usually associated with religious practice, are in reality activities of economic and financial character. While it is not the intention to interfere in the performance of religious practices it is considered expedient in the interest of the general public to place restrictions on such feasts which affect the finances of the persons holding the feasts and their family economy.' There need be no doubt but that the policy behind the Gujarat Obsequial Dinners (Control) Act, 1963 (Act No. 8 of 1964), s. 4 of which prohibits the giving or abetting of obsequial dinners to more than fifty persons, is the same.

authority of the State to restrict or prohibit them in any manner they like under the guise of administering the trust estate. Of course, the scale of expenses to be incurred in connexion with these religious observances may be and is a matter of administration of property belonging to religious institutions; and if the expenses on these heads are likely to deplete the endowed properties or affect the stability of the institution, proper control can certainly be exercised by State agencies as the law provides. We may refer in this connexion to the observation of Davar, J., in the case of *Jamshedji C. Tarachand* v. *Soonabai*,[1] and although they were made in a case where the question was whether a bequest of property by a Parsi testator for the purpose of perpetual celebration of ceremonies like Muktad, Baj, Yazashni, etc. which are sanctioned by the Zoroastrian religion were valid charitable gifts, the observations, we think, are quite appropriate for our present purpose (p. 209):

> '... if this is the belief of the community',–thus observed the learned Judge, 'and it is proved undoubtedly to be the belief of the Zoroastrian community–a secular Judge is bound to accept that belief–it is not for him to sit in judgement on that belief–he has no right to interfere with the conscience of the donor who makes a gift in favour of what he believes to be in advancement of his religion and the welfare of his community or of mankind ...'

These observations do in our opinion, afford an indication of the measure of protection that is given by Art. 26 (*b*) of our Constitution.'

As a result, the Bombay statute's attempt to infringe the liberty of management of religious trusts was rejected, and the Bombay legislature ultimately amended the offending section. Their Lordships of the Supreme Court said,[2]

> It is perfectly true, as has been stated by the learned counsel for the appellants, that it is an established maxim of the Jain religion that *deva dravya* or religious property cannot be diverted to purposes other than those which are considered sacred in the Jain scriptures. But apart from the tenets of the Jain religion, we consider it to be a violation of the freedom of religion and of the right which a religious denomination has under our Constitution to manage its own affairs in matters of religion, to allow any secular authority to divert the trust money for purposes other than those for which the trust was created ...

Thus, apart from information which may be pleaded and proved regarding the religious beliefs and practices of the group in question, the Constitution itself protects the commonly-held principle found in most religions that money dedicated to a religious purpose must not be diverted from it.

[1] (1907) 33 Bom. 122. [2] At p. 1193.

Whether this principle and its associated principles are honoured by a court which has jurisdiction to determine what is religious, and whether, being religious, the practice is protected by the Constitution, is naturally a question for speculation so long as adequate instances have not tested the court's inclinations and powers. We may look into the *positive* instance of the alleged right given to all Hindus to have free entry to religious institutions brought within a temple-entry statute, into the *negative* instance of Muslims' claim to slaughter cows sacrificially, and again into the *positive* instance of freedom of excommunication for religious reasons. These may be taken together.

Temple Entry, Cow-slaughter, and Excommunication

In *Sri Venkataramana Devaru* v. *State of Mysore*[1] the Madras Temple Entry Authorization Act, 1947, was attacked on the ground that the temple in question was not a public temple, and further that if it was a public temple the statute was invalid in so far as it authorized all Hindus freely to enter it, thereby infringing the freedom of the community to which the temple belonged to manage its own affairs in matters of religion. It was held that the temple, though it belonged to a community or denomination (Gowda Sāraswath Brahmins), *was* a public temple within the meaning of the Act, and that the freedom which the Constitution had anticipated in Art. 25 (2) (*b*), whereby temples should be thrown open to all Hindus, was subject to the other freedom guaranteed in Art. 26 (*b*), namely that the community should manage its own affairs in matters of religion. Religion includes practices, ceremonial law and conduct of worship. Each freedom must be enjoyed subject to the other. The result was a highly intelligent compromise, whereby all the religious objections of the community appeared to be preserved, while at the same time the benefit accorded to Harijans, and to others who though not Harijans would have been excluded because they were not members of the community, appeared not to have been diminished–for Temple Entry remained valid, save that the trustees and priests could exclude from the more sacred parts of the temple anyone they chose during times when the idol was supposed to be resting or

[1] (1957) 21 S.C.J. 382 = [1958] S.C.R. 895.

at times when those services were being conducted which only specially initiated persons were entitled to attend.[1]

The important point for our present purpose is not that the two demands, namely of the 'New' India and the 'Old', were reconciled happily, but that the Supreme Court recognized that it was possible for the trustees to prove, if necessary, the ritual requirements of the idol and its worship, whether from scriptures (*āgama-s* are specifically mentioned) or from evidence of the custom of the temple, and to insist successfully that these must be observed even by Hindus who had the benefit of the Act. But unfortunately it will not be possible for them to prove that the idol has no desire to be seen by Harijans. Apparently some room for conflict was allowed to remain. T. L. Venkaṭarāma Iyer, J., speaking for the Court, notices that if the sanctity of the inner shrine is violated a purification is called for, which everyone knows is a costly business; moreover he points out that a trustee who admits unentitled persons commits a breach of trust.[2] *At law* he can commit no breach of trust by admitting persons having a statutory right to enter. But if the unduly close presence of a Harijan would pollute the idol in the idol's own opinion (i.e. his trustees') the Act apparently burdens the idol (and thus his trustees) with the costs of purification at each statutorily-protected approach. The answer to this probably lies with the priests. They may put their heads together and find a cheap method of purification. The cheaper it is the better, for the state will not compensate them for the annoyance and expenditure which the approach of Harijans is likely to involve. The other case, namely the entry of non-members of the community to whom the temple belongs, is easier. These people had no rights to worship the idol previously, or could be excluded at the will and pleasure of the trustees. Now they can be excluded only if a genuine religious objection applies. In other cases their approach to the idol need not necessarily cause pollution (unless custom can be proved to the contrary) and no expenses are thrust upon the endowment.

It is important to bear in mind that the word 'worship' has

[1] On the right to enter and move about in a temple see also *Nar Hari* v. *Badrinath* in the Supreme Court (cited below, p. 489, n. 2).

[2] (1957) 21 S.C.J. 382 at 390, referring to *Sankaralinga* v. *Raja* (1908) 35 I.A. 176.

two implications in the context of Hinduism. The word covers *seva*, which means 'service', which is performed by the *pujārī-s* authorized by custom or grant;[1] and also *darśana*, which means, really, that the worshipper is presenting himself actually or notionally at the deity's 'durbar'. He obtains the 'sight' of the deity and is favoured with the deity's grace (*prasāda*) in return for his offering. The right to worship, as such, does not mean a right to perform *seva*. Harijans may thus stand and place their palms together before the idol, but the Constitution has not guaranteed that they may approach it within any fewer steps than any other class of Hindus not being *pujārī-s*. The *pujārī-s* have a legal right to keep the service of the idol to themselves whomsoever the Constitution or any valid enactment may admit to the temple buildings. The so-called 'holy of holies' will remain under the care of the customary ministrants, and no statute is supposed (at present) capable of removing this privilege proper to the idol or idols. This was explained by Gajendragadkar C.J., speaking for a bench of five judges of the Supreme Court in the *Satsang case* very recently. The main object of the legislation was to establish complete *social equality* between all sections of Hindus, for

> . . . we would like to emphasize that the right to enter temples which has been vouchsafed to the Harijans by the impugned Act in substance symbolizes the right of Harijans to enjoy all social amenities and rights, for let it always be remembered that social justice is the main foundation of the democratic way of life enshrined in the provisions of the Indian Constitution.[2]

The determination to seek social equality and justice is not pursued to the detriment of the rights of the idols to customary service, and litigation intended to exclude Harijans upon the allegation that their entrance to temples would interfere with the freedom of religion of the sects managing them was misconceived. The learned Chief Justice rightly commented[3] that since

[1] Gajendragadkar, C.J., at *Shastri Yagnapurushdasji* v. *Muldas* AIR 1966 S.C. 1119, 1127, col. 1, says 'It is only the Poojaris who are authorized to enter the said sacred portion of the temples and do the actual worship of the idols by touching the idols for the purpose of giving a bath to the idols, dressing the idols, offering garlands to the idols and doing all other ceremonial rites prescribed by the Swāminārāyan tradition and convention . . .'

[2] AIR 1966 S.C. 1119, 1135, col. 2.

[3] At the same page, col. 1.

1950 the whole social and religious outlook of the Hindu community has undergone a fundamental change, and the 'new' outlook is accepted widely. Muslims and Christians, however, not being entitled by statute to have *darśana* of an idol, are frequently excluded by trustees and their servants, though this does not necessarily conform to the most recent trends in Hinduism. That privilege is not taken from the sects and it may be a consolation in some quarters to be able to exercise an ancient privilege despite the winds of change. It must not be imagined that throwing open temples to the Harijans has had the effect of nullifying religious exclusiveness in its entirety. The *social* barrier has gone; the purely personal one remains. In Kerala, for example, women during their menstrual periods and persons 'under pollution arising out of birth or death in their families' (an entirely superstitious disqualification) are totally excluded from the entire temple and are placed upon a par with 'professional beggars when their entry is solely for the purpose of begging'.[1]

The case of the Muslim butchers was not so happy. Proof of the difficulties that would be suffered by the idol and the trustees and priests was abundant in *Venkataramana's case*. In the *Cow-slaughter cases*[2] the Muslims were not well served by their representatives, and no proof, or at any rate, no adequate proof was shown to support their case. The statutes which prohibited the slaughter of cattle had the indirect effect of depriving Muslim dealers in hides and guts, as well as butchers, of part or in some cases the whole of their livelihood. This was a consideration which did not weigh with the legislatures which were obsessed with the sanctity of the cow.[3] In addition to the argument in the Muslims' favour that their right to pursue their occupation had been taken away, the argument was raised that Muslims were entitled to slaughter a cow on a particular feast

[1] The Kerala Hindu Places of Public Worship (Authorisation of Entry) Act, 1965, sec. 4, authorizes the framing of Rules. See Rule 3 (published at [1966] K.L.T., Kerala Rules and Notifications, p. 72).

[2] *M. H. Quareshi* v. *State of Bihar* AIR 1958 S.C. 731; *A. H. Quraishi* v. *State of Bihar* AIR 1961 S.C. 448. These are discussed by V. K. S. Chaudhary at AIR 1962 Journal, 25–7. The Uttar Pradesh Prevention of Cow-Slaughter (Amendment) Act, 33 of 1958 was applied in *Bafati* v. *State* AIR 1964 All. 106.

[3] On this see above, p. 61. Luthera, cited above, pp. 136, 143.

day.[1] It was urged that their freedom to practise their religion had been infringed. Had it been proved to the court's satisfaction that Islam required the slaughter of the animal it is not impossible that the means would have been found to preserve the slaughter of cattle for religious purposes. But it was represented to the Court that Muslims could slaughter *camels* on the occasion or make gifts in charity as a substitute. Since an alternative was available the Court seized upon it to declare that slaughtering cows on this particular day was not an integral and essential part of the religion professed by the complainants, and that Art. 25 of the Constitution did not protect this observance. It seems highly likely that the true position is that Muslims are under a religious obligation to slaughter a camel or, failing that rare animal, a cow, or failing that to make the charitable donations: thus to take away an alternative is, or would seem to be, interference with religious freedom. However in the general interest, in order to subserve the sentimental requirements of the majority community, Muslims had to forgo one alternative and, from an Indian standpoint, this is not a deprivation of any moment. The distinction between belief and practice is probably not so interesting here as the recognition that the admitted presence of alternatives deprives the practice contended for of its urgency when conflicting religious interests had to be resolved in the search for the welfare of the nation.

We may now turn to the question of excommunication. It is a sanction most certainly to be reckoned with, where the community is sufficiently close-knit, as in *S. Varadiah Chetty* v. *P. Parthasarathy Chetty*,[2] a case of only a few years ago. There was a dispute over charities and accounts and a former Headman of the sub-sect was excommunicated and brought an unsuccessful complaint of defamation. P. Kunhamed Kutty, J., said:

> Undoubtedly, in the changing social order where individual liberty is recognized as a pre-eminent right, decisions taken on the basis of custom, usage and religious or caste sentiments have to be appreciated in terms of the changing times. This does not, however, mean that where an individual has done something wrong or prejudicial to the interests of his community the members of his community which, by virtue of custom or

[1] Bakr-Id (Baqarah-'Id, 'cow festival'), on which see T. P. Hughes, *Dictionary of Islam* (London, 1885), 'Īdu'l-aẓḥā (cf. *Koran* XXII. 33–8).

[2] [1964] 2 M.L.J. 433, 436.

usage, is competent to deal with such matters, cannot take a decision by common consent; and so long as such decision does not offend the law, it can be enforced by the will of the community.

In all States except Maharashtra and Gujarat and the portions of the old Bombay State that went to Mysore, excommunication as the weapon of caste discipline remains in full force, except for the prohibition of the practice of Untouchability in any form.[1] The scope of activity that can be enjoined or prohibited subject to the extreme penalty of excommunication is very large. The greater part of India is still rural, and in rural areas, especially those more remote from towns, social discipline is still upheld more by caste tribunals and their sanctions than by the courts. Castes can agree amongst themselves to avoid the courts altogether; to erect their own schedules of crime and punishment,[2] to keep their own marriage and divorce laws irrespective of what Parliament may enact;[3] and to punish acts which the law of the land allows. If the power of excommunication were taken from them the power to enforce lesser penalties would also be taken away. In the old Bombay State excommunication for any offence by any caste tribunal was prohibited by the Bombay Prevention of Excommunication Act, 1949.[4] The matter in *Sardar Syedna Taher Saifuddin* v. *Tyebbhai Moosaji Koicha*[5] went first before Shah, J., who upheld the statute, holding that the framing of the Act was such that exclusion of

[1] See p. 457, n. 2 above and n. 4 below. Note also the Himachal Pradesh Prevention of Excommunication Act, 8 of 1955. Elsewhere excommunication is valid: *Paduram* v. *Biswambar* AIR 1958 Or. 259.

[2] For the example of the Vāgrī community see above, p. 314, n. 6.

[3] On caste tribunals generally see articles by K. N. Thusu, S. G. Morab and S. K. Ganguly in *Man in India*, 45, pt. 2 (1965). The court after all inherited the panchayat's jurisdiction (*Dadaji* v. *Rukhmabai* (1886) 10 Bom. 301, 307, 310) and yet defies caste standards (*Mohan* v. *Smt. Shanti* AIR 1964 All. 21 and case cited at p. 358, n. 3 above). Above, p. 359.

[4] Act 42 of 1949. For its extension see Saurashtra Prevention of Excommunication Act, 5 of 1955, repealed by Bombay Prevention of Excommunication (Extension) Act, 1959. S.3 of the principal Act enacts that 'no excommunication of a member of any community shall be valid and shall be of any effect.' S.4 provides that, 'any person who does any act which amounts to or is in furtherance of the excommunication of any member of a community shall, on conviction, be punished with fine which may extend to one thousand rupees.'

[5] AIR 1953 Bom. 183 = (1952) 55 Bom. L.R. 1.

an excommunicated man from temples or from religious worship was not prevented by it, for the Act sought only to prevent and render void expulsions which deprived a person of rights and privileges which he was formerly entitled to enforce by a suit of a civil nature. In fact suits of a civil nature about religious rights are not foreign to the Indian legal system, so that the distinction would be very fine indeed. On appeal the case was heard by Chagla, C.J., and Bhagwati, J. Their Lordships once again upheld the statute. The Supreme Court subsequently reversed the decision[1] and overruled the expressions relative to the law which fell from the learned Chief Justice. In order to appreciate the significance we must look first at the complaint and then at the opinions of the Bombay High Court and the Supreme Court successively.

If we omit issues which do not concern us, the matter boiled down to this, that the plaintiff, a Dawoodi Bohra, claimed that orders of excommunication passed against him in 1934 and 1948 were rendered void and of no effect by the Act of 1949. It was held, almost certainly correctly, that if the Act validly prohibited and nullified excommunications it would terminate the excommunication of a previously excommunicated member of a community, and to that extent would have retrospective effect. It was urged that the Act was invalidated by the coming into force of the Constitution which by Art. 25 provided for freedom of conscience and profession, practice and propagation of religion (which we have already discussed), and by Art. 26 (which we have noticed in passing and shall refer to later), which protected the right of a religious denomination to manage its own affairs in matters of religion. Shah, J., as we have seen, took the view that the wording of the statute did not interfere with the plaintiff's religious rights, as he somewhat narrowly construed them. Chagla, C.J., speaking for the appellate court in Bombay said,[2]

> Then it is contended that the Act is *ultra vires* because it contravenes Arts. 25 and 26 of the Constitution. With regard to Art. 25, we had to consider a similar question in *State* v. *Narasu Appa Mali*.[3] What was challenged in that case was the Bombay Prevention of Hindu Bigamous Marriages Act, and Art. 25 was also relied upon in that case. We held in

[1] AIR 1962 S.C. 853. Luthera, cited above, pp. 98 ff.

[2] At 55 Bom. L.R. 19.

[3] See above, p. 444.

that case that in considering Art. 25 a sharp distinction must be drawn between religious faith and belief and religious practices. What the State protects is religious faith and belief. If religious practices run counter to public order, morality, health or a policy of social welfare upon which the State has embarked, then the religious practices must give way before the good of the people of the State as a whole. Here also, our view is that the right to excommunicate a member of a community is not part of religious faith and belief. At best, it can only be a religious practice . . .

. . . Now, the question is what exactly is the meaning of the expression 'managing its own affairs in matters of religion'. Does it mean that the religious denomination can manage its own affairs in such a manner as to deprive a member of that denomination of his legal rights and privileges? Surely, that cannot be the meaning to be given to the language used in the Constitution. . . . Further, it does not seem to us that when a religious denomination claims a right to expel or excommunicate a member, it is managing its own affairs in matters of religion. Religion has nothing whatever to do with the right of excommunication or expulsion. As we have said earlier while referring to Art. 25, it is more a question of religious practice than a matter of religious faith or belief, and the distinction between religious and religion is sharp and clear. Religion is a matter of a man's faith and belief. It is a matter concerning a man's contact with his creator. It has nothing whatever to do with the manner in which a practice is accepted or adopted as forming part of a particular religion or faith. Therefore, in our opinion, the defendant cannot claim the right conferred upon a religious denomination under Art. 26 to manage its own affairs in matters of religion in order to put forward the claim of excommunicating or expelling its members and thus depriving them of the rights and privileges which attach to the membership of that denomination.[1]

We have already seen that the narrow Bombay view of religion was not acceptable to the Supreme Court. It is no surprise to find, therefore, that in *Sardar Syedna Taher Saifuddin Saheb* v. *State of Bombay*[2] a much deeper concern for the religious integrity of the people of the former Bombay State was manifested. The Court was divided in opinion. Sinha C.J., dissenting, felt that the Act should have been upheld as it was in Bombay,

[1] 55 Bom. L.R. 20.

[2] AIR 1962 S.C. 853. The decision was widely disapproved by constitutional lawyers, on the grounds that it would encourage capricious and retrograde acts by religious leaders, masking conservative and even vengeful policies behind a façade of religion. The discussion by P. K. Tripathi at *Secularism* (cited above, p. 19), pp. 181 ff., is enlightening in this connexion. On the other hand D. Pathak's summary in his 'Freedom of Religion under the Constitution', *Law Review*, 18 No. 2 (1966), pp. 32–4, does not take a negative view of the case.

even though perhaps expressions of opinion *obiter* might not be acceptable to their Lordships. In his view the Act sought to fulfil individual liberty of conscience–a step, obviously, in the direction of freedom of religion in a modern cosmopolitan sense. Excommunication as a weapon is virtually dead, that is to say amongst religious communities outside the Roman Catholic fold, and excommunications in Scotland and Northern Ireland and mooted recently in America made strident headlines. If India is to modernize herself excommunication must go: or so the newly enfranchised Indian intellectual would suppose. The learned Chief Justice's viewpoint obviously sympathized with the movement which makes towards an inevitable future. He said,[1] '. . . though the Act may have its repercussions on the religious aspect of excommunication, in so far as it protects the civil rights of the members of the community it has not gone beyond the provisions of Art. 25 (2) (*b*) of the Constitution.' Das Gupta, J., speaking for the majority, opined that the Act might conceivably have been valid if it had prohibited excommunication for non-religious reasons. The majority held that the statute as phrased violated Art. 26 (*b*). The judgement of Ayyangar, J., is of more interest to us since it depicts the modern viewpoint of the majority of the judiciary:[2]

> '(Arts. 25 and 26) embody the principle of religious toleration that has been the characteristic feature of Indian civilization from the start of history, the instances and periods when this feature was absent being merely temporary aberrations. Besides, they serve to emphasize the secular nature of Indian Democracy which the founding fathers considered should be the very basis of the Constitution.' '. . . when once it is conceded that the right guaranteed by Art. 25 (1) is not confined to freedom of conscience in the sense of the right to hold a belief and to propagate that belief, but includes the right to the practice of religion, the consequences of that practice must also bear the same complexion and be the subject of a like guarantee.' 'The Act is concerned with excommunication which might have religious significance but which also operates to deprive persons of their civil rights.' 'The impugned enactment by depriving the head of the power and the right to excommunicate and penalizing the exercise of the power, strikes at the very life of the community by rendering it impotent to protect itself against dissidents and schismatics.'
>
> 'In my view by the phrase "laws providing for social welfare and reform" it was not intended to enable the legislature to "reform" a religion out of existence or identity. Art 25 (2) (*a*) having provided for

[1] At p. 865.

[2] At p. 871.

legislation dealing with "economic, financial, political or secular activity which may be associated with religious practices", the succeeding clause proceeds to deal with other activities of religious groups and these also must be those which are associated with religion. Just as the activities referred to in Art. 25 (2) (*a*) are obviously not of the essence of the religion, similarly the saving in Art. 25 (2) (*b*) is not intended to cover the basic essentials of the creed of a religion which is protected by Art. 25 (1).'[1]

At this stage it might be argued that provided the parties plead and prove that the practice is essentially religious the court will protect it to the extent that the constitutional guarantee is not qualified by the well-known formulae, 'subject to public order, morality and health', 'economic, financial . . . activity', 'social welfare and reform', 'throwing open of Hindu religious institutions . . .' This should ultimately affect the law relating to the definition of 'religious' in the context of religious and charitable trusts. But here we must notice the *obiter dicta* relating to 'superstition', which seem at first sight to strike an inharmonious note, and to confirm the narrow views evinced in the *samādhī* cases which we have discussed above.

In *Sardar Sarup Singh* v. *State of Punjab*[2] the Punjab Sikh Gurdwaras Act, 1925, was impugned on the ground that it prevented the direct election of officers on a universal denominational suffrage. It was upheld by the Supreme Court on the ground that this was not a matter of religion within Art. 26 (*b*). The contrast with rules relating to rites and ceremonies was pointed out: the latter would be protected. A religious denomination, said their Lordships, enjoys complete autonomy in the matter of deciding what rites and ceremonies are essential (and they emphasized the word 'essential'), according to the tenets of the religion they hold. The possibility that activities would be beyond constitutional protection as inessential to the religion was admitted.[3] The extraordinarily interesting case of *Durgah Committee, Ajmer* v. *Syed Hussain Ali*[4] concerned the validity of the Durgah Khawaja Saheb Act, 1955, which controls the administration of the trust associated with the tomb of Khwāja Moīn-ud-dīn Chishtī, the Sūfī of Ajmer, to which Hindus as well as Muslims make offerings and of which Hindus have at times been administrators. Previous decisions relating to this

[1] See pp. 873, 875. [2] AIR 1959 S.C. 860. [3] At p. 865, cf. 866.
[4] AIR 1961 S.C. 1402. Luthera, cited above, p. 121.

institution have shown that the trustee (*sajjāda-nashīn*) and the Khadims (ministrants) had divided the offerings to the detriment of the trust and to cheat the unwary.[1] The statute was directed to the benefit of the institution and the question of the membership of the managing committee was therefore vital. The Act provided for the offerings to be taken by the trustee. This was challenged on the ground, *inter alia*, that it infringed the freedom of management guaranteed by Art. 26 (*b*). The Supreme Court repeated what had been said in 1954 and again in 1958 by their Lordships to the effect that religion is *not* nothing else but a doctrine or belief; it might be more than an ethical code; it might prescribe rituals and observances, ceremonies and modes of worship which are regarded as integral parts of religion, 'and these forms and observances might extend even to matters of food and dress'. To this Gajendragadkar, J. (as he then was), added,[2]

> Whilst we are dealing with this point it may not be out of place incidentally to strike a note of caution and observe that in order that the practices in question should be treated as a part of religion they must be regarded by the said religion as its essential and integral part; otherwise even purely secular practices which are not an essential or an integral part of religion are apt to be clothed with a religious form and may make a claim for being treated as religious practices within the meaning of Art. 26. Similarly even practices though religious may have sprung from merely superstitious beliefs and may in that sense be extraneous and unessential accretions of religion itself. Unless such practices are found to constitute an essential and integral part of a religion their claim for the protection under Art. 26 may have to be carefully scrutinized; in other words, the protection must be confined to such religious practices as are an essential and an integral part of it and no other.

That this expression (uttered in 1961) was agreeable to the Supreme Court at large is proved by their being copied and repeated by Sinha, C.J., dissenting,[3] in the *Excommunication case* which was decided by the same Court at the beginning of 1962, and which we have already studied.[4] Though the majority did not take the learned Chief Justice's part in that appeal, they would not have denied the validity of the quotation. Mr.

[1] AIR 1961 S.C. 1402, 1406, 1409: *Report of the Durgah Khwaja Saheb (Ajmer) Committee of Enquiry* (October 13th, 1949), (New Delhi, Govt. of India, 1950), p. 63.

[2] At p. 1415, col. 2.

[3] AIR 1962 S.C. 853, at 864–5.

[4] Above, pp. 473 ff.

Justice Gajendragadkar made his view even more explicit, the following year, in *Tilkayat Shri Govindlalji Maharaj* v. *State of Rajasthan*,[1] a case which both disgusts and amuses the observer of Indian problems. There the Tilkayat, who was in fact the trustee of the rich temple, pretended that all its property and income were his own personally. The Rajasthan Nathdwara Temple Act, 1959, attacked by the Tilkayat whom it sought to control, was unsuccessfully impugned. The Rajasthan High Court had held that the Act was unconstitutional[2] because it improperly included private temples of which the Tilkayat was *shebait*; it attempted to vest direction of the affairs of the temple as well as of its property in the Committee; and thirdly, the provisions regarding the manner of disposing of the surplus income of the properties exceeded the limits of the legislature's jurisdiction. The decision was reversed in the Supreme Court. We are not concerned with all the technical issues, but with the consciousness on the Supreme Court's part that these wealthy pontiffs and their supporters really believed that their powers and status were a matter of religion.

There cannot be any doubt (we may interject) that the worshippers of the idol or idols really believe that by making donations which reach the Tilkayat's, or a similarly-placed individual's, pocket some spiritual benefit accrues to them, and his willingness to receive these donations, whether on the god's behalf or his own, is a condescension from which they derive religious satisfaction. This is a question of religion, and the pouring out of money proves its sincerity as nearly as any proof can. But the Supreme Court cannot accept that in modern India the affairs of religious communities can continue to be governed in this spirit. How do they avoid the fact of religious scruples standing in the way of reform? The learned Justice said that in deciding whether a given religious practice was an integral part of the religion or not, the test would always be whether it was regarded as such by the community following the religion. This question would always have to be decided by

[1] AIR 1963 S.C. 1638. Discussed by P. K. Tripathi at *Secularism* (cited above), pp. 188–92, where the point is made that apart from the (autocratic, pre-Constitution) *firmān* (decree) of the Udaipur Darbar the management of the temple's affairs was not so purely secular as to exclude the relevance of Artt. 25 and 26.

[2] AIR 1962 Raj. 196.

the Court and in doing so the Court might have to enquire whether the practice in question was religious in character and, if it was, whether it could be regarded as an integral or essential part of the religion, and the finding of the court on such an issue would always depend upon the evidence adduced before it as to the conscience of the community and the tenets of its religion. The result might well be that the secular had to be disentangled from the religious, and the Court might find itself in the position of rejecting as irrational attempts to call the one the other. The Tilkayat's right of management was not a religious practice, whatever might be the status of the Tilkayat in the eyes of the worshipping members of the sect.

At first sight these opinions would seem to conflict with the British and American precedents. In neither of those countries does the court determine whether practices are religious in the absolute sense, nor does it purport to sit in judgement upon the communities' own notions of the status of their practices,[1] deciding, for example, whether it would be *rational* to call one religious, or whether it should be discarded as *superstitious*. This jurisdiction is Indian, and, as some may think after perusing the material provided in this book, traditionally Indian. At first sight the Supreme Court's *obiter dicta* suggest a tyranny of intellectual Hinduism over the man-in-the-street's Hinduism, of a supremacy over questions of religion tailored to suit the policy of a cosmopolitanized nation. But another view of these opinions may be more nearly correct.

The Constitution, as understood by their Lordships, affords a limited freedom to religion and to religious practice. India traditionally tolerates divergencies in matters of religion and does not take up the position that one religion, or one sect, is entitled to patronage while the remainder are merely tolerated, nor does it take the position that the State should abstain from concern in all matters of religion. It does take the view, which pre-Constitution experience justified, that the State cannot be indifferent to religion; and that the balance between the claims of the religious *inter se*, between religion and the State, and between the individual and his sect must be maintained as a state function. This function is exercised by the courts. There-

[1] *Watson* v. *Jones* 80 U.S. 679 cited by Luthera at p. 38. *Thornton* v. *Howe* (1862) 31 Beav. 14; *Att.-Gen.* v. *Delaney* (1875) I.R. 10 C.L. 104.

fore the court must be able to distinguish between what is religious and what is not, and once it has established what is claimed to be religious it can proceed to determine whether the practice contended for comes within the limited freedom the Constitution allows. The first stage is to determine what is contended for, and it is open to litigants to prove the nature and content of the practice they defend from scriptures *or any other relevant and cogent evidence.* The second stage may involve a determination whether the practice is essential and integral to the religion. If it is an accretion, or an irrational or superstitious element in the ordinary senses of these words, it does not follow that it will not be essential. But the court will be in a position to decide on the evidence whether, being an accretion, superstitious, etc., it is nevertheless essential. If it is not essential, then it cannot claim protection against the State's enactments or regulations. The claim to be entitled to marry for the second or subsequent time during the lifetime of an undivorced wife is no doubt backed by religion, and it is neither irrational nor superstitious: but it is not an essential part of religion because the object intended to be served can be served otherwise without offence to the religion. Only the total bar of all alternatives would be an offence against the freedom of religion.

Thus we have not what it might seem, namely a conflict between a cosmopolitan concept of religion and a traditional Indian concept of religion, but a working out of a balance in such a way that the claims of a practice to be 'religious' naturally submit themselves to scrutiny if protection from the State is required. The freedom to believe is not touched. The freedom to act is guaranteed subject to such limitations as will make the continuance of social life in India possible.[1] This tentative conclusion may be revised after we have seen how the courts have dealt with the special but parallel subject of religious endowments, and how the Hindu public has reacted to enactment, or lack of enactment, in that highly typical context.

[1] Sinha, C.J. said at *Saifuddin Saheb* v. *State of Bombay* AIR 1962 S.C. 853 at p. 863, 'It was on . . . humanitarian grounds, and for the purpose of social reform, that so-called religious practices like immolating a widow at the pyre of her deceased husband, or of dedicating a virgin girl of tender years to a god to function as a *devadāsī* or of ostracizing a person from all social contacts and religious communion on account of his having eaten forbidden food or taboo, were stopped by legislation.'

14

RELIGIOUS ENDOWMENTS, PUBLIC AND PRIVATE

It would be possible[1] to argue that in dealing as they have with religious endowments of a public character the legislatures and the courts have taken a view of religion which is strikingly un-Indian, and have ignored the traditional Indian classifications. If this is correct, the provisional conclusion at the end of the last chapter must be revised, as the topic of religious endowments looms large within the sphere of the State's protection of religion in India. If this is false, our conclusion is of the greater strength. The argument that the authorities are departing from Indian ideas in conscious or unconscious imitation of the West–an argument greatly supported by passing allusions and hints in the important *Report of the Hindu Religious Endowments Commission* (1960–2) to which we shall make copious reference–is attractive and is one to which the present writer himself subscribed. Only when the whole canvas is surveyed can one form an impression of what is depicted: and this book has given an opportunity for a reappraisal. The result is, paradoxically, in favour of the whole matter retaining its native Indian flavour, and of the cosmopolitan elements being superficial and not determinative.

The great excitement regarding state regulation of public religious endowments–whether it be through a state corporation, through a commission with authority to manage or control

[1] This chapter contains (with additions and omissions and from a different angle) material provided in chapter 14 of D. E. Smith's symposium, *South Asian Politics and Religion* (Princeton University Press, 1966) combined with important new material which became available since that chapter was written, as well as the substance of a lecture delivered at the South Asia Institute, University of Heidelberg in July 1965.

numerous institutions or through a commission or committee set up for the individual institution alone–has dwarfed the other problems which in fact are not less important for the observer. Let us see first what the total range of religious endowments amounts to. Most important in point of number are the private temples and shrines; next, though of much shorter duration and significance come the trusts for charitable payments to the poor, of which we have already seen a specimen, or to Brahmins,[1] or for the performance of ceremonies whether at special places or not; one must mention next the grant or bequest to a public temple, whether to instal the idol (now somewhat rare)[2] or further to endow an existing idol; thereafter come the much less common creations of *maṭha-s* or the further endowment of such. Finally one can endow or further endow institutions which are neither temples nor *maṭha-s* (hereafter called *mutts*) but are institutions for worship or religious exercises or charitable activities, such as public feeding, each having its own constitution.[3]

Before we discuss the nature and extent of state interference with some (but not all) of these institutions we must come to understand what the public expects from them, and what the background is to the reforms which have been so thoroughgoing in some sectors of this sphere. The inconsistency between the two is very remarkable. The reformers appear to want to achieve something which the public is not interested, on the whole, to have. It would be easy to say that the reformers are westernized Hindus, whereas the bulk of the public are 'backward', and that the programme of reform is part of the 'education' of the nation. The present writer doubts whether, after all, this is really the case.

[1] See for example *Roopakula* v. *Sunkara* [1966] 1 An.W.R. 50; *Commr., M.H.R.C.E., Madras* v. *Narayana* AIR 1965 S.C. 1916. Derrett, *I.M.H.L.*, §. 780.

[2] *Bhupati* v. *Ram* (1910) 37 Cal. 128 F.B. Derrett, *I.M.H.L.*, §. 780. Mukherjea, cited above (p. 455, n. 1), p. 142.

[3] Derrett, *I.M.H.L.*, §§. 806–10. For examples see *V. Mariyappa* v. *B. K. Puttaramayya* AIR 1958 Mys. 93; *Gajanan* v. *Ramrao* AIR 1954 Nag. 212 (a *saṃsthānam*); *Poohari* v. *Commr., H.R.C.E.* AIR 1963 S.C. 510, 515 col. 1 (a '*sadāvarti*'); *Chandra* v. *Jnanendra* (1923) 27 C.W.N. 1033 (sacred grove). An institution called a *mutt* may not be one: *State of Madras* v. *Kunnakudi Melamatam* [1966] 2 S.C.J. 175 (institution to relieve poor pilgrims); *Adm. of the Shringeri Math* v. *Charity Commr., Bombay* AIR 1967 Bom. 194 (no instruction provided).

The Hindu view of life accepts the doctrine of *karma* and does not question the desirability of so living as to avoid rebirth. Prosperity in this life and success in the hereafter can be obtained, amongst other paths, by liberality to the poor, to Brahmins, and other deserving causes, and by donations to idols. The grace of the deity is believed to be available to sincere worshippers, whose sincerity is best shown by their generosity. Religious doctrines are taught by lines of teachers, and the maintenance of such doctrines and propagation of such religious views conduces to the approval of the deity or deities. Temples are houses for idols which represent the deity, and which have been 'brought to life' for this purpose by sacramental ceremonies carried out by competent authorities. The *śāstra* entirely determines whether or not an image of stone or bronze is a representative of the deity for purposes of worship.[1] Commonly the idol is called by the deity's name, and *is* the deity for practical purposes. There is no doubt but that orthodox śāstric learning denies that idols have any property.[2] The *śāstrī-s* do not countenance the further proposition that idols have legal personalities. Yet, for all that, the public insists upon giving gifts to the idol by way of the priests or other intermediaries, and it was accepted in many places and from a long time before the British period that the idol enjoyed the properties and disposed of them through his trustee or trustees. Indeed there are many inscriptions extant which show the idol actually making decisions and announcing them.[3] The legal personality of the idol was

[1] Kāṇe, *H.D.*, II, 896–903. Prānnāth Saraswatī, *Hindu Law of Endowments* (Calcutta, 1892), ch. 4.

[2] G.-D. Sontheimer, cited above (p. 147, n. 1). The fact is recognized at *Deoki* v. *Murlidhar* AIR 1957 S.C. 133. The case, which is of great general interest, establishes the proposition that the dedication to an idol is for the benefit of *worshippers*. Here the 'Old' and the 'New' India overlap: the 'Old' see dedication as intended to produce merit (hence benefit) for the donor; the 'New' sees it as intended to conduce to the beauty and religious atmosphere of the shrine (from the point of view of visitors, not all of whom will be donors).

[3] E.I. xxv, No. 34, pp. 318–26 at Kānchi (Conjeevaram), dated the equivalent of March 29th, 1359: 'This is according to the sacred order . . . In the month of Mesha of the year Vikārin . . . while We, in company with our consorts . . . were seated on the throne . . . in the *abhiṣeka-maṇḍapa*, on the representation of . . . who supervises the business of Our temple (or 'house') . . . We were pleased to assign to a Vaiṣṇavadāsa on whom We have

therefore a popular concept long before it became part of the Anglo-Indian law,[1] and the complaints which have been voiced judicially against this notion[2] are not entirely well-founded in legal history It is accepted in law that the idol thinks and acts through his trustee, who is usually called 'shebait' (from *seva*, 'worship').[3] The decision regarding what should be done in the idol's interest is taken by its *shebait*, and suits are brought and defended in the name of the idol. This has its difficulties when the question arises of taxing the idol's property and income. Curious debates have been entertained as to whether God Almighty can be taxed.[4] But, to everybody's relief, it is accepted that the property or income of a religious endowment can be taxed through the trustee, without having regard to the legal vesting of both in the deity.

One of the attractions of the religious endowment, especially the private endowment, was that the income was not assessed to income-tax to the extent that it was applied or finally set apart for application to the religious or charitable purpose (so the Income Tax Act, 11 of 1922, sec. 4(3)). But the recent statutory reform[5] provides that income shall be exempt from income-tax only to the extent of twenty-five per cent if the trust was created

bestowed the name of Brahma-tantra-svatantra-Jīyan the *maṭha* which had been set apart for him, the lands belonging thereto . . . so that he may propagate Our Rāmānuja-*darśana*, and after him, the disciples selected by him may, in succession, take possession of these and continue . . .' The convention still continues at Srirangam. Thus an idol's signature (!) can be forged: *Vadivelu* [1944] Mad. 685.

[1] The legal position is fairly stated by J. C. Ghose, *Law of Endowment*[2], p. 275, viz. that the proprietary title to the property is vested in the idol. Mukherjea, pp. 39–40, 140. Parliament recognizes this: an idol's gold is referred to at The Gold (Control) Act, 18 of 1965, s. 16 (4) (*b*).

[2] See the unusually phrased judgement of C. N. Laik, J., in *Commr. of I.-T., Calcutta* v. *Jogendra* AIR 1965 Cal. 570.

[3] Mukherjea, pp. 181 ff.

[4] See n. 2 above, also *Sri Sridhar* v. *I. T. Officer* AIR 1966 Cal. 494.

[5] Income-tax Act, 43 of 1961, sec. 11. An informative study is T. V. Viswanātha Aiyar's 'Taxation of Charities and Trusts' in *Proceedings of the Seminar . . . 1963* (Madras, Provincial Bar Federation, 1964), pp. 321–41. The author objects to both (*a*) and (*b*) above, in the first case because India, though secular, is not anti-religious and many religious communities would qualify, under the general law of charities, as 'public'; and in the second case because what is aimed at is the trust itself rather than the way it is administered.

before April 1st, 1962; while in the case of trusts created after that date no income is exempt if (*a*) the trust was created for the benefit of any religious community or caste (i.e. not for that of the Indian public, as such, irrespective of religion or caste); or (*b*) if under the terms of the trust any part of the income enures directly or indirectly for the benefit of the founder *or any relative of his*. This does not, of course, in any way hinder the dedication of property to a deity, but it does tend to remove one of the main incentives for such dedications. India as a State will not subsidize sectarian foundations nor shelter sources of income which masquerade as endowments, i.e. establishments for idols.

The endowment of a deity has various other functions besides the achieving of spiritual benefit for the worshippers.[1] Since Ṛgvedic times we have known of people who kept idols and loaned them to people for magical purposes, and[2] thereby, no doubt, made a substantial income from them. Many a private idol has been open to worship by the public or a section of the public, so that the trustee could collect the offerings.[3] The psychological point which emerges from the facts is simply this, that the *dharma* or spiritual consequence of a donation is fully obtained at the moment of relinquishing it in favour of the deity. What happens to the asset afterwards is no concern of the donor.[4] In the case of temples' endowments, and the idols them-

[1] See p. 484, n. 2. 'The dedication is a gift for a religious purpose and in a figurative sense is a gift to the deity as the ideal embodiment and symbol of the religious purpose' (*Champa* v. *Panchiram* AIR 1963 Cal. 551). 'The juridical person is the ideal embodiment of a pious idea and is the centre of the religious foundation . . . the image is . . . a compendious expression of the pious purpose' (*Upendra* v. *Anath* [1951] 1 Cal. 665, 672). The public have a 'greater and deeper interest' in the endowment than the *shebaits* have: *Venkataramana Ayyangar* (cited below), 40 Mad. 212 at p. 225, cited with approval at *Bishwanath* v. *Sri Thakur* AIR 1967 S.C. 1044.

[2] A. B. Keith at (1926) 30 C.W.N. xlviii–xliv, cited by Sontheimer, where cited, at p. 48, n. 8.

[3] Derrett, *I.M.H.L.*, §. 804. See *Koman* v. *Achuthan* (1934) 61 I.A. 405. A temple which began as a private temple may become a public temple by express or implied dedication: *V. Mahadeva* v. *Commr., H.R.E.B.* [1956] Mad. 624 (a case in which temples are discussed as 'business concerns').

[4] In mediaeval times the original founder might express exactly what should be done with the income and how the surplus should be spent (e.g. the Munirabad stone inscription of Vikramāditya (A.D. 1088), A.R.I.E., 483 of 1959/60, Hyderabad Arch. Ser., No. 5 [1922]). But individual donors would have no such notions.

selves, it is possible to argue that a broader sentiment has always existed, upon which not only the patrons or descendants of the founder but also the king may step in in default of such, or where they are negligent or prevented from taking action on behalf of the endowment. It is true that the *śāstra*, founding upon a *mīmāṃsā* doctrine that a limited or subservient ownership remains in the donor notwithstanding his gift until the merit be actually earned, left a legal basis upon which complaints could legitimately be pursued.[1] But this legal theory–no doubt relied upon in cases of gross abuse in ancient times–will not present itself to the mind of the individual worshipper.

As in human gifts to human beings, the one who receives a favour is the donor, so in the case of donations to a deity it is the deity who, whether he is pleased or not, assumes the obligation. The actual enjoyment of the object given can be left to the trustees, the priests,[2] and the touts and hangers-on who attach themselves to the temple as a business.[3] So 'mismanagement' of temple funds is part of the picture. The trustee is obliged by custom to spend the income on worship of the deity, and it is up to him how much he spends and how he spends it.[4] In the case

[1] See the discussion of Mitra-miśra, *Vīramitrodaya*, *Vyavahārādhyāya*, pp. 427–8, at V. N. Mandlik, *Hindu Law, Part II. The Vyavahāra Mayūkha*, etc., (Bombay, 1880), p. 337. Kāṇe, *H.D.*, II, p. 915.

[2] Mukherjea, pp. 229, 231. *Rama Rao* v. *Board of Commrs.*, *H.R.E.*, AIR 1965 S.C. 231 (*archaka-s* demand half of all offerings). In *Shahzad* v. *Raja Ram* AIR 1965 S.C. 254 the *pūjārī-s* claimed to be *shebaits*.

[3] Rāja Rāmmohun Roy in a pseudonymous work of 1820 (frequently published in the original and translation) attributed to him by S. N. Hay with adequate reason (*Dialogue between a Theist and an Idolater*, Calcutta, 1963) says (p. 123): '. . . all the presents made unto the images, as jewels, clothing, etc., the offerings of food, the refreshments presented in the afternoon, the morning oblations, etc., all these things are for these men. Moreover on festival days peculiar presents must be made to the images, and a great expense must be incurred at the great festivals, and at the performance of the ceremonies called Shwastyayan, Poorashcharan. etc., all this becomes the property of these covetous Pundits . . . Now men commit robbery, murder and theft for their profits' sake; what wonder is it, therefore, that these covetous Pundits deceive householders in order to derive advantage from it?' That jewels given to the deities should belong to the officiants, and that 'Pundits' should be leading offenders in deceiving the public seems odd: but the text remained uncontradicted in this respect notwithstanding its many editions.

[4] Derrett, *I.M.H.L.*, §. 787. *Kumaraswami* v. *Lakshamana* (1930) 53 Mad.

of a public temple the scale of worship and amenities for the worshippers will be a matter of custom and some fair notoriety: but until the recent statutes were implemented to control the endowments' administration no one knew how much money could be obtained for useful purposes from these quarters without any loss to the scale or glamour of daily or festal worship. When pressure was applied the facilities for worshippers were greatly extended, research institutes founded, and considerable amenities inaugurated for which payment has easily been forthcoming from the normal revenues of the institution. In one case, perhaps the most wealthy, a university has actually been founded and endowed. Where did the money go previously? Nobody bothered much, until this century saw a dramatic and continuous pressure to place the finances of such temples and *mutts* under secular control.

It is a fact that the institution which receives gifts is 'intended primarily for the propitiating of God by worshippers who go there seeking temporal and spiritual advantages'.[1] Vows are made in order to obtain a son or to recover from a disease. Gifts are made simply to acquire merit.[2] Businessmen afraid of losing their wealth take to religion and make lavish donations. What happens to the money is of small concern to them. Hence temples and *mutts* flourish, so long as the goose that lays the golden eggs is not killed. This *can* happen by mortgaging the temple's lands or the temple itself,[3] by leasing out the lands to relatives on long leases and at nominal rents, by taking all the profits and ploughing nothing back in the way of amenities for pilgrims, and so on. Temples decline when they are seen to be poor, for this means that few offerings are made in ratio to the trustees' or priests' cupidity, and if that is so the god cannot be

608. But note Mukherjea, J.'s, trenchant dictum at *Jogesh* v. *Sree Sree Dhakeswari* (1941) 45 C.W.N. 809, 816, col. 1.

[1] So the District Judge (uncontradicted) in a case that arose in 1947 (*Rama Rao*, p. 487, n. 2 above, at p. 234, col. 2).

[2] Sontheimer, pp. 71 ff., discusses possible motives. For a good instance see *Ramaswami* v. *Comm., H.R.C.E., Madras* AIR 1964 Mad. 317.

[3] *Mukundji (Thakur) Maharaj* v. *Goswami Persotam Lalji* AIR 1957 All. 77. It is possible to say that the alienation of the idol itself is (in some cases) *void*: *Sree Sree Iswar* v. *Surendra* (1941) 45 C.W.N. 665. Compare the facts in *Atyam* v. *P. Venkanna* AIR 1966 S.C. 629 and *Sundareswarar* v. *Marimuthu* AIR 1963 Mad. 369.

very efficacious or very grateful. A temple which starts as a good investment can rapidly go downhill if systematic exploitation of the income and alienation of the accumulated assets get out of hand. On the other hand there is no point in being a trustee of a wealthy temple if one cannot enjoy the perquisites and patronage which it gives. Social standing, enjoyment (in former days) of temple prostitutes, and the power to keep idle relatives or otherwise to advantage one's dependants–these were collateral aims, and very good reasons why particular families should constitute themselves monopolistic beneficiaries from the temporalities of the idol, the worship of which could be left to priests. Priests naturally became interested in the secular aspects.[1] *Pandas* or touts (pilgrims' guides) likewise began to have vested interests, and the more involved the sacred place and the larger its mythology, the better these people flourished. Quarrels between *shebaits*, priests and *pandas* over the distribution of their takings were common.[2] Schemes have had to be framed by rulers since long before the British period for the purpose of compromising conflicting claims, all conducted on a purely businesslike footing.[3] Again and again the *shebaits* claimed that the idol was God Almighty who would reward the generosity of the pilgrim a thousand-fold (*centuplum accipies*!), and when the coins were once within their grasp asserted that these were

[1] See p. 487 above. The law has recognized their hereditary right as property: *Raj Kali* v. *Ram Rattan* AIR 1955 S.C. 493.

[2] Typical was *Nar Hari* v. *Badrinath* [1953] 1 All. 42 S.C. = AIR 1952 S.C. 245. The most amusing example is at *Guru Estate* v. *Commr. I.-T., Bihar and Orissa* AIR 1963 S.C. 1452, where the Pandas at Jagannath (Puri) collected money under deeds executed by pilgrims and claimed the amounts were exempt under s. 4. (3) (i) or (ii) of the Income Tax Act, 1922, as religious or charitable funds. The business of a Panda at Gaya is thoroughly objectively handled at *Murari* v. *Narayan* AIR 1956 Pat. 345 and *Gopal* v. *Baiju* AIR 1958 Pat. 647, 648. For *Pandas* see also *Nand Kumar* v. *Ganesh* (1935) 58 All. 457.

[3] See the valuable collection of documents at N. Patnaik, 'Administration of Jagannath Temple in the Eighteenth Century', *Man in India*, 43 (1963), 214–17. Again Vaiśyas, Kṣatriyas and Brahmins were disputing regarding their rights attached to the famous Srisailam temple (Karnul Dist.). A copper-plate grant (at the Government Museum, Madras) bearing a date equivalent to February 13th, 1466, records the settlement. R. Sewell, *Lists of Inscriptions and Sketches of the Dynasties of Southern India* (list No. 3, New Imperial Ser., vol. 8) (Madras, 1884), No. 96, p. 15. Because non-Brahmins were involved the record is not in Sanskrit but in Old Telugu.

personal presents and belonged entirely to them.[1] Anglo-Indian judges have been sarcastic about this, but plainly because they did not understand the mentality at work. In *Venkataramana Ayyangar* v. *Kasturi*[2] Sheshagiri Ayyar, J., makes the matter plain enough.

> It is not necessary to labour further the point that the *archakas* can have no proprietary right in the offerings made to the Deity. In all the important temples in Southern India, devotees are called upon to pay a fixed sum for the *archanā*, the cost of the flowers, the remuneration of the person who recites the *archanā*, etc., and the *swarnapushpam* offered to the Deity. A practice which distributes a portion of the levy to the persons who bring the flowers, who recite the holy names, and who actually do the *pūjā*, will not be illegal. But any arrangement which recognizes the *swarnapushpam* as the property of the *archaka* will be obnoxious to religious precepts and purposes. If the *swarnapushpam* is regarded as the property of the Deity and if a portion of it is utilized to supplement the pay of the servants, there can be no objection to it. But such an arrangement can only be of a temporary character, subject to periodical re-adjustment with reference to the exigencies of the time.

Similarly the *mahant* or head of a *mutt* has been a source of perplexity. The members of the sect of whom he is the chief *ācārya* (teacher, confessor) are delighted to pay him his capitation present, and even vie with one another to show their obedience and devotion. He goes on money-collecting tours giving in exchange spiritual guidance to his disciples. Social prestige is available for a prominent devotee of the *mahant*, and the system keeps itself marvellously afloat. What interest does the *mahant* have in the profits of the *mutt's* assets and in the presents made to him? The law has made a hypocritical attempt to keep his interest within bounds, asserting that he is merely a trustee for the *mutt*.[3] But it is perfectly notorious that he in fact represents the *mutt*, that he has entire disposal over its assets subject to general controls which in practice were of very little effect until the recent legislation, and that he has never been ousted from personal enjoyment from any presents made to him as *mahant*.

[1] The most famous example is the Dakore (or Dahkor) Temple Case, *Manohar* v. *Lakhmiram* (1887) 12 Bom. 247 (see remarks at p. 265), and for the sequel *Shah* v. *Jamnadas* AIR 1965 Guj. 181. Mukherjea, p. 228.

[2] (1916) 40 Mad. 212 F.B. at p. 220.

[3] Derrett, *I.M.H.L.*, §. 820 and references there cited, also *Sudhindra* v. *Commr., H.R.C.E., Mysore* AIR 1963 S.C. 966. Mukherjea, pp. 333–6.

From where, then, does the opposition come, which seeks to make *shebaits* actually account for their idol's property, and would wish to make the *mahant* account for the expenditure of the *mutt's* wealth? The answer must lie in the distinction between the public temple and the *mutt* on the one side and the other components of the range of religious and charitable endowments on the other. As we shall see the vast number of private endowments is more or less uncontrolled by law: yet the reasons for dedicating property to an idol were much the same in the case of the private endowment as in the case of the public. The prestige of a family is aided (very markedly in Kerala) if it possesses a private temple. The possession of large funds by the idol gives the *shebaits* for the time being a disposition over funds which the personal law and the fiscal law also would not have allowed them had it passed by succession.[1] It is a perpetuity which grows in value, if wisely administered, and is a fine example of religion and expediency joining hands. Yet the law has not reformed private as it has public endowments.

The Constitution's provisions were cunningly drafted and have achieved a most suitable compromise. Art. 26 reads:[2]

> Subject to public order, morality and health, every religious denomination or any section thereof shall have the right–
> (*a*) to establish and maintain institutions for religious and charitable purposes;
> (*b*) to manage its own affairs in matters of religion;
> (*c*) to own and acquire moveable and immoveable property; and
> (*d*) to administer such property in accordance with law.

The founders were aware that closer control of the administration of public religious endowments, belonging, as the article says, to a 'religious denomination or any section thereof', which plainly excludes a family, was about to be achieved. There was no intention to hinder or hamper the spiritual side, but there was every hope of controlling the financial side, preventing

[1] No estate duty is payable because the deity cannot die. Some settlors actually appoint *shebaits* with a stipulated remuneration: *Nirmala* v. *Balai* AIR 1965 S.C. 1874. Cf. the facts and law in *Laxmidhar* v. *Rangabati* AIR 1967 Or. 90.

[2] D. D. Basu, *Commentary*, 4th edn., II, pp. 158 ff. On the whole topic of the Constitution in relation to religious endowments see 'Supplement' (pp. 359–75) by T. L. Venkaṭarāma Iyer in the second edn. of Mukherjea's work (1962) (which we have been citing here).

fraudulent alienations and peculation by *shebaits* and *mahants*, and turning a squalid institution masquerading as a religious organization into a respectable affair. The *mutts* that operated solely as money-making organizations, by engaging, through the *mahant*, in money-lending,[1] might be converted somehow into institutions more nearly resembling what *mutts* were in the beginning, colleges for the dissemination and development of sectarian learning and piety. The shameful scrambles and litigation over appointment to mahantships might then be somewhat diminished in volume or acerbity.[2] Each of the major States with the notable exception of West Bengal brought in statutes for the regulation of religious endowments, and we have seen that Bombay had an Act which was intended to be used, and indeed is used, for the better government of all public religious endowments of all communities. The central government produced a central Act called the Wakfs Act, since several times amended,[3] whereby all Muslim religious and charitable endowments can be brought within the control of Boards specially created for the purpose.

Thus the Constitution does not contemplate autonomy of religious groups in respect of their administration of their property. Religion may dictate how such property is acquired: but when acquired the law shall dictate how it is to be administered. The statutes aiming to control public temples and *mutts* have come under fire, and the following, briefly, is the result.

In the case of temples the statutes have survived to the extent that they provide for the registration of temples and a new system under which the properties are submitted to inventory, the expenditure is supervised, accounts are examined, and surpluses are applied to purposes of a charitable character. The

[1] *Mahant Ganeshgir* v. *Fatechand* (1934) 31 Nag.L.R. 282. B. S. Cohn, 'The role of the Gosains in the economy of eighteenth and nineteenth century Upper India', *Ind. Econ. Soc. Hist. Rev.*, 1, No. 4 (1964), pp. 1–8.

[2] A most instructive case is *Swamy Premananda* v. *Swamy Yogananda* [1965] K.L.T. 824, where the legal background, the squalid facts and the court's remedial powers are fully set out in the judgement of M. Mādhavan Nair, J. For another example of a contest for a *mutt* coupled with evidence of scandalous inadequacy in the *mahant* (who claimed he owned the Dera–they were Udāsīs–absolutely) see *Bhagwan* v. *Jairam* AIR 1965 Punj. 260.

[3] Muslim Wakfs Act, 29 of 1954 amended by central statutes (including Act 30 of 1959) of which the last is Act 34 of 1964.

shebaits, who have a right of property (not unnaturally!) in their office[1]–though the law has long restrained their itch to dispose of it for its market price[2]–and therefore could not be ousted without infringing the right of property guaranteed by Art. 19(1) (*f*), have after all been held bound to comply with the requirements of the statutes, since the motives of the latter were simply to provide for the more efficient conduct of the *shebaits*' own duties in the interests of the idols[3] which were, after all, inseparable from their own as *shebaits*. Thus public temples have been brought under active, if (one is told) not always perfectly efficient control, because the commissioners or their officers are in effect a layer of super-*shebaits*, whose sanction to proposed expenditure by the trustees is a valuable privilege, which exists, surely, in order to be exercised with discretion . . .[4] On the other hand the *mahants* have been more fortunate. We have already seen that the Supreme Court will not allow as constitutional any arrangement which in effect substitutes a commissioner or his officer for the *mahant*,[5] and so takes the management and responsibility for the *mutt* out of the *mahant's* hands, whereupon it would cease to be a *mutt*. The *mahant's* right of property in the *mutt's* assets comes to his aid, and his right to take the initiative in disposing of them cannot be taken away from him except by amending the Constitution appropriately,

[1] *Angurbala* v. *Debabrata* AIR 1952 S.C. 298; *Janki* v. *Koshalyanandan* AIR 1961 Pat. 293. R. N. Sarkar objects at AIR 1954 Journal, 91–4. Nevertheless the law remains: *Sree Kalimata* v. *Jibandhan* AIR 1962 S.C. 1330, 1333, col. 1. The authorities are discussed by T. L. Venkaṭarāma Iyer at Mukherjea, pp. 364–5.

[2] Derrett, *I.M.H.L.*, §. 793. See also *Jogesh* v. *Sree Sree Dhakeswari* (1941) 45 C.W.N. 809, 816; *Lakshmana* v. *Vaidyanatha* [1956] Mad. 1144; *Bairagi* v. *Sri Uday* AIR 1965 Or. 201 (void alienation of a family's idols).

[3] *Sri Jagannath* v. *State of Orissa* AIR 1954 S.C. 400 (Orissa Act 4 of 1939).

[4] Several functionaries seem to have been squeezed by the reforms: K. Rajayogananda Murthy, 'Hereditary *archakas* of temples in Andhra Pradesh', [1965] 2 An.W.R., *J.*, 16–17.

[5] See above, p. 465, n. 1 also *Sudhindra* v. *Commr., H.R.C.E.* AIR 1956 Mad. 491 (see p. 494 n. 4 below). Unfortunately, apart from the effect of the Seventeenth Amendment of the Constitution (1964) (which suspended the fundamental rights in respect of Assam Act 9 of 1961, which enabled lands belonging to religious institutions to be acquired) the Constitution was never intended to provide protection retrospectively: *Sri Jagadguru* v. *Commr., H.R.C.E. Hyderabad* AIR 1965 S.C. 502 (property rights of *mahant* validly taken away).

or by abolishing his right of property by statute. Moreover, over-eager officials must have full proof of the trustee's mismanagement before they adopt the drastic powers which the statutes vest in the Commissioners.[1] But the state's officers tread neatly round the toes of the venerable but suspicious pontiffs, and the submitting of *mutts* to modern systems of accounting cannot be prevented; the law presumes that the *mahant's* powers exist for the welfare, and not for the detriment, of his *mutt.*[2]

Meanwhile the Court's contempt for *pandas* and similar ministrants is unconcealed. They are a blot on the picture of what might otherwise be a dignified and reformed religious institution. We may approach the *Report of the Hindu Religious Endowments Commission*[3] and note the manner in which the members of the Commission, mostly lawyers of distinction, envisaged the further reform of the system which, to their minds, was still, for all the State statutes, far from satisfactory. But since they were sympathetic to the legal approach and in fact start from the standpoint which the law had then reached, the tone of the law must be looked at first.

The prototype of all the cases dealing with religious endowments in their fight against State supervision is *Commissioner of Hindu Religious Endowments, Madras* v. *Sri Lakshmindra Thirtha Swamiar, Shirur,*[4] which, decided in 1953, we have called *Lakshmindra's case* but is often referred to as 'the Shirur Mutt Case'. It will be remembered that the Constitution does not speak distinctly of *mahants.* These ambiguous characters have been given, as we have just seen, ample protection by the law, but the founders of the Constitution did not wish them to be viewed as in any way distinct from caste or denominational or sectarian heads functioning as part and parcel of a religious denomination. This was largely fictional, since the individuals, who differ very much in capacity and honesty, are frequently so far above their communities that, once they are appointed, they

[1] *Sri La Sri Subramanya Desiga Gnanasambanda Pandarasannadhi* v. *State of Madras* [1966] 2 An.W.R., S.C., 1 (S.C.)

[2] *Sri Sadasib* v. *State of Orissa* [1956] 19 S.C.J. 397 (Orissa Hindu Religious Endowments Act, 1952). *Sudhindra* v. *Commr., H.R.C.E.* AIR 1963 S.C. 966.

[3] Govt. of India, Ministry of Law (New Delhi), Manager of Publications, 1962. A favourable comment: S.C. Bhat at AIR 1964 Journal, 98–9.

[4] AIR 1954 S.C. 282. Above, p. 446. Luthera, pp. 117 f., 125. T. L. Venkaṭarāma Iyer, where cited, pp. 359, 362.

can be virtual dictators. They fulfil the need of the pious Hindu, felt especially in South India but equally acknowledged in the North and the East, to prostrate himself before a human being of professional otherworldliness. Genuine ascetics, true *sannyāsī-s*, are rarely met with. They exist in the Himalayas or remote places. But the substitute *sannyāsī*, who represents the genuine article, is available as the head of a religious sect, its 'pontiff', as he is often called, and is not infrequently treated as a deity by devotees. That the man may be a rascal is of no importance, and it is a commonplace that the Hindu worships the man *qua* professional ascetic, whilst at the same time despising him as probably bogus. The psychology behind this situation cannot be explored here.[1] Perhaps for this reason the Constitution maintained a discreet silence about *mahants*, and they were to take cover, if they could, behind the broad words we have set out above.

In this case, to put the celebrated affair briefly, the Commissioner of Hindu Religious Endowments was entitled under the Madras statute as then enacted[2] to take away from a *mahant* the actual administration of the *mutt* should certain circumstances materialize. The final sanction lay in a temporary or permanent expropriation of the luckless incumbent. Many judges would view the *mahant* with no favour: he is a rival prestige-figure who has seldom had to labour honestly to achieve his dubious position. But the *mahant* could count on the Supreme Court to judge between him and his intended supervisor by the light of the Constitution, and the result was highly satisfactory to him. The first point in his favour was his right of property, for he represented the *mutt* and the *mutt's* properties vested in him. Secondly he could take aid from a religious denomination's right to manage its own affairs, for the Court saw him as a representative of the denomination. This was a step that might have been more carefully considered in view of the attitude

[1] The remarkable case of the so-called *mahā-ṛṣi* who became spiritual guide to members of a well-known group of popular musicians while they contributed a proportion of their very large income to his 'mission' (1967) will appear to some readers to exemplify this situation admirably.

[2] Madras Hindu Religious and Charitable Endowments Act, 19 of 1951. The text is printed at Mukherjea, cited above, *first edition* (1952), pp. 505 ff. The current statute, Act 22 of 1959, is printed in the *second* edition, pp. clxxxx (*sic*) and following.

adopted by witnesses before the Hindu Religious Endowments Commission, namely that in fact the *mahant's* interests were often adverse to the community or 'denomination' which he was supposed to serve. However, the Supreme Court said,[1] through the mouth of B. K. Mukherjea, J., as he then was–the most learned member of the Court in the specific context of religious endowments, if not personally acquainted with conditions in South India whence the problem arose–

> Under Art. 26 (*b*), therefore a religious denomination or organization enjoys complete autonomy in the matter of deciding as to what rites and ceremonies are essential according to the tenets of the religion they hold and no outside authority has any jurisdiction to interfere with their decision in such matters.
>
> Of course, the scale of expenses to be incurred in connexion with these religious observances would be a matter of administration of property belonging to the religious denomination and can be controlled by secular authorities in accordance with any law laid down by a competent legislature; for it could not be the injunction of any religion to destroy the institution and its endowments by incurring wasteful expenditure on rites and ceremonies. It should be noticed, however, that under Art. 26 (*d*), it is the fundamental right of a religious denomination or its representative to administer its properties in accordance with law; and the law, therefore, must leave the right of administration to the religious denomination itself subject to such restrictions and regulations as it might choose to impose. A law which takes away the right of administration from the hands of a religious denomination altogether would amount to a violation of the right guaranteed under cl. (*d*) of Art. 26.

It is a matter of interest that the Muslim incumbents of Islamic institutions resembling *mutts* are not protected by such constitutional guarantees as are the *mahants*, because the law regards them as mere trustees with no right of property in the assets of the endowment.[2]

Investigation, Condemnation and Reform

As legislation to control the administration of Sikh temples had already been passed,[3] the institutions of the Sikhs were not

[1] At p. 291.

[2] *Hafiz* v. *U. P. Sunni Central Board* AIR 1965 All. 333 (the *mutawalli* is not like a *mahant*, being neither the head of a spiritual fraternity nor more than a servant of the founder of the wakf, in which he has no proprietary interest).

[3] Sikh Gurdwaras Act, Punjab Act 8 of 1925, supplemented by the Sikh Gurdwaras (Supplementary) Act, 24 of 1925, a central statute.

visited, but the Commission visited Buddhist and Jaina endowments and interested themselves in the institutions of the Lingayats, Ārya Samāj and Nirmals. 12,000 questionnaires were circulated, and 1,400 replies and 400 memoranda were received. They were on tour for 265 days outside Delhi. They visited 150 institutions in North India and 82 in South India. Verbatim evidence of witnesses ran into 3,000 foolscap pages. The *Report* itself starts with a very full and accurate historical introduction which sets the scene of the modern set-up fully and fairly. The *Report*, which we shall quote frequently below, comments,[1] 'With the passage of time and with the changing ideas of modern times a majority of these *mutts* have failed to maintain the standard of the olden days . . . In many cases the heads of the *mutts* have become essentially worldly and in some cases have been found by courts to be corrupt and immoral.' The *Report* proceeds to list and describe the statutory provisions for the correction of maladministration of endowments. The Regulations No. 19 of 1810 (Bengal), No. 7 of 1817 (Madras), No. 17 of 1827 (Bombay) indicated Government's concern for endowments, but Act 20 of 1863 dissociated Government from administration entirely. By Act 20 of 1877 s. 539 was inserted into the then Civil Procedure Code, which corresponds to s. 92 of the present Civil Procedure Code.[2] These provisions enable worshippers and others to take the initiative and with the consent of the Advocate General of the State to commence proceedings in the interest of the endowment.[3] Act 14 of 1920 attempted to extend the scope of judicial supervision where the members of the denomination or sect were prepared to take the initiative. This was not satisfactory since most frauds and instances of maladministration took place with the connivance of worshippers who might intimidate others who did not share the proceeds with them. The *Report* goes on to sketch the

[1] At p. 22.

[2] Derrett, *I.M.H.L.*, §. 802 and references there given. For an example of its use see *Bhagwan* v. *Jairam* AIR 1965 Punj. 260.

[3] The Advocate-General for political as well as expediential reasons may decline to do so and the courts are not agreed whether his administrative act is amenable to judicial review: *Raju* v. *Adv. Gen.* [1962] Mad. 722; *Abu* v. *Adv. Gen.* [1954] T.C. 369. Hence it is good to know that he can be bypassed where an idol's rights are concerned: *Bishwanath* v. *Sri Thakur* AIR 1967 S.C. 1044.

features of the Madras Hindu Religious and Charitable Endowments Act, Act 22 of 1959, which is the leading specimen of the current legislation which places the initiative squarely in the hands of Government as representing the interests of the public at large.[1] Hyderabad had a statute for all denominations, so had Bombay (which we have seen), so also Mysore, and the successor States are still governed by these statutes to the extents of the areas concerned. The remainder of Andhra, and the States of Bihar, Kerala, Madhya Pradesh, Orissa, Rajasthan and Uttar Pradesh have similar statutes.[2] The Uttar Pradesh statutes are of very limited scope and reflect the tenderness of the public there to trustees of such endowments. The *Report* expresses the opinion that no State should be without an appropriate statute. Bengal is an offender.[3] There important temples are treated as private property. Legislation in any case should be uniform for all communities and not be confined to Hindus.

The *Report* comments that private *mutts* are possible, but that all *mutts* should be treated as public,[4] and legislation would be needed to achieve this. The basis for this recommendation is rational:[5]

> Offerings are made by members of the public to temples as well as *mutts*. In the case of temples, they are made for the benefit of the deity out of devotion by the worshippers of the deity to the temple which is the property of a juristic person, namely, the deity. Such property has to be utilized for the spiritual benefit of the body of worshippers. This benefit may take the form of *sevas*, *pūjās*,[6] festivals, religious discourses, cultural activities including music, drama and dance conducive to [the] spiritual solace and enlightenment and activities designed to make the temple and its *dharmakartās*[7] useful, beneficial or elevating to the worshipping public. This property is obviously impressed with a public character inasmuch as the worshipping public is interested in it and should obviously be treated

[1] *Report*, pp. 26 ff.

[2] Printed at the end of the second edition of Mukherjea (cited above).

[3] *Report*, p. 30.

[4] *Report*, p. 36. But see the instance of a private *mutt* cited at p. 483, n. 3 above.

[5] *Report*, p. 36, para. 8.

[6] *Seva* and *pūjā* both mean 'worship'.

[7] For the various meanings of that word see Mukherjea, index, Derrett *I.M.H.L.* §. 790 and *Nanduri* v. *Sri Agasthesswaraswamivaru* AIR 1960 S.C. 622. The use of the word here seems inaccurate, and perhaps it is a misprint for *dharma-kāryas*?

as part of the set up. No absolute ownership in the strict sense in respect of offerings to the temple on behalf of *archakas*, *pūjāris*,[1] etc. should in our opinion be recognized.

Naturally where personal offerings are made out of veneration this would be another matter. But where offerings are made without specific designation they should be presumed to belong to the deity as a juristic entity. As for the disputed rights of the *mahants*, the considered opinion was that they should enjoy offerings as they like during their lifetimes but not dispose of them by will; after their deaths the properties should automatically vest in the *mutt*.[2]

The Commission note the squabbles that take place over whether a trust is private or public.[3] In order to avoid supervision the trustees do their utmost to prove that the trust is private. Vast sums are spent in litigation to this end. However, the public, the Commission says, inclines against endowments' being recognized as private unless there is strict proof, in other words they recommend that the burden of proof of an endowment's being private, should lie on those that assert it, a recommendation which may not perhaps be as practical as could be wished. The *Report* goes on to name a short list of temples where the public are invited to make offerings but the trustees claim that the idol and its temple are their private property:[4] a time-honoured situation for which the Commission had no sympathy. If necessary the Constitution itself should be amended in order to reform the law:

> '... even in cases where a temple is maintained within a residential place, if offerings are received from the public or a section thereof at the time of worship or devotion it should be treated as a public one and should cease to be treated as a private one.' 'Of course, if in any institution, a shebait, *archaka* or *pūjāri* engages in any religious service he may be adequately remunerated for such service.'[5]

The reader will notice that the concept of the *public* is uppermost in the Commission's minds. They think of the public's

[1] *Archaka* and *pūjārī* both mean 'priest', actual ministrant of the idol (above, p. 470, n. 1).

[2] P. 36, para. 9. This seems to be the law already: Derrett, *I.M.H.L.*, §. 820; Mukherjea, p. 335.

[3] At pp. 37–8.

[4] At pp. 40–1. Tarakeshwar Temple, W. Bengal; Dakshineshwara Temple near Calcutta; and the Nathdwara, Rajasthan (see above, p. 479).

[5] *Report*, p. 42. See above, p. 490, n. 2.

interests in the endowment, whereas nothing is surer than that the public as such never makes endowments, the public never worships: for as we have seen in our own studies the individual prostrates himself; for individual worship is the reverse side of group solidarity in social and financial terms, individual salvation in the 'other' world is the correlative of corporate cohesion in this. The Commission think of the public partly because they are appointed by the Government of India, partly because they are accustomed to think as public-spirited people, and partly (as we shall repeat) because the institutions they have visited are in these days open to be viewed as aspects of *India*, whereas previously they were only aspects of a *caste*, a section of the public, an area, or a royal family's prestige. It is in the light of this that we read their remarks:[1]

> Thus temples may be described as occult laboratories where certain physical acts of adoration coupled with certain systematized prayers, psalms, *mantras*[2] and musical invocations, can yield certain physical and psychological results as a matter of course, and if these physical processes are properly conducted, the results will accrue provided the persons who perform them are adequately equipped. One of the essentials for the proper conduct of rituals is the proper ordaining of the priest.[3] Also the efficacy of the prayers, *poojas*, *archanas*, *abhishekas*,[4] festivals, etc., very much depends on the expertness of the priestly agent employed in the physical process and ritualistic details. It is therefore essential that the correct approach and proper conditions should be rigidly followed to enable temples to fulfil their purpose . . . These ideas lead us to the irresistible conclusion that the *pūjās*, the rituals, the ceremonies and festivals in a temple must necessarily be conducted by persons fully qualified.

–because, we may interpolate, Hindus like the commissioners themselves may at any time visit the temple and wish to make offerings or participate in the festivities! In Kerala the extent of public participation in village temple festivals is very great, and temples are centres of public activity on a large scale. In the Madras State, for example, and farther north, this is by no means so marked, and continuing public interest in the

[1] At p. 42.

[2] Formulae used in worship (similar to litanies and the like).

[3] Priests are not ordained in Hinduism. It is a hereditary occupation.

[4] I.e. *pūjā-s*; *archana* means 'worship' (the work of the *archaka*); *abhiṣeka* literally means 'sprinkling' or 'coronation', inaugural ceremonies for the idol.

buildings and their endowments can be fitful and uncertain.[1]

The question of the ministrants' qualifications exercised the Commission greatly. They note the legal rules hindering the transfer of the *shebaiti*[2] with some satisfaction. These rules of course betray the fact that *shebaiti* is largely a source of financial profit. The actual worship in temples was found by the members of the Commission to be faulty, the *archaka-s* or *pūjārī-s* being efficient in nothing but 'extorting' money. 'Obviously they are hardly in a position to infuse a spirit of devotion and reverence in the devotees and worshippers who come to temples to seek Divine grace.'[3] The present writer would question this, since mumbled prayers and indistinct or incorrect formulae are often tolerated in places of worship (not excluding synagogues and churches) without loss to the reverence of the worshippers. However, it is certainly the case that the Commission found ignorance and incompetence wherever they went, except in the temples which they single out for praise, and they are delighted to find that schools for priests had been started in Madras anb Andhra. They would have been even more delighted had they learnt that in Kerala a scheme of education for intending temple priests is not only on the point of being put into effect but has every likelihood of being successful.[4] The *Report* waxes eloquent on the subject of the priests, and one extract will serve as a specimen of the whole:[5]

> . . . the priest there was a young boy of fifteen years of age who did not know even the name of the Deity, the type of worship to be performed or the *mantras* to be uttered. He had got by heart four lines of Sanskrit verse and with that equipment he carried with him a match-box with which he set fire to a piece of camphor, when any one visited the temple. His main

[1] *Inām* lands originally granted for the worship of an idol may even come to be alienated (subject to resumption) to a church! See *Roman Catholic Mission* v. *State of Madras* AIR 1966 S.C. 1457.

[2] At p. 44 (see above, p. 493, n. 2). At p. 50 they tell how *shebaits* are reported to have sold their rights to Muslim contractors!

[3] P. 47.

[4] Tripunithura Sanskrit College, near Ernakulam (Kerala). The crux is that modern education and priestly and general Sanskrit education must go together, or career-wise the candidate will have put his eggs in one basket. So the *Report*, p. 77.

[5] *Report*, p. 48.

interest was mainly to check whether a ticket had been purchased before a devotee went to the temple.

The *Report* goes on to admit the usefulness of hereditary rights to be *shebaits* or priests.[1] But none should act unless qualified. The proprietary right over the offerings should be abolished: but more than compensation would be available in return, for what is driving good men away from the profession, namely the absence of a minimum living wage, should be remedied. This of course would be possible only by means of comprehensive state control. The priests, in their view, should not be paid less than Rs. 60 (£3) a month. Where a temple cannot afford this a pool system might be adopted. The priests should be made to accept a code of conduct. They should give more services than they do, e.g. by giving discourses to the pilgrims.[2]

After struggles the *pandas* were eliminated at Tirupati. The satisfaction of the Commission is evident. However there would be no objection to genuine pilgrim-guides who hold certificates of proficiency or licences.[3]

The *Report* passes to the twin topics of mismanagement and misappropriation and the method to be adopted when once control has been established and some temples are found to have true surpluses (after paying for repairs, etc., which have hitherto so often been neglected).[4] In the Commission's view surpluses should be diverted from the temples which have them and should be devoted to restoration of crumbling or ruined temples, and the setting up and running of colleges in 'Hindu divinity'. Religious education and Sanskrit education could be fostered by this means. Discourses to the public on religious matters and mythology could be subsidized to good effect. The *shebaits*' and priests' objections to this can be overruled: they are only trustees and the courts' notion that they have proprietary rights in their offices or their takings is incorrect and must be amended.[5] The *Report* gives a long list of possible charitable purposes, e.g. hospitals, which could be served by surplus funds from rich

[1] At p. 58. [2] At the same place.

[3] *Report*, pp. 49–50, 60 ff., 167. The *Report* does not state in so many words that the Commissioners were themselves dunned by Pandas (as the present writer has been), but the lively animosity shown against these touts suggests nothing more likely.

[4] Chapter vii. [5] At pp. 97–9.

endowments. The law of *cy près* should be amended in India to correspond to certain amendments made in England by ss. 13 and 14 of the Charities Act, 1960.

On the subject of the succession to the headship of *mutts* the *Report* has much to say. Some think there should be a selection board to approve a *chela* (pupil) nominated by the previous *mahant*, but the Commission feel that in general each institution should follow its own custom, purified, however, from the curious abuses which have crept in in the interests of private greed:[1]

> The opinion of witnesses has been practically unanimous that the heads of mutts should have a sound knowledge of the language, in which the scriptures of the *sampradāya*[2] are written and also of the main tenets and books of that *sampradāya*. Though no academic qualifications as such can be laid down for such offices, a sound general education, together with a good knowledge of the regional language is considered desirable.

This strikes the western reader as comparable with an imaginary suggestion from a notable of, say, Worcester in England in, say, the early sixteenth century, that his bishop should be bound to know Latin and the breviary, and be able to speak English: sufficiently modest requirements, one would think, but apt to arouse the wrath of the clerical and perhaps even the secular authorities of the period. The *Report* notices that all reforming tendencies have been hindered by the Supreme Court's protecting the *mahants* by way of their (unfortunate) right of property in the endowment.[3] They are right to evince the suspicion that once the right of property ceases as a reality and as a theory the attractions of the hereditary or quasi-hereditary system of succession to mahantships will weaken. However, opinion does not entirely desert the wayward pontiffs in their hour of need:[4]

> . . . there is an equally strong volume of public opinion against any interference in the existing scheme of things. Indeed a number of witnesses are vehemently against Government interference with the management and administration of religious foundations. While there is general agreement on the need for supervisory control by Government with a view to

[1] See p. 95. That *sannyāsī-s*, especially those connected with *mutts*, should be well versed in Sanskrit is noted by M. Mādhavan Nair, J., at [1965] K.L.T. 833 (citing J. C. Ghose).

[2] 'Doctrinal tradition.' [3] P. 99. [4] P. 100.

seeing that the resources of the institutions are utilized on proper objects appertaining to them and that there is no misappropriation of funds, diversion of funds, breach of trust, alienation of property, etc., they feel that Government should not interfere in their day-to-day administration and management.

Political bias is feared, if the executive have any hand in the choice of *mahants*.

The *Report* mentions in passing that the *HSA* could be misinterpreted so as to give to the blood relations of a *sannyāsī* a right of inheritance in respect of the property he acquired after his *sannyāsa*, and *vice versa*, and that this would be incompatible with the intended status of a *mahant* who is usually a *sannyāsī*. It might in the view of the Commission be necessary to amend the *HSA* to clarify the position. In the meanwhile, as we have seen, a judicial decision[1] that the statute does not apply to *sannyāsī-s* has every likelihood of being followed, and will obviate the need to follow out this particular recommendation.[2]

The *Report* describes as a 'crime against society' that huge Jaina charitable endowments are left accumulating without being used except in private businesses.[3] It goes on to devote an entire chapter[4] to the irregularities and malpractices, mostly deposed to by hearsay, which disfigure the present state of Hindu religious institutions generally. First of all they recommend that the law of limitation should be changed, so that improperly alienated assets can be recovered without a limit of time.[5] This obviously wise recommendation is already in force in some regions with respect to alienations made subsequent to the coming into force of state supervision of endowments.[6] Next they recommend that the constitutional protection for the present trustees' right of property should be abolished. The likelihood that this will be put into effect seems considerable.

The Commission then applied its mind to a matter of interest

[1] *Sumer* v. *State of Rajasthan* AIR 1965 Raj. 2. Above, p. 332.

[2] *Report*, p. 102, para. 27. [3] P. 112. Above, p. 461. [4] Chapter x.

[5] At pp. 117, 182, para. 53. See Limitation Act, 1963, Art. 96. The need for the recommendation is well supported by (e.g.) *Gurandita Mal* v. *Amar* AIR 1965 S.C. 1966. Cf. the temporary effect of Public Wakfs (Extension of Limitation) Act, 29 of 1959, extending the period of recovery to August 15th, 1967.

[6] See Bombay Public Trusts Act, 1950, s. 52 A (Mukherjea, 2nd edn., p. liv).

to us in our present connexion. We have seen what were the essentials of the *Lakshmindra case*, and we have been observing the development of the Supreme Court's attitude to 'religion' and the freedom of religion in India. The *Report* adds that one who reads the Shirur Mutt Case (*Lakshmindra's case*), the Jain Temple Case (*Ratilal's case*)[1] and the Ajmer Mosque Case (*Durgah Committee, Ajmer*)[2] finds it difficult to resist the conclusion that what is said by Gajendragadkar, J., as he then was, at *Durgah Committee* v. *Syed Hussain Ali*[3] at p. 1415 is either an extension or an unavowed departure.[4] The passage includes what we have already quoted as an example of the Supreme Court's awareness of the need to distinguish between the essential parts of religion and other portions, and its awareness of the court's jurisdiction to determine whether an element is religious in the sense of essentially religious or not. The present writer is not aware of a discrepancy or a 'departure'. But from the point of view taken by the Commission it could fairly be said that the Supreme Court has wavered in accepting the possibility that matters which have a secular content and effect could be classified as religious. It is possible that objection was taken to the threat to declare a practice superstitious; but more probably the Commission was hostile to the constitutional protection of states of affairs nominally religious but actually secular, for in another place the *Report* makes it clear that a better distinction should be maintained between religion on the one hand and secular considerations on the other, and if necessary the Constitution should be amended to make this evident.[5] A further amendment should be needed, the Commission suggests, to prevent endowments' being classed as private when they received donations from the public.[6] The type of management has no bearing on this question, they contend: if members of the public resort to a temple it should be a public temple for this purpose. Gifts from members of the public to a *mahant* (i.e. not from his personal friends) are not, in their view, personal property, and the law should be amended to take account of this fact.[7]

The *Report* closes with a summary of recommendations,

[1] Above, p. 462. [2] Above, p. 477. [3] Above, p. 477.
[4] *Report*, pp. 114–15. [5] P. 146. [6] *Report*, p. 146.
[7] At pp. 36, 146.

which leaves us in no doubt but that if Hindu religious endowments of a public character are to be reformed in this spirit, which may well have animated the Founding Fathers of the Constitution, that Constitution itself must undergo numerous amendments for the purpose.

Are Private Endowments Exempt?

Meanwhile the abuses with regard to private endowments are mostly unnoticed or unsung. Evidently the worship of the deity in the family is more important than that in the public temple. But the latter has a feature which the former has not. The family which decides to secularize the property of its deity cannot be stopped from so doing, provided the act is that of all the body of the *shebaits* and of the family.[1] Now that the Hindu Succession Act has made a *shebaiti* pass in fragments to heirs like any property that cannot be disposed of by will[2] the chances that worship will be neglected[3] and that the idols' properties will be misappropriated have been greatly increased. It will soon be difficult, unless family arrangements are to be imputed for the purpose, to prevent an impossibility of the total shebait-body meeting to decide something in the idol's interest.[4] The State has not cared to make any positive provision for the preservation of the private trust, and has on the contrary so acted that its interests are likely to be endangered. But the public temple means patronage, and political patronage. By 'political patronage' is meant here not so much the likelihood that *mahants* will order their followers to vote for a particular candidate–though that is not unknown, despite the ban on appeals to religious affiliations in electioneering,[5] but rather the patronage and power which vast wealth gives and which can

[1] Derrett, *I.M.H.L.*, §. 789; also *Bairagi* v. *Sri Uday* AIR 1965 Or. 201, para. 28.

[2] Derrett, *I.M.H.L.*, §. 791. The *founder* can dispose of the *shebaiti* by his will: *Bai Zabu* v. *Amardas* [1967] 8 Guj. L.R. 281.

[3] The law already allows one who disbelieves in idol worship to be a shebait: *Raghunath* v. *Shyam* AIR 1961 Or. 157 (alekhdharmist)! Mukherjea, pp. 208–9.

[4] Derrett, *I.M.H.L.*, §. 795 (all *shebaits* must join for a disposition to be valid). Mukherjea, pp. 254–6 (delegation is impossible).

[5] Representation of the People Act, 1951, ss. 123 (3), 124 (5).

raise or lower the standing of individuals and groups, castes and sub-castes in the scale of inter-caste competition. This was something which everyone disliked, because if the wings of one's own patrons were clipped at the least the same could be said of others', and the clipping of other people's wings has the advantage that one cannot be outflown.

Nothing in the *Report* we have studied suggests that the members of the Commission were moved by such considerations. None of them were politicians in the usual sense. On the contrary we find that they unconsciously wished that *mahants* were like bishops, priests like ministers of religion, worship of idols like services, and *mutts* like cathedrals. There was even the suggestion that the ministrants in temples should take degrees in 'theology', a highly novel suggestion.[1] But notwithstanding this negative and positive evidence, the ultimate objection to the freedom of the *shebaits* of the great temples and of the *mahants* was not that it worked often adversely to the interests of the idols and the *mutts* but favourably to the temporary social and political interests of the *shebaits*, *mahants* and their favourites (though that was objectionable enough to one who had learnt to question the traditional principles of Indian piety), but rather that in a modern democracy there cannot be reserves of wealth and unpredictable power capable of being harnessed to forces incompatible with adult suffrage. The temples were an anachronism, not because they did not supply 'religion' in the western sense, nor because what went on there was a mockery of 'religion' as understood in the world at large; not because the 'staff' were ignorant and incompetent and unfit for the dignity of serving the deity, but because they stood for a focus of power, justification for which passed away when the British left and the soil of India became subject to the rule of the Indian people. Far too much had been dedicated to idols; far too much money came into the hands of those who did not earn it: the answer was not to burn the temples and to hang the *shebaits* and *mahants* (much as some hands itched to do this),[2] but to bring in the

[1] *Report*, pp. 74, 77 (the references to psalms, ordination and Holy Orders elsewhere are likewise no coincidences). Hinduism has not less than six *darśana-s*, but has no creed: the *Satsang case* (above p. 50).

[2] 'A Social Thinker' (M. P. Chatterjee?), in *Temples and Religious Endowments* (Calcutta, B. N. Neogi, 1951) expresses himself as follows: 'The

account-book and the ledger, and to call the refractory to heel by due process of law. This part of the revolution has been accomplished with exemplary charity, courtesy, and fore-thought, and is far too little appreciated for what it is. We need not be surprised that the *Report* urges that the work should be finished and the necessary measures taken to fulfil the programme.

What effect has this on religion? The writer would submit that it has little if any. The superintendence of the state over endowments has gone on, with little interruption, though with varying efficiency, from time immemorial. The Hindu kings and even some of their Muslim successors acted as patrons of temples and *mutts*, and saw to it that glaring anomalies were corrected.[1]

temples, the religious endowments as well as the income of the theological organizations, over which the right of the toilers is just and legal, must be utilized for the benefit of the toilers. No sentiment, no scruple, no law, no customs or usages should be allowed to stand as a bar in the fulfilment of this right (p. ii)'. 'This is an age of discovery, of science and industry and not of theology which with its superstitions stands as a great barrier to the progress and development of man and thereby retards the national awakening.' 'This theological morbidity must be supplanted by "Kshatra Sakti" to snub down cringing debasing effeminacy in all the branches of life so that a vigorous all-conquering spirit may be roused up in the breast of every youth (p. iv)'. 'In India the prelates or Mohunts acquire enormous wealth . . . They are too miserly for using it for any national utility. But their wealth is a gift of the toilers, and the high prelates are mere servants of the toilers (p. 3).' Theologians who can quote *śāstra-s* overlook the bread problem, 'as this is too distasteful to them' (p. 11). 'The temple is a religion-shop used as octroi office for collecting taxes (p. 12).' 'Now the shastric laws are fast changing. The second and third portions of theology, i.e. the devotional and the ritualistic portions, are getting completely changed and modified. This is inevitable. By the rolling of time, the taste and temperament of the people have changed. They have, in most cases, rejected the old modes of worship. All sorts of costly, time-killing, elaborate and cumbrous rituals they avoid, and they have supplanted these archaic rituals by shorter, simpler and cheaper ones. It is submitted that along with the second and the third portions of theology, the unsuitable portions of trust deeds and documents are to be modified or completely rejected . . . (p. 15).' The present writer agrees that, while the *karma-kāṇḍa* and *yoga-kāṇḍa* of Hinduism are weakening daily, the *bhakti* or *jñāna* aspect of Hinduism flourishes: it is natural that practices and institutions appropriate to the *karma-kāṇḍa* should be neglected or attacked.

[1] See above, p. 179, n. 4 and p. 181, n. 6. Also Kāṇe, *H.D.*, II, pp. 912–14, cites evidence from the *smṛti*-period up to the Peshwāī administration of the Deccan. On the *Śukranītisāra* see L. Gopal, *B.S.O.A.S.*, 25, no. 3 (1962), 532

The improved modern Indian versions of state control will 'purify' or 'refine' the image which public religious behaviour presents to observers, but can hardly affect the notion of religion held by the mass of the people. Indeed no such intention exists. The Commission would wish any Hindu visiting temples in any part of India to be impressed and to enjoy religious sentiments as fully as he could in any church or cathedral in Europe or elsewhere if he could imagine himself *pro tempore* a Christian; but however widely this wish is shared the actual religious aspirations of the people are not sought to be touched. The Hindu may still make his relinquishment in favour of the idol of his choice, and may still make his offering to the *mahant*; the way the money may be spent has to some extent been varied directly or indirectly by state control. The freedom of religion guaranteed by the Constitution has not stood in the way of this–for there was no reason why it should. There emerges no evidence that *mutts* or temples are any the worse for this legislation: on the contrary, once the notables swallowed the blow to their pride they realized that their security was enhanced, a worse fate had been avoided; and the well-being of their institutions is generally thought to have increased, notwithstanding the conflicts which sometimes arise between those who have a right to share in the administration.

The Position of Religion in Indian Law

Within the bounds of these two chapters we may ask ourselves what is the situation of religion as the State understands it in its day-to-day administration? Is it an entity which the law admits to parity with itself, immune from its supervision? The complex facts cannot, as we suggested at the outset, submit themselves to a neat and succinct formula. Complex facts represent a complex relationship.

The law is expressing in hard fact what the people, led by their most aware and best-equipped citizens, desire or think ideal with reference to these sensitive matters. Some un-Indian

n. 5. The objections which the ancient Hindu law had to ascetics who slipped from their vows of celibacy are fully endorsed by the Madras High Court in *Tiruvambala* v. *Manikkavachaka* (1915) 40 Mad. 177, 199 (quoted by Mukherjea, where cited, at p. 355).

doctrines have been found useful to express an Indian need; but they do not seem to represent in themselves a transplanted and so a non-indigenous idea. The present writer regrets his own haste in assuming that this was so: an error which reflects one perplexing character of Indian history.

There are areas where religious scruples are left entirely undisturbed by the law.[1] In the field of the personal laws the claim that religion has been interfered with turns out to be unsound, for the State has selected for the citizen an approved path from amongst several formerly possible paths, and has made it worth his while to keep to that path.[2] Where the legal support for religious doctrines has been relaxed or abandoned the opportunity for conscience to operate in matters of daily life has not been taken away or even impaired.[3] The religious beliefs of the people may not be insulted, nor may assemblies for worship be disturbed except at the risk of prosecution under the Penal Code.[4] The democratic tendency to resent reservations of facilities in public institutions has found expression in the temple-entry laws. These may interfere with the continuance of ancient customs of a religious character, but no human beings are deprived of their religion, for they can decamp and set up private institutions where they can worship in their own way.[5] If the idols themselves may be thought to be hard struck by this, the answer is that idols exist as a benefit for the deities' worshippers[6] and the idols' welfare is conclusively determined by way of the intention of the *shebaits*, whose ideas have been reformed by statute.[7] Those whose religious scruples include a belief in Untouchability have been prohibited from practising this: their remedy, if they continue in this belief, is to stay at home and to use only private facilities from which they can still exclude untouchables.[8] The caste notions which once had full play in public life (public life was virtually the balance between castes) are incompatible with the 'New' India, and everyone is agreed that public life can be regulated by majority rule.[9]

In the technical realm of religious bequests the courts deter-

[1] Above, p. 438. [2] Above, p. 448. [3] Above, p. 443.
[4] Above, p. 451. [5] Above, p. 469. [6] Above, p. 486, n. 1.
[7] Above, p. 455. [8] Above, p. 454.
[9] On the areas where the Constitution's bias against caste affect law and custom see above, p. 305, n. 4.

mine what is religious and are not afraid to call a belief superstitious, and thus unworthy to obtain public support.[1] They have every confidence in abundant learning on this subject. The result is that the caste-less society of the ideal state will not pay for individual eccentricities and will subsidize, in its own way (however trifling), only well-authenticated religious programmes. This does not hinder the individual's search for salvation. We have seen how public endowments are sought to be restricted: yet the current movement to invest the courts with jurisdiction to administer trusts created in so many words for *dharma* or an equally vague object testifies to a balancing demand for facilities for acquiring individual merit.[2] Even apart from the success this movement has had in one State, and the success it is likely (if not certain) to achieve when the topic comes up for general review, the scope for individuals to make what they visualize as religious bequests is very wide. The living person can make his donations, and he can direct his executors to pay, after his death, bequests to an institution of his choice: the State's aid is limited where the object of his intended benefaction is not accepted as religious by any substantial section of the public, the masters of every practical situation.[3] In determining what is religious and what activity can successfully appeal for the state's protection, the court looks into tradition, learning, books, *and* evidence of usage and opinion.[4] There is no

[1] Above, p. 480.

[2] Bequests for *dharma* or for 'salvation' are at present void for uncertainty: *Runchordas* v. *Parvatibai* (1899) 26 I.A. 71. Mukherjea, pp. 105–6. *Mohanlal* v. *Habibullah* AIR 1963 Pat. 430. But a powerful demand for the widening of the court's jurisdiction to frame schemes even for such vague trusts was made by A. S. Naṭarāja Ayyar at *Vyav. Nirṇ.* 4 (1955), 88 ff., and this is already accorded by s. 10 of the Bombay Act 29 of 1950 and by s. 3 of the Rajasthan Public Trusts Act, 42 of 1959 (Mukherjea, pp. xxxxi (*sic*), clxix), so that the testator's purpose may be achieved in those States. Patanjali Śāstrī, J., at *Veluswami* v. *Dandapani* [1947] Mad. 47, 55–6 points out *obiter* that as Hindus worship a Supreme Being a gift for the 'worship of God' ought to be valid under Hindu law, but this legal-theological point has not been ruled upon in a reported decision. In *obiter dicta* in *Shamboo* v. *Sardar* AIR 1967 J. & K. 52, where Hindus and Sikhs disputed about a shrine, it was suggested there might be a valid public and religious and charitable endowment not dedicated to any particular deity.

[3] Above, p. 458.

[4] Above, p. 467.

question (as at one time there seemed to be) of exalting book-religion at the expense of the faiths of the peasants.

When a community having definable religious opinions wishes to expel a member on the ground of an offence against the religion (which would itself be determined by the court in the manner or manners indicated above) it can do so, and the secular results of this expulsion are not to be allowed to stand in the way of the religious 'denomination's' authority to manage its own affairs in matters of religion.[1] But if the crux of the matter were merely superstition, as the court saw it, the right to expel could, if the State wished, be denied to all communities. Similarly we now find that when temples and *mutts* came to be placed in some states under executive supervision the claim that such a fate was a denial of freedoms guaranteed under Arts. 25 and 26 was negatived. Public control of public institutions will not be slackened because they subserve religious interests.

Thus the emphasis is on the word 'public'. Reforms needed equally in the field of private religious concerns are for the present postponed; they may or may not be practicable when the nation has more urgent tasks awaiting its attention. But throughout that sphere of thought where behaviour impinges on the public the public must lay down its conditions and impose its regulations. This it safely does as did the Hindu sovereigns of past ages, since it is (as it then was) accepted that the Government has both the right and the duty to balance conflicting interests, and the expression of religion in public has always been associated not so much, or primarily, with belief and faith but, as in Northern Ireland or the Island of Cyprus, with social affiliations, prestige, pressure-groupings, and matters properly subject, in their overt manifestations, to state regulation and control. And, as we shall see, neither Indian history in general nor Hinduism itself denies the validity of the State's jurisdiction in these regards.

[1] Above, p. 476.

15

THE FUTURE OF MUHAMMADAN LAW IN INDIA

Nowhere is the need for a delicate balance between the leading social interests so evident as in the thorny question of the need to reform Islamic, or as it is more realistically called, Muhammadan law in India. The name itself is a curiosity. Muhammadans (more properly Muslims) are those who follow the Prophet Muhammad, whether they are adherents of the numerically dominant school, the Hanafīs, or whether they are Shāfi'īs, or whether, on the contrary, they are followers of the Shī'ī (non-Sunnī) schools of Islamic law, such as the Ismā'īlīs, the Bohras, the Khojas, or even the supposedly unorthodox Ahmadīyas. There are also the Cutchi Memons,[1] who retain to some extent the private law of the Hindus, from amongst whom they originated. All these are Muhammadans, and their personal law is called, naturally, Muhammadan law by virtue of their religious affiliation. The term Islamic law is not incorrect, but could give the false impression that anywhere in South Asia the true Shariat (*shari'a*), or *fiqh*, the jurisprudence of Islam, was in force unamended.[2] The need for further amendment of what some have

[1] For these communities see A. A. A. Fyzee, *Outlines of Muhammadan Law*[3], London, 1964, pp. 62–74. This is the primary work of reference until the appearance of the forthcoming edition of F. B. Tyabji's *Muhammadan Law*.

[2] A leading textbook on the subject, Sir Roland Wilson's, was called *Anglo-Muhammadan Law*. A. A. A. Fyzee, *Cases in the Muhammadan Law of India and Pakistan* (Oxford, 1965), pp. xxi–xxxiv; also 'Recent developments in Muhammadan law in India', in Norman S. Marsh, ed., *Some Aspects of Indian Law Today* (London, Stevens, 1964), pp. 46 ff.; 'Muhammadan law in India', *C.S.S.H.*, 5 No. 4 (1963), pp. 401–15 or (1964) 66 Bom. L.R., *J.*, pp. 1–11; and 'The impact of English law on the Shariat in India', *Egyptian Rev. of Int. Law*, 18 (1962), pp. 1–27 or (1964) 66 Bom. L.R., *J.*, pp. 107–16, 121–8. M. C. Chagla in *Changes in Muslim Personal Law, a Symposium* (cited below, hereafter referred to as '*Changes*'), p. 93.

called, agreeably, Anglo-Muhammadan law, is urgently called for on purely practical and even humanitarian grounds, but the 'public' of India cannot find the necessary courage and skill to achieve it. It is feared that repercussions will result if what purports to be a secular State legislates–in a legislature in which Muslims are a minority–for the amendment of a system of private law which purports to be based on the commandments of God in his revelations through Muhammad in the Koran. The following arguments fall on deaf ears: that very little of the Muhammadan law actually depends on the Koran, that what does relates after all to the condition of Islamic society or even pre-Islamic society in the seventh century and not to modern India, that the greater part of the law was worked out by mediaeval jurists using their own methods of reasoning and not from first principles, still less from religious principles,[1] and that of that result only a fraction is actually in force in India (the rest having been already abolished),[2] and of that fraction a great part has been modified deliberately or accidentally by the judiciary through the period since 1772 when the East India Company first undertook directly to administer it.

The experts and the learned, amongst whom one must name Mr. M. C. Chagla and Mr. A. A. A. Fyzee as prominent Muslim lawyers, are agreed that reform is desirable[3] and that

[1] A point to be observed from N. J. Coulson, *A History of Islamic Law* (Edinburgh, 1964).

[2] M. Mujeeb in *Changes*, p. 7; Fyzee, *Cases* (cited above), p. xxii.

[3] M. C. Chagla (cited above). A. A. A. Fyzee's slightly more tentative remarks at 'Law and religion in Islam', *J.B.B.R.A.S.*, NS., 28, 1 (1953), pp. 29 ff., at p. 48, are followed by words of caution in his *Outlines*[3], p. viii: 'There is a tendency in certain quarters to criticize the conclusions reached by the classical authorities of Islamic law. It is undoubtedly true that the movement of society has rendered certain rules difficult to apply with equity. But valid criticism should be tempered with greater humility and hesitancy; it should be founded upon unremitting study of Arabic as a language and of law as a science, and illuminated with insight into the faith of man and the evolutionary processes in society. Without these safeguards, judicial valour cannot be exercised with benefit to the community.' The judge should leave reform to the legislature. We may for the present ignore Hindu scholars who have pressed for a uniform code of civil law (e.g. M. P. Jain, S. S. Nigam), but it is possibly justified to cite the arguments of Mangal Chandra Jain Kagzi, a law teacher of the University of Delhi, who belongs to a minority 'Hindu' community, in 'Advisability of legislating a uniform family law

certain reforms in particular cannot be postponed indefinitely. But the voices in favour of reform are automatically thought to be tinged with unorthodoxy, for it is an orthodox belief, in fact almost an article of faith, that the Muhammadan law is, or ought to be, part and parcel of the life of Muslims, and is therefore part of the Islamic religion. If Muslims do not follow the Shariat so much the worse for them; but pious Muslims cannot consent to the laws being modified.

It is pointed out that countries with overwhelmingly dominant Muslim majorities have enacted new laws, sometimes departing far from the Shariat, and even abrogating it in places, in those very fields of family law in which the attachment to the antiquated and peculiar Shariat rules remains strongest in India. This has no effect in India since it is answered that in so far as those countries have amended their laws that is their affair: the Muslim will continue to follow the Shariat, if he knows it, in his own life, and the State can make what arrangements it chooses. Thus, the experience and example of Pakistan, limited as it is, has no persuasive effect. Those who are keen to speak on this subject cannot speak except in favour of keeping the law unchanged, for amongst Indian Muslims the urge to contribute to this discussion is hardly found amongst those who are willing to criticize the sacred law of the people of the Prophet even if it remains in its adulterated Anglo-Muhammadan form. On the contrary there are movements to be noticed in Pakistan advocating a return to the traditional Islamic rules of law even in criminal contexts, whereas these had been abandoned in disgust more than a century ago.

But there is a way of proceeding which does receive respectful attention. The Constitution, to which the Muslim members of the Constituent Assembly gave their hearty support in all its elements, pledges the nation's faith to the creative effort required to substitute for the Hindu, Muhammadan, Parsi, Jewish and Christian laws a single Civil Code for all citizens. Just as caste is no longer accepted overtly as a factor in public life, and communalism has become an ugly word, so the personal laws are accepted as features of a transitional period. In the drafting of a Civil Code, therefore, lies the solution to

code', *Jaipur L.J.*, 5 (1965), pp. 192–200. His unqualified hostility to the Shariat Act ('the most regressive provision') is as unusual as it is justified.

this problem, and a few hints on the possible method to adopt for this purpose will not be out of place in this paper.[1]

'Secularism' has become in *some* quarters a fashionable word, and it is accepted as axiomatic that it means, in India, the co-existence of various religions under the benevolent supervision of the State. Dr. Rādhākrishnan said on August 21st, 1961, 'I want to state authoritatively that secularism does not mean irreligion.' When sectarian demands in the name of religion grew loud it was feared that secularism was in danger,[2] but it is not suggested that there is anything wrong with the demands as such: it is their being enforced upon members of other communities or sects which is objected to. It is said that freedom of religion amounts virtually to freedom from (someone else's) religion. It is also said that 'religious conditioning in childhood is tantamount to a violation of the adult's freedom of conscience', but this extraordinary notion does not amount to an assertion that religious teaching should be prohibited. Mr. M. C. Chagla edited a booklet embodying a symposium in memory of Jawaharlal Nehru, *Socialism, Democracy and Secularism.*[3] There Nehru is called a 'reverent agnostic' and Gandhiji (astonishingly) 'the greatest secularist of the age': because, of course, he was interested in the 'best' elements of all the higher religions. In the symposium Dr. Abū Sayeed Ayyūb, the Muslim editor of *Quest*, had the following revealing remarks to make:

> It is just as well that it [India] is not secular in the western sense of complete separation between Church and State, for it reserves to itself the right to intervene in the interest of necessary social reforms in matters which customarily come under the purview of religion. A good example of such wholesome deviation from western secularism is the Hindu Marriage Act. I hope the other religious communities of India will also be brought under the purview of this Act without undue delay. Whatever ancient scriptures might say, bigamy (not to speak of polygamy) shocks the moral sense of modern man. Ancient scriptures hardly kept the balance even as between man and woman, Brahmin and Sudra, Momin [Muslim]

[1] The present writer offered suggestions corresponding in part to what follows in 'The Indian Civil Code or Code of Family Law', *Law Quarterly* (Calcutta) 3 No. 3 (1966), pp. 137–44.

[2] 'R.H.' in *India News* (London), Jan. 21st, 1967. 'Secularism' being in favour, naturally all Hindu culture, including the Vedas, are said to be 'secular': an anonymous article entitled 'Secularism in Indian literature' in *India News*, Sept. 23rd, 1967.

[3] New Delhi (National Book Trust), 1965.

and Kafir, Christian and Heathen. No modern State can permit the perpetuation of such inequalities.

The Civil Code can therefore proceed as a feature of secularism and not as a method of reforming religious laws.

The Extent of the Problem

(*i*) *The personal law*

In keeping with the policy of this book it is not intended to enter into details of the law. These may be ascertained easily from the relevant textbooks. We do need, however, to grasp of what the personal law consists before we pass on to consider the cases in which even Muslims do not follow it. The two major schools, Sunnī and Shī'ī, do not complete the whole picture as Muslims in Kerala have the opportunity to prove that they are Shāfī'īs, i.e. followers of the school of the Imām Shāfī'ī, though the presumption is that they are Hanafīs, i.e. followers of the Imām Abū Ḥanīfa, whose doctrines are dominant in India. Followers of the other Sunnī schools are on the whole not found, and so Mālikī law and Hanbali law, adhered to by followers of the other great Imāms, can be neglected. In numerous details the Sunnī schools differ from each other, and all differ from the Shī'īs. The Shī'ī law in India is that of the Ithnā 'Asharī school, or of the numerically less important Ismā'īlis.[1] The Muhammadan law applied in India is based on the textbooks produced by Muslim scholars prior to the British period, and on the labours of British and later Indian students of Muhammadan law, who as translators or digesters of the law made their own subtle contribution to the subject. The topics selected for administration differ slightly from those listed for Hindus not because the list was different–it was one and the same for both–but because in course of time the elements of Muhammadan law thought necessary for applying the unquestioned items in the list expanded those limits by a kind of natural accretion and Justice, Equity and Good Conscience added others. Thus the personal law[2] is applied in the realm of Marriage, Dower

[1] For details of adherence to these schools and application of their laws see Fyzee, *Outlines*³, pp. 37–47, 77–8. It is to be noted that a Muslim has the option of changing his school without formality: *Fyzee*, p. 75.

[2] The implication that 'personal law' means 'law of one's personal *faith*, i.e. a law of peculiarly intimate concern' (suggested by M. C. Chagla at

(*Mahr*), Dissolution of Marriage, Parentage and Legitimacy, Guardianship, Maintenance, Gifts, *Wakf* (transfer to God for a charitable purpose), Pre-emption, Wills and Gifts made in Death-sickness, and Administration of Estates. It is at once evident that Dower and Gifts have a relation to the family law, but also appertain to the realm of transfer of property. While the *family* law may be reviewed for the purposes of a Civil Code (a process suspect in the eyes of orthodox Muslims) the regulation of property questions, and the technical rules regarding the type of estate that can be created and the manner in which transfers can be effectuated come within a different scope; the reservation in their favour in the general law at present operative with reference to Transfer of Property[1] and Testamentary Succession[2] may not ultimately claim the same privilege. It is very difficult to contend that religion prevents the transfer of an interest other than an entire interest,[3] or that conditions are void which are attached to a purported conditional transfer.[4] Dower relates to marriage, and it happens that the question of prohibition of dowries has already agitated Parliament. The Act of 1961 which is called the Dowry Prohibition Act[5] specifically exempts 'dower or mahr' in the case of persons to whom the Muslim Personal Law (Shariat) applies. The giving and taking of dower amongst Muslims is no abuse, nor is the giving and taking of *strīdhanam* in the same context amongst some Christians in Kerala.[6] The rule of Muhammadan law whereby a Muslim wife is entitled to dower from her husband has no counterpart in other personal laws, and

Changes) is quite unsound. As we have seen the personal law imputed to an individual has nothing to do with his actual beliefs or lack of beliefs.

[1] D. F. Mulla, *Transfer of Property Act, 1882*[5] (Bombay, Tripathi, 1966), p. 12.

[2] Indian Succession Act, 39 of 1925, ss. 211–13.

[3] On *Mushā* see Fyzee, *Outlines*[3], pp. 229 ff. (a gift of an undivided interest is inchoate at Hanafī law). In *Anjuman* v. *Nawab Asif* [1955] 2 Cal. 109 (Fyzee, *Cases*, pp. 357 ff.) it was held that life-interests can be created by any Muslim by gift or will. The decision was hailed as an advance.

[4] Fyzee, *Outlines*[3], pp. 212 ff.

[5] Derrett, *I.M.H.L.*, pp. 607–10.

[6] See a sequence of Notes: T. J. Mathew, 'Dowry Prohibition Act and the payment of Streedhanam', [1962] K.L.T., *J.*, 1 ff.; A. V. Moothedan (rejoining), 29 ff.; Derrett (summarizing), 43 ff.

the abolition of the rule would be an unnecessary affront to the community. On the other hand the possibility of any Muslim's making a special marriage under the Special Marriage Act (whereby the question of dower becomes inapplicable) indicates a way out of the difficulty to which we shall return.[1]

(ii) The deviations from the personal law

Granted that the personal laws of a Sunnī or Shi'ī Muslim can be ascertained from the books and from the case-law which has on the whole put them into force, it is by no means a matter of course that a Muslim should be governed by his personal law. It is usually assumed that for all practical purposes Muslims are governed by Muhammadan law since the Muslim Personal Law (Shariat) Act, 26 of 1937, was passed, when an attempt was made to draw the various sections of the largest minority community together.

The complications stem from the fact that large numbers of Muslims are governed, in the States which correspond, or partly correspond, to the former British India and in some other States, by customs which differ from the personal law. It is true that the great home of customary law, the Punjab, underwent a radical reform in that the Shariat Act abolished, to the extent that it was applicable, the privilege of local custom, but the Punjab and other areas must continue to recognize and enforce customary law, whether of regions, of castes, or even families, to the extent that that Act is not applicable either to persons or to property.[2] Islam itself made small room for custom.[3] In the former Hyderabad State the fundamental law of which was Islamic, custom could not be proved in derogation from the religious law.[4] Elsewhere custom was allowed, at Anglo-

[1] Below, pp. 533, 547.

[2] *Mian Saleh* v. *Sayyah Zawwar* (1943) 71 I.A. 14 illustrates this.

[3] Tahir Mahmood, 'Custom as a source of law in Islam', (1965) 7 *J.I.L.I.*, 102–6. Custom contravening an express text of the Koran or the *sunna* is void. It may however be used in order to interpret and apply legal rules on worldly affairs. Custom cannot derogate from law but it can supplement the sources of law when the intention of individuals has to be inferred (e.g. succession to the office of *mutawalli* or trustee of a *wakf*).

[4] *Begum Noorbanu* v. *Deputy Custodian General of Evacuee Property* AIR 1965 S.C. 1937, 1942.

Muhammadan law[1] or by statute[2] (because of the laxity with which the Shariat had been enforced by the Moghul and other Muslim rulers), to derogate from the book-law more or less similarly with its counterpart amongst Hindus, where custom, as we have seen, could, if validly proved, always derogate from the book-law; and moreover certain well-known and by no means insignificant commercial and other less well-known communities were known to be governed by Hindu law in respect of the property-rights of the family and/or testamentary or intestate succession as their customary law. Against this background it is perhaps best to commence a survey by seeing what the Shariat Act, 1937, actually attempted to do. We may refer to the text of the statute.[3]

1. (1) This Act may be called the Muslim Personal Law (Shariat) Application Act, 1937.

(2) It extends to the whole of India except the State of Jammu and Kashmir.

2. Notwithstanding any custom or usage to the contrary, in all questions (save questions relating to agricultural land) regarding intestate succession, special property of females, including personal property inherited or obtained under contract or gift or any other provision of Personal Law, marriage, dissolution of marriage, including *talaq*, *ila*, *zihar*, *lian*, *khula* and *mubaraat*, maintenance, dower, guardianship, gifts, trusts and trust properties, and *wakfs* (other than charities and charitable institutions and charitable and religious endowments) the rule of decision in cases where the parties are Muslims shall be the Muslim Personal Law (Shariat).

3. (1) Any person who satisfies the prescribed authority–

(*a*) that he is a Muslim, and

(*b*) that he is competent to contract within the meaning of section 11 of the Indian Contract Act, 1872, and

(*c*) that he is a resident of British India, may by declaration in the prescribed form and filed before the prescribed authority declare that he

[1] Fyzee, *Cases*, pp. xxviii–xxxi. *Kojas and Memons' Case*, Perry's Oriental Cases, 110–29.

[2] E.g. Oudh Estates Act, 1 of 1869. See *Raghuraj Chandra* v. *Subhadra* (1928) 55 I.A. 139, 145.

[3] The reader is warned that in Pakistan the Act applies to agricultural land and custom is totally abolished so far as Muslims are concerned: West Punjab Muslim Personal Law (Shariat) Application Act, 1948, supplemented by the Punjab Muslim Personal Law (Shariat) Application (Amendment) Act, 1951. See *Ghulam Sarwar* v. *Imtiaz Nazir* P.L.D. 1966 S.C. 559 and A. Gledhill, *Pakistan*[2] (London, Stevens, 1967), p. 279.

desires to obtain the benefit of the provisions of this section, and thereafter the provisions of section 2 shall apply to the declarant and all his minor children and their descendants as if in addition to the matters enumerated therein adoption wills and legacies were also specified.

The remainder of the statute is not of further interest, as it makes provision for the framing and publication of rules in furtherance of the purposes of the Act and repeals previous rules of law inconsistent with it.

The Act has by successive enactments at what may be referred to in each case as the 'relevant date' been extended to all parts of India, except Jammu and Kashmir.[1] The States' power to amend the central statute has been used to remove the words in the long brackets in section 2. Madras Act 18 of 1949 extends the application of the statute to agricultural land and removes from the section the exclusion of charities and endowments (a very important class of *wakf*). The result is that in some areas within the former British India the Act applies to agricultural land[2] but in many others, for want of a statute like the Madras Act, it does not. This is a very important limitation upon its use. A great many of those whom we might call from the legal point of view 'anomalous' Muslims are in fact commercial people whose wealth does not lie in agricultural land; but the agriculturalists of the Punjab who are Muslims (a small minority now) do indeed look to their lands for their livelihood. Muslims whose estates devolve by statute are likewise unaffected by this reform.[3] Further, we note the curious, but, as we shall see, suggestive, provisions of section 3, which leave it to the initiative of an individual Muslim to bind himself and his minor children and their descendants by the Shariat in respect of adoption (i.e. with the effect of renouncing any right to adopt which his customary law or local statute might otherwise give

[1] Merged States (Laws) Act, 59 of 1949 (see below); Part C States (Laws) Act, 30 of 1950; Miscellaneous Personal Laws (Extension) Act, 48 of 1959. The position in Pondicherry and the former Portuguese territories may be ignored for our present purposes.

[2] The Shariat Act was adopted in Madhya Bharat by Madhya Bharat Act 1 of 1953. It was not adopted by, e.g., Bihar. In Rajasthan, however, it had been applied by Ordinance 14 of 1949.

[3] In so far as any property still passes under the Oudh Estates Act (see above) or any similar enactment.

him), wills and legacies (i.e. so as to restrict his power to bequeath more than the allowable third to any heir or to bequeath any legacy to an heir at Koranic law). From this we draw the conclusion that as regards those topics a great many Muslims remain governed by their customary law, which in many cases closely resembles the un-codified Hindu law.

The position is further complicated by the discrepancies between the major communities of what we may call 'anomalous' Muslims. Originally the communities governed by customs resembling Hindu law in matters of inheritance and succession were the Khojas, the Cutchi Memons, Sunni Bohras of Gujarat, Molesalam Girasias of Broach, Halai Memons of Porbunder, and Mappillas or Moplahs of Kerala. Only some of these deserve special mention here.

Prior to 1937 in British India or the relevant date in other parts of India, Khojas were governed by the Hindu law of inheritance and succession;[1] after the relevant date they were governed by the Muhammadan law as to *intestate* succession, but retained (unless they took the optional step suggested in s. 3 of the Act) their customary right to will away the whole of their property. As to agricultural land the customary law prevails, except where the Shariat Act has been extended by later statutes. Some uncertainty prevails as to the Khojas' ability to give property by deed or will to unborn persons. The subjects of gifts and wills do indeed come within the scope of the Shariat Act, but that statute does not purport to repeal s. 5 of the Hindu Disposition of Property Act, 15 of 1916, which provides that where a State Government is of the opinion that the Khoja community in the State desire that that Act should be extended to them it may, by notification, declare that for 'Hindus' in the Act 'Khojas' should be read. The immediate effect of the Act of 1916 (which has not been modified in this respect by so recent a statute as the Miscellaneous Personal Laws (Extension) Act, 1959) was to enable Khojas to obtain the freedom then conceded to Hindus. The freedom was conceded subject to certain conditions set out in the Act, s. 3; and it is submitted that where the declaration has not been made the predicament of the

[1] *Advocate General of Bombay* v. *Muhammad Husen Huseni* (1866) 12 Bom. H.C.R. 323, Fyzee, *Cases*, pp. 504 ff. Mulla, *Hindu Law*[13], chapter xxvi, to be read subject to the Shariat Act, 1937.

Khojas remains similar to that of Hindus prior to 1916, notwithstanding anything contained in the Shariat Act.[1]

The Cutchi Memons have had an even more chequered career.[2] It was in their community that the device of individual option was first employed. Prior to 1920 the opinion had prevailed that the Cutchi Memons were governed by the Hindu law of the joint family as well as that of succession, but a decision of the Bombay High Court laid down that the law of the joint family had never applied to them by custom.[3] The Cutchi Memons Act, 46 of 1920 (amended by Act 34 of 1923) provided that a Cutchi Memon who was dissatisfied with the Hindu law of inheritance and succession, and desired to be governed by the Muhammadan law in these matters, might make a declaration in a prescribed form that he desired to obtain the benefit of the Act and thereafter the declarant and all his minor children and their descendants would be governed by Muhammadan law in matters of succession and inheritance. In 1937 (or the relevant date) the Shariat Act assimilated their situation to that of Khojas. By the Cutchi Memons Act, central Act 10 of 1938, the option to make a declaration was taken away, with the result that all Cutchi Memons were governed by the Hanafī school of Muhammadan law. The statute could not affect the devolution of agricultural land. The later Cutchi Memons Act, 25 of 1942, is not of significance for our purpose.[4]

One might suppose that the coming of the Act of 1938 on top of the Shariat Act would have sufficed to clarify the situation. Strangely not, since the States have taken more kindly to the one than the other, and the difference is obviously of some significance for the community. The Merged States (Laws) Act,

[1] The reader will note with interest that in *Ashrafalli Cassim* v. *Mahomedalli Rajaballi* [1947] Bom. 1 it was decided that a Khoja may still dispose of all his property by will, but trusts and *wakfs* created by him by his will must be governed as to their validity by the Muhammadan law. The *construction* of the will will be governed by Hindu law (their Lordships say that this will apply equally to a Cutchi Memon) but with regard to the making and execution of the will the Muhammadan law will apply. More inappropriate confusion it would have been difficult to conceive.

[2] S. R. Dongerkery, *The Law Applicable to Khojas and Cutchi Memons* (Bombay, 1929).

[3] *Haji Oosman* v. *Haroon* (1922) 47 Bom. 369.

[4] In *Cochin* the Cutchi Memons were subject to the Shariat since 1931.

central Act 59 of 1949 (which came into force on the 1st January, 1950) extended the Shariat Act to all 'merged States' within the Governors' Provinces and Chief Commissioners' Provinces. In the case of the former, which included the then States of Bombay and Madras, supplementary legislation by the then Provinces would be necessary. Madras extended the Cutchi Memons Act, 1938, to the former states of Pudukkottai, Banganapalle, and Sandur by Madras Act 35 of 1949 (the Act therefore applies to agricultural lands in those relatively small areas). We have seen how the Shariat Act was re-enacted with modifications in Madras by Act 18 of 1949. Now in Bombay both the Cutchi Memons Act, 1938 *and* the Shariat Act, 1937 were extended to the merged states of Baroda, Kolhapur, etc., considerable areas of territory, by Bombay Act 4 of 1950: in those areas both Acts would be applicable in respect of agricultural land. But there is no trace of a Bombay statute extending either of these Acts so as to be applicable in respect of agricultural land in the rest of the then Bombay State. These details testify to the confusion which persists, and apparently irks no one.

Meanwhile the Cutchi Memons are governed by the personal law in all matters, including testamentary and intestate succession, the only exceptions being those specified in the Shariat Act itself, to the extent that that Act has not been amended by any State statute. In Madras, unlike Bombay, it is still accepted that Cutchi Memons are governed by the Hindu law of the joint-family,[1] and no statute has been held to modify this fact. Moreover the Madras High Court has held that in the State of Mysore, which did not at the relevant time have an enactment corresponding to the Shariat Act, a Cutchi Memon could utilize his customary law, his will would be construed as if it were the will of a Hindu, and the testator had full testamentary power.[2] The peculiar position of Hyderabad impeded a similar decision there in a case to which we have alluded.

[1] *Abdul Hameed Sait* v. *Provident Investment Co.* AIR 1954 Mad. 961 FB (the point was not doubted). It is possible that in this little-known chapter of personal laws Fyzee's particulars at *Outlines*[3], pp. 72 ff. are not quite complete.

[2] *Abdul Sattar* v. *Abdul Hamid* [1945] Mad. 276. Fyzee doubts the correctness of the decision (*Outlines*[3], p. 74).

To discover the law governing a member of these communities it is obviously necessary to look into a number of criteria, in which the rule applicable in the High Court of the domicile, the local statutes and the central statutes in their amended or unamended condition have to be consulted. Nevertheless the most complicated situation among these 'anomalous' Muslims is not that of the Memons but of the Mappillas in Kerala. One would have expected the Shariat Act to have governed them equally with other Muslims. Once again the supposition would be too facile.

Mappillas were originally governed by marumakkattayam law, which embraced all aspects of the joint-family and succession.[1] A few families did not follow this system by custom. It must be recollected that the present State of Kerala consists of the Kasargode *tāluka* of the former S. Kanara District of the former Madras Presidency, the remainder of which District went to Mysore in the reorganization of 1956; the whole of the Malabar District which formerly belonged to Madras State; and the former Native States of Cochin and Travancore (with the exception of some areas of the latter which were given to Madras in 1956). Cochin and Travancore had their own laws relative to Mappillas, some of whom were Sunnīs following the Hanafī school and some Shāfi'īs.[2] When Kerala was created it was necessary for the laws of the three main components of the new State to be unified if possible in this respect as in many others. The inhabitants of the *Laccadives* are mostly Muslim and are governed by a category of marumakkattayam as their customary law: *Sheikriyammada Nalla* v. *Adm., Union Terr. of Laccadives* [1967] K.L.T. 395.

The history of legislation commences with the Mappilla Succession Act, Madras Act 1 of 1918: by this statute, the earliest in the series of statutes intended to 'Islamize' the personal law of Indian Muslims, the self-acquired properties of

[1] Hamid Ali, *Custom and Law in Anglo-Muhammadan Jurisprudence* (Calcutta, 1938). *Mammad Keyi* v. *Wealth Tax Officer, Calicut* [1965] K.L.T. 1238, 1246–7 F.B.

[2] The generality of Mappillas in S. Malabar are Shāfi'īs, but the presumption must be that Indian Muslims in general are Hanafīs: *Naha Haji* v. *Karikutty* [1966] K.L.T. 445; *Katheessa Umma* v. *Narayanath Kunhamu* AIR 1964 S.C. 275 (where the parties emanated from N. Malabar). Cf. *Aboobaker* v. *Kadeesa* [1966] K.L.T. 857 (case sent back for proof of school).

Mappillas governed by marumakkattayam or aliyasantāna[1] law were to descend according to the Muhammadan law. Under the Mappilla Wills Act, Madras Act 7 of 1928, the Mappillas who had previously been unable (as at pure marumakkattayam law) to dispose of property by will were admitted to the privilege accorded to Hindus under the Malabar Wills Act, 1898, of being able to dispose of their entire separate property by will. This statute now provided that the dispositions made by Mappillas to which the Act applied should be governed by the Muhammadan law. In 1932/3 the States of Travancore and Cochin legislated in the field. The Travancore Muslim Succession Act, 11 of 1108 (M.E.), provided that property in respect of which a deceased died intestate, not including *tārwād* property (i.e. the interest in the marumakkattayam family property), should devolve according to the Muhammadan law; and the Cochin Muslim Succession Act, 15 of 1108 (M.E.), was to the same effect.

The Mappilla Marumakkattayam Act, 1938, Madras Act 17 of 1939, applied to all Mappillas following the marumakkattayam law domiciled in Madras or having property in Madras. The statute largely follows the Madras statute dealing with Hindu marumakkattayis, regulating the management of the *tārwād*, giving a right to partition of the family property, and (what interests us more) providing (by s. 18) that succession to property obtained by an individual member should be governed by the Islamic law of inheritance. Thus the Mappillas were by 1939, like the Cutchi Memons of Madras, Hindus as to joint-family property (which was still very important), but Muslims as to separate property, both in respect of testamentary and intestate succession. What effect did the Shariat Act have on this situation? Judicial opinion has not been unwavering. The history of the subject was interestingly reviewed by a single judge of the Madras High Court in *M. Ayisumma* v. *V. P. B. Mayomoothy Umma*,[2] where it was held that where a man died after the Shariat Act but before the Mappilla Marumakkattayam Act of 1939 came into force his interests in *tārwād* property, whether or not he had exercised any right he might have to partition, would pass by Muhammadan law. This was

[1] Aliyasantāna is the variant of matriliny known in Mysore.

[2] AIR 1953 Mad. 425.

soon disapproved. In 1955 Rājamannar, C.J., and Panchapakesa Ayyar, J., held in *P. P. Abdurahiman Karnavan* v. *T. K. Avoomma*[1] that neither the central nor the Madras statute purported to make the Muslim personal law applicable to all matters relating to Muslims. Nor did it totally abrogate custom and usage in respect of matters other than those enumerated. The powers and property rights of Muslims dying intestate were not enlarged and neither enactment abolished the rights and incidents of a Mappilla marumakkattayam *tārwād*. A Full Bench of the same High Court held in 1958 in *Lakshmanan* v. *Kamal*[2] that the Shariat Act did not abolish or purport to abolish the rights and incidents of the Mappilla marumakkattayam *tārwād*.

The reason why Muhammadan law cannot apply to the interest in the marumakkattayam *tārwād* properties is simply that no *share* passes at death. The reasoning can be taken further. There are Hanafī Muslims in Madras (and probably in Andhra also) who are governed by the law of the Hindu joint family by custom. Just as Cutchi Memons remain entitled to follow a similar customary law in Madras, so other communities than Memons may claim to follow similar customs. In *M. Sandhukhan Rowther* v. *Ratnam*[3] the family was proved to have followed what for practical purposes was Hindu law. It was just such a family as the Shariat Act's promoters had hoped to affect. But Rājamannar, C.J. and Panchapakesa Ayyar, J., faced by the problem in 1957, after the *Abdurahiman case* had ventilated the situation of the Mappillas, held that it is only if there is a case of intestate succession that the provisions of the Shariat Act apply. If custom shows that survivorship operates as between the deceased and his surviving co-owners in the family, there would be no scope for the application of the Shariat Act! Where property could be the subject of intestate succession naturally custom could not be pleaded in derogation from the Muhammadan law. This situation is probably congenial to many Madrassi Muslims who are not Mappillas. But

[1] AIR 1956 Mad. 244.

[2] AIR 1959 Ker. 67 F.B. *Mammad Keyi* v. *Wealth Tax Officer, Calicut* [1965] K.L.T. 1238, 1246–7 F.B. Cf. *Mammad Keyi* v. *Asst. Controller, Estate Duty* [1962] Mad. 31.

[3] AIR 1958 Mad. 144.

the marumakkattayam *tārwād* is itself a dying institution and Mappillas like Hindus and Christians feel that separation of property must be the order of the day in Kerala. The story of the Mappillas must pass into another phase.

By s. 3 of the Sthanam Properties . . . Act, Kerala Act 28 of 1958, a *sthānamdār* who is a member of a Mappilla marumakkattayam family will not be followed by the next *sthānamdār* as at customary law, but the property of the *sthānam*[1] will be distributed on the members of the family *per capita* in a very curious manner. It is to be supposed that the *sthānam* property had been divided *per capita* immediately before the death of the last *sthānamdār* among himself or herself and all the members of the family then living (the shares being taken as separate property). His or her own hypothetical share would of course go to his or her heirs at Muhammadan law. But the distribution *per capita* is neither exactly marumakkattayam law nor Muhammadan law (needless to say). Beside this somewhat trifling piece of confusion we may place the doubts raised by the unexpected extension to Kerala as a whole of the Shariat Act itself by the Miscellaneous Personal Laws (Extension) Act, central Act 48 of 1959. It would of course have applied to agricultural lands throughout Kerala, a novelty so far as the Cochin and Travancore areas of Kerala were concerned, had not the Act itself excluded them. The Travancore and Cochin Muslim Succession Acts of 1932/3 were repealed (as supposedly otiose). Would the Kerala High Court take the Madras view that the Shariat Act had no bearing on the marumakkattayam family so long as it remained joint? If so the need to extend the Shariat Act was not urgent, that is to say, so far as family law is concerned: but the effect relative to other topics, such as marriage, divorce and *wakf* is obvious.

Two separate leaps forward were made in 1963. By the Mappilla Marumakkathayam (Amendment) Act, Kerala Act 32 of 1963, the name 'Mappilla' was deleted from the Madras statute (so far as Kerala is concerned) and the word 'Muslim' substituted. This was correct because the word 'Mappilla' or 'Moplah' can also signify a Christian in the Cochin area. Next

[1] For the meaning of *sthānam* see Derrett, *I.M.H.L.*, §. 579 and authorities there cited. The word here has no religious or, now, political or constitutional significance.

the statute was extended to Kerala and ceased to remain confined to the Malabar District and Kasargode. Further a new section was introduced, whereby if a member of a Mappilla *tārwād* died after September 3rd, 1962 having an interest in the *tārwād* his or her interest should devolve according to the Muslim Personal Law (Shariat) and not according to marumakkattayam law.[1] Shares taken under this provision are now freely partible by the persons entitled to them. The share that passes shall be the share that would have fallen to the member had a partition *per capita* been made immediately before his or her death among the members of the *tārwād* then existing. The law relating to the *tārwād* itself, its management and the rights and duties of members remains unaffected. By the Muslim Personal Law (Shariat) Application (Kerala Amendment) Act, Kerala Act 42 of 1963, the Shariat Act which had been in force in all Kerala since 1959 was amended. The reservation relating to agricultural land was removed from s. 2 of the Act. The new s. 2 which this Act substitutes reads as the Madras statute of 1949, with the exception that the original exclusion of 'charities and charitable institutions and charitable and religious endowments' (catered for at least in part by other statutes) is retained from the original Act, and is thus reintroduced into the Malabar area! The Act goes on to repeal the Madras enactment itself as in force in the Malabar District. The predicament of Mappillas domiciled in Madras City, for example, and having property in Madras State as now constituted and also in Kerala is an amusing example of the confusion of Indian law. As regards any matter not governed by any statute the law as understood by the High Court of the domocile should apply.[2] As regards a matter within the Madras statute the Madras High Court must apply the Madras statute, while the Kerala High Court must apply the Kerala statute. The jurisdiction of the courts may depend in some measure upon the situation of the land or lands, which are the subject of the dispute, and the forum in which the plaintiff chooses to bring his action.

[1] This imitated the reforms relating to marumakkattayam among Hindus carried out under the *HSA*, s. 7.

[2] Derrett, 'Private International Law and personal laws', (1965) 14 *I.C.L.Q.* 1370–5. *Virdhachalam* v. *Chaldean Syrian Bank* AIR 1964 S.C. 1425. Derrett, 'Conflicts of personal law and Kerala', [1966] K.L.T., *J.*, 52–9.

Enough has been said to show that only some Muslims formerly governed by Hindu law in respect of the joint-family, testamentary and intestate succession have been converted into followers of the personal law in these regards or some of them. In some cases they have been converted willy nilly. In others they have an option which a great many will not have exercised. About one community (Cutchi Memons) there is doubt whether they are still governed by the Hindu law in respect of the joint-family should they be domiciled in a State other than Maharashtra or Gujarat (the successors to the old Bombay Province), Madras, or the Hyderabad area of Andhra. Some High Courts may not accept the rule of relation to the law of the domicile and may incorrectly make a free choice between the Bombay and the Madras rulings on the subject, the outcome of which is problematical. In regard to Mappillas or Kerala Muslims it remains the case that all may have Muhammadan law applied to them in respect of adoption (a virtually non-existent topic so far as they are concerned), if they exercise their statutory option (which it may well be assumed they will not); in regard to wills and legacies they are already subject to the Muhammadan law in the Malabar District and Kasargode *tāluka*, but in those regards they have their statutory option in the other areas of Kerala. The failure of the Kerala legislature, such as it is, to cope with this anomaly is not to be attributed to ignorance; nor, more plausibly, to lack of legislative leisure; nor to a perverse desire to retain the traditional complexity of the subject, which does not daunt an Indian lawyer as seriously as it would daunt others; but to its small practical importance–there being far fewer Mappillas in Cochin and Travancore than in Malabar. However, we have disposed of the notion that all Muslims are governed as a matter of course by their personal law.

Some Complaints Against the Personal Law

A survey of the personal law is outside our limited space. The antiquated character of the system in regard to questions of transfer of property has already been hinted at. The discontent with the personal law experienced amongst Muslims who travel or are exposed to western influence is expressed more frequently in relation to the law of marriage and divorce and the law of succession than elsewhere. Antiquated rules relating to majority and guardianship and the contracting of marriage, dower and the like can be negotiated with a little forethought, but the main grievances are, not unnaturally, both intimate and, apparently, inexorable. It is quite sufficient for us to take three examples and to refer to the solutions adopted in other parts of the Muslim world. Brevity should be welcomed here for the experts on the subject, Prof. J. N. D. Anderson[1] and Prof. N. J. Coulson,[2] have between them written most extensively on the topic, and at long last their voices have found an echo in India herself.

Amendment by judicial legislation is hardly to be hoped for. The following remarks were made recently by the Madras High Court:[3]

> We have . . . to administer without in any way circumventing or deviating from the original texts, the law, as promulgated by the Islamic law-givers to suit the present-day conditions; and in doing so, it has to be remembered that Courts are not at liberty to refuse to administer any portion of those tenets even though in certain respects they may not sound quite modern.

Muslims exposed to, and inclined to admire the liberty of, the cosmopolitan world regard the permitted plural marriages of males as anomalous: it was an improvement upon the pre-Islamic customary law of the Arabs, but that did not stamp it with everlasting perfection. The power of the husband to divorce his wife unilaterally by pronouncing the word *talāk* is

[1] There is a bibliography of Anderson's writings on the subject at pp. 101–2 in his *Islamic Law in the Modern World* (New York University Press, 1959), but the following items may be added: 'The adaptation of Muslim law in Sub-Saharan Africa', in Hilda and Leo Kuper, edd., *African Law: Adaptation and Development* (Berkeley and Los Angeles, University of California Press, 1965), pp. 149–64 (taking a far from optimistic view of the future of amendment of Islamic law in the territories in question, so far as the populations' own public opinion is concerned); 'Codification in the Muslim world. Some reflections', *RabelsZ.*, 30, pt. 2 (1966), pp. 241–53 (expecting the general perseverance of the family law aspect of the Shariat); 'Recent reforms in the Islamic law of inheritance', (1965) 14 *I.C.L.Q.* 349–365; and (with N. J. Coulson) 'Islamic Law in contemporary cultural change', *Saeculum* 18 (1967), pp. 13–92 (the Indian predicament is not directly considered).

[2] *A History of Islamic Law* (cited above, p. 514, n. 1).

[3] *K. Veerankutty* v. *P. Kutti Umma* [1956] Mad. 1004, 1009.

derogatory to the status of women, and this is not in their eyes mitigated by the numerous devices known to the Shariat whereby a woman can be divorced, or virtually divorce herself, with her husband's prior or contemporaneous co-operation. The law of succession gives arbitrary shares to specified relatives, allows only a fraction of the estate to be bequeathed, regulates the classes of persons to whom bequests can in any case be made, and thus hinders developments which freedom or relative freedom of bequest have aided. Alongside this, and partly as a result of it, there exists the abuse known as the family *wakf*, in which property is dedicated to God but the income is used for the convenience of relatives or descendants of the settlor. The law of intestate succession did not know the device called 'representation', with the result that a surviving child can exclude grandchildren by a predeceased child, an awkward anomaly which no one can excuse.

Three methods have been adopted to overcome these and similar deficiencies. First, contrary rules have been culled from the corners of the juristic world known to Islam, and the State has insisted upon those rules being observed to the exclusion of the objectionable rules settled from the teachings of the major Imāms and their disciples. The resulting hotch-potch[1] is not true traditional Islamic law, but it is not tainted with a non-Islamic aroma. Secondly, the State has legislated to the effect that the Islamic rights shall not be used except with the consent of the State itself, or except upon compliance with conditions which the State lays down. Islamic principles can be invoked upon a high moral plane for the result thus aimed at. The grandchildren, for example, can be benefited by compulsorily deeming a legacy to have been given them by the deceased, so that justice is ultimately done. Thirdly, the system can be wholly or partly abolished, and rules more consistent with modern ideas can be enforced.

Indian experience, and that of Pakistan, is there to be studied by would-be reformers. India, in the Dissolution of Muslim Marriages Act, 8 of 1939, adopted rules from the Mālikī law and enabled wives to obtain matrimonial relief from their husbands in circumstances where the prevailing Hanafī law would not

[1] The comment, though not this expression, is suggested by Coulson at p. 199.

have helped them. In so far as the basis of the legislation was not non-Islamic the Act was successful and has aroused no opposition worthy of note.[1] Meanwhile undoubtedly the normal Indian pattern of interference with personal laws by statute was followed. All the while Muslims who knew of the facility and were inclined to use it were escaping from their personal law by marriages under the Special Marriage Acts. They voluntarily gave up their right to make plural marriages and their special rights of divorce, and submitted themselves to the 'general' régime. Their properties would pass under the Indian Succession Act and their powers of testamentary disposition were those of any non-Muslim, though perhaps somewhat more ample than those of a Hindu. Other Muslims were escaping the effects of the law of succession, where the personal law was indeed applicable to them and their properties, by entering to family arrangements, distributing the property in their lifetimes; and by settling funds *benami*,[2] by way of trusts and otherwise.

The method of allowing rights to be used subject to conditions laid down by the State was adopted, as we have seen, by government departments.[3] It was extensively used in Pakistan in the Muslim Family Laws Ordinance,[4] 1961. The same Ordinance also employed the method of direct legislation to amend the Islamic law, by providing for representation to apply in favour of grandchildren. It has been argued that the arrangements to control polygamy and divorce have much to recommend them in practice, but it is noticed that the legal rights have not themselves been taken away–it will be seen later that this is perhaps a practical way of proceeding, more to the taste of Indian Muslims, at any rate, than the Tunisian and similar methods which virtually abolish the Islamic rules, and consign them to the realm of conscience. It is also argued that the legislation with reference to grandchildren is not very practical, as it can produce unexpected side-effects in that chapter of the

[1] Fazlur Rahman at *Changes*, p. 74, also see below. The Dissolution of Muslim Marriages Act is reprinted at Fyzee, *Outlines*[3], pp. 462 ff. It is discussed in the same work at pp. 160 ff. The Act was amended for Pakistan by Ordinance 8 of 1961 (see n. 4 below), s. 13.

[2] On this institution see Derrett, *I.M.H.L.*, §§. 830–4, also *Sree Meenakshi* v. *I.-T. Commissioner* AIR 1957 S.C. 49.

[3] See above, p. 445.

[4] Ordinance 8 of 1961, reprinted at Fyzee, *Outlines*[3], pp. 471–6.

law.[1] This does not concern us vitally at the moment. What is important to discover is the juristic basis upon which the Shariat can be, in effect, amended.

The Objections to Reform

The most important objection to any reform of Islamic law in any of its derivative forms lies in the claim that only *ulama*, and in particular Muslim scholars specializing in *fiqh*, are competent to approve a proposal of this character.[2] The rustic Muslim will not relish a change in his family law unless it is approved by Muslim scholars who are not evidently biased in favour of cosmopolitanization of the community. Certain points of view are bound to prejudice the progress of reforms, however rational they sound to observers. The two chiefly objectionable notions are that religion is a matter of the conscience, between man and his God, and that rules of family law, transfer of property, and the like are therefore not religious, wherefrom it would follow that Parliament could legislate to amend or abolish the Shariat as and when it chose. This is the so-called 'secularist' approach, held by Mr. M. C. Chagla and others. As Dr. Subrahmanian has shown clearly in the Hindu context, the concept of 'secular' versus 'religious' may be valid in the West, but comes up against unexpected difficulties in India, where the two main religious communities profess, if they profess any religion, a religion which does not consider worldly or practical questions to be distinct from religion.[3] No definition of Islam, or of Hinduism for that matter, could proceed on the assumption that the family régime was not ultimately a religious question. In the case of Hindus, as we have seen, alternative approaches to *moksha* are there and are available to everyone. In the case of Muslims, the law as plainly laid down in the Koran or as indicated by the *sunna* of the Prophet and authoritatively interpreted by Imāms

[1] Coulson, 'Islamic family law, Progress in Pakistan', in J. N. D. Anderson, ed., *Changing Law in Developing Countries*, pp. 240–57; the same, *History of Islamic Law*, pp. 212 ff.; J. N. D. Anderson at (1965) 14 *I.C.L.Q.* 356 ff.; the same in *Changes in Muslim Personal Law* (below), pp. 83 f.

[2] Fazlur Rahman, where cited, pp. 74–5. Maulāna Saeed Ahmad Akbarābādī, at the same place, p. 19.

[3] N. Subrahmanian, 'Hinduism and secularism', *B. Inst. Trad. Cult.* (Madras), 1966, pt. 1, pp. 1–21.

who were personally acquainted with the *sunna* and with the conditions of life in the world in which the Prophet's teachings and examples were relevant and decisive, such law, to whatever extent it itself thinks proper to control the believer, is necessary to belief. It might be arguable that in India under the Sultans and Emperors the Shariat was more honoured in the breach, that the door of conversion to Islam was held rather wider open than would have been acceptable in some other parts of the Islamic world, and the price to be paid by the convert was lower. But it is the point of view of present-day Muslims whose sense of their religion and their community has sharpened since the beginning of the century which really counts. To adapt a comment of Donald E. Smith,[1] most scholars would hold that if for a thousand years Muslims have regarded a particular social practice as part of their religion, it *is* a part of religion, and we are wasting our breath if we try to tell them otherwise.

The second objectionable notion is that Islam, properly understood, requires (*a*) its fundamental principles to override the rules which are now anti-social, and (*b*) that individual rational interpretation of the sources, closed to the learned as well as the layman for many centuries, can be reopened in order to go back to first principles.[2] To this an evident answer could be that such activities, as those of the Central Institute of Islamic Research, founded in Pakistan in 1960, are hypocritical. The participants are really trying to found a new religion. Let them do so if they wish, but they cannot purport to speak for Muslims. The notion, often expressed in reference to Pakistan, that the *ulama* are chauvinistic reactionaries, merely expresses the thinker's alienation from the culture to which he still professes to belong. The present writer, fully aware of the essential difference between Islam and Hinduism, nevertheless totally admits the position of Maulāna Ihtishām ul Haq, who wrote, 'In Islam the provisions of the Holy Koran and the Sunna, be they in the form of basic principles or individual laws, are authoritative and final for all occasions and for all

[1] D. E. Smith, *South Asian Politics and Religion* (Princeton University Press, 1966), p. 9.

[2] This point of view is echoed in Maulāna Saeed Ahmad Akbarābādī (where cited) and in Justice M. H. Beg's contribution to G. S. Sharma, ed., *Secularism: its Implications for Law and Life in India* (Bombay, Tripathi, 1966).

epochs between the time of revelation and doomsday.'[1] But it happens that Islam is fully aware of what are called 'juristic tricks' whereby the literal provisions of the Shariat may be sidestepped by those who are entitled to do so.[2] The result is not that the law is divorced from conscience, but that conscience is legally quieted in its search for convenience. Legislation has no place in Islam, we are told: but this is not perfectly correct. Legislation cannot alter the Islamic law, but it can provide 'tricks' whereby, without purporting to abolish or even amend, without tampering with the streams of juridical development as known in the four main schools, without hypocritical appeals to the 'spirit' of the Islamic sources, social requirements which change can co-exist with the religious requirements which are themselves static. This is a position which Indian Muslims will be able to accept. But hardly if it is put to them as a reform of the personal law.

The doubts and fears of Indian Muslims in general respects are brought out by S. Abid Husain in his *Destiny of Indian Muslims*,[3] testifying to the tendency of prominent Muslims of the last generation to apply their minds to Islamic doctrines so as to make a compromise between reason and science on the one hand and religion, faith and tradition on the other. But the real hesitations in respect to the problem of reform of the personal law are admirably documented by Ziya-ul Hasan Faruqi in his

[1] Quoted by D. E. Smith, *South Asian Politics* . . . (cited above), pp. 42–3. Note also the remark of Professor Syed Hossein Nasr, an Iranian, whose contribution was not much appreciated at New Delhi, because it was scintillatingly frank and original (he accused Indian and other reformist Muslims of being mere imitators of Christians), but whose views deserve a much wider public than they then had: '. . . the *shariah* is the blueprint of the world, and if the world does not conform to the *shariah*, it is too bad for the world and not at all bad for the *shariah*. It is a very essential point that we forget. It is as if an engineer was constructing a building in conformity with a plan. If he makes . . . a real mistake, the building will crash on his head. This is really the Islamic conception, really the Muslim conception, of what law is.'

[2] An example is *Bazazia* cited by Fyzee, *Outlines*[3], p. 233. The topic is the subject of a thesis by the senior expert on Islamic law in the West: J. Schacht, 'Die arabische ḥiyal-Literatur . . .', *Der Islam*, 15 (1926), 211–32. Abū Ḥātim Maḥmūd ibn al-Ḥasan al Qazwīnī, *Das Kitāb al-ḥijal fil-fiqh* (*Buch der Rechtskniffe*), ed. and trans. J. Schacht (Hannover, 1924).

[3] London (Asia Publishing House), 1965, at, e.g., p. 64.

chapter entitled 'Indian Muslims and the ideology of the secular state' in D. E. Smith's *South Asian Politics and Religion.*[1] Mr. Faruqi deals briefly with the very interesting Symposium held at New Delhi on January 9th, 1964 on the occasion of the 26th International Congress of Orientalists. In the proceedings, published under the convenient title, *Changes in Muslim Personal Law,*[2] a full range of viewpoints was illustrated and information from the Middle East and Africa was surveyed. The participants did not conclude that Muhammadan law in India should be amended, but their contributions showed how difficult it was to agree even on an approach to the problem. We have, further, in Smith's *South Asian Politics and Religion* a chapter by Fazlur Rahmān, Director of the Central Institute of Islamic Research, Karachi, in which he appraises the Muslim Family Laws Ordinance of his own country, reviewing the arguments for this class of reform and the objections to it. In his view Muhammad was a seer-cum-reformer, and for that very reason he deprecates forced interpretations of the verses of the Koran to achieve social reform beyond what the Koranic period was able to attempt. But even his clear exposition fails to offer general practical propositions for reform.

The objections are not merely legal but also political. The majority has no competence morally or intellectually, though it has the *power* to do, in Parliament, for the community what it is unable at present to do for itself. Meanwhile Muslims are constantly told by well-wishers who are also Muslims that reform is inevitable: India cannot, says Saed Jaffer Hussain of the University of Delhi (copiously citing Anderson and Coulson),[3] be onlookers to the progress made in the other Muslim countries. And on the other hand the courts are claimed to have shown that Islamic law can move with the times and shows

[1] p. 535, n. 1 above.

[2] No editorial name is given, though it may have been produced under the supervision of Professor Humayun Kabir, then a Minister of the central Government. It was published by the Organizing Committee of the Congress, New Delhi, 1964 (and is available as pp. 79–101 of the *Proceedings* of the Congress, vol. I, New Delhi, 1966).

[3] 'Legal modernism in Islam: polygamy and repudiation', (1965) 7 *J.I.L.I.* 384–98. See also S. S. Nigam's plea for codification at (1963) 5 *J.I.L.I.*, 47–80.

some power of reforming itself.[1] The cases which are supposed to illustrate this alleged tendency turn out, on examination, to be worth little.[2] Nothing is to be hoped from judicial legislation. The glancing blows at the Muhammadan law made in connexion with pre-emption[3] and *wakfs*[4] have called forth plaintive comments: and the majority community, with its experience of mishandling Hindu law, is in no hurry to increase its burdens in the minority's interest.[5] The experience of the other countries of the Muslim world is overwhelmingly in favour of reform of some kind, but one cannot deny that no one of them is in India's position, and Pakistan's precedent is not entirely agreeable to Indian Muslims.

A Possible Solution

Thus the dilemma is complete, or so it would seem. So far as India is concerned there seems to be no compromise between those who believe that the personal law is sacred and cannot be amended, and those who believe that any law can be, and indeed often must be, amended by judicial and/or legislative

[1] S. M. Hasan at (1965) 7 *J.I.L.I.* 301–2; J. N. Saxena (1964) 6 *J.I.L.I.* 98 ff.

[2] *Valia* v. *Pathakkalan* AIR 1964 S.C. 275, if an advance, is a pathetic one; cf. *Maqbool* v. *Mst. Khodaija* AIR 1966 S.C. 1194 (where the archaic rules dominate); *Smt. Khatizabai* v. *Controller of Estate Duty* AIR 1960 Bom. 61 merely shows how ill the archaic *wakf-al-aulad* suits the general law. *Itwari* v. *Asghari* AIR 1960 All. 684 (Fyzee, *Cases*, pp. 188 ff.) if it is an advance (in the concept of 'cruelty' in matrimonial causes) is minimal and to hail it as an advance is to pronounce on the decrepitude of the system.

[3] Tahir Mahmood, 'Supreme Court's decision on pre-emption—a plea for reconciliation in Muslim law', [1965] 1 S.C.J., *J.*, 94–6. See above, p. 305, n. 4.

[4] Ziya-ul Hasan Faruqi, where cited, at p. 144. The Wakf (Amendment) Act, 1964, s. 2 (i), a harmless improvement of the law intended to control the management of charities, was necessitated by the decision in *Kassimiah Charities* v. *Secretary of the Madras State Wakf Board* AIR 1964 Mad. 18 that a secular dedication (for a school and dispensary) for the benefit of Muslims and non-Muslims alike though valid by Muhammadan law did not come within the Muslims Wakf Act, 1954.

[5] Chanchal Sarkar in his contribution to *Secularism: its Implications for Law and Life in India* (cited above) suggests that changes might well be initiated by Kashmir, which legislated on personal laws for itself and still retains competence to initiate legislation in that field.

modifications. Some say that enough amendment has already been made to justify further inroads on the ancient law in terms of social justice, and that the resistance to this on the part of the 'orthodox' is foolish. Others say that any amendment could practicably be carried out in the guise of a state law overriding all the former personal laws, consigning the former personal law of Muslims to the Muslims' own consciences. 'Let them, on that footing, carry out the prescribed rules of the Islamic law, perhaps better than ever before, on their own initiative, in the scope left to them by the State's legislation–or, if they do not wish to do this, then let them cease to blame the State for their failure to carry out the ancient precepts of the religion!' Meanwhile the peasantry and the uneducated believe that their personal law is a pledge of their religious integrity, and that to modify it, or to abolish it, is to throw them, as a community, into the melting-pot of the so-called secular state. Resistance to reform of Islamic law in India, even of the Anglo-Muhammadan law, will be justified if it is to be reformed by persons unqualified to consider the technical issues, unless[1] they are merely the agents of a Muslim conference of *ulama* who really know Islam and the Islamic law both as it is and as it ought to be. A unanimous report in favour of reform submitted by such an assembly could safely be acted upon by a complaisant Parliament. But Hindus' own fears about the integrity and efficacy of their own reforms; their own lack of certainty as to what function is served by reform in such a field; their lack of decisive vision into the nation's major objects and goals; their preference for 'pious words' and a 'holier-than-thou' attitude derived from the period of resentment of foreign rule: all these stand in the way of the majority's accepting the responsibility even if the undoubted trend in favour of social reform recognized on the part of objectively- and cosmopolitanly-minded Muslims were to give at last authoritative voice in a report by *ulama*. The dilemma seems on the point of settling into the normal asiatic response to crisis, inaction. Nothing will be done for an indefinite period.

Yet a lawyer's solution to the difficulty need not be ignored because of the lack of confidence on the part of the majority community. There is a way out of the difficulty which no one in India or Pakistan has thought of, so far as we know, and it

[1] As in the case of the Dissolution of Muslim Marriages Act.

should be explored before the problems evinced by the Delhi Symposium are accepted as insoluble. As we have seen, the main difficulty arises from the knowledge amongst the community that a Muslim is *entitled* by his religious law, as accepted by the law of the land, to do things which society no longer accepts as just. He may also do many things which society now considers archaic and inconvenient. Some Muslim societies have gone further than others, and perhaps further than India might be prepared to go, since an old-fashioned element persists in India which has lost its predominance in the more westernized Muslim countries. But it remains a fact that India as a multi-religious unity no longer has any reason for retaining some of the facilities which the personal law still affords to Muslims in India. Further, the religious law allows the Muslim to refuse to do what society in some cases believes he ought to do. If the religious law is to be respected, and the individual does not wish to escape, or has not escaped from it in time, into the no-man's-land of the Special Marriage Act, or if that no-man's-land is not wide enough to accommodate his particular need; and if on the other hand legislation abolishing the traditional rule cannot for the present be contemplated, what is the way out?

The French, not uncharacteristically, found the answer in at least one place which has come to the present writer's attention. They may well have employed it elsewhere. It is a matter of indifference whether they have, for once is often enough for our purposes. The Jews of Morocco, like the Muslims of India, reserved the right of divorce to the husband. Nevertheless the Jewish courts recognized the wife's right to be divorced in certain circumstances of grave danger to her or for some other weighty cause. This right on the part of the Jewish wife to secure a divorce from her husband grew gradually during an early period of what we might call semi-westernization, of partial exposure to the Gentile world, which gave married women a considerable freedom which could not but be envied in some quarters even of the very much stricter Jewish world. Yet nothing could enable the rabbis to grant to the wife a right of divorce which was the prerogative of the husband. If the rabbinical court declared that the wife was entitled to a divorce on account of her sufferings or other grave grounds and the husband, out of malice or other anti-social motive, refused to grant it (as his religious law might appear entirely to allow him to do) the French courts allowed the wife to sue her husband for damages.[1] The same situation could arise when the French civil court granted her a divorce but she was unable to marry again because the husband would not grant the 'bill of divorcement' (*get*) which the religious law required before she could be free to marry again within the community. The wife's injury entitled her to sue for damages. Now in India there is no tort in existence which will enable the wife in such circumstances to sue for damages. But there is no reason why one should not be introduced by legislation. By this method the religious law is left intact, and a wife who respects her religious law is not called upon to sue for the State's protection. But should she seek to take advantage of society's undoubted condemnation of plural marriages and failures to grant a divorce when required to do so, of capricious or malicious divorces, and of impractical and unsuitable legacies, foundations of family *wakfs*, and failure to provide for near relations, or should any other person injured (in society's view) by the capricious operation of the personal law wish to seek the State's protection, it should be perfectly possible for actions against the husband, or his estate in the hands of his heirs or legatees, so to level the balance, as to have the indirect effect of preventing the anti-social or unsocial use, or rather abuse, of the personal law. Just as in England the capricious willing away of one's property to the detriment of close relations can be rendered ineffective by their proper application under the Inheritance (Family Provision) Act, 1938, without the principle of free disposition of property by will having been directly infringed, so it should be possible, as a first step towards the formation of the Indian Civil Code, to create a right to damages or other appropriate relief if a Muslim husband, father, or testator abuses the rights accorded to him by his personal law. A man would not, for example, be prevented from marrying more than one wife concurrently by any such rule, but if the second marriage were without the consent of the first wife and operated to her detriment, she might be entitled to sue for so large a sum by way of damages for the injury done to her and by way of endowment against eventualities for the

[1] A. Zagouri, *Le divorce d'après la loi talmudique chez les marocains de confession israelite et les réformes actuelles en la matière* (Paris, L.G.D.J., 1958), p. 111.

future that few Muslim husbands or women contemplating marrying them would go through with that scheme. Likewise a husband who refuses a divorce in cases where society regards the wife as entitled to a divorce, should these fall outside the scope of the Dissolution of Muslim Marriages Act, may be sued in damages for the injury which the wife suffers in being kept tied to him and thus unable to remarry.

Such reforms would not be resented as tampering with the religious law,[1] and would provide a climate in which research could progress towards the projected Civil Code.

Confusion amongst the Personal Laws

While the sources of Muhammadan law are so diverse, the scope of the Muslim personal law is so uncertain, the capacity of the system to reform itself is so doubtful, the likelihood of Parliament's undertaking a reform of Muhammadan law is so problematical, and the probability that any reform will be widely ignored in practice is so high, the resultant dilemma is met by another of no shorter standing. The predicament of the Jewish personal law attracts little attention, but the actual rules of Parsi law are in many respects grossly out of date.[2] The law of succession of 'Indian Christians' differs in an important respect from that of other non-Parsis subject to the Indian Succession Act.[3] The discrepancies between the personal laws relating to Christians in Kerala and elsewhere[4] retain no justification. The Christian Marriage Bill which was based in shape at least upon the Hindu Marriage Act, 1955, seems to have come to nothing for no very clear reason: the project of codifying the law relating to marriage amongst Christians has not commended itself, at the last stage, to the legislature. The Indian Divorce Act is antiquated and needs to be overhauled, especially in view of the competition offered to it by the much more recent Special Marriage Act, 1954, with its own divorce Part (which is not without an eccentric feature).

[1] See opinion of Maulāna Saeed Ahmad Akbarābādī at *Changes*, p. 17.

[2] In particular secc. 50–6 of the Indian Succession Act.

[3] Sec. 33A of the Indian Succession Act.

[4] The Travancore Christian Succession Act remains in force notwithstanding the introduction of the Indian Succession Act into Travancore-Cochin in 1951: *Kurian Augusty* v. *Devassy Aley* AIR 1957 T.C.1.

The discrepancies between such rules as are agreed to prevail within the religious communities are often irrational. A Hindu can adopt, a Muslim (except by custom or local statute) cannot. Nor can a Christian. A Hindu can will away his property subject only to the rights of dependants. A Christian can will away everything irrespective of the rights of dependants. A Muslim cannot (subject to any valid custom to the contrary) dispose of more than his bequeathable fraction to legatees, and, in the major school of law, none of that fraction to heirs. A Muslim can create a perpetual *wakf* for his family. A Christian cannot, nor can a Parsi or a Jew. One could go on into further detail.[1] In this age it is easier to excuse anomalous rules on the grounds that the religion of those most nearly concerned requires that such provision should survive, than it is to deny to persons of different faiths similar conveniences should they wish to have them. Where reciprocity fails the law is at its weakest. For example, a Hindu can make a gift to a Muslim, and that is that. But if a Muslim makes a gift to a Hindu this transaction is governed by the Muhammadan law and is revocable. As if the 'religious' rule were not anomalous enough, it has actually been applied in industrial relations, so that it affects the availability of a Hindu employee's 'bonus'![2]

To make matters worse, there are gaps and interstices between the personal laws. There are people who are neither Hindus nor Muslims and there are those who appear to be both.[3] We have seen into what difficulties a Hindu falls if he

[1] Where a Christian is the *propositus*, dying intestate, his Hindu relations may inherit from him (*Siril* v. *Monga* AIR 1964 Ass. 58): but from a Muslim intestate governed in respect of succession by his personal law no non-Muslim may inherit, and under the *HSA* no one may inherit from a Hindu unless he is a Hindu (subject to the special exception, created by statute, for those heirs–but not their descendants–who have themselves been converted to another religion).

[2] *Someshwar* v. *Barkat Ullah* AIR 1963 All. 469.

[3] Hindus may be followers of the Āgā Khān and be Ismā'īlī Khojas: *Nur Ali* v. *Malka Sultana* P.L.D. 1961 (W.P.) Lahore 431, Fyzee, *Outlines*³, p. 69. K. M. Kapādia, 'The religious creeds among the Patidars of South Gujarat –a panoramic view', ch. 13 in T. K. N. Unnithan and others, ed., *Towards a Sociology of Culture in India* (D. P. Mukerji Volume) (New Delhi, Prentice Hall of India, 1965): Hindus who have adopted Muslim customs (including burial) are gradually becoming de-Islamized as they become richer. See also S. C. Misra, *Muslim Communities in Gujarat* (London, Asia Publishing House, 1964).

makes the supposedly unpatriotic move of being converted to another religion.[1] He is deprived of many conveniences and of not a few human rights, as that term is usually understood.[2] It is a curious fact that an illegitimate child has no right to be maintained at any personal law but the Hindu law;[3] the Criminal Procedure Code's provisions on the subject being only of an emergency and provisional nature, they are no substitute for a provision of the civil law. One such gap was sought to be plugged by Parliament when it amended the Hindu Adoptions and Maintenance Act, 1956, by providing for children to be adopted whose religion was not known.[4] Parliament's consciousness of the existence of such gaps has not been uniform. One gap, of a somewhat different description, was closed recently by an amendment of the Indian Succession Act;[5] on the other hand ignorance of the existence of Joint Family Law amongst Indians other than Hindus has caused much inconvenience,[6] with the result that Muslims have been held to be included within the word 'Hindu' in one context,[7] although such a curiosity of legal interpretation had been (rightly) refused in another. The family law of those who marry under the Special Marriage Act is markedly different from that of those who do not, and to make matters worse their *children*, whether or not they themselves marry or register their marriages under that statute, are also governed by a special régime departing in some particulars from the law of their religious community, if any. This can hardly continue indefinitely.

To make matters worse an individual can improve his position by changing his religion. A woman can, according to one judicial opinion, obtain a divorce from her Hindu husband by

[1] Muslims may even have Hindu law 'forms of marriage', if the present law relative to crossing the lines between the personal laws by conversion is to be consulted: *Moosa* v. *Haji* (1905) 30 Bom. 197.

[2] See above, p. 332.

[3] *Philomena* v. *Dara Nussarwanji* AIR 1943 Bom. 338.

[4] Act 45 of 1962.

[5] Indian Succession (Amendment) Act, 16 of 1962, amending secs. 211–13 (introducing the word 'Parsi' *inter alia*).

[6] See comments on Kerala litigation relative to the Wealth Tax Act, 27 of 1957, by Derrett at [1962] K.L.T., *J.*, 18–21 [1964] K.L.T., *J.*, 69–74, and [1966] K.L.T., *J.*, 71–3.

[7] *Biyyathumma* v. *Balan* [1966] K.L.T. 731 on the construction of the Agricultural Income-Tax Act, 1950, sec. 3 (3).

herself becoming a Muslim.[1] A Hindu or Muslim husband can obtain a divorce from his wife by himself becoming a Christian.[2] In this age such curiosities are little better than pathetic. The world is able to understand a situation in which the change of religion by one spouse without the other's consent could create such an atmosphere in the home that it would adversely affect the other's health and so give rise to grounds for divorce or lesser matrimonial relief, as for example on the footing of cruelty.[3] But we fail to grasp how law can justly unhinge a marriage which is not in danger on other grounds by means of a mere change of religion, unilaterally, on the part of one spouse. Worse still a Christian or Hindu or indeed any non-Muslim may, whilst married to a wife of his former religion, be converted to Islam, and marry a second, Muslim, wife, who may herself have been converted for the purpose.[4] He, and indeed she also, may then relapse into the former religious community–and this is one way in which legislation prohibiting polygamy can be evaded. Such a state of affairs cries out for legislative amendment. India's Parliament can surely supply, with every confidence, remedies such as will heal the divisions between the personal laws. Indeed it has done so, though with some complaint from Muslims. As we have seen[5] it has removed the discrepancies between the Muhammadan and the Hindu law relating to the validity of charitable endowments or gifts from non-Muslims to Muslim charities. The principle may be carried much further.

All this was foreseen when the project of the Indian Civil Code was envisaged by the Founding Fathers of the Constitution.

[1] For particulars of divorces under the Anglo-Muhammadan law and now under the Dissolution of Muslim Marriages Act, see Fyzee, *Outlines*[3], pp. 169–77.

[2] Native Converts Marriage Dissolution Act, 21 of 1866. The unsuitability of such laws is hinted at by Fyzee at the end of the section cited in the last footnote.

[3] Insistence upon a spouse's change of religion (even from Roman Catholicism to the Chaldean faith) may well be mental cruelty: *Elizabeth* v. *Paul* [1962] K.L.T. 857.

[4] Derrett, 'The convert's polygamous marriage', (1965) 67 Bom. L.R., *J.*, 71–4.

[5] See above, p. 439, n. 5. S. 66C, inserted by s. 21 of Act 34 of 1964.

The Indian Civil Code

The Civil Code promised in Art. 44 of the Constitution is, like the 'Hindu Code' of which we have spoken before, a misnomer, but a convenient one. The 'Hindu Code' does not codify in the usual sense of that term: many rules of the Anglo-Hindu law remain in force, and it is sometimes a question how the new and the old, but surviving, law are to be reconciled in practice. The Indian Civil Code will not be a civil code in the Continental sense. It will contain no rules of contract (which is governed by the Indian Contract Act) nor of tort or delict, which remains and will continue long to be uncodified. But Sir William Jones and those who followed him used to call the *corpora* of Hindu and Muhammadan law texts 'codes', and the expression 'code' to describe the body of the operative personal law recommended itself to Sir Hari Singh Gour amongst others. Thus the body of law which will sweep away the antiquated and discrepant mass of known and unknown vagaries which constitute (or are supposed to constitute) the personal laws of India will be quite aptly named Indian Civil Code, or, better still, 'Code of Family Law'.

Where angels fear to tread none of the wise are inclined to venture, and in that way a difficult but necessary task is indefinitely postponed. This however cannot be postponed for ever, and if an attractive formula is propounded the movement in favour of unification (which has some surviving political drive behind it) will overcome the inertia of timidity, whether on the part of the government or on the part of the minority communities. Their anxiety about their personal laws does not relate to the laws themselves (of which they cannot be better informed than the jurists, whose own knowledge, as we have seen, is somewhat tentative) but rather to their privileged position as minorities in a country ruled for practical purposes by a self-conscious majority which has hardly come to understand the nature and object of the celebrated Hindu 'tolerance'. But which formula will be likely to attract? It is submitted that certain requirements must be met, namely (i) a refusal to interfere with any right conferred at the present time by a religious law, whilst (ii) citizens are protected from abuse of those rights so that ultimately no member of any religious community or none is disadvantaged by such membership or non-membership. Moreover (iii) every step must be able to shelter under a precedent, the efficacy of which can be judged from experience. It is not the task of the present writer to sketch out the contents of this Code of Family Law, but lines upon which a blue-print might be envisaged can conveniently be submitted here.

It is a fact that concubinage as a recognized institution is dying out and the temporary marriage known as *mut'a*[1] is likewise in disfavour. But the co-existence of two classes of marriage is ancient and persistent. Even in Hindu law and custom there remain marriages of an inferior type which are solemnized with somewhat informal ceremonies and may be terminated with what amounts to a unilateral divorce in fact if not strictly in law.[2] Similarly on the plane of legislation there is the civil marriage in which Indians of any religion or none may be joined in matrimony, subject to a western-type divorce law and a law of inheritance which is not related to the needs of any particular religious community or its traditions; while on the other hand there is the Hindu Marriage Act which caters, or purports to cater, for Hindus not contemplating a non-traditional marriage. The facilities extended to all Indians by the Special Marriage Act cannot be taken away,[3] and the secular type of marriage, which can be called, for example, 'civil marriage', may form a part of the Marriage chapter of the Code. Grounds for matrimonial relief will surely be revised, and brought into line with the most approved grounds to be gathered from experience in India and other parts of the world. It is not necessary to suppose that spouses will ask for matrimonial relief inconsistent with the type of marriage into which they enter. If they celebrate a civil marriage they must not expect to exercise rights of divorce known only to particular religious laws, the Muslim husband must not expect to use his

[1] *Mut'a* (a word used in other senses also): Fyzee, *Outlines*³, pp. 112 ff.

[2] See above, p. 357.

[3] The question can arise whether the facilities offered by the Special Marriage Act are enough, for we find as a fact that women are converted to their proposed husband's religion, undergo the marriage ceremony appropriate to their new religion, but take a covenant from their husbands that they will not be called upon to live as a co-religionist with the family of the marriage–and such covenants are not against public policy (surprisingly): *Nizamul Haque* v. *Begum Noorjahan* AIR 1966 Cal. 465.

right of *talāk*, nor can the Hindu husband claim to marry a second wife on the grounds of the barrenness of the first, or failing the first wife's consent to divorce her, as some customs would still (apart from the Hindu Marriage Act's provisions for divorce on grounds) appear to allow.[1] A Hindu wife must not expect to be able to divorce her husband because he has changed his religion, or become a *sannyāsī*. Comparably, those who contemplate a traditional marriage are entitled to think in terms of a traditional matrimonial régime, and to retain rights to matrimonial relief suited thereto.

Another part of the Marriage chapter should provide for 'religious marriages'. For these the requirements may be as strict as those for the civil marriage, but subject to the concession that those whose former customary law allowed them to marry should be entitled to do so. Grounds for divorce should be provided, perhaps taking into account somewhat more of the public's traditional desires than was observed in 1955. On the other hand the right to divorce for cruelty, which now exists in one of the States should be extended to all. In addition to the grounds for divorce it should be provided, as at present, that customary laws entitling an individual to a divorce should remain in force, provided that the custom should be capable of strict proof, and should be continuous and not have been abandoned by the community, etc. The definition of 'custom' need not depart from the standard definition, save that it should be so defined as to enable any legal right (which was not previously obsolete) to be proved as a custom if it has not been abandoned. So far so good: no necessity has arisen to mention the name of any religious community. The existing grounds for divorce which are confined to Hindus, namely change of religion (*per se*) and *sannyāsa*, may safely be abolished, since they have no right to remain unless the facts alleged also constitute cruelty, whereupon the ground for divorce consisting in 'legal cruelty' will be a sufficient security for the petitioner. What, then, of the Muslim husband's right of *talāk*? This will be a customary right, and he can exercise it. What of his right to make plural marriages? This will be a customary right, and he can exercise it. Is then the Code to retain virtually a distinction for Muslims' advantage? No, for the Code should go on to provide for a new

[1] See above, p. 358.

right to relief in a matrimonial court on the ground of improper exercise of a customary right. A new tort should be adopted (as suggested above), whereby the wife aggrieved by her husband's *talāk* may sue not merely, as at present, for maintenance during the *iddat* period, but for maintenance *dum casta* until her remarriage, and for damages, which of course she will have to prove, for the injury done to her by the divorce. Likewise if her husband marries without her consent, she may sue, if she is damaged thereby, for damages as well as for the normal matrimonial reliefs. If she is entitled to a divorce whether under the 'civil marriage' régime or under the 'religious marriage' régime and she wishes to make a religious marriage and her former husband refuses to grant her the *talāk* (or, in the case of Jews, the *get*) required by the religious law before she is free to marry again, she may sue for damages for the injury he does her by maliciously refusing to grant the release. At Hindu customary law analogous situations may be found to exist which our present law ignores, so that the new tort may turn out to be a valuable adjunct to the armoury of matrimonial reliefs.

The topic of Succession is the next most difficult. The Muhammadan law inhibits the disposition of property by will, and it prides itself on the precision with which property passes by intestate succession to carefully chosen heirs and 'residuaries' who may take what is left over when the compulsory heirs have taken their shares. We have already seen to what embarrassment this gives rise, and we have noted that interference with the Koranic scheme can seem to infringe not merely the intellectual pride of the Muslim jurists but even their religion. A simple solution might seem, at first sight, to leave it to the conscience of the *propositus*. If he wishes to leave more than the Koranic proportion to legatees, and if he wishes to include heirs amongst his legatees, why not leave it to him? Ceylonese Muslims are entitled to leave all their property by will, and it does not seem as if fears of spiritual penalties have hampered their utilizing that right from time to time: why should Indian Muslims be more particular? Along the same lines Parliament might lay down in the Succession chapter of the Code that the property of an intestate should be divided in equal shares amongst his nearest relations (much upon the lines of the present class I of the Schedule of the Hindu Succession Act), and leave it to those relations whether their consciences prevent them from taking more than their Koranic entitlement, if any. But this is not realistic. One of the features of a system of personal laws is that the parties are entitled to bring suits to compel their relations to act within the borders of the religious law: so that if the entire family were not able to come to a family arrangement[1] by amicable agreement a suit based upon the specific rules of the personal law would have to be expected.

The correct solution would seem, therefore, to be along lines similar to those suggested for the Marriage chapter. A succession law for India, such as it is, exists already in the Indian Succession Act, to which even those not otherwise within the scope of its rules for distribution of estates are subject, as we have seen, by reason of marrying under the Special Marriage Act or being born of persons who have done so. The first stage would be to eliminate the special rules for Parsis and Indian Christians in favour of a modern and straightforward succession law, based upon the principles of nearness of blood and equality of the sexes, with perhaps a special reservation for the daughter-in-law in keeping with Indian conditions. Alternatively the daughter-in-law herself could be left to the maintenance chapter (which will deal with maintenance by living persons and out of their estates, as under the Hindu Adoptions and Maintenance Act) and she need not appear as a sharer at all. Further peculiarities of the present Hindu system could be examined to see whether they retain a rational basis and deserve to be kept: almost certainly (if predictions are to be believed) they will fail to pass this test, as they already fail to pass the test of conformity to the spirit of the *śāstra*. Thus the basic law of intestate succession will be provided. Alongside this general provision a special provision can be made, in reliance upon a precedent of interest to which we have already turned our attention.

The scheme whereby Muslims in India have been weaned away (with partial success) from their customary laws and have become subject to the Shariat began, and to a large extent continues, on a *voluntary* basis. We have seen how the Shariat did not and still does not apply to many Muslims in some respects

[1] On this useful institution see Derrett, 'Family arrangements in developing countries', in J. N. D. Anderson, ed., *Family Law in Asia and Africa* (London, Allen and Unwin, 1968).

unless they make a statutory declaration for the purpose. This leaves the onus on the individual to turn himself in legal terms from a 'customary' Muslim into a 'Shariat' Muslim. The pattern can be used in reverse. The somewhat hasty, and certainly transitional programme which the Shariat Act and its associated statutes represent must melt away in the face of the Civil Code. The principle of protecting the personal law must give way to the new principle of unifying family law without tampering with religion. The obvious means (in the present writer's submission) to achieve this end is to enforce the general law (suitably purified and brought up to date) except in such cases as the individual makes a statutory declaration to the effect that his estate shall be governed by the Shariat. The law of the Shariat can be codified, or simply left to be discovered by reference to the otherwise obsolete textbooks on Muhammadan law. Now if the individual does not make this declaration–and his relatives have the whole of his lifetime in which to persuade him to make it–there can be no objection to his, and their, being governed by the general law in this matter. It may be urged that this is too mechanical and that some people may not be able to drag themselves before the official in time, or he may not be able to be induced to make the journey to the village for the purpose. But there remains the testament. In his last hour the Muslim who has not made the statutory declaration can leave a will in which he requires his executor or executors to distribute his estate in accordance with the Shariat, and this is by no means contrary to the principles of the Civil Code: for the present writer, if he wishes to play a practical joke on his family, may require his executor to distribute his estate in strict accordance with the laws of Malta, or for that matter Quebec, and the English court must, if called upon, see that administration is carried out accordingly. Thus the 'Civil Code', or 'Code of Family Law', need not infringe upon the Shariat in any respect whatever.

The topic of Maintenance raises no problems. The divergencies between the personal laws are all subject to rationalization. The law of Adoption raises no problems. A good adoption law, modelled on the best available in the countries most acquainted with the institution can be enacted in the Adoption chapter. No Muslim not accustomed to adopt need adopt. He can ignore the facility. Hindus not wishing to adopt a daughter, or to adopt more than one son, need not do so. In fact great advantage will be taken of the institution, which serves purposes of a secular character near to the public's heart, irrespective of the spiritual purposes known to a large section of Hindus.[1] Hindus wishing to make a religious adoption may see that their choice and method conforms also to the new civil law, and two birds can be killed with one stone. The law relating to the joint-family remains, at first sight, a problem.[2] Because of the great difficulties in working the institution in practice it has often been urged that it should be abolished, or at least modified. The present situation, whereby it is left virtually unaffected, as an institution, by the reforms of 1956, cannot continue, as discrepancies are appearing between the various regions of India which the codifiers cannot have foreseen. The project of unification is only partly completed. There are Muslim joint-families, as we have seen; and it is not entirely safe to assume that no Christian joint-family exists, though these will disappear as the Indian Succession Act, introduced relatively recently in certain States, has its effect. The joint family has psychological origins, which persist although the economic motives which formerly strengthened it have greatly weakened. Those who are born joint may readily separate, so that in no sense is the institution a shackle or bar to progress. It is not possible to enact a joint-family law which would embrace Christians, Parsis, Muslims, Jews, and persons who have married under the Special Marriage Act or are children of persons who have so married; and the enactment of a joint-family law specifically for Hindus would seem to infringe the principle of secularism in the Code of Family Law. The way out of the difficulty, in keeping with the trend (or supposed trend) of the times would seem to be this: all heirs should take as sharers, 'tenants in common', absolutely.[3] But it should be open to fathers, on the births of their sons, to admit them to coparcenary status with themselves by a simple and inexpensive juridical act, such as a registered instrument, with which all India is completely familiar. The

[1] It is a commonplace, verifiable from any textbook of Hindu law that adoption under Jaina or Punjab customary law will be secular and would not be expected to serve religious purposes primarily or at all.

[2] See chapter 12 above.

[3] As under *HSA*, s. 19.

only persons likely to do this in fact will be Hindus now governed by Mitāksharā law. Next it should be open to sons succeeding to the property of their fathers to enter into coparcenary with each other by the same registered instrument. This will be used by Hindus now subject to Dāyabhāga law, and by those subject to Mitāksharā law as modified by the Hindu Succession Act who are dissatisfied with the situation under which they take as tenants in common and are bound to *treat* the property as joint-family property before the court may understand them to be subject to joint-family law in respect of it, a vague and unsatisfactory position. The law relating to the joint-family, its property and rights therein can then be codified upon the footing of convenience. If the joint family is indeed dying out it will die by failures to register the instruments, and eventually the sections can be deleted from the Code.

The law relating to religious endowments can be dealt with separately as befits the topic. Already, as we have seen, legislation directed to the removal of abuses on cross-communal lines is enacted or projected, and central legislation on the subject of appointment and succession, powers and rights of trustees is likely to meet little opposition on communal lines. The law relating to *benami* transactions is not essentially part of the family law, although it is frequently used between members of the same family. It cuts across communities and does not require to be codified. It may be ignored, remaining what it really is, namely a chapter of Indian equity. The Hindu law relating to *dāmdupat*[1] may simply be abolished.

Conclusion

The status of the Muhammadan law will have changed, and no Muslim will be governed by the Muhammadan law as such if these proposals or anything resembling them becomes law. But the right to follow the religious law will be safeguarded provided the person or persons most concerned take the necessary action. On that footing it cannot be said that the Muslims' personal law will have been either abolished or merged into the general mass: it will preserve its identity in a context inoffensive to the principle of the Civil Code. The object of the legislation will not

[1] See Derrett, *I.M.H.L.*, §§. 824–9.

be to make any particular attack upon any personal law, but to provide a workable and up-to-date general law such as the Constitution itself recognizes as a goal. To this all personal laws will have contributed something; the predicament of those that fall between personal laws will have been considered; and the anomalies attendant upon the two-centuries-old scheme of personal laws in their Anglo-Indian guise will have terminated. It is hoped that these wider aims will reconcile all hesitant parties to the step which, sooner or later, is bound to be made.

16
CONCLUSION

The movements for legal and social reform, continued by Hindus as much after Independence as before, including the probable motion towards the Indian Civil Code, suggest that Hinduism remains in this context a constant. The thread of history runs unbroken from before Aśoka to the grandchildren of the generation of Rādhākrishnan. The expression changes, the emphasis changes (from some standpoints it seems to improve), but the essence is the same. As the personal law drifts away and merges into a civil law the Hindu loses nothing which his religion would insist upon his keeping, and in legislating for other communities he feels no sense of touching the forbidden–it is not, to his mind, impious to lay hands upon what expediency may for the time being preserve from his interference. The distinctions between the imperative and the essential on the one hand and the accidental or inessential on the other seem to him real and justified. This is due to the character of Hinduism itself. The content of the Hindu religion shifts in balance, but the components remain the same as before. It is possible that the removal of legal props to the communities' identities may intensify awareness of spiritual rights, just as, some Britons believe, disestablishment of a religion tends to intensify the sincerity and interest of the communicants. But, whether or not this will result, the Hindu view of the function of the State is such that if it maintains a balance it performs a religious, not a 'secular' function: so that religion cannot be endangered by a step which rectifies imbalance. And the cause of the unity of India is a heavy weight in the scales, a weight which did not accumulate to its full force before as recently as 1950. It may be argued that this view of religion pays little regard to the attitude on the same subject on the part of non-Hindus. This would be plausible, if they were not merely non-Hindus but also non-Indians.

A contrast with Europe is instructive. The commonplace that the Church became rich, while the Brahmins rejected, as a caste, the responsibilities and the fruits of power, has been indicated sufficiently often to need no further emphasis. Another aspect of the contrast between Europe and India deserves to be pointed out. Europe learnt, painfully, through the century after 1540 or thereabouts that faith could be detached from behaviour, so that liberty of faith could be secured, provided behaviour did not *necessarily* derive from or rationally reflect it. Could it be said that this is what has happened and is about to happen in India? The evils of the dichotomy in Europe, followed out in America, do not encourage us to hope that it is. If this is about to develop, the *śāstra* (not to speak of the Shariat) has suffered a blow and the theory put forward in the course of this book is false. Let us take the supreme example and make the comparison.

Roman Catholics believed that the Pope was, after Jesus Christ, the Head on Earth of the Church. Therefore the Pope's decrees were binding upon every Christian in conscience, and it would be a mortal sin to contradict or contravene such decrees. This would be equally so whether the decrees were promulgated in spiritual or secular contexts, for the Church had its secular life which in fact supported its spiritual life. It was a sin to refuse to make restitution of a disputed object pending a suit about property in it before an ecclesiastical judge, and one who did not restore might be sentenced to excommunication. The reformed churches departed from the doctrine of the Western Catholic Church, and became actually or virtually independent. In England the extreme step was taken of first penalizing those that brought in, used or relied upon papal decrees, and of then declaring the king the only head of the Church of England by statute. Sir Thomas More, a lawyer and a theologian of no small standing, knew that this was wrong. Parliament could not change the nature of right and wrong. No one, to his mind, could be declared or made head of the Church who was not a cleric and purported to take his title from a secular body such as Parliament was. The religious law was superior ultimately to the secular law, and the latter derived its authority in large measure from the former. The statute, he believed, was repugnant and void. Sir Thomas More was tried and executed as a traitor; and the Reformation went on its bloody way. The unattractive compromise became a fact, and no amount of religion enables an individual to contravene his country's laws, whatever they are. This naturally comforts those who do not think too deeply.

In Europe it is accepted, however, that you are not free to do what you believe religion teaches you to do, but only what the State allows you to do. In America and Australia the same formula, *mutatis mutandis*, prevails. You can have what beliefs you choose, provided you do not act upon them in a manner contrary to that determined by the legislators (who may have any or no religion); and nice difficulties constantly arise, especially where the majority think it proper that everyone should do something which a religion forbids.[1] In Israel difficulties have arisen because the dominant religious faith does not recognize, and cannot see its way to recognizing, people as married whom the State is willing to see as a married couple, and some others as divorced whom the State would prefer to admit have been divorced.[2] Is the amendment or alteration of the so-called religious laws in India an example of this sort of clash between the State's aims and religion? There are those in India who, not better acquainted with their country's history than with the cosmopolitan atmosphere into which they are adhering or agglutinating (as we have described this temperament peculiar to India), would be prepared to accept that the conflict is of the same nature, in order the more easily to employ in India the hammer which seems to have cracked the nut in Europe.[3] But

[1] A useful survey of the problem in present-day America appears in M. Galanter's 'Religious freedoms in the United States: a turning point?', *Wisconsin Law. R.*, 1966, 2, pp. 217–96.

[2] Z. W. Falk, 'Religious law and the modern family in Israel', in J. N. D. Anderson, ed., *Family Law in Asia and Africa* (London, Allen and Unwin, 1968). G. Tedeschi, 'Transition from secular to religious matrimonial status and the retroactive application of the latter' and 'On the problem of marriage in the State of Israel', in *Studies in Israel Private Law* (Jerusalem, Kiryat Sepher, 1966).

[3] M. C. Chagla, at *Changes* (cited above, p. 537, n. 2), p. 13: 'Parliament is the ultimate arbiter in regard to what is social good, which is social justice and what is in the interest of the people as a whole'; p. 94: '. . . a

this would be to neglect the nature of Indian religion. The differences between Hinduism and Christianity and Islam as known in India have been exaggerated. The missionary and intolerant character of the two latter faiths may be correctly identified outside India, but that they possess these characteristics within India is more than doubtful. Muslims and Christians, whatever else they are, are *jāts* or *mazhabs*, 'faiths' or 'castes', and it is not surprising that both communities recognize caste within themselves, though their faiths specifically reject the notion. In other words in an India which is ruled by a Hindu majority the Hindu concept of religion as a *social* identification is accepted virtually by all. While the balance seems uncertain, the minorities are not afraid for their faiths, which any real persecution would strengthen rather than the reverse, but for their financial futures and prestige-ratings, which are values the majority themselves perfectly comprehend.

European religious manifestations have their own social overtones, but in another sense: the various churches are committed to the view that what is good for them is good for others. They seek to lay down standards not merely for themselves but for others. If something is not universally true it is not true at all. Not so the Indian outlook, which Muslims and Christians fully share with the dominant majority. Not only does the dominant religious complex start with the assumption that there are at least two paths to perfection, one social and the other strictly personal, but it preaches in its most influential holy book (and this is a rare specimen of *preaching* in Hinduism) that the several paths may at different times or in sequence or alternately be pursued by the same person. It is certain that India rejects the notion that *my* belief is superior to *yours*. For of course *my* belief is no more than *my* chosen path for the time being towards my own personal perfection.

From this it results that the patterns of action laid down by the

distinction must be drawn between the religious and secular aspect. The religious aspect cannot be touched. It is something personal to every Muslim . . . But the secular aspect is entirely different from the religious aspect. If the secular aspect of the law can be changed, then the only authority to change it is public opinion—in this country, Parliament, which represents public opinion, and in the election of which 50 million Muslims have as much a share as other fellow-citizens.'

State relate automatically to the framework within which the individual chooses his path or paths; the religion itself is not touched. By contrast the Tudor or Stuart Kings of England could not permit anyone to contemplate whether the pre-Reformation view of the Church's law could be right. The teaching of the Church, itself, left no alternative to a sincere living out of what the individual believed, and belief was crystallized in creeds and subordinate legislation of the Church's own legislatures. The King must prohibit this or his policies must fail. The Church called anyone who submitted to the King's laws a heretic, unless his adherence to the King was with mental reservations; and the King attempted to retaliate by preventing or penalizing mental reservations. At times the subject felt crushed between the millstones of the two tyrannies. The European Reformation left the subject with no choice: the Indian reformation is narrowing the field of choice, but no one contends that this precludes the subject from his religious goal. A keen examination of the Islamic faith may well be undertaken to find out what are the essentials of belief and practice, without which no Muslim can attain spiritual perfection: and if this is found out we can be sure that no Indian legislature will do anything to hinder progress along that path. In history Indian kings have prohibited sacrifices of animals in societies where the dominant faith found such sacrifices abhorrent; at the same time it was admitted that to prohibit other sacrifices which society recognized would be to court disaster. That is the counterpart of our modern position. The paths remain open to the individual ideally or theoretically. One can complain that the full choice in action is not left to the individual's option: we have seen why that is.[1] But it was never the case that the *śāstra* insisted upon one way, and one faith, or that public expression of that or any other faith was an inherent right. We have seen how the *śāstra* worked as a leaven in society, and not as a

[1] Above, p. 481. This is why P. K. Tripathi, Dean of the Faculty of Law, Delhi University, can say (in *Secularism: its Implications for Law and Life in India*, cited above, p. 19, n. 2) that in India all religions are patronized; the Indian constitution concentrates on the individual's liberty and the individual's welfare; freedom *from* religion is guaranteed as well, where his liberty and dignity (in a social sense) tended to be menaced; the individual is placed *above* religion; the freedom of religion is recognized only as incidental to his well-being and freedom generally.

straitjacket. There never was any question of a subject's being entitled to put his beliefs into practice if society objected, for all *adhikāra-s* came into existence within the sphere of a society, and when societies became numerous or complex the king kept the balance within or between them. The king's failing to do this could not be contemplated: it meant the end of *dharma-s* and the Rule of the Fish (*mātsya-nyāya*).

Now a doctrine is afoot that the philosophical and spiritual content of Hinduism is coming into its own while the *karma-kāṇḍa*, the chapters of the *śāstra* which provide for and regulate 'works', observances, acts done with intention of obtaining a reward, are gradually being abandoned by the majority. This may well be correct, and if it is, though many will not know it, Hinduism will be brought nearer to what the *Bhagavadgītā* prescribes as perfection – a future in which Indian Muslims and Christians must share to their profit and in which law will have played a valuable rôle.

BIBLIOGRAPHICAL NOTE

To obtain an impression of the place of law in the story of religion as a component in Indian public life it is desirable to start not with law nor with religion as the field of enquiry, but with general history, especially the history of institutions and Indian thought about those institutions. The field of enquiry can then conveniently be narrowed to embrace the history of social and economic life. It will then be time to look into the history of Indian religions. Thereafter we may proceed to consider the history of Indian law.

This will take the student to the topics of the legal systems—namely Hindu and Muhammadan law, for about the others no bibliography of any particular value exists.

This note may end with a short list of miscellaneous books and articles dealing with Indian society, the 'raw material', as it were, upon which, like surgeons, the legislators have operated and are about to operate.

History of Institutions

No one can afford to ignore the massive work of Mahāmahopādhyāya Dr. P. V. Kāṇe, the *History of Dharmaśāstra* (Poona, 1930–62), which embraces far more than the *śāstra* itself. Fortunately it has excellent indexes to each volume. A great boost was given to studies of Indian political theory by the discovery of Kauṭilya's *Arthaśāstra*. Text, translation and notes are now to be had in the excellent publication of R. P. Kāṅgle, *The Kauṭilīya Arthaśāstra*, 3 vols. (Bombay, 1960–5). V. R. Dīkshitār's *Maurya Polity* (Madras, 1932) paved the way for his *Gupta Polity* (Madras, 1952). A. S. Altekar's *State and Government in Ancient India*[4] (Delhi, etc., 1962) has the special merit of being the work of a fine historian with a legal training. Neither of these qualifications can be attributed without hesitation to the generality of writers on these themes. The prolific B. A. Saletore's

Ancient Indian Political Thought and Institutions (London, 1963) is a large compilation of conflicting opinions from earlier scholars seasoned with conjectures. Great, indeed vast knowledge does not certify sound judgement–but the problem is where to find sound judgement. The major work of L. Gopal, *The Economic Life of Northern India c. A.D. 700–1200* (Delhi, etc., 1965) is an example of its author's grasp of the fundamental sources and untiring industry. R. S. Sharmā's *Aspects of Political Ideas and Institutions in Ancient India* (Delhi, etc., 1959) contains studies which rate high in point of information and originality.

It is an error to suppose that the State in ancient India did not have an important sacral and ritual side, or that this side did not have a part to play. J. Gonda's 'Ancient Indian kingship from the religious point of view', *Numen*, 3 (1956), pp. 36–71, 122–55; 4 (1957) 24–58, 127–64, together with his and A. Basu's articles in *The Sacral Kingship* (Leiden, 1959) help to adjust the balance already overweighted in favour of politics and economics. J. C. Heesterman's *The Ancient Indian Royal Consecration* (The Hague, 1957) is another work of similar tendency.

The reader who needs a very rapid but reliable survey of ancient Indian political ideas may be recommended to use either V. P. Varma, *Studies in Hindu Political Thought*[2] (Benares, 1959) or J. W. Spellman, *Political Theory of Ancient India* (Oxford, 1964). A fuller and more leisurely treatment is that of the veteran U. N. Ghoshal, whose sense of balance and caution in judgement manifest themselves abundantly in his classic, *History of Indian Political Ideas* (Oxford, 1959).

History and Social and Economic Life

General histories are in a sense the best introduction. Above all for handiness, completeness, and exactness of tone stands the deservedly popular *Wonder that was India* by A. L. Basham (London, 1957 and several times reprinted). The vast historical encyclopaedia edited by R. C. Majumdār and A. D. Pusalker and others, the eight-volume *History and Culture of the Indian People* (Bombay, 1951–65) covers the Vedic Age onwards down to British Paramountcy and the Indian Renaissance. It deals with religious movements and social reforms, and even if the tone could be questioned, especially on more controversial matters, for weight of material and breadth of scope it will long remain unrivalled. R. C. Majumdār's *Ancient India* is a monumental and personal achievement (Benares, 1952). Of great value and convenience is a minor work by the doyen of Indian historians, K. A. Nīlakanta Śāstrī (hereafter referred to as K. A. N. Sastri), *Foreign Notices of South India from Megasthenes to Ma Hian* (Madras, 1939).

Kewal Motwani, India's foremost sociologist from the point of view of cultural continuity, did possibly his best work in *Manu: a Study in Hindu Social Theory* (Madras, 1934). A. W. P. Guruge's *Social Conditions of Ancient India as reflected in the Rāmāyaṇa* (Bombay, 1952) and D. P. Vora's *Evolution of Morals in the Epics* (Bombay, 1959) ably handle material less often exploited (though mention may be made of A. K. Sur's 'Sex and Marriage in the age of Mahābhārata', *Man in India*, 43 (1963), 42–54). Indra, *The Status of Women in Ancient India* (Delhi, 1955) and A. S. Altekar, *The Position of Women in Hindu Civilization from Pre-Historic Times to the Present Day* (Benares, 1938) handle a very popular theme. I. B. Horner, *Women under Primitive Buddhism* (London, 1930) and T. A. Baig, ed., *Women of India* (Delhi, 1958) represent the ends of the scale from the most scholarly to the most practical-optimistic, but both are excellent for their purposes. A compact work is S. Chattopādhyāya's *Social Life in Ancient India (in the background of the Yājñavalkya-smṛti)* (Calcutta, 1965), where the information is constantly backed by quotations in the original Sanskrit.

Histories dealing with single dynasties and with groups of dynasties give many dry facts, but set the scene in detail for the information on social and economic questions which they almost invariably provide. For this reason one may usefully consult K. A. N. Sastri, ed., *A Comprehensive History of India, II, Mauryas and Sātavāhanas* (Calcutta, 1957); R. Thapar, *Aśoka and the Decline of the Mauryas* (London, 1961); B. N. Puri, *India under the Kushanas* (Calcutta, 1963); K. A. N. Sastri, *History of South India from Prehistoric Times to the Fall of Vijayanagara*[3] (Bombay, 1966); A. S. Altekar, *The Rāṣṭrakūṭas and their Times* (Poona, 1934); M. V. Krishna Rao, *The Gaṅgas of Talkāḍ* (Madras, 1936); G. M. Moraes, *The Kadamba Kula* (Bomay, 1931); K. A. N. Sastri, *The Pāṇḍyan Kingdom* (London, 1929); K. A. N. Sastri,

The Cōḷas[2] (Madras, 1955); D. Desai, *The Mahāmaṇḍaleśvaras under the Cālukyas of Kalyāṇi* (Bombay, 1951); A. K. Majumdār, *Chaulukyas of Gujarat* (Bombay, 1956); N. Venkaṭarāmanayya, *The Eastern Cālukyas of Veṅgi* (Madras, 1950); J. D. M. Derrett, *The Hoysaḷas* (Madras, 1957); G. Yazdani, *Early History of the Deccan* (London, 1960).

More specifically on our themes are R. S. Sharmā's *Śūdras in Ancient India* (Delhi, etc., 1958), the leading work on the theme, and his *Indian Feudalism c. 300–1200* (Calcutta, 1965) which, whatever one thinks of the main contention, is a monument of careful use of inscriptions, the raw material of all histories of mediaeval times. D. R. Sastri's *Origin and Development of the Rituals of Ancestor Worship in India* (Calcutta, 1963) has a certain legal interest. A. Appadorai's *Economic Conditions in Southern India* (Madras, 1936) is matched by P. Niyogi, *Economic History of Northern India* (Calcutta, 1962); mention must also be made of S. K. Maity, *Economic History of N. India in the Gupta period* (Calcutta, 1957), B. N. Sharmā, *Social Life in N. India (A.D. 600–1000)* (Delhi, 1966) and also G. S. Dikshit, *Local Self-government in Mediaeval Karnataka* (Dharwar, 1964), which is almost exclusively based on inscriptions. The wealth of inscriptions surviving in the South relatively to the North accounts for admirable and reliable works on South Indian polity. B. A. Saletore, *Social and Political Life in the Vijayanagara Empire* (Madras, 1934) will be noted, as also the series of works by the veteran epigraphist-historian, T. V. Mahālingam, namely *Administration and Social Life under Vijayanagar* (March 1940); *Economic Life in the Vijayanagar Empire* (Madras, 1952), and the exceedingly valuable *South Indian Polity* (Madras, 1955).

History of Indian Religions

The great demand for information is being met by a flow of works both edifying and informative. It is superfluous to give a detailed bibliography when an excellent one is provided in a work which itself is an essential aid to the student: Kenneth W. Morgan, ed., *The Religion of the Hindus* (New York, 1953). The main works of Dr. S. Rādhākrishnan are listed there. The older works which are still of great use include M. Monier-Williams, *Brahmanism and Hinduism* (London, 1891); *Hinduism* (London,

1894); *Indian Wisdom*[4] (London, 1893); *Modern India and the Indians* (London, 1891); *Religious Thought and Life in India* (London, 1883); and the following works of J. N. Farquhar, *The Crown of Hinduism* (London, 1913); *Modern Religious Movements in India* (New York, 1915); *An Outline of the Religious Literature of India* (London, 1920); B. K. Goswāmi Shāstrī's *Bhakti Cult in Ancient India* (1923) has been published from Benares in 1965. Specimens of more recent works would include D. S. Sharmā, *Renaissance of Hinduism* (Benares, 1944); S. C. Chatterjee, *Fundamentals of Hinduism* (Calcutta, 1950); T. M. P. Mahādevan, *Outlines of Hinduism* (Bombay, 1956). A *tour de force* is W. Norman Brown's series of lectures in which the facts of Hindu religious life and the Sanskritic traditional are blended: *Man in the Universe: some Continuities in Indian Thought* (Berkeley, 1966). Some specialized studies, of value for our legal purposes, occur in J. Gonda, *Change and Continuity in Indian Religion* (Utrecht, 1965). If the present writer may say so, 'change and continuity' are the key words, or should be, in any indological study. S. K. Maitra's *Ethics of the Hindus* (Calcutta, 1956) reminds us that Hinduism is a *teaching*, as well as a comprehensive restatement of life.

But when all is said and done, the student does best to start with famous texts and to read them as *continua*, bearing in mind that each verse is influenced by its context, and each context by the theme of the section, and so on. The *Manu-smṛti* (or *Mānava-dharma-śāstra*) is one such book, and the translation of G. Bühler is regarded as the classic, though that by Burnell and Hopkins may be used for comparison. Another indispensable key to Indian moods and thought patterns is the *Bhagavadgītā*. The translation by Bhagvān Dās is much recommended, but that recently brought out by R. C. Zaehner in *Hindu Scriptures* (Everyman's Library, 944, 1966) is likely to achieve renown.

As for Islam, the works of B. Lewis, *The Arabs in History* (London, 1950) and H. A. R. Gibb, *Mohammedanism: an Historical Survey* (London, 1949) are regularly resorted to. But readers of this second book will require to study Aziz Ahmad's *Studies in Islamic Culture in the Indian Environment* (Oxford, 1964), especially chapter 5.

Bibliographical Note

History of Indian Law

The original texts of Hindu and Muhammadan law as applied in India tend to be difficult for the newcomer, but there is an advantage in seeing the sources directly: thus Colebrooke's translation of Jagannātha Tarkapañcānana's *Vivāda-bhaṅgārṇava* (known as Colebrooke's *Digest*) is an invaluable source. Other collections of importance are W. Stokes, *Hindu Law Books* (Madras, 1865) and S. Setlūr, *A Complete Collection of Hindu Law Books on Inheritance* (Madras, 1911).

The Constitution of India has its own history. A. B. Keith's *Constitutional History of India 1600–1935*² (London, 1937) is still useful for the earlier period. The leading work on the framing of the Constitution is Granville Austin, *The Indian Constitution: Cornerstone of a Nation* (Oxford, 1966). D. D. Basu's *Commentary on the Constitution of India*, now (1967) passing from its fourth into its fifth edition (5 vols.) is the principal source of information as to the *meaning* of the Constitution. M. P. Jain's *Indian Constitutional Law* (Bombay, 1962) is an established textbook; but M. V. Pylee, *Constitutional Government*² (Bombay, 1965) commands respect. On the Constitution and Indian law generally the handiest and most complete treatment is A. Gledhill, *The British Commonwealth. The Development of its Laws and Constitutions. India*² (London, 1964).

M. P. Jain, *Outlines of Indian Legal History*² (Bombay, 1966) has virtually superseded the barely readable *Background to Indian Law* (Cambridge, 1946) by G. C. Rankin but possibly not the very readable (if not very original) *Common Law in India* (London, 1960) by M. C. Setalvad, the former Attorney-General of India, whose *Role of English Law in India* (Jerusalem, 1966) covers post-Independence developments.

Donald E. Smith's *India as a Secular State* (Princeton, 1963) is in a class by itself. Though the presuppositions upon which it is based have been questioned, the range of material studied, the different facets of Indian life relevant to the theme, and the combination of historical grasp and sociological approach make it invaluable. Smith is concerned with the Constitution, recent and threatened legislation, and setting these against their proper backgrounds he brings the whole problem to life.

The bibliography of works dealing with the ancient and

mediaeval Hindu law is formidable, surprising in bulk and in confidence of reaching a forum (a confidence which has yet to be substantiated). R. B. Pāl's *Hindu Philosophy of Law in the Vedic and post-Vedic Times Prior to the Institutes of Manu* (Calcutta, N.D.) and *The History of Hindu Law in the Vedic Age . . .* (Calcutta, 1958), together with K. P. Jayaswāl, *Manu and Yājñavalkya, a Basic History of Hindu Law* (Calcutta, 1930) could be dismissed too lightly as subjective, for such work stands at the boundary between brilliance and guess-work. No such comment could be made of Kāṇe's *History of Dharmaśāstra*, to which we have already referred. Everything by N. C. Sen-Gupta is of great value, namely *Sources of Law and Society in Ancient India* (Calcutta, 1914); *Evolution of Ancient Indian Law* (London/Calcutta, 1953); 'Comparative view of law in ancient India', in G. S. Métraux and F. Crouzer, edd., *Studies in the Cultural History of India* (Agra, 1965), pp. 62–88.

U. C. Sarkar's *Epochs in Hindu Legal History* (Hoshiarpur, 1958) was itself epoch-making, as it attempted for the first time to depict Hindu law under a series of régimes. Not less outstanding is L. Sternbach's *Juridical Studies in Ancient Indian Law, I* (Delhi, etc., 1965). P. N. Sen's *The General Principles of Hindu Jurisprudence* (Calcutta, 1918) is not replaced by the much more readily available *Hindu Jurisprudence* (Calcutta, 1961) of K. R. R. Sastry. K. L. Sarkar's *Mimansa Rules of Interpretation as Applied to Hindu Law* is not superseded by Kāṇe's contribution on this subject in his fifth volume, valuable as that is, nor by the excellent, but foreshortened, *Mimamsa Jurisprudence* (*The Sources of Hindu Law*) (Allahabad, 1952) by A. S. Naṭarāja Ayyar. But by far the best introduction to *dharma-śāstra* for the European or American reader is R. Lingat's *Les Sources du Droit dans le Système traditionnel de l'Inde* (Paris, Mouton, 1967).

On custom and law one may recommend A. Steele, *Law and Custom of Hindu Castes* (Bombay, 1868); S. Roy, *Customs and Customary Law in British India* (Calcutta, 1911); P. V. Kāṇe, *Hindu Customs and Modern Law* (Bombay, 1950); M. P. Jain, 'Custom as a source of law in India', *Jaipur L.J.*, 3 (1963), pp. 96–130; and J. Jolly, *Hindu Law and Custom* (Calcutta, 1928). The last author's *Outlines of an History of the Law of Partition, Inheritance and Adoption* (Calcutta, 1885) was too ambitious a work judged by the standards of our day, but the material has been widely used and the book may be more widely available than more modern treatises.

S. C. Banerjee, *Dharma Sūtras: a Study in their Origin and Development* (Calcutta, 1962) is not well designed, but contains information, conveniently displayed, about an early stage in the development of the texts. C. Sankararāma Śāstrī's *Fictions in the Development of the Hindu Law Texts* (Adyar, 1926) made useful points even if the main contention remains unproven. S. Varadāchāriar, *The Hindu Judicial System* (Lucknow, 1949) remains the best treatment of the subject, though articles by L. Rocher expand our knowledge of individual aspects of the trial (see, e.g. 'Ancient Hindu Criminal Law', *J.O.R.* 24 (1955), pp. 15–34, also in *La Preuve* amongst the *Receuils de la Société Jean Bodin* and 'The theory of matrimonial causes according to the *dharmaśāstra*' in J. N. D. Anderson, ed., *Family Law in Asia and Africa* [London, Allen and Unwin, 1968]). S. C. Bagchi, *Juristic Personality of Hindu Deities* (Calcutta, 1933) is an admirable work of jurisprudence on a narrow theme. D. Mitter's somewhat antiquated *The Position of Women in Hindu Law* (Calcutta, 1909) retains its lead in point of fullness of treatment.

The greatest teacher of the wider aspects of Hindu law was R. V. Rangaswāmī Aiyaṅgar, amongst whose works the following can be recommended for their style, verve, breadth, and fervour: *Aspects of Social and Political System of Manusmṛti* (Lucknow, 1949) and *Some Aspects of the Hindu View of Life according to Dharmaśāstra* (Baroda, 1952); while there is considerable utility in his *Rājadharma* (Adyar, 1941) and *Indian Cameralism* (Adyar, 1949). R. C. Hazra, a teacher of *smṛti* and *purāṇa-s*, has published numerous articles on the meaning of *dharma* in *Our Heritage* from 1959 onwards.

Amongst the specialists' books of practical law, having a good historical background one may recommend R. Sarvādhikārī, *The Principles of the Hindu Law of Inheritance*² (Madras, 1922); G. D. Banerjee, *The Hindu Law of Marriage and Strīdhana*⁵ (Calcutta, 1923); and J. L. Kapur, *The Law of Adoption in India and Burma* (Calcutta, 1933).

The effect of British administration is seen most interestingly in the *Śukranīti* or *Śukranītisāra* (see L. Gopal at *B.S.O.A.S.*, 25, No. 3 (1962), pp. 524 ff.). See also Rudolph and Rudolph, 'Barristers and Brahmans in India: Legal Cultures and Social

Change', *C.S.S.H.*, 8 (1965), pp. 24–49. On the gradual disappearance of the Muhammadan law of crime in India see T. K. Banerjee, *Background to Indian Criminal Law* (Calcutta, etc., 1963). See also B. B. Misra, *The Central Administration of the East India Company* (Manchester, 1959); *The Judicial Administration of the East India Company in Bengal, 1765–1782* (Delhi, 1961). A. C. Patra, *The Administration of Justice under the East India Company in Bengal, Bihar and Orissa* (London, 1962) is not so distinguished a work. B. N. Pandey's *Introduction of English Law into India* (London, 1967) is the best study of Sir Elijah Impey's career. Articles throwing light on Indian attitudes to the subject include R. K. Misra, 'Some general implications of the influence of English law on the Indian society', *Jaipur L.J.*, 3 (1963), pp. 165 ff., and various articles contributed to the *Revista del Instituto de Derecho Comparado* (Barcelona), 8–9 (1957).

L. S. S. O'Malley's *Modern India and the West* (London, 1941) is a most valuable work, but not so valuable in its legal chapter.

For the Islamic legal materials consulted in India see Fyzee, *Outlines* (cited below), and in particular C. Hamilton, trans., *Hedaya* of Burhān ad-dīn al-Marghīnānī, second edition by Grady (London, 1870); and N. B. E. Baillie, *Digest of Moohummudan Law* I (London, 1875), II (London, 1896).

The Main Legal Systems

It is frequently necessary when coping with Indian legal materials of any age to consult a glossary: H. H. Wilson's *Glossary of Judicial and Revenue Terms* (London, 1855; Calcutta, 1940) is normally sufficient.

The best introduction to the history of the ancient indigenous system as it was when the British became responsible for it, showing how they took up their task and with what mixed results is to be found in the handy *Lectures in Hindu Law, the Genesis of the Personal Law* by K. V. Venkaṭasubrahmania Iyer (London, etc., Asia Publishing House, 1968).

To study Hindu law it is possible to avail oneself of two well-established (though not invariably accurate) publications, one increasingly popular, and one original and meritorious. D. F. Mulla's *Principles of Hindu Law*[13] (Bombay, 1966) and J. D. Mayne, *Treatise on Hindu Law and Usage*,[11] (Madras 1951, 1953) are the leading reference works. N. R. Rāghavāchāriar, *Hindu Law, Principles and Precedents*[5] (Madras, 1965) is particularly welcome amongst serious students. S. V. Gupte's *Hindu Law in British India*[2] (Bombay, 1947; *Supplement*, Bombay, 1955) is being replaced by the same author's *Hindu Law of Marriage* (Bombay, 1961) and *Hindu Law of Succession* (Bombay, 1963), so far as these go. J. D. M. Derrett, *Introduction to Modern Hindu Law* (Bombay, 1963) is a relatively succinct account. J. C. Ghose, *Principles of Hindu Law*[3] (Calcutta, 1917) utilizes texts fully.

R. N. Sarkar has published a work called *Hindu Code* (Calcutta, 1957). The general lines of the codification controversy are handled in J. D. M. Derrett, *Hindu Law Past and Present* (Calcutta, 1957). From the same city and in the same year appeared treatises on the four statutes making up the 'Hindu Code' by D. H. Chaudhari. T. P. Gopalakrishnan and others, *Codified Hindu Laws* (Allahabad, 1960) is much used.

A symposium containing no less than thirteen contributions to the discussions raised by the present state of the Hindu law is published in *Jaipur L.J.*, 5 (1965).

B. K. Mukherjea, *Hindu Law of Religious and Charitable Trust*[2] (Calcutta, 1962) is the classic work on the subject and supersedes older works in the field.

On the Indian Succession Act earlier works must likewise give place for the time being to P. L. Paruck's *The Indian Succession Act*[5] (Bombay, 1966).

To study Muhammadan law an even more attractive selection may be employed. R. K. Wilson's *Anglo-Muhammadan Law*[6] (London, 1930) is generally out of date but is useful for reference. Abdur Rahim's *Principles of Muhammadan Jurisprudence according to the Hanafi, Maliki, Shafi'i and Hanbali schools* (London/Madras, 1911), which does not concentrate on the Anglo-Muhhamadan law, is a source book for the courts. Syed Amir Ali, *Mahommedan Law*[4—5] (Calcutta, 1912, 1929) retains a high prestige. F. B. Tyabji, *Muhammadan Law: the Personal Law of Muslims*[3] (Bombay, 1940) is the practitioner's guide, but is written so as to be fit for any serious reader. A. A. A. Fyzee, *Outlines of Muhammadan Law*[3] (London, 1964) and *Cases in the Muhammadan Law of India and Pakistan* (Oxford, 1965) form a pair of teaching books by the best-known expert on Muhammadan law in South Asia. K. P. Saksena, *Muslim Law as Administered in India and Pakistan*[4] (Lucknow, 1963) is popular amongst practitioners.

Works on Indian Society

Nirad C. Chaudhuri, *The Autobiography of an Unknown Indian* (London, 1951; Bombay, 1964), and *The Continent of Circe* (London, 1965) are works to be read with caution, but not to be omitted. Home-truths and guesswork, scholarship and malice, anecdote and analysis mingle in these curious books. But if Mr. Chaudhuri is taken as evidence for the truth of Indian characteristics at which he carps the works have a scientific value. N. Subramanian's *Hindu Tripod (an Essay on Hinduism and Western Values)* (Madras, 1965) is a scholarly javelin thrown in much the same direction. A glimpse of a scholar's approach to the hagiography of *mahants* is to be seen in Professor V. Rāghavan's *The Jagadguru: interviews of visitors from abroad with H. H. Sri Chandrasekharendra Sarasvati Swamigal, Sankaracharya of Kanchi Kamakoti Peetha* (Madras, 1965). P. Spratt's attempt to attribute Hindu characteristics to narcissism and 'projective extroversion' is especially interesting as proof that such explanations are called for: *Hindu Culture and Personality* (Bombay, 1966).

Works attempting to explain India include D. Narain, *Hindu Character (a Few Glimpses)* (Bombay, 1957); D. P. Mukerji, *Modern Indian Culture*[2] (Bombay, 1948); P. Thomas, *Hindu Religions, Customs and Manners* (Bombay, 1949); and B. N. Varmā, ed., *Contemporary India* (London, 1964). See also M. L. Vidyārthi, *India's Culture through the Ages*[2] (Kanpur, 1952). K. Satchidānanda Mūrty, in *The Indian Spirit* (Waltair, 1965), contends that foreign interpretations of Indian culture overemphasize the 'spiritual' elements, attach too much importance to superficial and unrepresentative traditional materials, and overlook Hindu belief in the practical and the individual: the book manifests an up-to-date Hindu view of Hinduism.

B. Datta, *Hindu Law of Inheritance; an Anthropological Study* (Calcutta, 1957) seems to be a work *sui generis*. Works on social reform include S. Naṭarājan, *Century of Social Reform in India* (Bombay, 1959); C. H. Heimsath, *Indian Nationalism and Hindu Social Reform* (Princeton, 1964). Miscellaneous works on social aspects of law include A. Somerville, *Crime and religious beliefs in India* (Calcutta, 1966); P. Thomas, *Indian Women through the Ages* (Bombay, 1964); H. Chatterjee, *Studies in Some Aspects of Hindu Samskāras in Ancient India* (Calcutta, 1965). K. M. Kapādia's *Marriage and Family in India*[3] (Bombay, 1966) is an established work to which law and sociology have contributed.

Anthropological works suitable for background reading would include G. Morris Carstairs, *The Twice-born* (Bloomington, 1958); S. C. Dube, *Indian Village* (London, 1955); A. C. Mayer, *Caste and Kinship in Central India* (London, 1960); F. G. Bailey, *Caste and the Economic Frontier* (Manchester, 1957); McKim Marriott, ed., *Village India, American Anthropologist*, 57, 3, pt. 2, Memoir No. 83, 1955; E. R. Leach, ed., *Aspects of Caste in South India, Ceylon and North-West Pakistan* (Cambridge, 1962); Milton Singer, *Traditional India: Structure and Change* (Philadelphia, 1959); and the issues to date of *Contributions to Indian Sociology* (ed. by L. Dumont and D. Pocock, published by Mouton & Co., The Hague). T. Madan, *Family and Kinship* (London, Asia Publishing House, 1965), though actually devoted to the Pandits of Kashmir, deals incidentally with wider questions of traditional Indian society. C. v. Fürer-Haimendorf's *Morals and Merit* (London, Weidenfeld, 1967) offers a comparative study of values and social controls in South Asian societies, not all of them 'primitive'.

But the task of offering a bibliography of this kind is rendered otiose by the *Anthropological Bibliography of South Asia* by E. v. Fürer-Haimendorf (I. To 1955; II. 1955–9) (Paris/The Hague. 1958, 1964). However, while this present work was in the press L. Dumont's *Homo hierarchicus* (Paris, Gallimard, 1967) appeared. This is not only one of the most important works on the theory of caste (with an exhaustive bibliography) but also one which contains information on caste discipline and recent developments in the adjustment of social hierarchy to modern conditions, all relevant to our present theme. The author is personally acquainted with the people, and combines studies of śāstric theory with contemporary sociology.

INDEX OF STATUTES AND STATUTORY INSTRUMENTS

(*Note*. This index does not list separately the statutes of various territories, being based upon an alphabetical order. But from that order there are two exceptions. Firstly Regulations of the East India Company's Presidencies are not named here, but mostly referred to by their numbers; and secondly the word 'Indian' has been placed in brackets in some cases where the description, though properly part of the statute's title, is frequently omitted in practice. A warning is called for, to the effect that the name of the state which has enacted a particular state statute—as opposed to a central statute—may or may not be part of the title of the statute, so that it is not always advisable to search for a Madras statute under those commencing with the word 'Madras'. Amending statutes are not always listed below, where a reference to the principal Act serves also to draw attention to a place where its amending Acts are cited.)

INDEX OF CASES

Ankamma (B.) *v.* Bamanappa (B.) AIR 1937 Mad. 332 p. 395
Annamalai (A). Mudaliar *v.* Perumayee Ammal AIR 1965 Mad. 139 pp. 370, 384
Annapurnamma (P.) *v.* Appa Rao AIR 1963 A.P. 312 p. 376
Anon (1837) Morton 22 p. 297
Anukul Chandra *v.* Surendra [1939] 1 Cal. 592 p. 313
Apáji Narhar Kulkarni *v.* Rámchandra Rávji (1891) 16 Bom. 29 F.B. pp. 297, 306, 430
Appaji Jijaji Vaidya *v.* Mohanlal Raoji Gujar (1930) 54 Bom. 564 F.B. pp. 300, 309
Appaya *v.* Padappa (1899) 23 Bom. 122 p. 291
Aravamudha Aiyangar *v.* Ramaswami [1952] 1 M.L.J. 251 = [1953] Mad. 123 p. 297
Arun Kumar Patra *v.* Sudhanshu Bala AIR 1962 Or. 65 S.B.; AIR 1966 Or. 242 S.B. p. 392
Arunachala Moopanar *v.* Arumugha AIR 1953 Mad. 550 p. 300
Ashiruddin Ahmad *v.* The King AIR 1949 Cal. 182 p. 63
Ashrafalli Cassim *v.* Mahomedalli Rajaballi [1947] Bom. 1 p. 523
Asita Mohan *v.* Nirode AIR 1917 Cal. 292 p. 256
Athilinga Gounder *v.* Ramaswami Goundar [1945] Mad. 297 p. 308
Atmaram *v.* Bajirao (1935) 62 I.A. 139 p. 300
Atmaram *v.* King-Emperor AIR 1924 Nag. 121 p. 455
Att.-Gen. *v.* Delaney (1875) I.R. 10 C.L. 104 p. 480
Atyam Veerraju *v.* P. Venkanna AIR 1966 S.C. 629 p. 488
Ayi Ammal *v.* Subramania Asari AIR 1966 Mad. 369 p. 344
Ayisumma (M.) *v.* V. P. B. Mayomoothy Umma AIR 1953 Mad. 425 p. 526
Ayyappan *v.* Kurumpa Mema [1966] K.L.T. 514 p. 42
Azima Bibi *v.* Shamalanand (1912) 40 Cal. 378 P.C. p. 49
Aziz Bano *v.* Muhammad Ibrahim Husain (1925) 47 All. 823 p. 317

Baba *v.* Timma (1883) 7 Mad. 357 F.B. p. 425
Babarao *v.* Baburao AIR 1956 Nag. 98 p. 307
Bachiraju (P.) *v.* V. Venkatappadu (1865) 2 M.H.C.R. 402 p. 299
Bafati *v.* State AIR 1964 All. 106 p. 471
Bai Nani *v.* Chunilal (1897) 22 Bom. 973 p. 300
Bai Raman *v.* Jagjivandas Kashidas (1917) 41 Bom. 618 p. 298
Bai Zabu Khima *v.* Amardas [1967] 8 Guj. L.R. 281 p. 506
Baijnath Prasad Singh *v.* Tej Bali Singh (1921) 48 I.A. 195 p. 310
Bairagi Das *v.* Sri Uday Chandra AIR 1965 Or. 201 pp. 493, 506
Balaiah (B.) *v.* C. Lachaiah AIR 1965 A.P. 435 p. 435
Balusami Reddiar *v.* Balakrishna AIR 1957 Mad. 97 p. 306
Balwant Rao *v.* Baji Rao (1920) 47 I.A. 213 p. 39
Balwant Singh *v.* Rani Kishori (1898) 25 I.A. 54 p. 78
Bankey Lal *v.* Durga Prasad (1931) 53 All. 868 F.B. p. 314
Bappu (L.) Ayyar *v.* Renganayaki AIR 1955 Mad. 394 p. 429
Bebee Muttra, In the goods of (1832) Morton 191 p. 308
Begum Noorbanu *v.* Deputy Custodian General of Evacuee Property AIR 1965 S.C. 1937 p. 519

Indubai Pandhari *v.* Vyankati Vithoba (1965) 67 Bom. L.R. 612 p. 342
Isana Chandra's Case Morton-Montriou, xvi = 1 Ind. Dec., Old Ser., 399 p. 241
I.-T. Officer, Lucknow *v.* Bachu Lal Kapoor [1967] 1 S.C.W.R. 14 p. 429
Itwari *v.* Asghari AIR 1960 All. 684 p. 538

Jagamma *v.* M. Satyanarayana Murthi AIR 1958 An.P. 582 p. 314
Jagannath Churn *v.* Akali Dassia (1894) 21 Cal. 463 p. 291
Jagannath Pal *v.* Bidyanand (1868) 1 B.L.R., A.C., 114 p. 298
Jagannath Raghunath *v.* Narayan L. Shethe (1910) 34 Bom. 553 p. 304
Jagarnath Gir *v.* Sher Bahadur Singh (1934) 57 All. 85 pp. 312, 314
Jagdish Kumar *v.* Smt. Sita AIR 1963 Punj. 114 p. 392
Jagdish Lal *v.* Smt. Shyama Madan AIR 1966 All. 150 pp. 376, 392
Jagdish Pandey *v.* Rameshwar Chaubey AIR 1960 Pat. 54 p. 427
Jagubhai Hiralal *v.* Kesarlal Girdharlal (1925) 49 Bom. 282 p. 314
Jamiyatrám *v.* Bái Jamná (1864) 2 B.H.C.R. 11 p. 309
Jamshed A. Irani *v.* Banu (1960) 68 Bom. L.R. 794 p. 40
Jamshedji C. Tarachand *v.* Soonabai (1907) 33 Bom. 122 p 467
Janamma *v.* Joseph [1967] K.L.T. 105 p. 60
Janki Raman *v.* Koshalyanandan AIR 1961 Pat. 293 p. 493
Jaswantlal Linabhai *v.* Nichhabhai AIR 1964 Guj. 283 p. 430
Jatindra Nath Roy *v.* Nagendra Nath Roy (1931) 58 I.A. 372, 59 Cal. 576, AIR 1931 P.C. 268 pp. 116, 310
Jayaraj *v.* Mary AIR 1967 Mad. 242 F.B. p. 370
Jesa *v.* Kumbha AIR 1958 Raj. 186 p. 317
Jewa-jee *v.* Trimbuk-Jee (1842) 3 M.I.A. 138 p. 317
Jijoyiamba Bayi Saiba *v.* Kamakshi (1868) 3 M.H.C.R. 424 p. 254
Jina (P.) Magan *v.* Bai Jethi [1941] Bom. 535 p. 358
Jinnappa Mahadevappa *v.* Chimmava (1934) 59 Bom. 459 p. 310
Jnanendra Nath Roy, In the goods of (1922) 49 Cal. 1069 p. 44
Jogesh Chandra *v.* Sree Sree Dhakeswari (1941) 45 C.W.N. 809 pp. 488, 493
Jogul Kishore *v.* Sahib Sahai (1883) 5 All. 430 F.B. p. 297
Jotindra Mohun Tagore *v.* Ganendra Mohan Tagore (1872) 9 B.L.R. 377 P.C. p. 309
Jugal (M./S.) *v.* Commr. I.T., U.P. AIR 1967 S.C. 495 p. 430
Jugget Mohini *v.* Mst. Sokheemoney (1871) 14 M.I.A. 289 p. 296

Kadarbacha *v.* Rangasvámi (1863) 1 M.H.C.R. 150 p. 294
Kahandas Narrandas, *Re* (1881) 5 Bom. 154 p. 293
Kakumanu Pedasubhayya *v.* K. Akkamma AIR 1958 S.C. 1042 p. 312
Kalachund Chukurbuttee *v.* Jogul (1809) 1 S.D.A. (Cal.) 374 p. 296
Kalgavda Tavanappa Patil *v.* Somappa (1909) 33 Bom. 669 pp. 299, 309, 312
Kaliammal *v.* Muthu Pillai AIR 1966 Mad. 118 p. 307
Kalyani *v.* Krishnan [1966] K.L.T. 688 F.B. p. 42
Kamani Devi *v.* Sir Kameshwar Singh AIR 1946 Pat. 316 p. 299
Kameswara (D.) Sastri *v.* Veeracharlu (P.) (1910) 34 Mad. 422 p. 70
Kandasami Pillai *v.* Murugammal (1896) 19 Mad. 6 p. 297

Kanwal Ram *v.* H. P. Administration AIR 1966 S.C. 614 p. 355
Karsan Gojá, Reg. *v.* (1864) 2 B.H.C.R. 117 p. 293
Karthayini Amma *v.* Parukutty Amma AIR 1957 Ker. 27 p. 305
Kashinath, *i.e.* Cossinauth Bysack's Case (1826) Montriou, Hindu Will, p. 106 [see also IV Ind. Rep. 979 ff.] p. 309
Káshirám *v.* Bhadu (1870) 7 B.H.C.R., A.C.J., 17 p. 294
Kassimiah Charities *v.* Secretary of the Madras State Wakf Board AIR 1964 Mad. 18 p. 538
Kastoori (Smt.) Devi *v.* Chiranji Lal AIR 1960 All. 446 pp. 299, 315, 442
Kasubai *v.* Bhagwan [1955] Nag. 281 F.B., AIR 1955 Nag. 210 pp. 80, 297, 300
Katama Nachiar *v.* Srimut Rajah Moottoo (Rajah of Shivaganga) (1863) 9 M.I.A. 539 pp. 114, 424
Katheessa Umma *v.* Narayanath Kuhamu AIR 1964 S.C. 275 p. 525
Kattama Náchiár *v.* Dorasinga Tévar (1870) 6 M.H.C.R. 310 p. 292
Kaur Singh *v.* Jaggar Singh AIR 1961 Punj. 489 p. 345
Kaura (Mt.) Devi *v.* Mt. Indra Devi AIR 1943 All. 310 p. 313
Kayarohana Pathan *v.* Subbaraya Thevan (1915) 38 Mad. 250 pp. 297, 299, 313
Kedarmal Bharamal *v.* Surajmal Govindram (1908) 33 Bom. 364 p. 294
Kenchava *v.* Girimallappa Channappa (1924) 51 I.A. 368 p. 309
Kerutnaraen *v.* Mussamaut Bhobinesree (1806) 1 S.D.A. (Cal.) 213 p. 297
Keshav Hargovan *v.* Bai Gandi (1915) 39 Bom. 538 pp. 287, 362
Keyake Ilata K. Kanni *v.* Yadattil V. Achuda (1868) 3 M.H.C.R. 380 p. 290
Khageswar *v.* Aduti AIR 1967 Or. 80 pp. 355, 392
Khetramani Dasi *v.* Kashi Nath Das (1868) 2 B.L.R., A.C., 15 p. 298
Khwaja Muhammad Khan *v.* Husaini Begam (1910) 37 I.A. 152 p. 312
King-Emperor *v.* Bharat Bepari AIR 1921 Cal. 501(1) p. 63
Kirpal Singh *v.* Chandramani Devi AIR 1951 All. 507 p. 315
Kirpal (Mt.) Knar *v.* Bachan Singh [1957] 21 S.C.J. 438 p. 310
Kishenlal *v.* Mst. Prabhu AIR 1963 Raj. 95 p. 363
Kishori *v.* Mst. Chaltibai (1959) 22 S.C.J. 560 p. 73
Kistnochurn *v.* Ramnarain Morton-Montriou, 297 = 1 Ind. Dec., Old Ser. 178 p. 241
Kitab Ali Munshi *v.* Santi Ranjan AIR 1965 Trip. 22 p. 450
Kochu Govindan *v.* Lakshmi [1959] S.C.R. 63, AIR 1959 S.C. 71 p. 312
Kojahs and Memon's Case: Hirbae *v.* Sonabae (1847) Perry 110 pp. 294, 306, 520
Kokila *v.* K. M. Rajabather AIR 1957 Mad. 470 p. 427
Kolandai *v.* Gnanavaram [1943] 2 M.L.J. 664, AIR 1944 Mad. 156 p. 61
Kolandaivelu, *In re* (1917) 40 Mad. 1030 F.B. p. 342
Koman (M.) *v.* Achuthan Nair (1934) 61 I.A. 405 p. 486
Koshul *v.* Radhanath (1811) 1 S.D.A. (Cal.) 448 p. 296
Krishna Pada Dutt *v.* Sec. of State (1908) 12 C.W.N. 453 pp. 306, 313
Krishna Mudaliar *v.* Marimuthu Mudaliar [1939] 2 M.L.J. 423 p. 312
Krishnamurthi Ayyar *v.* Krishnamurthi Ayyar (1927) 54 I.A. 248 p. 310

Nar Hari Shastri *v.* Sri Badrinath Temple Committee [1953] 1 All. 42 S.C. = AIR 1952 S.C. 245 pp. 469, 489
Naragunty Lutchmeedavamah *v.* Vengama Naidoo (1861) 9 M.I.A. 66 p. 310
Narain Prasad *v.* Sarnam Singh (1917) 44 I.A. 163 p. 310
Narasammál *v.* Balarámáchárlu (1863) 1 M.H.C.R. 420 p. 293
Narasimharáv Krishnaráv *v.* Antáji (1865) 2 B.H.C.R. 61 p. 297
Narasimma Chariar *v.* Sri Krishna Tata Chariar (1871) 6 M.H.C.R. 449 p. 290
Narayan *v.* Laxman (1927) 51 Bom. 784 p. 411
Náráyan Sadánánd Bárá *v.* Bálkrishna (1872) 9 B.H.C.R. 413 p. 413
Narayan Prasad Choubey *v.* Smt. Prabhadevi AIR 1964 M.P. 28 p. 389
Narayan Das *v.* State AIR 1952 Or. 149 p. 63
Narayana (A.) Rao *v.* G. Venkatapayya AIR 1937 Mad. 182 p. 311
Narayana (A. M.) Sah *v.* A. Sankar Sah (1930) 53 Mad. 1 F.B. p. 300
Narayanaswami Reddiar *v.* Padmanabhan AIR 1966 Mad. 394 p. 358
Narayanaswami (K. V.) Iyer *v.* Ramakrishna (K. V.) Iyer AIR 1965 S.C. 289 p. 429
Narsi (G.) Reddi *v.* R. Rami Reddi [1964] 1 An.W.R. 261 pp. 297, 313
Nataraja (C. S.) Pillai *v.* C. S. Subbaraya Chettiar (1949) 77 I.A. 33 p. 310
Natarajan Chettiar *v.* Perumal Ammal AIR 1943 Mad. 246 p. 311
Natha *v.* Mehta Chhotalal AIR 1931 Bom. 89 pp. 299, 312, 313
Nathu Velji *v.* Keshawji Hirachand (1902) 26 Bom. 174 p. 291
Nilmadhub Doss *v.* Bishumber Doss (1869) 13 M.I.A. 85 p. 306
Nirmala *v.* Balai AIR 1965 S.C. 1874 p. 491
Nirodhini *v.* Nanda Sangma AIR 1945 Cal. 213 p. 305
Nizamul Haque *v.* Begum Noorjahan AIR 1966 Cal. 465 p. 547
Nundram *v.* Kashee Pandee (1822) 3 Sel. Rep. 232 p. 245
Nur Ali *v.* Malka Sultana P.L.D. 1961 (W.P.) Lahore 431 p. 543
Nusserwanjee *v.* Meer Mynoodeen (1855) 6 M.I.A. 134 p. 293

Off. Receiver *v.* Kassim Moosa Sait [1966] K.L.T. 985 p. 439

Padamavati (Sm.) *v.* Ramchandra Ananga Bhim AIR 1951 Or. 248 p. 306
Padman *v.* Hanwanta AIR 1915 P.C. 111 p. 312
Padmanabhan Moosad *v.* Parvathi [1967] K.L.T. 555 p. 300
Paduram Sahu *v.* Biswambar AIR 1958 Or. 259 p. 473
Paigi *v.* Sheonarain (1886) 8 All. 78 p. 290
Paili *v.* Krishna Panicker (1120/1944) 36 Cochin 300 F.B. p. 297
Palwanna Nadar *v.* Annamalai Ammal AIR 1957 Mad. 330 p. 410
Parbia Ram *v.* Smt. Thopli AIR 1966 H.P. 20 p. 355
Pattabhiramier *v.* Vencatarow Naicken (1870) 13 M.I.A. 560 p. 311
Pattayee *v.* Manickam AIR 1967 Mad. 254 p. 369
Peddamuttu *v.* Appu Rau (1864) 2 Mad. H.C.R. 117 p. 426
Peramanayakam *v.* Sivaraman AIR 1952 Mad. 419 F.B. pp. 403, 418
Perumal Chetti *v.* Province of Madras AIR 1955 Mad. 382 p. 313
Petit *v.* Jijibhai (1909) 11 Bom. L.R. 85 p. 40
Philomena Mendoza *v.* Dara Nusserwanji AIR 1943 Bom. 338 p. 544

Ravanna Koovanna *v.* Vana Pana Tirumalai AIR 1962 Mad. 500 = [1962] Mad. 974 p. 458

Rayaningaru (C. T.) *v.* Rajah Suraneni Vencata (1871) 6 M.H.C.R. 278 p. 310

Reg. *v.* Sambhu Raghu (1876) 1 Bom. 347 pp. 287, 358

Roman Catholic Mission *v.* State of Madras AIR 1966 S.C. 1457 p. 501

Roopakula *v.* Sunkara [1966] 1 An.W.R. 50 p. 483

Ruckmaboye *v.* Lulloobhoy Mottichund (1851–2) 5 M.I.A. 234 p. 308

Rukman Kanta *v.* Faquir Chand AIR 1960 Punj. 493 p. 372

Rukn ul Mulk *v.* R. Vishwanathan AIR 1950 Mys. 33 p. 423

Runchordas Vandrawandas *v.* Parvatibai (1899) 26 I.A. 71 p. 511

Rungama *v.* Atchama (1846) 4 M.I.A. 1 pp. 296, 304, 313

Rutcheputty *v.* Rajunder Narain (1839) 2 M.I.A. 133 p. 296

Sabitri (Smt.) Thakurain *v.* Savi (Mrs. F. A.) AIR 1933 Pat. 306 = 12 Pat. 359 pp. 299, 411

Sadananda *v.* Harinam AIR 1950 Cal. 179 p. 313

Sadanund, *see* Sudanund

Sahu Ram Chandra *v.* Bhup Singh (1917) 44 I.A. 126 p. 310

Saidullah Khan *v.* State of Bhopal AIR 1955 Bhopal 23 p. 449

Sakhu *v.* State [1951] Nag. 508 p. 355

Salemma *v.* Lutchmana Reddi (1897) 21 Mad. 100 p. 300

Sambasivam Pillai *v.* Sec. of State (1921) 44 Mad. 704 pp. 300, 313

Sambhu, *see* Reg. *v.* Sambhu.

Sambhu Chandra Dey *v.* Kartick Chandra (1926) 54 Cal. 171 p. 299

Sandhukhan (Mohamed) Rowther *v.* Ratnam AIR 1958 Mad. 144 p. 527

Sangápá *v.* Gangápá (1878) 2 Bom. 476 p. 290

Sankaralinga *v.* Raja (1908) 35 I.A. 176 p. 469

Sant Ram *v.* Labh Singh AIR 1965 S.C. 314 p. 305

Saraswathi (T.) Ammal *v.* Jagadambal AIR 1953 S.C. 201 pp. 305, 312

Saraswathi Ammal *v.* Anantha Shenoi [1965] K.L.T. 141 p. 299

Saraswathi Ammal *v.* Rajagopal Ammal AIR 1953 S.C. 491 pp. 458, 462

Sardar Sarup Singh *v.* State of Punjab AIR 1959 S.C. 860 p. 477

Sardar Syedna Taher Saifuddin *v.* Tyebbhai Moosaji Koicha AIR 1953 Bom. 183, (1952) 55 Bom. L.R. 1 p. 473

Sardar Syedna Taher Sarfuddin Saheb *v.* State of Bombay AIR 1962 S.C. 853 pp. 474–5, 478, 481

Sarubai *v.* Narayandas [1943] Bom. 314 p. 309

Sat Narain *v.* Behari Lal AIR 1925 P.C. 18 = 52 I.A. 22 p. 310

Saunadanappa *v.* Shivbasawa (1907) 31 Bom. 354 p. 294

Savlaram Kacharoo *v.* Yeshodabai Savlaram AIR 1962 Bom. 190 p. 394

Sayal (P. L.) *v.* Smt Sarla Rani AIR 1961 Punj. 125 p. 389

Sec. of State *v.* Adm. Gen., Bengal (1868) 1 B.L.R., O.C., 87 p. 304

Sec. of State *v.* Bombay Landing and Shipping Coy. (1868) 5 B.H.C.R. 23 p. 294

Sec. of State *v.* Rukhminibai AIR 1937 Nag. 354 p. 313

Seetha (Machingal P. Veettu) *v.* Machingal P. V. Kelu Menon AIR 1939 Mad. 564 p. 305

State of Madrass *v.* Kunnakudi Melamatam [1966] 2 S.C.J. 175 p. 483
Stríman Sadagópá *v.* Kristna Tatáchâriyár (1863) 1 M.H.C.R. 301 pp. 290, 291
Subba Rao (M.) *v.* Krishna AIR 1954 Mad. 227 p. 109
Subbanna (C.) *v.* C. Balasubbareddi AIR 1945 Mad. 142 F.B. p. 313
Subbarama Reddiar *v.* Saraswathi [1966] 2 M.L.J. 263 pp. 369, 399
Subbaraya Mudaliar *v.* Vedantachariar (1905) 28 Mad. 23 p. 290
Subbaya (K.) *v.* K. Ramakoteswara Rao AIR 1958 An.P. 479 p. 306
Subramania Ayyar *v.* Sabapathy Aiyar (1927) 51 Mad. 361 F.B. p. 305
Subramania (R.) Iyer *v.* Comm,, I.-T. AIR 1955 Mad. 623 p. 423
Subramaniam *v.* Kumarappa AIR 1955 Mad. 144 p. 293
Sudanund Mohapattur *v.* Bonomallee (1863) 1 Marshall 317 p. 309
Sudaram Patro *v.* Soodha Ram (1869) 11 W.R. 457 p. 291
Sudhindra *v.* Commr., H.R.C.E. AIR 1956 Mad. 491 p. 493
Sudhindra Thirtha *v.* Commr., H.R.C.E. AIR 1963 S.C. 966 pp. 490, 494
Sukumar Bose *v.* Abani Kumar AIR 1956 Cal. 308 p. 310
Sumer Chand *v.* State of Rajasthan AIR 1965 Raj. 2 p. 504
Sumrun Singh *v.* Khedun Singh (1814) 2 Sel. Rep., S.D.A. (Cal.) 147 p. 293
Sundarambal *v.* Suppiah AIR 1961 Mad. 323, [1963] 1 M.L.J. 106 p. 44
Sundareswarar (Sree S.B.V.) *v.* Marimuthu AIR 1963 Mad. 369 p. 488
Superintendent *v.* Corp. of Calcutta AIR 1967 S.C. 997 p. 289
Suraj Bunsi Koer *v.* Sheo Persad (1879) 6 I.A. 88 pp. 308, 310, 311, 418
Suraj Din *v.* Ram Chandra [1965] All. L.J. 665 p. 342
Surayya (T.) *v.* K. P. Balakrishnayya AIR 1941 Mad. 618 p. 299
Surayya (Y.) *v.* Y. Subbamma (1919) 43 Mad. 4 p. 313
Surendra Narayan *v.* Bhola Nath Ray Chaudhuri [1944] 1 Cal. 139 p. 313
Surjit Kumar *v.* Raj Kumari AIR 1967 Punj. 172 p. 395
Swamy Premananda *v.* Swamy Yogananda [1965] K.L.T. 824 p. 492
Swapna Mukherjee *v.* Basanta Ranjan AIR 1955 Cal. 533 p. 342
Syed Edulla *v.* Madras State Board [1966] 1 M.L.J. 17 p. 439

Tagore, Jotendromohun *v.* Gnanendramohun Tagore (1872) I.A. Sup. Vo. 47 p. 293
Tara Munnee Dossea *v.* Motee Buneanee (1864) 7 Sel. Rep. (Cal.) 273 p. 296
Tara *v.* Krishna (1907) 31 Bom. 495 p. 304
Tayawwa *v.* Chinnappa Mallappa AIR 1962 Mys. 130 p. 382
Tayumana Reddi *v.*Perumal Reddi (1862) 1 M.H.C.R. 51 p. 293
Teeluck Chunder *v.* Shama Churn (1864) 1 W.R. 209 p. 296
Teja Singh Subedar *v.* Sarjit Kaur AIR 1962 Punj. 195 p. 380
Thakoor (Mst.) Deyhee *v.* Rai Baluk Ram (1866) 11 M.I.A. 139 p. 299
Thakoorain Sahiba *v.* Mohun Lall (1867) 11 M.I.A. 386 pp. 299, 300, 310
Thakur Mohd. Ismail *v.* Thakur Sabir Ali AIR 1962 S.C. 1722 p. 439
Thangaswami (S. M. N.) *v.* Comm., I.-T., Madras AIR 1966 Mad. 103 p. 459
Thankammal *v.* Madhavi Amma [1966] K.L.T. 181 p. 42
The King (1814) 2 Strange N.C. 251 p. 312
Thirumaleshwara Bhatta *v.* K. Ganapayya AIR 1953 Mad. 132 p. 315

INDEX OF NAMES AND TOPICS

Basava, 178 n.
Basham, A. L., 59 n., 562
Basu, D. D., 321 n., 491 n., 566
Baynes, C. R., 277 n.
Bechert, H., 411 n.
Beg, M. H., 535 n.
Bengal, 116
Bhagavadgītā, the, 43, 46, 49, 70 n., 82, 565
Bhāgavatam, Śrīmad-, the, 67
bhakti, 15, 43, 46, 51
Bhandarkar, D. R., 207 n.
Bharatacandra Śiromaṇi, 254
Bhāruci, 128 n., 141 n., 152 n., 182 n., 189 n., 198, 214 n.
Bhāsa, 204 n.
Bhat, S. C., 494 n.
Bhaṭṭāchārya, B., 88 n., 99 n.
Bhaṭṭāchārya, D. C., 256 n.
Bhaṭṭāchārya, S., 27 n.
bhāvanā, 101
Bhavanātha, 134
Bhavaswāmī, 198, 204
Bhaviṣya-purāṇa, the, 98–9
Bhoja, 134 n., 204
bigamy, 338, 355 n., 358 n., 444
birth, right by, 135, 415, 417, 422, 434, 552–3
blackmail, 216–7, 295
Blackshield, A. R., 20
Bongert, Y., 176 n.
Borradaile, H., 256
Boulton, J. V., 30 n.
Brahmins, 80, 107, 119–20, 126, 159, 164, 165, 167, 172, 174, 178, 179, 182 n., 184, 189 n., 191 n., 192, 193, 210, 211, 230, 347–8, 362, 441, 450, 483; duties of, 183; feeding of, 38; gift to, 90; officiant, 67
Brahmo Samāj, 44
Bṛhadāraṇyakopaniṣad, 70 n., 82
Bṛhan-nāradīya-purāṇa, the, 90 n., 173
Bṛhaspati, 155, 157 n., 161 n., 184 n., 189, 190, 196 n., 199, 201 n., 208, 210, 215 n., 219, 431 n.
bribery, 221, 245 n.
British, and law, 227; dilemma of, 231 ff.; co-operation of with Indians, 268–9
Brown, C. P., 259 n.
Brown, W. Norman, 46, 61 n., 565
Buddhism, 27 n., 54
Buddhists, 52, 78, 102, 106 n., 308 n.
Buerkle, H., 29 n.
Bühler, G., 565
Burma, 319, 326
Burnell, A. C., 226 n., 261, 298, 401 n., 416 n., 565
Butler, Lord, 19

ca, 202 n.
Caṇḍeśvara, 183 n.
Canon law, 40 n., 160
Capoor, V. N., 31 n.
caritra, 15, 149, 154, 156–7
Carratelli, G. P., 27 n.
caste, 172–3, 177, 178, 182 n., 266, 290–1, 315 n., 350, 449, 500; and law, 32 n., 287, 313 n., 332, 359, 363; and penalties, 107, 220; belief in, 65–6; mixture of castes, 119, 175
caste-tribunals, 35, 82, 83, 291, see also *panchayat*
cāṭa, 202
Caturviṃśatimata, the, 204 n.
celebates, 168, 180, 410, 509 n.
Ceylon, Kandyan law in, 292; Sinhalese law in, 284; Tamil law in, 284 n.
Chagla, M. C., 29 n., 463, 464, 474, 513, 514, 516, 517 n., 557 n.
Chaṇḍāvarkar, N. G., 304
Chandrasekhara Ayyar, N., 298 n.
charity, 215 n., 460 ff., 502–3
Charters, 295
Chatterjee, H., 572
Chatterjee, S. C., 565
Chattopadhyay, A. K., 295 n.
Chattopādhyaya, S., 20, 563
Chaudhari, D. H., 570
Chaudhary, R. K., 154 n.